Ministry in America

Ministry in America

A Report and Analysis, Based on an In-Depth Survey of 47 Denominations in the United States and Canada, with Interpretation by 18 Experts

David S. Schuller,
Merton P. Strommen,
and Milo L. Brekke, Editors

A project of The Association of Theological Schools in the United States and Canada and of Search Institute

HARPER & ROW, PUBLISHERS
SAN FRANCISCO

Cambridge · London
Hagerstown · Mexico City
Philadelphia · São Paulo
New York 1817 · Sydney

MINISTRY IN AMERICA. Copyright © 1980 by The Association of Theological Schools in the United States and Canada and Search Institute. All rights reserved. Printed in the United States of America. No part of this book may be used or reproduced in any manner whatsoever without written permission except in the case of brief quotations embodied in critical articles and reviews. For information, address Harper & Row, Publishers, Inc., 10 East 53rd Street, New York, NY 10022. Published simultaneously in Canada by Fitzhenry & Whiteside Limited, Toronto.

FIRST EDITION

Designed by Patricia G. Dunbar

Library of Congress Cataloging in Publication Data
Main entry under title:

Ministry in America.

"A project of the Association of Theological Schools in the United States and Canada and of Search Institute."
1. Clergy—Office—Evaluation. 2. Clergy—United States. 3. Clergy—Canada.
4. Christian sects—United States. 5. Christian sects—Canada. I. Schuller, David S.
II. Strommen, Merton P. III. Brekke, Milo. IV. Association of Theological Schools in the United States and Canada. V. Search Institute.
BV660.2.M53   253   79-2990
ISBN 0-06-067721-X

---

80 81 82 83 84 10 9 8 7 6 5 4 3 2 1

Contents

III. Research Methodology

List of Figures
and Tables

I. Figures

II. Tables

Acknowledgments

We planned initially to acknowledge by name the people who made a significant contribution to this volume. When our beginning list passed 200, we reluctantly realized the impossibility of our hope. Simply, then, we express our thanks to the thousands who consider it a part of their ministry to give hours responding to questionnaires, interpreting findings, critiquing manuscripts, and writing letters to explain their conceptions of ministry. We wish to thank Jesse Ziegler and the leadership of the Executive Committee of the Association of Theological Schools (ATS) for their vision in identifying a fundamental need in ministerial education that needed to be addressed. We acknowledge the massive and sustained financial assistance of the Lilly Endowment; without the positive response of that staff and board, this project would never have been carried out. Special thanks are due to Charles G. Williams, Fred L. Hofheinz, and Robert W. Lynn. During the entire period of the study, the computer facilities of the Lutheran Brotherhood were offered without charge; we are in its debt for this courtesy. In all, the administration, faculties, and student bodies of some 160 seminaries in the United States and Canada participated, some repeatedly, in various stages of the study. We express our thanks to these colleagues, as we do to the leadership of approximately thirty denominations, whose leaders in departments of theological education and ministry assisted personally and by providing access to others.

A special word of thanks to the clergy in forty-seven different denominations who responded to our questionnaires and interviews and offered valuable encouragement and correction. It is with a deep sense of personal and professional loss that we acknowledge the death of two of our colleagues, Arthur M. Adams and Thomas C. Campbell. Arthur Adams was loved and respected by a full generation of students and colleagues at Princeton Theological Seminary and elsewhere as a churchman, theologian, and wise counselor. Tom Campbell's recent professional life included a professorship at Yale, the presidency of Chicago Theological Seminary, and the deanship at United Seminary of the Twin Cities. We are grateful to God, who called these two men to ministry, for their gifts of intellect and spirit, and for their sharing in these pages of what neither knew would be a final witness.

Finally, we the editors express gratitude to those who labored over months in bringing this book to completion. First of all to the authors of chapters—their work was a labor of love; to Deborah Schuller for painstaking checking of data, development of precis, and substantial rewriting of some denominational chapters; to Shelby Andress for dedicated and dogged copy editing; to Irene Strommen for uncounted evenings of editing and initial retyping; to Arlene Galloway for overseeing the smooth functioning of the assessment service; to typists at both ATS and Search Institute who typed draft after draft of some chapters.

We offer this book as a part of our collective ministry for the strengthening of the work of ministry in North America.

DAVID S. SCHULLER
The Association of Theological Schools

Introduction

Merton P. Strommen

The combined scholarly efforts of twenty authors and their assistants have made this unique book a reality. Its uniqueness resides in the nature of its data, the level of analyses that supplied information, and in general the fact that approximately 5,000 people helped write the chapters. By rating the importance of 444 descriptions of ministry, they provided a data base without precedence. Hence the descriptions of ministry found in this volume and the generalizations drawn by the authors about their denominational family draw on more than the authors' insights and personal observations. To years of experience in a church body that the authors have come to know as scholars and churchpeople, has been added the corroborating evidence of survey research data. Because the data are supplied by national random samples, the information can be generalized to seventeen major families of denominations.

This extensive collection of data is one outcome of the Readiness for Ministry Project—an ambitious venture begun by Jesse H. Ziegler, Executive Director of the Association of Theological Schools in the United States and Canada. Together with other educators, he sought a way of assessing the readiness of graduating seminary seniors to enter the professional ministry.

Merton P. Strommen is President of Search Institute and a member of the Readiness for Ministry Project team. He is the author of *Five Cries of Youth* and *A Study of Generations*, and editor of *Research on Religious Development*.

Generously funded by the Lilly Endowment, massive research efforts began in May 1973, under the direction of David S. Schuller, Associate Director of the Association of Theological Schools. Joining him in this effort were Milo L. Brekke and myself of Search Institute, a research agency formerly known as the Youth Research Center. This team of three, which added Daniel O. Aleshire in July 1975 and Francis Lonsway in the fall of 1976, provided the leadership and necessary continuity for what became a six-year project, 1973–1979.

WILLING COOPERATION

Well over 12,000 people participated in some aspect of the Readiness for Ministry Project. Thousands assisted in describing contemporary ministry, choosing and refining items for the Readiness questionnaire, ranking the descriptions of ministry in terms of their importance, naming clusters, developing and testing criterion-referenced instruments, and reviewing early drafts of this book. A profound sense of concern may have helped to motivate this remarkable willingness to help.

When we explained that this project was to assess the readiness of seminary students to enter the professional ministry, people were immediately interested. Congregation leaders said, "Whatever will result in more effective clergy, we're for it. Count on us to help." Laypeople concerned over the selection and training of clergy knew of clergy working below their potential, even as many knew of ones who were misfits in their position. Yet they gave their evaluations with full awareness of the enormous demands placed on clergy and of the vital role played by clergy in society. Similarly, faculty and students in seminaries across the continent gave unstintingly of their time in providing judgments about the needs of contemporary ministers. Ministers and priests in the full range of settings —parish, educational, hospital, residential, experimental—described their concepts of ministry by ranking the components of their work by level of priority.

BOOK PREPARATION

Two interim books report the identification of criteria and the development of assessment instruments that were the major outcomes of the first three years of this project. Volume I, *Readiness for Ministry: Criteria*, presents the criteria laity and clergy use when judging the effectiveness of a fledgling minister; Volume II, *Readiness for Ministry: Assessment*, describes the instruments developed by the research team for assessing the degree to which the criteria are found in students.

Assessment tools were introduced to the 200 seminaries of the Association of Theological Schools for use during the years 1977–1980 by entering as well as by graduating seminary students. The resulting profiles have aided students in setting educational goals, deciding where to serve, and establishing a program of continuing education. As noted in this book's chapter on the Orthodox Churches by Stanley Harakas, the assessment results have assisted faculties in their evaluation of the educational outcomes of their seminary curriculum.

This publication, in a sense, is a serendipitous outcome of the Readiness for Ministry Project, made possible by a grant and free computer time from the Lutheran Brotherhood of Minneapolis and supplemented by enormous contributions of personal time given by the denominational writers. It is based on the treasure of new information found in the ratings of importance that 5,000 randomly selected clergy and laity gave to 444 criterion statements. (The term *clergy* here includes not only parish clergy but also denominational officials, seminary professors, and seminary seniors.) Although these data were originally collected in order to supply the criteria needed for assessment purposes (and not to survey all religious groups in North America), they have been a valuable resource for this book. The survey data tell us how seminary oriented laity and clergy view ministry and order their priorities, thus showing how a large portion of religious America and Canada differ in their perceptions of ministry. Such data, when probed by means of the complex methods of multivariate analysis now possible, can answer what in the past have been unanswerable questions. Although the twenty authors found that the survey data information primarily confirmed observations and hunches they held with respect to their church body, they were at times pleasantly surprised and at other times puzzled or even disappointed.

Authors of the chapters on denominational families, selected in the spring and summer of 1976, began their study of the research data in the fall of that year. Each person was supplied documentation showing how his or her denominational family (1) organized its data into clusters (in contrast to the entire sample), (2) differed from other denominational families in the importance it accorded sixty of the sixty-four criterion characteristics (clusters 61–64 were not available in standard scores at this time), (3) differed from all others when responding to each of the 444 survey items, and (4) differed from all others on the basis of demographic variables. In addition, each author was supplied written comments by respondents of his or her denomination regarding what each felt was missing from the questionnaire.

Some of the authors, trained primarily as theologians, supplemented help from the editorial team of Schuller, Strommen, and Brekke with assistance given by one or more social scientists trained in the handling of such research data. Authors were asked to report faithfully the data from their groups; they were then free to contest the findings on the basis of what they knew about their church bodies. It is significant that the authors did recognize their denominations in the data and chose therefore to concentrate on showing how traditions and historical developments have shaped their churches' present perspectives on ministry.

First drafts of chapters became available for a series of manuscript review conferences: one held in Dayton and two in New York in the fall of 1977, and two in the spring of 1978 in Chicago. Seminary professors, parish clergy, and denominational executives were invited to attend these one-day conferences. Having read advance copies of each manuscript to be reviewed, these people, out of their interest in this project, gathered to critique the chapters in the light of the church body each knew. Once the chapters had been rewritten in more publishable form, the editors, with the help of research assistant Deborah Schuller, painstakingly checked the accuracy of every data-based statement. Great care was exercised to verify the author's appropriate use and interpretation of data. How the authors have chosen to interpret the meaning or significance of their data is of course their prerogative.

The process of several revisions (usually rewrites) was completed in September 1978.

USE AND QUALITY OF DATA

It is important to understand that all classifications of data reported in these chapters have been made empirically through cluster and factor analyses. (See Chapter 19 for explanation of methods.) This means that the opinions of the research team have not determined which items form each cluster or which clusters form each major factor or area of ministry. The data have been allowed to organize themselves. Furthermore, it should be recognized that today's computer capacities and software have opened the door for unprecedented analytic possibilities. Instead of analyses in which only one variable can be controlled at a time, multivariate analyses have been freely used, such as analyses in which the impact of up to thirty-eight variables are assessed simultaneously. Personal judgments were not involved in the derivation of the statistical data but, rather, were limited to such tasks as naming clusters and factors and interpreting score results.

Before reading the chapters, however, a reader may want assurance as to the reliability of the survey data. "How seriously did the 5,000 people take their task of answering 444 items? Might they have answered carelessly, out of disinterest or a sense of coercion?" Significantly, our survey data show relatively high measures of internal consistency (to assure one is measuring a single dimension)—one way of assessing reliability. The empirically derived clusters and families of clusters (factors) reflect ministry characteristics with sufficient clarity to be readily identified. A full accounting of research procedures used in this project is given in Chapter 19. (In this chapter, people familiar with Volume I, *Readiness for Ministry: Criteria,* will learn why certain refinements were introduced, altering some cluster names, mean (average) scores, and the basis for determining rank.)

Although massive in size and scope, the Readiness Project had certain restrictions that placed significant limitations on its data and these need to be mentioned. The first limitation has to do with the number of items that could be included in the questionnaire. Although literally thousands of criterion statements were considered, the number had to be trimmed to what a respondent could handle. Therefore, survey items were dropped that describe distinctive features of only one or two denominations or special programs within a congregation. Due to this limitation, Free Church respondents, for instance, were not able to find items in the questionnaire that describe their position on war, United Methodists failed to find items reflecting important concepts of "connectionalism" or "discipline," and some evangelicals looked in vain for items vital to them. Here, indeed, the study was limited. For this reason, denominations have been encouraged to do as the Lutherans have done—to develop additional items distinctive of denominational ecclesiology and theology and to include these with the Readiness Project items, in separate and parallel studies.

A second limitation resides in the fact that this study was carried out through the 200 seminaries of the Association of Theological Schools in the United States and Canada. Hence, the samples were limited to (1) denominations that had one or more seminaries in the professional accrediting association; (2) clergy who were seminary trained, which in the case of the Southern Baptist Convention eliminated almost one-half of its clergy; and (3) laity who were members of congregations served by clergy trained in a member seminary of the ATS. As a result, the random samples exclude portions of the religious community whose seminaries are not accredited, whose clergy are not seminary trained, and whose laity are found in congregations led by pastors without seminary training. This was not a limitation for the Readiness Project, however, because its purpose was to develop a way of assessing readiness to enter the professional ministry.

It is well known that a self-report is not always an indicator of real life. What people report may not always be so; what some avow as being of high importance to them may be no more than lip service to ideals espoused by their congregation. When this occurs, self-report is little more than normative rhetoric.

Although we do not know to what extent such slippage characterizes the data, we take seriously what laity and clergy do report as their expectations of contemporary ministry. Thus far, our validation studies do show a significant correlation between what people say and what they do. A strong case for construct validation (the fact that the findings are logical and recognizable) is emerging for this study from a variety of indices. Not least is the fact that twenty authors, in their responses, have given us confidence that the samples do indeed reflect distinctive features of their churches.

A word must be said about the black churches. As will be described in more detail in Chapter 19, we attempted to question a larger number of respondents in a number of the groups underrepresented in seminaries during the period of the study. Black representatives were among those oversampled. Unfortunately we were unable to secure responses from a sufficient number of black clergy and laity to warrant separate analysis and reporting. Each black respondent consequently has been totaled within in his or her own denominational group. Because an empirical analysis of responses of those in the African Methodist Episcopal Church and the African Methodist Episcopal Zion Church showed greatest affiliation with the larger family of the Presbyterian-Reformed churches, their data were included in that denominational family. During subsequent stages of development of assessment instruments, we were able to redress this initial weakness by consistently including black theological students, ministers, and faculty members.

A final limitation to be singled out resides in the fact that the data are cross-sectional and were collected at only one point in time; they cannot indicate trends or provide answers to "why?" Interpretations are limited to describing how people viewed ministry in the mid-1970s and to showing how groups differ in what they deem important emphases in ministry. One cannot make comparisons with previous years, extrapolate to the future, or make causal statements, although such would be ideal. Few studies supply data that do all that one would hope.

Some may consider the time lapse between the collection of data in 1974 and a publishing date in 1980 as another limitation. We do not view it as such. Data here are not being used as in an opinion poll where the value of the information is in being current, like the taking of one's temperature or assessing a candidate's preelection popularity. This research, rather than describing current feelings and moods, focuses on characteristics of ministry and the structure of people's concepts—elements that persist over time. Although profiles based on these characteristics may alter in shape as society changes, they do not vanish but continue in various shapes over time. We believe a similar study ten or twenty years from now will surface similar ministry characteristics to those being reported here; peaks and valleys formed by a profile will vary slightly with the times.

One additional comment. Lay and clergy samples used for this publication, although random, are, in the case of a few denominational families, smaller than we wanted. In the Christian Church (Disciples of Christ), for instance, too few laity participated in the survey to allow for meaningful comparisons between clergy and laity responses. In the case of the United Church of Canada, where this was also true, a second and larger sample was drawn and more responses secured. Interestingly, data from this cross-validation sample yielded essentially the same score results. Although the first-draft chapter on the United Church of Canada was based on data from the first sample, data from the second sample required few changes in what had been written.

Added confidence in our data resulted when responses from the Lutheran sample of 561 respondents were compared with data from a separate study involving 5,000 Lutherans. What Lindbeck reports in his chapter complements the conclusions reported in the book *Ten Faces of Ministry*,[1] which is based on the sample of 5,000. Our experience, and that of the twenty authors with these data, gives us confidence that what is reported here is a fair representation of ministry in the 1970s as perceived by a large portion of Christendom in North America.

THE MISSING CHAPTER

Unfortunately, one hoped-for chapter suffered as a casualty—for which an explanation seems required. To gain a more comprehensive view of the religious community in North America, we planned from the beginning to include the Jewish community. During the entire period of the Readiness for Ministry Project, Hebrew Union College—Jewish Institute of Religion was a member of the Association of Theological Schools. Following our basic guidelines, this meant we would sample the alumni and members of the Reform Jewish congregations served by these rabbis. We therefore contacted the dean of Hebrew Union, Kenneth Rossman, to "translate" the questionnaire from its pan-Christian form, maintaining the items in the original wording to the extent possible but making all necessary changes to enable the instrument to reflect the Jewish community's expectations of the young rabbi.

Using similar sampling procedures to those described in Chapter 19, we sent the questionnaire to selected rabbis and lay members of Jewish congregations. In spite of four follow-up contacts, the returns remained very small. With a warning as to the relatively small data base, we used the returns combined with those of the Unitarian-Universalist group. These two groups demonstrated mutual empirical similarities. These data are shown in the sixty-four profiles based on core cluster scores (Chapter 5) identified as Family 8, Jewish and Unitarian.

The data were shared with Robert L. Katz of the Hebrew Union, who was asked to write the Jewish chapter with the assistance of Francis Lonsway. The hope at that stage was that Rabbi Katz might provide insight into the meaning of the data from within the Jewish community.

A review panel expressed concern about the unity of the chapter and questioned the representativeness of the findings. Because the data base was too small to provide much confidence, we finally decided to withdraw the chapter. We are grateful to those who worked with the data and attempted to share the findings as well as to Rabbi Herbert Bronstein of Glencoe, Illinois, and Rabbi Sanford Seltzer of Boston, who aided in providing critical readings of the materials. Rabbi Seltzer raised several critical issues that finally tipped the decision in favor of dropping the chapter: (1) The heavily Christian auspices of the study and the weight of basically Christian concepts raise serious questions as to how faithfully the instruments could convey Jewish expectations regarding the rabbinate, and (2) The restriction of the sample to Reform Jews would raise questions both for their responses and for the broader Jewish community.

We are happy to share the results of the Jewish responses in the tables in Chapter 5, with a warning that the returns were smaller than expected; we are sorry that no chapter interpreting these data could be included.

OVERVIEW

This publication divides into three parts. The first, written by members of the research team, provides the rationale, definitions, and general orientation to ministry in the United States and Canada. It presents the philosophical and theological presuppositions underlying the Readiness for Ministry Project and describes how these are expressed in the research methodology.

Chapters 3, 4, and 5, which serve as basic references for the denominational chapters, supply structure and content from which the authors of denominational chapters draw.

Part II consists of a sequence of chapters written by churchpeople and scholars, highlighting distinctive perceptions of ministry found in thirteen denominational families. The data-based descriptions draw attention to the treasured accents of what each group views as a rich heritage. What the authors share reflects the multifaceted nature of ministries in North America.

Chapter 19, the principal chapter in the concluding section, explains for discerning readers how the foundational data were gathered and analyzed. Written by Milo Brekke, who carried primary responsibility for all research aspects of the project, it describes in some detail the care used in pressing for reliable, valid, and meaningful information. The data he made available to authors served to extend their normal powers of observation, enabling them to speak with greater confidence about the churches they know so well.

NOTE

1. Brekke, Strommen, Williams, *Ten Faces of Ministry* (Minneapolis: Augsburg, 1979).

I

How
Ministry Is
Perceived

1

Basic Issues in
Defining Ministry

David S. Schuller

An impressionistic scanning of ministry in North America over the past decade reveals that the concept of ministry has undergone significant change. Both the content and the forms of ordained ministries are being seriously reexamined. Unlike many other periods of significant change in models of ministry that the church has experienced, the pressures in the last decade came less directly from the surrounding culture and more intensely from the clergy themselves. Their internal questioning of their role was sometimes prompted by a fear of ineffectiveness, but was nevertheless a continued search for relevance. In many established church bodies, ministerial vocations decreased, and clergy left for other professional fields. In the words of one sympathetic observer, the minister appeared to be the "wounded healer." The predicament of the minister became as serious as that of people whom he or she would serve.

David S. Schuller, an ordained Lutheran clergyman, is Associate Director of The Association of Theological Schools in the United States and Canada and Administrative Director of the Readiness for Ministry Program. His writings include *The New Urban Society* and *Emerging Shapes of the Church*.

DEFINITIONS OF MINISTRY

Before there was broad acknowledgment of a common problem, many ministers felt that they were alone in experiencing doubts and frustrations. They tended to feel personally responsible for what appeared to be failures in their ministry. Yet when colleagues met, their old pattern of sharing success stories persisted. Loneliness and fear were thus driven further underground. Many concluded that if they were more dedicated, if they possessed greater faith, if they could increase their skills, then perhaps the sense of meaning and accomplishment would return.

In the midst of the erosion, one group found confidence in a rediscovery of biblical fundamentals. They sought to reestablish the biblical and theological foundations of ministry as these were preserved and interpreted in their tradition. They were called, after all, to be faithful, not successful. Scriptural imagery of struggle between church and world, faithfulness and apostasy, the eternal and the transitory provided the means for interpreting their own experiences and strengthening their resolve. Such ministers often felt more comfortable with images of the ministry initiated in an earlier day; they pursued patterns of ministerial work familiar to previous generations. Experimental forms of ministry frequently were rejected as fads or symptoms of accommodation. This group's response to a future that might overwhelm them was to turn to the past for scriptural and theological anchors that might keep them from being swept away. Before plunging ahead, they wanted to clarify anew the goals and purposes of ministry, the relation of ministry to the church, and the task of the ministry in relation to the world.

At the other end of the spectrum, another group turned to contemporary society, acknowledging the emergence of a society radically different from the industrial society that dominated the West in the period prior to World War II. Concepts and structures developed to serve the industrial revolution proved inadequate for addressing the issues that demanded solutions in the 1960s and 1970s. Arguing the inadequacy of pastoral images that emerged from a totally different context, this second group saw promise in viewing ministers as professionals among other contemporary professions.

Using the medical and legal professions as their models, this group desired both the technical specificity of content and the glowing status connoted by the word *professional*. A sense of inadequacy or inferiority was heightened as this group of ministers contrasted the more easily defined technical professions with the nebulous functions of "ministry." Ministers, for example, reported feelings of anxiety and frustration as they compared their seemingly undefined role in the sickroom with the clearly defined procedures of hospital staff.

In seeking to validate this claim for professionalism, its advocates note that the ministry clearly possesses the characteristics that distinguish a profession from other occupational fields. To be specific, the ministry utilizes a specialized body of knowledge that undergirds and informs its practice. It also involves a particular set of skills that can be taught and practiced under supervision. It entails an institutional setting through which service is rendered. A code of ethics defines the ministry and is monitored by fellow professionals. The minister functions as a responsible individual with an altruistic sense of service. These are characteristics of professionals in our society.

Those who led the movement to professionalize the ministry argued that such an interpretation addressed several root difficulties of ministry in the 1970s and beyond. For them, the key problem was that in a day of increasing professional specialization ministers continue to function and view themselves as generalists. Too much of their work escapes rigorous evaluation of peers and thus may become mediocre and amateurish. In contrast with professionals in medicine, law, or academe, many clergy appear unsure and self-deprecating. They suspect that they are less intelligent, that their education is not as good, and that their skills are not so highly developed. Professors in too many theological seminaries regularly lament the poor quality of students enrolled in their institutions in contrast to the more prestigious professional schools of the university. Voices in theological education call for raising the academic level of students admitted to schools of theology, hoping thereby to develop a ministry that will be more influential in the life of a community.

Central in this movement has been the concern to define as sharply as possible the competencies demanded in contemporary ministry. The traditional method of articulating a theology that can be "applied" in a local situation is completely reversed. The new question becomes "What are the specific competencies needed to meet the demands of contemporary ministry as these are actually experienced in the field?" The statement of competencies becomes the basis for specific educational programs, evaluation, and assessment.

A wide range of responses to the crises of ministry developed, then, that attempted to create new concepts for fashioning a unified vision of ministry. More clergy began to suspect that the problems faced by ministers were not those of individuals but primarily problems of the whole system. By the beginning of the 1970s, a variety of professional agencies offering psychological and managerial counseling skills turned their attention to ministers as a group needing help. While working for higher standards of accountability in ministerial practice, a new sympathy developed for the pain experienced by many contemporary ministers. A variety of new systems of personal and professional support were created to meet the need.

CLARIFYING THE GOALS OF MINISTRY

A major facet of confusion regarding contemporary ministry involves the goals of ministry and the implications those goals have for the clerical role. While church bodies differ in their definition of goals, a generalized response has developed within the churches of North America that accents the pastoral care of the individual. Even while the content of the minister's role remains communal, involving a group in worship or learning, the point of focus is on the individual. Much ministerial specialization in the last twenty years has involved increasing personal skills in counseling. To a great extent, the work of the ministry has involved individual contact in crisis situations.

Frustrations over the ineffectual quality of this individual response reached its climax during the 1960s. What were ministerial goals within society as a whole, as expressed in its organized forms? Some ministers compared their work to aiding individual casualties of warfare while ignoring or being unable to do anything about war itself. After years of work devoted to preaching, teaching, and the pastoral care of individuals, ministers and priests paused to ask what difference it all had made. Some began to fear they were going through motions, preaching prophetic sermons to people who were either helpless or unwilling to effect any change in the basic institutions of society. They feared that ministerial goals restricted to the individual made them unconscious agents for preserving the status quo, in which they kept people adjusted and content, while the establishment proved itself insensitive to human problems on a worldwide scale. The new problems of overpopulation, the redistribution of resources, war, hunger, pollution, and other violence did not easily yield to individual solutions. To preach an individual ethic of love and responsibility in a world community where the structures enforced, or at least perpetuated, inequity in opportunity, income, and housing appeared romantic or irresponsible.

Slowly then an answer emerged; this group affirmed that the goals of ministry must include the structures of society. Ministers should view themselves as change agents, not as people bandaging the victims of social structures. This affected more than those who espoused a moderate theological view. Some rejected the ideology and traditional responses of liberalism for a more radical stance. Many of the mechanisms for social improvement historically supported by the churches they rejected as attempts to make life more tolerable while leaving untouched the root problems. Clergy who agreed with this analysis began to ally ideologically and in practice with a radical or ultimately revolutionary stance. Liberation of the oppressed, ridding the world of exploitation, and identification with the hungry and the poor of the earth overshadowed concerns with helping the individual better adjust to an overdeveloped, affluent society.

Typically such clergy threw themselves into the arena of radical political activism with a new sense of freedom and commitment. Former clerical stereotypes symbolized by polite speech and somber dress were gleefully destroyed. Ministers found new allies outside the church; they learned new skills. Some left the ministry, formally or psychologically, to become community organizers. More fought in the area of civil rights, identifying with the poor and the oppressed. As time passed, however, they began to ask what special word or skill they possessed because they called themselves by the name of Christ. They saw organizations they had aided at birth becoming as oppressive and insensitive in their use of power as the structures they had replaced. As the excitement of revolt passed, familiar problems again merged: human ambition, bureaucratic intransigence, and the continuance of human needs.

In sharp contrast to those who defined the primary goals of ministry as centering in the public sphere stood others who claimed the chief goals of ministry concern the inner life of people. Many learned personally that if ministers were to be more than functionaries they must have developed their own inner spiritual life. Similarly, they perceived the ultimate task of ministry as focused on deepening people's own spirituality.

The interests of those who would give the answer of interior spirituality in recent years ranged from forms of Zen, yoga, or meditation, through various expressions of the human relations movement, to a renewed interest in Christian spirituality or mysticism. In spite of a variety of approaches, their goals focused on bringing the individual into touch with the springs of highest awareness and creativity in some transcendent fashion. Each approach offers a means for transcending the limitations of daily existence, of rising to new levels of awareness, and of more selfconsciously determining one's future. While few clergy sought a solution in one of the Eastern religions, a large number enrolled in group experiences designed to "get one in touch with oneself," to make one more sensitive to others, or to raise one's consciousness in regard to a particular issue.

Many clergy have used these experiences to fashion the character and content of their own ministry. For some this involved a theological pilgrimage from a classical, biblical theology to an eclecticism that borrows freely from a variety of Eastern religions and disciplines and insights from the behavioral sciences. Although initially these responses—public action or inner response—appear mutually exclusive, the most important dynamic remains the desperate search for the meaning and shape of ministry. One thinks of individuals who, while few in number, are symbols of this stance. They have personally incarnated these widely differing responses within their own ministry often within a relatively brief period.

TIME FOR SYNTHESIS

As we enter sympathetically into each of these typical responses to the dilemma of contemporary ministry, an echo of the truth and basic value of each stance becomes apparent. The problem, however, lies precisely in the vain attempt to build a final answer on partial truths, of seeking to encompass the richness of Christian ministry in a frozen moment of historical reaction.

What insights emerge from the ferment of the past generation's struggle to define ministry functionally for our day? Ministers will apparently need to live with a higher degree of tension and ambiguity as the normal way of life. A sense of peace and stability may be a delusion and a false expectation. Some clergy talk longingly of becoming personally "freed up" in order to be able to serve more fully. Only slowly is the truth learned: Ministry "happens" most authentically in the midst of suffering and ambiguity. One's own human predicament forms part of the response of ministry. Clergy frequently delude themselves by thinking that one is prevented from genuine ministry by the underbrush of false cultural expectations, organizational demands, and the general nitty gritty of "running a church." These excuses vanish with the realization that those very misunderstandings, intrusions, and tedious expectations present the moment and context for ministry. The dream of first removing the problem so that ministry might take place gives way to the vision of robustly seizing the problem as the best way of beginning to minister.[1]

Our day has become wary of the glib answer. People have been disappointed too many times; they have followed too many who would sell packaged hope. None of the painless solutions worked. They no longer listen to suggestions shouted from the sidelines. Only the one who has experienced the pain, the frustrations, the struggle of living fully in a moment such as ours—and has both glimpsed meaning and has personally heard the word of hope—dare speak to us. Only those who have been wounded may speak of healing. Only those who have come to grips with their own loneliness are able to enter into the loneliness of another. This is not to romanticize the pain of ambiguity or loneliness; it is not an encouragement for a superficial swapping of stories of personal distress. It affirms the answer pastorally fashioned by Henri Nouwen[2] of the minister as the one who acknowledges his or her own humanity and uses that awareness as a vehicle of ministry.

The Readiness for Ministry Project arose in this period of struggle. Some theological students were hesitant about entering certain parochial ministries, being ignorant of the expectations held by the laity of their church body but usually fearing the worst. Lay leaders in turn were occasionally

bewildered as some young clergy seemed to ignore community expectations and plunge into activities that did not include the primary objectives
of the church. Theological schools often felt uncomfortable in seeking to
educate young clergy in ways that changed their perceptions of the goals
and objectives of ministry, with the result that service within a congregation or parish of the related church became extremely difficult. It was hard
to define with any degree of assurance the positions held by the various
groups that made up the life of the church in a given place. From the
beginning of the project, it was therefore necessary to seek to hear accurately each sector of the church and to allow for a variety of expressions
of models of ministry within the criteria that eventually developed.

Since the initiative for the project lay with The Association of Theological Schools in the United States and Canada, the decision was made to
focus on "readiness for professional ministry."

Readiness for professional ministry is a concept that can apply to church
leadership of any age or position. In this project, the term denotes the
qualities, abilities, and knowledge of the beginning minister that make
him or her able to do the work of ministry acceptably and to continue
growing toward professional maturity outside of the formal instructional
setting and the protected status of "student." Readiness thus represents
a kind of "takeoff point" on the preparation curve. It will have varying
meanings in different religious groups and subcultures.

Readiness is to be distinguished from the larger concept of "effectiveness in ministry." The latter has meanings that vary at different stages of
one's career. A neophyte pastor is usually evaluated by somewhat different norms than those applicable to ministers fifteen years into their careers. Moreover, the further a minister moves along in his or her career,
the more factors other than seminary education begin to impinge on
potential effectiveness. Beyond the crucial early years, other influences on
the minister's job performance probably loom larger than the quality of
theological education.

At the same time we assume that the professional life of ministers is
developmental.[3] Thus the competencies to begin ministry in an ordained
capacity are not different in kind from those expectations one has of clergy
with ten years' experience. One expects a higher degree of competence at
given periods; the definition of the competency remains essentially the
same.[4]

As a result, the expectations of beginning clergy as provided by the
clergy and laity of forty-seven denominations across North America provide a significant insight into understanding their general concept of ministry.

NOTES

1. James E. Dittes creatively develops this idea in *The Church in the Way* (New York: Scribner's, 1967).

2. Henri J. M. Nouwen, *The Wounded Healer: Ministry in Contemporary Society* (New York: Doubleday, 1972).

3. The strategy of the Project was based on the following major assumptions.

First, the professional life of ministers is developmental. Readiness to begin the practice of ministry differs in degree from the competency to be expected of experienced ministers. The project focuses primarily on an identification of criteria and the development of ways of assessing readiness to begin the practice of ministry.

Second, it is not the prerogative of the research team to define ministry for any religious group, yet some delimitation of what constitutes ministry for this project is necessary at the outset. Therefore, carefully executed procedures are needed by which the people of God can express their various understandings of ministry by the criteria that they describe and rank in importance. The meaning they bring to ministry must determine the criteria for readiness for ministry.

Third, criteria for assessing readiness can be identified empirically. People in seminaries and denominations do use criteria, whether consciously or inadvertently, consistently or haphazardly, in making private and public judgments regarding the readiness of seminary graduates and new clergy to enter the ministry. Procedures must allow for identification of these criteria from descriptive evidence freely provided by the various evaluator groups.

Fourth, criteria to be identified are the criteria actually being used in present formal and informal assessments by the people of God. This is the case even though the criteria actually being used by any individual or group may or may not coincide with historic confessions or other credal statements, if any, of the respective denominations.

Fifth, the full range of theological and denominational thought will be represented in random samples of evaluators across all denominations. Random sampling may have selected only one seminary to represent several seminaries of a denomination. Nevertheless, the many persons from the several groups of evaluators chosen through those seminaries and their graduates can be assumed to be representative of the full range of theological and denominational thought.

Sixth, views of readiness will vary somewhat systematically on the basis of certain variables. People can be expected to view readiness differently depending on such factors as the denomination, evaluator group, particular setting for ministry, the sex of the minister, and the race of the minister in relation to that of the community of faith he or she is attempting to serve. Therefore, criteria for readiness cannot be ranked well in isolation from these factors.

Seventh, types and families of criteria can be identified. The number of criteria is not infinite. There are limits to each universe of criteria and objective ways of discovering those limits. Nevertheless, the numbers of criteria in use are very large. But they are interrelated to such a degree that by use of sophisticated statistical procedures types of criteria and families can be identified empirically.

Eighth, all criteria will not be common to all denominations. Identification of the lowest common denominator of criteria among denominations will not suffice. Likewise, all criteria will neither be recognized nor used by all denominations or all evaluator groups.

Ninth, relative importance of criteria will have to be identified by user populations. It is also not within the prerogatives of the research team to evaluate the relative importance, relevance, or appropriateness of criteria of readiness for ministry. Rather, the research team must develop and execute effective procedures for enabling and assisting the many evaluator groups to make those judgments.

Tenth, within each denomination, the relative number of each type of evaluator will partially determine the hierarchy of criteria identified. Criteria judged most important by one evaluator group (for example, laypeople) may not be judged most important by another (for example, seminary faculty). Therefore, the relative size of each evaluator group will determine in part the overall rank ordering of criteria for each denomination and all combined.

Because there are no natural, objective guidelines for setting those proportions, they must be set arbitrarily. As a general rule, laypeople (non-ordained members of the religious group) and professionals (the combination of faculty, seniors, denominational officials, and other clergy) will be equally represented (50-50).

4. It was clear in our early investigation that people do not have a *different* set of expectations for the young minister. They seem to conceive of a threshold: a person is expected to possess a minimal package of theological understandings and skills. Beyond this, laity demonstrate a tolerance for certain deficiencies in young ministers, in the belief that he or she is still maturing professionally.

In terms of the study's design, the first continent-wide questionnaire was sent to a sample of alumni of seminaries (and to the laity served by them), regardless of age or length of service. The second-round questionnaire was sent to a similar sample, with the exception that laity surveyed were restricted to those in congregations served by clergy who had begun their work in ministry during the last several years. The report received from respondents to both questionnaires indicated that they responded in terms of ministry in general over against a restricted response regarding the ministerial expectation of a young minister. Thus while our expectation was to focus on readiness to begin the practice of ministry, reports from clergy and laity indicated they were primarily providing information about ministry in general.

2

Identifying
the Criteria
for Ministry

David S. Schuller

Our task was to develop criteria for contemporary ministry that were specific and concrete enough to be used as a basis for assessing readiness to begin service in an ordained capacity. We needed to aid laity and clergy alike in elaborating on gross generalizations that had served adequately in a simpler past. We sought to move beyond the view that what the average church was looking for in its minister was simply a "man of God" who could "preach well" and was "interested in serving people."

In designing the project, we saw the need for developing a clear picture of what contemporary ministry entails while avoiding what theologians and ministers fear, namely, a market analysis where the implied question crudely phrased is "What kind of minister do people want to purchase these days? What does the most popular model look like?" We share the concern of many that we not lose sight of the biblical affirmations that the ministry is a gift God gives his church, that a minister called by God receives his directions from a source other than popular demand. We were concerned lest a church be built on norms derived from constituent votes. The word *prophetic* best says what our critics fear may be lost. They ask, "How can we expect to educate men and women who will serve as prophets to their generation—in the train of prophets, apostles, and martyrs—if their theological education and ministry is shaped on the basis of popular expectations and demands?"

We have proceeded, then, recognizing the values both of understanding the ministry as a gift of God and also as a human profession. On the one side, there is a transcendent quality that exists beyond any given culture. Christian ministry exists prior to any individual currently filling the office. It is rooted in God's intention and call. In tension with this exists the human dimension, a community forming and shaping the ministry in light of its culture. The call of God must be authenticated within the Christian community. Ministry is in danger when it is cut loose from the understanding of either its transcendent or its cultural dimensions. Most churches have tried to incorporate the insights of Ephesians 4. God gives gifts of ministry . . . to the community . . . for its upbuilding. Therefore the minister is never only the hired functionary of the local church, carrying out the wishes of the group. He or she proclaims an empowering Word anchored in the events related to the life, death, and resurrection of Jesus Christ.

From the beginning of the project's design, the research team has been sensitive to this danger of reducing ministry to its human dimension, of highlighting sociological and psychological issues while slighting the more elusive theological dimensions. Therefore, while deliberately pressing to describe the work of the ministry as concretely and specifically as possible, we eagerly invited biblical, theological, and historical input to assure the description of contemporary ministries that would stand the test of theological critique. It was for this reason that theological professors (biblical, historical, and so on) were involved in developing the pool of items that were used to form the survey questionnaire. They were also included as one sector of the professional group of ministers surveyed.

We used procedures that would enable us to hear the whole "people of God" as represented in the churches of North America. We sought to provide concrete building blocks in the form of specific questionnaire items that were sufficiently varied that everyone could fashion his or her model of ministry. The primary purpose underlying the revision and addition of items, which resulted in a second questionnaire, was to expand the range of items so that a broader spectrum of people might more accurately describe what they feel is necessary for one to serve in a full-time pastoral ministry.

The research team initially feared that a grouping of criteria items might yield only the desire for a "nice guy" to serve as a minister. However, a reading of the core dimensions (see Chapter 5) quickly makes clear that this did not happen. Ministers and laity alike tend to build certain biblical and theological insights into the great variety of dimensions used to evaluate the contemporary minister. While many do not use classical theological concepts in portraying their expectations of a minister, the items forming core criteria are not without the transcendental dimension. The study does not propose a new gospel of empiricism that seeks to make popular opinion normative for the church. Rather, it seeks to present a clear picture of where people are in their understanding of ministry and to use their expectations as preliminary criteria.

But how valid are these findings for the future? Those who most strongly sense the need for developing a new concept of ministry, one that prepares men and women for an emerging future, are restive about too much concern with models of ministry that they feel are already relatively useless or moribund. The researchers made a conscious choice at the inception of the program not to build an assessment for beginning ministry on the basis of futuristic literature. While remaining appreciative of its function, we found it too speculative and diffuse to serve as a foundation for judgments regarding professional practice in a given profession. Dialogue should continue with those making projections regarding the future shape of ministry in order to raise implications it contains for contemporary ministry and theological education.

In this project, our goal was to probe the realities of ministry as they currently exist and not to subtly impose our values, for example, regarding models of ministry. Some have questioned the important position we seem to ascribe to denominations. We do not intend to champion denominational influence nor to agree it is a vestige of an earlier historical period. We are seeking to determine how laity and clergy alike respond as to the benefits and disadvantages of denominational structures on those engaged in ministry. Similarly, the heavier accent in the questionnaire on congregational or parochial ministry reflects the fact that the predominance of ministry taking place today is still found within the local church in the community setting.

IDENTIFYING RANGE OF CRITERIA

The first stage of the project was to identify what people see, hear, and sense that causes them to feel a given act of ministry has been effective or ineffective. For many people, these criteria remain hidden in the back of their brains, often held more subconsciously than self-consciously. This is true for church leaders as well as laity. It came as a repeated shock to find how many leaders in church bodies when examining a person for ordination lacked articulated criteria, relying instead on intuition and a "general feeling" about the person and his or her abilities.

We, therefore, sought to use procedures that would help bring these subconsciously held criteria into verbal forms. One of our most helpful means was the use of "critical incidents." We asked people across the spectrum of church life to recall a specific moment when an ordained clergy ministering to them was either highly effective or clearly ineffective. Over 1,200 people responded to this request, providing the details of what they recalled and giving the reasons why they judged the minister's actions as effective or ineffective. By analyzing these written accounts, we were able to identify where people tend to see ministry taking place and what serves as the basis for their judgments regarding effectiveness. These became a major source of questionnaire items.

In order to assure a complete systematic understanding of ministry in the 1970s, we read and classified thousands of criterion statements. Many of these came from a search of literature that surveyed both ministry and practice in the related helping professions.[1] These obviously covered a broad spectrum as to degree of specificity, sensitivity to theological concerns, and breadth of view regarding "ministry."

Following the initial screening processes,[2] we developed a pretest questionnaire that was composed of some 850 specific items. This pretest was completed by over 2,000 people randomly selected from among all forty-seven denominations of religious bodies represented in the Association of Theological Schools (ATS). Our sampling procedures sought a balance in which half the respondents were from the clergy and half from the laity. The clergy category consisted of four groups: seminary professors, clergy active in the field, denominational leaders, and senior seminary students. Weighting procedures were used that enabled each person—layperson or clergy, from a large or very small denomination—to have equal voice in describing his or her conception of ministry. Because of concern with the special issues of ministry related to minority groups and women, disproportionately large numbers of such groups were invited to participate (for example, Hispanic-American clergy and laity, women clergy, and black clergy).

We asked each person to evaluate the degree of importance each of the 850 items holds for the specific situation in which they were experiencing ministry; for example, a small rural church setting, a chaplaincy in a large general hospital, a ministry in an inner-city congregation. People were further requested to evaluate the completeness of the criteria and make specific suggestions of additional criteria germane to their ministerial context or denomination. Our working classification design was then redesigned in order to reflect the suggestions, which numbered in the thousands. In summary, the written comments of 2,000 people responding in the pretest provided answers as to the classification design's completeness, balance, and theological adequacy. Furthermore, analyses of the pretest data answered major procedural questions as to whether or not meaningful clusters of individual items would form.

During the spring of 1974, a revised questionnaire of 444 items was completed. We attempted to make the items specific and behavioral—actions that could be seen and heard—and yet phrased on the level that people normally use in making judgments about ministers. The actual level of specificity varied as can be seen in these items selected at random:

- When teaching, is able to keep his or her students interested
- Speaks from the pulpit about political issues
- Has thought through a counseling approach that is consistent with own theology
- Prays with laity in small groups
- Often belittles a person in front of others

This second questionnaire contained the most useful items from the earlier instrument augmented by many of the additions suggested by respondents. Using this revised questionnaire, 5,169 randomly selected persons participated in a second continent-wide survey in 1974 from which 4,995 usable answer sheets were secured. The professional respondents included 444 professors in theological schools, 441 senior seminary students, 1,917 seminary graduates who were in active ministry, and 322 denominational officials responsible for some phase of ministry, usually at a district level. The lay respondents consisted of 1,871 randomly selected persons, members of congregations of the forty-seven denominations.

While it was useful to discover how people evaluated each of the 444 items in terms of importance for their ministerial situations, it was more important to determine whether or not these items formed larger patterns. The pressing question was this: "Are there larger configurations or constructs present in people's minds when they respond to items describing particular skills, faith commitments, theological understandings, and certain personality characteristics?"

To answer this question, two independent mathematical models were used: cluster and factor analysis. In organizing the results of the individual responses, we sought methods that would avoid presenting data on the basis of preconceived categories. While we built an initial structure in order to organize the hundreds of individual items, our concern was to discover what natural organizing principles were in the minds of our respondents. We preferred to share the data on the basis of the way clergy and laity naturally conceive of ministry. Our two methods operate on the basis of the consistency of response of people to particular sets of ideas. Suppose individuals are asked to respond to their degree of liking or disliking a whole series of sports that include baseball, sailing, swimming, mountain climbing, bowling, canoeing, racquet ball, jogging, water skiing, and tennis. People probably respond in a similar way to sailing, swimming, canoeing, and water skiing. Some may express a great liking for the set; others only medium enjoyment; and yet others, a genuine dislike. But there would probably be some consistency of response because they are all water sports. (Perhaps a subgroup would revolve about those involving a boat in contrast to those involving immersion in the water.)

In cluster analysis (homogeneous keying), the computer is able to determine such patterns of response. Thus it selects three items, from perhaps several hundred, on which there is consistency of response on the part of people without consideration as to the content of the items. (They tend to respond to all three items in the same way.) The computer then selects other items to add to the group as long as each addition adds to the reliability of the set. This process continues until no more items will increase the reliability. Thus clusters will vary considerably in length from two or three items to several dozen. We used two separate methods as an additional safeguard, to assure that we were accurately reflecting the underlying dimensions or concepts that people had in their minds.

Through the use of these two sensitive methods, we were able to ascertain how people think about ministry in their own particular contexts. Clusters of items develop, then, when people respond to them in a similar fashion. Some, for example, may have felt that all items of a certain type were very important for ministry in their context; others may have responded in a uniformly lukewarm fashion to the same items. Whenever people responded in a consistent fashion to a similar set of items, their patterns of response formed a cluster.

When the responses of the total group of respondents were cluster and factor analyzed, approximately fifty clusters were identified. The same procedure was used a second time, utilizing only the responses of the laity, and a third time for the responses of professionals (clergy and seminarians). The result was a total of approximately 150 clusters from the three groups, namely, from the total group, the laity, and the clergy.

We then had to determine the extent to which clusters from laity and professionals were similar clusters—portraying similar underlying dimensions—and which were unique. In analyzing the 150 clusters for uniqueness, the research team used four guidelines: (1) Use total group clusters wherever lay and clergy clusters were so similar that essentially the same cluster was formed from a total group analysis; (2) From similar clusters, select those that are richest in detail; (3) Select clusters most unidimensional, those that appear to revolve around a single dimension; and (4) Choose clusters that are meaningful, that portray a desirable characteristic of ministry.

Of the 150 clusters made available to the research staff, 64 clusters were distinguished as identifiably separate ones that could be called *core clusters*. We found that each of these clusters had an underlying dimension that represents a criterion commonly used by people across all forty-seven denominations when making judgments about ministers. These 64 criteria represent a level of generalization above the description of individual items.

The processes used to identify clusters also yielded a measure of their perceived importance. By averaging the scores of all items in a cluster, we determined the importance of each dimension to the thousands of people surveyed. This ranking of each of the sixty-four clusters gives us an estimate of what is generally seen as absolutely essential down to what is viewed as detrimental or disqualifying for a priest or minister. The sixty-four clusters and the specific items that comprise them are discussed in Chapter 5.

To review, we systematically moved from the level of 1,200 descriptions of ministry to 850 items to 444 items that our study found formed the best descriptions. Ultimately these formed sixty-four clusters of criteria that describe dimensions of ministry. We still needed to know whether these sixty-four criteria or dimensions formed a pattern in people's thinking. To answer this question, we proceeded to a second level of analysis using the same procedures noted earlier. We analyzed the cluster criteria, permitting the data to organize themselves into families of clusters. From this final level of analysis, eleven major themes or areas of ministry emerged that provide an understanding of how criteria relate to one another. These eleven areas of ministry are analyzed in Chapter 3. Figure 2-1 provides an overview of the steps described here.

What are the most significant characteristics that people across denomi-

FIGURE 2-1
**Sequence of Steps from General Descriptions
of Ministry Through Organization by Factors**

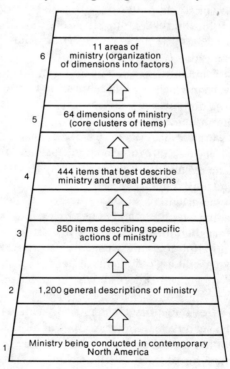

6   11 areas of ministry (organization of dimensions into factors)

5   64 dimensions of ministry (core clusters of items)

4   444 items that best describe ministry and reveal patterns

3   850 items describing specific actions of ministry

2   1,200 general descriptions of ministry

1   Ministry being conducted in contemporary North America

national lines are looking for in their young priests or ministers? Ranking at the top is a construct or dimension whose items point to the label "service without regard for acclaim." This cluster of items describes an individual who is able to accept his or her personal limitations, and who, believing the gospel, is able to serve without concern for public recognition. This is reinforced by the second highest factor, namely, that of personal integrity; this describes one who is able to honor his or her commitments by carrying out promises despite all pressures to compromise. Ranking third is a factor that has to do with Christian example. The cluster describes one whose personal belief in the gospel manifests itself in generosity, and in general, a Christian example that people in the community can respect. The total group of clergy and laity allot fourth place to the characteristic of acknowledging limitations and mistakes, and recognizing the need for continued growth and learning. Ranking fifth is a cluster that has to do with the minister as a leader in community building. The items in this cluster focus on actions that will build a strong sense of community within a congregation. It includes taking time to know parishioners well and developing a sense of trust and confidence between him- or herself and the members of the parish.

If you reflect on these top five criteria, you will notice that four lie within the area of the clergy's personal commitment and faith and center in the minister or priest as a person. The last of the group describes a particular leadership skill. When we examine the clusters that rank sixth through tenth, we see other major ministerial roles. The sixth cluster describes the responsible functioning of one who shows competence and responsibility by completing tasks, by being able to handle differences of opinion, and by recognizing the need to continue to grow in pastoral skills. The seventh ranked dimension describes the minister as a perceptive counselor, as one who reaches out to people under stress with a perception, sensitivity, and warmth that is freeing and supportive. This is followed by a cluster that focuses on the minister as a person who manifests a positive approach, remaining calm under pressure while continuing to affirm people. The ninth ranking criterion focuses on a theocentric biblical ministry, a drawing attention to God's Word and Person in preaching, teaching, and leading worship. The final cluster amplifies a note previously sounded by focusing on the minister who enables counseling.

Going to the opposite end of the list of characteristics or dimensions, what constructs rank lowest? Which criteria draw the most severe judgment from both clergy and laity?

Significantly the three lowest in rank do not deal with a lack of any particular skill but rather focus on the minister as a person. The minister who would be characterized by these criteria was ranked lowest by the respondents. The harshest criticism centers on what people describe as undisciplined living, a construct centered on being involved in illicit sexual relationships and other self-indulgent actions that irritate, shock, or offend. The second most serious negative[3] describes a self-serving ministry, a minister who avoids intimacy and repels people with a critical, demeaning, and insensitive attitude. This is a large cluster. It includes items that describe such actions as belittling a person in front of others, using one's ministerial role to maintain a sense of superiority, and being quick to condemn people whose words or actions are seen as questionable. The third most serious set of problems cluster around expressions of professional immaturity and actions that demonstrate immaturity, insecurity, and insensitivity when buffeted by the demands and pressures of the profession.

All of the analyses to this point deal with the data gathered from respondents in all forty-seven denominations. Although some observers question the viability of denominations in today's church, most persons respond to the ministry of a particular church body. Thus, a young person is unlikely to plan simply to become a priest or minister of the holy Christian church as it manifests itself in the Eastern or Western tradition. Instead one intends to be ordained as a Roman Catholic priest, a United Methodist minister, or a Lutheran pastor. Our final analyses then addressed the question of the models of ministry operative within specific denominational families. In these analyses, the responses of laity and professionals were examined separately for each family of denominations. The details of these procedures are provided in Chapter 4.

No issue has been raised more frequently during this study than the question of what the characteristics or criteria represent. How normative are they? Is the entire endeavor detrimental to a biblical view of ministry in its use of procedures that seem to resemble market analysis? Are we denying the possibility of a truly prophetic ministry by asking people what they want in a minister? From the beginning, we insisted that the project not suggest that popular opinion should become normative for the church. The data are descriptive—they present a clear picture of people's understanding of ministry. When we arrive at this point in our thinking, it becomes clear that our categories of "normative" as opposed to "descriptive" are inadequate. We assiduously want to avoid any ultimate definition of ministry that arises from popular expectation that may uncritically reflect a sensate culture. People may look for a ministry that supports the economic and social status quo, that pronounces a benediction on their prejudices and assures them that affluence is a sign of God's blessing. Our materials and procedures cannot provide a norm for ministry that demands its source in God and its definitions arising from the Scriptures and its critical shaping by the community of faith. To the extent that the items and clusters of the project reflect such understandings of ministry, they become more than simple description. But that judgment about the value of what is being described must be made by churches, seminaries, and other groups that weigh the descriptions against their biblical, theological norm.

For example, our data show that for better or worse a larger number of people see ministry to the individual facing personal stress as more important than ministry extended to the general community outside the church. Each church body must make a normative judgment about this descriptive fact. For those who see a need to express a word of judgment and grace to the social structures as well as to individuals, a challenge of high proportions still exists within the churches, according to our findings.

In the Readiness for Ministry Project, our goal has been to probe the realities of ministry as they currently exist. We have used procedures that have minimized the influence of the research team, seeking instead means for enabling individuals to portray the models of ministry they hold in their own lives.

After we secured the basic data for each of the seventeen families of denominations, we selected a person from each church body who was theologically aware of the unique dimensions of ministry alive in his or her tradition. We asked these authors honestly to portray the profiles of ministry that emerged from the responses of the clergy and laity of that group, but then to enter into active dialogue with the data. These authors are varied in their experience in handling empirical data; they differ in the reliance they are ready to place on the procedures of the behavioral sciences that generated the data. While trying to organize the materials in a readable form, we also seek to make clear what the data are and how the authors analyze and respond to their materials.

We have found sharp portraits of church bodies emerging from these materials. Some long-held impressions are verified. Some stereotypes are challenged. Overall, one gains a sense of the struggles of the ministry in the last third of this century, yet also of its vitality.

GLOSSARY OF TERMS

Cluster analysis. A mathematical method for detecting patterns of consistency among responses to items in the questionnaire. One of two methods used to organize the data of this study into characteristics or dimensions.

Dimensions (or *criteria, characteristics, core clusters*). One of sixty-four descriptions of facets of ministry composed of items from the questionnaire. Items were organized into dimensions by statistical methods.

Factor. A group of dimensions that describe a major area of ministry. Statistical analyses grouped the sixty-four dimensions into eleven major factor areas.

Factor analysis. One of two mathematical methods utilized by the research team that enable responses of participants to organize into patterns (or "clusters") from an empirical base. Only clusters generated by both factor and cluster analysis were retained for consideration.

Family of denominations.   One of the seventeen groupings into which the forty-seven denominations in the study were arranged. These groupings were determined partially by consideration of history and significance, partially by empirically demonstrated similarity. A complete list of denominations within each family is given in Chapter 4.

Item.   One of the 444 statements about ministry in the questionnaire evaluated by 4,995 persons. Items were then empirically grouped into dimensions on the basis of response patterns.

Laity.   Persons in this study who were not ordained clergy or who were not members of one of the four subgroups included in "professionals."

Professionals   (also *clergy*). Persons in this study belonging to one of the following four groups: professors in theological schools or seminaries; senior seminary students; seminary graduates in active ministry (for three or fewer years); and denominational officials responsible for some phase (usually judicatory) of ministry.

Rating.   The evaluation people gave each item:

	From	To
Highly important, essential or mandatory	+2.51	+3.00
Quite important, a major asset	+1.51	+2.50
Somewhat important, a minor asset	+0.51	+1.50
Neither important nor unimportant	−0.50	+.050
Somewhat detrimental, a minor hindrance in ministry	−1.50	−0.51
Quite detrimental, a major hindrance in ministry	−2.50	−1.51
Highly detrimental, harmful, could destroy the effectiveness of ministry	−3.00	−2.51

NOTES

1. Robert J. Menges was requested to conduct a major portion of the literature review. See his *Assessing Readiness for Professional Practice,* Occasional Paper of the Center for the Teaching Professions (Evanston, Ill.: Northwestern University, 1973).

2. In this chapter, a brief overview of our method is provided to enable the reader to understand and assess the materials presented. For a more detailed description of method, see Chapter 19.

3. Because of the large number of non-Catholic respondents who scored the items in "Priestly Commitments" (CC 41) as not applying to their denomination, Core Cluster 41 technically ranks second lowest for the total group. Roman Catholic respondents, however, valued this in the second highest category, with a 1.68.

3

Eleven Major
Areas of Ministry

Daniel O. Aleshire

What is the function of the minister in the modern community? The answer is that it is undefined. There is no agreement among denominational authorities, local officials, seminaries, professors, prominent laymen, ministers or educators as to what it should be.

—Mark May, *The Education of American Ministers* (1934)

Some things change. Many who look at May's statement today will by conviction change "laymen" to "laypeople." Many will respond to "modern community" with connotations of declining inner city and burgeoning suburb, while May likely thought of residential central cities. Many will think of "minister" in less male terms and, likely, less "mainline Protestant only" terms than May might have.

Some things persist. Forty-five years have not brought an agreed-on definition of ministry. "What is the function of the minister in the modern community?" is still an earnest question. That ministry is a treasure

Daniel O. Aleshire was, at the time of this writing, a research scientist with Search Institute and a member of the Readiness for Ministry Project team. He is now on the faculty of the Southern Baptist Theological Seminary, Louisville, Kentucky.

in earthen vessels is agreed on. But just what the treasure is, and how the vessel should be formed and adorned, are still contested issues.

Some things are new. May's question was raised at a time when "professional" was a term seldom associated with ministry. But this term, and the areas of technical competence it reflects, have found a home in current concepts of ministry. With its coming, a new question is murmured. Henri Nouwen comments on "The question that is brought to ministers' minds with an increasing urgency is 'What is there beyond professionalism—is ministry just another specialty in the many helping professions?' "[1] Is there something in the treasure in the vessel that transcends the function and form of other treasures?

The Readiness for Ministry Project's investigation of the concepts of ministry addressed both the persisting question, "What are the functions?" and the emerging question, "What of ministry transcends the functions?" Furthermore, the people who provided the data are precisely those who May hoped might one day express some mutual agreement: denominational officials, local officials, seminary professors, laypeople, and ministers.

MAJOR THEMES IN MINISTRY EXPECTATIONS

This chapter explores the fabric and hue of ministry expectations emerging from the broadest level of analysis of the Readiness for Ministry data. Broad themes were formed by grouping core clusters (empirically derived sets of survey items) through the use of a factor analytic process.[2] This approach allowed all of the approximately 5,000 people who responded to the questionnaire to participate in the definition of themes. A factor was formed for each separate theme running through the core clusters. Thus each factor's reason for existence is that it describes a theme that no other factor describes. Each factor is calculated so that the theme it identifies is as distinctive as possible from the other themes. The sixty-four core clusters factored into eleven major themes. Table 3-1 summarizes the eleven themes.

This chapter also traces the similarities and differences found among the participants' perceptions of ministry. The agreements and disagreements are determined by comparing ratings of importance given by various subgroups. Table 3-2 contains a list of the variables that were used to identify subgroups from which systematic patterns of variation might be traced.

The chapter describes the eleven ministry themes in terms of the ratings of importance given them. The first part deals with the factors that receive the highest ratings of importance; the second part, those in the mid-range of the rating possibilities; and the third part with the two factors rated as undesirable or detrimental to ministry.

TABLE 3-1
Eleven Major Themes in the Readiness for Ministry Data

**I. The following themes are rated, across the entire sample, as "quite important"
(that is, receiving a rating between 2.49 and 1.50 on a scale from +3.0 to −3.0).**

Theme Title and Description	*Average Rating*	*Rank*
Open, Affirming Style (Factor 4) A style of ministry that reflects a minister who is positive, open, flexible; who behaves responsibly to persons as well as to tasks.	2.18	1
Caring for Persons under Stress (Factor 9) Psychologically informed counseling skills that are made readily available to people experiencing stress and delivered with minister's own empathetic involvement.	1.98	2
Congregational Leadership (Factor 8) An administrative style that implies shared leadership, that builds persons into a cooperative community, that is efficient, and that properly utilizes conflict.	1.97	3
Theologian in Life and Thought (Factor 10) Broad general knowledge and theological understanding built on careful thought and reflection; and conscious examination of minister's own life.	1.88	4
Ministry from Personal Commitment of Faith (Factor 2) An approach to ministry that reflects a deep personal faith commitment, is centered in strong biblical affirmation, and emphasizes evangelistic and mission goals.	1.82	5
Development of Fellowship and Worship (Factor 5) The ability to promote a sense of mutuality in the entire worshiping community, to preach with competence and sensitivity, and to lead worship in esthetically sensitive ways.	1.79	6
Denominational Awareness and Collegiality (Factor 11) Basic knowledge and prudent appreciation of collegial openness in relation to one's denominational identification.	1.65	7

TABLE 3-1 — *CONTINUED*

II. The following themes are rated, across the entire sample, as "somewhat important" (that is, receiving an average rating between 1.49 and 0.00 on a scale from +3.0 to −3.0).

Theme Title and Description	Average Rating	Rank
Ministry to Community and World (Factor 1) An active concern for oppressed people and social issues evidenced by aggressive political leadership, promotion of understanding of issues, and championship of unpopular causes.	1.32	8
Priestly-Sacramental Ministry (Factor 7) A ministry reflecting priestly commitments and stressing the sacramental and liturgical aspects of the faith and the celibacy of the priest.	0.24	9

III. The following themes are rated, across the entire sample, as "undesirable" or "detrimental." ("Undesirable" is the meaning of a rating between −1.50 and −0.51, and "detrimental" is the meaning of ratings between −2.50 and −1.51, on the scale from +3.0 to −3.0).

Theme Title and Description	Average Rating	Rank
Privatistic , Legalistic Style (Factor 6) A style of ministry that precludes involvement in community programs or politics; reflects a legalistic orientation to ethical issues, and dominates decision-making processes.	−1.25	10
Disqualifying Personal and Behavioral Characteristics (Factor 3) A self-serving ministry characterized by undisciplined living, irresponsibility, professional immaturity, and pursuit of personal advantage.	−1.80	11

UNDERSTANDING TWO DIMENSIONS

Complex data such as the Readiness for Ministry data contain a variety of dimensions. This chapter, however, will discuss the findings with reference to only two of these dimensions.

TABLE 3-2
Summary of Variables Used to Identify Patterns of Variation in Responses to the Readiness for Ministry Survey Questionnaire

Variable	*Categories Within the Variable*
Denominational family	Participants were assigned to one of seventeen denominational families depending on their denominational affiliation
Frequency of attendance at worship or mass	Daily; more than once a week; about once a week; two or three times a month; less than once a month
Evaluator group	Seminary professor or administrator; lay member of congregation; parish pastor; denominational official; seminary student
Laity and Professional (clergy)	This variable redefined the "Evaluator group" into two categories: lay people and clergy. Clergy includes all groups listed for "Evaluator group" except lay members
Size of parish attended	Less than 50; 50–199; 200–499; 500–999; 1000–2499; 2500–4999; 5000–9999; 10,000 and over
Occupation	Clerical; craft or blue-collar; laborer; operative (for example, delivery agent); private household worker; professional; manager-owner; sales worker; service worker; semiprofessional; farmer
Education	Eighth grade or less; some high school/trade school; high school/trade school graduate; some college; college graduate; some graduate or professional school; seminary graduate; master's; graduate beyond master's; doctorate
Ministry context	Twelve ministry contexts were identified as the settings in which recent seminary graduates usually serve. Respondents were asked to identify the ministry context they were thinking of as they responded to the questionnaire: Grass-roots General Practice; Homogeneous, Urban-Suburban; Ethnic Congregation; Transitional Community; Inner-City Struggle;

TABLE 3–2 — *CONTINUED*

Variable	Categories Within the Variable
	Subsidized Mission; Prospering Urban-Suburban Congregation; Educational or Youth Ministry in a Parish; Educational Ministry—Academic; Ministry in and to the Community; Therapeutic Ministry in an Institution; Evangelism; and Other
Income	Thirteen categories beginning with "Under $3,000" and ending with "$40,000 or more"
Sex	Respondents identified themselves as either male or female
Age	Respondents identified their current age
Size of community	Respondents characterized the community in which they resided by size categories ranging from "Open country" to "1,000,000 or over"
Region	Respondents indicated their location in one of five Canadian regions or eight U.S. regions

Note: This list shows the variables in rank order of the average amount of variance they account for in analyses across the eleven second-order factors. Several other variables were also evaluated, but their average contribution was so small (less than one-half of 1 percent of the variance) that they are not included above. These variables are race; whether or not the rater was a relative of a minister; and, if Roman Catholic, whether order or diocesan ministry setting. Full discussion of variables is included in Chapter 19.

The first has already been mentioned and shown in Table 3-1; namely, the rating of importance. Each person responded to the items in the Readiness for Ministry questionnaire by indicating how highly he or she values the activity or behavior described by a particular item; for example, "highly important," "quite important," and so on through various levels to "detrimental." These rating categories were assigned places on a ± 3.00 scale:

	From	To
Highly important, essential or mandatory	+2.51	+3.00
Quite important, a major asset	+1.51	+2.50
Somewhat important, a minor asset	+0.51	+1.50
Neither important nor unimportant	−0.50	+0.50
Somewhat detrimental, a minor hindrance in ministry	−1.50	−0.51
Quite detrimental, a major hindrance in ministry	−2.50	−1.51
Highly detrimental, harmful, could destroy the effectiveness of ministry	−3.00	−2.51

The numbers can be averaged together to form a score for the item based on all participants' responses. The resulting score can be related back to logical response categories. For example, an average rating of $+1.93$ means that the item is seen as "quite important" (the response category for $+2.0$ on the scale) among the 5,000 participants. The rating of importance always has a direct link to the logical categories that people have used to evaluate the items.

The second dimension is less obvious than the rating of importance and has no direct tie to the response categories. This dimension deals with the centrality of a core cluster to the factor in which it has been grouped. In the tables showing the factors, the degree to which any one cluster is associated with the factor theme is indicated by how close to the top a cluster is listed. The first cluster shown in a factor is the most central to the theme of the factor. The last cluster shown is the least central— although it is still more closely related to the theme in which it appears than to any other. The clusters between the first and the last are more central than the last, but less central than the first. The dimension of centrality is important for the interpretation of factor themes. Since clusters close to the top are more crucial to the meaning of the theme, they should have greater influence in interpretation. (Note: the position of clusters in a factor is empirically determined by their factor loading. See Chapter 19 for a description of the factor analytic procedure that supplies this information.)

AREAS OF MINISTRY PERCEIVED AS MOST IMPORTANT

Which of the eleven themes portray the most valued aspects of ministry? Do they define functions—things the minister or priest should do? Or do they speak of character, faith, and personhood—things the minister or priest should be? This first section deals with the themes that receive, on the average, a rating of "quite important." This rating represents the second highest rating category provided by the questionnaire. However, since none of the eleven factors is rated in the highest category, the factors discussed in this section comprise the most highly rated themes. Seven of the eleven factors received the "quite important" rating, suggesting that no one dimension is viewed as singularly important. The 5,000 participants rate these themes with almost equal importance. (Only about half a point of difference exists between the average rating of the highest factor [$+2.18$] in this section and the lowest [$+1.65$].)

The factors clearly include dimensions of both function and character. Some emphasize personal and faith dimensions, while others define skills and competencies. Still others blend the two into inseparable units. Together, they present a perception of what is important in ministry that reflects both historical tradition and contemporary lifestyle; and that combines function and personhood into an embracing, holistic expression of ministry.

Open, Affirming Style (Factor 4)

"Above reproach," "sensible," "dignified," "temperate," "hospitable," "gentle," "not quarrelsome," "not a lover of money," and "well thought of by others"[3]—compare these terms with characteristics such as "Positive approach," "responsible functioning," "flexibility of spirit," "personal integrity," and "acceptance of clergy role." The first series was compiled by the writer of I Timothy to identify the premiere personal qualities for one who would undertake the role of pastoral overseer (bishop). It conveys ancient insight to the task of ministry and, perhaps, a sense of some very fundamental human dimensions. The second list, compiled by the 5,000 people who responded to the Readiness for Ministry questionnaire, is not unlike the first. The terms of the second are more complex, less straightforward; but the similarity of meaning is striking. The clusters whose names are included in Table 3-3 form the highest rated of the eleven themes, a factor that has been entitled "Open, Affirming Style."

The theme that attracts this top rating is only partially communicated by the title given it. It is a dimension of ministry that is more than a "style," more than "openness," more than "affirming," and even more than the impact of the three yoked together. This theme weaves into a common fabric ideas about the function of ministry and the qualities of style and approach that transcend the function. It is a theme of ministry in which the priest or minister not only "works at further development of pastoral skills" but also "helps others see the best in people" and "shows a good mixture of seriousness and joy." It includes both an approach to ministry functions in which a minister "does not avoid tasks of ministry he or she does not enjoy" and an approach to life in which he or she maintains "personal integrity despite pressures to compromise." This theme portrays style in the foreground and function in the background. The factor's high rating indicates that, while the expectation of ministry or priesthood in North America includes competence in functions, it is also highly sensitive to the character and spirit of the person who carries out these functions.

The theme is not only the highest rated of the eleven but it also collects the most unanimous agreement. Males and females, laity and professionals, Protestants and Catholics, old and young—all tended to rate the items that comprise the clusters in this factor in very much the same manner. The variations in ratings cannot be accounted for by systematic patterns in subgroup responses (only 2.2 percent of the variance can be accounted

TABLE 3-3
Factor 4: Open, Affirming Style

Core Cluster No.	Name and Description	Average Rating[a]
44	*Positive Approach* Handling stressful situations by remaining calm under pressure while continuing to affirm persons	2.25
43	*Fidelity to Tasks and Persons* Showing competence and responsibility by completing tasks, relating warmly to persons, handling differences of opinion, and growing in skills	2.29
42	*Personal Responsibility* Honoring commitments by carrying out promises despite pressures to compromise	2.43
45	*Flexibility of Spirit* Adaptability, balance, free sharing of views, and welcoming of new possibilities	2.11
47	*Acceptance of Clergy Role* Having made peace with personal ambitions and the ministerial profession, and avoiding use of the authority of the ministerial role to dominate arguments or gain personal advantage	1.88
36[b]	*Acknowledgment of Limitations* Acknowledging limitations and mistakes, and recognizing the need for continued growth and learning	2.35
46[c]	*Valuing Diversity* Strong enough acceptance and valuation of diversity in people and ideas to face the risks involved in changes	1.97
	Factor average	2.18

[a]This is the average rating of the total group of respondents.

[b]This cluster is grouped with the first five in the analysis of the responses from laity only.

[c]This cluster is grouped with the first five in the analysis of the responses from clergy only.

for by variables such as sex, denominational family, age, and several others).[4] There is some tendency for clergy to rate the clusters higher than laity, and for persons thirty-five to sixty-five years old to rate clusters higher than do those either younger or older.[5] But the most compelling documentation regarding this factor is the high degree of consensus about its central importance.

The factor is both affirming and disconcerting. It is affirming in that a social science questionnaire of the twentieth century has unearthed a perception of ministry not unlike that in a biblical record of the first century. There is a sense in which this factor touches something deep—not just a "today-yes-tomorrow-no" public opinion. It is disconcerting in that it presents a theme that could be used as yet another pedestal on which clergy are to live their public lives. It is disconcerting, too, because much of the education process intended to prepare persons for ministry does not deal directly with concerns included in this factor: character, personhood, and style.

Whether affirming or disconcerting, or perhaps both, the factor stands as a significant statement about ministry made by one of the largest audiences ever consulted on the subject. By the agreed-on importance they expressed, the statement has been made pervasively.

Caring for Persons Under Stress (Factor 9)

Perhaps no other contemporary phenomenon has invaded the practice of ministry with the impact that pastoral care has acquired during the past three decades. Its contemporary significance is attested to by the high rating of importance given the "Caring for Persons under Stress" factor (see Table 3-4). This theme, which describes professional skills related to counseling, is rated virtually the same as Factor 8, "Congregational Leadership" (+1.98 for Factor 9 versus +1.97 for Factor 8).

Although the very high rating is based on the responses of both laity and clergy,[6] the structure of the clusters and the factor emerge from the clergy. Clergy apparently perceive these items and clusters as more cohesive units than do laity. The differences between some of the clusters in this theme are very subtle—reflecting issues probably salient to sophisticated ministerial professionals but not so evident to laity. Like the "Open, Affirming Style" theme, this factor attracts widespread agreement. When the responses of all clergy are analyzed to detect subgroups with varying opinions of the factor's importance, no interpretable group patterns emerge.[7] On clusters where there is a meaningful difference in clergy and laity ratings, clergy give the higher ratings.[8] Females rate some of the clusters higher than do males.

This theme defines both competence in counseling and empathetic involvement. "Perceptive Counseling," the highest loading cluster, deals with the ability to hear, understand, and appreciate a person's problems. "Enabling Counseling" outlines technical competencies that help people who are experiencing stress to perceive and deal with their problems. The

TABLE 3-4
Factor 9: Caring for Persons under Stress

Core Cluster No.	Name and Description	Average Rating
21	*Perceptive Counseling* Reaching out to persons under stress with a perception, sensitivity, and warmth that is freeing and supportive	2.26[a]
26	*Cominstry to the Alienated* With skill and understanding, reaching out through the congregation to the estranged, beleaguered, or isolated	1.50
23	*Caring Availability* Responding with deep care and sensitivity to hurting people in crisis situations	2.20
22	*Enabling Counseling* Using high levels of understanding and skill in aiding persons to work through serious problems	2.23
25	*Involvement in Caring* Becoming personally involved in the mutual exchange among persons who seek to learn through suffering	1.73
	Factor average	1.98

Note: This factor structure results from the analysis of responses from clergy only. No similar structures emerge from responses of laity alone.

[a]Although the factor structure is determined by clergy, the average ratings are based on the responses of both laity and clergy.

other clusters define skills necessary for helping the alienated and the hard to help. There is also a dimension describing availability to people in need. This factor makes as clearly stated an expression of professional skill as made by any of the eleven factors.

It is interesting to note that one core cluster that deals with counseling is conspicuously absent. Cluster 24, "Counseling as Pastor," is dominated by statements such as "helps people use the resources of faith in coping with personal problems" and "has thought through a counseling approach that is consistent with own theology." Even though the cluster deals with counseling, it grouped into Factor 2, "Ministry from Personal Commitment of Faith," rather than in this factor. The absence of this cluster underscores the more technical, psychological nature of Factor 9, "Caring for Persons under Stress."

Congregational Leadership (Factor 8)

"Congregational Leadership" is another factor, like "Caring for Persons under Stress," which is formed from the clergy perceptions of ministry. It identifies the leadership skills necessary to enable the members of the congregation or parish to be leaders and ministers. A major portion of this factor deals with sharing ministry and developing a community that nourishes and sustains that ministry. A cluster dealing with utilization of conflict also finds a home in this theme, as does a cluster that describes "Efficient Administration." Table 3-5 shows the clusters in this factor.

H. Richard Niebuhr advanced a thesis in the mid-1950s that the emerging role of the professional minister in North America was as "Pastoral Director." The architectural symbol of this emerging model is the pastor's

TABLE 3-5
Factor 8: Congregational Leadership

Core Cluster No.	Name and Description	Average Rating
57	*Sharing Congregational Leadership*　Active employment of lay leadership—regardless of sex—in establishing and executing an overall parish strategy	2.07
55	*Building Congregational Community*　Actions that will likely build a strong sense of community within a congregation	2.34
58	*Effective Administration*　Handling administrative responsibilities with understanding, efficiency, and careful planning	1.74
56	*Conflict Utilization*　Understanding conflict theologically and being able to utilize conflict as a means for airing differences and stressing concern and understanding	2.11
59	*Responsible Staff Management*　From a theological foundation, showing a sensitivity to staff feeling and needs by careful handling of staff policies and issues	1.58
	Factor Average	1.97

Note: The structure in this factor emerges from the responses of clergy only, but average ratings are based on responses of both laity and clergy.

office in the church building. From the office, the pastor "directs the activities of the church . . . studies and does some of his pastoral counseling." The work of the pastoral director is first "that of building and 'edifying' the church." To accomplish that task, Niebuhr asserts that a required skill is the ability to "administer the church as a church."[9]

The ministry skills and activity in this factor bear an uncanny resemblance to the description Niebuhr proposes for the pastoral director. If one combines this factor with the "Caring for Persons under Stress" factor, the likeness increases. These two factors are rated equally high (less than .01 point between their average ratings) and maintain a unique position as the skills considered most important for the contemporary practice of ministry.

Like the other factors discussed so far, this factor attracts great agreement among the raters. What disagreement there was, was relatively small and took the following forms. Clergy fifty-one years of age and older rate this factor highest. The lowest rating comes from the clergy under fifty-one years of age who are considering the ministry contexts of evangelism or therapeutic ministry in an institution. Generally, clusters are rated more highly by older respondents than by younger ones; and, where there is a significant difference, clergy rate those clusters as more important than do laity.

Theologian in Life and Thought (Factor 10)

Factor 10 encompasses elements of style and approach that are highly valued among the study's participants. It is similar to Factors 8 and 9 in that, once again, the structure emerges from the responses of clergy. The clusters in this factor are shown in Table 3-6.

One facet of this factor is the minister's reasonable acceptance of his or her humanity. The highest loading cluster conveys the importance of ministers acknowledging their own humanity and accepting counsel from others. There is a positive acceptance of human limitations in these clusters, but they do not imply license to excuse one's self from dealing with personal faults and correctable failures. This theme also identifies the importance of priests and ministers practicing their ministry without regard for acclaim. The concept is not, as the reader might first suspect, a masochistic "I've suffered so unnoticed." Rather, it is one where a minister laughs easily at him- or herself, serves others willingly, and recognizes emotional and physical limitations.

Respondents have greater differences of opinion on this factor than on the others discussed thus far. For example, clergy rate each cluster in this factor significantly higher than do laity. The ministry context that the respondent had in mind as he or she was rating the items also provides

TABLE 3-6
Factor 10: Theologian in Life and Thought

Core Cluster No.	Name and Description	Average Rating
38	*Acknowledgment of Own Vulnerability* Openly facing the ambiguities of life, the struggles of faith, and the disappointments of ministry	1.42
30	*Use of Broad Knowledge* Alert to the world around, sensitively using a broad base of information to stimulate people to become thinking Christians	1.92
29	*Theological Reflection* Having developed definite theological positions, nevertheless regularly evaluating them in the light of experience and current theological trends	1.90
34	*Service in Humility* Relying on God's grace, serves others without seeking personal reputation for success or infallibility	2.52
28	*Clarity of Thought and Communication* Sharpening already keen intelligence through continual theological study and careful attention to clarity of thought and expression	2.18
39[a]	*Acceptance of Counsel* Seeking to know God's will through the counsel and ministry of others	1.35
	Factor average	1.88

[a]The responses of laity related Cluster 39 to Cluster 38, and so Cluster 39 is included in this factor. The first five clusters emerge as a factor from the ratings of professionals alone.

some systematic variation of responses. Generally, the core clusters in this factor are rated as somewhat less important in smaller, predominantly homogeneous urban or suburban congregations than in larger congregations or in specialized ministry settings such as academic ministry, youth ministry, or an inner-city struggling mission. Three of the six clusters in the factor are rated significantly more important by people attending larger parishes than those attending smaller ones (less than 500 members).

In the midst of these variations, however, one core cluster (CC) attracts virtually no systematic difference in ratings. It is the most highly rated of the sixty-four core clusters—"Service in Humility" (CC 34). It defines an approach to ministry in which the priest or minister relies on God's grace and serves others without seeking a personal reputation for success or infallibility.

These variations in the ratings confirm some observers' suspicions. Some groups are not anxious for the minister to affirm his or her humanity. The minister or priest as the imitation of Christ is still a basic expectation for some people. The factor ratings also confirm the hunch that tension remains, for some, between the life of commitment in faith and the life of thought. Laity, for example, rate the clusters "Being Informed by Theology" and "Stimulating Use of Broad Knowledge" much lower than do clergy.

Ministry from a Personal Commitment of Faith (Factor 2)

None of the seven factors in this part of the chapter precipitates as much disagreement among respondents as does Factor 2. Some groups endorse it with authority. Others find it a collection of language and piety so foreign to their religious commitment that they are suspicious of it.

What is the content of a factor that attracts and repels with such force? The cluster that most intimately reflects the theme includes items such as "Shows sensitivity to the leading of the Holy Spirit" and "Holds that, in the midst of serious problems, God is at work." The theme characterizes a style of ministry that emerges from a personal faith commitment, holds a firm belief in the Bible as final authority, and emphasizes the evangelistic and mission goals of God's people. It is a theme that endorses personal example setting and "above reproach" behavior. It is a ministry that affirms the importance of prayer by actively praying with and for others. Table 3-7 summarizes the clusters in this factor.

For some, such a theme is a key to effective ministry. Lutheran, Presbyterian-Reformed, Southern Baptist, Evangelical A and B, and Free Church respondents who attend worship more than once a week judge this theme to be very important in ministry. For others, the theme is more questionable. For example, United Methodist, Anglican-Episcopal, United Church of Christ, Christian-Disciples, Roman Catholic, and United Church of Canada respondents who attend mass or worship once a week or less rate this factor as less important than the group just mentioned.

The differences in rating this factor, unlike most of the factors discussed thus far, are not variations due to laity-clergy status. Rather, two variables seem to identify the pattern in the variation, namely, denominational family and frequency of attendance. One can account for over 25 percent of the variance by noting respondent's denominational affiliation and frequency of attendance at mass or worship. In every cluster in this factor, people who attend mass or worship more frequently rate the clusters as

TABLE 3-7
Factor 2: Ministry from Personal Commitment of Faith

Core Cluster No.	Name and Description	Average Rating
37	*Commitment Reflecting Religious Piety* Profound consciousness of God's redeeming activity in life, living out a sense of call to Christ's mission with freedom and courage	2.20
31	*Affirmation of Conservative Biblical Faith* A biblically based faith, and a firm belief in the Bible as final authority	1.97
2	*Theocentric-Biblical Ministry* Drawing attention to God's Word and Person when preaching, teaching, and leading worship	2.24
61	*Evangelistic Witness* Witnessing to Jesus Christ by sharing own faith and encouraging others to do so	1.88
62	*Accepting Mutual Intercession* Openness to ministry of other people while actively praying with and for others	1.70
40	*"Born-Again" Christianity* Religious experience that manifests itself in verbal expression regarding God's activity in daily life	0.02
12	*Encouragement of World Mission* Stimulating a congregational response to world need that is reflective, theologically based, and sacrificial	1.95
17[a]	*Assertive Individual Evangelism* Aggressive approach to strangers and the unchurched, hoping to convert some to Christianity	1.03
35[a]	*Christian Example* Personal belief in the gospel that manifests itself in generosity and a life of high moral quality	2.42
6[a]	*Encouragement of Spiritual Sensitivity* Offering a spiritually sensitive ministry that awakens a sense of forgiveness, freedom, and renewal in the congregation	1.93

TABLE 3–7 — CONTINUED

Core Cluster No.	Name and Description	Average *Rating
24[b]	*Theologically Oriented Counseling* Using theologically sound counseling approaches to help people cope with personal problems, using resources of faith	2.17
	Factor average	1.82

[a]These clusters group together with the first seven clusters in the analysis of responses from laity alone.

[b]This cluster groups together with the first seven clusters in the analysis of responses from professionals alone.

more important than people who attend mass or worship less frequently. A third variable, the age of respondents, adds another consistent variation. On most clusters in this factor, the rating of importance increases with the age of respondents. Fifty-year-olds (across church bodies) tend to rate the clusters as more important than do thirty-year-olds.

The interpretative possibilities regarding these three variables are so intriguing they are hard to resist. But it is important they be resisted. Since the data are descriptive, they can tell which variables relate to response patterns, but they cannot identify causes for the relationship. For example, one could argue from these data that: (1) as persons age, they perceive this theme as more important; (2) older respondents reflect the attitude of an earlier period of North American ministry that is not now shared by their younger peers. However, neither argument could be substantiated by the data.

We have noted the differences characterizing perceptions of this theme. However, it is important to note that, for the theme to exist at all, there must be agreement that it is a facet of ministry. Furthermore, this theme has been rated, on the average, "Quite Important, a Major Asset." Averages can occur for a variety of reasons. Water can have an "average" temperature of lukewarm because very hot water was mixed with near freezing water. One can have an "average" temperature of lukewarm because lukewarm water was mixed with more lukewarm water. But, if the "average" temperature is hot, it can only be because relatively hot water was mixed with relatively hot water. Ratings of importance are the same. A high importance rating is only possible when a large majority are in agreement with each other. Thus, although this factor reflects more variance than is true for the other themes in this section, the factor stands as testimony that a majority of people who participated in this study see this theme as valid, important, and appropriate for professional ministry.

Development of Fellowship and Worship (Factor 5)

Factor 5 represents one of the more salient of the minister's skills. While he or she may be a good counselor and administrator, those skills will be most evident only to subgroups of the congregation. But "Competent Preaching and Worship Leading"—which is the most central cluster in this theme—will be evident to anyone attending worship or mass. The theme also includes "liturgical sensitivity in worship," the ability "sensitively and effectively to interpret the teaching of the Gospel in contemporary life," and the ability to lead worship in ways that involve the congregation in sharing, praying, singing, and participating together. The entire factor is shown in Table 3-8.

If the skills described in this theme are more obvious to the congregation than other skills, as has just been asserted, then the sixth-place rank of this theme raises an interesting question. Do North American churches really value administrative and counseling skills more than preaching and worship leading skills? Are preaching and worship leading viewed as less important skills than counseling and administration?

These data are point-in-time estimates of the importance participants ascribed to questionnaire items. They cannot identify trends. But the data raise a question that likely deserves serious reflection among people and church bodies that emphasize the preaching ministry of the church: "Is there a shift away from preaching and worship leading as primary ministry functions? If forced to choose, would congregations prefer a minister who is a good counselor and administrator although poor preacher, or one who is a good preacher although poor administrator and counselor?"

As a whole, Factor 5 is rated similarly by most respondents. There is some tendency for persons considering ministry in nontraditional parish contexts (for example, an institutional therapeutic context) to rate this factor as less important. Respondents from more liturgical traditions tend to place greater importance on the theme than people from less liturgical traditions—although this difference is very slight. The ratings of importance on three of the clusters increase as respondents' age increases.

The ratings identify this ministerial skill as important, agreed-on, and necessary, particularly for the individual who will function in the local church pastorate. But the rank order of themes suggest that other skills are viewed as more important than this one.

Denominational Awareness and Collegiality (Factor 11)

This brief factor, formed by professional responses, consists of only two clusters. The clusters are derived from analysis of the responses clergy made. The theme suggests prudent appreciation for denominational tradi-

TABLE 3-8
Factor 5: Development of Fellowship and Worship

Core Cluster No.	Name and Description	Average Rating
5	*Competent Preaching and Worship Leading* Holding attention while preaching and being well in command of all aspects of a service	1.87
3	*Relating Well to Children and Youth* Showing sensitivity and skill in ministering to children and youth as individuals	2.04
7	*Liturgical Sensitivity* Appreciative and competent in the use of what is pastorally suitable and inspiring in a worship service	1.63
1	*Relating Faith to Modern World* Sensitive interpreting and teaching the gospel in contemporary life	2.20
9[a]	*Sacramental-Liturgical Ministry* Orientation toward worship, and stressing the sacramental and liturgical aspects of the faith	1.07
4[b]	*Encouragement of Mutuality in Congregation* Developing a congregational sense of being a family of God where there is mutual sharing, worship, and broad participation	1.93
	Factor average	1.79

[a]Double loading — this cluster is loaded with equal strength both in this factor and in Factor 7, "Priestly-Sacramental Ministry." Issues related to this cluster will be discussed in the section dealing with Factor 7.

[b]This cluster groups with the others in the analysis of responses from professionals alone.

tion and awareness of the denomination's polity and history. Items in the cluster state behaviors such as "usually follows directives from denominational leaders" and gives a "calm, rational explanation when a request contrary to denominational regulations cannot be granted." The two clusters are shown in Table 3-9.

Factor 11 is rather uniformly rated by most clergy. Well over two-thirds rate the factor at or slightly above the average rating of 1.65. Respondents who differ from the average rating tend to place less importance on the theme. There is no systematic pattern that categorizes those differing with the majority. One noticeable tendency is that the ratings of importance increase as age of respondents increases.

TABLE 3-9
Factor 11: Denominational Awareness and Collegiality

Core Cluster No.	Name and Description	Average Rating
32	*Denominational Knowledge* Knowing both the shaping context and current position of denomination's political and theological stance	1.54
49	*Denominational Collegiality* Acceptance of denomination's directives and regulations while maintaining a collegial relationship with superiors and staff	1.76
	Factor average	1.65

MINISTRY THEMES WITH POSITIVE BUT DISPUTED RATINGS

The two themes reported in this section are rated, across the entire sample, as "Somewhat Important." Such a rating assigns these themes to the positive side of the rating scale, but to the lowest rating category within the positive range.

The two factors reveal two contested issues in the practice of faith: One issue deals with the essence of ordained ministry, and the second issue concerns the role of the church in the world. By stating definite positions, the themes give people a clear context for agreement or disagreement; there is both. The agreement and disagreement about ordained ministry is related to the respondents' denominational tradition. But the dynamics influencing the ratings dealing with the second issue are subtle and, at times, bewildering.

Ministry to the Community and World (Factor 1)

While the biblical tradition clearly reflects many consistent themes, it also reflects some interesting contrasts. For example, positions regarding religiously motivated political action appear to vary. The prophets of the Old Testament were quite political. Jeremiah, Amos, Hosea—all had ministries in which they frequently interpreted the word of Yahweh in political terms. But the New Testament reflects a less politicized concept of ministry. Neither Jesus nor Paul model politically assertive ministries—at least in ways that right social inequalities and change faulty political systems.

(Of course, their teaching and style of life provide a precedent for politically active ministry. But their practice of ministry was not aggressively political.) This biblical contrast persists in contemporary perceptions of ministry. Some people view political action as central to authentic ministry. Others contend that ministry must be to persons, not to structures or social issues.

"Ministry to Community and World" portrays a ministry area of aggressive political leadership coupled with an active concern for the oppressed. It is an area of ministry characterized by openness to new ideas and in personal style, and giving pastoral service to all people. Respondents who see this theme as highly important are endorsing activities such as "Works to improve community service to older persons," "Explores theological issues underlying current social movements," and "Insists that political struggle is a rightful concern of the church." The theme clearly identifies an area of ministry that is socially conscious, issue-oriented, concerned for the oppressed, and actively seeking to rectify social injustices—particularly by means of political action. The clusters that group together to form this theme are included in Table 3-10.

"Aggressive Political Leadership" (CC 18) is the most central cluster in the factor. This theme includes both a concern for social wrongs and wronged people, and the assertion that political action is an appropriate means of dealing with these issues. Although Core Cluster 18 is the most central to the theme, it is the least highly rated of the nine clusters in this factor.

The theme attracts widely differing ratings of importance. Our analyses suggest that some systematic patterns account for a significant part of the differences. One pattern emerges when we identify which respondents rate this factor highest and which lowest.[10]

The variables that identify these groups are denominational family, level of education, and evaluator group.[11] Additional analyses indicate two other variables are associated with consistent rating patterns: the ministry context under consideration and the size of the parish the raters attend.

People who rate this theme as important can be characterized by the following description. They attend either very small (less than fifty members) or relatively large (500–5,000 members) parishes, have high levels of education, live in the more urban or metropolitan areas, are clergy but not serving as parish pastors, and view ministry in the context of an ethnic congregation, transitional congregation, or staff role in a large, prospering congregation. People who rate this theme as less important tend to be members of medium-sized congregations (200–299 members), live in very small towns or open country, and are laity or clergy who serve as parish pastors.

The descriptions of high and low rating respondents yield some insight about minister-priests and political activities. People generally appear to

TABLE 3-10
Factor 1: Ministry to Community and World

Cluster No.	Name and Description	Average Rating
18	*Aggressive Political Leadership* Working actively, sometimes using the pressure of community groups, to protest and change social wrongs	−0.32
16	*Active Concern for the Oppressed* Knowledgeably and earnestly working in behalf of minority and oppressed peoples	1.12
14	*Promotion of Understanding of Issues* Developing, using, and encouraging theological, sociological, and psychological understandings in ministry	1.39
15	*Support of Community Causes* Active participation in social structures to improve the community	1.19
13	*Initiative in the Development of Community Service* Working for improvement and sometimes originating community service to persons with special needs	1.83
50	*Support of Unpopular Causes* A confident, vigorous participation in community affairs, willing to risk loss of popularity in support of a cause	1.74
8	*Ecumenical and Educational Openness* Openness to cooperation with people whose theology, culture, or educational methods are different	1.57
33[a]	*Interest in New Ideas* Deep involvement with current thinking and openness to testing new or current ideas	0.50
11[a]	*Pastoral Service to All* Reaching out in ministering to persons of all classes, whether members or not	1.92
	Factor average	1.32

[a]These two clusters factor with the first seven clusters in the analysis of responses from clergy alone.

think it important that ministers be sensitive to social evil and oppression. They also endorse political involvement for certain kinds of ministers in certain settings. For example, respondents consider it important for an associate staff member in a large congregation or the single staff member of a subsidized inner-city mission to be politically active. But political activity does not seem to be as widely endorsed for other ministers in other settings. A politically active ministry is not rated as important for the small-town parish pastor who serves a 250-member congregation.

It may be that respondents are saying that the pastor of the small parish has all he or she can do without extensive political involvement. Or the data may be saying that many respondents do not agree that the minister's proper response to social evil is political action. Or the dynamic may be that people think political activity is a proper clergy activity, but only when the political activities address the life of the congregation (inner-city ethnic congregation, large congregation with community influence, and so on). The reasons remain elusive.

Priestly-Sacramental Ministry (Factor 7)

Factor 7 (Table 3-11) is clearly the most denomination-specific of the eleven. The ratings of importance follow very systematic denominational patterns. Of the variance in responses, 67 percent can be accounted for by respondents' denominational affiliation.

The most central core cluster to this theme (CC 41) includes items of special interest to Roman Catholics: for example, "Regularly receives the Sacrament of Penance," "Places importance on the daily celebration of Mass," and "Expresses devotion to the Blessed Sacrament." The second cluster embraces priesthood in a larger context. Its items can be affirmed by participants from groups, with a formalized liturgical tradition (that is, Roman Catholics, Orthodox, Anglican-Episcopal, and Lutheran). The third cluster in the factor returns to the particular Roman Catholic emphasis of the first one. It is the only cluster in any of the eleven factors that relates negatively to a theme. "Mutuality in Family Commitments" is seen as more strongly negatively associated with (celibate) priesthood than positively related to any of the other ten factors.

The group who rate this theme most highly are Roman Catholic clergy and laity, followed by Orthodox, Anglican-Episcopal, and Lutheran groups, in that order. Most Protestants rate the theme very low, although black, American Indian, Asian, and those who marked "Other" for racial background rate the theme as somewhat more important than do white and Hispanic Protestants. The lowest ratings of all come from white and Hispanic Baptists, Evangelicals, Free Church members and "Other Protes-

TABLE 3-11
Factor 7: Priestly-Sacramental Ministry

Cluster No.	Name and Description	Average Rating
41	*Priestly Commitment* Taking seriously the sacramental life and priestly vows	−2.03
9	*Sacramental-Liturgical Ministry* Orientation toward worship and stressing the sacramental and liturgical aspects of the faith	1.07
48[a]	*Mutual Family Commitment* Agreement in the minister's deep commitment to family and the family's commitment to his or her vocation	1.83
	Factor average	0.24

[a]Core Cluster 48 loads negatively in this factor. It is the only core cluster of the sixty-four that is more strongly identified negatively with a factor than positively.

tants." (All statements referring to race or ethnic origin are based on respondents' self-reports.)

This factor receives the lowest average rating of the nine factors that are rated in the "importance" range. It is mandatory, however, to dissect that average rating into its very high rating among Roman Catholics and others from more liturgical groups, and its relatively low rating by mainline Protestants and very low rating by evangelical Protestants.

The variation in ratings seems clearly related to a theology of ordained ministry. For those who view ministry as priestly and sacramental, the theme receives a high rating of importance. But for those less liturgical, radical reformation Protestants, "sacramental" and "liturgical" are judged as less important concepts in ministry.

THEMES VIEWED AS DETRIMENTAL OR UNDESIRABLE

The Readiness for Ministry data suggest that several themes are unanimously evaluated as an important part of professional ministry. A few themes are judged less unanimously—and their importance depends on a respondent's denominational background or particular view of ministry. This third section deals with two themes judged, across the sample, as more negative than positive. Not all people perceive them as negative. Some people from some traditions see some of these characteristics as important and desirable. But the majority judgment is that the two themes deal with questionable, if not dysfunctional, ministry activities.

Privatistic, Legalistic Style (Factor 6)

Factor 6 combines a rather unique set of clusters that link together personal qualities, leadership style, and a concept of ministry. Together, these clusters form a theme that is rated by the total group of respondents as "Undesirable" and is summarized in Table 3-12.

The most central cluster in the factor describes a concept of ministry asserting that the "betterment of society is not a responsibility of the congregation" and doubting that "any good (comes) from social or political change." The theme includes the description of a leadership style that tends to bypass disciplined planning, "encourages decisions that favor buildings over people," and "plans projects without considering financial requirements." Other clusters in this theme identify behaviors such as using "the pulpit to express personal irritation" and trying "to pressure

TABLE 3-12
Factor 6: Privatistic, Legalistic Style

Cluster No.	Name and Description	Average Rating
20	*Total Concentration on Congregational Concerns* A ministry that avoids directly confronting social change	−1.42
27	*Law Orientation to Ethical Issues* Emphasis on God's demands and condemnation as a basis for solving personal problems	−1.00
60	*Intuitive Domination of Decision Making* Bypassing the disciplined task of planning and deciding for the congregation what decisions should be made	−1.32
19[a]	*Precedence of Evangelistic Goals* Strong belief that efforts for the betterment of society are of minor importance by comparison with the evangelization of all humankind	−0.94
10[b]	*Alienating Activity* Alienation of self and congregation by public and private stances that are critical and manipulative	−1.54
	Factor average	−1.25

[a]Cluster 19 groups with the first three in analyses based on responses of the clergy alone.

[b]Cluster 10 groups with the first three in analyses based on responses of the laity alone.

people into affirming faith in God." The theme also includes a cluster (CC 19) holding that "The church's task of proclaiming the Gospel by preaching and teaching overshadows in importance the task of helping to eliminate the physical suffering of people."

There are some systematic variations in the ratings of this theme—but the variations reflect only marginal movement above or below the "Undesirable" rating. For all but a few church bodies, clergy tend to rate the theme as more undesirable than laity. (This is true for each of the five clusters in this theme.) Across church bodies, females view these clusters as more undesirable than males, and younger respondents view them more negatively than do older respondents. Although some individuals find positive features of ministry in this theme, most respondents see the image of ministry it portrays as undesirable.

Disqualifying Personal and Behavioral Characteristics (Factor 3)

While there were some who saw positive features in Factor 6, the total group evaluation becomes more unanimously critical of Factor 3, "Disqualifying Personal and Behavioral Characteristics." This theme reflects very little systematic variation. The only consistent pattern is a tendency for clergy to rate clusters as slightly more detrimental than laity. Other variables such as a respondent's sex, age, the ministry context being considered, size of parish attended, frequency of attendance, and denominational family contribute very minimally to establishing patterns of variations. These clusters evoke widespread agreement. The behaviors and characteristics described by this theme are considered detrimental to ministry.

Table 3-13 summarizes the clusters in this factor. The most central of negatively rated clusters is also the largest of the sixty-four core clusters. It includes thirty items that are in the cluster more because they describe behaviors viewed as detrimental to ministry than because of any internal logical theme. Items range from "Often belittles a person in front of others" to "Uses ministerial role to maintain a sense of superiority." It embraces how the minister responds to pressure (for example, "Looks for another call or parish appointment the moment things do not go well" and "Becomes moody when pressures increase"); how he or she relates to people ("Tends to be abrupt and impatient when talking with people" and "Pays less attention to the thinking of women than the thinking of men"); and how he or she feels about him- or herself ("Talks as though unable to forgive self" and "Tends to be pessimistic"). Other clusters in this theme describe undisciplined and self-indulgent actions that shock or offend (CC 53), irresponsibility to the congregation, professional immaturity, and pursuit of personal advantage (CC 64, 52, and 63).

TABLE 3-13
Factor 3: Disqualifying Personal and Behavioral Characteristics

Cluster No.	Name and Description	Average Rating
54	*Self-Protecting Ministry* Avoiding intimacy and repelling people by a critical, demeaning, and insensitive attitude	−2.02
53	*Undisciplined Living* Undisciplined and self-indulgent actions that irritate, shock, or offend	−2.08
64	*Irresponsibility to the Congregation* Through independence and lack of discipline, not placing oneself in a position of responsibility to the religious community to be served	−1.63
52	*Professional Immaturity* Actions that demonstrate immaturity, insecurity, insensitivity, and being buffeted by the demands and pressures of the profession	−1.89
63	*Pursuit of Personal Advantage* Personal insecurity, expressed in grandiose ideas and manipulative efforts to gain or to keep personal advantages	−1.59
51[a]	*Secular Lifestyle* Parting company with some ministerial stereotypes by participating in a secularized lifestyle	−1.57
	Factor average	−1.80

[a]Cluster 51 groups with the other five on the basis of analyses of responses from clergy alone.

The most negatively rated cluster (CC 53) describes behaviors such as "Occasionally involved in extramarital affairs or illicit sexual relationships" and "Lives beyond personal means." These two items illustrate a unique feature of this theme. It is not just a collection of salient "sins" like "illicit sexual relationships." It also includes such behaviors as living beyond one's means. In one sense, that may be a moral issue; but in another sense it may be a statement about lifestyle.

The theme states by negation the expectation that ministers and priests be whole and healthy persons. They are expected to be people whose security is not based on a self-image propped up by the ministerial role, or others' unconditional acceptance of his or her views, or the trappings of material success. The theme thus suggests an expectation that, just as ministers and priests should abide by an accepted moral code, they should also exhibit characteristics many would associate with psychological health.

SUMMARY AND DISCUSSION

The first part of this chapter describes the seven most highly rated ministry themes. They encompass a variety of ministry skills, competencies, and approaches as well as personal characteristics and faith. They reflect an inclusive vision of ministry in which several things are important. Niebuhr notes that the term many use to describe the kind of person needed for pastoral posts is "the all-around man" (woman).[12] The high ratings of importance of these ministry themes, and the generally high degree of agreement among raters, confirm the "all-around" terminology.

This aggregate of themes likely leaves the minister or priest with the sense of a heavy load: "How can I be personally and professionally competent in all these areas?" "Should I even seek to be?" "Don't these themes reflect unrealistic expectations from which people need to be freed?" But in the midst of the questions, one must also ask, "Do the themes suggest quality and grace, wisdom and love, caring and competence?" To the extent that they do, they must be respected as meaningful goals toward which the maturing minister or priest should grow.

The themes are, similarly, of no universal comfort to the institutions who train ministers. Can "Positive Approach" or "Responsibility to Tasks and Persons" or "Religious Commitment" be taught at a seminary? Not very easily, and maybe not very much. Educational institutions can more handily deal with themes that identify valued skills. But the expectations go beyond skills. Theological education that teaches only skills and ideas has not fully prepared people for careers of ministry where personhood and faith are judged equally as important as skills and ideas.

Laity and clergy should beware of the abundance of themes reflecting very high expectations. Few ministers or priests can excel in all the areas where expectations are high. Laity must not allow unrealistic expectations of ministry to become normative.

The themes discussed in the second part of the chapter evoke ratings of less importance than do the themes in the first section. Both themes state positions that some rate very important, while others rate them as unimportant or detrimental. In some ways, both themes present partial pictures of the issues they define. For example, far more defines the uniqueness of Roman Catholic priesthood than the expressions of devotion in Core Cluster 41 and the practice of celibacy, as is implied by negation in Core

Cluster 48. Similarly, there is more to "Ministry to Community and World" than unearthing issues, showing concern, and generating political action. Other styles of ministry to the community and world (for example, belonging to civic groups and working with nonpolitical church agencies to deal with social problems) are not included. These partial pictures likely contribute to the attraction of polarized ratings, as well as the basic positions inherent in the themes.

The third part describes themes that are seen, generally with great agreement, as undesirable or detrimental. There is a sense in which these most negatively viewed themes are similar to the most positively viewed themes. The most highly rated themes portray a merger of certain qualities of personhood and character with a certain competence in ministry skills. The themes evaluated as most detrimental reflect a similar merger of personal qualities (this time, negative qualities) and ministry activities that reflect incompetence in real practice. The personal self is not separated from the professional self at either the positive or negative ends. The patterns in the data imply an integrated perception of ministry not unlike the Christian concept of incarnation. The message of grace and righteousness is incarnated in the life of one who is called to share grace and to urge followers to righteousness. There is, of course, tension between the completeness of the truth the minister or priest proclaims and the incompleteness with which any embodiment occurs. But to contend that the minister or priest need not embody the truth of the proclamation is likely as faulty as to contend that the embodiment must be perfect in order to have the qualification to proclaim.

There is another sense in which the factors described in the third part of the chapter are similar to those discussed in the first part. These themes in both parts are characterized by widespread agreement among participants, although, to be sure, there are some differences.

Responses frequently vary as a function of denominational family. People over thirty-five tend to rate many clusters as more important than do people under thirty-five. The importance given some clusters varies on the basis of the ministry context being considered. Laity and clergy frequently differ. But, even with the variations produced by these dimensions, a pervasive degree of agreement remains. Much of this volume is devoted to the task of explicating the unique expressions of ministry among church bodies in North America. That uniqueness, however, must be viewed as a meaningful extension from a basic commonality.

Eleven themes of ministry are presented in this chapter. It may be of value to note the picture of ministry portrayed by the factors as a whole.

Factors 1, 2, 5, 7, 8, 9, and 11 identify content areas in the function of ministry—what the minister or priest does. One might expect the priest or minister to develop skills in these areas. They are themes that identify major areas of the minister's work: "Leading Worship," "Ministering to

FIGURE 3-1
Diagram of Readiness for Ministry Themes

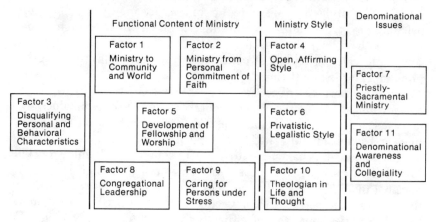

Spiritual Needs," "Ministering to Community and World," "Ministering to Persons under Stress," and "Leading the Congregation." Factors 4, 6, and 10 describe personal and professional styles—how the minister or priest does the tasks of ministry. They are likely indicators of personhood and character. For example, he or she may go about the functions with an "open, affirming style" or with a more "privatistic, legalistic style." In contrast to these areas of ministry content and style, Factor 3 defines behavior and characteristics that disqualify an individual from effective ministry.

Together, the themes form a holistic picture of ministry. The very expansiveness of that picture is both threatening and attractive. Expectations of ministers are many—perhaps too many. Most expectations are high—perhaps too high. But the picture is realistic. The expectations do exist, and they define the setting in which ministry in North America is practiced.

NOTES

1. Henri Nouwen, *Creative Ministry* (New York: Doubleday, 1978), p. xxi.
2. The methods of procedure are discussed in detail in Chapter 19.
3. Abstracted from I Timothy 3:11 ff. (Revised Standard Version).
4. This information was provided by the automatic interaction detection (AID) analyses. This analytic approach, as well as other approaches used to identify the group variations, are discussed in Chapter 19, under the subsection heading "Identifying Significantly Different Subgroups."
5. These findings emerged from the Analyses of Variance, also described in detail in the subsection of Chapter 19 mentioned in Note 4.

6. The distinction between laity and clergy is not necessarily a distinction between unordained and ordained people. "Clergy" includes respondents who identified themselves as denominational officials, seminary professors, seminary students, or parish clergy.

7. This is the result of another series of automatic interaction detection (AID) analyses; see Note 4.

8. This difference was significant at P<.005. In this chapter, any mention of difference or variation is based on statistical significance at least at the .005 level.

9. H. Richard Niebuhr, *The Purpose of the Church and Its Ministry* (New York: Harper & Row, 1956), pp. 79–94.

10. This is another application of AID, described in Note 4.

11. Table 3-2 describes the subcategories in each of these variables.

12. Niebuhr, *The Purpose of the Church*, p. 84.

4

Models of Ministry

Merton P. Strommen

Denominations as well as individuals differ in their concepts of what constitutes an effective ministry. Some are convinced that the primary emphasis of ministry should be on the encouragement of spiritual sensitivity—commitment, forgiveness, freedom, and renewal—while others believe that the essence of ministry lies in a stress on the liturgical and sacramental elements; still others maintain that the chief concern of ministry should be in the field of social action. Some denominational families prefer to combine all three emphases. In several denominational families, laity prefer an accent on meeting spiritual needs, and clergy prefer an accent on meeting social needs. These differences, highlighted by profiles on data from the Readiness for Ministry Project, are discussed and interpreted by the authors of subsequent chapters.

In order to document the fact of varying models of ministry, this chapter compares seventeen denominational families on their responses as to the importance of 64 ministry characteristics (described in Chapter 5). Although commonalities appear, there are marked differences in the perceived importance of a number of ministry characteristics. These differences signal the existence of differing goals and purposes in people's concept of ministry. The plotting of profile differences on a continuum, as we have done, not only highlights impressive commonalities among denominational families regarding what they expect of a beginning minister but also shows the dramatic differences in what the denominational families are seeking through ministry.

This chapter introduces the following chapters on denominational families. It identifies models of ministry, contrasts between clergy and laity, and ministry commonalities as established by the research data. Illustrations of different approaches to ministry are drawn, not only from the data but also from comments of the denominational writers.

To avoid unnecessary complexity, this chapter limits its information to comparisons that meet a rigorously high standard. Differences between denominational families and between laity and professionals are reported when Scheffe's test of significance—a correction factor that is introduced in the analysis to eliminate the possibility of concluding that differences that occur by chance are significant—shows an extremely low probability of these differences occurring by chance. The primary standard is this: Whatever falls below a .0001 probability (1 chance in 10 thousand) is deemed significant and of practical importance. Such a demanding requirement for statistical significance allows only the striking differences to surface. When no significant differences occurred using this criterion the standard was lowered to a probability of .001 to avoid the error of ignoring significant differences at that level. In the few instances where this was done, the level of .001 is indicated. (See profiles given in Chapter 5.)

FOUR APPROACHES TO MINISTRY

Four discernible models function in the minds of people to shape their understanding of ministry. Each model or concept influences the priorities that people give to a range of generally accepted functions and qualities of ministry. Significantly, these models follow denominational lines. In fact, denominational differences account for more variance in how people view ministry than all other variables considered in our analyses, such as sex, age, laity and clergy status, size of church, region, ministry setting, ethnic background, or frequency of church attendance. Major denominations can be classified on the basis of their concept of the clergy's task.

Before identifying the four models of ministry, we describe how the denominational families were formed and how their scores were derived for making comparisons.

Classifying Denominations

Although members of forty-seven denominations did participate in the criterion-ranking survey from which these research data were drawn, the extreme variation in size of denominations (for example, Swedenborgian and Roman Catholic) made classification a necessity. The task was accomplished in the following manner: Staff members of the Association of Theological Schools drew on their experience with denominations of the participating seminaries to classify the forty-seven church bodies into 15 categories; two of these 15 categories served as catch-alls for denominations that could not be classified into any one of the thirteen major families. Later, a factor analysis of denominations was made to determine how the denominations would group empirically when the organizing principle was their concept of ministry. It was hoped that such an empirical classification of denominations would provide a less arbitrary, yet equally meaningful, classification of denominational families. The results proved to be more extreme than expected. Some empirically formed denominational families made immediate sense; others were puzzling because they did not fit any existing rationale. It was recognized, however, that agreement between denominations on how ministry was viewed did not necessarily presuppose theological or ecclesial agreement.

Due to the radical classification resulting from factor analysis, it seemed best to use its information only for reclassifying denominations hidden in the two miscellaneous categories, or for dividing the too-large group of Evangelicals. The empirical classification of denominations resulted in these two changes: Evangelical church bodies were separated into two groups (hereafter known in this book as Evangelical A and Evangelical B). People of Unitarian persuasion and those embracing the Jewish faith were combined on the basis of a common concept of ministry; the African Methodist Episcopal and the African Methodist Episcopal Zion denominations became part of the Presbyterian-Reformed family; and Christian Churches and Churches of Christ and the North American Christian Convention formed a separate group called the Christian Churches (not Disciples).

With the factor analysis of denominations serving as a basis for modifying the original classification of denominations, a revised list (see Table 4-1) of seventeen denominational families was formed. In this new reclassification, the totals for each "family" sample are fairly uniform.

Deriving and Comparing Scores

Given this new classification, the next task was to score individuals within each of the denominational families on each of the sixty-four core criterion clusters. Such data would enable us to answer the basic question, "Is ministry perceived differently by certain denominational families than by others? If so, in what ways?"

It may be remembered that respondents in the 1974 Readiness for Min-

TABLE 4-1
Families of Denominations as Revised Through Factor Analysis

Denominational Family	*No. of Laity*	*No. of Professionals*	*Total in Family*
1. *Anglican-Episcopal Churches*	92	167	259
Anglican Church of Canada			
Episcopal Church			
2. *American-Canadian Baptist Family*	59	265	324
American Baptist Churches in the USA			
Baptist Federation of Canada			
3. *Southern Baptists*	106	148	254
4. *Christian Church (Disciples of Christ)*	17	94	122
5. *Orthodox Church*	48	74	122
Greek Orthodox Archdiocese of North and South America			
Orthodox Church in America			
6. *Evangelical B*	107	266	373
Church of God (Anderson, Ind.)			
Church of the Nazarene			
Church of the New Jerusalem (Swedenborgian)			
Churches of God, General Conference			
Evangelical Congregational Church			
Evangelical Covenant Church of America			
Seventh-day Adventists			
7. *Free Church Family*	121	199	320
Brethren Church (Ashland, Ohio)			
Church of the Brethren			
General Conference Mennonite Church			
Mennonite Brethren Churches in North America			
Mennonite Church			
Religious Society of Friends			
8. *Jewish and Unitarian*	60	66	126
Union of American Hebrew Congregations (Reform)			
Unitarian Universalist Association			

TABLE 4-1 — *CONTINUED*

Denominational Family	No. of Laity	No. of Profes- sionals	Total in Family
9. *Lutheran Churches*	340	221	561
American Lutheran Church			
Lutheran Church in America			
Lutheran Church—Missouri Synod			
10. *United Methodist Church*	89	229	318
11. *Presbyterian-Reformed Family*	203	413	616
African Methodist Episcopal Church			
African Methodist Episcopal Zion Church			
Associate Reformed Presbyterian Church (General Synod)			
Christian Reformed Church			
Cumberland Presbyterian Church			
Moravian Church in America			
Presbyterian Church in Canada			
Presbyterian Church in the US			
Reformed Church in America			
United Presbyterian Church in the USA			
12. *Roman Catholic Church (Order)*	42	120	162
13. *Roman Catholic Church (Diocesan)*	297	133	430
14. *United Church of Christ*	65	135	200
15. *United Church of Canada*	95	168	263
16. *Evangelical A*	95	333	428
Baptist General Conference			
Baptist Missionary Association of America			
Conservative Baptist Associa- tion of America			
Evangelical Free Church of America			
North American Baptist Conference			
17. *Christian Churches (Not Disciples)*	35	93	128
Christian Churches and Churches of Christ			
North American Christian Convention			
Totals	1,871	3,124	4,995

istry survey rated the importance of 444 criterion items as they relate to the ministry context each respondent knew best. In giving an answer, respondents used a verbal scale that also served as a numerical scale:[2]

	From	To
Highly important, essential or mandatory	+2.51	+3.00
Quite important, a major asset	+1.51	+2.50
Somewhat important, a minor asset	+0.51	+1.50
Neither important nor unimportant	−0.50	+0.50
Somewhat detrimental, a minor hindrance in ministry	−1.50	−0.51
Quite detrimental, a major hindrance in ministry	−2.50	−1.51
Highly detrimental, harmful, could destroy the effectiveness of ministry	−3.00	−2.51

By using the numerical ratings of each item, it was possible to derive an average score for a cluster of items that would indicate the importance respondents accorded the characteristic being described. For instance, a high score on the core cluster "Assertive Individual Evangelism" (CC 17), would indicate that its items were rated as being highly important; a low score would indicate that its items were rated less important, even to the point of being undesirable. By means of this procedure, it was possible to derive scores for each characteristic (for all who participated in the survey). These scores were weighted so that laity and professionals within each family of denominations spoke with equal voice, regardless of the number participating. The average of these weighted scores became the score for a "family," thus allowing for comparisons between the seventeen families as reclassified.

To facilitate comparisons, all scores on the sixty-four core clusters were standardized so that a score of 50 would represent the average response for the 4,995 respondents to each set of items. Thus, the average score for Core Clusters 34 and 54 was 50, even though the actual grand mean (or average) for "Service in Humility" (CC 34) is 6.20 and for "Self-Protecting Ministry" (CC 54) is 1.70. This standardization of scores, through the use of a floating average, eliminates the relative difference in rank between core clusters. In doing so, however, it provides a way of making precise comparisons between denominational families. By equalizing the core clusters and holding them constant, we can focus on the issue of determining how denominational families differ in what they consider important in ministry.

It is helpful to know that the difference between a standard score of 45 and 50 is one-half a standard deviation (a measure of score distributions). In this project, such a difference in standard scores, roughly speaking, can happen by chance only once in 10 thousand times (although admittedly this rule of thumb varies by size of group and the variability of scores).

At this point, we are ready to consider the question, "What are the four models of ministry that characterize denominational families?" An inspection of the sixty-four profiles (Figures 5-1 to 5-64) given in Chapter 5 show four identifiable patterns that suggest four differing emphases in ministry.

Model 1: Spiritual Emphasis

The first and most striking profile pattern is formed by the way in which denominational families rank dimensions in the factor entitled "Ministry from Personal Commitment to Faith." Nine of its eleven dimensions or core criterion clusters show striking profile contrasts and clear evidence of a distinct pattern. In the dimensions listed in Table 4-2, highest importance is usually given by Southern Baptists and by the Evangelical A and Evangelical B families. Secondary peaks in importance tend to occur for American-Canadian Baptist, Free Church, Lutheran, Presbyterian-Reformed, and Christian (not Disciples) families. Lowest priorities are given these characteristics by Jewish and Unitarian respondents, who tend to view these emphases as more detrimental than helpful. Higher than the Jewish and Unitarian, but still among those least interested in these dimensions one usually finds the Anglican-Episcopal, Christian (Disciples), and United Church of Christ families.

The profiles or graphs (all sixty-four of which appear in Chapter 5) are highly reliable estimates of how denominational families vary in their approach to each aspect of ministry. Differences between groups that cannot be attributed to chance (more than once in 10 thousand) are indicated to the right of each profile. For each profile, precise measures of variability are shown in the upper right-hand corner.

Two observations are now in order. First, very close agreement between laity and clergy characterizes the first six profiles listed in Table 4-2. There is no variation in scores except for what random error might produce (see Figure 4-1). Second, in the remaining five profiles the laity of several denominational families, more than the clergy, accord high importance to "Affirmation of Conservative Biblical Faith" (CC 31), "Assertive Individual Evangelism" (CC 17), "Evangelistic Witness" (CC 61), "Precedence of Evangelistic Goals" (CC 19), and " 'Born-Again' Christianity" (CC 40). Most consistently, the denominational families where laity value these emphases more than do clergy, are Lutheran, United Methodist, Presbyterian-Reformed, Roman Catholic (Order and Diocesan), and United Church of Christ. Their clergy are likely to be less evangelistically assertive in their ministry than many laypeople want them to be.

The best illustration of how the eleven profiles form a discernible pat-

TABLE 4-2
Dimensions That Form Model 1: Spiritual Emphasis

Core Cluster Title	Core Cluster No.	Laity-Clergy Probability	No. of Significant Family Contrasts[a]
Encouragement of Spiritual Sensitivity	6	NS[b]	46
Theocentric-Biblical Ministry	2	NS	30
Commitment Reflecting Religious Piety	37	NS	33
Christian Example	35	NS	35
Secular Lifestyle (viewed as a hindrance)	51	NS	54
Theologically Oriented Counseling	24	NS	20
Affirmation of Conservative Biblical Faith	31	.000013	56
Assertive Individual Evangelism	17	.00011	76
Evangelistic Witness	61	.000076	41
Precedence of Evangelistic Goals	19	.000036	56
"Born-Again" Christianity	40	.000003	58

[a]The number of denominational families whose scores contrast with each other at a probability level of significance of less than .0001.

[b]NS = Not significant.

tern is given in the profile scores on Core Cluster 31 ("Affirmation of Conservative Biblical Faith"). This profile, Figure 4-2, shows which denominational families give this characteristic highest importance, which families form secondary peaks, and which groups shy away from the statement embodied by its items. In this profile, one also sees which laypeople differ sharply with their clergy on the importance of this characteristic.

Importance of a Spiritual Emphasis

No set of comparisons shows a higher number of statistically significant differences between denominational families than the eleven profiles that graphically portray Model 1. As indicated in Table 4-2, the number of contrasts that cannot be credited to chance ranges from 20 to 76, with the average of 46. However, one should note that the Jewish and Unitarian group, in "Affirmation of Conservative Biblical Faith" (CC 31), for example, disagrees with every other denominational family (or, accounts for sixteen of the fifty-six statistically significant differences). This great

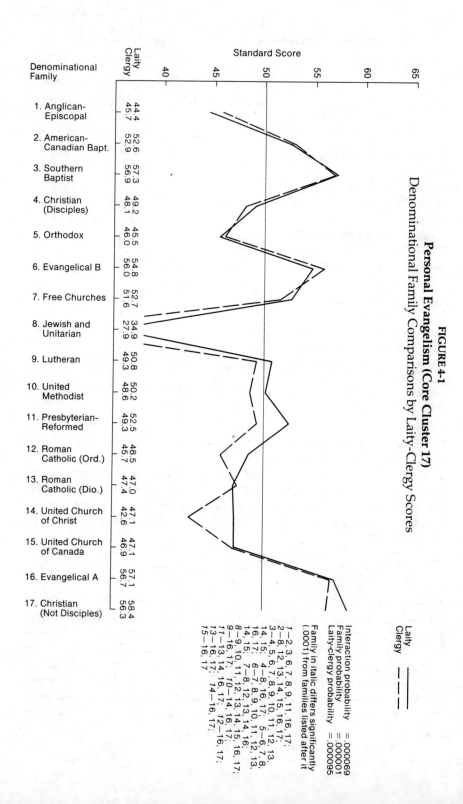

FIGURE 4-1
Personal Evangelism (Core Cluster 17)
Denominational Family Comparisons by Laity-Clergy Scores

Standard Score

Denominational Family

	Laity	Clergy
1. Anglican-Episcopal	44.4	45.7
2. American-Canadian Bapt.	52.6	52.9
3. Southern Baptist	57.3	56.9
4. Christian (Disciples)	49.2	48.1
5. Orthodox	45.5	46.0
6. Evangelical B	54.8	56.0
7. Free Churches	52.7	51.6
8. Jewish and Unitarian	34.9	27.9
9. Lutheran	50.8	49.3
10. United Methodist	50.2	48.6
11. Presbyterian-Reformed	52.5	49.3
12. Roman Catholic (Ord.)	48.5	45.7
13. Roman Catholic (Dio.)	47.0	47.4
14. United Church of Christ	47.1	42.6
15. United Church of Canada	47.1	46.9
16. Evangelical A	57.1	56.7
17. Christian (Not Disciples)	58.4	56.3

Laity ———
Clergy – – –

1—2, 3, 6, 7, 8, 9, 11, 16, 17;
2—8, 12, 13, 14, 15, 16, 17;
3—4, 5, 6, 7, 8, 9, 10, 11, 12, 13,
14, 15; 4—8, 16, 17; 5—6, 7, 8,
16, 17; 6—7, 8, 9, 10, 11, 12, 13,
14, 15; 7—8, 12, 13, 14, 16;
8—9, 10, 11, 12, 13, 14, 15, 16, 17;
9—16, 17; 10—14, 16, 17;
11—13, 14, 16, 17; 12—16, 17;
13—16, 17; 14—16, 17;
15—16, 17

Interaction probability = .0000069
Family probability = .000001
Laity-clergy probability = .000095

Family in italic differs significantly
(.0001) from families listed after it

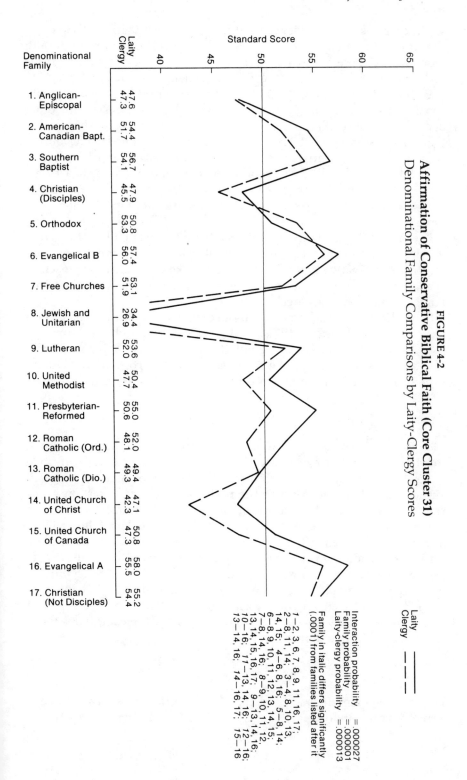

FIGURE 4-2

Affirmation of Conservative Biblical Faith (Core Cluster 31)
Denominational Family Comparisons by Laity-Clergy Scores

Denominational Family	Laity	Clergy
1. Anglican-Episcopal	47.6	47.3
2. American-Canadian Bapt.	54.4	51.7
3. Southern Baptist	56.7	54.1
4. Christian (Disciples)	47.9	45.5
5. Orthodox	50.8	53.3
6. Evangelical B	57.4	56.0
7. Free Churches	53.1	51.9
8. Jewish and Unitarian	34.4	26.9
9. Lutheran	53.6	52.0
10. United Methodist	50.4	47.7
11. Presbyterian-Reformed	55.0	50.6
12. Roman Catholic (Ord.)	52.0	48.1
13. Roman Catholic (Dio.)	49.4	49.3
14. United Church of Christ	47.1	42.3
15. United Church of Canada	50.8	47.3
16. Evangelical A	58.0	55.5
17. Christian (Not Disciples)	55.2	54.4

Standard Score: 40 45 50 55 60 65

Laity ———
Clergy ‒ ‒ ‒

Interaction probability = .000027
Family probability = .000001
Laity-clergy probability = .000013

Family in italic differs significantly (.0001) from families listed after it

1—2, 3, 6, 7, 8, 9, 11, 16, 17;
2—8, 11, 14; 3—4, 8, 10, 13;
14, 15; 4—6, 8, 16; 5—8, 14;
6—8, 9, 10, 11, 12, 13, 14, 15;
7—8, 14, 16; 8—9, 10, 11, 12,
13, 14, 15, 16, 17; 9—13, 14, 16;
10—16; 11—13, 14, 16; 12—16;
13—14, 16; 14—16, 17; 15—16

variation gives ample evidence that denominational families disagree on the importance of ministry arising from the personal commitment of faith described by these dimensions. (See Chapter 5 for a listing of the items and profiles of the scores for each of the dimensions listed in Table 4-2.)

By way of illustration, Richards, in his chapter on the Anglican-Episcopal family, comments on how his church body contrasts with other denominational families in its accent on human interrelationships rather than on theocentric matters. Likewise, Campbell, in his chapter on the United Church of Christ family, indicates that clergy and laity of his church body are less likely than other denominational groups to affirm a conservative biblical faith, to believe in assertive individual evangelism, or to ask a narrowly conceived religious commitment of those whom they serve.

In contrast, Songer, writing for the Southern Baptist family, affirms that his church body wants ministers to verbalize their religious experience, to affirm a conservative biblical faith, and to take an assertive approach to evangelism. The same desired emphasis characterizes the denominational families classified as Evangelical A and B.

Some denominational groups, out of conviction, favor the "Encouragement of Spiritual Sensitivity" (CC 6), a "Theocentric-Biblical Ministry" (CC 2), and an emphasis on "Commitment Reflecting Religious Piety" (CC 37); other denominational families, also out of conviction, favor an expression of ministry in which other characteristics are highlighted.

Ethical Living

Closely associated with the dimension of spiritual emphasis are strong convictions regarding exemplary living by the pastor. A secular lifestyle is seen by some as a powerful hindrance to an effective ministry. If certain virtues are lacking, the faith of the pastor is called into question. Conversely, in the more liturgically oriented denominational families less importance is placed on the minister's setting an example in faith and life. In addition to rejecting the traditional stereotypes of puritanism, some families even add the wish that their clergy not appear too pious. Examples of these strong contrasts in points of view are found in the profiles of "Christian Example" (CC 35) and "Secular Lifestyle" (CC 51). Interestingly, laity and clergy within each denominational family are in full agreement as to how powerfully a pastor's way of life contributes to, or hinders, an effective ministry.

Evangelism

Three of the dimensions in Ministry Model 1 reflect an evangelistic concern: "Assertive Individual Evangelism" (CC 17), "Evangelistic Witness"

(CC 61), and "Precedence of Evangelistic Goals" (CC 19). These aggressive approaches to evangelism are closely identified with verbal expressions of faith that characterize " 'Born-Again' Christianity" (CC 40). It is with respect to these dimensions that denominational families differ most radically. (See Table 4-2 for the number of family contrasts.) Some give high priority to the evangelistic emphasis described by these dimensions, whereas others view it as a hindrance to an effective ministry. Hubbard's chapter on Evangelical A and B families underscores the high expectation of Evangelicals that a beginning minister be active in evangelism; however, Becker's chapter shows that education has become the preferred approach of the Christian (Disciples) family.

Model 2: Sacramental-Liturgical Emphasis

A second distinctive pattern is found in the ways in which denominational families view the characteristics of the "Priestly-Sacramental Ministry" (Factor 7). Striking peaks of importance are registered here on the profiles of three families—Roman Catholic (Order and Diocesan), Orthodox, and Anglican-Episcopal ("Priestly Commitment," CC 41, and "Sacramental-Liturgical Ministry," CC 9). A less distinct pattern emerges for the cluster entitled "Denominational Collegiality" (CC 49). On this characteristic, several other families of denominations join with the sacramental and liturgically oriented church bodies. Those who accord higher than average importance to this ministerial dimension include the Evangelical B, Lutheran, United Methodist, and Presbyterian-Reformed families. Their scores are also significantly above those of the Jewish and Unitarian, United Church of Christ, and Christian (not Disciples) families. (Table 4-3 and Chapter 5 provide documentation.)

TABLE 4-3
Dimensions That Form Model 2: Sacramental-Liturgical Emphasis

Core Cluster Title	Core Cluster No.	Laity-Clergy Probability	No. of Significant Family Differences[a]
Priestly Commitment	41	.000055	60
Sacramental-Liturgical Ministry	9	.000332	56
Denominational Collegiality	49	.000106	25

[a]The number of denominational families whose scores contrast with each other at a level of significance of less than .0001.

Sacramental-Liturgical Ministry

The profile given as an illustration of Model 2 highlights the priestly character of ministry in these three expressions of the universal Christian church (see Figure 4-3). Ministry in these families of denominations involves taking seriously the sacramental life and priestly vows (CC 41).

Descriptions of the sacramental-liturgical emphasis in ministry are especially evident in the chapter by Harakas, who describes Orthodox congregations as being viewed primarily as a eucharistic community. By virtue of ordination, clergy are called to a singular focus on the transcendent and holy. Their most important task is to lead the sacramental worship. As is also typical in the Roman Catholic and Anglican-Episcopal families, major importance is attached to the priest's function of administering the sacraments.

Strikingly, such an approach to ministry stirs as many significant family differences as does the "Spiritual Emphasis" of Model 1. This concept of ministry, held with deep conviction and reverence, distinguishes these three denominations from Protestant families. (See Chapter 5 for a listing of items and profiles for each of the core clusters.)

A fourth profile accents a distinctive requirement of Roman Catholic clergy, namely, celibacy. The differing expectations of these clergy on "Mutual Family Commitment" (CC 48) is dramatically evident. Here, however, they are not joined by Orthodox and Anglican-Episcopal members whose feelings regarding the clergy's obligations to spouse and children parallel those of all others.

Model 3: Social Action Emphasis

A discernible, but far less obvious, model of ministry is discussed in the chapters on the Christian (Disciples), United Church of Christ, and United Church of Canada. Becker characterizes the Christian (Disciples) family as being especially concerned about a ministry to community and world. Campbell, although noting an absence of strong social activism, sees that the United Church of Christ does affirm a ministry to community and world. Fennel, author of the chapter of the United Church of Canada, is troubled that in his church body concern for such a ministry seems to have superseded an emphasis on increasing the community of faith.

Significantly, in these denominational families and in the Jewish and Unitarian family one finds less enthusiasm for the type of spiritual emphasis found in Model 1. Score averages for these four families (and for the Anglican-Episcopal) are among the lowest on dimensions of Model 1, and strikingly so on "Affirmation of Conservative Biblical Faith" (CC 31) and " 'Born-Again' Christianity" (CC 40).

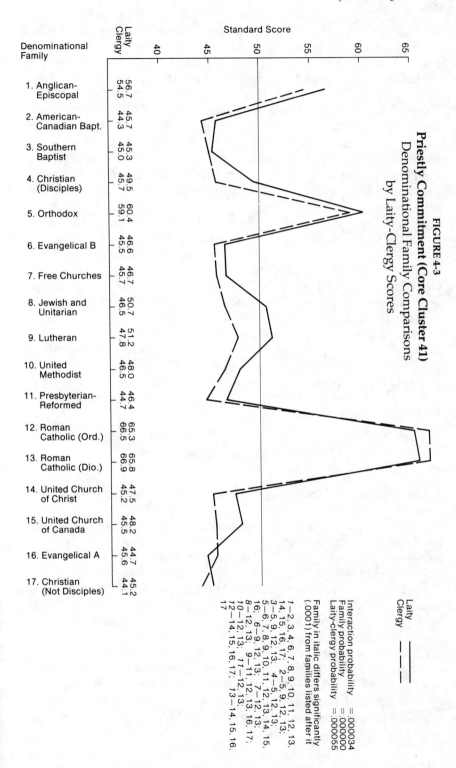

FIGURE 4-3
Priestly Commitment (Core Cluster 41)
Denominational Family Comparisons
by Laity-Clergy Scores

Denominational Family		Laity	Clergy
1.	Anglican-Episcopal	56.7	54.5
2.	American-Canadian Bapt.	45.7	44.3
3.	Southern Baptist	45.3	45.0
4.	Christian (Disciples)	49.5	45.7
5.	Orthodox	60.4	59.1
6.	Evangelical B	46.6	45.5
7.	Free Churches	46.7	45.7
8.	Jewish and Unitarian	50.7	46.5
9.	Lutheran	51.2	47.8
10.	United Methodist	48.0	46.5
11.	Presbyterian-Reformed	46.4	44.7
12.	Roman Catholic (Ord.)	65.3	66.5
13.	Roman Catholic (Dio.)	65.8	66.9
14.	United Church of Christ	47.5	45.2
15.	United Church of Canada	48.2	45.5
16.	Evangelical A	44.7	45.6
17.	Christian (Not Disciples)	45.2	44.1

Laity ———
Clergy – – –

Interaction probability = .000034
Family probability = .000000
Laity-clergy probability = .000055

Family in italic differs significantly
(.0001) from families listed after it

1—2, 3, 4, 6, 7, 8, 9, 10, 11, 12, 13,
14, 15, 16, 17; 2—5, 9, 12, 13;
3—5, 9, 12, 13; 4—5, 12, 13;
5—6, 7, 8, 9, 10, 11, 12, 13, 14, 15,
16; 6—9, 12, 13; 7—12, 13;
8—12, 13; 9—11, 12, 13, 16, 17;
10—12, 13; 11—12, 13;
12—14, 15, 16, 17; 13—14, 15, 16,
17

Social concern characterizes this third model of ministry, but it is not clearly etched in a profile pattern for Factor 1, "Ministry to Community and World" for both laity and clergy. Although high importance is accorded such ministerial factors as "Support of Unpopular Causes" (CC 50), "Promotion of Understanding of Issues" (CC 14), "Support of Community Causes" (CC 15), "Interest in New Ideas" (CC 33), and "Aggressive Political Leadership" (CC 18), the peaks are usually formed by the clergy but not by the laity of the Christian Church (Disciples), United Church of Christ, United Church of Canada, and the Jewish and Unitarian family. Moreover, although their scores are among the highest, they are not statistically higher than those of other mainline denominations.

Nevertheless, in these families there is a discernible emphasis on social concern, which finds its primary documentation in individual items, where differences do reach statistical significance. This approach to ministry is most evident in the priorities of clergy; it is shown in a negative reaction to "Precedence of Evangelistic Goals" (CC 19) and to a "Law Orientation to Ethical Issues" (CC 27). Clergy and laity from these four denominational families (plus Anglican-Episcopal) are the most negative toward the approaches characterized in these two core clusters. In a sense, this model of ministry involves a sensitivity to people and a willingness to break with traditional approaches as well as an openness to new ideas on a helpful ministry. The profile "Interest in New Ideas" (see Figure 4-4), given as an illustration of this model, may be useful to the reader. It is part of Factor 1, "Ministry to Community and World" and illustrates an openness of style often labeled *liberal*.

Model 4: Combined Emphases

The fourth and least distinctive model of ministry combines the emphases of the first three models. Some denominational families take pride in such a balanced approach to ministry. Lindbeck observes that Lutherans emphasize sin and forgiveness but not revivalistic techniques; they emphasize the sacraments but do not consider ministry as being essentially sacramental or liturgical.

The United Methodist Church is today especially conscious of its social responsibility, and this is evident in its respondents' scores on "Ministry to Community and World." Yet it continues a liturgical interest, given the fact of roots in Anglicanism.

Presbyterian-Reformed churches experience a cleavage in emphasis, a championing of two emphases. A greater proportion of laity than of clergy want an emphasis on evangelism and personal religious experience, whereas more of the clergy than laity want to emphasize community causes and social concerns. This laity-clergy division is particularly sig-

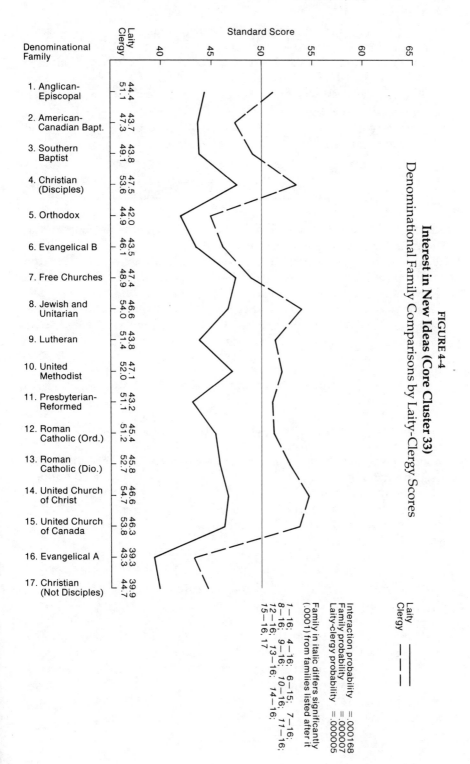

FIGURE 4-4
Interest in New Ideas (Core Cluster 33)
Denominational Family Comparisons by Laity-Clergy Scores

nificant, because the Presbyterian-Reformed Churches have had a tradition of strong lay leadership since the days of John Knox.

One might view these denominational families as reflecting a balanced approach to ministry, one in which the emphases of Models 1 and 3 are both taken seriously. Their authors, however, prefer to present their denominational families as distinctive embodiments of unique traditions as well as denominations that share a great many commonalities with other mainline Protestant groups.

CLERGY-LAITY CONTRASTS

Although clergy and laity agree on many aspects of what is important in a ministry, they contrast sharply on others. One-third (twenty-one) of the sixty-four core cluster profiles dramatize this disagreement. Nine of the contrasts center in a "Ministry to Community and World" (Factor 1); five relate to a minister's need to be a "Theologian in Life and Thought" (Factor 10); and the remaining seven form a miscellany of areas. These disagreements serve to identify the kinds of tension that a beginning minister might well expect to surface within a parish.

Ministry to Community and World

Laypeople, as a general rule, place far less importance than do clergy on ministries outside of the congregation. As illustrated in Table 4-4, all nine dimensions in this factor elicit contrasting scores between laity and clergy. Certain denominational families are quite supportive of outside ministries, and others are not. As a result, there exist, in addition to the laity-clergy contrasts, a number of contrasts between families. An illustration of these dramatic differences is found in the profile of scores on "Aggressive Political Leadership" (CC 18); see Figure 4-5.

"Support of Unpopular Causes" (CC 50) finds its strongest advocates in the Jewish and Unitarian family, whose ratings of this ministerial function are well above those of the Orthodox, Roman Catholic (Order and Diocesan), and Evangelical A families. Their differences in scores cannot be attributed to chance errors. This ministerial activity or characteristic clearly creates a dividing line between the most liberal and the more conservative of the denominational families.

"Promotion of Understanding of Issues" (CC 14) is another ministerial function that provokes enormous contrasts between clerical and lay expectations. Generally, notably less interest is expressed by laity in a minister's attempting to understand sociological, psychological, and

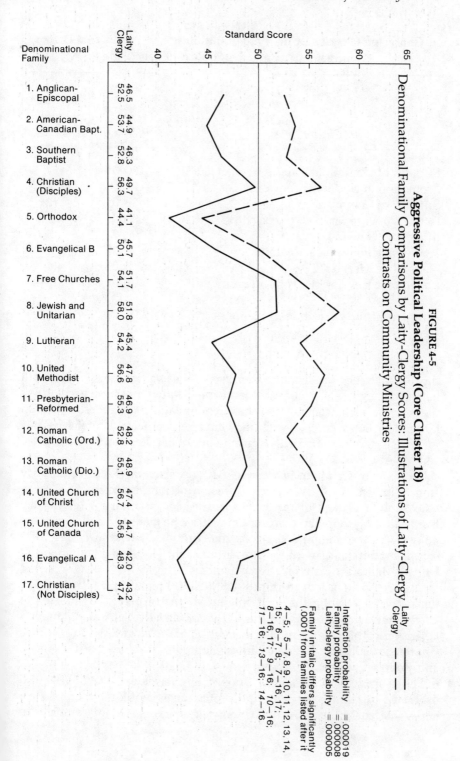

FIGURE 4-5

Aggressive Political Leadership (Core Cluster 18)

Denominational Family Comparisons by Laity-Clergy Scores: Illustrations of Laity-Clergy Contrasts on Community Ministries

Laity ——————
Clergy – – – –

Interaction probability = .000019
Family probability = .000008
Laity-clergy probability = .000005

Family in italic differs significantly
(.0001) from families listed after it

4—5; 5—7,8,9,10,11,12,13,14,
15; 6—7,8; 7—16,17;
8—16,17; 9—16; 10—16;
11—16; 13—16; 14—16

Denominational Family	Laity	Clergy
1. Anglican-Episcopal	46.5	52.5
2. American-Canadian Bapt.	44.9	53.7
3. Southern Baptist	46.3	52.8
4. Christian (Disciples)	49.7	56.3
5. Orthodox	41.1	44.4
6. Evangelical B	45.7	50.1
7. Free Churches	51.7	54.1
8. Jewish and Unitarian	51.8	58.0
9. Lutheran	45.4	54.2
10. United Methodist	47.8	56.6
11. Presbyterian-Reformed	46.9	55.3
12. Roman Catholic (Ord.)	48.2	52.8
13. Roman Catholic (Dio.)	48.9	55.1
14. United Church of Christ	47.4	56.7
15. United Church of Canada	44.7	55.8
16. Evangelical A	42.0	48.3
17. Christian (Not Disciples)	43.2	47.4

TABLE 4-4

Characteristics of a Ministry to Community and World That Draw Contrasting Lay and Professional Expectations

Core Cluster Title	Core Cluster No.	Laity-Clergy Probability	No. of Significant Family Contrasts[a]
Support of Unpopular Causes	50	.000014	4
Promotion of Understanding of Issues	14	.000008	8
Support of Community Causes	15	.00001	12
Active Concern for the Oppressed	16	.00001	7
Interest in New Ideas	33	.000005	13
Aggressive Political Leadership	18	.000005	21
Pastoral Service to All	11	.000059	4
Initiative in Development of Community Services	13	.00007	7
Ecumenical and Educational Openness	8	.00009	5

[a]Significant at a probability level of less than .0001.

theological issues. Specifically, members of the Evangelical A family, both laity and clergy, tend to show the least appreciation for this matter, differing significantly from eight other denominational families: Christian (Disciples), Free Church, Jewish and Unitarian, Lutheran, United Methodist, Presbyterian-Reformed, Roman Catholic (Diocesan), and United Church of Christ.

"Support of Community Causes" (CC 15) also draws a lower priority from members of the Evangelical A denominations, especially their laity, who show a marked disinterest in this aspect of ministry. Joining the Evangelical A group in preferring a minister who tends to isolate his or her ministry from community issues are the Orthodox, whose lower priorities contrast significantly with the evaluation of the Jewish and Unitarian and United Methodist denominational families.

"Active Concern for the Oppressed" (CC 16) points up another emerging pattern. Showing the least interest in that aspect of "Ministry to Community and World" are the Orthodox and Evangelical A families. Characteristically higher in their evaluation of such a ministry are the Free Church, Jewish and Unitarian, United Methodist, Presbyterian-Reformed, and Roman Catholic (Diocesan) families.

The characteristic of having "Interest in New Ideas" (CC 33) is also evaluated differently by laity and professionals, with enormous differences that could occur by chance only at an extremely low probability level of .000005. This characteristic is reflected by a deep involvement with current thinking and an openness to testing new and avant-garde ideas. Of importance is the fact that the contrast is not only between the overall clergy-laity expectations or between Evangelical A denominations and most other denominational families; but the contrast exists also in the differing valuations placed by the clergy and laity within some denominational families on "Interest in New Ideas." For instance, in denominational families that have traditionally emphasized the importance of having a learned clergy, their ministers differ most from their laity in valuing more highly the quality of being open to current ideas. (A likely reason is the liberal accent of several items found in the cluster.) These denominational families are the Anglican-Episcopal, Jewish and Unitarian, Lutheran, Presbyterian-Reformed, United Church of Christ, Roman Catholic (Order and Diocesan), and United Church of Canada.

"Aggressive Political Leadership" (CC 18) poses one of the greatest chasms between clergy and their laity, a chasm that varies by denominational family with differences as large as ten standard scores, or one standard deviation (the distance between the fifteenth and eighty-fifth percentile on a scale). Resistance is greatest among Orthodox and Evangelical A laity; support is greatest among the Free Church and Jewish and Unitarian families. The sharpest contrast between clergy and laity surfaces in the responses of American-Canadian Baptist, Lutheran, United Methodist, Presbyterian-Reformed, and United Church of Christ families. (The profile pattern for this ministry characteristic typifies the patterns formed by the dimensions of Factor 1, "Ministry to Community and World.") Showing least interest in this area of ministry are the Orthodox, Evangelical A, and Christian (not Disciples) families.

"Pastoral Service to All" (CC 11) is a quality of ministry typified by clergy who are already reaching out in a ministry to people of all classes, whether members of the congregation or not. The characteristic involves giving pastoral service to all people with needs, encouraging all classes of people to join one's congregation, and ministering to people in prison as well as to their families. Those placing less importance on this characteristic are found in the Orthodox, Jewish and Unitarian, and Roman Catholic (Order) families, in some contrast to which are the members of Evangelical B denominations. Their significantly higher ranks show them to be the most disposed to an open-door policy for all people.

"Initiative in Development of Community Services" (CC 13) finds less interest among the Evangelical A denominations, which consist primarily of conservative Baptists. They differ significantly from at least one-half of the denominational families in the lower priority they give to a minister's working for improvement in their community and at times originating a new service for persons with special needs. Their scores differ from: Southern Baptists, Free Church, Jewish and Unitarian, United Methodist,

Presbyterian-Reformed, United Church of Christ, and United Church of Canada.

"Ecumenical and Educational Openness" (CC 8) is a personal quality favored least by Evangelical A denominations. Evidencing more interest in such a ministerial stance are the Christian (Disciples), Free Church, United Methodist, Presbyterian-Reformed, and United Church of Christ families. Clergy and laity in these denominations place a higher value on working cooperatively with people who may be culturally and theologically different.

Summary

No area of ministry draws as sharp a disagreement between clergy and laity as the importance of "Ministry to Community and World." Laity's idea of the clergy's task leads them to relegate extracongregational ministries to the category "OK—if there's time," whereas clergy place them much higher on their totem pole of values. One group that does not view community leadership as an appropriate task of their clergy is the Orthodox. Their sacramental concept of ministry calls the priest to a narrower focus. In his chapter on the Orthodox Churches, Harakas acknowledges this fact and gives an explanation of why, in his opinion, such ministries are the responsibility of the laity.

Clearly, when attention is centered on whether or not to emphasize the needs of people in community and world differing models of ministry appear. Denominational families place differing priorities on a community-oriented ministry; laity and clergy also vary in profiles of interest. On the nine characteristics that comprise this factor, laity show levels of interest lower than clergy, but basically parallel to those of clergy.

Theologian in Life and Thought

Laity generally consider it of less importance that a beginning minister seek to be a theologian in life and thought. Their expectations fall well below those of their clergy in every denominational family. Exceptions are the Free Church and Jewish and Unitarian laity, who are in accord with their clergy to a far greater degree than any other denominational family. For the most part, however, laity neither expect nor encourage clergy to probe deeply into theological issues. They assume that what needs to be known has been already learned at seminary. This sense among laity that clergy have "arrived" with respect to what they need to know theologically is illustrated in a profile (see Figure 4-6) that highlights the clergy-laity contrasts typical of the core clusters in this section. Following are the six

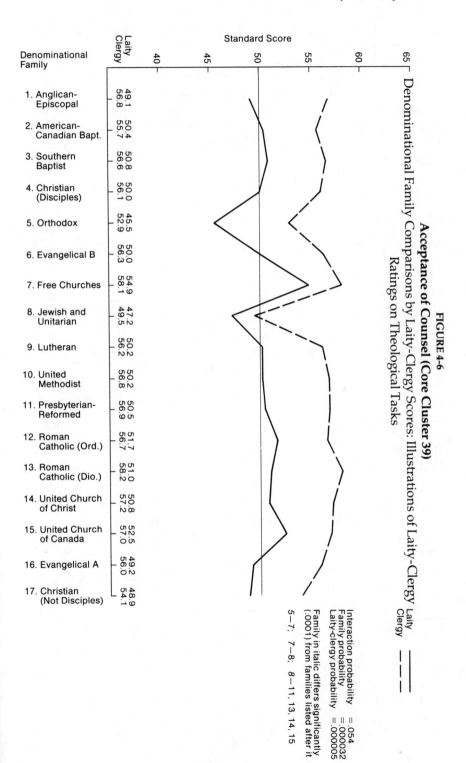

FIGURE 4-6

Acceptance of Counsel (Core Cluster 39)

Denominational Family Comparisons by Laity-Clergy Scores: Illustrations of Laity-Clergy Ratings on Theological Tasks

Standard Score

Denominational Family	Laity	Clergy
1. Anglican-Episcopal	49.1	56.8
2. American-Canadian Bapt.	50.4	55.7
3. Southern Baptist	50.8	56.6
4. Christian (Disciples)	50.0	56.1
5. Orthodox	45.5	52.9
6. Evangelical B	50.0	56.3
7. Free Churches	54.9	58.1
8. Jewish and Unitarian	47.2	49.5
9. Lutheran	50.2	56.2
10. United Methodist	50.2	56.8
11. Presbyterian-Reformed	50.5	56.9
12. Roman Catholic (Ord.)	51.7	56.7
13. Roman Catholic (Dio.)	51.0	58.2
14. United Church of Christ	50.8	57.2
15. United Church of Canada	52.5	57.0
16. Evangelical A	49.2	56.0
17. Christian (Not Disciples)	48.9	54.1

Laity ———
Clergy — — —

Interaction probability = .054
Family probability = .000032
Laity-clergy probability = .000005

Family in italic differs significantly (.0001) from families listed after it

5—7; 7—8; 8—11, 13, 14, 15

characteristics that comprise the factor entitled "Theologian in Life and Thought." (See Table 4-5.)

"Clarity of Thought and Communication" (CC 28) and "Theological Reflection" (CC 29) are valued by fewer laity than clergy. Although these core clusters do rank in the top one-third of ministerial expectations, it should be noted that they were generated by the response of clergy, who seem to associate private intellectual efforts with the communication of insights and to place theological positions within an experiential context. Apparently, laity are less enamored by ministers, who carefully develop distinct theological positions and who then evaluate these positions in light of experience and current theological trends. The differences in how laity, as against clergy, value this characteristic bespeaks a differing perception of the ministerial role. Significantly, there is no denominational family whose scores in these first two characteristics (CC 28 and CC 29) differ from any other family. This difference of perception holds true across the board.

"Use of Broad Knowledge" (CC 30) tends to be favored not only by clergy as a group, but also by the Jewish and Unitarian family, in contrast to the Evangelical A family. Aside from this difference between two denominational groups (significant at a probability of .001), the notable contrast is between laity and clergy, with laity valuing less that beginning ministers have a broad base of knowledge for stimulating people to become thinking believers.

"Acknowledgment of Own Vulnerability" (CC 38), which laity view as a less important quality in beginning ministers, may point up some of their lack of realism regarding clergy. As indicated in Figure 5-38, laity are either less likely to acknowledge the full humanity of clergy or are less inclined toward the stance of openly acknowledging one's struggles of

TABLE 4-5

Characteristics of Theologian in Life and Thought That Draw Contrasting Lay and Clergy Expectations

Core Cluster Title	Core Cluster No.	Laity-Clergy Probability	No. of Significant Family Contrasts[a]
Clarity of Thought and Communication	28	.000027	0
Theological Reflection	29	.000009	0
Use of Broad Knowledge	30	.000026	1
Acknowledgment of Own Vulnerability	38	.000014	3
Acceptance of Counsel	39	.000005	6

[a]Significant at a probability level of less than .001.

faith and feelings as to life's ambiguities. Less appreciative of this personal openness are the laity and clergy of Evangelical B denominations. They value this quality significantly less than do clergy and laity of the Lutheran, Presbyterian-Reformed, and United Church of Christ families.

"Acceptance of Counsel" (CC 39), the last dimension related to the minister's being a "Theologian in Life and Thought," involves the characteristic of seeking to know God's will through the counsel and ministry of others. The failure of some to appreciate the human side of clergy is reflected in the proneness of laity to view this stance as less necessary. The contrast of their scores with what professionals consider important is strikingly documented in the profile given as Figure 4-6. Notable, too, is the high value given this kind of openness by both clergy and laity of the Free Church family, who contrast significantly with Eastern Orthodox and Jewish-Unitarian. Also differing from the Jewish-Unitarian family in the higher priorities they give to seeking God's will through others are members (especially clergy) of the Presbyterian-Reformed, Roman Catholic (Diocesan), United Church of Christ, and United Church of Canada families.

Additional Laity-Clergy Contrasts

Seven additional characteristics show laity-clergy contrasts that suggest differing concepts of what is important in a ministry (Table 4-6). These center on no single area of ministry but represent, rather, a miscellany of ministerial areas.

"Enabling Counseling" (CC 22) is a ministerial competence that laity appreciate less than do their clergy. The importance of having high levels of skill and understanding in aiding people to work through serious problems is less apparent to lay respondents. Most appreciative of such skills appear to be the laity of the Christian (Disciples) family, Jewish and Unitarian, and United Church of Christ; these laity seemingly agree with their clergy in the estimates they give regarding the importance of this ministerial task. However, denominational variations are not sufficiently large to be significant.

"Valuing Diversity" (CC 46) is a quality that laity generally also value less than clergy. They are less desirous than clergy that a beginning minister show appreciation for diversity in people and ideas. Neither are they as interested in the risk involved in possible change. Most resistance to such a characteristic is exhibited by the Orthodox respondents. Contrasting with them in a greater appreciation of this characteristic are the Christian (Disciples), Free Church, Jewish and Unitarian, and United Church of Christ families.

TABLE 4-6
Miscellaneous Ministerial Characteristics That Show Marked Contrast in Clergy-Laity Expectations

Core Cluster Title	Core Cluster No.	Laity-Clergy Probability	No. of Significant Family Contrasts[a]
Enabling Counseling	22	.000016	0
Valuing Diversity	46	.000013	4
Relating Well to Children and Youth	3	.000007	0
Encouragement of World Mission	12	.000009	18
Denominational Knowledge	32	.000011	18
Accepting Mutual Intercession	62	.000013	16
Law Orientation to Ethical Issues	27	.000008	27

[a]Significant at probability level of less than .0001.

"Relating well to Children and Youth" (CC 3) is a dimension in which the usual order is reversed. Laity accord greater importance than do clergy to the beginning minister's ability to relate well to children and youth. This reversal in score level is particularly significant in a day when, as denominations deemphasize youth work, laity have become increasingly dismayed over what is happening to their youth.

"Encouragement of World Mission" (CC 12) shows differences between clergy and laity that vary considerably by denominational family. Generally, laity accord less importance to a global view of one's mission responsibility, with the most notable exception appearing for those of Evangelical B denominations, who, with their clergy, give significantly higher priorities than do the Anglican-Episcopal, Orthodox, Jewish and Unitarian, and Roman Catholic (Order) families. The Jewish and Unitarian group is the family most undervaluing the items that describe a response to world need (including the need for evangelism) that is reflective, sacrificial, and theologically based. It differs significantly in this regard from the other sixteen denominational families.

The lesser interest of laity in a beginning minister's being informed, knowledgeable, and open to information from other sources applies also to ministers being conversant with the polity as well as the political and theological stance of their denomination. Not surprisingly, "Denominational Knowledge" (CC 32) is given lowest priority by a family of churches that does not view itself as a centrally organized denomination. The Christian (not Disciples) family demonstrates its sense of not being a denomination by the extremely low ratings given this core cluster. The highest evaluation of this characteristic is given by the Presbyterian-Reformed family.

The quality of being open to the ministry of other people while actively praying with and for others ("Accepting Mutual Intercession," CC 32) is especially valued by the clergy. They, more than laity, realize and appreciate the support and encouragement this gives a beleaguered cleric. Such a quality is not common to the Jewish and Unitarian members who participated in the Readiness for Ministry Project.

"Law Orientation to Ethical Issues" (CC 27) represents a stance toward people that evokes great variations of response in almost every way (see Figure 4-7). Laity take a harder line with respect to how ethical issues should be approached. Many more laity than clergy expect the minister to condemn, to give solutions, and to make judgments on matters such as suicide. Those least oriented toward such an approach are professionals and laity of the Jewish-Unitarian families. Less inclined also toward taking a strong stand on these matters are the Anglican-Episcopal and United Church of Christ respondents, who score significantly lower than the Orthodox, Evangelical B, and Evangelical A families.

COMMONALITIES IN MINISTRY

Our discussions of ministry models and clergy-laity contrasts may leave the impression that commonalities with respect to perceptions of ministry are few and far between. Actually, that is not the case. Commonalities are the dominant characteristic of twenty-seven of the sixty-four core cluster criteria. Of these, twelve are perceived very similarly irrespective of denominational family or clergy-laity status. They are seen as carrying the same weight in facilitating or hindering an effective ministry. An additional fifteen are viewed quite similarly, meaning commonalities outnumber the differences. Where is one likely to find these commonalities?

Common agreement tends to center in the importance of an "Open, Affirming Style" (Factor 4), in "Caring for Persons under Stress" (Factor 9), and in the abilities needed to give effective "Congregational Leadership" (Factor 8). Across the spectrum of denominational families, these are the areas where expectations of a beginning minister are most likely to be similar.

Characteristics Showing Greatest Commonality

Greatest similarity in perception as to what ought to characterize ministers is found among the six personal qualities of Table 4-7 and the six minis-

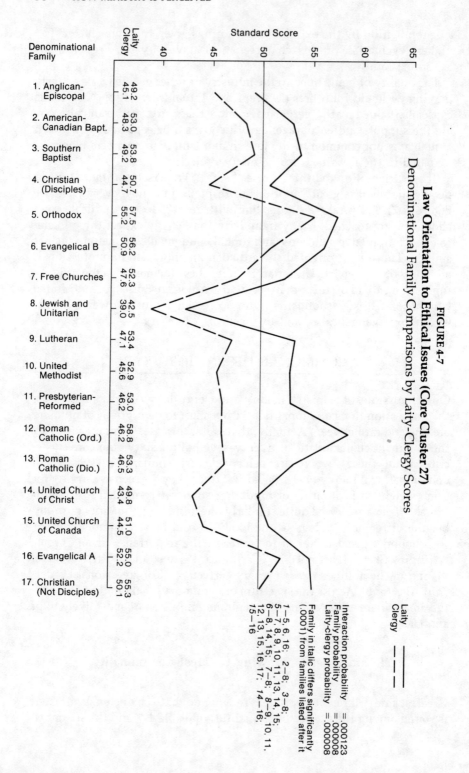

FIGURE 4-7
Law Orientation to Ethical Issues (Core Cluster 27)
Denominational Family Comparisons by Laity-Clergy Scores

Denominational Family	Laity	Clergy
1. Anglican-Episcopal	49.2	45.1
2. American-Canadian Bapt.	53.0	48.3
3. Southern Baptist	53.8	49.2
4. Christian (Disciples)	50.7	44.7
5. Orthodox	57.5	55.2
6. Evangelical B	56.2	50.9
7. Free Churches	52.3	47.6
8. Jewish and Unitarian	42.5	39.0
9. Lutheran	53.4	47.1
10. United Methodist	52.9	45.6
11. Presbyterian-Reformed	53.0	46.2
12. Roman Catholic (Ord.)	58.8	46.2
13. Roman Catholic (Dio.)	53.3	46.5
14. United Church of Christ	49.8	43.4
15. United Church of Canada	51.0	44.5
16. Evangelical A	55.0	52.2
17. Christian (Not Disciples)	55.3	50.1

Laity ———
Clergy — — —

Interaction probability = .000123
Family probability = .000008
Laity-clergy probability = .000008

Family in italic differs significantly (.0001) from families listed after it
1—5, 6, 16; 2—8; 3—8;
5—7, 8, 9, 10, 11, 13, 14, 15;
6—8, 14, 15; 7—8; 8—9, 10, 11,
12, 13, 15, 16, 17; 14—16;
15—16

TABLE 4-7
**Personal Qualities That Seventeen Denominational Families Agree
Are Either Highly Important or Most Detrimental to Ministry**

Rank in Importance	Core Cluster Title	Core Cluster No.	No. of Significant Family Contrasts
Highly Important			
	Fidelity to Tasks and Persons	43	0
	Positive Approach	44	0
	Flexibility of Spirit	45	0
Most Detrimental			
	Alienating Activity	10	0
	Professional Immaturity	52	0
	Self-Protecting Ministry	54	0

Note: Laity-clergy probabilities were not significant on these dimensions.

terial functions of Table 4-8. Each of these characteristics is viewed similarly, irrespective of denominational family. Although the precise measures of variance do record some variation between laity and clergy, on three of the functions the profiles are relatively flat. Commonality, the dominant feature of these ministry characteristics, is clearly evident in the illustrative profile on "Positive Approach" (CC 44) in Figure 4-8.

The six personal qualities about which there is widespread agreement emerge as ones that are seen as either the most detrimental or highly important to a pastoral ministry. Apparently there is little argument regarding their significance in helping or hindering a ministry. No significant differences were found between any of the seventeen denominational families in the high rating of importance they give to "Fidelity to Tasks and Persons" (CC 43), "Positive Approach" (CC 44), and "Flexibility of Spirit" (CC 45). Clergy and laity are in complete agreement with regard to the facilitating quality of these dimensions.

Commonality is also the dominant feature of denominational attitudes toward the ministry-defeating qualities of "Alienating Activity" (CC 10), "Professional Immaturity" (CC 52), and "Self-Protecting Ministry" (CC 54). Clergy and laity alike view these as major hindrances to an effective ministry.

Paralleling these six qualities are six commonly viewed ministerial functions (Table 4-8).

Denominational perceptions of ministry are essentially the same when prioritizing key tasks of "Building Congregational Community" (CC 55), "Relating Faith to Modern World" (CC 1), "Competent Preaching and

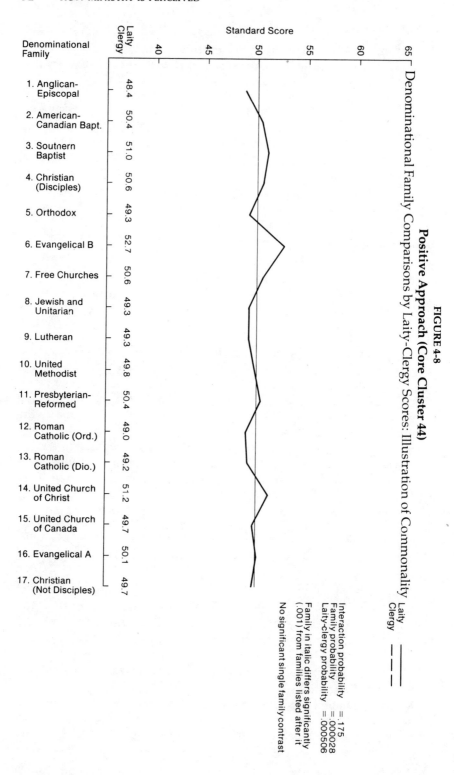

FIGURE 4-8

Positive Approach (Core Cluster 44)

Denominational Family Comparisons by Laity-Clergy Scores: Illustration of Commonality

Standard Score

Denominational Family	Laity Clergy
1. Anglican-Episcopal	48.4
2. American-Canadian Bapt.	50.4
3. Southern Baptist	51.0
4. Christian (Disciples)	50.6
5. Orthodox	49.3
6. Evangelical B	52.7
7. Free Churches	50.6
8. Jewish and Unitarian	49.3
9. Lutheran	49.3
10. United Methodist	49.8
11. Presbyterian-Reformed	50.4
12. Roman Catholic (Ord.)	49.0
13. Roman Catholic (Dio.)	49.2
14. United Church of Christ	51.2
15. United Church of Canada	49.7
16. Evangelical A	50.1
17. Christian (Not Disciples)	49.7

Laity ————
Clergy – – –

Interaction probability = .175
Family probability = .000028
Laity-clergy probability = .000506

Family in italic differs significantly
(.001) from families listed after it

No significant single family contrast

TABLE 4-8

Ministerial Functions Viewed Most Similarly by Laity and Professionals in Seventeen Denominational Families

Core Cluster Title	Core Cluster No.	Laity-Clergy Probability
Building Congregational Community	55	NS[a]
Relating Faith to Modern World	1	NS
Competent Preaching and Worship Leading	5	NS
Involvement in Caring	25	.000157
Comininstry to the Alienated	26	.000048
Responsible Staff Management	59	.000062

Note: No family contrasts were significant at the .0001 level.
[a]Not significant.

Worship Leading" (CC 5), "Involvement in Caring" (CC 25), "Cominstry to the Alienated" (CC 26), and "Responsible Staff Management" (CC 59). Commonality is their dominant feature. However, laity accord less importance to the last three ministerial functions, a difference which is statistically significant. As is already evident, laity are less concerned about ministries to the outsider—the lonely and alienated.

To summarize, the twelve dimensions of Tables 4-7 and 4-8 are viewed alike by all denominational groups. Of these, only three show differences between the scores of laity and clergy. In these aspects of ministry, we have the greatest similarity in perception.

Similar Characteristics with More Differences

Fifteen additional characteristics are viewed alike except for a few exceptions that either point up distinctive emphases of certain denominational families or identify slight but consistent differences between laity and clergy. Although these differences are real, they are muted in comparison to those discussed in the section on contrasts. Commonality is still their dominant characteristic. Admittedly, for some, the line between commonality and contrast is a thin one, because we are indeed dealing with a continuum.

Personal Qualities

The nine characteristics shown in Table 4-9 are personal qualities that are viewed quite similarly, except for a few differences that merit some comment.

TABLE 4-9
Personal Qualities Drawing Quite Similar Expectations but with Some Notable Exceptions

Core Cluster Title	Cluster No.	Laity-Clergy Probability	No. of Significant Family Contrasts[a]
Positive Qualities			
Service in Humility	34	.000033	0
Personal Responsibility	42	.000039	3
Acknowledgment of Limitations	26	.000048	1
Acceptance of Clergy Role	47	NS	2
Negative Qualities			
Intuitive Domination of Decision Making	60	.000028	0
Total Concentration on Congregational Concerns	20	.000107	0
Undisciplined Living	53	.000093	3
Pursuit of Personal Advantage	63	.000106	0
Irresponsibility to the Congregation	64	.000075	0

[a]Significant at .00001 level.

"Service in Humility" (CC 34), an interesting facet of Factor 10 ("Theologian in Life and Thought") ranks first in importance of all sixty-four core clusters. Its presence in this factor indicates that ministers' efforts to be theologians are associated in people's minds with a service orientation; scholarly interests are valued and pursued primarily in order that ministers may more effectively serve people. As characterizes all the dimensions of this factor, laity place a slightly lower value than do clergy on this characteristic for a beginning minister.

"Personal Responsibility" (CC 42) which ranks second highest in importance among the sixty-four core criteria, shows differences between three sets of denominational families. Evangelical B denominations give higher importance to this quality in a beginning pastor than do the Roman Catholic (Order and Diocesan) groups. Here again is further evidence of what is seen in other profiles, that in church bodies holding a high view of ordination, where the priest carries out a sacramental ministry, laity demand less of their clergy on matters relating to their personal qualities.

"Acknowledgment of Limitations" (CC 36) draws a beyond-chance difference in scores between two families of denominations—Evangelical B, and Jewish and Unitarian. The Evangelical B family considers it more important that beginning ministers frankly acknowledge their limitations and mistakes.

"Acceptance of Clergy Role" (CC 47) is another commonly desired characteristic that Evangelical B denominations view as greater in importance. They contrast with the Anglican-Episcopal family and Roman Catholic (Diocesan) family in not wanting beginning ministers to use the authority of their clergy role to wield authority or gain personal power.

"Intuitive Domination of Decision Making" (CC 60) is a personal quality more troubling to laity served by Roman Catholic (Order) priests than those of any other group. They, and to a lesser degree, United Church of Canada laity, contrast significantly with their clergy in seeing this type of leadership as a negative feature in beginning ministers. This quality, ranked fifty-fifth by the entire sample, draws its most unfavorable rank from these laity and, interestingly, from Orthodox clergy.

"Total Concentration on Congregational Concerns" (CC 20) shows its major exception in the scores of laity being less likely to view such a stance toward ministry as detrimental. But this is not true for all denominational groups. Clergy and lay perceptions coincide in several of the families—Anglican-Episcopal, Southern Baptist, Orthodox, Evangelical B, Free Church, Jewish and Unitarian, and Christian (Disciples). In one family (Evangelical A), a switch occurs as the clergy show a greater inclination toward noninvolvement than their laity.

"Undisciplined Living" (CC 53) is another characteristic viewed differently among some of the laity served by the Roman Catholic (Order) family. Its lesser concern over self-indulgent living among clergy contrasts with how this quality of life is viewed within Southern Baptist, Free Church, and Evangelical A denominational families. Members in these latter groups more adamantly view this characteristic (which ranks sixty-third among the sixty-four) as being detrimental to the office of the ministry.

Items in "Pursuit of Personal Advantage" (CC 63) describe the actions of clergy whose personal insecurities are expressed in grandiose ideas and manipulative efforts to gain personal advantages. Although laity are slightly more tolerant of this negative quality, denominational families (clergy and laity) do not vary in their low evaluation of this characteristic.

Laity also are the more tolerant of a ministerial leader who acts irresponsibly toward his or her congregation ("Irresponsibility to the Congregation," CC 64). Offenses such as being intoxicated, committing the congregation to a program without authority, scolding, and sleeping late draw sharper negative valuations from professional clergy. But, again, denominational families do not vary in their estimate of how much such irresponsible conduct hinders an effective ministry. These two qualities are commonly viewed alike.

Ministerial Functions

The final six characteristics that, except for some distinctive differences, tend to be viewed similarly are shown in Table 4-10. Commonality, rather than contrast, still remains their dominant theme.

"Perceptive Counseling" (CC 21), a highly desired competence, is viewed similarly by the seventeen families. However, laity give a lower priority to this ability.

"Caring Availability" (CC 23) finds its highest expectations among Evangelical B denominations. They especially want their pastor to be ready and available to assist hurting people in crisis situations. Significantly lower in their ranking of this service are members of the Anglican-Episcopal and Lutheran families. Although they accord high importance to this eleventh-ranked characteristic, their expectation of a beginning minister is a bit below the average and statistically different from Evangelical B.

"Conflict Utilization" (CC 56) is valued less by laity of all denominational families. They accord less importance than do their clergy to this ministerial competence. Although sampling error probably accounts for most of such variations in laity scores, one must note the suggestion of greater appreciation for this skill among Jewish and Unitarian laity and among both laity and clergy of the United Church of Christ.

"Sharing Congregational Leadership" (CC 57) shows a notable exception in the differing expectations of clergy and laity. Clergy are consistently more sensitive to the need for the kind of pastoral leadership that shares responsibility with laity. It is noteworthy that both Roman Catholic (Order) clergy and laity consider it of lesser importance that lay leadership be employed in a congregational ministry. They differ significantly with Evangelical B, Free Church, United Methodist, Presbyterian-Reformed, United Church of Christ, and United Church of Canada families, who accord greater value to this approach to a congregational ministry.

"Encouragement of Mutuality in Congregation" (CC 4) draws lower ratings from the Anglican-Episcopal family than typify most other denominational families. There is less expectation within this communion that a beginning minister work for a congregational sense of family characterized by mutual sharing, worship, and broad participation. Similarly inclined, and also contrasting with Evangelical B denominations, are members of the Orthodox and the Jewish and Unitarian families.

"Effective Administration" (CC 58) is another ministerial characteristic on which the laity and clergy scores interlace to reflect how their perceptions vary by denominational family. Interestingly, among the Jewish and Unitarian groups, with their greater concern for the intellectual gifts of clergy or rabbi, an efficient administration is seen as less important to a beginning minister. They differ significantly in their lower evaluation of

TABLE 4-10
**Ministerial Functions Drawing Quite Similar Expectations
but with Greater Differences Between Groups**

Core Cluster Title	Core Cluster No.	Laity-Clergy Probability	No. of Significant Family Contrasts[a]
Perceptive Counseling	21	.000021	0
Caring Availability	23	.000088	2
Conflict Utilization	56	.000037	0
Sharing Congregational Leadership	57	.000020	6
Encouragement of Mutuality in Congregation	4	NS[b]	7
Effective Administration	58	NS	5
Liturgical Sensitivity	7	NS	3

[a]Significant at .0001 level.
[b]Not significant.

this ministerial competence from several other denominational families (Southern Baptists, Evangelical B, United Methodist). Tending also to consider this function as of less importance are both the Free Church and Anglican-Episcopal families, who differ significantly in their perception with the Evangelical B family.

Similarly, Evangelical A representatives are less concerned about a worship leader's "Liturgical Sensitivity" (CC 7). Their lesser interest in this characteristic contrasts with their counterparts, Evangelical B denominations, and with those in Presbyterian-Reformed and Roman Catholic (Diocesan) congregations.

CONCLUDING REFLECTIONS

It is a rare person who does not intuitively sense differences between denominations of churches in their approach to ministry. Even though the clues picked up are subtle and seemingly fragmentary, one gains an undeniable impression of varying cultures as they are reflected in such things as the vocabulary people use, the style of architecture, the type of music, liturgical appointments, and sermon emphases. Underlying theological presuppositions do surface to find expression in what an outsider sees, hears, and senses.

Although paper-and-pencil data are far less sensitive than a person's intuitive perceptors, measures used in the Readiness for Ministry Project successfully show nuances of varying denominational perspectives on ministry. Profiles of denominational family scores on sixty-four core clusters show patterns reflecting four basic concepts or models of ministry. In graphic and sometimes quite dramatic form, these profiles show how ministry is differentially perceived.

Although major areas of commonality do exist and although sixty-four commonly used criteria can be identified, it is apparent that differing concepts of ministry, profound and deep, do exist. What one group of laity and clergy deem of highest importance, another group finds a bit embarrassing. Such differing perspectives center in three major areas: "Ministry from Personal Commitment of Faith," "Ministry to Community and World," and "Priestly-Sacramental Ministry." Without question, priorities differ with respect to how these aspects of ministry are perceived. The result is four distinctive models of ministry.

Of the seventeen variables considered in the various multivariate analyses, we found that differences introduced by denomination account for the largest portion of variance. No other grouping results in such marked differences in the priorities people give various kinds of ministry.

A second major source of variation relates to the perception of clergy and laity. As seen earlier, dramatic differences exist in how the two groups view the areas "Ministry to Community and World" and "Theologian in Life and Thought." The degree to which these values are differentially perceived is visibly apparent on the profiles related to these aspects of ministry. Although other single characteristics often draw rather contrasting scores, no other area shows such consistent differences in value.

These contrasts in perceptions signal the need for clergy who consider theirs a prophetic ministry to recognize the weight of opinion and tradition that surrounds many current evaluations by laity. Some tasks viewed as highly important by clergy are discounted by as many laity.

While acknowledging the fact of differing perceptions of importance, one needs, at the very same time, to acknowledge the areas where remarkable commonality occurs. Least variation occurs between denominational families with respect to "Open and Affirming Style" (Factor 4), "Caring for Persons under Stress" (Factor 9), and "Effective Congregational Leadership" (Factor 8). There is quite universal agreement between laity and clergy in congregations on the North American continent regarding the importance of such ministries. Commonality is the dominant characteristic with respect to the perception of ministry held in these areas.

When the initial data on differing models of ministry were shared with several denominational leaders, one smiled and said, "This study will set the ecumenical movement back twenty years!" However, a careful reading of the core findings contradicts this opinion; what is shared here can enhance the churches' search for greater unity. While it may destroy illusions of superficial ecumenical sameness, it inspires hope by highlighting the rich diversity and heritages that churches can share with one another.

As the four models discussed in this chapter suggest, denominational families who affirm a common allegiance to the same Lord, differ sharply in how they define their priorities in ministry. Representatives of the Free Church family, for instance, expressed a frustration over items that carry overtones of an ordained clergy whose function is alien to their concept of ministry. Representatives of the Southern Baptist Churches and the Orthodox Churches found the concept of a "denominational family" disturbing—but for very different reasons. The Baptists were concerned lest readers sense a unity on the denominational level that would deny the autonomy of the individual congregation. The Orthodox were concerned lest their accent on roots dating back to apostolic times be denied by the designation of "a denomination." Real and treasured concepts of ministry distinguish one denominational family from many others.

Readers will perhaps come to experience, as did the researchers, a new appreciation for the insights and sensitivities of each group as it views itself in the larger mosaic of the holy Christian church. Here we are aided by the authors of the denominational chapters, who help us see the fundamental integrity of the approach that characterizes their church body. What may appear initially as erosion or accommodation can be viewed more sympathetically as an attempt faithfully to serve a world vastly changed from the first century. What one is apt to read initially as cultural evasion and a dogged clinging to tradition can be seen as a faithfulness to one's heritage and as an attempt to use its gifts in ministry today.

In the following chapters, you are invited to hear the voices of some 5,000 representatives of churches across North America talk about their vision of ministry and priesthood, trying to be faithful to the past while serving in the present. These expressions can form agendas for clergy and laity in local congregations. On a regional and national level, they can inform strategies being devised for educating new men and women for ministry in the coming decades.

5

Sixty-four Core
Clusters and
Their Profiles

Deborah R. Schuller

One of the most significant groups of data compiled in this study is the set of sixty-four characteristics that laity and clergy indicate are the major concepts they use in assessing the quality of ordained ministry. These characteristics, or dimensions of ministry, arose empirically by the steps described in Chapter 2. They were generated by two mathematical processes that analyze the responses of people to the hundreds of items provided in the questionnaire. Throughout this book, references to the core clusters, by number or by name, are made. The tables in this chapter list the specific items that comprise each of the sixty-four clusters, as well as the value attached to those items by the respondents to the questionnaire. Frequent references are made in Part II to clusters distinctive to each denominational family. These were derived from a separate analysis of the responses of ministers and laity of only that single church body or family of churches.

The items of each of the sixty-four clusters form a unity because people responded in a similar fashion to them. Respondents may have seen all of the items as extremely important or as relatively unimportant; the key is a consistency of response among a large number of people. The clusters

Deborah R. Schuller, formerly a member of the Search Institute staff, is currently engaged in advanced study at York University in Toronto, Ontario.

are presented in a sequence as they developed from factor and cluster analyses of the data. Identification is provided as to the group—clergy, laity, or total group—who initially generated the cluster. The mean presented is the response of the total group to that cluster, even though it may have originated from the response of the laity or the clergy.

The term *load,* which is used in the tables, indicates how strongly the given item contributes to the characteristic identified in the cluster. The higher the load (the closer to 1.00), the greater the importance of that item in delineating the characteristic. The characteristic represents the dimension that underlies the items. To aid in the use of the clusters, the research team has written titles and brief, one-sentence descriptions. These attempt to reflect the cluster as accurately and objectively as possible. At times they represent a degree of interpretation. Thus, in using the core cluster the "given" remains the list of items. The title is at best a form of short-hand, a label to remind one of the fuller description.

Items below the asterisks in this chapter's tables relate to more than one cluster and have been assigned to the given cluster on the basis of functional relevance and a load equal to or greater than .45.

Means are based on the following ratings from the questionnaire:

	From	To
Highly important, essential or mandatory	+2.51	+3.00
Quite important, a major asset	+1.51	+2.50
Somewhat important, a minor asset	+0.51	+1.50
Neither important nor unimportant	−0.50	+0.50
Somewhat detrimental, a minor hindrance in ministry	−1.50	−0.51
Quite detrimental, a major hindrance in ministry	−2.50	−1.51
Highly detrimental, harmful, could destroy the effectiveness of ministry	−3.00	−2.51

READING THE PROFILES

This chapter also includes sixty-four full-page figures, one for each of the core clusters. They show how laity differ from clergy, and how denominational families differ from each other, in the importance they accord each ministry characteristic. In the case of negative characteristics, the profiles show the degree to which each characteristic is viewed as detrimental to an effective ministry.

The ratings of importance each person gave the items of a cluster were translated into a composite standard score. Averaged into overall scores for laity and clergy of each denominational family, they are plotted on graphs for visual inspection. The actual scores are given across the lower portion of the figure, above the denominational families. The average of all responses to the items of that cluster is a score of 50, the midpoint between top and bottom of the figure. The scores of laity and clergy for a particular church or family show how that group differs from the average of all responses.[1]

The distance between clergy-laity scores or between denominational groups cannot always be the basis for drawing conclusions about real differences. If the sample is small and its people varied greatly in their responses, the differences graphed may be due to error variance (see Chapter 19). The list on the right of each figure thus shows which families contrast with which other families in ways that cannot be attributed to chance. Numbers listed on the left are the families that contrast statistically with those on the right.[2]

To the general question "What is it people are looking for in their ministers?" this chapter provides the most comprehensive answer. These sixty-four characteristics describe the configuration of expectations of Christians in North America. But contained within this general pattern of expectations are both common affirmation and great diversity, as the figures indicate. Differences in history, biblical interpretation, understanding of the ministerial role, the relation of the "one set apart" to the rest of the religious community and to the world outside—all these affect the way in which church bodies, their clergy and laity, differ in their portrait of the minister.

NOTES

1. Standard scores show how much an individual's or group's score differs from the average of some other group. The group against which comparison is made is called a *norm* or *standard* group.

A standard score, therefore, shows a group's degree of deviation from a *standard of comparison*. In this chapter, a standard score of fifty represents the average of the comparison group. Each standard score point (or unit) equals one-tenth of a standard deviation from that average. Standard scores greater than fifty are above the average of the comparison or standard group; standard scores less than fifty are below the average of the comparison group. If an individual or group gets a standard score of fifty, their answers on the dimensions under assessment are the same as the average for the comparison group.

A standard score of sixty is one standard deviation above average and a standard score of forty is one standard deviation below average. For any group that is like the comparison group, one can expect 95 percent of the people to receive standard scores between thirty and seventy, slightly less than 70 percent to receive standard scores between forty and sixty, and about 40 percent to receive standard scores between forty-five and fifty-five. Though individuals may receive standard scores beyond the forty to sixty range, one rarely finds the *average* standard score of a *group* of 100 people to be outside that range. To do so the group would need to be quite different from the comparison group with respect to the dimension under assessment.

Standard scores also show how a person's or group's score on one test compares with their score on another quite different test, where the metrics or scales of the two measures are different. (For example, the range of scores on one test may be from ten to 100 with an average of seventy, and the range of scores on another test may be from thirty-five to eighty-five with an average of fifty-five. It is obvious that a score of sixty-five could not mean the same for both tests.)

When the scores on both tests are changed to standard scores, the averages of both become fifty, and a standard deviation from the average is ten points for both tests. Resulting standard scores then mean the same for both tests and comparisons can be made between scores on both tests.

2. The *test for interaction* shows the probability that for the criterion under consideration people on the average do not differ simultaneously by their clergy or lay status and by denominational family, and that the amount of clergy/laity difference does not vary significantly by denomination. The *test for family* shows the probability that for the criterion under consideration people in one denominational family, regardless of whether clergy or laity, on the average do not differ from those of another denominational family or set of denominational families. The *test for clergy and lay differences* shows the probability that the clergy on the average do not differ from the laity by a particular amount regardless of denominational family.

For the first characteristic (Figure 5-1) this says in general: (1) There are six chances in 100 that denominational family and laity-clergy status are not related jointly to "Relating Faith to Modern World" (i.e., one might get this degree of difference due to sampling procedures without their being a real relationship in the population). (2) There are twenty-seven chances in one million that one's denominational family is not related to this issue of relating faith to the modern world. (3) There are twenty-four chances in one hundred that one's position as laity or clergy is not related to this issue.

TABLE 5-1
Core Cluster 1: Relating Faith to Modern World
(sensitive interpretation and teaching of the gospel in contemporary life)

Load	Item No.	Item	Mean
.71	44	Presents the Gospel[a] in terms understandable to the modern mind	2.555
.65	41	Helps laypeople relate Christian teachings to current issues and human needs	2.454
.56	48	Helps people determine religious educational needs in the congregation	1.903
.44	45	Explains any changes introduced into the worship service	1.778
		* * *	
.45	49	When teaching, is able to keep students interested	2.302
		Grand mean	2.20

[a]Wording of items conforms here to usage of the 46 Christian denominations, although a parallel Jewish form was also provided. See the introduction for details.

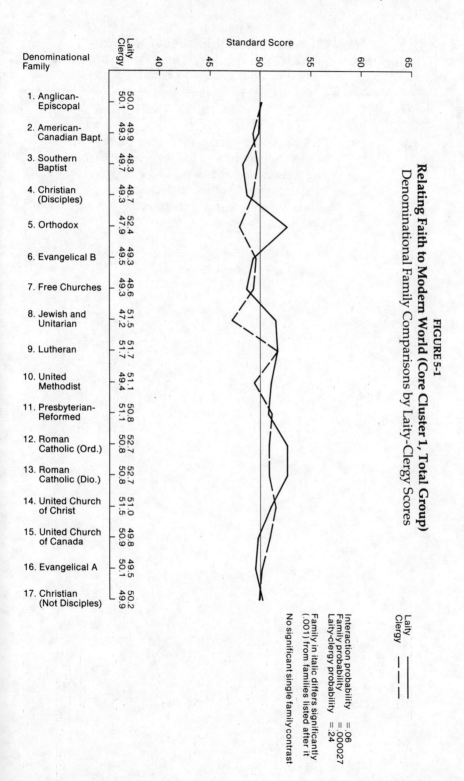

FIGURE 5-1
Relating Faith to Modern World (Core Cluster 1, Total Group)
Denominational Family Comparisons by Laity-Clergy Scores

Denominational Family	Laity	Clergy
1. Anglican-Episcopal	50.0	50.1
2. American-Canadian Bapt.	49.9	49.3
3. Southern Baptist	48.3	49.7
4. Christian (Disciples)	48.7	49.3
5. Orthodox	52.4	47.9
6. Evangelical B	49.3	49.5
7. Free Churches	48.6	49.3
8. Jewish and Unitarian	51.5	47.2
9. Lutheran	51.7	51.7
10. United Methodist	51.1	49.4
11. Presbyterian-Reformed	50.8	51.1
12. Roman Catholic (Ord.)	52.7	50.8
13. Roman Catholic (Dio.)	52.7	50.8
14. United Church of Christ	51.0	51.5
15. United Church of Canada	49.8	50.9
16. Evangelical A	49.5	50.1
17. Christian (Not Disciples)	50.2	49.9

Standard Score

Laity ————
Clergy — — —

Interaction probability = .06
Family probability = .000027
Laity-clergy probability = .24

Family in italic differs significantly
(.001) from families listed after it

No significant single family contrast

TABLE 5-2
Core Cluster 2: Theocentric-Biblical Ministry
(drawing attention to God's Word and Person when preaching,
teaching, and leading worship)

Load	Item No.	Item	Mean
.60	50	Guides people by relating the Scriptures to their human condition	2.176
.58	46	Uses biblical insights to guide members in making ethical or moral decisions	2.141
.50	43	Leads worship so it is seen as focusing on God	2.425
		* * *	
.45	47	When he is through preaching, you are conscious of Jesus Christ	2.232
		Grand mean	2.24

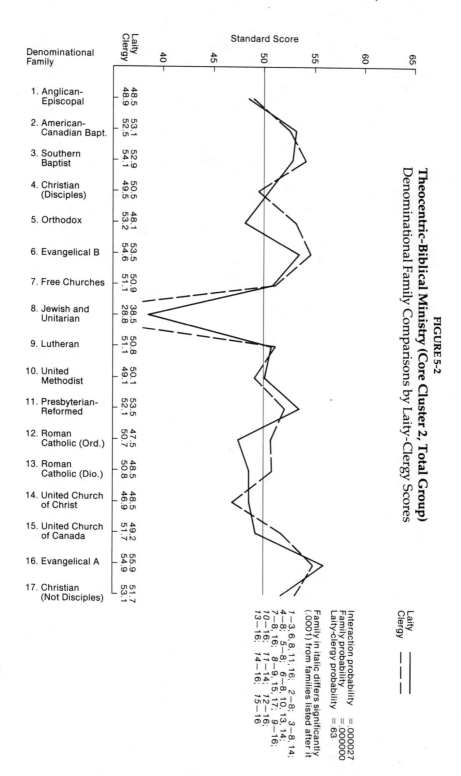

FIGURE 5-2

Theocentric-Biblical Ministry (Core Cluster 2, Total Group)
Denominational Family Comparisons by Laity-Clergy Scores

Denominational Family	Laity	Clergy
1. Anglican-Episcopal	48.5	48.9
2. American-Canadian Bapt.	53.1	52.5
3. Southern Baptist	52.9	54.1
4. Christian (Disciples)	50.5	49.5
5. Orthodox	48.1	53.2
6. Evangelical B	53.5	54.6
7. Free Churches	50.9	51.1
8. Jewish and Unitarian	38.5	28.8
9. Lutheran	50.8	51.1
10. United Methodist	50.1	49.1
11. Presbyterian-Reformed	53.5	52.1
12. Roman Catholic (Ord.)	47.5	50.7
13. Roman Catholic (Dio.)	48.5	50.8
14. United Church of Christ	48.5	46.9
15. United Church of Canada	49.2	51.7
16. Evangelical A	55.9	54.9
17. Christian (Not Disciples)	51.7	53.1

Laity ———
Clergy — — —

Interaction probability = .000027
Family probability = .000000
Laity-clergy probability = .63

Family in italic differs significantly
(.0001) from families listed after it

1–3, 6, 8, 11, 16; 2–8; 3–8, 14;
4–8; 5–8; 6–8, 10, 13, 14;
7–8, 16; 8–9, 15, 17; 9–16;
10–16; 11–14; 12–16;
13–16; 14–16; 15–16;

TABLE 5-3
Core Cluster 3: Relating Well to Children and Youth
(showing sensitivity and skill in ministering to children and youth
as individuals)

Load	Item No.	Item	Mean
.66	77	Treats children as thinking individuals	2.268
.62	99	Is effective in working with students and other young adults	2.175
.57	68	Sees youth as part of the congregation rather than a programmatic appendage	2.597
.56	89	Demonstrates the skills needed to teach small children effectively	1.473
.54	74	Helps the congregation keep in touch with disinterested youth	2.030
.53	51	Conducts worship services in a way that is meaningful for children	1.728
		Grand mean	2.04

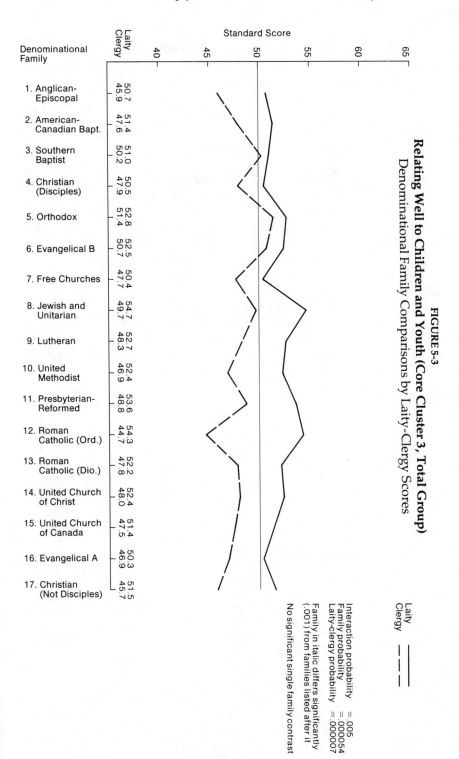

FIGURE 5-3

Relating Well to Children and Youth (Core Cluster 3, Total Group)
Denominational Family Comparisons by Laity-Clergy Scores

Standard Score

Denominational
Family

	Laity	Clergy
1. Anglican-Episcopal	50.7	45.9
2. American-Canadian Bapt.	51.4	47.6
3. Southern Baptist	51.0	50.2
4. Christian (Disciples)	50.5	47.9
5. Orthodox	52.8	51.4
6. Evangelical B	52.5	50.7
7. Free Churches	50.4	47.7
8. Jewish and Unitarian	54.7	49.7
9. Lutheran	52.7	48.3
10. United Methodist	52.4	46.9
11. Presbyterian-Reformed	53.6	48.8
12. Roman Catholic (Ord.)	54.3	44.7
13. Roman Catholic (Dio.)	52.2	47.8
14. United Church of Christ	52.4	48.0
15. United Church of Canada	51.4	47.5
16. Evangelical A	50.3	46.9
17. Christian (Not Disciples)	51.5	45.7

Laity ———
Clergy – – –

Interaction probability = .005
Family probability = .000054
Laity-clergy probability = .000007

Family in italic differs significantly
(.001) from families listed after it

No significant single family contrast

TABLE 5-4

Core Cluster 4: Encouragement of Mutuality in Congregation
(developing a congregational sense of being a family of God where there
is mutual sharing, worship, and broad participation)

Load	Item No.	Item	Mean
.58	101	Encourages and stimulates a singing congregation	1.643
.50	90	Provides opportunities for fuller, richer, participation of congregation in shared prayers	1.713
.49	73	Leads worship in a manner that inspires joy	2.223
.45	100	Provides opportunities within the congregation for personal growth and spiritual enrichment	2.419
.44	85	Preaches funeral sermons that acknowledge personal grief	1.426
.40	95	Becomes a part of the daily life, work, and play of the people served	2.175
		Grand mean	1.93

60658

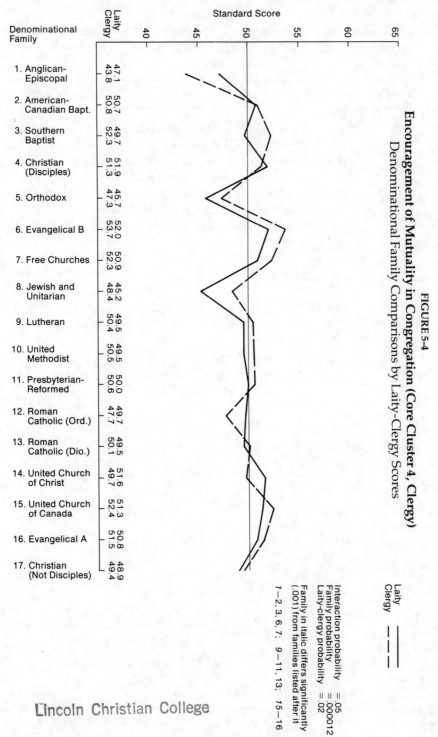

FIGURE 5-4
Encouragement of Mutuality in Congregation (Core Cluster 4, Clergy)
Denominational Family Comparisons by Laity-Clergy Scores

Standard Score

Denominational Family	Laity Clergy
1. Anglican-Episcopal	47.1 / 43.8
2. American-Canadian Bapt.	50.7 / 50.8
3. Southern Baptist	49.7 / 52.3
4. Christian (Disciples)	51.9 / 51.3
5. Orthodox	45.7 / 47.3
6. Evangelical B	52.0 / 53.7
7. Free Churches	50.9 / 52.3
8. Jewish and Unitarian	45.2 / 48.4
9. Lutheran	49.5 / 50.4
10. United Methodist	49.5 / 50.5
11. Presbyterian-Reformed	50.0 / 50.6
12. Roman Catholic (Ord.)	49.7 / 47.7
13. Roman Catholic (Dio.)	49.5 / 50.1
14. United Church of Christ	51.6 / 49.7
15. United Church of Canada	51.3 / 52.4
16. Evangelical A	50.8 / 51.5
17. Christian (Not Disciples)	48.9 / 49.4

Laity ————
Clergy – – –

Interaction probability = .05
Family probability = .000012
Laity-clergy probability = .02

Family in italic differs significantly
(.001) from families listed after it

1–2, 3, 6, 7; 9–11, 13; 15–16

TABLE 5-5
Core Cluster 5: Competent Preaching and Worship Leading
(holding attention while preaching and being well in command of all aspects of a service)

Load	Item No.	Item	Mean
.63	70	When preaching, holds the interest and attention of congregation	2.455
.47	65	Conducts smoothly all the religious rites that occur in the local setting	1.519
.42	55	Handles disturbances during worship in ways that both maintain the dignity of the service and minister to needs of people	1.657
		Grand mean	1.87

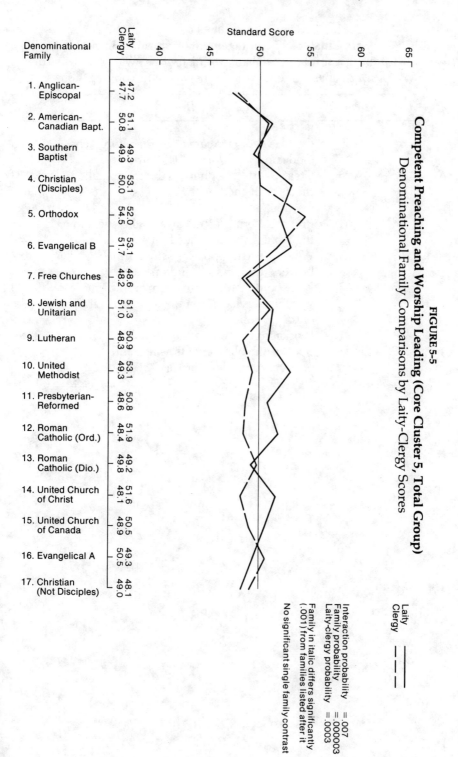

FIGURE 5-5

Competent Preaching and Worship Leading (Core Cluster 5, Total Group)

Denominational Family Comparisons by Laity-Clergy Scores

Standard Score

Denominational Family	Laity	Clergy
1. Anglican-Episcopal	47.2	47.7
2. American-Canadian Bapt.	51.1	50.8
3. Southern Baptist	49.3	49.9
4. Christian (Disciples)	53.1	50.0
5. Orthodox	52.0	54.5
6. Evangelical B	53.1	51.7
7. Free Churches	48.6	48.2
8. Jewish and Unitarian	51.3	51.0
9. Lutheran	50.9	48.3
10. United Methodist	53.1	49.3
11. Presbyterian-Reformed	50.8	48.6
12. Roman Catholic (Ord.)	51.9	48.4
13. Roman Catholic (Dio.)	49.2	49.8
14. United Church of Christ	51.6	48.1
15. United Church of Canada	50.5	48.9
16. Evangelical A	49.3	50.5
17. Christian (Not Disciples)	48.1	49.0

Laity ———
Clergy — — —

Interaction probability = .007
Family probability = .000003
Laity-clergy probability = .0003

Family in italic differs significantly
(.001) from families listed after it

No significant single family contrast

TABLE 5-6
Core Cluster 6: Encouragement of Spiritual Sensitivity
(offering a spiritually sensitive ministry that awakens a sense of
forgiveness, freedom, and renewal in the congregation)

Load	Item No.	Item	Mean
.76	59	Enables people to sense the gift of forgiveness God conveys through his Word	2.473
.75	96	Creates an atmosphere in the congregation that is enlivened by the gospel spirit of freedom and love	2.173
.64	64	Preaches sermons that awaken listeners to their sinfulness and need for a Savior	1.541
.60	53	When preaching, places self, as much as hearers, under God's judgment	2.197
.53	67	Will spontaneously change plans during a worship service in response to the leading of the Spirit	0.690
.51	91	Works for renewal in the Church	2.096
.39	57	Speaks of biblical events as real and important not dead history	2.231
		Grand mean	1.93

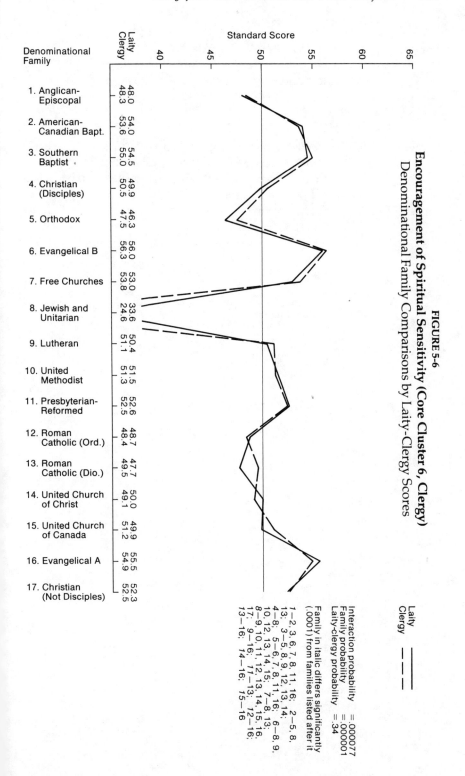

FIGURE 5-6

Encouragement of Spiritual Sensitivity (Core Cluster 6, Clergy)
Denominational Family Comparisons by Laity-Clergy Scores

Denominational Family		Laity	Clergy
1. Anglican-Episcopal		48.0	48.3
2. American-Canadian Bapt.		54.0	53.6
3. Southern Baptist		54.5	55.0
4. Christian (Disciples)		49.9	50.5
5. Orthodox		46.3	47.5
6. Evangelical B		56.0	56.3
7. Free Churches		53.0	53.8
8. Jewish and Unitarian		33.6	24.6
9. Lutheran		50.4	51.1
10. United Methodist		51.5	51.3
11. Presbyterian-Reformed		52.6	52.5
12. Roman Catholic (Ord.)		48.7	48.4
13. Roman Catholic (Dio.)		47.7	49.5
14. United Church of Christ		50.0	49.1
15. United Church of Canada		49.9	51.2
16. Evangelical A		55.5	54.9
17. Christian (Not Disciples)		52.3	52.5

Standard Score: 40 45 50 55 60 65

Laity ———
Clergy — — —

Interaction probability = .000077
Family probability = .000001
Laity-clergy probability = .34

Family in italic differs significantly
(.0001) from families listed after it

1–2, 3, 6, 7, 8, 11, 16; 2–5, 8,
13; 3–5, 8, 9, 12, 13, 14;
4–8; 5–6, 7, 8, 11, 16; 6–8, 9,
10, 12, 13, 14, 15; 7–8, 13;
8–9, 10, 11, 12, 13, 14, 15, 16,
17; 9–16; 11–13; 12–16;
13–16; 14–16; 15–16

TABLE 5-7
Core Cluster 7: Liturgical Sensitivity
(appreciative and competent in the use of what is pastorally
suitable and inspiring in a worship service)

Load	Item No.	Item	Mean
.56	93	Demonstrates an appreciation for music which is liturgically and pastorally suitable	1.570
.50	94	Celebrates worship services in a professional yet personal manner	2.065
.37	79	Shows competence in use of the arts in worship	1.264
		Grand mean	1.63

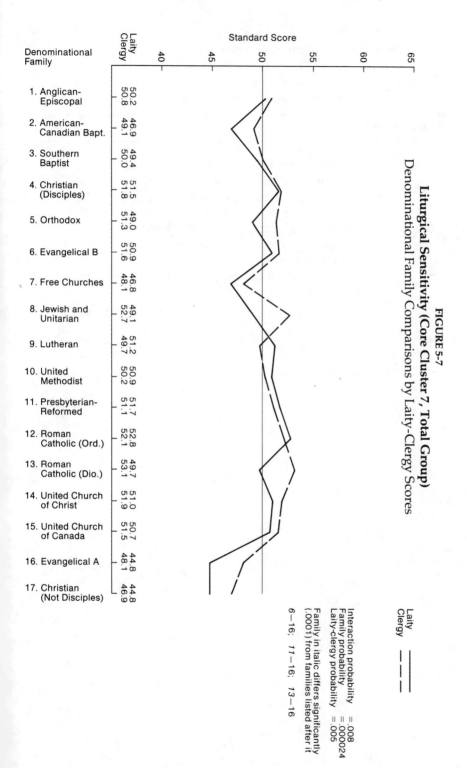

FIGURE 5-7

Liturgical Sensitivity (Core Cluster 7, Total Group)
Denominational Family Comparisons by Laity-Clergy Scores

Denominational
Family

Standard Score

Laity
Clergy

	Laity	Clergy
1. Anglican-Episcopal	50.2	50.8
2. American-Canadian Bapt.	46.9	49.1
3. Southern Baptist	49.4	50.0
4. Christian (Disciples)	51.5	51.8
5. Orthodox	49.0	51.3
6. Evangelical B	50.9	51.6
7. Free Churches	46.8	48.1
8. Jewish and Unitarian	49.1	52.7
9. Lutheran	51.2	49.7
10. United Methodist	50.9	50.2
11. Presbyterian-Reformed	51.7	51.1
12. Roman Catholic (Ord.)	52.8	52.1
13. Roman Catholic (Dio.)	49.7	53.1
14. United Church of Christ	51.0	51.9
15. United Church of Canada	50.7	51.5
16. Evangelical A	44.8	48.1
17. Christian (Not Disciples)	44.8	46.9

Laity ——
Clergy – – –

Interaction probability = .008
Family probability = .000024
Laity-clergy probability = .005

Family in italic differs significantly
(.0001) from families listed after it

6–16; 11–16; 13–16

TABLE 5-8
Core Cluster 8: Ecumenical and Educational Openness:
Openness to Pluralism
(openness to cooperation with people whose theology, culture,
or educational methods are different)

Load	Item No.	Item	Mean
.59	82	Participates in ecumenical projects with ministers of other denominations	1.567
.59	56	Develops educational ministries with persons of other races and cultures	1.086
.58	71	Has thought through a theological stance regarding cooperation with other denominations	1.773
.51	66	Supports responsible persons trying new educational methods or ideas	1.842
		Grand mean	1.57

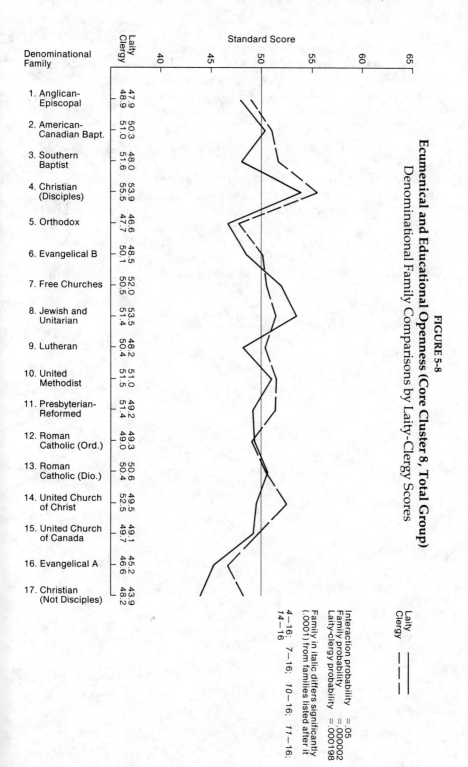

FIGURE 5-8

Ecumenical and Educational Openness (Core Cluster 8, Total Group)

Denominational Family Comparisons by Laity-Clergy Scores

Denominational Family	Laity	Clergy
1. Anglican-Episcopal	47.9	48.9
2. American-Canadian Bapt.	50.3	51.0
3. Southern Baptist	48.0	51.6
4. Christian (Disciples)	53.9	55.5
5. Orthodox	46.6	47.7
6. Evangelical B	48.5	50.1
7. Free Churches	52.0	50.6
8. Jewish and Unitarian	53.5	51.4
9. Lutheran	48.2	50.4
10. United Methodist	51.0	51.5
11. Presbyterian-Reformed	49.2	51.4
12. Roman Catholic (Ord.)	49.3	49.0
13. Roman Catholic (Dio.)	50.6	50.4
14. United Church of Christ	49.5	52.5
15. United Church of Canada	49.1	49.7
16. Evangelical A	45.2	46.6
17. Christian (Not Disciples)	43.9	48.2

Laity ——————

Clergy — — —

Interaction probability = .05
Family probability = .000002
Laity-clergy probability = .000198

Family in italic differs significantly
(.0001) from families listed after it

4–16; 7–16; 10–16; 11–16;
14–16

TABLE 5-9
Core Cluster 9: Sacramental-Liturgical Ministry
(orientation toward worship, and stressing the sacramental and
liturgical aspects of the faith)

Load	Item No.	Item	Mean
.63	76	Considers his professional ministry as sacramental	0.832
.61	63	Is primarily worship oriented—sees self as first and foremost a liturgist	−0.302
.58	54	Never deviates from traditional orders of worship	−1.089
.57	92	Understands and appreciates the dogmatic and liturgical foundations of prayer	1.440
.49	61	Explains the meaning of worship and liturgy	1.913
		* * *	
.52	78	Teaches the meaning of sacraments	1.894
		Grand mean	1.07

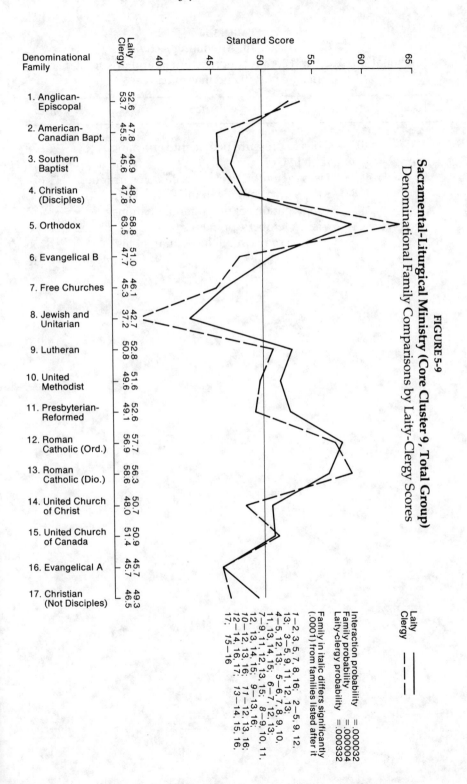

FIGURE 5-9

Sacramental-Liturgical Ministry (Core Cluster 9, Total Group)
Denominational Family Comparisons by Laity-Clergy Scores

Denominational Family	Laity	Clergy
1. Anglican-Episcopal	52.6	53.7
2. American-Canadian Bapt.	47.8	45.5
3. Southern Baptist	46.9	45.6
4. Christian (Disciples)	48.2	47.8
5. Orthodox	58.8	63.5
6. Evangelical B	51.0	47.7
7. Free Churches	46.1	45.3
8. Jewish and Unitarian	42.7	37.2
9. Lutheran	52.8	50.8
10. United Methodist	51.6	49.6
11. Presbyterian-Reformed	52.6	49.1
12. Roman Catholic (Ord.)	57.7	56.9
13. Roman Catholic (Dio.)	56.3	58.6
14. United Church of Christ	50.7	48.0
15. United Church of Canada	50.9	51.4
16. Evangelical A	45.7	45.7
17. Christian (Not Disciples)	49.3	46.5

Laity ———
Clergy — — —

Interaction probability = .000032
Family probability = .000004
Laity-clergy probability = .000332

Family in italic differs significantly
(.0001) from families listed after it

1—2, 3, 5, 7, 8, 16; 2—5, 9, 12,
13; *3*—5, 9, 11, 12, 13;
4—5, 12, 13; *5*—6, 7, 8, 9, 10,
11, 13, 14, 15; *6*—7, 12, 13;
7—9, 11, 12, 13, 15; *8*—9, 10, 11,
12, 13, 14, 15; *9*—13, 16;
10—12, 13, 16; *11*—12, 13, 16;
12—14, 16, 17; *13*—14, 15, 16;
17; 15—16

TABLE 5-10
Core Cluster 10: Alienating Activity
(alienation of self and congregation by public and private stances
that are critical and manipulative)

Load	Item No.	Item	Mean
.70	103	Tries to pressure people into affirming faith in God	−1.678
.64	102	Uses the pulpit to express personal irritation	−1.674
.59	108	Keeps own congregation "apart" from congregations of other denominations	−1.533
.58	104	Visits members' homes only when requested	−1.302
.53	105	Seldom prays in public without notes	−1.536
		Grand mean	−1.54

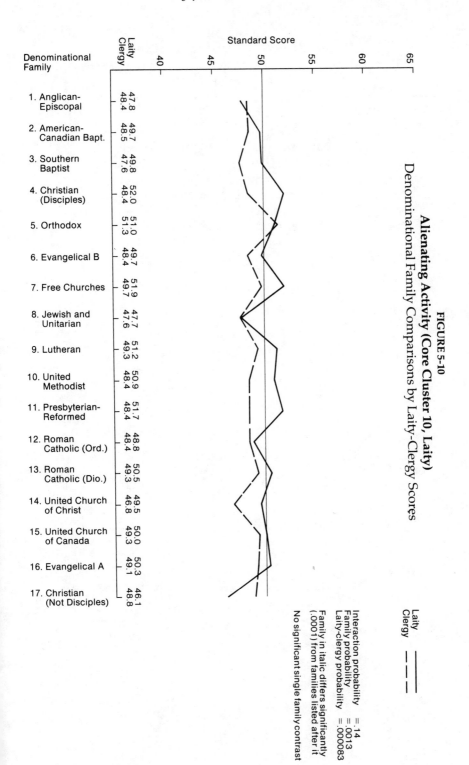

FIGURE 5-10
Alienating Activity (Core Cluster 10, Laity)
Denominational Family Comparisons by Laity-Clergy Scores

Denominational Family	Laity	Clergy
1. Anglican-Episcopal	47.8	48.4
2. American-Canadian Bapt.	49.7	48.5
3. Southern Baptist	49.8	47.6
4. Christian (Disciples)	52.0	48.4
5. Orthodox	51.0	51.3
6. Evangelical B	49.7	48.4
7. Free Churches	51.9	49.7
8. Jewish and Unitarian	47.7	47.6
9. Lutheran	51.2	49.3
10. United Methodist	50.9	48.4
11. Presbyterian-Reformed	51.7	48.4
12. Roman Catholic (Ord.)	48.8	48.4
13. Roman Catholic (Dio.)	50.5	49.3
14. United Church of Christ	49.5	46.8
15. United Church of Canada	50.0	49.3
16. Evangelical A	50.3	49.1
17. Christian (Not Disciples)	46.1	48.8

Laity ———
Clergy – – –

Interaction probability = .14
Family probability = .0013
Laity-clergy probability = .000083

Family in italic differs significantly
(.0001) from families listed after it

No significant single family contrast

TABLE 5-11
Core Cluster 11: Pastoral Service to All
(reaching out in ministering to persons of all classes,
whether members or not)

Load	Item No.	Item	Mean
.62	147	Gives pastoral service to all people with needs	2.325
.59	154	Encourages all classes of people to join the congregation	2.097
.42	152	Ministers to persons in prison and their families, whether members of the congregation or not	1.348
		Grand mean	1.92

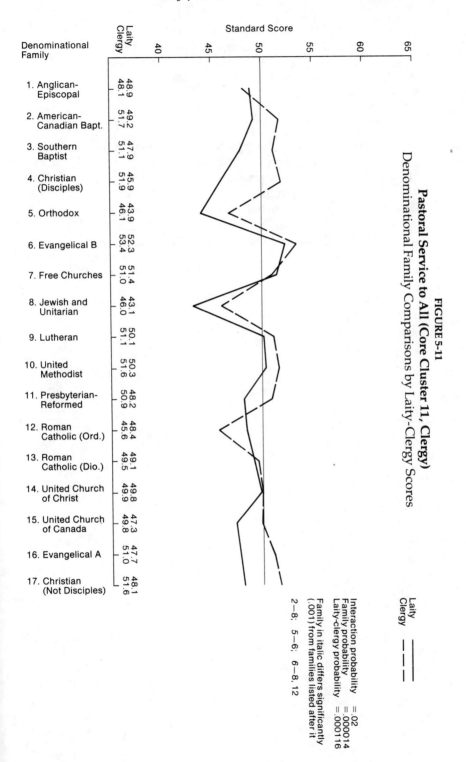

FIGURE 5-11

Pastoral Service to All (Core Cluster 11, Clergy)

Denominational Family Comparisons by Laity-Clergy Scores

Laity
Clergy — — —

Interaction probability = .02
Family probability = .000014
Laity-clergy probability = .000116

Family in italic differs significantly
(.001) from families listed after it

2–8; 5–6; 6–8, 12

Denominational Family

	Laity	Clergy
1. Anglican-Episcopal	48.9	48.1
2. American-Canadian Bapt.	49.2	51.7
3. Southern Baptist	47.9	51.1
4. Christian (Disciples)	45.9	51.9
5. Orthodox	43.9	46.1
6. Evangelical B	52.3	53.4
7. Free Churches	51.4	51.0
8. Jewish and Unitarian	43.1	46.0
9. Lutheran	50.1	51.1
10. United Methodist	50.3	51.6
11. Presbyterian-Reformed	48.2	50.9
12. Roman Catholic (Ord.)	48.4	45.6
13. Roman Catholic (Dio.)	49.1	49.5
14. United Church of Christ	49.8	49.9
15. United Church of Canada	47.3	49.8
16. Evangelical A	47.7	51.0
17. Christian (Not Disciples)	48.1	51.6

Standard Score: 40, 45, 50, 55, 60, 65

TABLE 5-12
Core Cluster 12: Encouragement of World Mission
(stimulating a congregational response to world need that is
reflective, theologically based, and sacrificial)

Load	Item No.	Item	Mean
.68	146	Stimulates congregation to new interest and support for world missions	1.785
.54	110	Presents a theological basis for the mission of the Church	2.018
.49	120	Urges parish to respond to critical needs in the world through sacrificial giving	1.689
.44	147	Gives pastoral service to all people with needs	2.325
		Grand mean	1.95

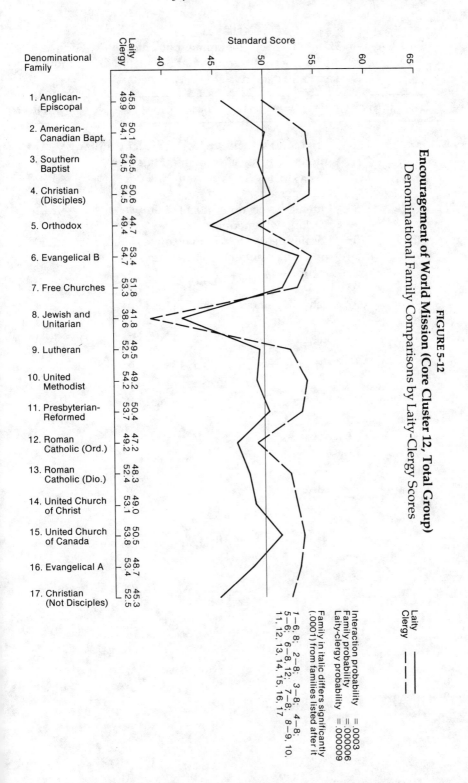

FIGURE 5-12

Encouragement of World Mission (Core Cluster 12, Total Group)

Denominational Family Comparisons by Laity-Clergy Scores

Denominational Family	Laity	Clergy
1. Anglican-Episcopal	45.8	49.9
2. American-Canadian Bapt.	50.1	54.1
3. Southern Baptist	49.5	54.5
4. Christian (Disciples)	50.6	54.5
5. Orthodox	44.7	49.4
6. Evangelical B	53.4	54.7
7. Free Churches	51.8	53.3
8. Jewish and Unitarian	41.8	38.6
9. Lutheran	49.5	52.5
10. United Methodist	49.2	54.2
11. Presbyterian-Reformed	50.4	53.7
12. Roman Catholic (Ord.)	47.2	49.2
13. Roman Catholic (Dio.)	48.3	52.4
14. United Church of Christ	49.0	53.1
15. United Church of Canada	50.5	53.8
16. Evangelical A	48.7	53.4
17. Christian (Not Disciples)	45.3	52.5

Laity ——
Clergy – – –

Interaction probability = .0003
Family probability = .000006
Laity-clergy probability = .000009

Family in italic differs significantly
(.0001) from families listed after it
1–6; 2–8; 3–8; 4–8;
5–6; 6–8,12; 7–8; 8–9,10,
11,12,13,14,15,16,17

TABLE 5-13
Core Cluster 13: Initiative in Development of Community Services
(working for improvement and sometimes originating community
service to persons with special needs)

Load	Item No.	Item	Mean
.62	114	Originates activities which consider youths' interests and awaken their enthusiasm	2.173
.61	111	Works to improve community services to older persons	1.730
.52	113	Often goes beyond the call of duty in working with people	2.020
.45	118	Locates people to whom he might refer individuals not helped by community agencies	1.604
		* * *	
.42	109	Actively works for justice in the local community	1.627
		Grand mean	1.83

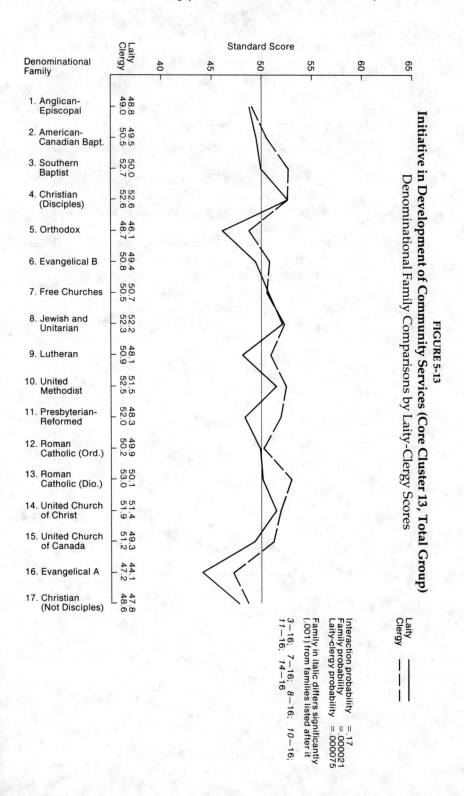

FIGURE 5-13

Initiative in Development of Community Services (Core Cluster 13, Total Group)

Denominational Family Comparisons by Laity-Clergy Scores

Denominational Family	Laity	Clergy
1. Anglican-Episcopal	48.8	49.0
2. American-Canadian Bapt.	49.5	50.5
3. Southern Baptist	50.0	52.7
4. Christian (Disciples)	52.6	52.6
5. Orthodox	46.1	48.7
6. Evangelical B	49.4	50.8
7. Free Churches	50.7	50.5
8. Jewish and Unitarian	52.2	52.3
9. Lutheran	48.1	50.9
10. United Methodist	51.5	52.5
11. Presbyterian-Reformed	48.3	52.0
12. Roman Catholic (Ord.)	49.9	50.2
13. Roman Catholic (Dio.)	50.1	53.0
14. United Church of Christ	51.4	51.9
15. United Church of Canada	49.3	51.2
16. Evangelical A	44.1	47.2
17. Christian (Not Disciples)	47.8	48.6

Laity ⎯⎯⎯
Clergy ⎯ ⎯ ⎯

Interaction probability = .17
Family probability = .000021
Laity-clergy probability = .000075

Family in italic differs significantly (.001) from families listed after it

3–16; 7–16; 8–16; 10–16; 11–16; 14–16

TABLE 5-14
Core Cluster 14: Promotion of Understanding of Issues
(developing, using, and encouraging theological, sociological, and
psychological understandings in ministry)

Load	Item No.	Item	Mean
.63	138	Demonstrates understanding of the influence of social and psychological forces on people	1.590
.63	131	Explores theological issues underlying current social movements	1.344
.50	132	Helps youth identify their gods and evaluate their adequacies	1.661
.47	145	Identifies sociological characteristics of congregation and community	1.239
.47	125	Invites professionals from the community to participate in congregational programs or services	1.098
		Grand mean	1.39

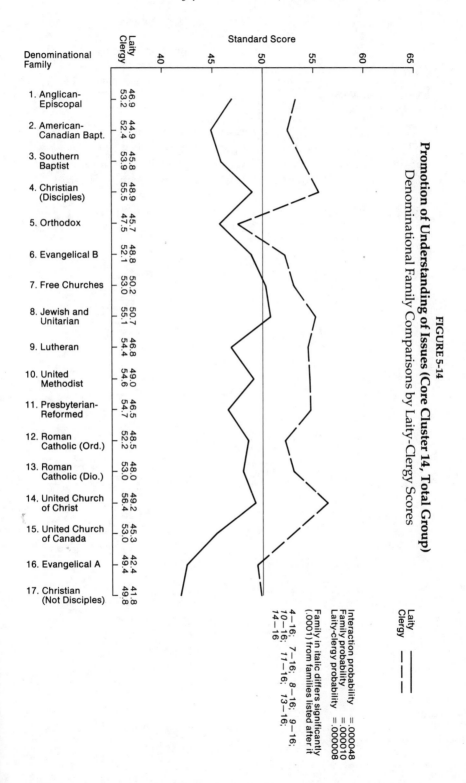

FIGURE 5-14

Promotion of Understanding of Issues (Core Cluster 14, Total Group)

Denominational Family Comparisons by Laity-Clergy Scores

Denominational Family	Laity	Clergy
1. Anglican-Episcopal	46.9	53.2
2. American-Canadian Bapt.	44.9	52.4
3. Southern Baptist	45.8	53.9
4. Christian (Disciples)	48.9	55.5
5. Orthodox	45.7	47.5
6. Evangelical B	48.8	52.1
7. Free Churches	50.2	53.0
8. Jewish and Unitarian	50.7	55.1
9. Lutheran	46.8	54.4
10. United Methodist	49.0	54.6
11. Presbyterian-Reformed	46.5	54.7
12. Roman Catholic (Ord.)	48.5	52.2
13. Roman Catholic (Dio.)	48.0	53.0
14. United Church of Christ	49.2	56.4
15. United Church of Canada	45.3	53.0
16. Evangelical A	42.4	49.4
17. Christian (Not Disciples)	41.8	49.8

Laity ——
Clergy — — —

Interaction probability = .000048
Family probability = .000010
Laity-clergy probability = .000008

Family in italic differs significantly
(.0001) from families listed after it
4—16; 7—16; 8—16; 9—16;
10—16; 11—16; 13—16;
14—16

TABLE 5-15
Core Cluster 15: Support of Community Causes
(active participation in social structures to improve the community)

Load	Item No.	Item	Mean
.62	144	Actively supports efforts to improve educational programs of the community	1.383
.56	140	Serves on task forces or committees to improve conditions at school or in the neighborhood	1.127
.50	158	Works with different community factions	1.068
		Grand mean	1.19

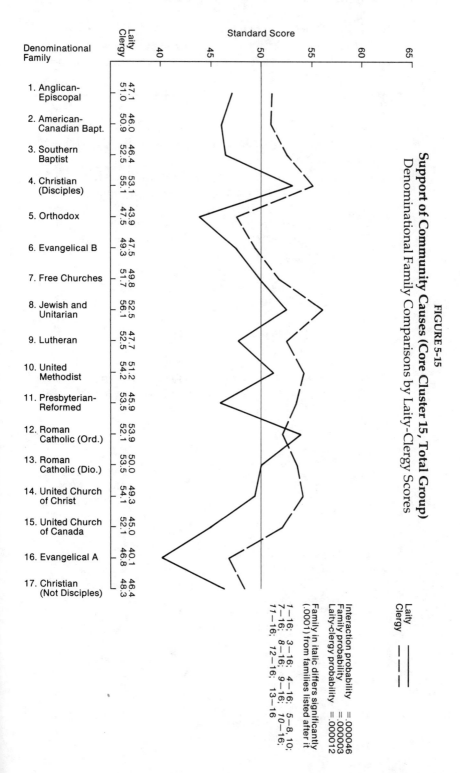

FIGURE 5-15

Support of Community Causes (Core Cluster 15, Total Group)

Denominational Family Comparisons by Laity-Clergy Scores

Denominational Family	Laity	Clergy
1. Anglican-Episcopal	47.1	51.0
2. American-Canadian Bapt.	46.0	50.9
3. Southern Baptist	46.4	52.5
4. Christian (Disciples)	53.1	55.1
5. Orthodox	43.9	47.5
6. Evangelical B	47.5	49.3
7. Free Churches	49.8	51.7
8. Jewish and Unitarian	52.5	56.1
9. Lutheran	47.7	52.5
10. United Methodist	51.2	54.2
11. Presbyterian-Reformed	45.9	53.5
12. Roman Catholic (Ord.)	53.9	52.1
13. Roman Catholic (Dio.)	50.0	53.5
14. United Church of Christ	49.3	54.1
15. United Church of Canada	45.0	52.1
16. Evangelical A	40.1	46.8
17. Christian (Not Disciples)	46.4	48.3

Laity ——————
Clergy — — — —

Interaction probability = .000046
Family probability = .000003
Laity-clergy probability = .000012

Family in italic differs significantly
(.0001) from families listed after it

1–16; 3–16; 4–16; 5–8, 10;
7–16; 8–16; 9–16; 10–16;
11–16; 12–16; 13–16

TABLE 5-16
Core Cluster 16: Active Concern for the Oppressed
(knowledgeably and earnestly working in behalf of minority and oppressed peoples)

Load	Item No.	Item	Mean
.64	155	Works toward racial integration in the community	1.138
.59	161	Uses authoritative information and facts to meet racism and prejudice in congregation and community	1.326
.54	129	Works to integrate people of varying educational, ethnic, and cultural backgrounds into the congregation	1.502
.54	157	Acquaints self with the history and aspirations of minority groups and other oppressed people	1.168
.45	160	Makes individuals aware of their possible part in causing world poverty	1.163
		* * *	
.45	148	Recommends that the parish cut off financial support for institutions (hospitals, missions, etc.) that discriminate against minorities	−0.166
		Grand mean	1.12

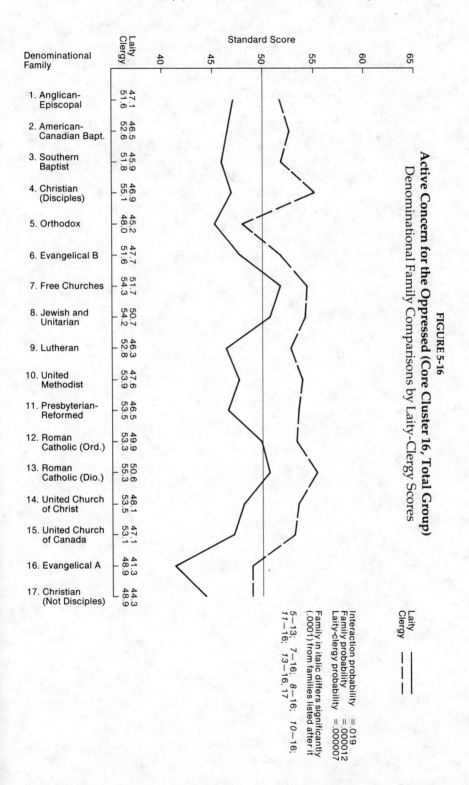

FIGURE 5-16
Active Concern for the Oppressed (Core Cluster 16, Total Group)
Denominational Family Comparisons by Laity-Clergy Scores

Denominational Family	Laity	Clergy
1. Anglican-Episcopal	47.1	51.6
2. American-Canadian Bapt.	46.5	52.6
3. Southern Baptist	45.9	51.8
4. Christian (Disciples)	46.9	55.1
5. Orthodox	45.2	48.0
6. Evangelical B	47.7	51.6
7. Free Churches	51.7	54.3
8. Jewish and Unitarian	50.7	54.2
9. Lutheran	46.3	52.8
10. United Methodist	47.6	53.9
11. Presbyterian-Reformed	46.5	53.5
12. Roman Catholic (Ord.)	49.9	53.3
13. Roman Catholic (Dio.)	50.6	55.3
14. United Church of Christ	48.1	53.5
15. United Church of Canada	47.1	53.1
16. Evangelical A	41.3	48.9
17. Christian (Not Disciples)	44.3	48.9

Laity ——
Clergy — — —

Interaction probability = .019
Family probability = .000012
Laity-clergy probability = .000007

Family in italic differs significantly (.0001) from families listed after it

5—13; 7—16; 8—16; 10—16;
11—16; 13—16, 17

TABLE 5-17
Core Cluster 17: Assertive Individual Evangelism
(aggressive approach to strangers and the unchurched, hoping to
convert some to Christianity)

Load	Item No.	Item	Mean
.75	135	Frequently approaches strangers to ask about the condition of their souls	−1.177
.68	116	Visits unchurched people to share the faith	1.704
.59	123	Priorities in use of time indicate the belief that the one and only way to build an ideal world society is to convert everyone to Christianity	−0.508
.57	150	Seeks to bring everyone to know God's love in Jesus Christ	2.356
		Grand mean	1.03

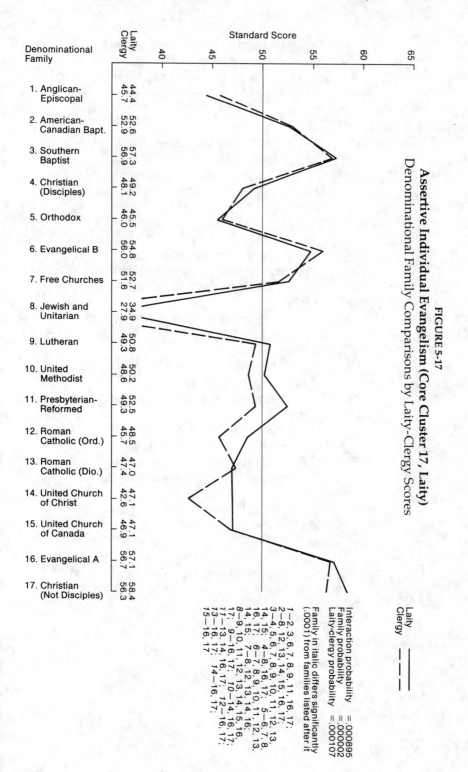

FIGURE 5-17

Assertive Individual Evangelism (Core Cluster 17, Laity)

Denominational Family Comparisons by Laity-Clergy Scores

Denominational Family	Laity	Clergy
1. Anglican-Episcopal	44.4	45.7
2. American-Canadian Bapt.	52.6	52.9
3. Southern Baptist	57.3	56.9
4. Christian (Disciples)	49.2	48.1
5. Orthodox	45.5	46.0
6. Evangelical B	54.8	56.0
7. Free Churches	52.7	51.6
8. Jewish and Unitarian	34.9	27.9
9. Lutheran	50.8	49.3
10. United Methodist	50.2	48.6
11. Presbyterian-Reformed	52.5	49.3
12. Roman Catholic (Ord.)	48.5	45.7
13. Roman Catholic (Dio.)	47.0	47.4
14. United Church of Christ	47.1	42.6
15. United Church of Canada	47.1	46.9
16. Evangelical A	57.1	56.7
17. Christian (Not Disciples)	58.4	56.3

Interaction probability = .000895
Family probability = .000002
Laity-clergy probability = .000107

Family in italic differs significantly
(.0001) from families listed after it

1—2, 3, 6, 7, 8, 9, 11, 16, 17;
2—8, 12, 13, 14, 15, 16, 17;
3—4, 5, 6, 7, 8, 9, 10, 11, 12, 13;
4—8, 16, 17;
5—4, 6, 7, 8, 9, 10, 11, 12, 13;
6—7, 8, 9, 10, 11, 12, 13;
7—8, 12, 13, 14, 15, 16;
8—9, 10, 11, 12, 13, 14, 15, 16,
17;
9—16, 17; 10—14, 16, 17;
11—13, 14, 16, 17;
13—16, 17; 12—16, 17;
15—16, 17. 14—16, 17.

Laity ——
Clergy – – –

TABLE 5-18
Core Cluster 18: Aggressive Political Leadership
(working actively, sometimes using the pressure of community
groups, to protest and change social wrongs)

Load	Item No.	Item	Mean
.65	128	Insists that political struggle is a rightful concern of the Church	0.146
.64	119	Participates in an effort to remove an incompetent or ineffective official from school, church, union, or government	−0.328
.63	117	Speaks from the pulpit about political issues	−0.148
.63	142	Uses principles and methods of social organization for political change	−0.660
.62	115	Organizes groups to change civil laws which seem in the light of Scripture to be morally wrong	0.504
.62	124	Encourages nonunion laborers to organize	−1.640
.61	143	Is willing to risk arrest to protest social wrongs	−0.730
.61	136	Works to make sure that all people are free to buy property in areas of their choice	−0.748
.58	130	Pressures public officials on behalf of the oppressed	0.122
.57	137	Organizes study groups in congregation or community to discuss public affairs	0.024
.57	151	Organizes action groups in the congregation to accomplish directly some political or social goal	−0.432
.51	122	Declares a willingness to run for public office in the community (school board, city council, etc.)	−0.904

* * *

.49	126	Takes an informed position on controversial community issues	1.235
		Grand mean	−0.32

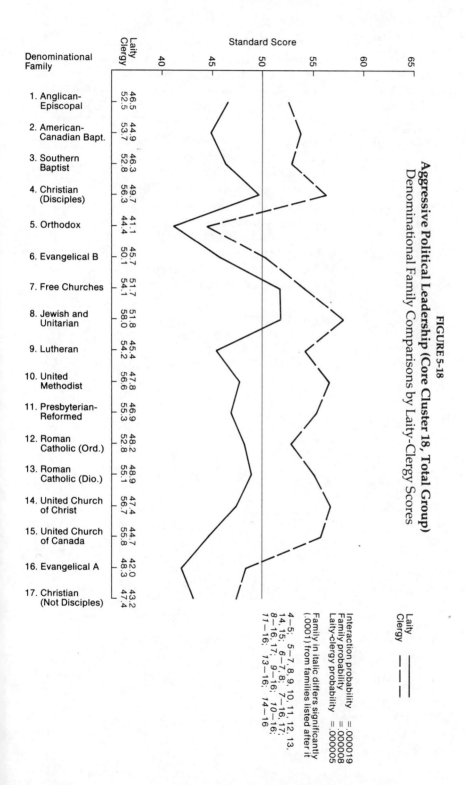

FIGURE 5-18

Aggressive Political Leadership (Core Cluster 18, Total Group)
Denominational Family Comparisons by Laity-Clergy Scores

Denominational
Family

	Laity	Clergy
1. Anglican-Episcopal	46.5	52.5
2. American-Canadian Bapt.	44.9	53.7
3. Southern Baptist	46.3	52.8
4. Christian (Disciples)	49.7	56.3
5. Orthodox	41.1	44.4
6. Evangelical B	45.7	50.1
7. Free Churches	51.7	54.1
8. Jewish and Unitarian	51.8	58.0
9. Lutheran	45.4	54.2
10. United Methodist	47.8	56.6
11. Presbyterian-Reformed	46.9	55.3
12. Roman Catholic (Ord.)	48.2	52.8
13. Roman Catholic (Dio.)	48.9	55.1
14. United Church of Christ	47.4	56.7
15. United Church of Canada	44.7	55.8
16. Evangelical A	42.0	48.3
17. Christian (Not Disciples)	43.2	47.4

Laity ———
Clergy – – –

Interaction probability = .000019
Family probability = .000008
Laity-clergy probability = .000005

Family in italic differs significantly
(.0001) from families listed after it

4–5; 5–7, 8, 9, 10, 11, 12, 13,
14, 15; 6–7, 8; 7–16, 17;
8–16, 17; 9–16; 10–16;
11–16; 13–16; 14–16

TABLE 5-19
Core Cluster 19: Precedence of Evangelistic Goals
(strong belief that efforts for the betterment of society are of minor
importance by comparison with the evangelization of all humankind)

Load	Item No.	Item	Mean
.67	134	Holds that the church's task of proclaiming the gospel by preaching and teaching overshadows in importance the task of helping to eliminate physical sufferings of people	−0.554
.67	135	Frequently approaches strangers to ask about the condition of their souls	−1.177
.61	123	Priorities in use of time indicate the belief that the one and only way to build an ideal world society is to convert everyone to Christianity	−0.508
.56	121	Insists that clergy should stick to religion and not concern themselves with social, economic, and political questions	−1.178
		Grand mean	−0.94

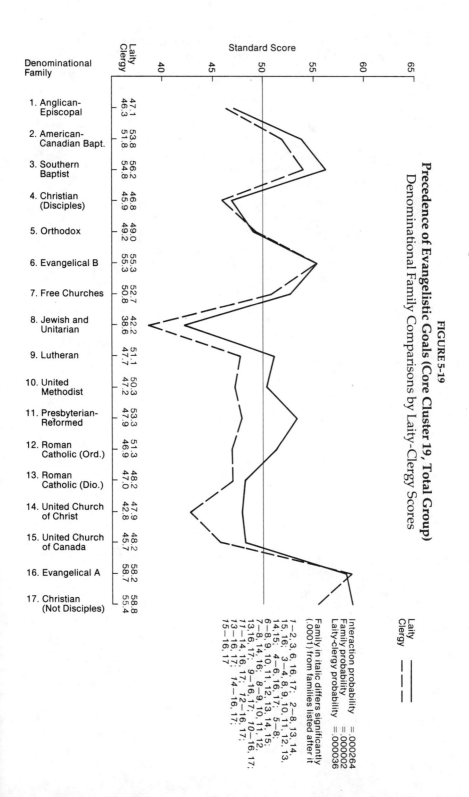

FIGURE 5-19

Precedence of Evangelistic Goals (Core Cluster 19, Total Group)
Denominational Family Comparisons by Laity-Clergy Scores

TABLE 5-20

Core Cluster 20: Total Concentration on Congregational Concerns

(a ministry that avoids directly confronting social change)

Load	Item No.	Item	Mean
.73	164	Often expresses doubt about any good coming from social or political change	−1.546
.70	165	Does not participate in community programs for fear of alienating members of the congregation	−1.491
.70	162	Insists that the betterment of society is not a responsibility of the congregation	−1.667
.53	163	Acts as though the church should provide a haven of safety in the midst of change	—0.926
		Grand mean	−1.42

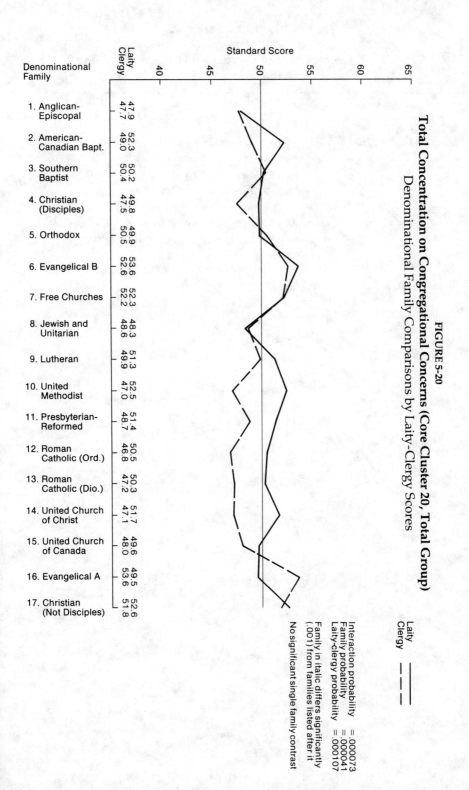

FIGURE 5-20

Total Concentration on Congregational Concerns (Core Cluster 20, Total Group)
Denominational Family Comparisons by Laity-Clergy Scores

Denominational Family	Laity	Clergy
1. Anglican-Episcopal	47.9	47.7
2. American-Canadian Bapt.	52.3	49.0
3. Southern Baptist	50.2	50.4
4. Christian (Disciples)	49.8	47.5
5. Orthodox	49.9	50.5
6. Evangelical B	53.6	52.6
7. Free Churches	52.3	52.2
8. Jewish and Unitarian	48.3	48.6
9. Lutheran	51.3	49.9
10. United Methodist	52.5	47.0
11. Presbyterian-Reformed	51.4	48.7
12. Roman Catholic (Ord.)	50.5	46.8
13. Roman Catholic (Dio.)	50.3	47.2
14. United Church of Christ	51.7	47.1
15. United Church of Canada	49.6	48.0
16. Evangelical A	49.5	53.6
17. Christian (Not Disciples)	52.6	51.8

Laity ———
Clergy – – –

Interaction probability = .000073
Family probability = .000041
Laity-clergy probability = .000107

Family in italic differs significantly
(.001) from families listed after it

No significant single family contrast

TABLE 5-21
Core Cluster 21: Perceptive Counseling
(reaching out to persons under stress with a perception, sensitivity,
and warmth that is freeing and supportive)

Load	Item No.	Item	Mean
.73	267	When conversing with a person, listens for feeling tones as well as words	2.490
.67	269	Will at times convey warmth and concern for a grief-stricken person by silence and physical presence	2.373
.64	263	Effects a relationship with counselees in which a problem is addressed with honesty and reality	2.419
.52	264	After his visits, persons fearful of death often feel less anxious	2.054
.52	268	Helps organize members ready to help others in times of illness and trouble	1.943
		Grand mean	2.26

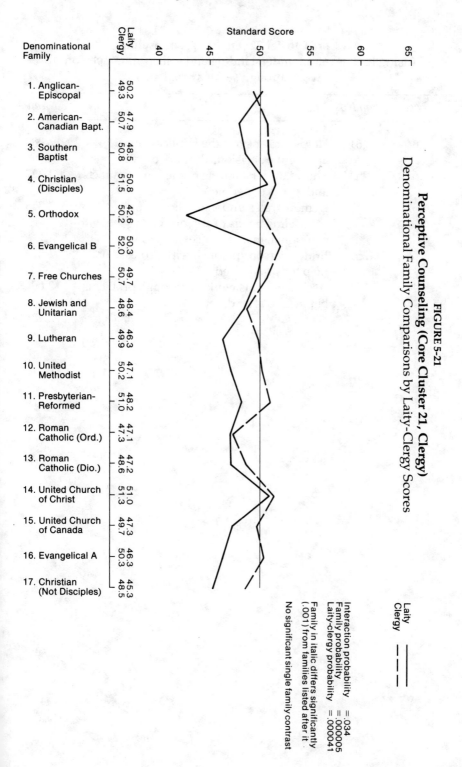

FIGURE 5-21

Perceptive Counseling (Core Cluster 21, Clergy)
Denominational Family Comparisons by Laity-Clergy Scores

Denominational
Family

	Laity	Clergy
1. Anglican-Episcopal	50.2	49.3
2. American-Canadian Bapt.	47.9	50.7
3. Southern Baptist	48.5	50.8
4. Christian (Disciples)	50.8	51.5
5. Orthodox	42.6	50.2
6. Evangelical B	50.3	52.0
7. Free Churches	49.7	50.7
8. Jewish and Unitarian	48.4	48.6
9. Lutheran	46.3	49.9
10. United Methodist	47.1	50.2
11. Presbyterian-Reformed	48.2	51.0
12. Roman Catholic (Ord.)	47.1	47.3
13. Roman Catholic (Dio.)	47.2	48.6
14. United Church of Christ	51.0	51.3
15. United Church of Canada	47.3	49.7
16. Evangelical A	46.3	50.3
17. Christian (Not Disciples)	45.3	48.5

Laity ———
Clergy – – –

Interaction probability = .034
Family probability = .000005
Laity-clergy probability = .000041

Family in italic differs significantly (.001) from families listed after it

No significant single family contrast

TABLE 5-22
Core Cluster 22: Enabling Counseling
(using high levels of understanding and skill in aiding persons to
work through serious problems)

Load	Item No.	Item	Mean
.64	261	Helps persons test the implications of alternative decisions they are considering	2.080
.63	252	Shows understanding of the inner conflicts and drives of people	2.327
.57	280	Demonstrates understanding of the counseling needs of persons distressed with emotional, marital, or sexual problems	2.355
.56	259	Brings persons in touch with professional help they may need	2.374
.48	254	Assists persons working through problems before and after divorce	2.002
		Grand mean	2.23

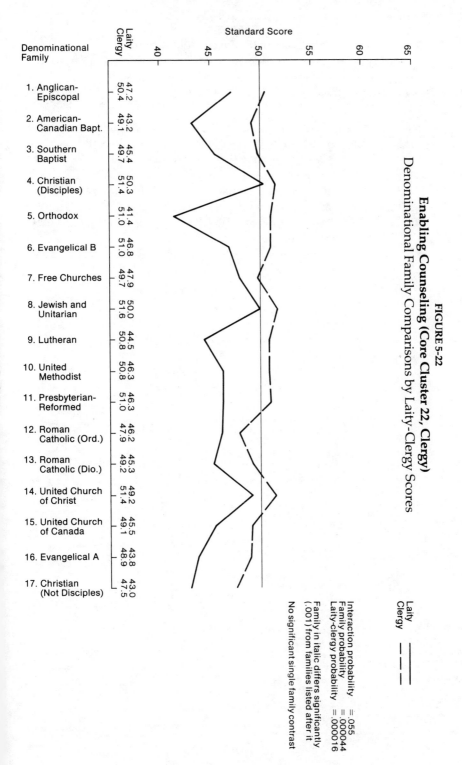

FIGURE 5-22

Enabling Counseling (Core Cluster 22, Clergy)

Denominational Family Comparisons by Laity-Clergy Scores

Denominational Family	Laity	Clergy
1. Anglican-Episcopal	47.2	50.4
2. American-Canadian Bapt.	43.2	49.1
3. Southern Baptist	45.4	49.7
4. Christian (Disciples)	50.3	51.4
5. Orthodox	41.4	51.0
6. Evangelical B	46.8	51.0
7. Free Churches	47.9	49.7
8. Jewish and Unitarian	50.0	51.6
9. Lutheran	44.5	50.8
10. United Methodist	46.3	50.8
11. Presbyterian-Reformed	46.3	51.0
12. Roman Catholic (Ord.)	46.2	47.9
13. Roman Catholic (Dio.)	45.3	49.2
14. United Church of Christ	49.2	51.4
15. United Church of Canada	45.5	49.1
16. Evangelical A	43.8	48.9
17. Christian (Not Disciples)	43.0	47.5

Standard Score: 40 45 50 55 60 65

Laity
Clergy — — —

Interaction probability = .055
Family probability = .000044
Laity-clergy probability = .000016

Family in italic differs significantly
(.001) from families listed after it

No significant single family contrast

TABLE 5-23
Core Cluster 23: Caring Availability
(responding with deep care and sensitivity to people in crisis situations)

Load	Item No.	Item	Mean
.58	278	Provides a parental type of counseling for youth or students out of touch with parents	1.898
.56	273	Goes immediately to minister to people in crisis situations	2.318
.47	256	Responds graciously when called for help at an inconvenient time	2.285
.45	275	Moves slowly and softly with people who are hurting	2.293
		Grand mean	2.20

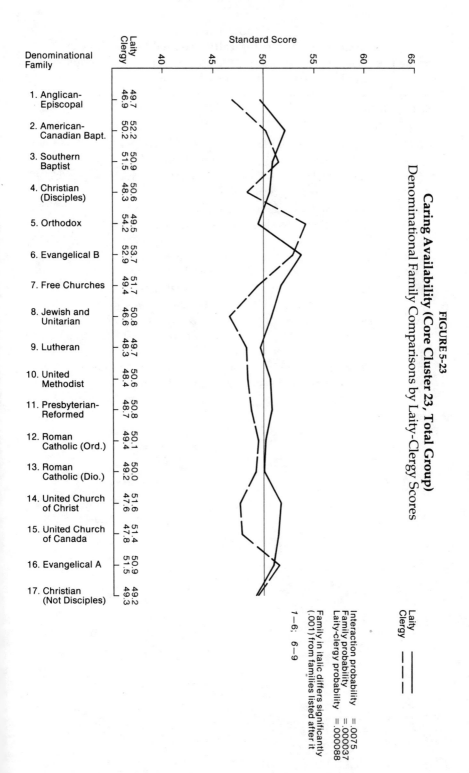

FIGURE 5-23

Caring Availability (Core Cluster 23, Total Group)

Denominational Family Comparisons by Laity-Clergy Scores

Denominational Family	Laity	Clergy
1. Anglican-Episcopal	49.7	46.9
2. American-Canadian Bapt.	52.2	50.2
3. Southern Baptist	50.9	51.5
4. Christian (Disciples)	50.6	48.3
5. Orthodox	49.5	54.2
6. Evangelical B	53.7	52.9
7. Free Churches	51.7	49.4
8. Jewish and Unitarian	50.8	46.6
9. Lutheran	49.7	48.3
10. United Methodist	50.6	48.4
11. Presbyterian-Reformed	50.8	48.7
12. Roman Catholic (Ord.)	50.1	49.4
13. Roman Catholic (Dio.)	50.0	49.2
14. United Church of Christ	51.6	47.6
15. United Church of Canada	51.4	47.8
16. Evangelical A	50.9	51.5
17. Christian (Not Disciples)	49.2	49.3

Laity ———

Clergy — — —

Interaction probability = .0075
Family probability = .000037
Laity-clergy probability = .000088

Family in italic differs significantly
(.001) from families listed after it

1—6; 6—9

TABLE 5-24
Core Cluster 24: Theologically Oriented Counseling
(using theologically sound counseling approaches to help people cope
with personal problems, using resources of faith)

Load	Item No.	Item	Mean
.69	271	Helps people use the resources of faith in coping with personal problems	2.408
.66	266	Helps people recognize ways God may be working in their lives	2.220
.66	274	Shows a degree of skill in finding theologically sound solutions to pastoral problems	1.907
.65	262	Through his/her ministry, people are led to deepened spiritual growth and commitment	2.477
.65	260	When counseling, will sometimes confront person with the need to believe	1.838
.63	249	Counsels on matters of wrong-doing with the intent of conveying an awareness of God's forgiveness	2.233
.52	279	Has thought through a counseling approach that is consistent with own theology	2.143
		Grand mean	2.17

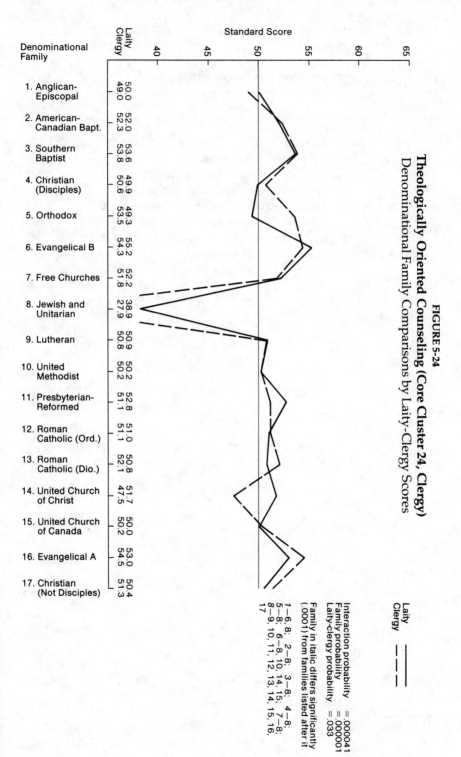

FIGURE 5-24
Theologically Oriented Counseling (Core Cluster 24, Clergy)
Denominational Family Comparisons by Laity-Clergy Scores

Denominational Family	Laity	Clergy
1. Anglican-Episcopal	50.0	49.0
2. American-Canadian Bapt.	52.0	52.3
3. Southern Baptist	53.6	53.8
4. Christian (Disciples)	49.9	50.6
5. Orthodox	49.3	53.5
6. Evangelical B	55.2	54.3
7. Free Churches	52.2	51.8
8. Jewish and Unitarian	38.9	27.9
9. Lutheran	50.9	50.8
10. United Methodist	50.2	50.2
11. Presbyterian-Reformed	52.8	51.1
12. Roman Catholic (Ord.)	51.0	51.1
13. Roman Catholic (Dio.)	50.8	52.1
14. United Church of Christ	51.7	47.5
15. United Church of Canada	50.0	50.2
16. Evangelical A	53.0	54.5
17. Christian (Not Disciples)	50.4	51.3

Standard Score: 40, 45, 50, 55, 60, 65

Laity ———
Clergy – – –

Interaction probability = .000041
Family probability = .000001
Laity-clergy probability = .033

Family in italic differs significantly
(.0001) from families listed after it

1—6, 8; 2—8; 3—8; 4—8;
5—8; 6—8, 10, 14, 15; 7—8;
8—9, 10, 11, 12, 13, 14, 15, 16,
17

TABLE 5-25
Core Cluster 25: Involvement in Caring
(becoming personally involved in the mutual exchange among
persons who seek to learn through suffering)

Load	Item No.	Item	Mean
.66	246	Engages people who have struggled through a problem to help those now facing it	1.854
.64	248	In counseling, shares own beliefs, opinions, suggestions without forcing them on a person	2.139
.57	247	Tries to learn the meaning of suffering from a person who suffers	1.783
.45	251	Can help a terminally ill patient deal with the question of shortening or prolonging life through rejecting or accepting medical care	1.147
		Grand mean	1.73

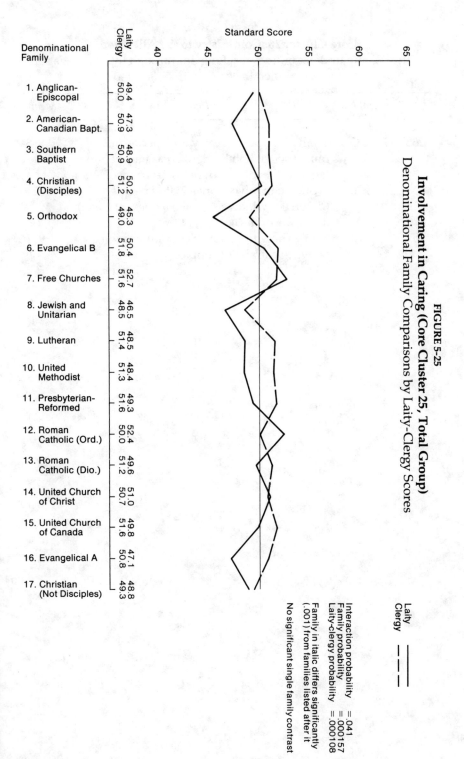

FIGURE 5-25

Involvement in Caring (Core Cluster 25, Total Group)
Denominational Family Comparisons by Laity-Clergy Scores

TABLE 5-26
Core Cluster 26: Coministry to the Alienated
(with skill and understanding, reaching out through the congregation
to the estranged, beleaguered, or isolated)

Load	Item No.	Item	Mean
.65	265	Trains groups that carry out specialized ministries (rehabilitation, crisis intervention, legal and medical aid, financial counsel, etc.)	0.098
.59	276	Works to involve more isolated people (divorced, widowed, singles, migrants, etc.) in the life of the congregation	2.021
.51	270	Knows how to establish communication between estranged couples	1.931
		Grand mean	1.50

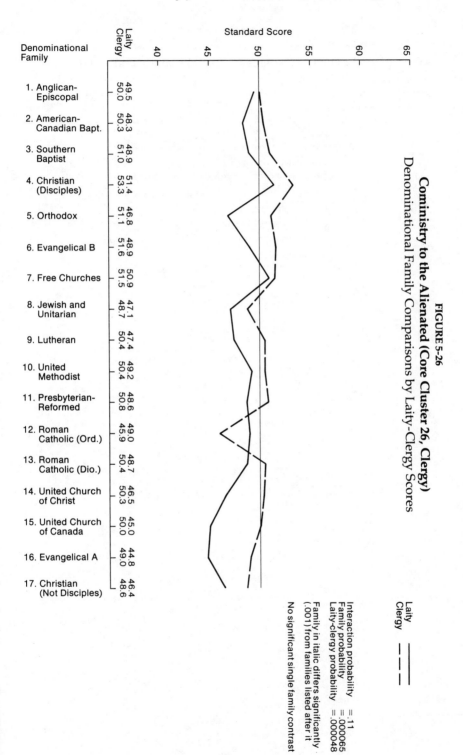

FIGURE 5-26

Coministy to the Alienated (Core Cluster 26, Clergy)

Denominational Family Comparisons by Laity-Clergy Scores

Denominational Family	Laity	Clergy
1. Anglican-Episcopal	49.5	50.0
2. American-Canadian Bapt.	48.3	50.3
3. Southern Baptist	48.9	51.0
4. Christian (Disciples)	51.4	53.3
5. Orthodox	46.8	51.1
6. Evangelical B	48.9	51.6
7. Free Churches	50.9	51.5
8. Jewish and Unitarian	47.1	48.7
9. Lutheran	47.4	50.4
10. United Methodist	49.2	50.4
11. Presbyterian-Reformed	48.6	50.8
12. Roman Catholic (Ord.)	49.0	45.9
13. Roman Catholic (Dio.)	48.7	50.4
14. United Church of Christ	46.5	50.3
15. United Church of Canada	45.0	50.0
16. Evangelical A	44.8	49.0
17. Christian (Not Disciples)	46.4	48.6

Laity
Clergy — — —

Interaction probability = .11
Family probability = .000065
Laity-clergy probability = .000048

Family in italic differs significantly
(.001) from families listed after it

No significant single family contrast

TABLE 5-27
Core Cluster 27: Law Orientation to Ethical Issues
(emphasis on God's demands and condemnation as a basis
for solving personal problems)

Load	Item No.	Item	Mean
.73	255	Treats suicides as deaths outside the Kingdom of God	−1.575
.67	281	Draws attention to God's condemnation whenever wrongdoing is confessed privately	−0.952
.53	250	Tries to provide solutions for all personal problems presented	0.122
		Grand mean	−1.00

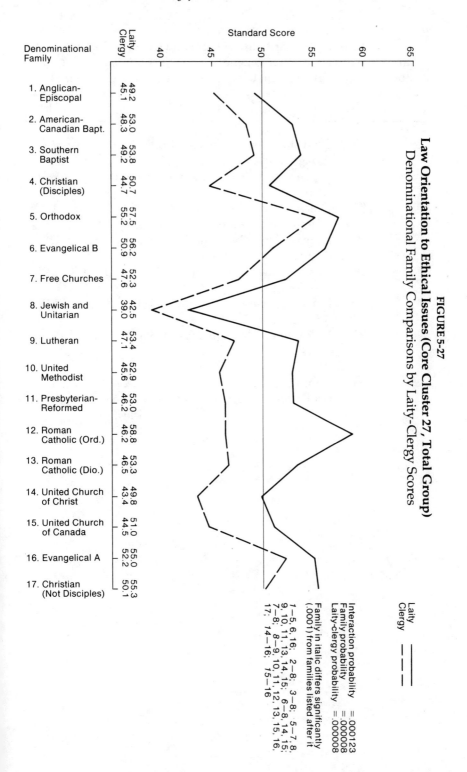

FIGURE 5-27

Law Orientation to Ethical Issues (Core Cluster 27, Total Group)
Denominational Family Comparisons by Laity-Clergy Scores

Denominational Family	Laity	Clergy
1. Anglican-Episcopal	49.2	45.1
2. American-Canadian Bapt.	53.0	48.3
3. Southern Baptist	53.8	49.2
4. Christian (Disciples)	50.7	44.7
5. Orthodox	57.5	55.2
6. Evangelical B	56.2	50.9
7. Free Churches	52.3	47.6
8. Jewish and Unitarian	42.5	39.0
9. Lutheran	53.4	47.1
10. United Methodist	52.9	45.6
11. Presbyterian-Reformed	53.0	46.2
12. Roman Catholic (Ord.)	58.8	46.2
13. Roman Catholic (Dio.)	53.3	46.5
14. United Church of Christ	49.8	43.4
15. United Church of Canada	51.0	44.5
16. Evangelical A	55.0	52.2
17. Christian (Not Disciples)	55.3	50.1

Laity ———
Clergy – – –

Interaction probability = .000123
Family probability = .000008
Laity-clergy probability = .000008

Family in italic differs significantly
(.0001) from families listed after it

1–5, 6, 16; 2–8; 3–8; 5–7, 8;
9, 10, 11, 13, 14, 15; 6–8, 14, 15;
7–8; 8–9, 10, 11, 12, 13, 15, 16;
17; 14–16; 15–16.

TABLE 5-28

Core Cluster 28: Clarity of Thought and Communication
(sharpening already keen intelligence through continual theological
study and careful attention to clarity of thought and expression)

Load	Item No.	Item	Mean
.69	285	Own statements of belief reflect careful thought and evaluation	2.480
.63	284	Explains complex issues in understandable terms	2.264
.53	286	Quickly grasps the basic issues in complicated matters	1.928
.51	290	Increases own theological competence through research and study	2.417
.48	298	Demonstrates combination of both thinking and doing	2.357
.46	295	Learns from experiences by reflecting on their significance	2.204
.46	297	Makes fine, intellectual distinctions when necessary	1.544
		* * *	
.45	296	Continues theological education through reading professional books and journals	2.225
		Grand mean	2.18

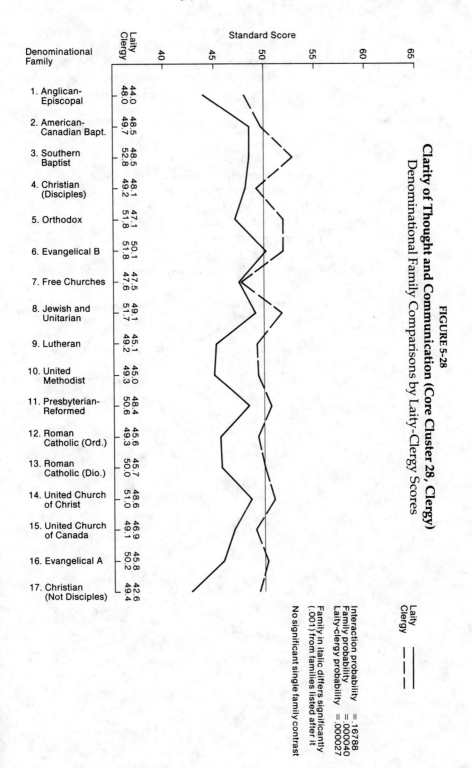

FIGURE 5-28

Clarity of Thought and Communication (Core Cluster 28, Clergy)
Denominational Family Comparisons by Laity-Clergy Scores

Denominational Family	Laity	Clergy
1. Anglican-Episcopal	44.0	48.0
2. American-Canadian Bapt.	48.5	49.7
3. Southern Baptist	48.5	52.8
4. Christian (Disciples)	48.1	49.2
5. Orthodox	47.1	51.8
6. Evangelical B	50.1	51.8
7. Free Churches	47.5	47.6
8. Jewish and Unitarian	49.1	51.7
9. Lutheran	45.1	49.2
10. United Methodist	45.0	49.3
11. Presbyterian-Reformed	48.4	50.6
12. Roman Catholic (Ord.)	45.6	49.3
13. Roman Catholic (Dio.)	45.7	50.0
14. United Church of Christ	48.6	51.0
15. United Church of Canada	46.9	49.1
16. Evangelical A	45.8	50.2
17. Christian (Not Disciples)	42.6	49.4

Laity ——————
Clergy — — —

Interaction probability = .16788
Family probability = .000040
Laity-clergy probability = .000027

Family in italic differs significantly
(.001) from families listed after it

No significant single family contrast

TABLE 5-29
Core Cluster 29: Theological Reflection
(having developed definite theological positions, nevertheless regularly
evaluates them in the light of experience and current theological trends)

Load	Item No.	Item	Mean
.56	324	Regularly reflects theologically on own ministerial experience	1.747
.53	325	Acknowledges the heritage and current contribution Jews provide to an understanding of Christianity	1.581
.51	327	Has thought out a theological position concerning matters such as divorce, abortion, suicide, etc.	2.030
.48	307	Is clear about the theology that guides and informs his ministry	2.343
.46	306	Evaluates current trends in theological thought	1.778
		* * *	
.51	326	Understands processes by which one arrives at ethical decisions	1.919
		Grand mean	1.90

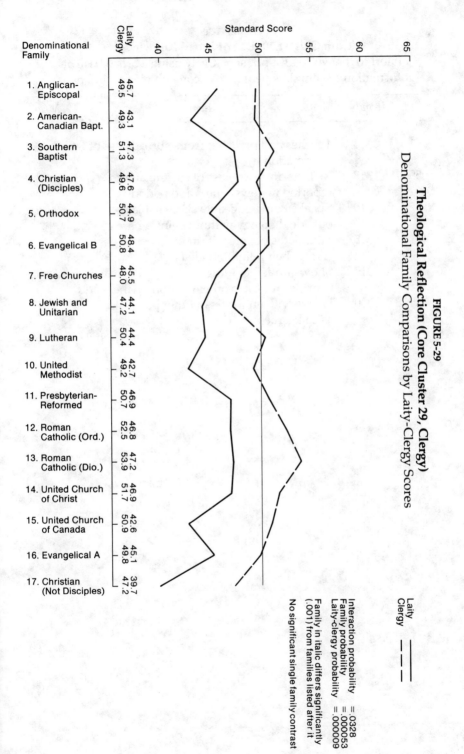

FIGURE 5-29

Theological Reflection (Core Cluster 29, Clergy)

Denominational Family Comparisons by Laity-Clergy Scores

Denominational Family	Laity	Clergy
1. Anglican-Episcopal	45.7	49.5
2. American-Canadian Bapt.	43.1	49.3
3. Southern Baptist	47.3	51.3
4. Christian (Disciples)	47.6	49.6
5. Orthodox	44.9	50.7
6. Evangelical B	48.4	50.8
7. Free Churches	45.5	48.0
8. Jewish and Unitarian	44.1	47.2
9. Lutheran	44.4	50.4
10. United Methodist	42.7	49.2
11. Presbyterian-Reformed	46.9	50.7
12. Roman Catholic (Ord.)	46.8	52.5
13. Roman Catholic (Dio.)	47.2	53.9
14. United Church of Christ	46.9	51.7
15. United Church of Canada	42.6	50.9
16. Evangelical A	45.1	49.8
17. Christian (Not Disciples)	39.7	47.2

Laity ——
Clergy — — —

Interaction probability = .0328
Family probability = .000053
Laity-clergy probability = .000009

Family in italic differs significantly (.001) from families listed after it

No significant single family contrast

TABLE 5-30
Core Cluster 30: Use of Broad Knowledge
(alert to the world around, sensitively using a broad base of
information to stimulate people to become thinking Christians)

Load	Item No.	Item	Mean
.61	314	Teaches and preaches from a broad base of information	2.199
.59	318	Reflects an awareness of current affairs reported in newspapers and periodicals	1.933
.57	310	Speaks knowledgeably about subjects outside theology without being a bore	1.794
.51	315	Stimulates people within the parish to clarify their religious beliefs	2.125
.50	317	Shows understanding of young people who express interest in other religions of the world	1.852
45	330	Works with members of other professions as colleagues	1.617
		Grand mean	1.92

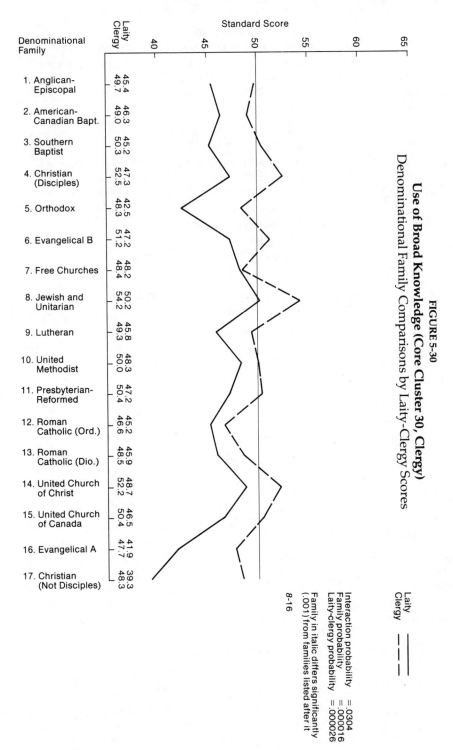

FIGURE 5-30

Use of Broad Knowledge (Core Cluster 30, Clergy)
Denominational Family Comparisons by Laity-Clergy Scores

Standard Score

Denominational Family	Laity	Clergy
1. Anglican-Episcopal	45.4	49.7
2. American-Canadian Bapt.	46.3	49.0
3. Southern Baptist	45.2	50.3
4. Christian (Disciples)	47.3	52.5
5. Orthodox	42.5	48.3
6. Evangelical B	47.2	51.2
7. Free Churches	48.2	48.4
8. Jewish and Unitarian	50.2	54.2
9. Lutheran	45.8	49.3
10. United Methodist	48.3	50.0
11. Presbyterian-Reformed	47.2	50.4
12. Roman Catholic (Ord.)	45.2	46.6
13. Roman Catholic (Dio.)	45.9	48.5
14. United Church of Christ	48.7	52.2
15. United Church of Canada	46.5	50.4
16. Evangelical A	41.9	47.7
17. Christian (Not Disciples)	39.3	48.3

Laity
Clergy ———

Laity ———
Clergy — — —

Interaction probability = .0304
Family probability = .000016
Laity-clergy probability = .000026

Family in italic differs significantly
(.001) from families listed after it

8-16

TABLE 5-31
Core Cluster 31: Affirmation of Conservative Biblical Faith
(a biblically based faith, and a firm belief in the Bible as final authority)

Load	Item No.	Item	Mean
.73	308	Interprets the authority of Scripture as being in the Gospel message	1.751
.71	293	Affirms that Jesus Christ is the Son of God	2.564
.65	287	Treats the Bible, interpreted by the Church, as the final authority in all matters of faith	1.295
.61	294	Gives evidence of continued and thorough study of the Scriptures	2.483
.59	313	Acknowledges the presence and activity of a personal devil (Satan)	1.144
		* * *	
.46	321	Demonstrates knowledge of Scripture	2.608
		Grand mean	1.97

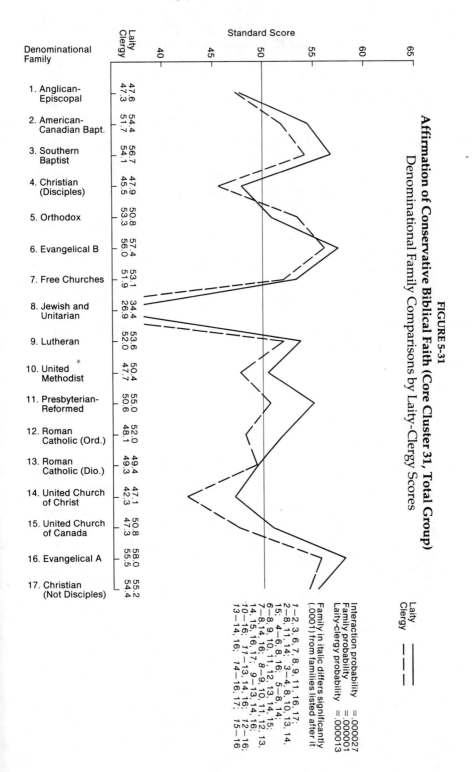

FIGURE 5-31

Affirmation of Conservative Biblical Faith (Core Cluster 31, Total Group)

Denominational Family Comparisons by Laity-Clergy Scores

Denominational Family

1. Anglican-Episcopal
2. American-Canadian Bapt.
3. Southern Baptist
4. Christian (Disciples)
5. Orthodox
6. Evangelical B
7. Free Churches
8. Jewish and Unitarian
9. Lutheran
10. United Methodist
11. Presbyterian-Reformed
12. Roman Catholic (Ord.)
13. Roman Catholic (Dio.)
14. United Church of Christ
15. United Church of Canada
16. Evangelical A
17. Christian (Not Disciples)

Laity / Clergy

	Laity	Clergy
1	47.6	47.3
2	54.4	51.7
3	56.7	54.1
4	47.9	45.5
5	50.8	53.3
6	57.4	56.0
7	53.1	51.9
8	34.4	26.9
9	53.6	52.0
10	50.4	47.7
11	55.0	50.6
12	52.0	48.1
13	49.4	49.3
14	47.1	42.3
15	50.8	47.3
16	58.0	55.5
17	55.2	54.4

Standard Score
40 45 50 55 60 65

Laity ———
Clergy – – –

Interaction probability   = .000027
Family probability   = .000001
Laity-clergy probability   = .000013

Family in italic differs significantly
(.0001) from families listed after it

1—2, 3, 6, 7, 8, 9, 11, 16, 17;
2—8, 11, 14; 3—4, 8, 10, 13, 14,
15; 4—6, 8, 16; 5—8, 14;
6—8, 9, 10, 11, 12, 13, 14, 15;
7—8, 14, 16; 8—9, 10, 11, 12, 13,
14, 15, 16, 17; 9—13, 14, 16;
10—16; 11—13, 14, 16; 12—16;
13—14, 16; 14—16, 17; 15—16

TABLE 5-32
Core Cluster 32: Denominational Knowledge
(knowing both the shaping context and current position of
denomination's political and theological stance)

Load	Item No.	Item	Mean
.60	323	Is conversant with the polity and official statements of own denomination	1.918
.56	316	Knows the historical circumstances that shaped confessional statements of the denomination	1.159
		Grand mean	1.54

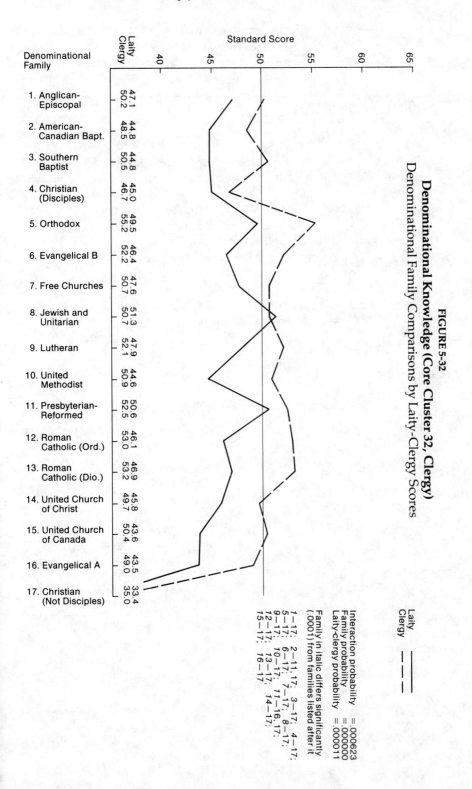

FIGURE 5-32

Denominational Knowledge (Core Cluster 32, Clergy)
Denominational Family Comparisons by Laity-Clergy Scores

Denominational Family	Laity	Clergy
1. Anglican-Episcopal	47.1	50.2
2. American-Canadian Bapt.	44.8	48.5
3. Southern Baptist	44.8	50.5
4. Christian (Disciples)	45.0	46.7
5. Orthodox	49.5	55.2
6. Evangelical B	46.4	52.2
7. Free Churches	47.6	50.7
8. Jewish and Unitarian	51.3	50.7
9. Lutheran	47.9	52.1
10. United Methodist	44.6	50.9
11. Presbyterian-Reformed	50.6	52.5
12. Roman Catholic (Ord.)	46.1	53.0
13. Roman Catholic (Dio.)	46.9	53.2
14. United Church of Christ	45.8	49.7
15. United Church of Canada	43.6	50.4
16. Evangelical A	43.5	49.0
17. Christian (Not Disciples)	33.4	35.0

Laity ——
Clergy – – –

Interaction probability = .000623
Family probability = .000000
Laity-clergy probability = .000011

Family in italic differs significantly
(.0001) from families listed after it

1—17; 2—11, 17; 3—17; 4—17;
5—17; 6—17; 7—17; 8—17;
9—17; 10—17; 11—16, 17;
12—17; 13—17; 14—17;
15—17; 16—17

TABLE 5-33
Core Cluster 33: Interest in New Ideas
(deep involvement with current thinking and openness to testing
new or current ideas)

Load	Item No.	Item	Mean
.64	328	Advocates a "liberation theology" because of its implication for oppressed people	−0.288
.59	303	Regularly attends the theater and cinema (from G to X)	−1.186
.58	288	Encourages the belief that some other religions of the world make worthwhile contributions to humanity	1.427
.54	289	Consistently uses own inner life as one means for testing ideas and interpreting events	1.250
.48	292	Buys and reads a wide range of popular books and magazines	0.808
		Grand mean	0.50

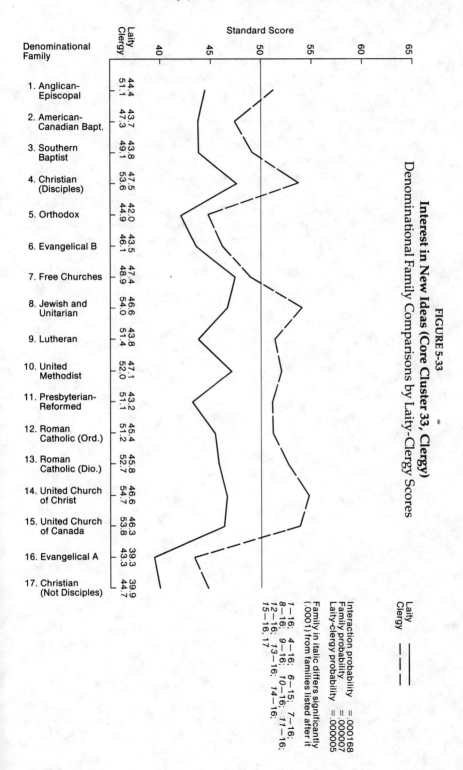

FIGURE 5-33

Interest in New Ideas (Core Cluster 33, Clergy)

Denominational Family Comparisons by Laity-Clergy Scores

Denominational Family	Laity	Clergy
1. Anglican-Episcopal	44.4	51.1
2. American-Canadian Bapt.	43.7	47.3
3. Southern Baptist	43.8	49.1
4. Christian (Disciples)	47.5	53.6
5. Orthodox	42.0	44.9
6. Evangelical B	43.5	46.1
7. Free Churches	47.4	48.9
8. Jewish and Unitarian	46.6	54.0
9. Lutheran	43.8	51.4
10. United Methodist	47.1	52.0
11. Presbyterian-Reformed	43.2	51.1
12. Roman Catholic (Ord.)	45.4	51.2
13. Roman Catholic (Dio.)	45.8	52.7
14. United Church of Christ	46.6	54.7
15. United Church of Canada	46.3	53.8
16. Evangelical A	39.3	43.3
17. Christian (Not Disciples)	39.9	44.7

Laity ———
Clergy – – –

Interaction probability = .0001168
Family probability = .000007
Laity-clergy probability = .000005

Family in italic differs significantly
(.0001) from families listed after it

1–16; 4–16; 6–15; 7–16;
8–16; 9–16; 10–16; 11–16;
12–16; 13–16; 14–16;
15–16, 17

TABLE 5-34
Core Cluster 34: Service in Humility
(relying on God's grace, serves others without seeking personal
reputation for success or infallibility)

Load	Item No.	Item	Mean
.69	336	Serves others willingly with or without public acclaim	2.560
.68	335	Recognizes own emotional and physical limitations	2.541
.57	333	Laughs easily even at self	2.151
.54	338	Believes the Gospel she/he preaches	2.837
		Grand mean	2.52

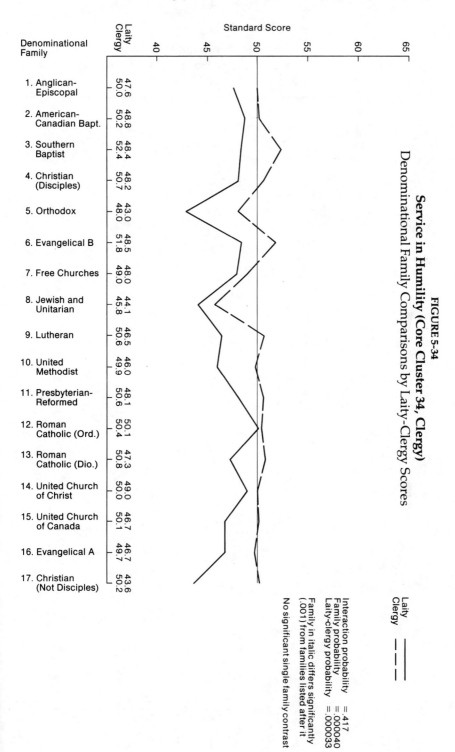

FIGURE 5-34
Service in Humility (Core Cluster 34, Clergy)
Denominational Family Comparisons by Laity-Clergy Scores

TABLE 5-35
Core Cluster 35: Christian Example
(personal belief in the Gospel that manifests itself in generosity
and a life of high moral quality)

Load	Item No.	Item	Mean
.67	376	Sets a Christian example that people in the community respect	2.504
.57	373	Behaves morally in a way that is above reproach	2.215
.48	338	Believes the Gospel she/he preaches	2.837
.46	374	Provides a personal witness to the Gospel by his/her own generosity	2.112
		Grand mean	2.42

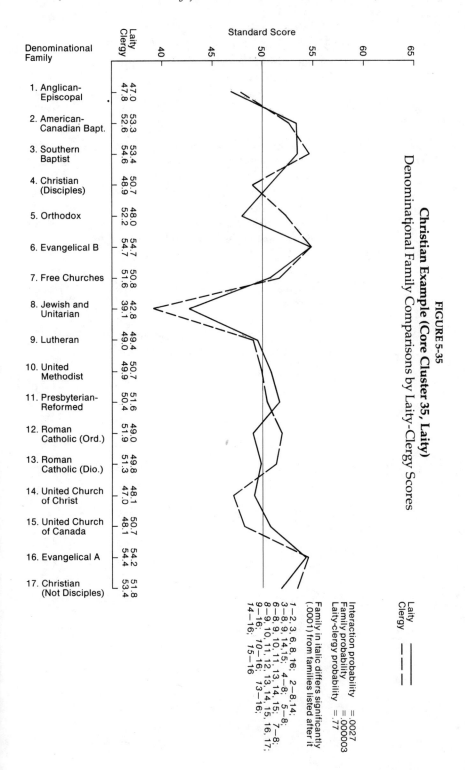

FIGURE 5-35
Christian Example (Core Cluster 35, Laity)
Denominational Family Comparisons by Laity-Clergy Scores

TABLE 5-36
Core Cluster 36: Acknowledgment of Limitations
(acknowledging limitations and mistakes, and recognizing the need
for continued growth and learning)

Load	Item No.	Item	Mean
.67	359	Says willingly, "I don't know," regarding subjects beyond own knowledge or competence	2.491
.66	361	Acknowledges own need for continued growth in faith	2.609
.66	363	Shows sufficient awareness of own inadequacies to know when help is needed	2.365
.58	365	Apologizes when he/she has offended a person	2.512
.53	357	Acknowledges own mistakes to congregation's governing board (or superior)	1.775
.47	360	Approaches life as one who believes the forces of good are greater than the forces of evil	2.373
		Grand mean	2.35

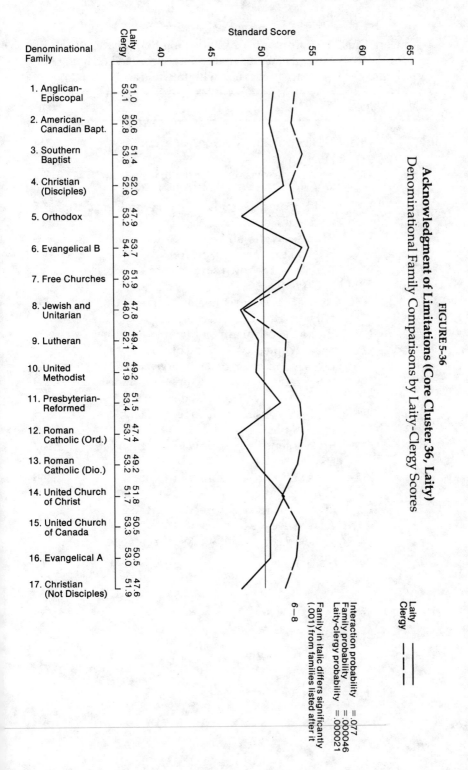

FIGURE 5-36
Acknowledgment of Limitations (Core Cluster 36, Laity)
Denominational Family Comparisons by Laity-Clergy Scores

Denominational Family	Laity	Clergy
1. Anglican-Episcopal	51.0	53.1
2. American-Canadian Bapt.	50.6	52.8
3. Southern Baptist	51.4	53.8
4. Christian (Disciples)	52.0	52.6
5. Orthodox	47.9	53.2
6. Evangelical B	53.7	54.4
7. Free Churches	51.9	53.2
8. Jewish and Unitarian	47.8	48.0
9. Lutheran	49.4	52.1
10. United Methodist	49.2	51.9
11. Presbyterian-Reformed	51.5	53.4
12. Roman Catholic (Ord.)	47.4	53.7
13. Roman Catholic (Dio.)	49.2	53.2
14. United Church of Christ	51.8	51.7
15. United Church of Canada	50.5	53.3
16. Evangelical A	50.5	53.0
17. Christian (Not Disciples)	47.6	51.9

Laity ——
Clergy — — —

Interaction probability = .077
Family probability = .000046
Laity-clergy probability = .000021

Family in italic differs significantly
(.001) from families listed after it

6—8

TABLE 5-37
Core Cluster 37: Commitment Reflecting Religious Piety
(profound consciousness of God's redeeming activity in life, living out
a sense of call to Christ's mission with freedom and courage)

Load	Item No.	Item	Mean
.77	343	Shows sensitivity to the leading of the Holy Spirit	2.214
.75	332	Shows the mission of Christ to be first in own life	2.421
.75	334	Holds that in the midst of serious problems, God is at work	2.395
.73	362	Expresses profound hope because of a belief in the Kingdom of God	2.405
.72	369	Acknowledges own sin and confesses this to God	2.391
.72	337	Appears to be sustained by a sense of God's call when the going gets rough	2.334
.71	340	Views the call or appointment to a parish, once accepted, as a calling of God	1.957
.70	372	Lives with a sense of daily forgiveness	2.147
.68	348	Interprets the decision to enter the ministry as a personal call from God	1.899
.64	358	Expresses desire for all to recognize the reign of the Lord	1.905
.63	370	Spends time daily in private prayer and meditation	2.382
.60	364	Uses Scripture as a source of spiritual nourishment	2.446
.57	353	Lives with a sense of freedom in the Gospel	2.048
.43	351	Acknowledges own inability to arrive at some decisions without deep prayer and thought	1.947
		Grand mean	2.20

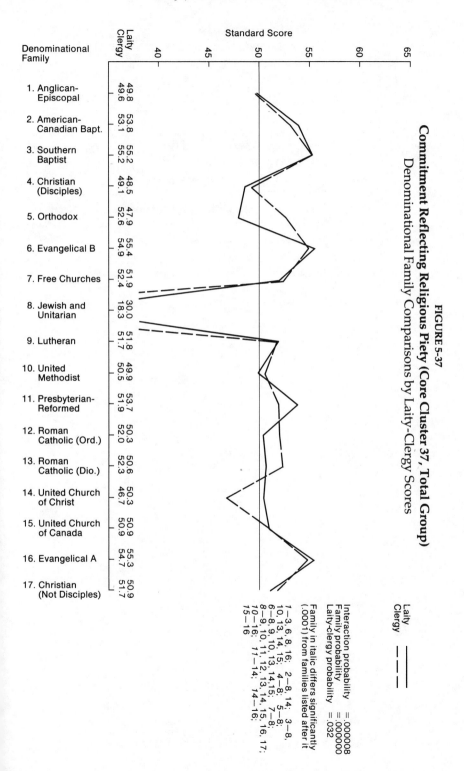

FIGURE 5-37

Commitment Reflecting Religious Piety (Core Cluster 37, Total Group)

Denominational Family Comparisons by Laity-Clergy Scores

Denominational Family	Laity	Clergy
1. Anglican-Episcopal	49.8	49.6
2. American-Canadian Bapt.	53.8	53.1
3. Southern Baptist	55.5	55.2
4. Christian (Disciples)	48.5	49.1
5. Orthodox	47.9	52.6
6. Evangelical B	55.4	54.9
7. Free Churches	51.9	52.4
8. Jewish and Unitarian	30.0	18.3
9. Lutheran	51.8	51.7
10. United Methodist	49.9	50.5
11. Presbyterian-Reformed	53.7	51.9
12. Roman Catholic (Ord.)	50.3	52.0
13. Roman Catholic (Dio.)	50.6	52.3
14. United Church of Christ	50.3	46.7
15. United Church of Canada	50.9	50.9
16. Evangelical A	55.3	54.7
17. Christian (Not Disciples)	50.9	51.7

Laity
Clergy – – –

Interaction probability = .000008
Family probability = .000000
Laity-clergy probability = .032

Family in italic differs significantly
(.0001) from families listed after it

1—3, 6, 8, 16; 2—8, 14; 3—8,
10, 13, 14, 15; 4—8; 5—8;
6—8, 9, 10, 13, 14, 15; 7—8;
8—9, 10, 11, 12, 13, 14, 15, 16, 17;
10—16; 11—14; 14—16;
15—16

TABLE 5-38
Core Cluster 38: Acknowledgment of Own Vulnerability
(openly facing the ambiguities of life, the struggles of faith,
and the disappointments of ministry)

Load	Item No.	Item	Mean
.77	345	Openly admits to times of doubt and struggle over own personal faith	1.331
.70	331	Talks openly about own experiences of fear and frustration	1.257
.64	356	Doesn't try to hide the fact that he/she worries	1.377
.60	339	Acknowledges there are times when he/she gives in to temptation	1.973
.54	352	Admits privately that the ministry has its disappointments	1.164
		Grand mean	1.42

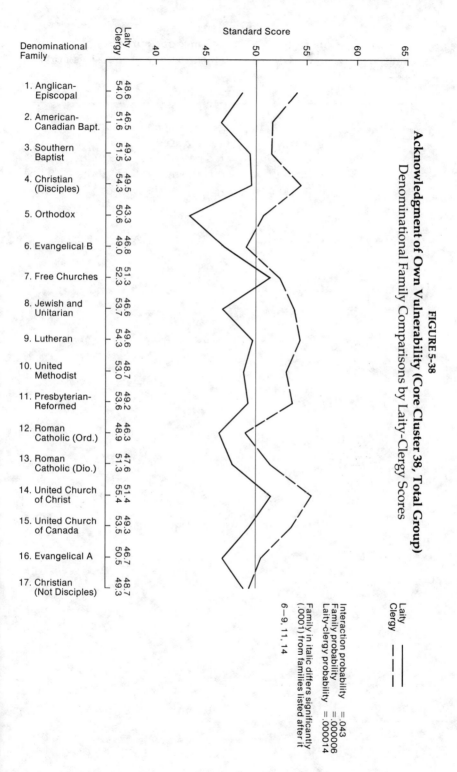

FIGURE 5-38

Acknowledgment of Own Vulnerability (Core Cluster 38, Total Group)

Denominational Family Comparisons by Laity-Clergy Scores

Denominational Family	Laity	Clergy
1. Anglican-Episcopal	48.6	54.0
2. American-Canadian Bapt.	46.5	51.6
3. Southern Baptist	49.3	51.5
4. Christian (Disciples)	49.5	54.3
5. Orthodox	43.3	50.6
6. Evangelical B	46.8	49.0
7. Free Churches	51.3	52.3
8. Jewish and Unitarian	46.6	53.7
9. Lutheran	49.6	54.3
10. United Methodist	48.7	53.0
11. Presbyterian-Reformed	49.2	53.6
12. Roman Catholic (Ord.)	46.3	48.9
13. Roman Catholic (Dio.)	47.6	51.3
14. United Church of Christ	51.4	55.4
15. United Church of Canada	49.3	53.5
16. Evangelical A	46.7	50.5
17. Christian (Not Disciples)	48.7	49.3

Laity   ———
Clergy   — — —

Interaction probability = .043
Family probability = .000006
Laity-clergy probability = .000014

Family in italic differs significantly
(.0001) from families listed after it

6—9, 11, 14

TABLE 5-39
Core Cluster 39: Acceptance of Counsel
(seeking to know God's will through the counsel and ministry of others)

Load	Item No.	Item	Mean
.58	355	Seeks the thinking of other people as one way of knowing God's will	1.372
.55	347	Confides in a trusted person(s)	1.524
.46	352	Admits privately that the ministry has its disappointments	1.164
		Grand mean	1.35

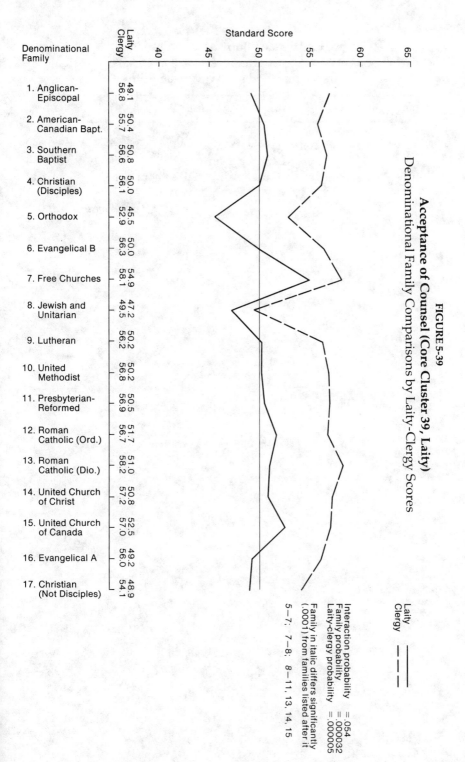

FIGURE 5-39
Acceptance of Counsel (Core Cluster 39, Laity)
Denominational Family Comparisons by Laity-Clergy Scores

Denominational Family	Laity	Clergy
1. Anglican-Episcopal	49.1	56.8
2. American-Canadian Bapt.	50.4	55.7
3. Southern Baptist	50.8	56.6
4. Christian (Disciples)	50.0	56.1
5. Orthodox	45.5	52.9
6. Evangelical B	50.0	56.3
7. Free Churches	54.9	58.1
8. Jewish and Unitarian	47.2	49.5
9. Lutheran	50.2	56.2
10. United Methodist	50.2	56.8
11. Presbyterian-Reformed	50.5	56.9
12. Roman Catholic (Ord.)	51.7	56.7
13. Roman Catholic (Dio.)	51.0	58.2
14. United Church of Christ	50.8	57.2
15. United Church of Canada	52.5	57.0
16. Evangelical A	49.2	56.0
17. Christian (Not Disciples)	48.9	54.1

Laity ———
Clergy — — —

Interaction probability = .054
Family probability = .000032
Laity-clergy probability = .000005

Family in italic differs significantly
(.0001) from families listed after it

5–7; 7–8; 8–11, 13, 14, 15

TABLE 5-40
Core Cluster 40: "Born-Again" Christianity
(religious experience that manifests itself in verbal expression
regarding God's activity in daily life)

Load	Item No.	Item	Mean
.70	354	Refers to self as a "born-again" Christian	0.290
.65	344	Speaks of being "sanctified"	−0.794
.61	377	In social conversation, talks about what the Lord has done recently in own life	0.612
		Grand mean	0.02

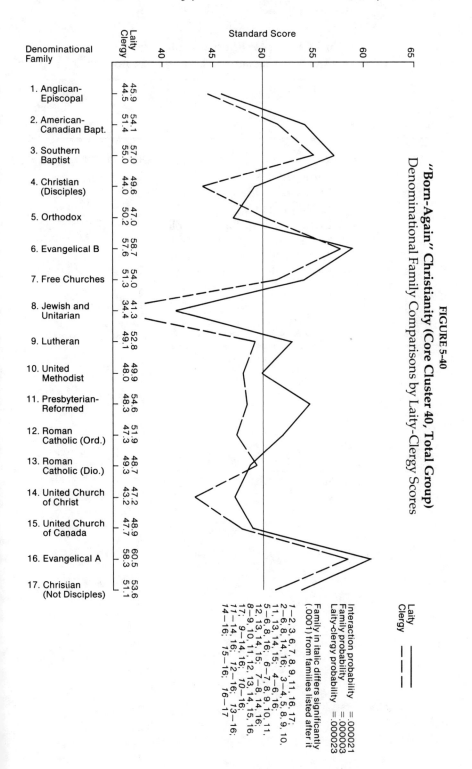

FIGURE 5-40

"Born-Again" Christianity (Core Cluster 40, Total Group)
Denominational Family Comparisons by Laity-Clergy Scores

Standard Score

Denominational Family		Laity	Clergy
1. Anglican-Episcopal		45.9	44.5
2. American-Canadian Bapt.		54.1	51.4
3. Southern Baptist		57.0	55.0
4. Christian (Disciples)		49.6	44.0
5. Orthodox		47.0	50.2
6. Evangelical B		58.7	57.6
7. Free Churches		54.0	51.3
8. Jewish and Unitarian		41.3	34.4
9. Lutheran		52.8	49.1
10. United Methodist		49.9	48.0
11. Presbyterian-Reformed		54.6	48.3
12. Roman Catholic (Ord.)		51.9	47.3
13. Roman Catholic (Dio.)		48.7	49.3
14. United Church of Christ		47.2	43.2
15. United Church of Canada		48.9	47.7
16. Evangelical A		60.5	58.3
17. Christian (Not Disciples)		53.6	51.1

Laity ⎯⎯⎯
Clergy ⎯ ⎯ ⎯

Interaction probability   = .000021
Family probability   = .000003
Laity-clergy probability   = .000023

Family in italic differs significantly
(.0001) from families listed after it

1–2, 3, 6, 7, 8, 9, 11, 16, 17;
2–6, 8, 14, 16; 3–4, 5, 8, 9, 10,
11, 13, 14, 15; 4–6, 16;
5–6, 8, 16; 6–7, 8, 9, 10, 11,
12, 13, 14, 15; 7–8, 14, 16;
8–9, 10, 11, 12, 13, 14, 15, 16,
17; 9–14, 16; 10–16;
11–14, 16; 12–16; 13–16;
14–16; 15–16; 16–17

TABLE 5-41

Core Cluster 41: Priestly Commitment

(taking seriously the sacramental life and priestly vows)

Load	Item No.	Item	Mean	Roman Catholic Mean[a]
.85	367	Receives the Sacrament of Penance regularly	−2.234	1.84
.81	349	Places much importance on daily celebration of Mass	−2.134	2.26
.79	383	Expresses devotion to the Blessed Sacrament	−1.781	2.31
.71	386	As a priest, is able to manage his personal finances in a spirit of poverty	−1.953	1.69
		Grand mean	−2.03	1.68

[a]The four items that comprise this cluster are obviously of greater importance to Catholics than to non-Catholics. The extremely low scores generated by the total group are artifactual. Thus, for reasons of relevance, total means for Roman Catholics are included in this core cluster.

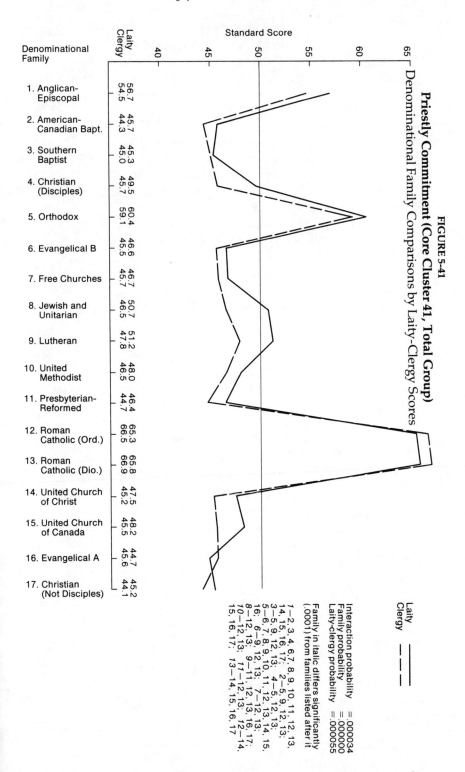

FIGURE 5-41

Priestly Commitment (Core Cluster 41, Total Group)

Denominational Family Comparisons by Laity-Clergy Scores

Denominational Family	Laity	Clergy
1. Anglican-Episcopal	56.7	54.5
2. American-Canadian Bapt.	45.7	44.3
3. Southern Baptist	45.3	45.0
4. Christian (Disciples)	49.5	45.7
5. Orthodox	60.4	59.1
6. Evangelical B	46.6	45.5
7. Free Churches	46.7	45.7
8. Jewish and Unitarian	50.7	46.5
9. Lutheran	51.2	47.8
10. United Methodist	48.0	46.5
11. Presbyterian-Reformed	46.4	44.7
12. Roman Catholic (Ord.)	65.3	66.5
13. Roman Catholic (Dio.)	65.8	66.9
14. United Church of Christ	47.5	45.2
15. United Church of Canada	48.2	45.5
16. Evangelical A	44.7	45.6
17. Christian (Not Disciples)	45.2	44.1

Laity ——

Clergy – – –

Interaction probability = .000034
Family probability = .000000
Laity-clergy probability = .000055

Family in italic differs significantly
(.0001) from families listed after it

1—2, 3, 4, 6, 7, 8, 9, 10, 11, 12, 13,
14, 15, 16, 17; 2—5, 9, 12, 13;
3—5, 9, 12, 13; 4—5, 12, 13;
5—6, 7, 8, 9, 10, 11, 12, 13, 14, 15,
16; 6—9, 12, 13; 7—12, 13;
8—12, 13; 9—11, 12, 13, 16, 17;
10—12, 13; 11—12, 13; 12—14,
15, 16, 17; 13—14, 15, 16, 17

TABLE 5-42
Core Cluster 42: Personal Responsibility
(honoring commitments by carrying out promises despite pressures to compromise)

Load	Item No.	Item	Mean
.63	513	Maintains personal integrity despite pressures to compromise	2.548
.57	505	Keeps own word—fulfills promises	2.747
.54	510	Works independently without prodding or supervision	2.257
.38	514	Relates warmly and nondefensively to ministers who are either predecessors or successors	2.182
		Grand mean	2.43

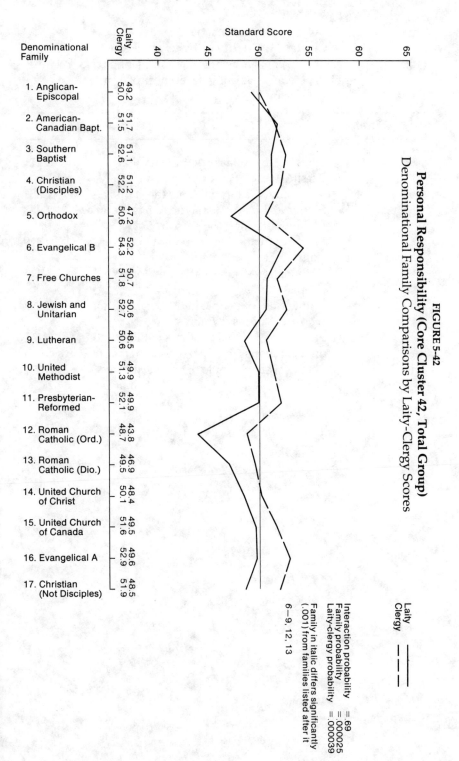

Personal Responsibility (Core Cluster 42, Total Group)
Denominational Family Comparisons by Laity-Clergy Scores

FIGURE 5-42

Denominational Family	Laity	Clergy
1. Anglican-Episcopal	49.2	50.0
2. American-Canadian Bapt.	51.7	51.5
3. Southern Baptist	51.1	52.6
4. Christian (Disciples)	51.2	52.2
5. Orthodox	47.2	50.6
6. Evangelical B	52.2	54.3
7. Free Churches	50.7	51.8
8. Jewish and Unitarian	50.6	52.7
9. Lutheran	48.5	50.6
10. United Methodist	49.9	51.3
11. Presbyterian-Reformed	49.9	52.1
12. Roman Catholic (Ord.)	43.8	48.7
13. Roman Catholic (Dio.)	46.9	49.5
14. United Church of Christ	48.4	50.1
15. United Church of Canada	49.5	51.6
16. Evangelical A	49.6	52.9
17. Christian (Not Disciples)	48.5	51.9

Laity ―――
Clergy ― ― ―

Interaction probability = .69
Family probability = .000025
Laity-clergy probability = .000039

Family in italic differs significantly
(.001) from families listed after it

6–9, 12, 13

TABLE 5-43
Core Cluster 43: Fidelity to Tasks and Persons
(showing competence and responsibility by completing tasks, relating
warmly to persons, handling differences of opinion,
and growing in skills)

Load	Item No.	Item	Mean
.66	468	Does not avoid tasks of ministry that he/she does not enjoy	2.225
.65	465	Generally finishes what he/she starts	2.381
.61	467	Shows ability to offer an opposing view without attacking the person	2.438
.61	466	Works at further development of pastoral skills	2.429
.56	469	Demonstrates honest affection for other people	2.414
.50	464	Is not afraid of people in the congregation who are "success symbols"	2.222
.45	473	Shares the feelings of others without letting own emotions cloud personal judgment	2.141
.44	474	Relates well to people of varied cultures	2.101
		Grand mean	2.29

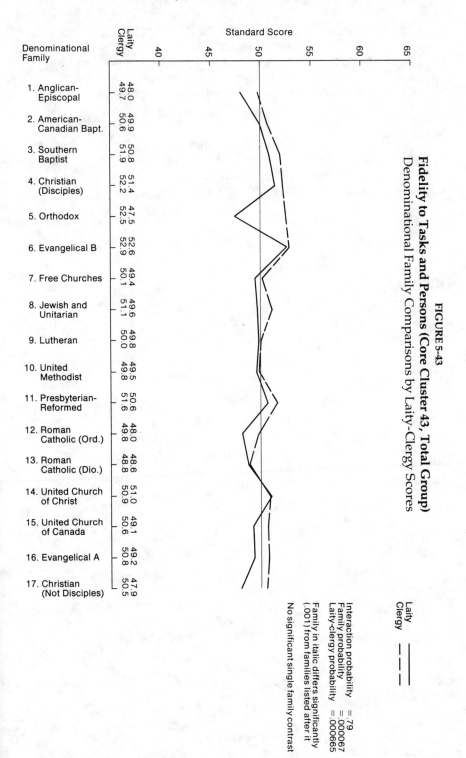

FIGURE 5-43

Fidelity to Tasks and Persons (Core Cluster 43, Total Group)
Denominational Family Comparisons by Laity-Clergy Scores

Denominational Family	Laity	Clergy
1. Anglican-Episcopal	48.0	49.7
2. American-Canadian Bapt.	49.9	50.6
3. Southern Baptist	50.8	51.9
4. Christian (Disciples)	51.4	52.2
5. Orthodox	47.5	52.5
6. Evangelical B	52.6	52.9
7. Free Churches	49.4	50.1
8. Jewish and Unitarian	49.6	51.1
9. Lutheran	49.8	50.0
10. United Methodist	49.5	49.8
11. Presbyterian-Reformed	50.6	51.6
12. Roman Catholic (Ord.)	48.0	49.8
13. Roman Catholic (Dio.)	48.6	48.8
14. United Church of Christ	51.0	50.9
15. United Church of Canada	49.1	50.6
16. Evangelical A	49.2	50.8
17. Christian (Not Disciples)	47.9	50.5

Laity ——
Clergy – – –

Interaction probability = .79
Family probability = .000067
Laity-clergy probability = .000665

Family in italic differs significantly
(.001) from families listed after it

No significant single family contrast

TABLE 5-44
Core Cluster 44: Positive Approach
(handling stressful situations by remaining calm under pressure, while continuing to affirm persons)

Load	Item No.	Item	Mean
.51	501	Acts calmly during times of stress	2.289
.45	500	Remains positive and constructive toward cantankerous members	2.141
.40	502	Helps others see the best in people	2.341
		Grand mean	2.25

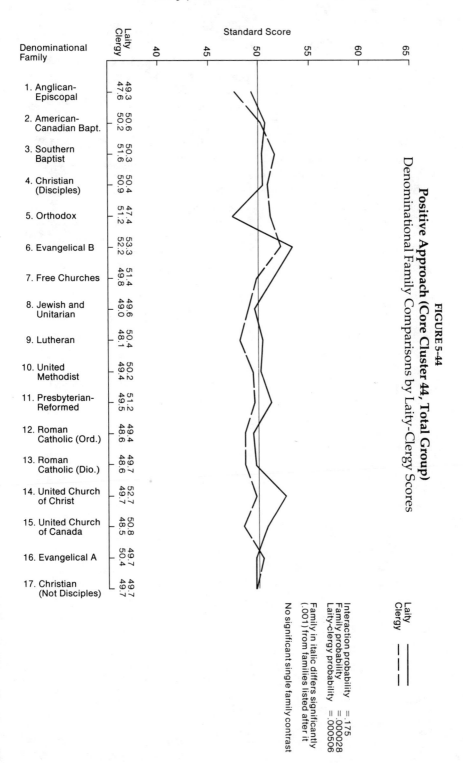

FIGURE 5-44
Positive Approach (Core Cluster 44, Total Group)
Denominational Family Comparisons by Laity-Clergy Scores

Denominational Family	Laity	Clergy
1. Anglican-Episcopal	49.3	47.6
2. American-Canadian Bapt.	50.6	50.2
3. Southern Baptist	50.3	51.6
4. Christian (Disciples)	50.4	50.9
5. Orthodox	47.4	51.2
6. Evangelical B	53.3	52.2
7. Free Churches	51.4	49.8
8. Jewish and Unitarian	49.6	49.0
9. Lutheran	50.4	48.1
10. United Methodist	50.2	49.4
11. Presbyterian-Reformed	51.2	49.5
12. Roman Catholic (Ord.)	49.4	48.6
13. Roman Catholic (Dio.)	49.7	48.6
14. United Church of Christ	52.7	49.7
15. United Church of Canada	50.8	48.5
16. Evangelical A	49.7	50.4
17. Christian (Not Disciples)	49.7	49.7

Laity ——
Clergy – – –

Interaction probability = .175
Family probability = .000028
Laity-clergy probability = .000506

Family in italic differs significantly (.001) from families listed after it

No significant single family contrast

TABLE 5-45
Core Cluster 45: Flexibility of Spirit
(adaptability, balance, free sharing of views, and welcoming of
new possibilities)

Load	Item No.	Item	Mean
.68	483	Expresses own ideas freely	1.920
.59	485	Adapts well to new situations or circumstances	2.295
.59	482	Shows a good mixture of seriousness and joy	2.257
.56	484	Bounces back after negative experiences	2.270
.55	481	Is usually eager to try out new possibilities	1.804
		Grand mean	2.11

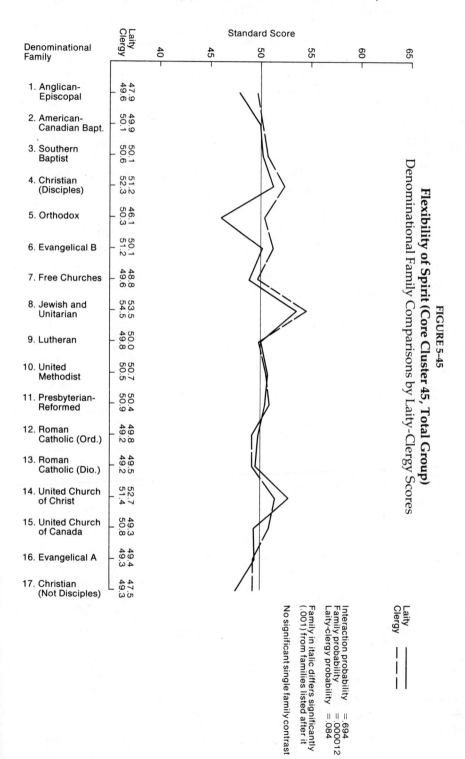

FIGURE 5-45

Flexibility of Spirit (Core Cluster 45, Total Group)

Denominational Family Comparisons by Laity-Clergy Scores

Denominational Family	Laity	Clergy
1. Anglican-Episcopal	47.9	49.6
2. American-Canadian Bapt.	49.9	50.1
3. Southern Baptist	50.1	50.6
4. Christian (Disciples)	51.2	52.3
5. Orthodox	46.1	50.3
6. Evangelical B	50.1	51.2
7. Free Churches	48.8	49.6
8. Jewish and Unitarian	53.5	54.5
9. Lutheran	50.0	49.8
10. United Methodist	50.7	50.5
11. Presbyterian-Reformed	50.4	50.9
12. Roman Catholic (Ord.)	49.8	49.2
13. Roman Catholic (Dio.)	49.5	49.2
14. United Church of Christ	52.7	51.4
15. United Church of Canada	49.3	50.8
16. Evangelical A	49.4	49.3
17. Christian (Not Disciples)	47.5	49.3

Laity ———
Clergy — — —

Interaction probability = .694
Family probability = .000012
Laity-clergy probability = .084

Family in italic differs significantly (.001) from families listed after it

No significant single family contrast

TABLE 5-46
Core Cluster 46: Valuing Diversity
(strong enough acceptance and valuation of diversity in people and ideas to face the risks involved in changes)

Load	Item No.	Item	Mean
.60	495	Accepts people whose lifestyles differ from his/her own	2.155
.58	488	Encourages members to value diversity of cultures, personal experiences, ideas, etc.	1.756
.40	499	Accepts the risk involved in change	1.993
		Grand mean	1.97

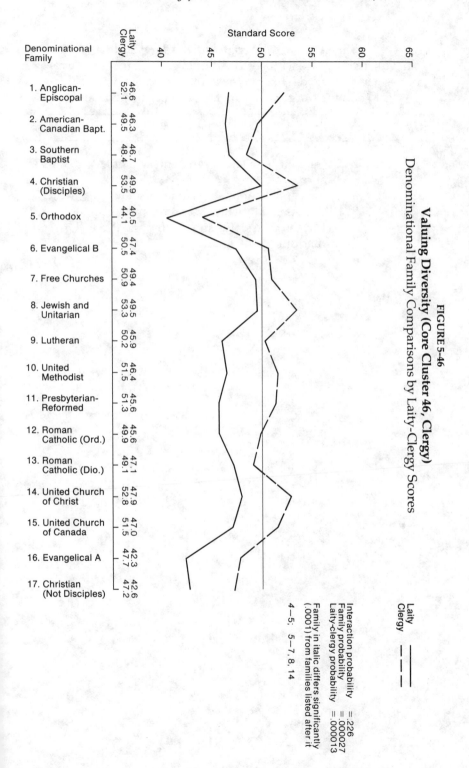

FIGURE 5-46

Valuing Diversity (Core Cluster 46, Clergy)

Denominational Family Comparisons by Laity-Clergy Scores

TABLE 5-47

Core Cluster 47: Acceptance of Clergy Role
(having made peace with personal ambitions and the ministerial
profession and avoiding use of the authority of the ministerial role
to dominate arguments or gain personal advantage)

Load	Item No.	Item	Mean
.70	492	Responds to heated arguments without raising voice	1.937
.62	493	Doesn't hide or push own clergy identity	1.971
.42	508	Accepts comfortably the discrepancy between own status and income and those of some other professions	1.754
		Grand mean	1.88

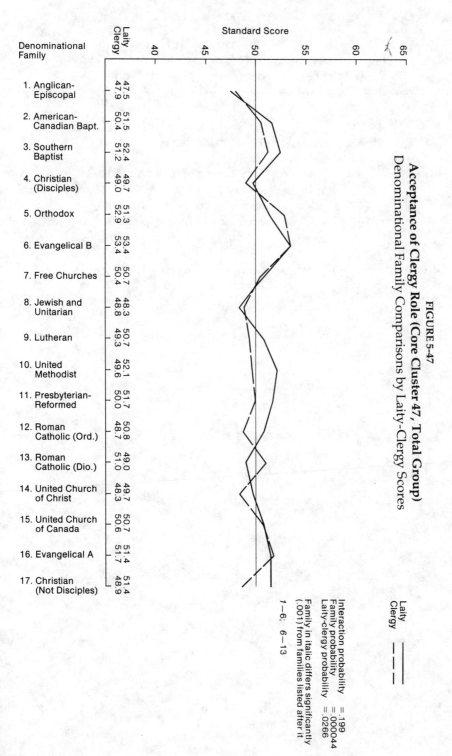

Denominational Family	Laity	Clergy
1. Anglican-Episcopal	47.5	47.9
2. American-Canadian Bapt.	51.5	50.4
3. Southern Baptist	52.4	51.2
4. Christian (Disciples)	49.7	49.0
5. Orthodox	51.3	52.9
6. Evangelical B	53.4	53.4
7. Free Churches	50.7	50.4
8. Jewish and Unitarian	48.3	48.8
9. Lutheran	50.7	49.3
10. United Methodist	52.1	49.6
11. Presbyterian-Reformed	51.7	50.0
12. Roman Catholic (Ord.)	50.8	48.7
13. Roman Catholic (Dio.)	49.0	51.0
14. United Church of Christ	49.7	48.3
15. United Church of Canada	50.7	50.6
16. Evangelical A	51.4	51.7
17. Christian (Not Disciples)	51.4	48.9

Standard Score

40   45   50   55   60   65

FIGURE 5-47

Acceptance of Clergy Role (Core Cluster 47, Total Group)
Denominational Family Comparisons by Laity-Clergy Scores

Laity —————
Clergy – – – –

Interaction probability   = .199
Family probability   = .000044
Laity-clergy probability   = .0266

Family in italic differs significantly
(.001) from families listed after it

1–6; 6–13

TABLE 5-48
Core Cluster 48: Mutual Family Commitment
(agreement in the minister's deep commitment to family
and the family's commitment to his/her vocation)

Load	Item No.	Item	Mean
.88	512	Schedules regular time to be alone with family	1.952
.88	511	Spouse is sympathetic and committed to minister's vocation	1.818
.86	497	Keeps commitments to own children as consistently as professional appointments	1.846
.62	463	Shows own family really means something to her/him	2.264
.46	476	Approaches appropriate board when present income is not adequate	1.268
		Grand mean	1.83

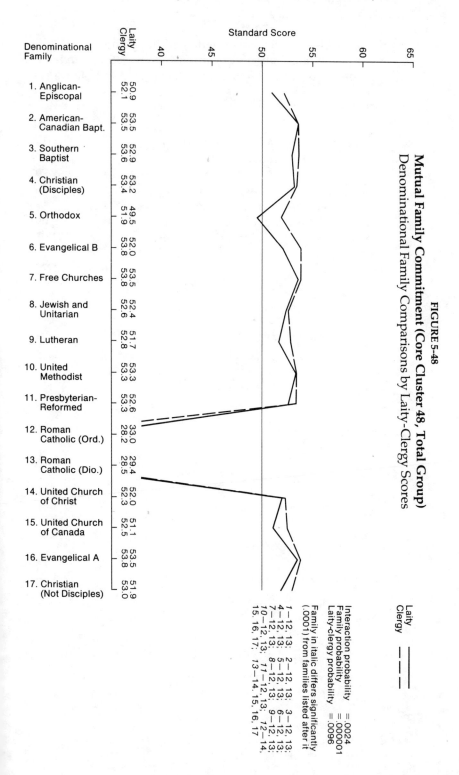

FIGURE 5-48

Mutual Family Commitment (Core Cluster 48, Total Group)
Denominational Family Comparisons by Laity-Clergy Scores

Denominational Family	Laity	Clergy
1. Anglican-Episcopal	50.9	52.1
2. American-Canadian Bapt.	53.5	53.5
3. Southern Baptist	52.9	53.6
4. Christian (Disciples)	53.2	53.4
5. Orthodox	49.5	51.9
6. Evangelical B	52.0	53.8
7. Free Churches	53.5	53.8
8. Jewish and Unitarian	52.4	52.6
9. Lutheran	51.7	52.8
10. United Methodist	53.3	53.3
11. Presbyterian-Reformed	52.6	53.3
12. Roman Catholic (Ord.)	33.0	28.2
13. Roman Catholic (Dio.)	29.4	28.5
14. United Church of Christ	52.0	52.3
15. United Church of Canada	51.1	52.5
16. Evangelical A	53.5	53.8
17. Christian (Not Disciples)	51.9	53.0

Laity ——
Clergy — — —

Interaction probability = .0024
Family probability = .000001
Laity-clergy probability = .0096

Family in italic differs significantly
(.0001) from families listed after it

1—12, 13; 2—12, 13; 3—12, 13;
4—12, 13; 5—12, 13; 6—12, 13;
7—12, 13; 8—12, 13; 9—12, 13;
10—12, 13; 11—12, 13; 12—13, 14,
15, 16, 17; 13—14, 15, 16, 17

TABLE 5-49
Core Cluster 49: Denominational Collegiality
(acceptance of denomination's directives and regulations while
maintaining a collegial relationship with superiors and staff)

Load	Item No.	Item	Mean
.69	509	Usually follows directives from denominational leaders	1.111
.60	506	Gives calm, rational explanation when a request contrary to denominational regulations cannot be granted	1.793
.56	470	Works cooperatively with superiors	2.094
.53	507	Promotes good working relationships with staff professionals	2.039
		Grand mean	1.76

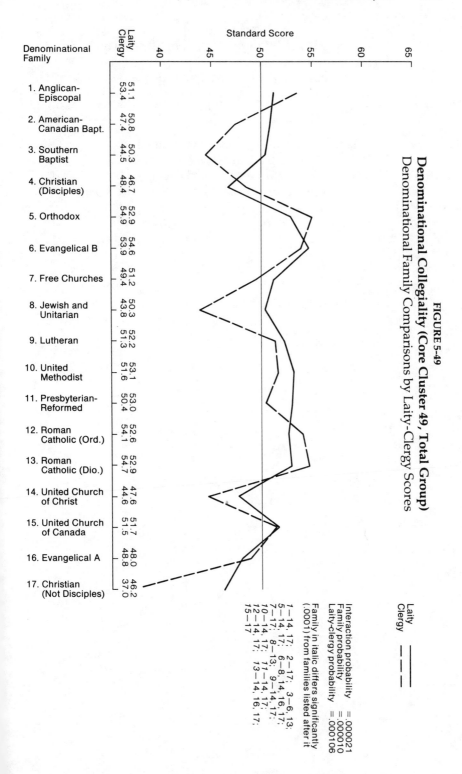

FIGURE 5-49

Denominational Collegiality (Core Cluster 49, Total Group)
Denominational Family Comparisons by Laity-Clergy Scores

Standard Score

Denominational Family	Laity	Clergy
1. Anglican-Episcopal	51.1	53.4
2. American-Canadian Bapt.	50.8	47.4
3. Southern Baptist	50.3	44.5
4. Christian (Disciples)	46.7	48.4
5. Orthodox	52.9	54.9
6. Evangelical B	54.6	53.9
7. Free Churches	51.2	49.4
8. Jewish and Unitarian	50.3	43.8
9. Lutheran	52.2	51.3
10. United Methodist	53.1	51.6
11. Presbyterian-Reformed	53.0	50.4
12. Roman Catholic (Ord.)	52.6	54.1
13. Roman Catholic (Dio.)	52.9	54.7
14. United Church of Christ	47.6	44.6
15. United Church of Canada	51.7	51.5
16. Evangelical A	48.0	48.8
17. Christian (Not Disciples)	46.2	37.0

Laity ——————
Clergy — — — —

Interaction probability   = .000021
Family probability   = .000010
Laity-clergy probability   = .000106

Family in italic differs significantly
(.0001) from families listed after it

1–14, 17;   2–17;   3–6, 13;
5–14, 17;   6–8, 14, 16, 17;
7–17;   8–13;   9–14, 17;
10–14, 17;   11–14, 17;
12–14, 17;   13–14, 16, 17;
15–17

TABLE 5-50
Core Cluster 50: Support of Unpopular Causes
(a confident, vigorous participation in community affairs, willing to risk loss of popularity in support of a cause)

Load	Item No.	Item	Mean
.58	498	Participates vigorously in community causes as a private citizen	1.258
.54	499	Accepts the risk involved in change	1.993
.53	504	Supports an unpopular cause, if own belief indicates it is right	1.789
.52	503	Expresses own stand on issues	1.928
		Grand mean	1.74

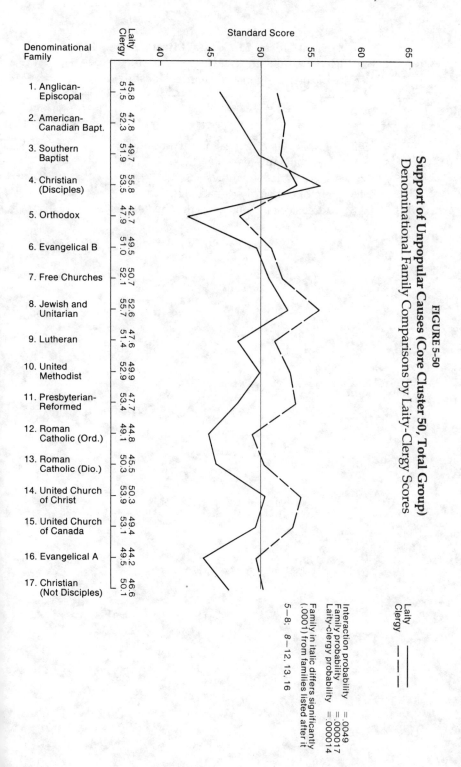

FIGURE 5-50

Support of Unpopular Causes (Core Cluster 50, Total Group)
Denominational Family Comparisons by Laity-Clergy Scores

Denominational Family	Laity	Clergy
1. Anglican-Episcopal	45.8	51.5
2. American-Canadian Bapt.	47.8	52.3
3. Southern Baptist	49.7	51.9
4. Christian (Disciples)	55.8	53.5
5. Orthodox	42.7	47.9
6. Evangelical B	49.5	51.0
7. Free Churches	50.7	52.1
8. Jewish and Unitarian	52.6	55.7
9. Lutheran	47.6	51.4
10. United Methodist	49.9	52.9
11. Presbyterian-Reformed	47.7	53.4
12. Roman Catholic (Ord.)	44.8	49.1
13. Roman Catholic (Dio.)	45.5	50.3
14. United Church of Christ	50.3	53.9
15. United Church of Canada	49.4	53.1
16. Evangelical A	44.2	49.5
17. Christian (Not Disciples)	46.6	50.1

Laity
Clergy   — — —

Interaction probability = .0049
Family probability = .000017
Laity-clergy probability = .000014

Family in italic differs significantly
(.0001) from families listed after it

5–8; 8–12, 13, 16

TABLE 5-51
Core Cluster 51: Secular Lifestyle
(parting company with some ministerial stereotypes
by participating in a secularized lifestyle)

Load	Item No.	Item	Mean
.78	543	Enjoys visiting local nightclubs and cocktail lounges	−1.717
.75	569	Occasionally gambles	−1.665
.68	556	Smokes heavily (tobacco) in public	−1.228
.67	526	Occasionally tells jokes that hearers consider dirty	−1.667
		Grand mean	−1.57

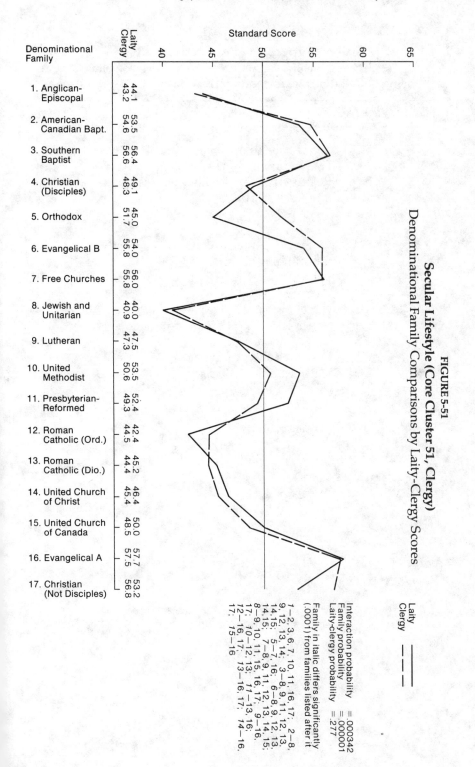

FIGURE 5-51

Secular Lifestyle (Core Cluster 51, Clergy)

Denominational Family Comparisons by Laity-Clergy Scores

Denominational Family	Laity	Clergy
1. Anglican-Episcopal	44.1	43.2
2. American-Canadian Bapt.	53.5	54.6
3. Southern Baptist	56.4	56.6
4. Christian (Disciples)	49.1	48.3
5. Orthodox	45.0	51.7
6. Evangelical B	54.0	55.8
7. Free Churches	56.0	55.8
8. Jewish and Unitarian	40.0	40.9
9. Lutheran	47.5	47.3
10. United Methodist	53.5	50.6
11. Presbyterian-Reformed	52.4	49.3
12. Roman Catholic (Ord.)	42.4	44.5
13. Roman Catholic (Dio.)	45.2	44.4
14. United Church of Christ	46.4	45.4
15. United Church of Canada	50.0	48.5
16. Evangelical A	57.7	57.5
17. Christian (Not Disciples)	53.2	56.8

Laity ——
Clergy — — —

Interaction probability = .0000342
Family probability = .000001
Laity-clergy probability = .277

Family in italic differs significantly (.0001) from families listed after it

1–2, 3, 6, 7, 10, 11, 16, 17; 2–8, 9, 12, 13, 14; 3–8, 9, 11, 12, 13, 14, 15; 5–7, 16; 6–8, 9, 12, 13, 14, 15; 7–8, 9, 11, 12, 13, 14, 15; 8–9, 10, 11, 15, 16, 17; 9–16, 17; 10–12, 13; 11–13, 16; 12–16, 17; 13–16, 17; 14–16, 17; 15–16

TABLE 5-52
Core Cluster 52: Professional Immaturity
(actions that demonstrate immaturity, insecurity, insensitivity, and being buffeted by the demands and pressures of the profession)

Load	Item No.	Item	Mean
.79	523	Tends to be cold and impersonal	−2.212
.74	530	Frequently shows favoritism	−1.943
.73	529	Rejects criticism as evidence of disrespect for ministerial office	−1.967
.72	521	Pouts publicly when things don't go own way	−2.275
.67	534	Worries excessively about what others think of him/her	−1.754
.67	531	Shows little concern for individuals outside the parish	−1.752
.64	525	Under pressure is likely to violate own principles and conform to expectations of congregation	−1.804
.63	528	Measures own worth by the salary received	−1.706
.63	533	Makes impulsive decisions	−1.618
		Grand mean	−1.89

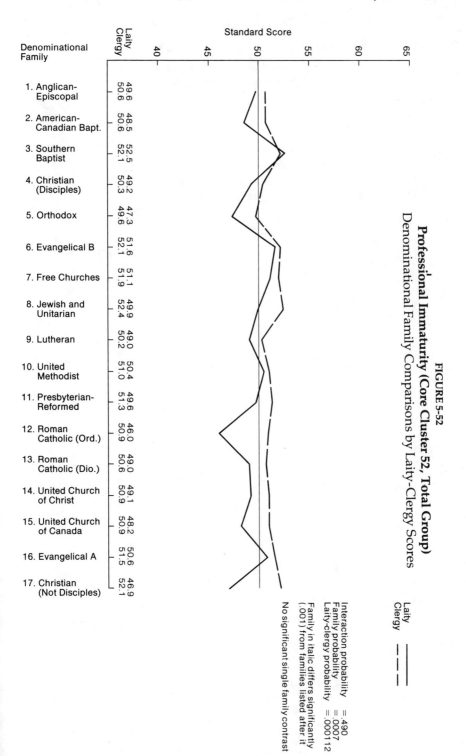

FIGURE 5-52

Professional Immaturity (Core Cluster 52, Total Group)
Denominational Family Comparisons by Laity-Clergy Scores

Denominational Family	Laity Clergy		
1. Anglican-Episcopal	49.6 50.6		
2. American-Canadian Bapt.	48.5 50.6		
3. Southern Baptist	52.5 52.1		
4. Christian (Disciples)	49.2 50.3		
5. Orthodox	47.3 49.6		
6. Evangelical B	51.6 52.1		
7. Free Churches	51.1 51.9		
8. Jewish and Unitarian	49.9 52.4		
9. Lutheran	49.0 50.2		
10. United Methodist	50.4 51.0		
11. Presbyterian-Reformed	49.6 51.3		
12. Roman Catholic (Ord.)	46.0 50.9		
13. Roman Catholic (Dio.)	49.0 50.6		
14. United Church of Christ	49.1 50.9		
15. United Church of Canada	48.2 50.9		
16. Evangelical A	50.6 51.5		
17. Christian (Not Disciples)	46.9 52.1		

Laity ———
Clergy — — —

Interaction probability = .490
Family probability = .0007
Laity-clergy probability = .000112

Family in italic differs significantly
(.001) from families listed after it

No significant single family contrast

TABLE 5-53
Core Cluster 53: Undisciplined Living
(undisciplined and self-indulgent actions
that irritate, shock, or offend)

Load	Item No.	Item	Mean
.61	566	Occasionally involved in extramarital affairs or illicit sexual relationships	−2.517
.61	560	Lives beyond personal means	−2.026
.57	563	Displays irritating mannerisms	−1.693
		Grand mean	−2.08

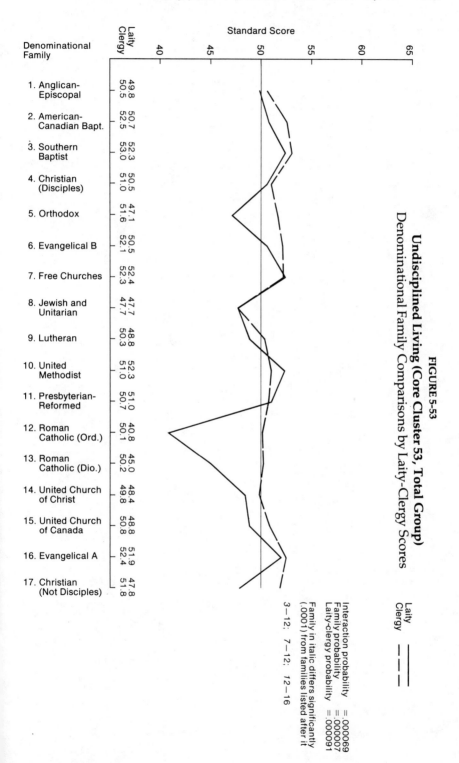

FIGURE 5-53

Undisciplined Living (Core Cluster 53, Total Group)

Denominational Family Comparisons by Laity-Clergy Scores

Denominational Family	Laity	Clergy
1. Anglican-Episcopal	49.8	50.5
2. American-Canadian Bapt.	50.7	52.5
3. Southern Baptist	52.3	53.0
4. Christian (Disciples)	50.5	51.0
5. Orthodox	47.1	51.6
6. Evangelical B	50.5	52.1
7. Free Churches	52.4	52.3
8. Jewish and Unitarian	47.7	47.7
9. Lutheran	48.8	50.3
10. United Methodist	52.3	51.0
11. Presbyterian-Reformed	51.0	50.7
12. Roman Catholic (Ord.)	40.8	50.1
13. Roman Catholic (Dio.)	45.0	50.2
14. United Church of Christ	48.4	49.8
15. United Church of Canada	48.8	50.8
16. Evangelical A	51.9	52.4
17. Christian (Not Disciples)	47.8	51.8

Laity ———
Clergy – – –

Interaction probability = .000069
Family probability = .000007
Laity-clergy probability = .000091

Family in italic differs significantly
(.0001) from families listed after it

3–12; 7–12; 12–16

TABLE 5-54

Core Cluster 54: Self-Serving (Self-Protecting) Behavior
(avoiding intimacy and repelling people by a critical,
demeaning, and insensitive attitude)

Load	Item No.	Item	Mean
.82	573	Often belittles a person in front of others	−2.558
.80	565	Tends to be abrupt and impatient when talking with people	−2.109
.79	562	Uses ministerial role to maintain a sense of superiority	−2.285
.79	561	Is quick to condemn people whose words or actions seem questionable to him/her	−2.187
.77	559	Uses sermons to attack certain members in the congregation or community	−2.448
.76	572	Fails to provide leadership at times when congregation is looking for direction	−2.215
.75	558	People are afraid to come to him/her for counseling on problems and problem situations	−2.310
.75	552	Appears to believe own opinion as a minister should be accepted without question	−2.107
.74	539	Discusses with members of the congregation what has been said in confidence	−2.662
.72	548	Rarely, if ever, visits the sick and shut-ins	−2.342
.71	541	Preaches and teaches in a way that is abstract and unrelated to life	−2.162
.68	557	Looks for another call or parish appointment the moment things do not go well	−2.055
.68	567	Seeks personal preferential treatment because of identity as clergy	−1.994
.68	546	Becomes moody when pressures increase	−1.807

TABLE 5–54 — *CONTINUED*

Load	Item No.	Item	Mean
.65	571	Unable to adjust to the habits of others who share in the living situation (wife, children, fellow priests)	−1.975
.65	574	Talks as though unable to forgive self	−1.923
.65	553	Cannot apply learnings from books	−1.880
.65	554	Pays less attention to the thinking of women than the thinking of men	−1.816
.65	547	Dominates group discussion	−1.790
.64	570	Gives impression that if a job is to be done right, he/she must do it	−1.857
.64	555	Tends to be pessimistic	−1.759
.62	544	Acts as though there is only one right way to do most things	−1.878
.61	536	Cannot let go of details and delegate responsibility	−1.769
.60	535	Seems oblivious to people because of being engrossed in "higher things"	—2.057
.58	537	Publicly shows impatience with people who resist change	−1.770
.57	568	Places great importance on own status and position	−1.882
.57	540	Takes criticism of parish programs personally	−1.620
.54	542	Gives the impression of being always busy and in a hurry	−1.587
.53	545	Regards other vocations as "better" than the ministry	−1.882
		Grand mean	−2.02

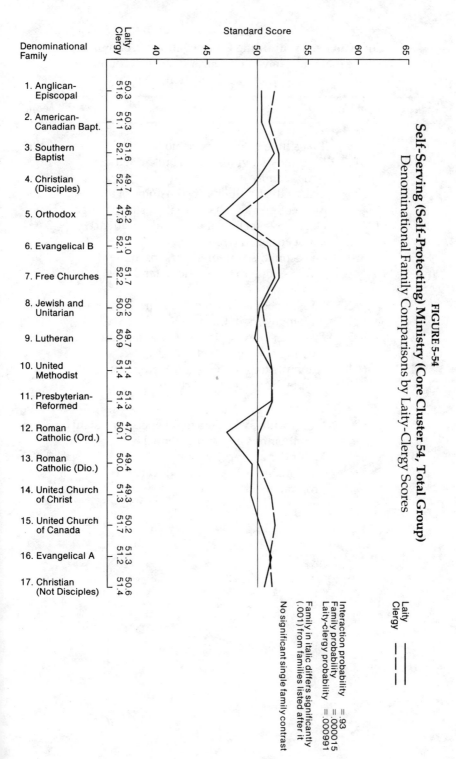

FIGURE 5-54

Self-Serving (Self-Protecting) Ministry (Core Cluster 54, Total Group)
Denominational Family Comparisons by Laity-Clergy Scores

Denominational Family	Laity	Clergy
1. Anglican-Episcopal	50.3	51.6
2. American-Canadian Bapt.	50.3	51.1
3. Southern Baptist	51.6	52.1
4. Christian (Disciples)	49.7	52.1
5. Orthodox	46.2	47.9
6. Evangelical B	51.0	52.1
7. Free Churches	51.7	52.2
8. Jewish and Unitarian	50.2	50.5
9. Lutheran	49.7	50.9
10. United Methodist	51.4	51.4
11. Presbyterian-Reformed	51.3	51.4
12. Roman Catholic (Ord.)	47.0	50.1
13. Roman Catholic (Dio.)	49.4	50.0
14. United Church of Christ	49.3	51.3
15. United Church of Canada	50.2	51.7
16. Evangelical A	51.3	51.2
17. Christian (Not Disciples)	50.6	51.4

Laity ———
Clergy — — —

Interaction probability = .93
Family probability = .000015
Laity-clergy probability = .000991

Family in italic differs significantly
(.001) from families listed after it

No significant single family contrast

TABLE 5-55
Core Cluster 55: Building Congregational Community
(actions that will likely build a strong sense of community
within a congregation)

Load	Item No.	Item	Mean
.71	678	Takes time to know parishioners well	2.483
.63	674	Promotes activities which build a sense of parish family	2.354
.63	676	Learns the traditions and customs of the local congregation before suggesting change	2.289
.62	679	Develops a feeling of trust and confidence between self and members	2.654
.59	680	Seeks out discontented persons in the congregation to try to understand their complaints	2.078
.55	712	Causes people to feel they are needed in the ongoing work of the parish	2.442
.51	685	Evaluates how well parish programs are meeting people's needs	2.310
.45	691	Attempts to find the real reasons why people drop out of church	2.231
		* * *	
.52	670	Meets with lay leaders to set goals consistent with their mission and potential	2.498
.45	681	Maintains an appreciation for the relationship between the budget and program needs	2.107
		Grand mean	2.34

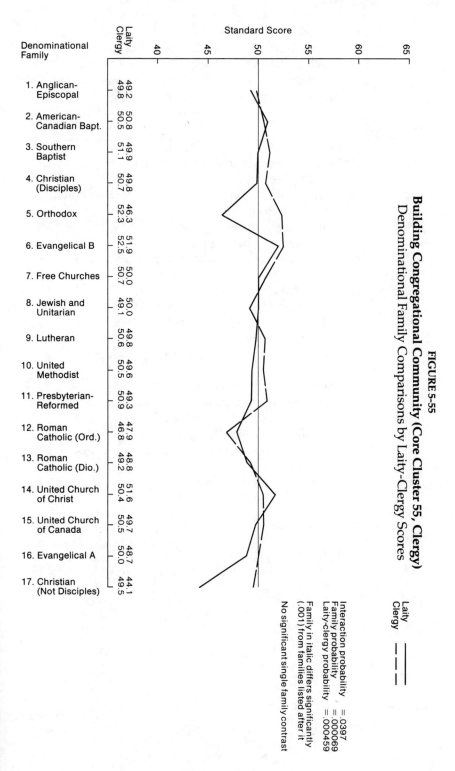

FIGURE 5-55

Building Congregational Community (Core Cluster 55, Clergy)
Denominational Family Comparisons by Laity-Clergy Scores

Denominational Family	Laity	Clergy
1. Anglican-Episcopal	49.2	49.8
2. American-Canadian Bapt.	50.8	50.5
3. Southern Baptist	49.9	51.1
4. Christian (Disciples)	49.8	50.7
5. Orthodox	46.3	52.3
6. Evangelical B	51.9	52.5
7. Free Churches	50.0	50.7
8. Jewish and Unitarian	50.0	49.1
9. Lutheran	49.8	50.6
10. United Methodist	49.6	50.5
11. Presbyterian-Reformed	49.3	50.9
12. Roman Catholic (Ord.)	47.9	46.8
13. Roman Catholic (Dio.)	48.8	49.2
14. United Church of Christ	51.6	50.4
15. United Church of Canada	49.7	50.5
16. Evangelical A	48.7	50.0
17. Christian (Not Disciples)	44.1	49.5

Laity ——
Clergy — — —

Interaction probability = .0397
Family probability = .000069
Laity-clergy probability = .000459

Family in italic differs significantly
(.001) from families listed after it

No significant single family contrast

TABLE 5-56
Core Cluster 56: Conflict Utilization
(understanding conflict theologically and being able to
utilize conflict as a means for airing differences
and stressing concern and understanding)

Load	Item No.	Item	Mean
.66	709	Creates opportunities for people to air their differences	1.679
.65	701	In a conflict situation, makes sure opinions of the minority are heard	2.259
.64	696	In group discussion, stimulates many, not just a few, to participate	2.331
.58	698	Protects group discussions from domination by one or two	2.066
.58	675	On occasion, will bring conflict out into the open in a constructive way	2.081
.56	704	Helps others feel it is all right to disagree with a minister	1.822
.56	714	Distinguishes between surface and serious tensions	2.150
.54	686	On controversial issues, concentrates on helping all to understand the issues	2.277
.53	717	In conflict situations lets people know where he stands in a way that does not alienate them	2.218
.52	693	Has an understanding of conflict as it relates to own theology	1.845
.49	718	Helps people know why changes are being made and what they will be	2.400
		* * *	
.51	682	Shows skill in moving people from anger to creative action	2.213
.47	671	In general discussion can identify the heart of the matter	2.193
		Grand mean	2.11

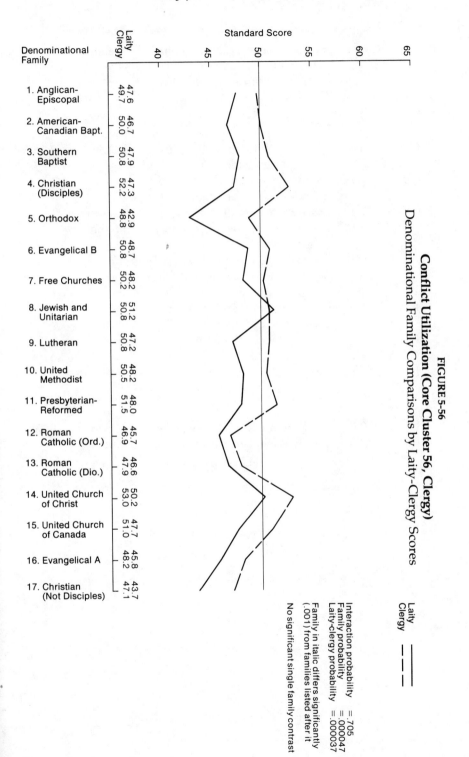

FIGURE 5-56

Conflict Utilization (Core Cluster 56, Clergy)
Denominational Family Comparisons by Laity-Clergy Scores

Denominational Family	Laity	Clergy
1. Anglican-Episcopal	47.6	49.7
2. American-Canadian Bapt.	46.7	50.0
3. Southern Baptist	47.9	50.8
4. Christian (Disciples)	47.3	52.2
5. Orthodox	42.9	48.8
6. Evangelical B	48.7	50.8
7. Free Churches	48.2	50.2
8. Jewish and Unitarian	51.2	50.8
9. Lutheran	47.2	50.8
10. United Methodist	48.2	50.5
11. Presbyterian-Reformed	48.0	51.5
12. Roman Catholic (Ord.)	45.7	46.9
13. Roman Catholic (Dio.)	46.6	47.9
14. United Church of Christ	50.2	53.0
15. United Church of Canada	47.7	51.0
16. Evangelical A	45.8	48.2
17. Christian (Not Disciples)	43.7	47.1

Laity ———
Clergy – – –

Interaction probability = .705
Family probability = .000047
Laity-clergy probability = .000037

Family in italic differs significantly (.001) from families listed after it

No significant single family contrast

TABLE 5-57

Core Cluster 57: Sharing Congregational Leadership
(active employment of lay leadership—regardless of sex—in
establishing and executing an overall parish strategy)

Load	Item No.	Item	Mean
.66	695	Shares leadership with lay leaders chosen by the congregation	2.350
.62	703	Encourages elected lay leaders to make major decisions affecting the congregation	1.879
.60	700	Discourages use of stereotyped sex roles in assigning responsible positions within the congregation	1.758
.51	699	Seeks adequate congregational support before launching innovative projects	2.229
.49	694	Ties innovations to the needs of the parish	1.851
.46	697	Considers an overall parish strategy before planning individual projects	2.055
.45	704	Helps others feel it is all right to disagree with a minister	1.822
.44	670	Meets with lay leaders to set goals consistent with their mission and potential	2.498
		* * *	
.48	729	Works to broaden the base of participation in the decision-making process of the parish	2.235
		Grand mean	2.07

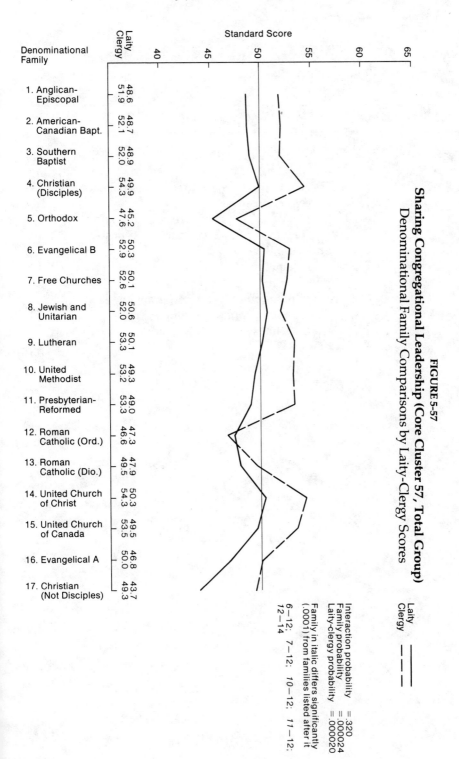

FIGURE 5-57

Sharing Congregational Leadership (Core Cluster 57, Total Group)
Denominational Family Comparisons by Laity-Clergy Scores

Denominational Family	Laity	Clergy
1. Anglican-Episcopal	48.6	51.9
2. American-Canadian Bapt.	48.7	52.1
3. Southern Baptist	48.9	52.0
4. Christian (Disciples)	49.9	54.3
5. Orthodox	45.2	47.6
6. Evangelical B	50.3	52.9
7. Free Churches	50.1	52.6
8. Jewish and Unitarian	50.6	52.0
9. Lutheran	50.1	53.3
10. United Methodist	49.3	53.2
11. Presbyterian-Reformed	49.0	53.3
12. Roman Catholic (Ord.)	47.3	46.6
13. Roman Catholic (Dio.)	47.9	49.5
14. United Church of Christ	50.3	54.3
15. United Church of Canada	49.5	53.5
16. Evangelical A	46.8	50.0
17. Christian (Not Disciples)	43.7	49.3

Laity ———
Clergy — — —

Interaction probability = .320
Family probability = .000024
Laity-clergy probability = .000020

Family in italic differs significantly (.0001) from families listed after it
6–12; 7–12; 10–12; 11–12; 12–14

TABLE 5-58
Core Cluster 58: Effective Administration
(handling administrative responsibilities with understanding,
efficiency, and careful planning)

Load	Item No.	Item	Mean
.60	702	Administers the church office in an orderly and efficient way	2.040
.59	713	Has the planning skills that would make for success in business	1.558
.55	672	Sees that parish records are kept up to date	1.910
.55	684	Understands a financial statement of assets and liabilities	1.819
.53	725	Sees that church property is neat and in good repair	1.448
.51	692	Anticipates building and program needs through long-range planning	1.827
.43	707	Clarifies lines of authority in administrative matters	1.616
		Grand mean	1.74

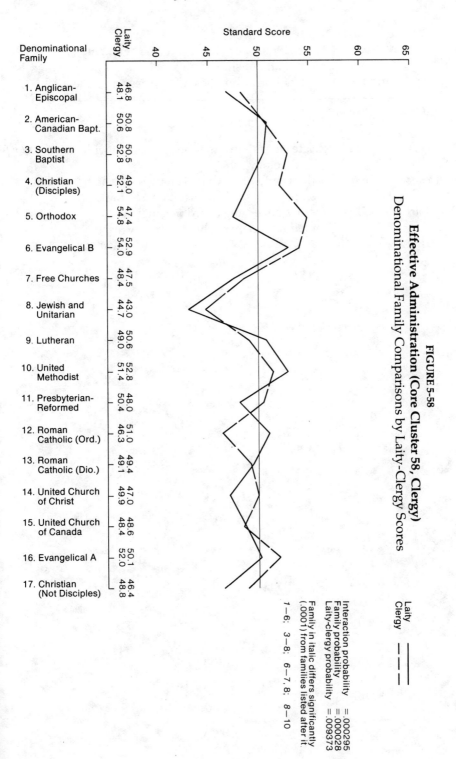

Denominational Family	Laity Clergy
1. Anglican-Episcopal	46.8 / 48.1
2. American-Canadian Bapt.	50.8 / 50.6
3. Southern Baptist	50.5 / 52.8
4. Christian (Disciples)	49.0 / 52.1
5. Orthodox	47.4 / 54.8
6. Evangelical B	52.9 / 54.0
7. Free Churches	47.5 / 48.4
8. Jewish and Unitarian	43.0 / 44.7
9. Lutheran	50.6 / 49.0
10. United Methodist	52.8 / 51.4
11. Presbyterian-Reformed	48.0 / 50.4
12. Roman Catholic (Ord.)	51.0 / 46.3
13. Roman Catholic (Dio.)	49.4 / 49.1
14. United Church of Christ	47.0 / 49.9
15. United Church of Canada	48.6 / 48.4
16. Evangelical A	50.1 / 52.0
17. Christian (Not Disciples)	46.4 / 48.8

FIGURE 5-58

Effective Administration (Core Cluster 58, Clergy)

Denominational Family Comparisons by Laity-Clergy Scores

Laity ——
Clergy ― ― ―

Interaction probability = .000295
Family probability = .000028
Laity-clergy probability = .009373

Family in italic differs significantly (.0001) from families listed after it

1—6; 3—8; 6—7, 8; 8—10

TABLE 5-59
Core Cluster 59: Responsible Staff Management
(from a theological foundation, showing a sensitivity to staff feelings and needs by careful handling of staff policies and issues)

Load	Item No.	Item	Mean
.70	711	Relates to staff in a manner consistent with own theology	1.608
.68	687	Is direct and positive in dealing with a staff member whose services must be terminated	1.625
.61	715	Presses governing board or congregation for fair treatment of church employees	1.520
		Grand mean	1.58

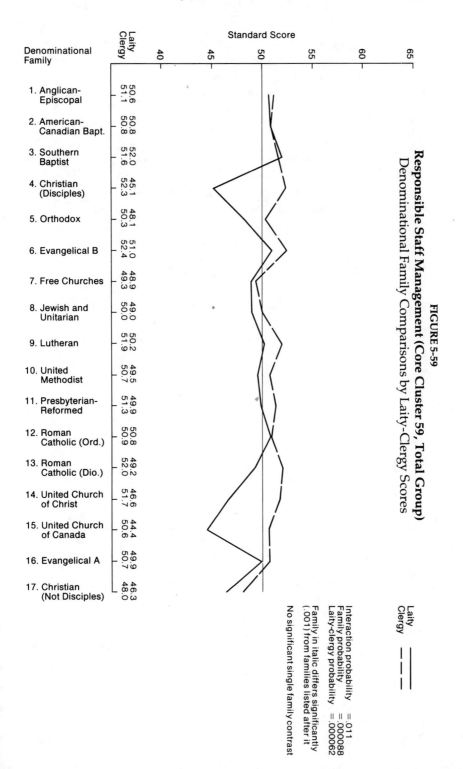

FIGURE 5-59

Responsible Staff Management (Core Cluster 59, Total Group)
Denominational Family Comparisons by Laity-Clergy Scores

Denominational Family	Laity	Clergy
1. Anglican-Episcopal	50.6	51.1
2. American-Canadian Bapt.	50.8	50.8
3. Southern Baptist	52.0	51.6
4. Christian (Disciples)	45.1	52.3
5. Orthodox	48.1	50.3
6. Evangelical B	51.0	52.4
7. Free Churches	48.9	49.3
8. Jewish and Unitarian	49.0	50.0
9. Lutheran	50.2	51.9
10. United Methodist	49.5	50.7
11. Presbyterian-Reformed	49.9	51.3
12. Roman Catholic (Ord.)	50.8	50.9
13. Roman Catholic (Dio.)	49.2	52.0
14. United Church of Christ	46.6	51.7
15. United Church of Canada	44.4	50.6
16. Evangelical A	49.9	50.7
17. Christian (Not Disciples)	46.3	48.0

Laity ———
Clergy — — —

Interaction probability = .011
Family probability = .000088
Laity-clergy probability = .000062

Family in italic differs significantly (.001) from families listed after it

No significant single family contrast

TABLE 5-60
Core Cluster 60: Intuitive Domination of Decision Making
(bypassing the disciplined task of planning and deciding for
the congregation what decisions should be made)

Load	Item No.	Item	Mean
.71	705	Acts as though planning is less necessary in the church than in other institutions	−1.302
.69	710	Glosses over differences among people to give the impression of unity	−1.201
.68	706	Encourages decisions that favor buildings over people	−1.586
.65	708	Relies primarily on charisma and intuition in planning parish activities	−1.173
.61	727	Plans projects without considering financial requirements	−1.496
.51	726	Seeks to be viewed as the ultimate authority in the parish	−1.135
		Grand mean	−1.32

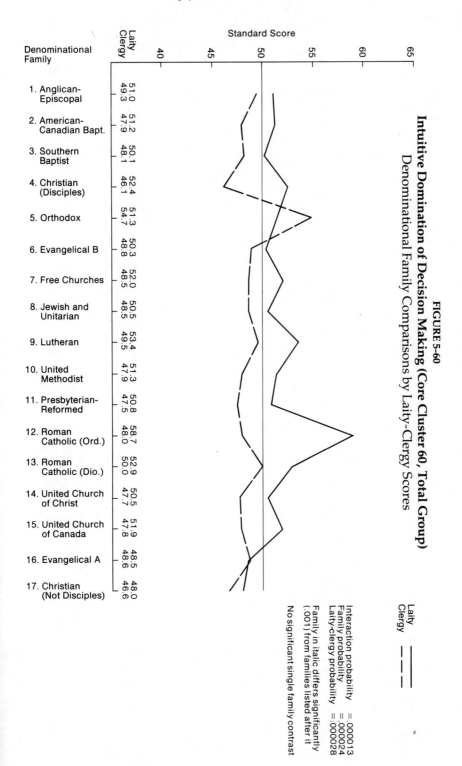

FIGURE 5-60

Intuitive Domination of Decision Making (Core Cluster 60, Total Group)
Denominational Family Comparisons by Laity-Clergy Scores

Denominational Family	Laity	Clergy
1. Anglican-Episcopal	51.0	49.3
2. American-Canadian Bapt.	51.2	47.9
3. Southern Baptist	50.1	48.1
4. Christian (Disciples)	52.4	46.1
5. Orthodox	51.3	54.7
6. Evangelical B	50.3	48.8
7. Free Churches	52.0	48.5
8. Jewish and Unitarian	50.5	48.5
9. Lutheran	53.4	49.5
10. United Methodist	51.3	47.9
11. Presbyterian-Reformed	50.8	47.5
12. Roman Catholic (Ord.)	58.7	48.0
13. Roman Catholic (Dio.)	52.9	50.0
14. United Church of Christ	50.5	47.7
15. United Church of Canada	51.9	47.8
16. Evangelical A	48.5	48.6
17. Christian (Not Disciples)	48.0	46.6

Laity ————
Clergy — — —

Interaction probability = .000013
Family probability = .000024
Laity-clergy probability = .000028

Family in italic differs significantly
(.001) from families listed after it

No significant single family contrast

TABLE 5-61
Core Cluster 61: Evangelistic Witness
(witnessing to Jesus Christ by sharing own faith
and encouraging others to do so)

Load	Item No.	Item	Mean
.63	47	When he is through preaching, you are conscious of Jesus Christ	2.232
.62	62	People are converted as a result of his/her ministry	1.646
.51	81	Leads worship in a way that people feel the closeness of God	2.387
.51	69	Helps laypeople feel confident in sharing their faith with nonmembers	2.237
.45	75	Quotes much Scripture from memory when preaching and teaching	0.540
		* * *	
.41	42	Preaches with authority	2.009
		Grand mean	1.88

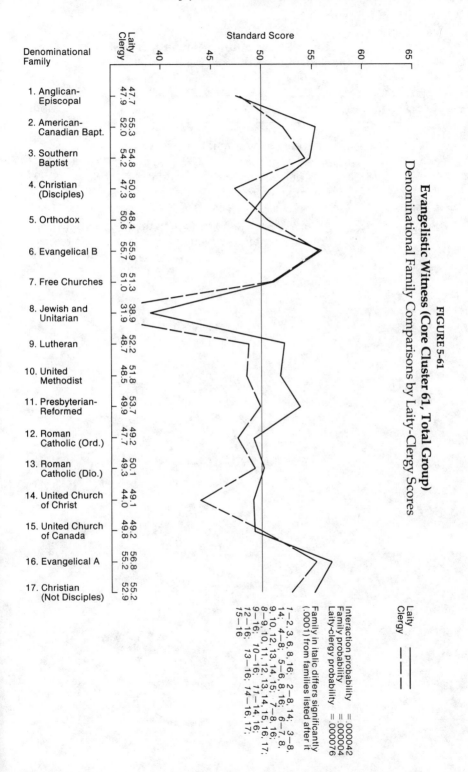

Denominational Family	Laity Clergy
1. Anglican-Episcopal	47.7 / 47.9
2. American-Canadian Bapt.	55.3 / 52.0
3. Southern Baptist	54.8 / 54.2
4. Christian (Disciples)	50.8 / 47.3
5. Orthodox	48.4 / 50.6
6. Evangelical B	55.9 / 55.7
7. Free Churches	51.3 / 51.0
8. Jewish and Unitarian	38.9 / 31.9
9. Lutheran	52.2 / 48.7
10. United Methodist	51.8 / 48.5
11. Presbyterian-Reformed	53.7 / 49.9
12. Roman Catholic (Ord.)	49.2 / 47.7
13. Roman Catholic (Dio.)	50.1 / 49.3
14. United Church of Christ	49.1 / 44.0
15. United Church of Canada	49.2 / 49.8
16. Evangelical A	56.8 / 55.2
17. Christian (Not Disciples)	55.2 / 52.9

FIGURE 5-61

Evangelistic Witness (Core Cluster 61, Total Group)

Denominational Family Comparisons by Laity-Clergy Scores

Laity ——————
Clergy — — —

Interaction probability = .000042
Family probability = .000004
Laity-clergy probability = .000076

Family in italic differs significantly
(.0001) from families listed after it

1—2, 3, 6, 8, 16; 2—8, 14; 3—8,
14; 4—8; 5—6, 8, 16; 6—7, 8,
9, 10, 12, 13, 14, 15; 7—8, 16;
8—9, 10, 11, 12, 13, 14, 15, 16, 17;
9—16; 10—16; 11—14, 16;
12—16; 13—16; 14—16, 17;
15—16

TABLE 5-62

Core Cluster 62: Accepting Mutual Intercession

(openness to ministry of other people while actively
praying with and for others)

Load	Item No.	Item	Mean
.63	384	Actively engages in intercessory prayer on behalf of others	1.703
.62	385	Accepts the ministries of another pastor or Christian friend	1.998
.54	380	Prays with laity in small groups	1.562
.53	487	Accepts people who talk about their dramatic religious experiences	1.520
		Grand mean	1.70

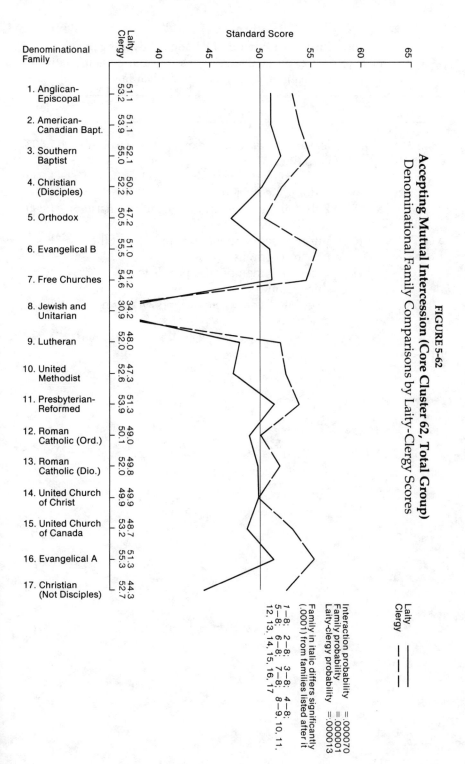

FIGURE 5-62

Accepting Mutual Intercession (Core Cluster 62, Total Group)
Denominational Family Comparisons by Laity-Clergy Scores

Denominational Family	Laity	Clergy
1. Anglican-Episcopal	51.1	53.2
2. American-Canadian Bapt.	51.1	53.9
3. Southern Baptist	52.1	55.0
4. Christian (Disciples)	50.2	52.2
5. Orthodox	47.2	50.5
6. Evangelical B	51.0	55.5
7. Free Churches	51.2	54.6
8. Jewish and Unitarian	34.2	30.9
9. Lutheran	48.0	52.0
10. United Methodist	47.3	52.6
11. Presbyterian-Reformed	51.3	53.9
12. Roman Catholic (Ord.)	49.0	50.1
13. Roman Catholic (Dio.)	49.8	52.0
14. United Church of Christ	49.9	49.9
15. United Church of Canada	48.7	53.2
16. Evangelical A	51.3	55.3
17. Christian (Not Disciples)	44.3	52.7

Laity ———
Clergy – – –

Interaction probability = .000070
Family probability = .000001
Laity-clergy probability = .000013

Family in italic differs significantly
(.0001) from families listed after it

1—8; 2—8; 3—8; 4—8;
5—8; 6—8; 7—8; 8—9, 10, 11,
12, 13, 14, 15, 16, 17

TABLE 5-63
Core Cluster 63: Pursuit of Personal Advantage
(personal insecurity expressed in grandiose ideas and manipulative
efforts to gain or to keep personal advantages)

Load	Item No.	Item	Mean
.73	517	Is usually upset by unexpected demands on own time	−1.802
.71	519	Seeks constant reassurance that he/she is doing a good job	−1.349
.68	518	Entertains ambitions and dreams inconsistent with the ministerial calling	−1.890
.65	516	Strongly seeks public acclaim for what the parish accomplishes	−1.383
.63	515	Frequently manipulates people to get things done	−1.736
.55	520	Uses intellect to avoid dealing with own emotions	−1.370
		Grand mean	−1.59

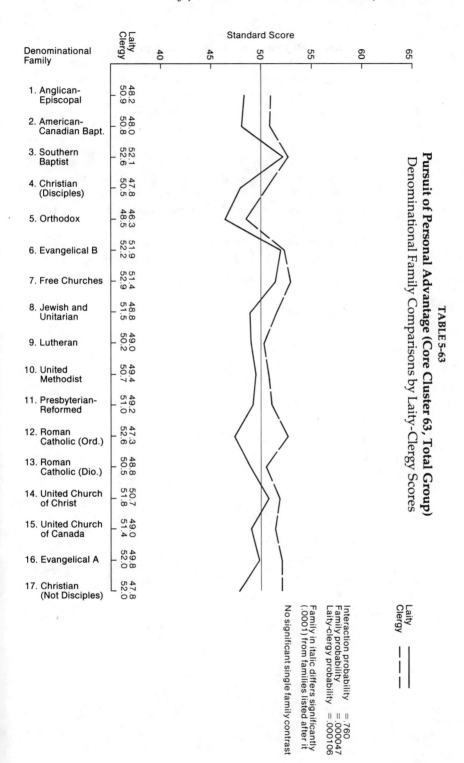

TABLE 5-63

Pursuit of Personal Advantage (Core Cluster 63, Total Group)
Denominational Family Comparisons by Laity-Clergy Scores

Denominational Family	Laity	Clergy
1. Anglican-Episcopal	48.2	50.9
2. American-Canadian Bapt.	48.0	50.8
3. Southern Baptist	52.1	52.6
4. Christian (Disciples)	47.8	50.5
5. Orthodox	46.3	48.5
6. Evangelical B	51.9	52.2
7. Free Churches	51.4	52.9
8. Jewish and Unitarian	48.8	51.5
9. Lutheran	49.0	50.2
10. United Methodist	49.4	50.7
11. Presbyterian-Reformed	49.2	51.0
12. Roman Catholic (Ord.)	47.3	52.6
13. Roman Catholic (Dio.)	48.8	50.5
14. United Church of Christ	50.7	51.8
15. United Church of Canada	49.0	51.4
16. Evangelical A	49.8	52.0
17. Christian (Not Disciples)	47.8	52.0

Laity ————
Clergy – – –

Interaction probability = .760
Family probability = .000047
Laity-clergy probability = .000106

Family in italic differs significantly
(.0001) from families listed after it

No significant single family contrast

TABLE 5-64
Core Cluster 64: Irresponsibility to the Congregation
(through independence and lack of discipline, not placing
oneself in a position of responsibility to the
religious community to be served)

Load	Item No.	Item	Mean
.67	564	Is occasionally intoxicated	−2.270
.62	575	Commits congregation to a program without consulting his superior (or governing board)	−1.870
.62	551	Frequently scolds the congregation in sermons	−1.687
.51	538	Works and sleeps late	−0.705
		Grand mean	−1.63

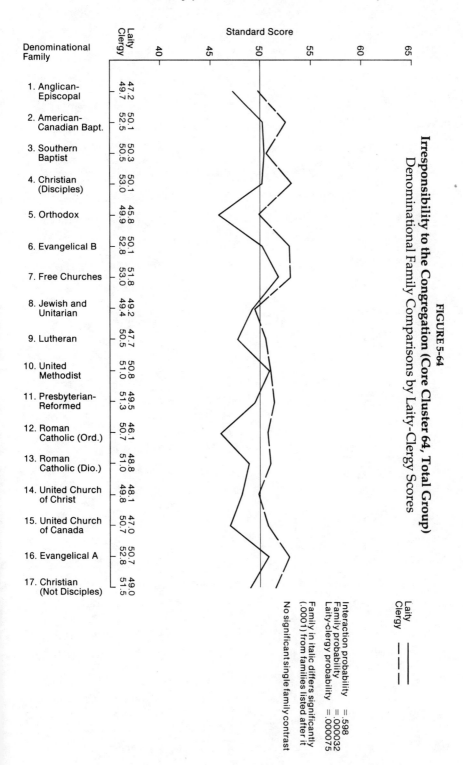

FIGURE 5-64

Irresponsibility to the Congregation (Core Cluster 64, Total Group)

Denominational Family Comparisons by Laity-Clergy Scores

Denominational Family	Laity	Clergy
1. Anglican-Episcopal	47.2	49.7
2. American-Canadian Bapt.	50.1	52.5
3. Southern Baptist	50.3	50.5
4. Christian (Disciples)	50.1	53.0
5. Orthodox	45.8	49.9
6. Evangelical B	50.1	52.8
7. Free Churches	51.8	53.0
8. Jewish and Unitarian	49.2	49.4
9. Lutheran	47.7	50.5
10. United Methodist	50.8	51.0
11. Presbyterian-Reformed	49.5	51.3
12. Roman Catholic (Ord.)	46.1	50.7
13. Roman Catholic (Dio.)	48.8	51.0
14. United Church of Christ	48.1	49.8
15. United Church of Canada	47.0	50.7
16. Evangelical A	50.7	52.8
17. Christian (Not Disciples)	49.0	51.5

Laity ——————
Clergy — — —

Interaction probability = .598
Family probability = .000032
Laity-clergy probability = .000075

Family in italic differs significantly
(.0001) from families listed after it

No significant single family contrast

II

Churches and Denominational Families

6

Anglican-Episcopal
Churches

David E. Richards

David Richards opens his chapter with a description and brief examination of the ten most highly valued ministerial characteristics held by the Anglican-Episcopal family. After his examination of these Anglican-Episcopal conceptions of the priesthood, he moves successively into the response of this family within each of the seven major sections of the questionnaire used in this study, and he notes those dimensions where Anglican-Episcopal respondents differ significantly from the total group.

In marked contrast to those denominational families whose primary expectations focus on transcendent dimensions of faith and priesthood, Anglican-Episcopal clergy and laity are concerned primarily with the quality of a young priest's interpersonal relationships. The relation of priest to parishioners and the ability to create and sustain a community of faith are central issues.

Richards expresses concern about historic accents in the role of priesthood that, according to these data, appear diminished in the Anglican-Episcopal family; a lower-than-average valuation of the Scripture as a source of ethical guidance, withdrawal from vigorous social involvement, and resistance to the

David E. Richards serves as Executive Director of the Office of Pastoral Development of the House of Bishops, the Episcopal Church. He has previously served as Suffragan Bishop in the Diocese of Albany, New York, and was Bishop of Central America from 1957 through 1968.

use of religious terminology and Christian symbols in pastoral counseling.

In his conclusion, he explains his projections of some of the long-range outcomes of current ministerial expectations, some of which he views as opposing or contradicting. The ideal priest, he judges, appears to be a meek, self-effacing individual who lacks ego strength. Simultaneously, however, people idealize the priest and expect pastoral expertise across a wide diversity of fields. Richards stresses various dilemmas that need to be at least partially resolved for effective ministry in the near future.

The data of this denominational family come from the responses of persons in the Episcopal Church in the United States and the Anglican Church of Canada.

The original intention of the Readiness for Ministry Project was to develop means to assess the quality of theological education generally available in North America today. It was clear to the initiators of the study "that the quality of that education can be assessed best by determining the degree to which those who experience such education are indeed prepared for the practice of ministry."

The data generated from this project provide information about how Anglicans and Episcopalians evaluate various criteria that could be used in assessing a beginning minister. The data reflect what current feelings are—not what they ought to be. Some findings that surface could be viewed as complimentary to the Anglican-Episcopal family, others as negative. The data include primarily statements of attitudes toward and expectations of beginning ministers. A careful study of the data should give a clear benchmark of what Anglican-Episcopal respondents deem most and least important in ministry today.

In this chapter, I shall first analyze the conceptions of priesthood held by the clergy and laity of the Anglican-Episcopal Churches. We shall then analyze their responses within the seven taxonomic sections of the Readiness for Ministry questionnaire, being alert to points at which the Anglican-Episcopal Churches differ significantly from those of other denominations. Differences in response of clergy and laity will also be examined. In each section, we shall begin to reflect on the implications of the findings for the future of this church body.

What are the major constructs of ministry underlying the expectations of Anglicans and Episcopalians as they conceive of their priests and ministers? In order to hear the voice of this ecclesiastical family, I shall examine the configurations of ideas that develop from the responses of clergy and laity of this group. As Anglican-Episcopal respondents express their model of ministry in contrast to other church families, to what do they grant highest priorities?

The ten clusters that rank highest of the sixty-three clusters formed solely on the basis of Anglican-Episcopal responses throw into sharp focus the distinctive characteristics of this family. The major concepts describing the Anglican-Episcopal priest are cast in heavily human and relational terms. In contrast to some denominational families, the prime accents are not on theocentric issues or issues of faith but, rather, on the quality of human interrelations. The role of worship and particular accents of a spiritual ministry are subsumed within the play of person-to-person interaction. (See Table 6-1.)

The most highly rated of the Anglican-Episcopal clusters has to do with the relationship between the priest and parishioners. Laity and professionals are especially concerned that the priest develop a sense of trust between him- or herself and members of the parish. A minister is expected to have more than a cursory acquaintance with his or her parishioners. This notion is reinforced by the expectation that the priest cause "people to feel they are needed in the ongoing work of the parish." The relationship between priest and parishioners is exemplified further within this cluster by an emphasis on the priest's explaining in advance to the congregation about changes that are to occur within the parish. The ability of the priest to create in his parishioners a sense of trust and a sense of being important, informed members of a defined community is crucially important to the Anglican-Episcopal concept of ministry.

The theme of the priest-parishioner relationship, reinforced in the second-ranking cluster, is articulated more distinctly by Anglican-Episcopal clergy than by their laity. This cluster deals with the priest's relationship to parishioners in a broad guiding and counseling role. A sensitivity to the quality of human relationships is primary; thus, when a priest is counseling, he or she is to listen for feeling tones, as well as to the actual words. The minister is to be aware of the limitations of his or her own role and to be willing and knowledgeable about the process of referral to other professional counselors. This guiding and counseling role is further manifested by an approach wherein persons are helped to weigh the implications of alternate decisions.

The human dimension of any relationship between priest and parishioner is central. It appears to be posited on a genuine respect for the parishioner's ability to resolve problems. The emphasis is not on the priest as an omniscient answer giver; but rather, on the priest as a conveyor of strength by his or her physical and emotional presence, as a helper of individuals by enabling them to reach their own solutions.

This concern with interpersonal relations is manifested in the third-ranking cluster, which broadens to emphasize the relations of parishioner to parishioner (not just priest to parishioner) in a large community of faith. Anglican-Episcopal respondents look for a priest who will create an atmosphere within the parish of freedom, joy, and love. Within this context, worship is seen as an important means of creating such a community of faith.

TABLE 6-1
**Comparison of Highest-Ranking Core Clusters
with Highest-Ranking Anglican-Episcopal Clusters**

Core Clusters of Total Group			Anglican-Episcopal Clusters		
Rank Order	Title	Grand Mean	Rank Order	Title	Grand Mean
1	*Service in Humility* (CC 34) Relying on God's grace, serves others without seeking personal reputation for success or infallibility	2.52	1	Development of personal relationship with parishioners characterized by trust, confidence, and concern	2.49
2	*Personal Responsibility* (CC 42) Honoring commitments by carrying out promises despite pressures to compromise	2.43	2	In guiding-counseling roles, receptive to inner feelings of parishioners, respectful of their right to make decisions, and aware of when other professional help is needed	2.41
3	*Christian Example* (CC 35) Personal belief in the Gospel, that manifests itself in generosity and a life of high moral quality	2.42	3.5	Creation of a community of faith through worship in which an atmosphere of freedom, joy, and love is alive	2.30
4	*Acknowledgment of Limitations* (CC 36) Acknowledging limitations and mistakes and recognizing the need for continued growth and learning	2.35	3.5	Dependable, uncompromising under pressure, remains calm and positive under stress	2.30
5	*Building Congregational Community* (CC 55) Actions that will likely build a strong sense of community within a congregation	2.34	5	Mature acceptance of emotional and physical limitations; able to acknowledge mistakes without undue personal threat	2.28

TABLE 6-1 — *CONTINUED*

Core Clusters of Total Group			Anglican-Episcopal Clusters		
Rank Order	Title	Grand Mean	Rank Order	Title	Grand Mean
6	*Fidelity to Tasks and Persons* (CC 43) Showing competence and responsibility by completing tasks, relating warmly to people, handling differences of opinion, and growing in skills	2.29	6	Through leading worship and preaching, enables people to sense God's presence and spiritual gifts	2.27
7	*Perceptive Counseling* (CC 21)　Reaching out to persons under stress with a perception, sensitivity, and warmth that is freeing and supportive	2.26	7	Ability to help parishioners use resources of faith in coping with serious problems	2.26
8	*Positive Approach* (CC 44)　Handling stressful situations by remaining calm under pressure, while continuing to affirm persons	2.25	8	In ministering during crisis situations, provides sensitive personal counseling and ministry of other people	2.25
9	*Theocentric-Biblical Ministry* (CC 2) Drawing attention to God's Word and Person when preaching, teaching and leading worship	2.24	9.5	Shares leadership functions with laity in goal setting, decision making, and broadening the leadership group	2.24
10	*Enabling Counseling* (CC 22)　Using high levels of understanding and skill in aiding persons to work through serious problems	2.23	9.5	Is personally sustained through serious difficulties by a sense of God's calling, Christ's mission, and the leading of the Holy Spirit	2.24

Of equal importance to the preceding is the concern articulated by Anglican-Episcopal respondents with regard to the personal character of the priest. This cluster parallels closely the core cluster dealing with personal responsibility (CC 42). Central for Anglican-Episcopal respondents in what they deem important in a beginning minister is that he or she fulfill promises made and maintain personal integrity in the face of outside pressures. The uniqueness of their cluster centers in the addition of an expectation that a minister act calmly during periods of stress and remain positive when dealing with problem people. They do not share the expectation (which appears in a comparable core cluster) of an ability to work independently without prodding or supervision. Some might see a parallel in this to the traditional gentleman officer, who fulfills his promises, maintains his integrity, acts calmly during stress, and deals in a positive way with cantankerous people.

A person who is able to establish this relationship of trust, who can create a sense of community, is also someone who recognizes his or her own human vulnerability. The fifth most important cluster describes a priest who is aware of personal emotional inadequacies and physical limitations. Such a person is able to laugh at him- or herself and to acknowledge mistakes before those to whom he or she might be accountable.

The focus of concern shifts in the sixth-ranking cluster to a more direct expression of spirituality as it manifests itself in worship and the historic expression of the Christian faith. This sixth Anglican-Episcopal cluster is the first where one finds an emphasis on theological and Christological concepts. While their highest-ranked clusters accent relationships between priest and parishioners or the specific qualities of a priest, this cluster deals with the relationship of a parishioner to God. Such relationship manifests itself in worship where a person feels the closeness of God. It includes the work of the minister, who enables a parishioner to sense the gift of God's forgiveness.

These two streams of concern, the one dealing with interpersonal relationships and the other with divine and human dimensions, intersect in a relatively small cluster, ranking as seventh in importance to Anglicans and Episcopalians. The integrating characteristic of this cluster revolves about the priest's role in helping people to recognize ways in which God is working in their lives. As one who is close to people during their moments of stress and tragedy, the priest helps them use the resources of faith to meet their problems.

The locus of the eighth cluster is the giving of help to people in crisis situations. The heart of this concept is availability of the priest, his or her ability to go immediately to people experiencing a crisis situation. This cluster includes as well an emphasis on marshalling the ministering help of other people who themselves have struggled through personal tragedies. Such persons, together with the priest, may effectively help a parishioner in similar moments of stress. Included in the cluster is an emphasis on dealing gently with people in need and advising in such a way that personal decision is not violated or trampled on. This cluster illustrates themes that run constantly through the Anglican-Episcopal clusters: the priest's personally sensitive relationship with parishioners, respect for an individual's choice of action, and the involvement of all in a sharing community.

Leadership within such a community is highlighted in the ninth-ranked cluster, showing that Anglican-Episcopal respondents are particularly sensitive to how parish leadership is shared with laity. It is defined in the specifics of goal setting and involvement of laity when making major decisions. Their responses show appreciation of the priest who works to broaden the base of participation in the decision-making process of the parish and who allows people freedom in carrying out assigned responsibilities.

Seen as equally important to the previous cluster is the cluster (tenth in our examination) that concerns the spiritual sustenance of the priest, particularly during times of stress. This sustaining force is found in a sense of call from God himself and only secondarily in an appointment to a specific parish. A theological foundation undergirds this concept: the call of God, the leading of the Holy Spirit, and the making of Christ's mission first in one's life.

MINISTRY TO THE RELIGIOUS COMMUNITY

As might have been expected, in the Anglican-Episcopal tradition major importance is attached to the priest's functions as a minister of the sacraments. (See Table 6-2.) What appears to be distinctive and especially valued is the function of what we might refer to as "liturgical management." It is appreciated when the priest or minister plans ahead for Sunday worship, taking the time to inform or instruct worshippers regarding any changes or new elements that are to be introduced into the worship design. It seems clear that Anglican-Episcopal parishioners are not open to spontaneous interventions and changes in planned liturgical worship.

There is correspondingly less accent on the role of preaching. Anglican-Episcopal respondents differ significantly from others in not placing as high a value on a preacher's ability to hold the attention and interest of a congregation (Item 70).

Whereas in other denominations, worshippers expect ethical guidance based on Scripture, members of the Anglican and Episcopal Churches do not especially value this use of Scripture. In this, they differ particularly from the Southern Baptist, Evangelical B, Presbyterian-Reformed, and Christian (not Disciples) families in their response to a "Theocentric Min-

TABLE 6-2
**Selected Items from "Ministry to the Religious Community"
in Which Anglican-Episcopal Judgment of Highest Importance
Differs Significantly from That of
All Other Denominations**

Item No.	Item	Percent Judging "Highly Important"	
		Anglican-Episcopal Family	All Other Denominations
46	Using biblical insights to guide members in making ethical or moral decisions	30	43
47	When he is through preaching, you are conscious of Jesus Christ	44	56
50	Guides people by relating the Scriptures to their human condition	32	46
62	People are converted as a result of his/her ministry	23	36
64	Preaches sermons that awaken listeners to their sinfulness and need for a Savior	12	35
69	Helps laypeople feel confident in sharing their faith with nonmembers	32	47
70	When preaching, holds the interest and attention of the congregation	38	54
76	Considers his professional ministry as sacramental	43	20
78	Teaches the meaning of sacraments	48	40

Note: Significance is at or below the .0001 level.

istry" (CC 2). In some churches, it is clearly understood that Scripture dictates expected behaviors. This is not quite so clearly understood in the Anglican-Episcopal Churches. Hence, the question "What, exactly, is our most valued and appreciated use of Scripture?" Only 32 percent of the Anglican-Episcopal respondents felt it was highly important that a priest "guide people by relating the Scriptures to their human condition" (Item 50). Over one-half see great value in using Scripture as a source of spiritual nourishment (although this ranks significantly below responses from those in other denominations). Apparently a more devotional, rather than ethical, use of Holy Scripture is desired. This must be viewed within a transdenominational context in which Anglican-Episcopal respondents tend to rank any direct use of Scripture lower than does the total group.

We note from recent studies that a high percentage of Anglican-Episcopal theological students and possible ordinands are attending non-Anglican-Episcopal seminaries. In these seminaries, it is likely that they are learning to see Scripture as a more valued guide to specific ethical questions and moral behavior. As graduates from these schools enter the Anglican-Episcopal parish ministry, they may find themselves differing from their peers in how they use the Holy Scriptures. They may present a concept of scriptural use that differs from what has been traditionally established or practiced in Anglican-Episcopal parishes.

It becomes clear from the data in this section that Anglican-Episcopal respondents prefer well-planned and well-ordered worship, with little emphasis on Scripture as a guide to ethics, and more emphasis on their use of Scripture in spiritual nurture. After asking ourselves exactly what our view is of Scripture and how we make use of it, we might well ask also, if it is not our source of moral and ethical guidance, what *do* we use as a basis for measuring the morality of our judgments and behaviors?

Clergy and laity respond with a high degree of unanimity to concerns related to ministries within the religious community. The one exception has to do with a ministry to children and youth. In this realm, Anglican-Episcopal laity (together with the laity of other denominational families) express a much higher expectation than do their clergy (CC 3). Laypeople view this characteristic of ministry as being far more important than do ordained clergy.

MINISTRIES TO THE COMMUNITY AND TO THE WORLD

Data from this section tell us something about how the ministers and members of the Anglican-Episcopal Churches expect a beginning priest to act toward outsiders. (See Table 6-3.) They apparently do not fully appreciate behaviors that indicate concern and compassion for the unchurched and for world mission. Anglican-Episcopal respondents are not against the

TABLE 6-3

**Selected Items in "Ministry to Community and World" in Which
Anglican-Episcopal Judgment of Highest Importance Differs
Significantly from That of All Other Denominations**

Item No.	Item	Percent Judging "Highly Important"	
		Anglican-Episcopal Family	All Other Denominations
116	Visits unchurched people to share the faith	13	34
114	Originates activities which consider youths' interests and awaken their enthusiasm	26	35
123	Priorities in use of time indicate the belief that the one and only way to build an ideal world society is to convert everyone to Christianity	7	12
147	Gives pastoral service to all people with needs	52	59
146	Stimulates congregation to new interest and support for world missions	16	31
150	Seeks to bring everyone to know God's love in Jesus Christ	55	72

Note: Significance is at or below the .0001 level.

unchurched, nor do they talk down world mission (on the contrary, they are inclined to talk it up), but in actuality, Anglicans and Episcopalians really do not expect their clergy to give these interests, concerns and activities a very high priority.

In common with other mainline denominations, Anglican-Episcopal respondents place only mild importance on wanting their pastor to give pastoral service to all (CC 11), to take initiative in development of community services (CC 13), and to reflect an emphasis on mission-mindedness (CC 12). But they do not take an extreme posture of resistance to community involvement, as evidenced by the fact they do not particularly favor

"Total Concentration on Congregational Concerns" (CC 20). They do not pit a spiritual, Gospel-proclaiming ministry against stressing community service and political change. In general, clergy are more likely to see value in supporting community causes (CC 15), expressing an active concern for the oppressed (CC 16), and exerting a degree of aggressive political leadership (CC 18).

What is suggested here is a kind of passivity toward certain vital issues in our society, and throughout the world. While we know that such issues as loneliness, isolation, and hunger exist, we—at the same time—accept an attitude of passivity. We appreciate the clergyperson who is less dynamic on social issues. This could mean that in the Anglican-Episcopal Churches active, overtly compassionate clergy stand out. Sometimes they are valued as token activists and ecclesiastical social workers and may even be well supported, especially while, for example, working on earthquake relief in the Philippines, or Guatemala. But on the home front their active services may not be sought after or appreciated. This becomes particularly true where the priest would be involved in actively pursuing social or political change at the perceived expense of helping individuals in need.

MINISTRIES TO PERSONS UNDER STRESS

The White House Conference on Mental Health (1965) pointed out that a high percentage of people under stress turn first of all to clergy. Through clergy, those with deep psychological problems may ultimately be referred to mental health professionals. Data related to this section seem to indicate that Anglican-Episcopal members value in beginning clergy a counseling approach that generally makes no reference to religious terminology and Christian symbols.

While acknowledging the counseling role as a legitimate part of priesthood, Anglican-Episcopal respondents are reticent about an overt spiritual dimension in the counseling process. Their responses are significantly different from other church bodies in their reduced enthusiasm for such items as "Shows a degree of skill in finding theologically sound solutions to pastoral problems" (Item 274) or "When counseling, will sometimes confront person with the need to believe" (Item 260). More than 80 percent of the Anglican-Episcopal respondents endorse as important the idea that clergy offer counsel "in a way that respects a person's freedom to choose his own course of action." Counseling seems to be valued in terms of the psychological comfort that is given.

Such counseling help, however, is generally offered in response to requests made during times of crisis, including inconvenient periods such as holidays or late at night. Clergy responses to such requests are necessary and good. What is not known is the degree to which Anglican-Episcopal clergy aggressively intervene in a crisis. It is possible that privacy and individuality have been overly respected, to the extent that clergy will not enter a situation until asked to do so. Confrontation and aggressive pastoral and personal outreach may not be an inherently Anglican-Episcopal style. Unfortunately, this means that people who are controlled by certain social restraints grapple alone with intense emotional, spiritual, or moral needs until forced by the utter urgency of their situation to ask for outside help. A way to offset this would be to make clergy more conscious of the value of early intervention in crisis—or what we might think of as preventive pastoral care—as contrasted with custodial pastoral intervention.

THE MINISTER AS THEOLOGIAN AND THINKER

With respect to the priest as a theologian and thinker, Episcopalians share some points of view with other denominations.

The Anglican-Episcopal responses do not differ significantly from the total group with regard to five of the six dimensions or core clusters included in this section of the questionnaire. In ranking the issues related to "Clarity of Thought and Communication" (CC 28), both laity and clergy assign mildly less priority than do most other groups, but not to a statistically significant extent. However, they do differ sharply and significantly with seven other families of denominations by according less importance to "Affirmation of Conservative Biblical Faith" (CC 31). This provides an interesting insight into the Anglican-Episcopal Churches. There is a strong affirmation of Jesus Christ as the Son of God and a positive response to treating the Bible, when interpreted by the church, as the final authority in matters of faith. There is also an equally clear desire for Anglican-Episcopal clergy to give evidence of continued and thorough study of the Scriptures. But the group sharply rejects a literal interpretation of the Scriptures by giving a significantly lower-than-average response to the item regarding "the presence and activity of a personal devil (Satan)" (Item 313).

Distinctively, Anglican-Episcopal respondents value a clergyperson's use of his or her own inner life experiences and personal reference points as a tool in ministry, rather than of sharply defined denominational moral expectations. Those moral expectations simply are not stated. Anglican-Episcopal respondents seem to resist an externally defined ethic that can be clearly labeled Anglican-Episcopal. Thus they differ significantly from other denominations in their much lower ranking of such items as "Clearly identifies to parishioners the denomination's moral expectations" (Item 312) or "Is conversant with the polity and official statements of own denomination" (Item 323).

Just stating the problem in this way suggests that, in fact, the Anglican-Episcopal Churches are held together more by social and cultural bonds than by an intensely embraced theology. A relatively high percentage of their responses endorse a ministry that encourages "members to acknowledge one another as the Body of Christ, even though they hold divergent theological views" (Item 322). In this they are in basic agreement with many other churches. And they do not consider it important that the beliefs of a priest beginning his or her ministry reflect the teachings of the denomination. It is clear from the responses in this section that unity can be maintained in spite of theological diversity. Anglican-Episcopal respondents are particularly suspicious of theological consensus if it derives from a theological base that could be used in a legalistic fashion. They see far less value than many other ministers and laypeople in having their clergy possess an articulated theological position on matters such as divorce, abortion, and suicide (Item 327).

If moderation is the key term to describe the Anglican-Episcopal Churches then apparently the price members pay is that their denominational theological standards and expectations are not clearly expressed apart from canons and the Prayer Book. It is a matter of record that these can be changed by mutual agreement arrived at through democratic parliamentary action. Hence, the theological base appears to change from time to time, to the great distress of some and the great satisfaction of others.

THE MINISTER'S PERSONAL COMMITMENT TO FAITH

It is easier to describe how the minister's commitment to faith is *not* perceived in the Anglican-Episcopal Churches than it is to describe accurately how such a commitment *is* perceived. The faith commitment of any person is viewed as an elusive element. Under the very best of circumstances, it is difficult to articulate just what the Anglican-Episcopal Churches want and where they expect their ministers to stand in this regard. In general, their formulas for faith are contained in the Prayer Book. It may be that a quiet assumption is made that those formulas indeed represent the point where all Anglican-Episcopal ministers stand. Since the common understanding of faith commitment is based on the Prayer Book (*lex orandi, lex credendi*: "As we pray, so we believe"), more can be said by stating what they feel is *not* included in this arena.

To illustrate, Anglican-Episcopal respondents are less inclined than others to attribute deployment and placement of clergy within a particular congregation as being under the specific direction of God. They feel that it is appropriate to have faith that God calls to the ordained ministry in the first instance; after that, however, the exact place where one serves is perceived as dictated by many other factors. This suggests a concept of faith commitment in which God's hand tends not to be seen in daily events or in the management of personal lives. Episcopalians do not readily rely on biblical texts to give guidance in decision making.

A stronger humanistic undercurrent is apparent. Spending time daily in private prayer and meditation (Item 370) is not judged so highly important as in other denominations, nor do many feel a priority in a young priest's encouraging "selected young people to consider the ministry as a vocation" (Item 350).

In various other denominations, clergy are expected to model faith commitment for their constituencies. Not only are they expected to set moral examples, but they must also set faith and believing examples. Although it is a hard element to assess, the expectation is that ministers should be faith and life "exemplars."

In responding to the general dimension of "Christian Example" (CC 35), Anglican-Episcopal clergy and laity are alike in the lower-than-average rank they assign this characteristic. The Anglican-Episcopal response is significantly lower than that of all three Baptist groups and the Evangelicals. But they see more value in example than does the Jewish and Unitarian grouping. They set significantly less value on a priest's serving as a Christian example in the community (Item 376), witnessing through his or her generosity (Item 374), or behaving in a way that is above reproach (Item 373).

Hand in hand with this response goes a tendency to reject the traditional stereotype of puritanism among clergy. Anglican-Episcopal clergy are allowed to smoke publicly and drink socially. If they fail to uphold certain social and moral standards, they may still be tolerated in the ministry. Even though it might precipitate a move to another community, the lapse or "slip" may not be seen as cause for being forced out of the ministry, nor out of the church. It is almost as though members do not wish to see their clergy as being too perfect in terms of their personal lifestyles. They prefer that their clergy be open and honest about who they really are and what they are like. In terms of the descriptions of secularity offered in the questionnaire, Anglican-Episcopal respondents do not see puritanical standards as important as most Protestants generally do.

Finally, the characteristics dealing with priestly commitments uniquely mark the Anglican-Episcopal Churches, along with the Orthodox Churches and the Roman Catholic Church. A great deal of diversity within the church is obvious, as priests and laypeople evaluate the importance of regularly receiving the Sacrament of Penance, of daily celebrating Holy Communion, of expressing devotion to the Blessed Sacrament, and of managing personal finance in a spirit of poverty. Thus while a large enough group positively values these items to distinguish the Anglican-Episcopal Church from Protestant churches, the Anglican-Episcopal group itself spreads across the full range of responses, from seeing such action as virtually indispensable, to those who feel they hinder effective ministry.

THE MINISTER AS PERSON AND LEADER

A strong contrast appears between what members of the Anglican-Episcopal Churches ideally desire in a minister and what is seen and judged on the basis of actual performance. It seems to me that 80 percent of Anglican-Episcopal respondents idealize expectations of clergy in terms that are difficult to fulfill. Normal ego needs seem to be denied as having any validity, and, in the name of humility, stereotypes emerge that seem to favor incompetence and militate against professional skills and status.

In this section are noted some of the highly endorsed items that describe desired characteristics of a minister in the Anglican-Episcopal Churches. (The extremely high degree of importance attached to these characteristics is not usually significantly different from that attached by the total group; however, they are worthy of attention, because 90 percent or more of Anglican-Episcopal respondents judge these characteristics as "quite" or "highly" important.) First, the minister "serves others willingly with or without public acclaim" (Item 336). While thus serving, the ideal minister "shows sufficient awareness of own inadequacies to know when help is needed" (Item 363). Because he or she is clear about inadequacies, it follows that the minister "recognizes own emotional and physical limitations" (Item 335). A minister is desired who "acknowledges own sin and confesses this to God" (Item 369). In addition to asking God's forgiveness, the norm is that the minister is one who "apologizes when he/she has offended a person" (Item 365). Under these circumstances, it follows naturally that he or she "acknowledge own need for continued growth in the faith" (Item 361).

In dealing with organizations and in rendering pastoral services, the pattern of self-abnegation continues. The "good" minister "seeks additional information when ideas are not clear" (Item 304), "knows when referral to a specialist is needed" (Item 277), and "brings people in touch with professional help they may need" (Item 259). He or she "says willingly, 'I don't know' regarding subjects beyond own knowledge or competence" (Item 359) and "advises in a way that respects a person's freedom to choose his own course of action" (Item 272).

What is described here is the profile of a beginning clergyperson clearly endorsed by over 90 percent of the Anglican-Episcopal respondents and—if the sample is truly representative of the entire church—it is a view of ministers held by about two and a half million Episcopalians in the United

States. I fear this is a pattern of humility that can be supported best by persons with low self-image and modest skills and abilities. It is not the image of aggressive leadership. In the name, perhaps, of collaborative management, it is highly prized (88 percent) when the minister "shares leadership with lay leaders chosen by the congregation" (Item 695) and "meets with lay leaders to set goals consistent with their mission and potential" (Item 670).

Some of these things are not wrong in themselves, but as a number of passive-dependent behaviors cluster together to form a profile or an image of what ideally is expected of an Anglican-Episcopal minister, the resulting picture is likely to keep out of the ministry persons who feel that a little acclaim is appropriate, that a sturdy ego relishes strength rather than owning up to limitations, and that mastery of professional skills reduces dependence on other professionals.

Apparent inconsistencies emerge as I further analyze this and other portions of the data. While the minister is expected to be humble and self-effacing, he or she must at the same time show some amazing strengths. Again, I cite items that were rated as "quite important," or "highly important" by at least 90 percent of the Anglican-Episcopal respondents. For example, the "good" minister is expert and competent in developing a "feeling of trust and confidence between self and members" (Item 679). He or she "effects a relationship with counselees in which a problem is addressed with honesty and reality" (Item 263) and "promotes activities which build a parish family" (Item 674). These items suggest a strong leader who makes things happen and boldly takes both organizational and spiritual leadership in people's lives. "Through his/her ministry, people are led to deepened spiritual growth and commitment" (Item 262). The "good" pastor "helps people use the resources of faith in coping with personal problems" (Item 271) and "presents the Gospel in terms understandable to the modern mind" (Item 44).

This idealized view of the functions, behaviors, and temperament of the person called to ministry suggests extremely high standards for selection and a quality of training sufficient to produce expertise in a variety of fields. It is an excellent picture.

However, there is further contrast as one picks up notes of negative evaluation and underlying criticism. One suspects that most of the respondents have had some negative experiences that have engendered a view of the ministry that is not complimentary. For 90 percent of the sample to agree on these observations is a piece of data that in itself cannot be ignored. Laity may have known a minister who "Uses sermons to attack certain members in the congregation or community" (Item 559); "Discusses with members of the congregation what has been said in confidence" (Item 539); "Often belittles a person in front of others" (Item 573); "People are afraid to come to him/her for counseling on problems and problem situations" (Item 558); "Occasionally involved in extramarital affairs or illicit sexual relationships" (Item 566); and "Rarely, if ever, visits the sick and shut-ins" (Item 548).

The preceding items relate to behaviors that are both objectionable and present. However, these are happily balanced by other behaviors that are of a more positive and redeeming nature. The following items concerning behaviors (and the temperament and personality that go along with them) are very highly rated and more desirable in clergy: "Demonstrates honest affection for other people" (Item 469); "Loves and cares for each member as a person not as a statistic" (Item 480); "When conversing with a person, listens for feeling tones as well as words" (Item 267); "Takes time to know parishioners well" (Item 678); "Treats children as thinking individuals" (Item 77); "Sees youth as part of the congregation rather than a programmatic appendage" (Item 68); "Maintains personal integrity despite pressures to compromise" (Item 513); and "Keeps own word—fulfills promises" (Item 505). Here we see a definition of excellence in terms of certain human qualities that would greatly enrich any ministry.

In addition to these humane and loving characteristics, it is clear that qualities of spiritual and religious strength and optimism are also prized highly. The following related items point in this direction and are rated by 80 percent or more of respondents as "quite" or "highly" important: "Approaches life as one who believes the forces of good are greater than the forces of evil" (Item 360); "Expresses profound hope because of a belief in the Kingdom of God" (Item 362); "Believes the Gospel she/he preaches" (Item 338); "Holds that in the midst of serious problems, God is at work" (Item 334); and "Own statements of belief reflect careful thought and evaluation" (Item 285).

In reflecting on these various "profiles" that emerge, we see some painful contradictions in expectations. It would appear that many Anglican-Episcopal respondents expect their clergy to be humble and passive and to avoid any show of aggressiveness that might be construed as "worldly." Humble, self-effacing clergy are desired. However, combined with this pattern is the expectation that vigorous leadership will be evident, pastoral and organizational skills will abound, and behavior will be assertive and forceful. These two things do not fit easily together; and this may explain why some clergy have an extremely difficult time pleasing their parishioners and performing successfully. Regretfully, there appears to be a high level of awareness regarding faulty performance, and this could be interpreted to mean that strong feelings of judgment and condemnation are focused on clergy whose behaviors invite criticism. Clergy get caught in the crossfire of mixed signals sent to them about the kinds of people and the type of leadership the church calls for in the ordained ministry.

This is not a new insight. It confirms the 1968 findings of the General Division of Research and Field Study.[1] In this empirical research study, over 800 clergy completed time-use diaries. Results show that clergy work 66.7 hours per week. The biggest block of time—10 hours—is devoted to administration. Church organizations take 5.5 hours per week. On the whole, clergy feel that they spend more time on activities that are least important (and activities they generally like to do least) than they spend on functions that are seen as most important, such as hospital visiting, parish calling, counseling, and teaching. These acts of service take altogether only 12.8 hours per week. Items that are ranked as least important take a total of 23.1 hours per week.

The message here seems to be that clergy feel called to ministry for one type of function but are likely to spend their time and energy performing quite a different function. The care of souls is one thing. Making a parish a howling success is another. The perpetual dilemma is how to combine the sensitivities of a gentle, loving, thoughtful, theologically reflective, deeply spiritual pastor (which the church would like to have) with the attributes of an excellent organizer, a person who is skilled in group development and management, and a person who is competent to provide aggressive leadership (which the church actually calls for). Elements of this dilemma emerge in the data in terms of the contradictory profiles that I have identified.

However, more work needs to be done by more people to examine the data and develop from it the insights that will aid in interpreting accurately to applicants the view of ministry held in the Anglican-Episcopal Churches, the strengths and the temperament ministry requires in this day and age, and the kind of training that makes one truly ready for effective and joyous ministry in the twenty-first century.

NOTE

1. David Covell, "The Priest and His Problems" [monograph] (New York: Executive Council of the Episcopal Church, 1969).

7

American-Canadian Baptist Family

Leon Pacala

Leon Pacala introduces his chapter by pointing out the many historical similarities between American (U.S.) and Canadian Baptists and the relation of these two groups to the entire body of Baptists. Since the empirical responses of American and Canadian Baptists reflect a great deal of similarity, these two groups are examined in this study as a single unit. Rather than explain how these Baptists differ from the total sample group, Pacala opts to examine the clusters that form on the sole basis of American-Canadian Baptist data. He can then compare the manner in which this denominational family (as opposed to the entire transdenominational group) conceptualizes ministry. Pacala organizes these clusters according to seven major dimensions of ministry (as based on the seven major sections of the questionnaire used in this study) from which those clusters were derived. On this framework, he places his reading of the concept and style of ministerial leadership as indicated in the data from American-Canadian Baptists.

Central to their conception of ministry is the conviction that the church is the primary agent of ministry. Ordained leadership functions not on the basis

---

Leon Pacala is President of Colgate Rochester Divinity School/Bexley Hall/Crozer Theological Seminary, Rochester, New York. He has taught philosophy and religion at the university level and served as Dean of Arts and Sciences, Bucknell University, Lewisburg, Pennsylvania, before assuming his present position in 1973.

of any intrinsic authority or office, but, rather, in the name of and on behalf of the congregation. Thus, a high value is placed in the personal embodiment of Christian commitment, values, and standards of conduct viewed as marks of the regenerated life. Conversely, this group is more negative than some other denominations about personal conduct of ministers that is at variance with the life of faith.

The author points to the emphasis on conversion in Baptist theology as the reason for higher expectations for ministerial concern and involvement in social and political spheres. American and Canadian Baptist laity and ministers appear less prone than others to fix sharp demarcations between regeneration of life within the church and the world at large.

Baptists comprise the largest Protestant family in the Western hemisphere. They are also the most fragmented, for no one theological or ecclesiastic tie unites the more than 26 million people who claim the name of Baptist.

If there is a common bond among Baptists, it is the freedom that characterizes and qualifies their religious experience. Baptists understand religious faith as a "personal relation between the human soul and God. Into this relation, nothing may intrude. . . . Liberty of conscience, freedom from creedal bondage, freedom from doctrinal interpretation, the local church autonomy—these constitute Baptist ecclesiastical democracy."[1]

Baptist insistence on religious freedom has been the source of much ecclesiastic fragmentation and countless forms of church polity; it has served as a sanction for Baptist groups to spawn endlessly; it has formed an acceptable rationale for schisms. Consequently, the denominational name now embraces a wider spectrum of beliefs and practices than can be found in any other church family. Baptists claim to be the "recognized democrats of the Protestant world" and maintain with fervent pride the heritage of religious freedom that stems from this religious self-understanding.

Because of historical similarities between the American Baptist Churches in the USA and the Baptist Federation of Canada, the designers of the Readiness for Ministry Project combined the data gathered from these two denominations. The histories of the two Baptist groups have much in common, and until approximately a decade ago the national border had relatively little denominational significance for the two. The two groups were shaped by many of the same historical and religious forces throughout their formative periods. There were times when much of the leadership of the American Baptists came from Canada. During the first one-third of this century, for example, major portions of the faculties of such American Baptist seminaries as Colgate-Rochester, Crozer, and Chicago were Canadian.[2] As a result, American Baptists have enjoyed a closer kinship with Canadian Baptists than with any other Baptist denomination.

For purposes of this study, it is significant to point out that the ties between American and Canadian Baptists are not merely historical in nature. They also share much in common as regards their church polities. When American Baptists adopted their current official name in 1950, they did so with the commitment to hold the name in trust for Christians "of like faith and mind who desire to bear witness to the historical Baptist convictions *in a framework of cooperative Protestantism*" (my emphasis). The Baptist Federation of Canada, which consists of four federated member bodies, also has a commitment to cooperative church ventures. Such a commitment sets Canadian and American Baptists apart from most other Baptist groups.[3]

In addition to their unique commonalities, these two Baptist groups join with all Baptists in supporting issues that stem from a commitment to religious freedom, issues that are of peculiar significance in the study of ministerial leadership. The emphasis that all Baptists place on religious freedom inevitably poses many problems of church polity, none of which are more complex than those pertaining to the organization and exercise of ecclesiastic authority and power. If power is understood as the ability to affect others regardless of their consent and if authority is the right to exercise such power, then the problem of authority and power remains a fundamental concern for Baptists.[4]

As the data show, this central concern carries far-reaching implications for the ordained ministry among Baptists. Given the absence of any single authoritative, ecclesiastic norm for ministry, the data hold peculiar value for Baptists and thus may represent as authoritative a definition of ministry as is possible to have within the Baptist polity. In other words, in a system in which religious freedom is the basic operative and unifying principle, the distinction between descriptive and prescriptive results of such a study as the Readiness for Ministry Project may be minimal indeed. With the loss of that important distinction, Baptists are constantly threatened by the practical effects of their polity. If for no other reason, then, the Readiness for Ministry Project requires the most serious consideration on the part of all Baptists.

AMERICAN-CANADIAN BAPTIST CRITERIA FOR MINISTRY

The data in this chapter were derived from a total of 324 American-Canadian Baptists who responded to the 444 items of the Readiness for Ministry questionnaire. While the ratio of laity to clergy response is one to four, answers are weighted; consequently we hear equally from ministers and laypeople. The responses to the individual items are ordered by technical mathematical procedures, so that the data organized to produce clusters of responses, each reflecting a central characteristic of ministry that the responses of these 324 people indicate to be significant. These clusters are developed from items arranged within seven larger dimensions of ministry—all empirically found by American-Canadian Baptists to be significant for ministry.

The seven categories of ministry on which the following analysis is based are

1. Ministries to the Religious Community
2. Ministries to Community and World
3. Ministries to Persons under Stress
4. The Minister as Theologian and Thinker
5. The Minister's Personal Commitment of Faith
6. The Minister as a Person
   a. Negative or dysfunctional characteristics
   b. Positive or supportive characteristics
7. The Minister as Leader

It should be noted that, whereas the core clusters are relevant to all denominations, the number and specific character of denominational clusters vary from one denominational family to another, depending on the values assigned by each church constituency to the 444 items that produce the data base. These items are rated according to a scale of −3 to +3. From a factor analysis of these ratings, the clusters are formed, each with a "grand mean" or average, indicating the value placed on each cluster by the denomination in question. These grand means can be interpreted according to the following scale:

	From	To
Highly important, essential or mandatory	+2.51	+3.00
Quite important, a major asset	+1.51	+2.50
Somewhat important, a minor asset	+0.51	+1.50
Neither important nor unimportant	−0.50	+0.50
Somewhat detrimental, a minor hindrance in ministry	−1.50	−0.51
Quite detrimental, a major hindrance in ministry	−2.50	−1.51
Highly detrimental, harmful, could destroy the effectiveness of ministry	−3.00	−2.51

The American-Canadian Baptist data produce sixty-two clusters that, taken together, represent a comprehensive profile of American-Canadian Baptists' expectations of their ministers. The American-Canadian Baptist clusters are presented in Table 7-1 in their rank order. I have taken the

TABLE 7-1
Rank Order of American-Canadian Baptist Clusters

American-Canadian Baptist Clusters Rank Order	Cluster Description	Grand Mean
1	Exemplifies Christian commitment in attitudes and standards of conduct in personal life and community relations	2.56
2	Clearly demonstrates the biblical and theological grounds for ministry	2.55
3	Possesses sufficient confidence of self and commitment to ministry to recognize personal limitations and inadequacies without impairing ability to serve others	2.53
4	Maintains a ministry characterized by a profound sense of hope which is rooted in the biblical affirmation of the reality of God's kingdom	2.51
5	Places high priority upon personal family life and finds in family relationships an embodiment of the wholeness of ministry	2.47
6	Exercises pastoral care with sympathy, respect, and professional competence	2.44
7	Ministers fully to persons faced with crises, grief, or other human needs	2.42
8	Sustains a personal discipline of spiritual formation which includes prayer, meditation, and dependence upon God's grace and forgiveness	2.37
9	Shares ministerial leadership with laity of church and encourages full participation of the congregation in the ministry of the church	2.37
10	Preaches a Christ-centered gospel which is understandable to the modern mind	2.36
11	Fulfills responsibilities of ministry with seriousness and yet with joy and good humor	2.35

TABLE 7–1 — *CONTINUED*

American-Canadian Baptist Clusters Rank Order	Cluster Description	Grand Mean
12	Exemplifies personal discipline, initiative, maturity, and integrity in all professional responsibilities	2.31
13	Places high priority upon knowing all parishioners well and on nurturing a relationship of trust with them	2.29
14	Demonstrates the ability to be positive, affirmative, adaptive, and effective throughout the range of demanding and often difficult situations comprising the context of ministry	2.25
15	Integrates the various functions of ministry in such fashion that counseling is carried on as a form of the proclamation of God's love and guided by theological understanding of ministry	2.23
16	Emphasizes Christian stewardship and assists the congregation in maintaining a sense of responsibility for the financial support and use of the financial resources of the congregation	2.21
17	Encourages fullest participation of all groups in the life of the congregation and possesses the skill to nurture and sustain such participation	2.15
18	Deals with complex matters of faith in understandable terms	2.14
19	Deals with conflict creatively by anticipating and intervening as needed to preserve personal freedom and autonomy, on one hand, and unity of fellowship, on the other	2.12
20	Works effectively with all members of the congregation and seeks opportunities to increase the ability to maintain these relationships	2.10
21	Informs and shapes the practice of ministry at all levels by broadly based knowledge and disciplined reflection	2.09

TABLE 7-1 — *CONTINUED*

American- Canadian Baptist Clusters Rank Order	*Cluster Description*	*Grand Mean*
22	Proclaims the Word of God authoritatively in ways whereby the needs and conditions of the congregation are addressed	2.08
23	Maintains a ministry of caring concern for all people in need	2.08
24	Responds to persons according to their needs rather than some imposed or hoped-for "religious" objective or response	2.07
25	Regardless of situations or opportunities, maintains openly an integrity of belief and personal identity	2.06
26	Works from a perspective in which the theological, ecumenical, and social concerns of the gospel are effectively expressed	2.03
27	Shapes worship freely according to the leading of the Spirit and the joy the Holy Spirit inspires	2.03
28	Exercises leadership in a manner that nurtures the growth and well-being of the congregation by creative acceptance of individual differences and conflicts that are present	2.02
29	Possesses the personal maturity to relate easily and effectively with people of diverse backgrounds, personalities, social status, and religious orientation	2.01
30	Is sensitive to the needs, roles, and autonomy of the various people and groups within the congregation and is especially effective in working with children, youth, and lay leadership	2.00
31	Maintains an ongoing program of study and research and applies theological and historical knowledge to contemporary religious situations	1.99

TABLE 7-1 — *CONTINUED*

American-Canadian Baptist Clusters Rank Order	Cluster Description	Grand Mean
32	Accepts diversity of people, lifestyles, and ideas as creative rather than threatening possibilities	1.98
33	Encourages the congregation to translate its commitment to the gospel into acts of loving concern for people of all classes and needs	1.89
34	Exercises administrative responsibilities for staff and financial resources of the congregation in ways that are consistent with theological beliefs	1.84
35	Exercises administrative responsibilities for the business life of the church in ways that are consistent with sound management principles	1.71
36	Leads the congregation to experience worship as the celebration of the community of faith and the wholeness of life	1.71
37	Uses a variety of resources for worship as means of opening up the congregation to the living reality of God	1.70
38	Encourages an understanding of and orientation to the world as the locus of God's activity	1.67
39	Actively supports laity in their understanding of community needs and the means of effectively addressing these needs	1.64
40	Encourages, trains, and supports laity in ministering to persons in stress and need	1.60
41	Directs preaching to conversion to Jesus Christ	1.59
42	Freely and openly acknowledges to the congregation the human nature and limitations of minister's personal faith and spiritual experiences	1.55

TABLE 7–1 — *CONTINUED*

American-Canadian Baptist Clusters Rank Order	Cluster Description	Grand Mean
43	Utilizes the most effective resources, inside and outside the church, in serving the diverse needs of the congregation and community	1.49
44	Stresses the significance of an understanding of the theological and intellectual roots for faithful adherence to the gospel	1.46
45	Conceives ministry as including personal involvement in the life, concerns, and needs of the community	1.38
46	Seeks to understand, to care, and to minister to minority groups and all oppressed people	1.12
47	Uses and interprets diversity of liturgical and art forms in worship, but does not consider the minister as primarily a liturgist	1.00
48	Supports community service agencies and actively seeks to transform social, political, and educational institutions in carrying out scriptural mandates of ministry	0.98
49	Understands and values the nature and significance of the sacraments for the community of faith and ministry	0.68
50	Becomes involved in public issues regardless of personal consequences, especially those involving prejudice, racism, and political and economic injustice	0.64
51	Participates in cultural activities, especially art and theater	0.20
52	Conceives of ministry as primarily evangelism dealing with conversion of individuals to Christianity	−0.44
53	Conceives of the minister as the ultimate authority in all parish matters	−1.32

TABLE 7-1 — *CONTINUED*

American-Canadian Baptist Clusters Rank Order	*Cluster Description*	*Grand Mean*
54	Stresses order to the detriment of freedom in public worship and congregational life	−1.57
55	Refrains from participation in social concerns or community programs for fear of compromising the basic goals of ministry	−1.65
56	Believes that a minister's effectiveness or spiritual life is dependent on daily use of sacraments and established forms of spiritual disciplines	−1.72
57	Seeks public acclaim to the detriment of maintaining personal and professional integrity in relations with others	−1.75
58	Shapes relations with others on the basis of personal benefits to be derived from such relationships	−1.81
59	Carries on official duties so compulsively that individuals and their needs are not taken seriously	−1.92
60	Personal lifestyle conflicts with minimal standards of behavior considered compatible with ministry	−2.06
61	Fails to honor confidentiality in pastoral relations and is unable to use criticism constructively	−2.11
62	Values professional status and position so highly that effective ministry to individuals is sacrificed	−2.14

liberty of presenting them in terms of a descriptive generalization, attempting in this way to communicate something of the distinctive characteristics and nuances of American-Canadian Baptist expectations reflected in the clusters.

CONCEPT AND STYLE OF MINISTERIAL LEADERSHIP

A quick analysis of the American-Canadian Baptist clusters reveals that 68 percent of the clusters are considered by these Baptists as "highly" or "quite" important. In the study of the total group of forty-seven denominations, a similar percentage of core clusters bear such high rankings (64 percent). However, these Baptist clusters differ at two points. A larger percentage of the highest-ranked clusters is to be found in those sections of ministerial attributes pertaining to the minister's "Personal Commitment of Faith" (12 percent for American-Canadian Baptists, 7 percent for the total group) and to the "Minister as a Leader" (19 percent of the American-Canadian Baptist clusters, 12 percent of the total group). American-Canadian Baptists place a relatively higher value on these two categories of ministerial leadership.

These differences are significant. The emphasis on the minister's personal commitment of faith reflects a form and style of leadership that is *representational in nature.* American-Canadian Baptists expect ministers to embody those attributes of faith and life characteristic of the "priesthood of all believers." As stated in an American Baptist study paper, the ordained ministry "is, in effect, an acted parable, a gracious similitude or likeness of the life of the church as it is called to unite the Word of God and the work of God." The authority and status of ministers are rooted in this paradigmatic or representational role.

The data characterize this form of leadership. American-Canadian Baptists place the highest priority on the cluster that describes the personal embodiment of Christian commitment, values, and standards of conduct acceptable to the congregation (rank order of 1). Conversely, personal lifestyles that conflict with what is believed to be the marks of a regenerated life are considered the most detrimental to ministerial leadership—Baptist Clusters (A-CBC) 60, 61, 62. The high values placed on leadership reflecting hope, joy, spiritual discipline, and personal integrity (as reflected in clusters with rank orders of A-CBC 4, 6, 8, 11, and 12) further confirm this form of leadership.

This conclusion is borne out by the responses of American-Canadian Baptists to individual items that comprise the clusters of ministry characteristics. The 10 items on which there exists greatest consensus among these Baptists as to the fundamental importance of each include the following: "Believes the gospel she/he preaches" (Item 338), "Affirms that Jesus Christ is the Son of God" (Item 293), and "Maintains personal integrity despite pressures to compromise" (Item 513). Conversely, the greatest impediments to ministerial leadership are involvement in extramarital and illicit sexual relations (Item 566) and breaking of confidences disclosed to the minister by members of the congregation (Item 539). American-Canadian Baptists are not guilty, however, of an exaggerated and false sense of ministerial holiness. They recognize that ministers are fully human and have the same spiritual needs as others. Acknowledgment and confession of sin is one of the highest-ranked items (Item 369).

The data illumine other aspects of this representational style of leadership. American-Canadian Baptists place unusually high significance on the minister's personal family life. (See Table 7-2.) This criterion is ranked fifth highest, with a grand mean of 2.47. It is obvious from these data that Baptists look on the relationship between ministers and their families as paradigms of the relations that should exist in congregations.

American-Canadian Baptists expect ministers to reflect the unique emphases of Baptist piety. The evangelism that has been an important part of Baptist traditions is recognized in the "conversion" emphasis of ministerial leadership (A-CBC 41). One rather surprising bit of data is the relatively low rating placed on the cluster that specifically defines ministry in terms of an evangelism that is conceived primarily as "conversion of individuals to Christianity." This cluster has a rank of only 52, with a grand mean of −0.44. There is no doubt but that this modest ranking reflects American-Canadian Baptist reservations about defining evangelism as set in opposition to ministry in the social and political realms. It should not be interpreted, however, as suggesting that evangelism is a relatively minor aspect of American-Canadian Baptist ministerial leadership.

An analysis of the American-Canadian Baptist cluster readily confirms this interpretation. (See Table 7-3.)

American-Canadian Baptist response to these items is significantly different from those of the total group. Fifty-nine percent of the latter consider Item 123 on conversion detrimental; 44 percent of the

TABLE 7-2
American-Canadian Baptist Expectations of Minister's Personal Family Life

Item No.	Items in American-Canadian Baptist Cluster 5	Mean
497	Keeps commitments to own children as consistently as professional appointments	2.53
512	Schedules regular time to be alone with family	2.46
511	Spouse is sympathetic and committed to minister's vocation	2.43

TABLE 7-3
American-Canadian Baptist Cluster 52
(Items Relating to Evangelism)

Item No.	Items in American-Canadian Baptist Cluster 52	Mean
123	Priorities in use of time indicate the belief that the one and only way to build an ideal world society is to convert everyone to Christianity	0.14
134	Holds that the church's task of proclaiming the gospel by preaching and teaching overshadows in importance the task of helping to eliminate physical sufferings of people	0.00
135	Frequently approaches strangers to ask about the condition of their souls	−0.68
121	Insists that clergy should stick to religion and not concern themselves with social, economic, and political questions	−1.08

American-Canadian Baptists are of the same opinion. Conversely, 33 percent of the American-Canadian Baptists consider it "very important," compared to 23 percent of the total group. Such data confirm a serious regard for evangelism of this type among many American-Canadian Baptists, but reflect a very serious reservation among most Baptists about leadership that conceives of such evangelism simply or primarily as a matter of caring for individual souls—in the spiritual sense—without concern for the social, economic, and political conditions of existence.

Finally, the moralism that runs as a very clear thread throughout the American-Canadian Baptist clusters can be understood in terms of the representational role of ministers. There are very significant differences between Baptist responses and those of the total group to items dealing with gambling, intoxication, frequenting of bars, and public smoking. For example, 74 percent of all American-Canadian Baptists consider smoking in public as "highly" or "quite" detrimental to ministerial leadership; only 46 percent of the total group are of this opinion. Conversely, less than 10 percent of the American-Canadian Baptists think it makes no difference, whereas 30 percent of the total group discount its significance.

This section of the analysis can be concluded with the observation of a concurrence between American-Canadian Baptist data and an emerging pattern of moral criteria becoming established in our society. The U.S. Supreme Court has ruled that the propriety of some forms of social conduct should be judged by local standards of taste. This may indeed be a legal or judicial implication or outcome of the U.S. democratic system. A similar set of expectations is clearly at work among American-Canadian Baptists. Given the local autonomy of the congregation, the representational nature and style of ministerial leadership implied in American-Canadian Baptist polity serves in a very direct and significant manner to define the norms of Church leadership.

The second general characteristic of the American-Canadian Baptist clusters is the emphasis found in these data on the minister as a leader. Of those American-Canadian Baptist clusters with grand means of 1.51 or higher, proportionately one-third more of the American-Canadian Baptist clusters than those of the total group focus on this general aspect of ministry. This proportion highlights the importance that American-Canadian Baptists accord to the role of minister as leader.

It may seem paradoxical for Baptists, given their commitment to democratic polity, to place such high priority on the leadership capability of ministers. The key to understanding these data, however, is to recognize the type of leadership they imply. To generalize, this type of leadership is *functional* in nature and style.

Central to the conception of ministry for all Baptists is the belief that the primary agent of ministry is the church. In this context, the church is understood quite literally as the congregation comprising the "priesthood of all believers." Ministers function in this context, neither by virtue of a distinct order with its intrinsic and objective authority, nor an office with its unique rights, but on the basis of a function that is exercised in the name of and in behalf of the congregation. It is a form of leadership that is marked by delegated authority, the exercise of which is measured not by formally defined powers but by the effectiveness with which the basic functions are performed. Hence, Baptists value leadership that is informal (as distinct from formally defined powers), pragmatic, and efficient.

The data present an outline of this form of leadership. It is nonsacramental in nature (A-CBC 3, 48, 56), is reflective of the authority of a Scriptural and spiritual basis of church life (A-CBC 2, 4, 10, 27, 37, 54, 53), and is ultimately measured by the effectiveness with which it enhances the life and work of the congregation.

Enhancement of congregational life is the most persistently recurring theme running throughout the following American-Canadian Baptist clusters: priorities of leadership are centered on encouraging lay leadership (A-CBC 9, 39), nurturing relations with congregational members (A-CBC 13, 20), sustaining initiative and responsibility for congregational life among parishioners (A-CBC 16, 17), aiding the growth and well-being of the congregation (A-CBC 28), training and supporting laity in the witness and ministry of the church (A-CBC 40).

American-Canadian Baptists value pastoral more highly than priestly effectiveness (A-CBC 6, 7, 23, 24). They expect this pastoral leadership, however, to be exercised with professional competence (A-CBC 6, 15) and administrative skill and effectiveness (A-CBC 34, 35). They expect this leadership also to reflect those professional abilities that are implied in the effective exercise of preaching (A-CBC 2, 10, 22), teaching (A-CBC 18), and intellectual capacities and discipline (A-CBC 2, 21, 31, 44). Functional leadership implies such personal qualities as self-confidence (A-CBC 3), flexibility and acceptance of diversity of people and viewpoints (A-CBC 14, 32), good humor (A-CBC 11), impeccable integrity (A-CBC 25), maturity (A-CBC 29), and sensitivity to a wide range of human predicaments (A-CBC 30).

Furthermore, American-Canadian Baptists value leadership that is ecumenical (A-CBC 26) and not narrowly ecclesiastic in scope (A-CBC 23). Above all, they prize leadership that is oriented to the spiritual needs of the congregation (A-CBC 22) but that also serves the full spectrum of the needs of society and oppressed peoples everywhere (A-CBC 21, 33, 39, 45, 46, 48, 50, 51). As indicated earlier, these latter characteristics are probably more significant than almost any others in distinguishing American-Canadian Baptists from their other Baptist brothers and sisters.

Two somewhat surprising results revealed by these data need to be given special attention. The first concerns ministry to children and youth. Unlike the total group, there is no American-Canadian Baptist cluster that deals specifically with this form of ministry. (Such a cluster does appear in the data for the total group comprised of all denominational families, where it has a rank order of 19 and a grand mean of 2.04.) To American-Canadian Baptists, working with children and youth is one element in a broader expectation that ministers be able to relate to all groups that comprise the congregation. For example, the one cluster that does focus on children and youth draws a rank order of 30. (See Table 7-4).

In all three items in the American-Canadian Baptist Cluster 30, a greater percentage of the total group accords highest value (that is, "highly important") to these items than do American-Canadian Baptists. Further-

TABLE 7-4

American-Canadian Baptist Cluster 30
(Items Focusing on Children and Youth)

Item No.	Items in American-Canadian Baptist Cluster 30	Mean
68	Sees youth as part of the congregation rather than a programmatic appendage	2.54
86	Encourages youth to rethink and restate ageless truths for themselves	2.22
89	Demonstrates the skills needed to teach small children effectively	1.23

more, in responding to another individual item that relates to conducting worship in ways meaningful to children (Item 51), only 12 percent of the American-Canadian Baptists consider this "highly important" compared with 28 percent of the total group of forty-seven denominations.

One can only guess at the reasons for these differences concerning elements of ministerial leadership. One is tempted to conclude that the Baptist belief in "believer's baptism" as the basis of the church may lead to the tendency to distinguish between first- and second-order groups within the congregation and to define priorities of ministerial leadership accordingly. What these particular data may suggest is a prevalent ambiguity in American-Canadian Baptist practice and polity regarding the exact status of nonadults within the congregation of believers.

A second aspect of these data merits special interpretation. Of those clusters dealing with ministerial functions that are most directly ecclesiastic in nature and that are classified under the heading "Ministries to the Religious Community," the top-rated American-Canadian Baptist cluster under that heading ranks tenth overall, with a grand mean of 2.36. For the total group, the highest ranked core cluster of this type stands ninth overall, but with a grand mean of 2.24. Both the American-Canadian Baptist cluster and the core cluster reflect the same general theme of relating faith to the modern world. However, the items comprising these two clusters differ in a significant manner. For the total group, this cluster emphasizes clear, understandable communication of the gospel, primarily through teaching and meeting the educational needs of the congregation. For American-Canadian Baptists, the emphasis is on a Christ-centered gospel, which is proclaimed with authority, and presented in terms understandable to the modern mind. This difference between perceptions of American-Canadian Baptists and of the total group as to what constitutes the effort to relate the Christian faith to the modern world is startling. It emphasizes the priority that preaching has in the cultic life of American-Canadian Baptists and implies leadership that is both professionally trained and charismatically gifted. This emphasis suggests the continuation of a classic form of preaching ministry that has been characteristic of Baptists throughout their history. However, this American-Canadian Baptist cluster appears only tenth in rank order, followed by clusters of a complementary nature in their emphasis with rank orders of 22, 26, 27, and 30. It suggests that this form of charismatic leadership may be giving way in priority to another kind of leadership—one that is more interpersonally oriented and capable of supporting, maintaining, and cultivating the congregation through other forms of pastoral ministry.

In addition to what we can learn from the American-Canadian Baptist clusters, it is important to note the significant differences that appear in their responses to individual items. The greatest number of significant differences between American-Canadian Baptists and other groups is found in items that are included in the following three sections, or broad areas of ministry: "Ministries to the Religious Community," "Ministries to Community and World," and the "Minister's Personal Commitment for Faith." The responses of American-Canadian Baptists are significantly different from all others for 24 percent, 23 percent, and 36 percent of all items, respectively, in these areas or sections.

Regarding the nature and style of ministry to the religious community, the significant differences in items show that more American-Canadian Baptists stress the authority of the Bible, the evangelical orientation of preaching for conversions (6 percent of the American-Canadian Baptists and 15 percent of the total group consider this detrimental); freedom to conduct worship according to the leading of the Holy Spirit (15 percent of the American-Canadian Baptists judge this to be undesirable, 32 percent of the total group find it so); and the nonsacramental, nonsacerdotal nature of ministry.

Symbolic of such difference in the Baptist data is the response to Item 61, "Explains the meaning of worship and liturgy." Of the total group, 28 percent value this as "highly important," only 12 percent of the American-Canadian Baptists are of this opinion. Why this difference? Undoubtedly part of the responses of these Baptists is affected by inclusion of the term *liturgy*, which would not be considered important by Baptists who place greater value on freedom or informality of worship. But more significantly, Baptist piety is not essentially rationalistic; it is rather, deeply experiential and confessional. The need for explanation, therefore, would naturally receive a lower priority in American-Canadian Baptist contexts.

Finally, one-half of all respondents in the study consider it detrimental for a minister to view himself or herself "primarily as a change agent in the church" (Item 97). Only one-third of the American-Canadian Baptists are of this opinion. In fact, 32 percent of American-Canadian Baptists, as against 22 percent of the total group, consider this "quite" or "highly" important. These responses by American-Canadian Baptists are further indication of the informal, spontaneous, nonsacramental style of leadership so highly valued.

Significant differences are found in Baptist expectations of ministers in the roles they play in the community and the world. In contrast to the total group, smaller percentages of American-Canadian Baptists consider it detrimental for ministers to organize groups to change civil laws; to speak from the pulpit about political issues; to declare willingness to run for public office; to consider political struggle as a rightful concern of the church; to work for freedom for all to buy property in areas of their choice; to work toward racial integration; and to speak prophetically out of the conviction that the church is the conscience of humanity. On this last item, 72 percent of the American-Canadian Baptists, as against 59 percent of all others, consider it to be "highly" or "quite" important.

Again, a generalization can be made regarding these data. American-Canadian Baptists, with their conversional theology, tend not to fix sharp demarcations between the regeneration of life within the household of faith and the world at large. They look to their ministers for qualities that will better enable the congregation to carry out its mission to the world at large. Thus, 82 percent of the American-Canadian Baptists and only 68 percent of the total group consider it very important that ministers visit the unchurched for the purpose of sharing the church's faith. Likewise, 82 percent of these Baptists and 71 percent of the total group place an equally high value on ministerial support of world mission.

As in the case of the total clusters, the greatest percentage of significantly different responses to individual items by American-Canadian Baptists is found in those expectations concerning the personal faith and commitment of ministers. These differences confirm what has already been said regarding Baptist clusters. They confirm the style of Baptist leadership that is rooted in a conception of ministry as a calling rather than an office, that reflects the confessional basis on which leadership is rooted, rather than formal, ecclesiastic or sacramental authority. Baptists place high value on the right to leadership that is the result of reflecting in one's personal life significant signs of the regeneration and renewal brought about by faith. Ministry is not a guild with its own self-imposed standards by which professional activity can be measured. It is a function to which one is called and appointed by the congregation, and in the final analysis it is measured by the degree to which it represents the life and faith of the congregation. In the absence of any objective, formal or established order of authority that defines ministry, the most significant and widely accepted sanctions and norms for ministry among American-Canadian Baptists are to be found in what ministers believe and the manner in which they reflect these beliefs in their leadership.

In general, American-Canadian Baptist laity and clergy share a common perception of the ministry and its defining norms. The data reveal that responses of laity differ from those of the clergy by five or more standard scores in 8 of the 64 core clusters. Clergy, more highly than laity, value leadership that is aggressively political, emphasizes theological reflection and intellectual understanding of issues, actively works in behalf of the oppressed, and utilizes a high degree of professional knowledge and skill in enabling counseling. However, laity place a higher significance on leadership that relates well to children and youth. Laity take greater exception than do clergy to leadership that dominates decision making, have a greater preference for leadership that concentrates on the congregation without involvement in social change, and place higher significance on verbal expressions or confessions of God's activity in their personal experience. In their attitudes toward denominational structures, clergy place more importance on knowing the theological and political stance of the denomination, but laity are much more accepting of denominational directives and expectations. In general, the data do not reveal any greater clergy-laity differences among American-Canadian Baptists than among other denominations of similar polity and structure.

CONCLUSION

These data are both reassuring and disturbing. One finds in them strong evidence of a consistency between American-Canadian Baptist beliefs and polity. The functional and representational conceptions and styles of leadership can be understood, and rightly so, as implications of the democracy of which Baptists are so proud.

But this consistency may have a dark side. In the absence of formalized, objective, officially recognized ecclesiastic authority, ministerial leadership too often falls prey to the pragmatic principle that "success is its own norm." A functional and representational ministry constantly risks being measured only by congregational consensus and confirmation and may lack the saving recourse of some transcendent basis or means of evaluation. The Readiness for Ministry Project is important to an understanding of American-Canadian Baptists, for it represents a most comprehensive profile of congregational expectations. As such, it offers the opportunity to evaluate those expectations that would otherwise work their way with unparalleled effectiveness into becoming Baptist polity.

The data point to emerging issues that will loom increasingly large on the horizons of the American-Canadian Baptist family. For example, the extraordinary emphasis placed by these Baptists on the minister's family life and the support of the spouse poses yet unrecognized issues for American-Canadian Baptists, that of separating family and spouse roles from the professional life and expectations of ministers.

The data gathered by the Readiness for Ministry Project contribute significantly to the understanding of contemporary denominations and represent a milestone in the empirical studies of religious bodies. For American and Canadian Baptists, they make it possible to assess the profile of their expectations of ministers within the broader spectrum of other denominational views.

As all important studies do, the Project raises many questions for which there are no answers. The data are based, for example, on the assumption that ministry is a singular reality, monolithic in form: They reveal a great deal about parish ministry but very little about other forms of ministry. In addition, there is nothing in the data that makes it possible to discern whatever significant differences may exist between American and Canadian Baptist churches concerning norms of effective ministry. These two church communities share much in common, but there may be latent or emerging differences that need to be discerned. Furthermore, there is a need to determine whatever differences—whether rooted in social, economic, or geographic sources—may exist within each of these church bodies. The American Baptist Churches, USA, includes a growing body of Black Baptists. It is important to know whether the criteria of Black Baptists differ from those held by others within this Baptist family.

Finally, additional research is needed in order to fully understand American and Canadian expectations of ministry as they are shaped by beliefs that are distinctively Baptist in nature. For example, it would be significant to discover the range of attitudes of American and Canadian Baptists regarding the means whereby the authority of Scripture is to be observed in ministerial practices. A similar question exists concerning the exercise of ministry rooted in the reality and work of the Holy Spirit. If these transcendent realities are the sources of authority to which American and Canadian Baptists appeal, further study is needed of the implications of these beliefs for ministry.

The limitations of the present study do not detract from its value. As it stands, it enables American and Canadian Baptists to ask themselves: Is this conception of ministry faithful to our Baptist witness? To the extent that the data make it possible to pose this key question with clarity and perspective, they are significant instruments in the churches' unending quest for self-understanding.

NOTES

1. William B. Lipphard, quoted in O. K. Armstrong and Marjorie M. Armstrong, *The Indomitable Baptists* (Garden City, N.Y.: Doubleday, 1967), p. 372.

2. Winthrop S. Hudson, *Union Seminary Quarterly Review* 32 (1977), p. 177.

3. American Baptists constitute the eighteenth largest denomination in the United States, with 1,350,000 members in 5,888 churches (1979). The Baptist Federation of Canada is the eighth largest Canadian denominational group, with 129,762 members in 1,117 churches. (See Constant H. Jacquet, Jr., ed., *Yearbook of American and Canadian Churches* [Nashville, Tenn.: Abingdon, 1979].)

4. This is the central thesis of Paul M. Harrison's study of American Baptists, *Authority and Power in the Free Church Tradition* (Princeton, N. J.: Princeton University Press, 1959).

8

Southern Baptists

Harold S. Songer

This chapter defines ministerial expectations for the largest of the Protestant church bodies in North America, a group that prides itself on its congregational autonomy and yet manifests powerful centripetal forces.

In his analysis, Songer employs two different units of data: (1) the responses of Southern Baptists and the other denominational families to the core clusters, as well as significant contrasts with these other denominations, and (2) conceptions of ministry that emerge in unique clusters formed only by Southern Baptist responses.

A sharp profile of similarities to and contrasts with other denominations appear from the two different grids of comparison. Southern Baptist expectations are similar to those of other denominations in many respects; however, Southern Baptists do register statistically significant differences from other denominations in approximately one-third of the core areas discussed. The most significant contrasts concern three different dimensions: (1) an open and verbal acknowledgment of religious experience; (2) encouragement and maintenance of a relevant biblical faith, as manifested by treating the Bible

Harold S. Songer is Assistant Provost, Director of Professional Studies, and Professor of New Testament Interpretation at Southern Baptist Theological Seminary in Louisville, Kentucky. His writings include "James" in *The Broadman Bible Commentary* and *Colossians: Christ Above All.*

*as authoritative; and (3) an active concern for the unchurched, showing itself
in an assertive style of personal evangelism. This aggressive stance in evangelism is the distinction that most often sets Southern Baptists apart from many
denominational groups. Those three denominational families who do not differ
significantly from the Southern Baptists in evangelism (Evangelical A and B
groups and the Christian Church [not Disciples]) do differ significantly from
Southern Baptists in social action and involvement. The highest expectation
of Southern Baptists is commitment to Christ. Southern Baptists interpret this
commitment as entailing both aggressive individual evangelism and social
action—both perceived as biblically grounded and quite compatible each with
the other. It is important to note that these data are based on seminary-trained
clergy only, thus excluding the large number of Southern Baptist clergy who
lack this training, as well as laity of the congregations served by pastors not
trained in seminaries.*

Entrance into the pastoral ministry among Southern Baptists is under
the congregational control of individual churches. A local church can
ordain a person for ministry without seeking either approval or recommendation from another church and can select any available person as
pastor.[1] People who are accustomed to hierarchical or official regulatory
structures among churches may ask how such congregational autonomy
can result in enough similarity among churches to sustain a denomination.
The answer to this question is in understanding the powerful centripetal
forces operating in Southern Baptist life, which are quite visible in, and
to some extent typified by, the massive cooperative financial support—
nearly $200 million in 1978—given by the more than 35 thousand Baptist
churches for missionary, benevolent, and educational enterprises. Less
obvious, but offering a much deeper perception of the denomination's
unity, is the understanding of ministry that exists among Southern Baptists. This chapter focuses on how Southern Baptists perceive readiness for
pastoral ministry. Or, put in terms more familiar to the denomination, the
question is "What do church members and other ministers expect of a
preacher who has just completed seminary training?" The answer will be
pursued from the responses of more than 5,000 people (both clergy and
laity) who participated in the Readiness for Ministry Project.[2] People were
asked, for example, whether visiting unchurched people to share the faith[3]
was considered to be "highly important," "quite important," "somewhat
important," "undesirable," or "detrimental" for a beginning minister.
Predictably, 99.2 percent of the Southern Baptists' responses fell in the
"important" range, with 67.3 percent identifying this as "highly important."[4] Among other denominations, however, only 31 percent of the
responses rated this item as "highly important."[5]
Although such responses to the individual items in the survey are
interesting, the most fascinating dimension of the research has been the

isolation of basic areas of expectation for beginning ministers by clustering the related responses into groups. These key areas, called *core clusters*[6] in the Readiness for Ministry findings, reveal what expectations the beginning minister will face in his or her denomination. This basic understanding of what persons in forty-seven denominations anticipate from ministers can be used in two ways to illuminate the distinctive dimensions of the Southern Baptist understanding of ministry. First, the areas of expectation for ministers can be examined from the standpoint of the attitudes of different denominational groups. This approach, which allows Southern Baptists to be compared with other denominations in 60 crucial areas, is taken in the first part of the chapter. Second, another set of expectations, developed by using only the responses of Southern Baptists, can be compared with the core clusters. This approach delineates the distinctive Southern Baptist understanding of readiness for ministry with even more precision and is followed in the second part of this chapter.

SOUTHERN BAPTIST EXPECTATIONS FOR MINISTRY COMPARED WITH THE EXPECTATIONS OF OTHER DENOMINATIONS

How do Southern Baptist expectations for beginning ministers compare with those of other denominations? When the basic areas of expectation are looked at from the perspective of this question, the sixty areas or clusters of expectation fall into two categories: In about one-third, or twenty-two areas, Southern Baptists significantly contrast with other denominations, and in the remaining two-thirds (thirty-eight areas) they are in general agreement with other groups. Table 8-1 displays the denominations in each family and indicates, by reference to the core cluster number, how Southern Baptists compare with other groups in each key area of expectation.[7]

In order to gain the best perspective on the Southern Baptist expectations for ministers in comparison with other denominations, the areas where Southern Baptists contrast with other groups are examined first. Then, using this data as a base, the remaining thirty-eight areas are discussed.

Category 1: Areas of Expectation for Ministers with Significant Contrasts between Southern Baptists and Other Denominations

Southern Baptists register highly significant differences from other denominations in their expectations for beginning ministers in twenty-two of the sixty clusters. Although every area of contrast is interesting,

TABLE 8-1

Contrasts and Agreements of Other Denominational Families with Southern Baptists

Family Name	Significant Contrast with Southern Baptists Indicated (5.0 Standard Scores or More)	Core Clusters Likelihood of Significant Contrast with Southern Baptists Approached (At Least 4.0 Standard Scores but Less Than 5)	Very Close Agreement with Southern Baptists (2.0 Standard Scores or Less)
Anglican-Episcopal Churches	2, 4, 6, 9, 17, 19, 31, 35, 37, 40, 41, 51	12, 24, 27, 28, 49	1, 7, 8, 10, 11, 13, 14, 15, 16, 18, 21, 22, 25, 26, 30, 32, 33, 34, 36, 38, 39, 45, 46, 47, 48, 50, 54, 55, 56, 57, 59, 60
American-Canadian Baptist Family	—	17	1, 2, 3, 4, 5, 6, 7, 8, 9, 10, 11, 12, 13, 14, 15, 16, 18, 20, 21, 22, 23, 24, 25, 26, 27, 28, 30, 32, 33, 34, 35, 36, 37, 38, 39, 41, 42, 43, 44, 45, 46, 47, 48, 49, 50, 51, 53, 54. 55, 56, 57, 58, 59, 60
Christian Church (Disciples of Christ)	17, 19, 31, 40	6, 8, 33, 35, 37, 51	1, 3, 4, 5, 7, 9, 10, 11, 12, 13, 20, 21, 23, 25, 29, 32, 34, 36, 38, 39, 42, 43, 44, 45, 48, 49, 53, 54, 55, 56, 57, 58, 60

Orthodox Churches	6, 9, 17, 40, 41	4, 11, 12, 18, 19, 27, 32, 34, 39, 46, 51	1, 3, 15, 16, 20, 22, 23, 26, 36, 43, 44, 47, 50, 55, 56, 58
Evangelical B	49	—	1, 2, 3, 4, 6, 7, 8, 10, 13, 14, 15, 16, 17, 18, 19, 21, 22, 23, 24, 25, 26, 27, 28, 29, 30, 31, 32, 33, 34, 35, 36, 37, 39, 41, 42, 43, 44, 45, 46, 47, 48, 50, 51, 52, 53, 54, 55, 56, 57, 59, 60
Free Church Family	17	16	1, 3, 4, 5, 6, 7, 8, 9, 11, 12, 13, 14, 15, 20, 21, 22, 23, 24, 26, 27, 30, 32, 33, 34, 35, 36, 38, 39, 41, 42, 43, 44, 45, 47, 48, 50, 51, 52, 53, 54, 55, 56, 57, 60
Jewish and Unitarian Family	2, 6, 12, 17, 19, 24, 27, 31, 35, 37, 40, 51, 58	4, 8, 9, 11, 15, 30, 34, 39, 46, 53	1, 3, 5, 7, 10, 13, 18, 20, 21, 28, 38, 42, 43, 44, 48, 49, 52, 54, 55, 56, 57, 60

TABLE 8-1 — CONTINUED

Family Name	Significant Contrast with Southern Baptists Indicated (5.0 Standard Scores or More)	Core Clusters Likelihood of Significant Contrast with Southern Baptists Approached (At Least 4.0 Standard Scores but Less Than 5)	Very Close Agreement with Southern Baptists (2.0 Standard Scores or Less)
Lutheran Churches	6, 9, 17, 19, 35, 40, 41, 51	49	3, 4, 5, 7, 8, 10, 11, 12, 13, 14, 15, 16, 18, 20, 21, 22, 25, 26, 27, 30, 33, 34, 36, 38, 39, 42, 43, 44, 45, 46, 47, 48, 50, 54, 55, 56, 57, 58, 59
United Methodist Church	17, 19, 31, 37, 40	9, 49, 51	1, 3, 4, 5, 7, 8, 10, 11, 12, 13, 14, 16, 20, 21, 22, 23, 25, 26, 30, 32, 38, 39, 42, 43, 45, 46, 47, 48, 50, 52, 53, 54, 55, 56, 57, 58, 59, 60
Presbyterian-Reformed Family	9, 17, 19, 51	40, 41, 49	1, 2, 3, 4, 5, 8, 10, 11, 12, 13, 14, 15, 16, 18, 20, 21, 22, 23, 24, 25, 26, 27, 29, 30, 33, 34, 36, 38, 39, 42, 43, 44, 45, 46, 47, 48, 50, 52, 53, 54, 55, 56, 57, 59, 60

Roman Catholic Church (Order)	6, 9, 17, 19, 41, 48, 51, 53	2, 31, 37, 40, 42, 49	3, 5, 8, 10, 13, 14, 18, 20, 22, 23, 25, 27, 29, 30, 32, 33, 34, 39, 44, 45, 46, 59
Roman Catholic Church (Diocesan)	6, 9, 17, 19, 31, 37, 40, 41, 48, 49, 51	53	3, 4, 5, 10, 11, 12, 13, 14, 16, 20, 21, 22, 23, 25, 26, 27, 29, 30, 34, 36, 38, 39, 44, 45, 46, 47, 55, 57, 59
United Church of Christ	2, 6, 17, 19, 31, 35, 37, 40, 51	24, 27, 33, 53	1, 3, 4, 5, 7, 8, 10, 11, 12, 13, 16, 20, 21, 23, 25, 26, 28, 29, 32, 34, 36, 39, 41, 43, 44, 45, 48, 49, 50, 54, 55, 57, 60
United Church of Canada	17, 19, 31, 35, 37, 40, 51	6, 24, 28, 47, 52, 58	1, 3, 4, 5, 10, 11, 12, 13, 14, 15, 20, 21, 22, 23, 30, 32, 34, 36, 38, 39, 41, 44, 45, 46, 50, 54, 55, 56, 57, 60
Evangelical A	13, 15	18, 33	1, 2, 3, 4, 5, 6, 9, 10, 11, 12, 17, 20, 21, 22, 23, 24, 25, 31, 32, 35, 36, 37, 38, 39, 42, 43, 44, 45, 47, 48, 49, 51, 52, 53, 54, 55, 58, 59, 60
Christian Church (not Disciples)	32	14, 18, 28, 29, 33, 49, 59	1, 2, 3, 4, 5, 9, 10, 11, 17, 19, 20, 23, 25, 27, 31, 35, 38, 39, 41, 42, 44, 45, 47, 48, 51, 54, 60

the importance of an expectation for understanding Southern Baptists in their distinctiveness varies in terms of how many other denominations are in contrast. When the twenty-two clusters where contrast occurs are looked at from the standpoint of the number of denominations contrasting with Southern Baptists, three patterns emerge. The first pattern is one in which Southern Baptists, along with many other denominations, are in contrast with only a few groups; the second finds Southern Baptists in contrast with some others and, at the same time, in close agreement with nearly the same number of denominations. Finally, there is the third and most revealing pattern, in which Southern Baptists contrast with many or most others and agree with very few denominations.

Pattern 1: Southern Baptists and Many Other Denominations in Contrast with a Few Others

The eleven specific dimensions of expectations for ministers that find Southern Baptists in agreement with many other denominations and in contrast with a few embrace various aspects of ministry, which can be discussed under four headings: support of community and world causes, encouragement of spiritual growth and Christian community, responsible lifestyle, and denominational relationships.

Support of Community and World Causes

Southern Baptist ministers and those in most other denominations agree in their expectations that clergy actively participate in social structures to improve the community (Core Cluster, or CC, 15) and work for—sometimes even originating—community services to people with special needs, such as youth or senior citizens (CC 13). But, as closely related as these areas are, a difference in the responses is clear. Southern Baptist laity have slightly higher expectations in the latter of these areas than the former, which suggests that Southern Baptists are more favorably inclined toward their ministers' initiating and improving community services when specific and visible groups are involved than they are inclined for their ministers to participate in more general programs of community betterment. What is crucial, however, is that Southern Baptists do have higher expectations in both areas and are in significant contrast with the four Baptist groups in the Evangelical A family—the general, missionary, conservative, and North American Baptists. The two other Baptist bodies—American Baptist Churches in the USA and the Baptist Federation of Canada—are in general agreement with Southern Baptists, but their less intense expectations for these aspects of a minister's functioning do not throw them into significant contrast with the Evangelical A group. The differences among Baptist bodies in how ministry is conceived point to the need for moving away from the imprecise lumping of denominations together simply because the term *Baptist* appears in the groups' self-designation. At this and at other points, Southern Baptists have expectations for ministers that are significantly different from those of other Baptist bodies.

Another characteristic of ministry that Southern Baptists intensely anticipate from their ministers is stimulating a congregational response to world need that is reflective, theologically based, and sacrificial (CC 12). This encouragement of the church to fulfill its world mission is an area in which Southern Baptists have traditionally understood themselves to be very strong. Actually, the denomination's expectations are in significant contrast with only one group—the Jewish and Unitarian family—and show very close agreement ($\pm$ 2 standard scores) with the majority of all others. This rather surprising register of expectations by Southern Baptists is thrust into more prominence by the variation between the responses of laypeople and clergy. In nearly every denomination the clergy have higher expectations for beginning ministers, and the gap is substantial in the case of Southern Baptists. The existence of this gap in expectations may hold profound implications for the cooperative financial support by churches for mission endeavors in the near future.

Encouragement of Spiritual Growth and Christian Community

Southern Baptists' expectations that their ministers help people cope with their personal problems and lead people to deeper spiritual commitment (CC 24) are moderately high—along with Evangelical groups A and B— and in contrast with the less intense expectations of the Jewish and Unitarian group.

Stated negatively, Southern Baptist clergy agree with most of their colleagues in other denominations in feeling it undesirable that a minister emphasize God's demands and condemnation as a basis for solving personal problems (CC 27). What is most revealing is the radical division between the expectations of clergy and laity. Although Southern Baptists do not approach the cleavage that exists in some families, Southern Baptist laypeople indicate greater willingness to accept a legalistic orientation to ethical problems than their ministers want to give.

Southern Baptists—along with most other denominations—want their ministers to work to develop a congregation's sense of being a family of God where a mutual sharing, worship, and broad participation exist (CC 4). This contrasts significantly with the less intense expectation registered by the Anglican-Episcopal family.

Responsible Lifestyle

All denominations disapprove of a minister's self-indulgent actions that irritate or offend (CC 53)—such as living beyond one's means or having an illicit affair. Southern Baptists register a high level of disapproval (with their clergy and laity in close agreement), but contrast significantly only with the Roman Catholic (Order) family.

Another dimension of a responsible lifestyle is agreement between the minister's commitment to his or her own family and that family's commitment to the minister's vocation (CC 48). The contrasts that exist in expectations are what one would expect—the celibate priesthood causes Roman Catholics to contrast with every other family.

The final area of expectations reflecting a responsible lifestyle is that the minister handle administrative responsibilities with understanding, efficiency, and careful planning (CC 58). Southern Baptists' rating of such administrative ability differs sharply only from the lower assessment registered by the Jewish and Unitarian family. Southern Baptists, with their strong anticipations for ministers' functioning efficiently as administrators, are in close agreement with almost one-half of the other denominational families; the strongest expectations, however, are present in the Evangelical B group.

Denominational Relationships

The last category, in which Southern Baptists contrast with a few but are in agreement with many other denominational families, concerns the minister's relationship with his or her denomination. Southern Baptists feel it is important for a minister to know both the history and the current stance of his or her denomination (CC 32), but they stand between the extremes of very high or low assessment and agree closely ($\pm$ 2 standard scores) with other denominational families. The expectations of clergy are generally higher than those of the laity, and Southern Baptist ministers are 5.7 standard scores higher in their rating than are the laity. This contrast in expectations, which exists in several groups, probably reflects the focus of the clergy on a denominational identity and that of the laity on an identity focused more specifically in a single congregation.

Southern Baptists generally expect their ministers to show loyalty to their denomination—accepting its directives and regulations and maintaining cooperative relationships with its leaders (CC 49). Again, Southern Baptists are between the extremes, contrasting significantly with the upward swings of the Evangelical B group and the Catholic (Diocesan) families. The most interesting data emerge at the point of the low expectations of clergy compared with the much higher ones of the laity among Southern Baptists. When this pattern is compared with the one discussed in the preceding paragraph, it would seem that Southern Baptist laypeople expect of young ministers loyalty to their denomination more than an understanding of it. The clergy, however, expect the young ministers to understand the denomination more than they expect them to be loyal or cooperative.

Pattern 2: Southern Baptists in Contrast to and Agreement with Approximately an Equivalent Number of Other Denominations

In five areas of expectation for beginning ministers, Southern Baptists register significant contrast with other denominations and, at the same time, are in close agreement with almost the same number. Southern Baptists have very mild expectations regarding two of these characteristics and very high expectations for the other three.

The two dimensions of ministry which Southern Baptists rate quite low relate to the minister's priestly commitment (CC 41) and to the minister's sacramental-liturgical orientation, with a ministry that focuses on worship and stresses the sacramental aspects of faith (CC 9). Standing in close agreement with Southern Baptists in their low assessment of both of these areas are all other Baptist groups, the Christian (Disciples), the Free Church family, and the Christian (not Disciples) family. In both of these areas of expectation—sacramental-liturgical orientation and priestly commitment—high value is assigned by the Anglican-Episcopal, Orthodox, Lutheran, and both Roman Catholic families. These latter denominational families tend to contrast in Core Cluster 41, "Priestly Commitment," with the group (including Southern Baptists) that attaches a low significance to "Sacramental-Liturgical Ministry" (CC 9). The Presbyterian-Reformed family contrasts significantly with Southern Baptists in expectations for sacramental-liturgical ministry, but not at the point of priestly commitment.

The three areas of expectation for ministers where Southern Baptists register an opposite evaluation, feeling such areas to be important for a beginning minister include: (1) having a theocentric-biblical ministry that will draw attention to God's Word and Person in preaching, teaching, and leading worship (CC 2); (2) setting a Christian example by living a life that the community will respect and that is above reproach (CC 35); and (3) possessing a deep religious commitment that reflects an awareness of God's redeeming activity in life and a sustaining sense of God's call to the task of ministry (CC 37).[8] Agreeing closely with Southern Baptists in these three areas are all other Baptist groups (the American-Canadian Baptist family and the Baptist churches in Evangelical A) and the bodies included in the Evangelical B group—Church of God (Anderson, Indiana), Church of the Nazarene, and others. In their high expectations for a biblical ministry, Southern Baptists are joined by the Presbyterian-Reformed and the Christian (not Disciples) families, who attach a similar degree of importance to setting a Christian example.

However, significantly less intense expectations in these three areas are present among the Anglican-Episcopal, Jewish and Unitarian, and United Church of Christ groups. These same denominational families, with the addition of the Lutheran, contrast significantly with Southern Baptists on Christian example. With regard to commitment reflecting religious piety, these same denominational families have significantly less intense expectations than Southern Baptists; two other families that show less intense expectation than Southern Baptists in this area of expectation are the United Methodist and Roman Catholic (Diocesan).

In interpreting the stance of Southern Baptists in regard to their high expectations for a beginning minister to have what could be termed a spiritual rather than a priestly orientation in ministry, it is important to note two things. First, the less intense expectations of several denominations for ministers to set a Christian example do not imply low or negative expectations. What the data indicate is that Southern Baptists are significantly more concerned than many other groups with these aspects of ministry and thus have expectations that are significantly more intense than the groups that contrast with them. The relative importance or rank of these concerns or expectations in relation to others held by Southern Baptists emerges in the second part of this chapter. Second, a relationship exists in the understanding of Southern Baptists between the two sets of expectations just discussed. The issue is one of what qualifies or certifies the validity of ministry; for Southern Baptists it is not liturgy, sacrament, or ordination—it is divine call, devout life, and biblical base.

Pattern 3: Southern Baptists and a Few Others in Contrast with Many Other Denominations

Southern Baptists show significant contrasts with most other denominations in six specific expectations for their ministers. These six expectations relate to three areas of ministerial functioning: open acknowledgment of religious experiences, encouragement and maintenance of a relevant biblical faith, and active concern for the unchurched.

Open Acknowledgment of Religious Experiences

In sharp contrast to most other denominations, Southern Baptists want their ministers to verbalize their religious experience and to speak naturally in social situations about God's activity in their daily lives (CC 40). Very high expectations are also registered by the Evangelical groups A (which includes four other Baptist bodies) and B. Nine denominational families have sharply less intense expectations of ministers in this area and stand in significant contrast to Southern Baptists: Anglican-Episcopal, Christian Church (Disciples), Orthodox, Jewish and Unitarian, Lutheran, United Methodist, Roman Catholic (Diocesan), United Church of Christ, and United Church of Canada.

For a Southern Baptist, to speak of one's faith is a crucial dimension of the Christian's responsibility to be a witness for Christ in one's life; and the epitome of refusal to be a good witness is the open denial of religious experience implied by a secularized lifestyle (CC 51)—enjoying local nightclubs and lounges, gambling, heavy smoking in public, and telling jokes hearers consider dirty. Most denominational families want the beginning minister not to exhibit such behavior, but Southern Baptists react more intensely than many others and register extremely strong negative reactions to a secularized lifestyle, contrasting with the responses of the following denominational families: Anglican-Episcopal, Jewish and Unitarian, Lutheran, Roman Catholic (Order), United Church of Christ, and United Church of Canada.

Encouragement and Maintenance of a Relevant Biblical Faith

Southern Baptists want their ministers to affirm a biblical faith (CC 31), proclaiming Christ as God's Son, treating the Bible as authoritative, and showing evidence of a continued study of the Scriptures. The high expectation of Southern Baptists in this regard contrasts significantly with seven other denominational family groups: Anglican-Episcopal, Christian Church (Disciples), Jewish and Unitarian, United Methodist, Roman Catholic (Diocesan), United Church of Christ, and United Church of Canada.

Much the same pattern of disagreement exists in a closely related area of expectation—that ministers encourage spiritual renewal (CC 6) by enabling persons to sense the gift of forgiveness, by creating congregational atmosphere enlivened by the gospel spirit of love and freedom, and by preaching to awaken persons to their sinfulness and need for a Savior. Southern Baptists have significantly higher expectations than do persons from the Anglican-Episcopal, Orthodox, Jewish and Unitarian, Lutheran, Roman Catholic (both Order and Diocesan), and United Church of Christ denominational families.

Active Concern for the Unchurched

How Southern Baptists expect their ministers to function in the area of evangelism represents the area of expectation in which Southern Baptists contrast with the largest number of other groups. Southern Baptists expect ministers to have an assertive style of evangelism (CC 17), taking the initiative in approaching strangers or the unchurched and seeking to convert them to Christianity. Only three other denominational families register such intense expectations: Evangelical A (with its four other Baptist bodies—Baptist General Conference, Baptist Missionary Association of America, Conservative Baptist Association of America, North American

Baptist General Conference), Evangelical B, and Christian Churches (not Disciples).

The crucial nature of this area of expectation for understanding Southern Baptists in relation to other denominations stands out boldly when the assessments of the remaining thirteen families are examined. Every other denominational group but one (American-Canadian Baptist) stands in significant contrast with Southern Baptists at this point. And, to make the denominational contrasts even crisper, it should be noted that very little disparity exists within the families between laity and clergy.

The only exception to the polarities of close agreement or significant contrast with Southern Baptists is posed by the American-Canadian Baptist family, which includes the American Baptist Churches in the USA and the Baptist Federation of Canada. These two Baptist bodies are the only ones not in significant contrast with Southern Baptists at any point in expectations for ministers; thus it is interesting that the widest variation between Southern Baptists and the American-Canadian Baptist family occurs at this point.[9]

Clearly, this assertive style of evangelism—approaching strangers to ask about the condition of their souls, visiting the unchurched to share the faith, believing that the way to an ideal world is the conversion of people, and seeking to bring all to know God's love in Christ—constitutes a watershed in the difference between what Southern Baptists and most others expect of beginning ministers.

Closely related to the expectation just discussed is the minister's having a strong belief that efforts to improve society are of minor importance when compared with efforts to evangelize the world (CC 19); and, as would be anticipated, Southern Baptists—in close agreement with the same three groups as in Core Cluster 17 (assertive evangelism)—register very strong feelings that evangelistic goals are of great importance for their ministers. Ten denominational groups stand in distinct and significant contrast, making the precedence of evangelistic goals another crucial aspect of ministry in which Southern Baptists are different from most others.[10]

But the conclusion must not be drawn that evangelism by itself is the key to understanding Southern Baptists' conception of ministry. The strong and important emphasis that Southern Baptists have at this point is crucial, but needs to be set in the larger context that will be constructed in the following section.

Category 2. Areas of Expectation for Ministers with No Significant Contrasts Between Southern Baptists and Other Denominations

In thirty-eight aspects of expectation for beginning ministers, no significant contrasts exist between Southern Baptists and other denominations.

In about one-half or seventeen of these aspects of ministry, contrasts exist between other groups; and rather general agreement exists among all denominations in the remaining twenty-one areas.

Group 1: Areas of Expectation for Ministers with Significant Contrast Among Other Denominations

Significant contrasts emerge among other denominational groups in seventeen specific expectations for beginning ministers. Such situations—especially when a contrasting group is one with which Southern Baptists are in frequent crucial agreement at other points—throw additional light on the unique pattern of expectations held by Southern Baptists. These seventeen expectations pinpoint what is anticipated from ministers in three areas of their functioning: candid acceptance of one's role and humanity as a minister, sensitive and informed style of ministry, and realistic ministry to the socially oppressed or culturally different.

Candid Acceptance of One's Role and Humanity as a Minister

In this area, beginning ministers face the expectations that they will openly acknowledge their limitations and mistakes (CC 36), candidly confess personal struggles of faith and the disappointments of ministry (CC 38), actively seek counsel from others as to God's will (CC 39), and demonstrate being comfortable with the role of minister and its financial implications (CC 47). In each of these aspects of the minister's functioning, Southern Baptists register very close agreement with the expectations of three-fourths of the other denominational families. But the Evangelical B group—which was closely allied with Southern Baptists in those crucial areas where Southern Baptists were in contrast with most others—is in significant contrast with one or more others in three out of four of these expectations (CC 39, acceptance of counsel, is the exception). Southern Baptists, however, stand between the polarities and in close agreement with the majority of the other denominational groups.

Sensitive and Informed Style of Ministry

This group of seven expectations further clarifies the difference in expectations between Southern Baptists and others. In five aspects of ministerial functioning, Southern Baptists stand between the extremes in agreement with from two-thirds to more than three-fourths of the others, while the Evangelical B group registers somewhat more intense expectations, throwing its denominations into contrast with one or more others, in the areas of liturgical sensitivity (CC 7), pastoral service to all (CC 11), ready availability in crisis (CC 23), personal responsibility expressed in resistance to pressure to compromise (CC 42), and active employment of lay leadership (CC 57). To be sure, the difference between Evangelical B and the Southern Baptists (along with most others) is not vast in these five areas; but the former group is in contrast with one or two others in each instance, while Southern Baptists are not.

In the two remaining expectations in the area of a sensitive and informed style of ministry, Southern Baptists again stand between the extremes and in agreement with the majority of others in wanting a beginning minister to make stimulating use of a broad knowledge of current events and subjects other than theology (CC 30) and to demonstrate involvement with an openness to current ideas (CC 33). What is significant for understanding Southern Baptists is that the Evangelical A family (with its four Baptist groups—General, Missionary, Conservative, and North American) registers a very low intensity of expectations in comparison with others, contrasting with ten other families (62.5 percent) at the point of openness to current ideas.

Realistic Ministry to the Socially Oppressed or Culturally Different

Six specific expectations face the beginning minister in this area, which focuses on dimensions of social concern: openness to working cooperatively with the culturally and theologically different (CC 8), promotion of the fuller understanding of social and cultural issues (CC 14), work and activity in behalf of minorities and the oppressed (CC 16), aggressive political leadership against social wrongs (CC 18), realistic tolerance of cultural or social diversity (CC 46), and a willingness to support unpopular causes (CC 50). Southern Baptists are neither the leaders nor the laggards in the intensity of their expectations for beginning ministers in these areas, but again stand between the extremes. But the Evangelical A family with its four Baptist groups, previously conspicuous because of its close agreement with Southern Baptists on evangelism, is now prominent because of its significantly low expectations in five out of six of these aspects of ministry—tolerance for diversity being the exception. Southern Baptists, who register a substantially higher intensity of expectations for their ministers in the five areas under discussion than does the Evangelical A group, are not in significant contrast with any other group, and agree closely ($\pm$ 3 standard scores) with the majority of others in every case.

Group 2: Areas of Expectation for Ministers with General Agreement Among All Denominations

In twenty-one of the sixty areas of expectation for beginning ministers, the outstanding feature is the substantial agreement that exists among all denominations. When perceived as a whole, these twenty-one areas establish a crucial vantage point for surveying the differences that exist in expectations between Southern Baptists and other denominations by identifying common ground and pinpointing the boundaries of contrasts. What is at once apparent when these areas are viewed together is that the basic focus of the agreement among denominations is in terms of the kind of person the minister is. The stress is on the minister's qualities of sensitivity to people and situations, the minister's willingness to accept others and care for them both personally and as a congregational fellowship, and the minister's professional balance and poise in conducting worship and creating an appropriate tone for fellowship and caring in the congregation.

Some of the twenty-one expectations focus directly on the personal character of the minister, such as the anticipation that the minister be willing to serve others with or without public acclaim (CC 34), that the minister function responsibly (CC 43) and possess a realistic flexibility of spirit (CC 45), and that he or she maintain a person-centered relationship with the staff (CC 59) and relate personally to both children and youth (CC 3). This focus on personhood is also made negatively—the beginning minister should neither alienate (CC 10) nor dominate individuals and groups (CC 60); should not display professional immaturity (CC 52) by, for example, showing favoritism or by measuring his or her worth by the salary received; and should not use the office of minister to avoid intimacy by means of a critical or insensitive attitude (CC 54).

Other expectations in this group of twenty-one, in which response across all denominations tends to fall within a narrow range of agreement, stress the qualities of the minister as they emerge in situations where people are hurting or could easily be hurt. Positively, the minister is expected to reach out and support persons under stress (CC 21) or who are isolated and alienated (CC 26), to be skilled in helping people with serious problems (CC 22), and to be involved personally with people in mutual learning through suffering (CC 25). The minister is also expected to maintain his or her own balance under stress and hostility (CC 44), as well as to assist people in conflict to learn from the experience while maintaining respect for their opponents (CC 56).

The five remaining areas of expectations in which there is agreement among denominational families deal more explicitly with the minister's function as it is traditionally conceived. The minister should enable people to understand and apply their faith in modern life (CC 1), should command respectful attention while preaching or leading worship (CC 5); he or she should be theologically informed (CC 29) and be able to communicate and interpret with clarity to laypeople (CC 28). Approached negatively, this is to say that the minister is expected not to concentrate totally on concerns of the congregation and thereby avoid confronting the need for social change (CC 20).

The Southern Baptists' Expectations for Ministry: Contrasts and Agreements

When the sixty key areas of expectation for beginning ministers are viewed as a whole, the most fascinating feature is the interplay and pattern of agreement and contrast that exists among the denominational families. For Southern Baptists, the degree of commonality with other denominations is greater—although not necessarily more important—than the difference, as no significant contrasts exist between Southern Baptists and any other group in thirty-eight of the sixty areas of expectation. And it should be noted that in twenty-one of the sixty no significant differences among any of the denominational families emerge. Generally speaking, the agreement between Southern Baptists and others focuses on four dimensions of expectations for ministers: that the minister function well in the traditional role of the clergy, such as in preaching and explaining the faith in a relevant way;[11] that the minister be a caring, sensitive person who nurtures congregational fellowship and life;[12] that the minister demonstrate faith by example in service and in personal character;[13] and that the minister demonstrate concern for improving society by appropriate action.[14]

This commonality, however, sketches only general areas rather than pinpointing specifics, and the differences among denominations emerge only as the dimensions of expectation are more finely delineated. In twenty-two aspects of expectation for ministers, significant contrasts do exist between Southern Baptists and one or more other denominational families, and the pattern formed by these contrasts between Southern Baptists and other denominational groups reveals what is distinctive in the Southern Baptist expectations for beginning ministers.

The first highly distinctive dimension of Southern Baptists' conception of readiness for ministry relates to the evangelistic stance of the denomination. At the point of expecting ministers to express an aggressive approach to the unchurched and seek to convert others to Christianity (CC 17), the high valuation placed on such an approach by Southern Baptists throws them into significant contrast with twelve of the sixteen other families, which together include 31 denominations. The other expectations with a high number of contrasts between Southern Baptists and others point in the same general direction. Southern Baptists want their ministers to believe deeply that the evangelization of all persons has clear priority over efforts to improve society (CC 19). The denomination expects its ministers to converse naturally and easily with others about what God has done in their own lives, referring to themselves as "born again" (CC 40). Or, stated inversely, the denomination reacts strongly against a secularized lifestyle in a minister (CC 51), interpreting it as the epitome of a lack of evangelistic concern and experience.

Moving in this same vein are the denomination's strong anticipations that their ministers will encourage a congregational spirituality that emphasizes God's love and forgiveness to sinners (CC 6) and will stress that Jesus is God's Son and that the Scripture is authoritative (CC 2, 31) rather than emphasize the liturgical aspects of the faith (CC 9). The denomination also expects a minister to demonstrate a personal piety that flows from a sense of divine call (CC 37) rather than a priestly commitment (CC 41); and to set a personal Christian example (CC 35).

All of these areas of expectations for ministers point to a style of evangelism and personal spirituality treasured and appreciated by Southern Baptists with an intensity that throws them into significant contrast with all of the other denominational families except the American-Canadian Baptist; and, as has been noted, the only contrast that Southern Baptists approach with regard to this group is at the point of an assertive individual evangelism (CC 17).[15] Every case of contrast in all of these areas related to evangelism and personal spirituality points in the same direction, as Table 8-2 shows. The other denominations are in remarkable agreement in their contrasts with Southern Baptists; all the significantly contrasting groups have much less desire that their ministers display the evangelistic piety Southern Baptists expect in their ministers, but a greater desire that their ministers stress the sacramental (CC 9) and priestly (CC 41) ministry.

A stress on evangelism and a particular style of spirituality, however, is only one of the two dimensions of the distinctive Southern Baptist expectations for ministers. The second emerges when the contrasts between Southern Baptists and the three denominational families that closely agree with them on evangelism are examined (see Table 8-2). The Evangelical A group, with its four other Baptist groups (Baptist General Conference, Baptist Missionary Association of America, Conservative Baptist Association of America, and North American General Baptist Conference) significantly contrast with the Southern Baptist denomination in two expectations. Both pinpoint the same area, social concern and involvement—Southern Baptists have significantly higher expectations that their ministers take the initiative in developing community services (CC 13) and in actively supporting efforts for community improvement (CC 15). That this difference between Southern Baptists and Evangelical A runs deep is clear from the significant contrast approached in two other areas of expectation that point in the same direction; namely that beginning ministers be deeply involved with current ideas (CC 33), and that they show aggressive political leadership (CC 18).

The two remaining families in general agreement with Southern Bap-

TABLE 8-2

Significant Contrasts Between Southern Baptists and Other Denominational Families

(less or more intense expectations than Southern Baptists)

Area of Expectation[b]	Number of Families in Contrast with Southern Baptists	Denominational Families[a]															
		Anglican-Episcopal Churches	American-Canadian Baptist Family	Christian Church (Disciples)	Orthodox Church	Evangelical B	Free Church Family	Jewish-Unitarian Family	Lutheran Churches	United Methodist Church	Presbyterian-Reformed Family	Roman Catholic Church (Order)	Roman Catholic Church (Diocesan)	United Church of Christ	United Church of Canada	Evangelical A	Christian Church (Not Disciples)
Assertive Individual Evangelism (17)	12	less		less	less		less	less	less	less	less	less	less	less	less		
Precedence of Evangelistic Goals (19)	10	less		less					less	less	less	less	less	less	less		
Talks Openly of Religious Experience (40)	9	less		less	less			less	less	less			less	less	less		

Item												
Avoids Secular Lifestyle (51)	8	less			less	less	less	less	less	less	less	less
Encouragement of Spiritual Sensitivity (6)	7	less			less	less	less	less	less	less	less	
Affirmation of a Biblical Faith (31)	7	less	less		less	less		less	less	less		
Stress on Sacramental-Liturgical Ministry (9)	6	more	more		more	more	more	more				
Commitment that Reflects Piety (37)	6	less			less	less		less	less	less		
Priestly Commitment (41)	5	more	more		more	more	more	more				
Sets a Christian Example (35)	5	less			less	less			less	less		
Stress on Theocentric and Biblical Ministry (2)	3	less	less		less				less			
Mutual Family Commitment (48)	2						less	less				
Denominational Collegiality (49)	2			more			more					
Promotes Mutuality in the Congregation (4)	1	less										
Encouragement of World Missions (12)	1				less							

TABLE 8-2 — *CONTINUED*

Denominational Families[a]

Promotes Development of Community Services (13)	1														less	
Supports Community Improvement (15)	1														less	
Theologically-Oriented Counseling (24)	1						less									
Legalistic Approach to Ethical Issues (27)	1						less									
Demonstrates Knowledge of Denomination (32)	1															less
Avoids Undisciplined Living (53)	1										less					
Administrative Ability (58)	1						less									
Total number of contrasts with each denominational group	12	0	4	5	1	1	13	8	5	4	8	11	9	7	2	1

[a] For a full listing of the groups in each family, see Table 4-1.

[b] Numbers in parentheses refer to core clusters; see Chapter 5 for a full description of each core cluster.

tists on assertive evangelism contrast more sharply with them at the point of expectations related to denominational concerns. Evangelical B rises significantly at the point of denominational collegiality (CC 49); and the Christian Church (not Disciples) registers significantly less important the expectation that a minister know the history and current stance of his or her denomination (CC 32).

What is distinctive in Southern Baptists' expectations for ministers in comparison with other denominations emerges in a pattern that is both simple and consistent. When Southern Baptists agree with others on social concerns, there is sharp contrast at the point of personal evangelism (thirteen denominational families); and when Southern Baptists are in agreement with others on evangelism, the tendency is for tension and contrast to exist in the area of social concern or action (three families).

With regard to this distinctive Southern Baptist concept of expectation for beginning ministers, three comments should be made. First, this distinction is not normally experienced in its unity by those outside the denomination. From the standpoint of other denominational families, Southern Baptists are conspicuous by their differences rather than by their similarities insofar as expectations for ministers are visible in functioning ministers. Consequently, laypeople and ministers of most other denominations tend to see Southern Baptists as aggressive, evangelical activists who verbalize and stress intensely a style of biblical spirituality usually associated with extreme theological conservatism. These obvious contrasts between Southern Baptists and others seize attention, and thus too little notice is taken of the denomination's similarities with others, which include openness to current ideas and social concern. Ironically, it is precisely these commonalities with the majority of denominations that cause the few families that agree with Southern Baptists on evangelism to view Southern Baptists as too liberal and as tending to move toward theological compromises that blunt evangelistic concern by stressing social involvement.

The second thing that needs to be noted is that the general agreement between Southern Baptists and others at the point of social concern should not be interpreted to mean that the denomination's sense of concern is of the same kind that exists in other groups. The congregational control that results in a minister's vulnerability to dismissal when large numbers of a church's membership disagree sharply with the pastor's actions or positions has resulted in most Southern Baptist pastors' adopting a selective and gradualistic approach on controversial issues. The general stance of the denomination on social issues is not to be understood, therefore, on the basis of the position of one individual church, but rather from the official statements of the agencies of the denomination, such as the Christian Life Commission, which have been quite progressive.[16]

The third observation about Southern Baptists' unique expectation for both evangelism and social action is that it has been isolated by noting how Southern Baptists differ from other groups. However, acknowledging the existence of such a distinct expectation does not indicate the degree of value that Southern Baptists place on this particular expectation. How Southern Baptists rank personal evangelism or dimensions of social action has not been taken into account, and basically this approach to the Southern Baptists' expectations is followed in the next section of this chapter.

SOUTHERN BAPTIST AREAS OF EXPECTATION FOR MINISTRY COMPARED WITH THOSE FROM THE TOTAL GROUP OF DENOMINATIONS

Sixty-four core areas of expectation for beginning ministers emerge in the analysis of the data from the forty-seven denominations surveyed in the Readiness for Ministry Project. When the identical process of cluster and factor analysis is applied to the data coming only from the responses of Southern Baptists, forty-eight areas of expectation emerge that are unique to Southern Baptists.[17] These forty-eight areas from the one denomination can be compared to the sixty-four of the entire group of families in two ways. First, the two groups of expectations can be compared to determine similarities and differences in areas of expectation, and, second, the two groups of expectations can be compared on the basis of the degree of importance assigned to areas of expectation.

Similarities and Differences in Areas of Expectation

The sixty-four core areas of expectation drawn from the forty-seven denominations are arranged in the research of the project into thematic sections.[18] These seven categories describe aspects of the minister's life or work, such as "Ministries to the Religious Community," and provide an excellent framework for comparing the sixty-four core and forty-eight Southern Baptist clusters of expectation.

Section 1: Ministries to the Religious Community

Five areas of expectation emerge from the Southern Baptists' responses in this section, as indicated in Table 8-3; and each of the five shows both similarities to and differences from core expectations.[19]

The first two Southern Baptist expectations correspond somewhat to the transdenominational core expectations of the encouragement of spiritual renewal (CC 6) and congregational mutuality (CC 4), but with the specific inclusion (unlike the core clusters) of children and youth. Here,

TABLE 8-3
**Comparisons Between Southern Baptist and Core Cluster Responses in
"Ministries to the Religious Community"**

Southern Baptist Cluster No.	*Southern Baptist Mean*	*Southern Baptist Cluster*	*Related Core Cluster No.*	*Total Group Mean*
1	2.25	*Concern for Spiritual Growth* Enabling all to achieve a deeper spiritual life through personal growth and the realization of forgiveness	6	1.93
2	2.21	*Promotion of Nurturing Mutuality* Encouraging the mutuality, nurture, and evangelistic witness of the entire congregation	4	1.93
3	2.05	*Evangelical Preaching and Worship Leading* Communicating in preaching and worship God's presence in judgment and grace in a professional manner	2 5	2.24 1.87
4	1.71	*Competent Leader of Worship* Leading worship in which music and prayer contribute to the dignity of worship and the needs of people	5 7	1.87 1.63
5	1.20	*Openness in Style* Willing to introduce innovations in worship and to cooperate with other denominations on the basis of a considered theological stance	8	1.57

the Southern Baptist understanding of how the minister should function reflects the denomination's special concern for children and youth in the light of its evangelical stance. Among Southern Baptists, all people become members of the church by voluntarily joining the church on the basis of a personal decision to become a Christian, and this makes the minister's concern for children and youth an important dimension of expectations related to spiritual growth and congregational mutuality.

Southern Baptist expectations related to preaching and worship (Southern Baptist Clusters, or SBC, 3 and 4) include the items in the corresponding core cluster on competent preaching and worship leading (CC 5); but the family's intense concern for an evangelistic style of preaching emerges in the emphasis—lacking in the core cluster—that the minister preach so as to awaken listeners to their sinfulness and need for a savior, to place both the minister and hearers under God's judgment, and to leave persons conscious of Jesus Christ.

Southern Baptists expect their ministers to demonstrate some ecumenical openness (SBC 5), but the denomination's experiences and perception of cooperation with other groups result in an expectation different from the corresponding core cluster in this area (CC 8) by pinpointing two items the denomination associates with ecumenical influence—using the arts in worship and having group discussion of the sermon.

Section 2: Ministries to the Community and World

Seven Southern Baptist expectations emerge in the general area of "Ministries to the Community and the World," and all but one are quite similar (although not identical) to core clusters, as Table 8-4 indicates. The exception is the Southern Baptist expectation of how ministers should function at the point of precedence of evangelistic goals (SBC 9) which is close enough to the corresponding core cluster (CC 19) to bear the same title, but the stress is quite different. The core expectation delineates a ministerial attitude that is somewhat negative toward efforts to improve society, including such items as the insistence that a minister stick to religion and leave politics alone. The Southern Baptist expectation focuses on evangelistic goals in such a way as to embrace social action without including the negative dimensions of the core cluster, yet by featuring the affirmation that the way to build an ideal society is to convert everyone to Christianity.[20] Southern Baptists thus expect their beginning ministers to function so as to affirm both the priority of evangelism and the necessity of social action. There is a notable absence from the denomination's cluster of an item that implies that social action in the political realm is not desirable. It reinforces the affirmation of social action and evangelism that emerges from the comparison of Southern Baptist expectations with those of other denominations. Further validation of the denomination's position comes into view in its assessment of an attitude of resistance to community involvements (SBC 12) by ministers: Southern Baptists react negatively, ranking such an attitude between detrimental and undesirable.

Section 3: Ministries to Persons under Stress

The Southern Baptist expectations related to this dimension of the minister's functioning are similar to the core expectations for the most part (see Table 8-5). The denomination's evangelistic concern shines through in its expectation that ministers be spiritual counselors through whom counselees are "led to deepened spiritual growth and commitment."[21]

TABLE 8-4

**Comparisons Between Southern Baptist and Core Cluster Responses
in "Ministries to Community and World"**

Southern Baptist Cluster No.	Southern Baptist Mean	Southern Baptist Cluster	Related Core Cluster No.	Total Group Mean
6	1.48	*Responsible Citizenship* Demonstrates informed community citizenship by contact with local political life and encourages others to be responsive to community needs	15	1.19
7	1.28	*Promotion of Understanding of Issues* Develops, uses, and encourages theological, sociological and psychological understandings in ministry	14	1.39
8	1.19	*Sensitivity to Social Problems* Understands and is sensitive to the problems of the oppressed and minority groups and actively seeks to share this sensitivity with others	No precise correlation with core cluster items	
9	0.62	*Precedence of Evangelistic Goals* Believes that the evangelization of all people has priority over but does not cancel efforts in the area of social action	19	−0.94
10	0.48	*Social Concern* Works to integrate social minorities into the congregation, has the respect of social outcasts, and seeks to relieve the problems of the oppressed	16	1.12
11	0.20	*Community Involvement* Supports efforts to improve the community by serving on committees, by organizing action and study groups, and by seeking to remove ineffective officials	13	1.83
12	−1.59	*Resistance to Community Involvement* Avoids direct confronting of social change in a theologically conservative ministry	20	−1.42

TABLE 8-5
**Comparisons Between Southern Baptist and Core Cluster Responses
in "Ministries to Persons under Stress"**

Southern Baptist Cluster No.	Southern Baptist Mean	Southern Baptist Cluster	Related Core Cluster No.	Total Group Mean
13	2.51	*Spiritual Counseling* Conducting a ministry to people with problems or in difficulty from the perspective of faith	24	2.17
14	2.35	*Competent Counseling* Counseling that reflects both professional expertise and appreciation for the freedom of persons	21	2.26
15	2.15	*Professional Ministry to Troubled Persons* Providing appropriate ministry in counseling and/or referral for persons with serious marital, emotional, or personal problems	22	2.23
16	1.46	*Ministry to the Suffering* Ministering with sensitivity and care to the dying, bereaved, and suffering	25	1.73

Section 4: The Minister as Theologian and Thinker

The expectations of the Southern Baptist Convention with regard to a stimulating use of theological knowledge (SBC 19) are similar to the total group's core clusters; but all of the other expectations in this area are distinctive (see Table 8-6). Southern Baptists' expectations focus on their ministers' demonstrating continuing professional growth (SBC 17), while the related core cluster stresses current functioning.

The denomination has a concern for balance that does not emerge clearly in the core expectations. Southern Baptists want their ministers to have both intelligence and curiosity (SBC 22), both biblical and denominational knowledge (SBC 18), and both professional and general knowledge (SBC 21). They also want their ministers to affirm both evangelism and social action (SBC 20). This stress on balance may reflect the denomination's painful struggles in coming to deal realistically with the massive social and cultural changes that the South has experienced.

TABLE 8-6

**Comparisons Between Southern Baptist and Core Cluster Responses
in "Minister as Theologian and Thinker"**

Southern Baptist Cluster No.	Southern Baptist Mean	Southern Baptist Cluster	Related Core Cluster No.	Total Group Mean
17	2.35	*Professional Development* Continuing professional growth as an outcome both of study and reflection on experience	28	2.18
18	2.22	*Balanced Biblical and Denominational Knowledge* Possessing a balanced knowledge of both Scripture and one's denomination	29 32	1.90 1.54
19	1.99	*Stimulating Use of Theological Knowledge* Encouraging people in their quests for truth from a base of personal conviction and knowledge, while encouraging mutuality and acceptance	29 30	1.90 1.92
20	1.70	*Professional Balance* Maintaining an informed professional balance between evangelism and social action as well as in controversial issues	No precise correlation with core cluster items	
21	1.70	*Professional and General Knowledge* Possessing and appropriately using both technical-professional and general cultural knowledge	30	1.92
22	1.56	*Disciplined Intelligence and Curiosity* Demonstrating a disciplined use of intelligence in the context of analyzing issues and having a broad awareness	28	2.18

Section 5: The Minister's Personal Commitment of Faith

The expectation felt to be most essential to effective ministry among Southern Baptists emerges in this group of expectations, namely, religious commitment (SBC 23), as Table 8-7 shows. The items that form this expectation are as follows: "Shows the mission of Christ to be first in own

TABLE 8-7

Comparisons Between Southern Baptist and Core Cluster Responses in "The Minister's Personal Commitment of Faith"

Southern Baptist Cluster No.	Southern Baptist Mean	Southern Baptist Cluster	Related Core Cluster No.	Total Group Mean
23	2.71	*Religious Commitment* Ministering from an awareness of God's providential presence and out of a deep awareness of God's call to ministry and a specific church	37	2.20
24	2.63	*Christian Example* Maintaining a Christian life that is a worthy and respected example; being nourished by the biblical revelation	35	2.42
25	2.51	*Healthy Spirituality* Living with responsible awareness of limitations; having a disciplined routine of prayer, awareness of God's redeeming power, and openness toward the help others can provide	37 38	2.20 1.42
26	2.51	*Service in Humility* Relying on God's grace, serving others without seeking a personal reputation for success	34	2.52
27	1.70	*Acknowledgment of Own Humanity* Honestly and openly confessing personal weaknesses and spiritual struggles	38	1.42
28	1.34	*Acceptance of Counsel* Seeking to know God's will through the counsel and ministry of others	39	1.35
29	−3.01	*Priestly Commitments* Taking seriously the sacramental life and priestly vows	41	−2.03

life" (Item 332); "Shows sensitivity to the leading of the Holy Spirit" (Item 343); "Views the call or appointment to a parish, once accepted, as a calling of God" (Item 340); "Interprets the decision to enter the ministry as a personal call from God" (Item 348); and "Appears to be sustained by a sense of God's call when the going gets rough" (Item 338). Southern Baptists place the highest priority on the minister's obedient awareness of the presence of God in his or her life, wanting the minister to understand not only entrance into, but also faithful continuance in, ministry as God's intention or call. This expectation for beginning ministers correlates closely with the second-ranked one among Southern Baptists for their ministers—that he or she be a respected example of Christian life (SBC 24).

The five remaining Southern Baptist expectations are similar to the core clusters, and the duplication of the highest-ranked core expectation—"service in humility" (CC 34)—highlights the weight that Southern Baptists give to the inner and outer dimensions of evangelical piety that emerge in the denomination's stress on religious commitment and personal example.

Section 6 (A and B): The Minister as a Person (Positive and Negative)

Southern Baptists have very definite ideas about what kind of person the minister should be. And, although some of the denomination's expectations (SBC 30, 31, 34, 37) are similar to the core clusters "Personal Responsibility" (CC 42), "Flexibility of Spirit" (CC 45), "Acceptance of Clergy Role" (CC 47), and "Denominational Collegiality" (CC 49), (SBC 30, 31, 34, 37, respectively), a distinctive Southern Baptist emphasis emerges in the remainder (see Table 8-8). How the minister relates to people in situations of potential or actual conflict is crucial for Southern Baptists because of the autonomy of local congregations in which disagreements between people can easily be transposed into issues about policy that demand formal congregational attention. Southern Baptists thus expect their ministers to maintain professional balance in conflict (SBC 32), to be able to adapt to trying situations (SBC 33), and to show professional maturity by letting others lead when appropriate (SBC 35). This expectation for professional maturity neatly illustrates the denominational family's concerns by placing emphasis on letting others run the show when they are in charge, but tempers the withdrawal this might indicate with the item "Works independently without prodding or supervision" (Item 510).

The Southern Baptist expectation that ministers display a mature social identity (SBC 36) has no close counterpart in the core clusters. The expectation represents the denomination's concern for their ministers to be mature people who can maintain significant relationships in a broad social spectrum without neglecting crucial dimensions of their responsibilities.

TABLE 8-8
TABLE 8-8
Comparisons Between Southern Baptist and Core Cluster Responses in "The Minister as a Person (Positive)"

Southern Baptist Cluster No.	Southern Baptist Mean	Southern Baptist Cluster	Related Core Cluster No.	Total Group Mean
30	2.63	*Personal Responsibility* Honors commitments by keeping promises, spending time with family and not yielding to pressures to compromise	42 48	2.43 1.83
31	2.31	*Flexibility of Spirit* Demonstrates a healthy flexibility of spirit in bouncing back, adapting to the new, and relating to highly successful people without being threatened	45	2.11
32	2.18	*Balance in Conflict* Maintains professional balance by being honest and objective in situations of opposition	43 44	2.29 2.25
33	2.12	*Disciplined Adaptability* Has adaptability that demonstrates itself in relating to persons with cultural differences, not avoiding unenjoyable tasks, and sharing feelings without personal bias	43 46	2.29 1.97

Southern Baptists also have strong feelings about what their ministers should not be, and the five expectations related to this are all evaluated as undesirable and highly detrimental to ministry (see Table 8-9). The first two expectations as to how the minister should not function pinpoint insensitivity to others (SBC 38) and personal insecurities displayed in relationships with others (SBC 39). These negative anticipations for ministers simply represent the other side of the denomination's expectation that ministers be mature, adaptable, balanced people (SBC 36, 35, 33, 32), as discussed earlier. The expectation dealing with a rigid and insensitive style, for example, focuses on matters such as paying more attention to men than women, being unable to apply learning from books, displaying

TABLE 8-8 — *CONTINUED*

Southern Baptist Cluster No.	Southern Baptist Mean	Southern Baptist Cluster	Related Core Cluster No.	Total Group Mean
34	2.08	*Acceptance of Clergy Role* Demonstrates healthy attitude toward his or her role as a minister	47	1.88
35	2.07	*Professional Maturity* Demonstrates maturity in letting others lead when appropriate, works independently, and accepts the risk of change	43	2.29
36	1.98	*Social Identity* Displays maturity of social identity in roles by participating vigorously in community affairs, keeping commitments to his or her children, and conversing easily with those of opposite sex	No precise correlation with core cluster items	
37	−0.05	*Denominational Collegiality* Demonstrates a relationship of professional integrity with the denomination by cooperating or explaining rationally reasons for not doing so	49	1.76

pessimism, scolding the congregation, and giving the impression of always being busy.

Southern Baptists register their most intensely negative feelings with regard to the minister's living an undisciplined and egotistic life (SBC 42). The style of life pinpointed involves having illicit sexual affairs, using the ministerial role to maintain superiority, placing great stress on one's status, being intoxicated, and seeking preferential treatment on the basis of one's clergy status. The denomination's feelings about a secular and self-serving lifestyle (SBC 40) are nearly as intense; and the items included are similar to those in the related core clusters (CC 51, 52), including such

TABLE 8-9

**Comparisons Between Southern Baptist and Core Cluster
Responses in "The Minister as a Person (Negative)"**

Southern Baptist Cluster No.	Southern Baptist Mean	Southern Baptist Cluster	Related Core Cluster No.	Total Group Mean
38	−1.83	*Rigid and Insensitive Style* Publicly displays rigidity and insensitivity in regard to the thought, feelings, and needs of others	54	−2.02
39	−2.07	*Professional Immaturity* Acts in way that demonstrates immaturity, insecurity; is buffeted by the responsibilities of ministry	52	−1.89
40	−2.11	*Secular and Self-Serving Lifestyle* Displays behavior associated with a secular life and a desire to have things his or her own way	51 54	−1.57 −2.02
41	−2.13	*Vocational Maladjustment* Reveals maladjustment to ministerial vocation by misuse of time and neglect of family; sees other vocations as better; and is unable to adjust to other people	No precise correlation with core cluster items	
42	−2.19	*Undisciplined and Egotistic Lifestyle* Displays self-indulgent and egotistical behavior that offends or irritates, such as sexual affairs, use of alcohol, stress on self-importance, abrupt and thoughtless condemnation of others, and living beyond one's means	53 54	−2.08 −2.02

items as visiting nightclubs and lounges (Item 543), gambling (Item 564), being publicly impatient with those who resist change (Item 537), and being moody (Item 546).

Southern Baptists have quite negative evaluations of behavior that indicates maladjustment to the ministerial vocation, such as allowing job responsibilities to take priority over family or regarding other vocations as better than the ministry. The positive counterpart of this is the very high Southern Baptist expectation that ministers feel it is God's intention for them to be both in the ministry, generally, and working at the task at hand, specifically (SBC 23).

Section 7: The Minister as Leader

This section is unique in that it contains an equal number of core and Southern Baptist clusters, while in the other six sections fewer Southern Baptists than total group clusters emerge. This points to the very intense concerns that Southern Baptists have with leadership. The distinctive concerns of the denomination emerge in two ways: first, in the importance attached to the area in general by the large number of clusters (see Table 8-10); and second, in the specific expectations related to leadership that shows respect for people (SBC 44) and exhibits a sense of responsibility (SBC 48). Leadership premised on respect for persons is, for Southern Baptists, leadership that is shared with capable laypeople without regard for sex, that includes openness to evaluate programs realistically, and that treats the lay leadership as people who are worth knowing in themselves. Responsible leadership points out the implications or values implied in congregational decisions and authentically helps others to feel that it is appropriate to disagree with a minister. The congregational polity and autonomy of Southern Baptist churches is clearly reflected in these expectations.

Comparison of Expectations by Rank Order

The distinctive Southern Baptist expectations for beginning ministers have emerged with some clarity as the denomination's expectations have been examined, but the fuller picture becomes visible only when the internal ranking and relative importance of this denomination's expectations are assessed. The expectations—both core and Southern Baptist—are ranked in terms of the average (grand mean) of the items in the expectation, on the basis of a seven-point scale. Three represents "highly important"; 2, "quite important"; 1, "somewhat important"; 0, neither important nor unimportant; −1, "somewhat" detrimental or "undesirable"; −2, "quite detrimental"; and −3, "highly detrimental," harmful to effective ministry. The crucial breaking point in the scale is thus at 0 point, where the assessment of an expectation moves from a positive (desirable) to a negative evaluation.

The most interesting comparisons between core and Southern Baptist expectations are in the highest and lowest-ranked clusters, and the following discussions focus on these groups.

TABLE 8-10
**Comparisons Between Southern Baptist and Core Cluster Responses
in "The Minister as Leader"**

Southern Baptist Cluster No.	Southern Baptist Mean	Southern Baptist Cluster	Related Core Cluster No.	Total Group Mean
43	2.43	*Community Building* Actively promotes and encourages mutual concern and appreciation in the congregation	55	2.34
44	2.32	*Leadership with Respect for People* Demonstrates a style of leadership that appropriately recognizes the skills, needs, resources, and viewpoints of others	57	2.07
45	2.12	*Administrative Skill* Shares skill in administration by sensitive awareness of budget and program needs, clarifying channels of authority, and dealing with complaints and conflicts	58	1.74
46	2.11	*Managerial Skill* Displays accepted management skills in office operation, financial reporting, and staff personnel supervision	58 59	1.74 1.58
47	1.90	*Sharing Congregational Leadership* Actively employs lay leadership in the formation of programs for and in the work of the church	No precise correlation with core cluster items	
48	1.90	*Responsible Leadership* Leads responsibly by pointing out implications of decisions, allowing others to disagree; and ties innovations to parish needs	56 57	2.11 2.07

Comparison of Expectations of the Highest Rank

The ten expectations for beginning ministers that are given the highest rank and represent the qualities that are judged as most desirable and indispensable in ministers are listed in Table 8-11. In analyzing the rela-

TABLE 8-11
Comparisons Between Highest-Ranking (Top Ten) Southern Baptist Clusters and Core Clusters

Southern Baptist Expectations			*Total Group Core Expectations*		
Rank Order	*Name*	*Grand Mean*	*Rank Order*	*Name*	*Grand Mean*
1	Religious Commitment (SBC 23)	2.71	1	Service in Humility (CC 34)	2.52
2.5	Christian Example (SBC 24)	2.63	2	Personal Responsibility (CC 42)	2.43
2.5	Personal Responsibility (SBC 30)	2.63	3	Christian Example (CC 35)	2.42
3.3	Healthy Spirituality (SBC 25)	2.51	4	Acknowledgment of Limitations (CC 36)	2.35
3.3	Service in Humility (SBC 26)	2.51	5	Building Congregational Community (CC 55)	2.34
3.3	Spiritual Counselor (SBC 13)	2.51	6	Fidelity to Tasks and Persons (CC 43)	2.29
4	Community Building (SBC 43)	2.43	7	Perceptive Counseling (CC 21)	2.26
5.5	Competent Counseling (SBC 14)	2.35	8	Positive Approach (CC 44)	2.25
5.5	Professional Development (SBC 17)	2.35	9	Theocentric-Biblical Ministry (CC 2)	2.24
6	Leadership with Respect for People (SBC 44)	2.32	10	Enabling Counseling (CC 22)	2.23

Note: Clusters with identical grand means are given a similar rank order number; for example, 2.5.

tionships between these top ten core and Southern Baptist expectations, it is important to remember that precise correspondence between the expectations does not exist. What must be conceptualized, therefore, is not a mechanical listing of the clusters in rank order vis-à-vis one another but the larger patterns that exist. The first, and most obvious, is the striking agreement in assigning top priority—the first three clusters in each group —to expectations that the minister be a person of Christian faith and character. This assessment, agreed on by both groups, means that the kind of person the beginning minister is as a committed and functioning Christian is seen as more crucial for the beginning minister than professional skills. This does not mean that the minister's professional skills are of no consequence because expectations in this area are generally assessed as important,[23] but it does mean that professional skill in itself is not what has first priority in expectations for ministers among Southern Baptists.

The second pattern to be noted is the shift in emphasis that occurs among the highest ranked expectations in their common stress on the minister's total quality as a person. The expectation that a minister serve with humility is the highest-ranked core cluster, but the third-ranked Southern Baptist expectation. For Southern Baptists, the most highly ranked expectation is religious commitment that puts the mission of Christ first in one's life, shows sensitivity to the leading of the Spirit, and is related to the minister's belief that God has called him or her into the ministry. The stress on what may be termed the "inner dimensions" of personal commitment to Christ and ministry also emerges in the third-ranked Southern Baptist expectation that the minister demonstrate spirituality by relying on prayer and being aware of God's redeeming power. To be sure, Southern Baptists agree with other groups in expecting exemplary Christian lives from their ministers and give this expectation second rank; but in comparison with others Southern Baptists register a definite shift in emphasis from the primacy of the outer to the inner dimensions of piety.[24]

The remaining expectations of the highest rank in both the core and Southern Baptist groups focus more on functional aspects of ministry, but not so sharply that the minister's being may be neatly divided from his or her doing. These very highly ranked expectations for ministers clearly deal with function from the perspective of the kind of person the minister is. This emphasis is consistent in these highest ranked clusters, but not in functionally oriented expectations of the middle range.[25] Southern Baptists, for example, expect their ministers to be counselors who lead persons to deepened spiritual growth (SBC 13), to be professionals who show continuing growth from study and prayerful reflection on experience (SBC 17), to be catalysts for mutual spiritual concern and appreciation in the congregation (SBC 43), and to be leaders who are sensitive to the needs and points of view of others (SBC 44).

But this emphasis on personal spirituality and commitment—as crucial as it is for Southern Baptists—must not be pressed so far as to obscure the general agreement in emphasis that exists between the top ten expectations in each group. When the top ten are viewed from the standpoint of the sections used in the Readiness for Ministry research design, the agreement is striking. Not only do the top ten of both groups occur in the same sections, but their relative distribution is correlated, as illustrated in Table 8-11.

Comparison of Expectations of the Lowest Rank

The expectations of the lowest rank, which articulate how people feel ministers should *not* function, focus mainly on the minister's morality, relationships, and attitudes. Seven Southern Baptist[26] and ten core expectations are assessed as representing undesirable or detrimental features, as shown in Table 8-12. When these two groups are compared, it is striking that the common denominator of intense negative expectations for ministers is in the area of relationships that exhibit a negative attitude.

Southern Baptists and other denominational families have intensely negative reactions to personal immorality, and there is virtually no difference in emphasis between the lowest-ranked expectation of the Southern Baptists and that of other denominational families.

SUMMARY

The Southern Baptist denomination's expectations for its beginning ministers are similar to those of other denominations in many respects. Within the sixty-four core expectations, Southern Baptists are in basic agreement with nearly all denominations in about one-third of the areas and in fairly close agreement with many other denominations in another one-third, although other denominations contrast significantly. Strong similarity also exists between the core and the Southern Baptist expectations at both ends of the spectrum: The personal qualities of the minister—both positive and negative—constitute the areas where the most intense reactions are registered.

But contrasts do exist between Southern Baptists and every other denominational family. Generally speaking, the outstanding difference is in the area of personal evangelism. Southern Baptists expect their ministers actively and personally to seek to bring others to a knowledge of Jesus Christ. It is this area of expectation that most often finds Southern Baptists in significant contrast with other denominational groups. Only three other denominational families agree with Southern Baptists in evangelism; and the tendency is for these to be in contrast or tension with Southern Baptists in the areas of social involvement and action that Southern Baptists assess highly—but not so highly as personal evangelism—in both the core and denominational clusters. Southern Baptists thus expect their ministers to be active in both personal evangelism and social action. Aggressive evangelism is the most visible difference between Southern Baptists and the other large denominations, judged from the perspective of non-Southern Baptists. For the denomination itself, however, the most intense expectation of the minister is commitment to

TABLE 8-12
**Comparisons Between Lowest-Ranking Southern Baptist Cluster (7)
and Core Cluster (10) Responses**

Southern Baptist Expectations			*Total Group Core Expectations*		
Rank Order	*Name*	*Grand Mean*	*Rank Order*	*Name*	*Grand Mean*
			55	Intuitive Domination of Decision Making (CC 60)	−1.32
			56	Total Concentration on Congregational Concerns (CC 20)	−1.42
			57	Alienating Activity (CC 10)	−1.54
42	Total Concentration on Congregational Concerns (SBC 12)	−1.59	58	Secular Lifestyle (CC 51)	−1.57
43	Rigid and Insensitive Attitude (SBC 30)	−1.83	59	Pursuit of Personal Advantage (CC 63)	−1.59
44	Priestly Commitment (SBC 29)	−2.01	60	Irresponsibility to the Congregation (CC 64)	−1.63
45	Professional Immaturity (SBC 39)	−2.07	61	Professional Immaturity (CC 52)	−1.89
46	Secular and Self-Serving Lifestyle (SBC 40)	−2.11	62	Self-Protecting Ministry (CC 54)	−2.02
47	Vocational Maladjustment (SBC 41)	−2.13	63	Priestly Commitment (CC 41)	−2.03
48	Undisciplined and Egotistic Lifestyle (SBC 42)	−2.19	64	Undisciplined Living (CC 53)	−2.08

Christ. And to Southern Baptists, this commitment both assumes and calls for aggressive evangelism and efforts to improve society: expectations that have rather consistently been viewed as alternatives—frequently as mutually exclusive ones—in American religious life.[27]

The beginning minister among Southern Baptists thus faces expectations that are traditionally in tension, and he or she must cope with whatever stress is created by the expectation for a ministry that includes both aggressive personal evangelism and active social concern. Whether Southern Baptists have expectations for their ministers that are in irrevocable opposition and thus face either fragmentation or transition to one emphasis or the other may be debated, but the current conviction of the denomination is that the two expectations are biblical and must be held concurrently. This is the crucial distinctive of Southern Baptist expectations for ministry: The one who would minister must lead people to God in the name of Christ and then must lead them to walk with God by making their faith visible in social concern and action.[28]

NOTES

1. The ordaining of a person to the pastoral ministry among Southern Baptists traditionally involves formal interrogation by a council authorized by the church in each instance. Such a council usually includes several local Southern Baptist pastors, as well as some deacons (laypeople with specific administrative and/or spiritual responsibilities) from the authorizing church.

2. For the procedures, see Chapter 19.

3. Item 116 in the Readiness for Ministry questionnaire.

4. The range of responses is as follows: "highly important," 67.3 percent; "quite important," 25.2 percent; "somewhat important," 6.7 percent; and "undesirable," .8 percent.

5. The response range among all others is "highly important," 31 percent; "quite important," 36.9 percent; "somewhat important," 24.9 percent; and "undesirable," 7.2 percent.

6. For a discussion of cluster analysis and the list of items in the core clusters, see Chapter 5.

7. For the procedures, see Chapter 19.

8. For the specific items in these clusters, see Chapter 5.

9. American Baptist Churches of the USA register lower in intensity of expectations by 4.7 standard scores (laity) and 4.0 standard scores (clergy) for an average of 4.35, and 5 standard scores indicate the usual level of significant contrast.

10. It should be noted that this cluster does not feature a rejection of social concern, as does Cluster 20.

11. Clusters included in this category are CC 1, 5, 7, 28, 29, 30, and 33.

12. The clusters included are CC 3, 8, 10, 11, 21, 22, 23, 25, 44, 55, and 56.

13. Clusters in this category are CC 34, 36, 38, 39, 42, 43, 45, 47, 52, and 54.

14. Clusters CC 14, 16, 18, 20, 26, 46, 50, and 57 are included.

15. See Note 9.

16. This paragraph is deeply indebted to the illuminating study of John Lee Eighmy, *Churches in Cultural Captivity: A History of the Social Attitudes of Southern Baptists* (Knoxville: University of Tennessee Press, 1972).

17. For the procedure, see Chapter 19.

18. The working taxonomy is discussed fully in Chapter 19.

19. For titles and item content of core clusters, see Chapter 5.

20. This item is included in Core Cluster 19, but has a mean of only −0.51 versus a Southern Baptist mean of 1.10.

21. This emphasis is included in "Theologically Oriented Counseling" (CC 24).

22. This item is Core Cluster 42, "Personal Responsibility"; but Southern Baptists place the item in a social rather than individual context.

23. The grand mean in core clusters and Southern Baptist clusters for expectations that relate to professional skills are generally between "somewhat important" (1) and "quite important" (2).

24. Core Cluster 37, "Commitment Reflecting Religious Piety," which is quite similar to Southern Baptist Cluster 23, has a grand mean of 2.19 and a rank order of 12.

25. Examples are Core Clusters 1, 13, 15, 47, and 58.

26. The Southern Baptist Cluster 37, with the rank order of 41, "Denominational Loyalty," has a grand mean of −1.05 but is not included in the group because the cluster does not represent a low assessment of expectations or loyalty to the denomination by its members. The first two items in the cluster are positive for Southern Baptists: "Usually follows directives from denominational leaders" (Item 509) and "Gives a rational reason when one cannot comply with a denominational request" (Item 506). But the next item is "Regularly wears clerical collar or other distinctive clothing" (Item 486), and although this is denominational loyalty it is negative for Southern Baptists, is given a mean of −2.85 and results in the total cluster's being conceived of negatively from the viewpoint of the grand mean, −1.05. If the third item, dealing with distinctive clothing, is omitted, the grand mean is positive: 0.70.

27. Kenneth Cauthen, *Impact of American Religious Liberalism* (New York: Harper & Row, 1962) pp. 3–37.

28. Southern Baptists are generally perceived as restricting their activism to certain traditional moral issues, with little concern for such issues as industrial pollution. This popular conception must be challenged. The statements of the Southern Baptist Convention agencies take firm stands on matters related to industrial pollution, euthanasia, abortion, drug abuse, and racial prejudice, among other things. To be sure, the loudest voices are heard in areas clearly understood to be issues of morality, such as pornography, but among the larger and more sophisticated churches, specific action has been taken in social action areas that are not traditionally associated with Southern Baptists. In any case, the study does not identify the particular kind of social action that is in view. Baptists are selective in terms of the social action issues that they are most aggressively involved in, and the selectivity varies rather widely among churches of the denomination. This tends to diffuse and scatter the influence more than in a denomination with greater hierarchical unity.

9

Christian Church
(Disciples of Christ)

Edwin L. Becker and David S. Schuller

This chapter analyzes responses from members of the Christian Church (Disciples of Christ) from two vantage points. In the first section, the authors proceed sequentially through the seven basic parts of the study's questionnaire, comparing the clusters formed by Disciples' responses with those core clusters formed by the responses of the total group. In this manner, the most highly valued of all the ministerial expectations held by the Disciples can be analyzed, as well as those distinctive characteristics of this denomination extracted from a comparison of it with the total group. In the second section, Disciples' responses are compared to the core clusters with those of the other sixteen denominational families.

The historical evolution of this denomination continues to inform its character. The Christian Church, born on the American frontier, still possesses a concept of ministry in which the twin principles of voluntarism and congregational polity are evident. These result in the demand that its ministers be both skillful in meeting the personal needs of church and possess the capacity to keep a congregation intact and vital.

Edwin L. Becker is Professor of Sociology of Religion, Christian Theological Seminary, Indianapolis, and an ordained minister in the Christian Church (Disciples of Christ). The author of *Responding to God's Call*, he has conducted studies of the church in developing countries and of urban policy in the United States.

Pragmatic tests of meeting congregational needs make the Disciples' minister particularly vulnerable to "grass-roots" opinion. While orthodoxy and denominational loyalty are not sensitive issues, the practical test of actual competence remains the fundamental question.

Ranking highest among Disciples' qualifications for ministry is personal honesty. Nearly as important is skill as a counselor. While placing heavy accent on the minister as a person and on his or her own faith commitment, the Disciples place an even higher premium on leadership than do other denominational families. Disciples differ distinctly from other denominations in attaching more importance to a ministry outside the walls of the church. Supporting such a broad concept of ministry to the community is an above-average emphasis on a minister's being open to new ideas from a wide variety of sources, to his or her valuing diversity, and to facilitating greater understanding of issues. Finally, Disciples warmly endorse a certain openness in leadership style within a congregation; at the same time, they resist certain dimensions of denominational loyalty.

The number of responses from Disciples to the Readiness for Ministry questionnaire is not sufficient to permit a comparison of Disciples laity with Disciples clergy. The denomination is analyzed as one bloc.

There was a time when the Christian Church (Disciples of Christ) could and did boast that it was the largest religious body originating on the North American continent. Taking form in the United States during the early and mid-nineteenth century, the Disciples' concept of ministry was strongly influenced by voluntarism, which modified nearly every Protestant denomination's polity, in practice if not in theory. Called by Sidney Mead "the evangelical conception of ministry," it was characterized by self-reliance and tested by the question of the pragmatist, "Does it work?"[1]

The Disciples movement began and spread in western Pennsylvania and west of the Appalachians; in both areas, there had been no tradition of an established religion. The founders were Presbyterian ministers who broke with their parent denominations, which at that time were rigidly sectarian, to proclaim Christian unity based on the Scriptures. They were convinced that a simple, noncreedal, and rational interpretation of Scripture would enable Christians to transcend their sectarian loyalties and come together into one Christian fellowship. Within a free-enterprise religious market, these pastors and their early followers competed successfully along the frontier, winning established congregations to their point of view, as well as forming new ones. By preaching, debating, and writing, they gained attention and commitment. For several decades, they had no sponsoring body, but were truly entrepreneurs of the faith.

Notable among these early leaders was Alexander Campbell, editor, publicist, preacher, and founder of a college and of several journals. He was tremendously influential in determining the style and rationale for the new movement out of which came the Christian Church (Disciples of Christ). The concept of ministry that he enunciated was set firmly within a context of rugged congregationalism. Ministers were made, ordained, and called by local congregations. According to Alexander Campbell, "The call to the ministry consisted neither in a personal ambition on the part of the one called, a mandate from the Holy Spirit, nor a transmission of authority from a sacerdotal system; but in a social compact with the church."[2]

The call to ministry as a "social compact" is an important ingredient in understanding the nature of Disciples ministry to this day. Clarence Lemon, who knew the Disciples denomination well, wrote that "to Campbell and his followers, the social contract was between the local congregation and the minister. There was no presbytery, or connectionalism, to which the clergy had obligation. Thus any congregation might ordain a minister, without much regard to fitness, education or, at times, even character. The premise for securing and ordaining ministers left the whole matter to congregational individualism and gave free play to the personal ambitions of individual preachers."[3] Potential ministers are to this day called "candidates"; they are elected by vote of the members and hold only the office that the congregation recognizes and grants to them.

Langdon Gilkey has suggested, correctly, that the Disciples were a sect of the Enlightenment.[4] Its members never downgraded education for their ministers and were as active as any nineteenth-century American evangelical church in establishing colleges. Neither did they elevate the work of the Holy Spirit to a central position in determining the call to ministry nor attribute to it a primary role in the formation of the church. In these ways, the Disciples could be distinguished from those other important evangelical churches whose suspicions of education accompanied their attacks on a hierarchy.

The staunch voluntarism and congregationalism have persisted through most of the life of the denomination and have undergone major change only in recent decades. As a result of a process known by the denomination as "restructure," important modifications have been made in its system, changes that have reflected a corporate understanding of the nature of the church. Even today the congregation continues to exercise final authority in the call of a minister to its pulpit. The validity of ordination is ensured by the inclusion of laity from two sponsoring congregations in the laying on of hands.

However, no longer do congregations act on their own. Ministerial "standing"—granted to women as well as to men—is not with congregations, but with regional offices of the church under terms set by the regional body. Ordination standards are established at the regional level of the denomination. It is doubtful, nevertheless, whether this shift of responsibility for certification of ministers from a local congregation to the regional level has decisively changed the concept of the minister as a religious leader who is primarily responsible to a congregation and whose qualifications are determined by the needs of the congregation where he or she works. The "social compact" between a minister and a congregation continues to be the determining factor in establishing a ministry, even though quite radically different procedures have been introduced to "credential" a minister. The author of a recent comprehensive survey of ministry among the Disciples has stated,

The Christian Church is an organization characterized by the voluntary association of members and groups, lay control, aversion to clerical or hierarchical authority, and a corporate ministry dependent on the maintenance of a spirit of cooperation and consensus. All of these factors require political skills for effective ministry and that requirement runs throughout the whole structure of the denomination and all forms of ministry. Political skill in this context means the ability to establish a constituency of support and trust among the members of the congregation in addition to shaping and reshaping consensus among the membership. . . . Within the Christian Church, the office of pastoral minister, as office, contains little formative power today. The capacity for influence and change lies in the interrelationship of trust and support between pastor and people.[5]

Voluntarism and congregationalism remain significant ingredients in a Disciples concept of ministry.

This brief summary of the Disciples' understanding of the status of a minister suggests that substantive expectations for ministry are tied directly to the expectations a congregation has for itself. Concepts of ministry and of the purpose and nature of the congregation are bound together. A congregation sees a minister first and foremost as its own leader and only secondly as an embodiment of some larger concept of the church's purpose. The successful minister acknowledges this fact and deals with the ensuing tensions between the expectations of the local congregation and his or her own personal commitments, which often are shaped by broader theological and cultural influences.

Disciples' responses to the survey imply sufficient uniqueness to warrant separate designation as one of the seventeen denominational families. Because the replies to the questionnaire are so few, particularly on the part of the laity, no attempt has been made to analyze lay and ministerial responses separately. The following tables and discussion present the findings of the survey insofar as they point up qualities and skills expected by Disciples in the beginning minister. The basis of organization of the discussion is the seven taxonomic sections of the questionnaire. Factor analysis of the responses to the items in each section for the total group of respondents (across all seventeen denominational families) produces sixty-four core clusters or dimensions of expectations. This same method of analysis is then applied to the responses of Disciples, resulting in clusters unique to this denominational family. (See Chapter 4 for a fuller description of core clusters and denominational clusters.)

MINISTRIES TO THE RELIGIOUS COMMUNITY

As the Disciples' responses to questions concerning ministries to the religious community are analyzed, eight clusters emerge. (See Table 9-1.) When these clusters are compared with the core criteria, four emerge as unique. The first and highest-ranking cluster in this area of ministry focuses on worship. While bearing some resemblance to one of the core clusters ("Competent Preaching and Worship Leading," core cluster, or CC, 5), its basic accent is different. The Disciples' cluster revolves around leading worship in a way that helps people to feel the closeness of God. It includes the elements of interesting preaching and worship celebrated in a professional, yet personal manner. From pioneer days onward, Disciples have accented worship and the weekly celebration of the Lord's Supper. The weekly service is led by lay elders so that this central feature of worship can be observed even in the absence of an ordained minister.

Secondly, the Disciples demonstrate an interest in the educational ministry of their pastors, particularly as this touches the education of laity. They are concerned that lay teachers be trained and that the minister help laypeople confidently to share their faith. This concept includes helping the congregation keep in touch with disinterested youth.

The third unique dimension involves a versatile quality of leadership. It displays itself in the skills needed to relate thoughtfully to youth and children as well as to the whole congregation in worship.

Finally, the respondents identify a concern for an open and spontaneous style of ministry. This would be evident in nondefensiveness on the part of a minister, in openness to members of his or her congregation, and in participation with other ministers in ecumenical projects.

With these four characteristics providing a general framework or context of this denominational family's expectations, note can be made (in Table 9-2) that Disciples differ from the total group of the remaining denominational families in attaching significantly *less* importance to certain items in "Ministries to the Religious Community."

The historic mission of the denomination reflects itself in the much greater importance attached to a minister's having thought through a theological stance in cooperating with other denominations, to participating in ecumenical projects, and to a type of preaching that acknowledges the special personal needs of the hearers.[6]

TABLE 9-1
Christian Church (Disciples of Christ) Clusters Relating to
"Ministries to the Religious Community"

Disciples Cluster No.	Disciples Cluster	Disciples Grand Mean	Disciples Rank Order
1	*Competent in Preaching and Worship* Prepares well for preaching and worship that is both interesting and creates a feeling of God's presence	2.36	13
2	*Education of Laity* Assists laypersons to become confident teachers of their faith both within and outside the congregation	2.17	18
3	*Bible in Daily Life of Church Members* Makes use of biblical resources when guiding persons in their personal decisions and in matters affecting public ceremonies of the church	2.11	21
4	*Innovative-Supportive Educational Leadership* Employs effective and interesting methods in own teaching ministry and encourages students and other teachers in new experiences	1.91	27

MINISTRIES TO THE COMMUNITY AND WORLD

In common with other denominational families, the Disciples place less accent on ministries extending to the broader community and world than on those person-to-person ministries within the congregation. Table 9-3 presents the five Disciples clusters in this second area. The Disciples, however, show a special sensitivity to the importance of keeping people aware that their own needs and the needs of others in the world are inseparable. While attaching the same sense of importance to "Aggressive Political Leadership" (CC 18), a political issue characteristic has developed that describes active speaking and organizing in the political sphere based on a study of the issues in the light of Scripture.

Disciples differ from other Christian bodies by disagreeing with the

TABLE 9-1 — *CONTINUED*

Disciples Cluster No.	Disciples Cluster	Disciples Grand Mean	Disciples Rank Order
5	*Versatile Leadership* Has sufficient variety of skills to relate well to youth and children, as well as the total congregation through worship and music	1.88	28
6	*Sensitive and Contemporary* Can use both traditional and contemporary materials effectively, including the arts, to communicate the gospel in teaching and in worship	1.77	30
7	*Open and Spontaneous Style* Can participate without defensiveness, as demonstrated in dialogue with congregational involvement in ecumenical projects and by changing worship in response to the Spirit	1.56	32
8	*Witnesses to the Gospel* Through preaching and worship, is able to bring people to Jesus Christ	1.15	37

idea that "Clergy should stick to religion and not concern themselves with social, economic, and political questions" (Item 121). Similarly, they are more likely to insist that "Political struggle is a rightful concern of the church" (Item 128). An aggressive pursuit of converts is not part of their pattern; they are less likely than average "to ask strangers about the condition of their souls" (Item 135).

A sense of this group's priorities for the mission of the church emerges in Table 9-4 when we see its members place a statistically *higher* importance on specific items in "Ministries to Community and World."

MINISTRIES TO PERSONS UNDER STRESS

In viewing "Ministries to Persons under Stress," the Disciples responses do not form any expectations that differ from those enunciated by the core

TABLE 9-2

Items from "Ministries to the Religious Community" That the Christian Church (Disciples of Christ) Ranks Significantly Lower in Importance Than Other Denominational Families

| | | Percent of Respondents Who Rate Items as "Important" | |
| | | | |
Item No.	Item	Disciples	All Other Denominational Families
42	Preaches with authority	67	78
47	When he is through preaching, you are conscious of Jesus Christ	75	86
64	Preaches sermons that awaken listeners to their sinfulness and need for a Savior	42	63
75	Quotes much Scripture from memory when preaching or teaching	7	22
78	Teaches the meaning of sacraments	68	78
92	Understands and appreciates the dogmatic and liturgical foundations of prayer	32	53

Note: Significance at or below the .001 level. "Important" includes all those answers included in the response categories "very important" and "quite important."

clusters. (See Table 9-5.) In general, clergy and parishioners alike endorse the importance of a minister as a resourceful, sensitive, informed counselor. In agreement with other denominational families, a desire for a minister who expresses a spiritual and theological dimension when counseling is indicated. Note the two Disciples clusters (16 and 17) that heavily underscore the desire for a strong theological undergirding to a minister's counseling. The first focuses sharply on the integration of one's theology with counseling skills. The second indicates the possibility of forgiveness and spiritual growth eventuating from the person's ministry.

A slight pattern of difference arises in a few other points. This group does not want a minister who tries to provide solutions for all problems. They want pastoral help to be given with no spiritual strings attached. They place significantly lower emphasis than does the total group on "When counseling, will sometimes confront person with the need to be-

**Christian Church (Disciples of Christ) Clusters Relating to
"Ministries to the Community and World"**

Disciples Cluster No.	Disciples Cluster	Disciples Grand Mean	Disciples Rank Order
9	*Concern for Others* Keeps people aware that their own needs and the needs of others in the world are inseparable; that by being open to others they learn about themselves	1.96	25
10	*Political Issue Ministry* Will take personal risks in political activity based on a study of the issues in light of Scripture	0.90	38
11	*Involvement for Social Justice* By speaking, teaching, organizing will attempt to involve the congregation in programs to secure justice for the oppressed	0.88	39
12	*Ministry of Confrontation* Expresses concern for oppressed people by confronting public officials	0.60	40
13	*Social Action Leadership* Joins with others in social action to effect change that he or she finds theologically justified	0.32	41

lieve" (Item 260). They do feel it is important that clergy train groups to carry out specialized ministries.

THE MINISTER AS THEOLOGIAN AND THINKER

In the broad area of the "Minister as Theologian and Thinker," too, the general expectations emerging from the core clusters tend to be reflected by Disciples responses as well. In Table 9-6, one Disciples cluster (22) emerges in a somewhat unique form, although its basic ingredients are familiar. The cluster pivots about a minister's knowledge of the historical

TABLE 9-4

Items from "Ministries to the Community and World" That the Christian Church (Disciples of Christ) Ranks Significantly Higher in Importance Than Other Denominational Families

		Percent of Respondents Who Rate Items as "Important"	
Item No.	*Item*	*Disciples*	*All Other Denominational Families*
118	Locates people to whom he might refer individuals not helped by community agencies	71	59
128	Insists that political struggle is a rightful concern of the church	41	29
136	Works to make sure that all people are free to buy property in areas of their choice	27	19
137	Organizes study groups in congregation or community to discuss public affairs	42	22
139	Urges members to be both informed and responsive to community needs	86	73
140	Serves on task forces or committees to improve conditions at school or in the neighborhood	59	36
141	Shows concern about liberation of oppressed people	72	56
142	Uses principles and methods of organization for political change	32	18
149	Makes contact with the political thought and life in the community	57	38
151	Organizes action groups in the congregation to accomplish directly some political or social goal	23	17
153	Provides community leadership in ways that awaken trust	83	69

TABLE 9-4 — *CONTINUED*

Item No.	Item	Percent of Respondents Who Rate Items as "Important"	
		Disciples	All Other Denominational Families
155	Works toward racial integration in the community	71	52
156	Speaks prophetically out of a conviction that the Church is the conscience of humanity	77	60
158	Works with different community factions	56	37

Note: Significance is at .001 level. "Important" includes all those answers included in the response categories "very important" and "quite important."

development of the church and of his or her own denomination. It includes the highly valued quality of continued theological growth through research and study.

A generally sophisticated, liberal expectation for the Disciples ministry is reflected in four items in which the denominational family ranks significantly higher than other families. These higher expectations include regularly attending the theater and cinema (Item 303), advocating a "liberation theology" (Item 328), working collegially with members of other professions (Item 330), and using one's "own inner life as one means for testing ideas and interpreting events" (Item 287).

The group expresses lower expectations in a series of items reflecting certain traditional biblical teachings: the affirmation of Jesus Christ as the Son of God (Item 293); acknowledgment of the presence and activity of a personal devil (Satan, Item 313); and treatment of the Bible, "interpreted by the Church, as the final authority in all matters of faith" (Item 287). One suspects that the qualification regarding "interpreted by the Church" heavily influences the very low rating of the last item (only 10 percent of Disciples, versus 40 percent of the remaining group consider this "highly important"; and nearly one-half—48 percent—of the Disciples consider it "detrimental" to effective ministry). For the other group of items, all reflect a distancing from any statement that ascribes too much authority

TABLE 9-5
Christian Church (Disciples of Christ) Clusters Relating to "Ministries to Persons under Stress"

Disciples Cluster No.	Disciples Cluster	Disciples Grand Mean	Disciples Rank Order
14	*Paraprofessional Counselor* A resourceful, sensitive, informed counselor to people under stress with insight to know when to refer persons for professional help	2.59	2
15	*Empathetic Ministry* Supportive and freeing to people experiencing stress by listening carefully and sensitively	2.57	3
16	*Counseling from a Theological Base* Counsels persons out of own theology of ministry as well as with skills	2.36	12
17	*Counseling as a Christian Minister* Responds positively to calls for help and senses a spiritual theological objective when counseling	2.32	16
18	*Cominis try to Individuals* Develops groups of people within the church to minister to their own needs and to particular needs of persons in the community	1.93	26
19	*Exercise of Pastoral Authority* In counseling situations, is able to exercise his or her ministerial authority in appropriate ways that will help people faced with crucial decisions	1.63	31

to the denomination. Thus the group ranks lower in importance a dovetailing of the minister's own beliefs and the teaching of the denomination with the task of identifying the denomination's moral expectations to parishioners. Yet Disciples respondents perceive as more important than other groups the need to encourage members to acknowledge one another as the Body of Christ, even though they hold divergent theological views.

TABLE 9-6
**Christian Church (Disciples of Christ) Clusters Relating to
"The Minister as Theologian and Thinker"**

Disciples Cluster No.	*Disciples Cluster*	*Disciples Grand Mean*	*Disciples Rank Order*
20	*Theological Clarity* Able to state theological doctrines clearly and ready to help persons find answers to religious questions	2.38	10
21	*A Theological and Ethical Resource* Expresses complex theological matters in understandable language; can help persons clarify their own theological and ethical thinking	2.35	14
22	*Theologically Informed* Studies regularly to keep up-to-date theologically and to enlarge own understanding of the Scripture and the history of the church	2.18	17
23	*A Learned Minister* Widely read in contemporary literature and in social issues; able to incorporate that learning into preaching and teaching	1.96	24
24	*Trusts Experience* Has own life together theologically and ethically so as to be open to a wide variety of issues and experiences without becoming victimized by popular fads	1.40	35

THE MINISTER'S PERSONAL COMMITMENT OF FAITH

While the basic shape of the Disciples' expectations for ministers is similar to that of other denominational families, in many cases the expectations themselves are somewhat lower. (See Table 9-7.) One cluster of expectations, derived from Disciples responses (Disciples Cluster 28), differs from Core Cluster 39, "Acceptance of Counsel." "Handling of Personal Dissatisfaction" has as its locus for the Disciples the ability to confide in a

TABLE 9-7
Christian Church (Disciples of Christ) Clusters Relating to
"The Minister's Personal Commitment of Faith"

Disciples Cluster No.	Disciples Cluster	Disciples Grand Mean	Disciples Rank Order
25	*A Personal Faith* It is obvious that the Gospel is known as "good news" for the minister personally and therefore he/she continues to grow in faith	2.54	4
26	*Recognition of One's Own Needs* Sincerely acknowledges his/her own spiritual dependence and can ask for and receive forgiveness	2.40	7
27	*Ministry as Calling* Knows his/her call to ministry to be clearly from God, a calling shared by the spouse; nurtures the calling by practice of spiritual discipline	2.04	23
28	*Handling of Personal Dissatisfaction* Can acknowledge own problems with the ministry and can talk with trusted persons about frustrations and doubts	1.47	33
29	*Religious Language* Talks about own Christian life in particularistic terms and tells of experiences with God that set him/her apart from others (see CC 40)	−1.19	42
30	*Priestly Disciplines* Regular in practice of religious disciplines associated with one's ordination (see CC 41)	−2.80	44

trusted person. The other two items in the cluster permit an interesting glance into Disciples thinking. The two items linked or associated empirically in this cluster include "Admits privately that the ministry has its disappointments" and "Actively tries to change the traditional shape of ministry to fit the future better."

When the Christian Church (Disciples of Christ) response is analyzed on the level of the individual items, in only one instance does it stand significantly higher than those of other denominational families. This is related to personal doubt: "Openly admits to times of doubt and struggle over own personal faith" (Item 345). But as Table 9-8 demonstrates, frequently this denominational family's expectations are significantly lower in items relating to personal piety.

TABLE 9-8
Items from "Minister's Commitment of Faith" That the Christian Church (Disciples of Christ) Ranks Significantly Lower in Importance Than Other Denominational Families

		Percent of Respondents Who Rate Items as "Important"	
Item No.	Item	Disciples	All Other Denominational Families
340	Views the call or appointment to a parish once accepted, as a calling of God	65	91
343	Shows sensitivity to the leading of the Holy Spirit	65	80
344	Speaks of being "sanctified"	6	21
348	Interprets the decision to enter the ministry as a personal call from God	52	76
354	Refers to self as a "born-again" Christian	13	37
358	Expresses desire for all to recognize the reign of the Lord	59	77
369	Acknowledges own sin and confesses this to God	87	91
377	In social conversation, talks about what the Lord has done recently in own life	15	32
384	Actively engages in intercessory prayer on behalf of others	60	74

Note: Significance is at .001 level. "Important" includes all those answers included in the response categories "very important" and "quite important."

THE MINISTER AS A PERSON (POSITIVE)

As Disciples reflect on the positive personal characteristics they consider important in their ministers, their responses indicate they use six major dimensions in their thinking. Three of these are distinctly different from those formed by the rest of the denominational families in North America who participated in this project. (See Table 9-9.)

TABLE 9-9

Christian Church (Disciples of Christ) Clusters Relating to "The Minister as a Person (Positive)"

Disciples Cluster No.	Disciples Cluster	Disciples Grand Mean	Disciples Rank Order
31	*Personal Honesty* Can express feelings honestly with strength to resist pressures to compromise	2.60	1
32	*Responsible Spouse and Parent* Is loving and supportive of members of own family	2.48	6
33	*Self-Understanding* Can recognize own feelings toward difficult tasks and persons, and is able to handle them so that they do not interfere with the practice of ministry	2.39	8
34	*Self-Direction* Will take controversial stands as a Christian, granting the same rights to those who differ	2.15	19
35	*Realistic Acceptance of Clergy Status* Has own material needs in order and under control, not overly concerned about other people's opinions	1.47	34
36	*Response to Authority* Relates to persons in authority and other clergy without resentment or envy, distinguishing between what cannot and what should and can be changed	1.35	36

The Disciples Cluster 31 ("Personal Honesty") is of special significance because it is the highest-ranked cluster among the Disciples (grand mean of 2.60). It is composed of four items. (See Table 9-10.) This is an interesting dimension in which honesty is the underlying variable for expressing affection, fulfilling promises, and maintaining personal integrity. Such honesty becomes a key to adaptability.

Disciples Cluster 33 ("Self-Understanding") shares many of the same items with Core Cluster 43 ("Fidelity to Tasks and Persons"). But this Disciples cluster centers in the further development of pastoral skills. It incorporates the theme of working in difficult or stressful areas of ministry while behaving calmly, positively, and in a rational manner toward other people. It combines the essence of two core clusters, "Fidelity to Tasks and Persons" (CC 43) and "Positive Approach" (CC 44) and shows how they are differentiated.

Another cluster dealing with a realistic acceptance of one's clergy status (Disciples Cluster 35) is unique. It shares only a single item with the core cluster of a similar title, "Acceptance of Clergy Role" (CC 47). The Disciples cluster centers on the minister's not drawing attention to self, relating this to an acceptance of the discrepancy clergy may experience with regard to their income and status and that of other professions and also relating this to the ability to live on the level of one's parishioners.

Three of the ten highest-ranked characteristics concern the person of the minister. Disciples want a minister who is, above all, honest—honest with his or her own feelings, honest with people, honest and responsible in dealing with his or her own family, and growing in pastoral skills in such

TABLE 9-10
**Christian Church (Disciples of Christ) Cluster 31, Ratings
Relating to "Personal Honesty"**

Factor Load	Item No.	Item	Disciples Mean
.57	469	Demonstrates honest affection for other people	2.51
.57	505	Keeps own word—fulfills promises	2.78
.53	485	Adapts well to new situations or circumstances	2.43
.38	513	Maintains personal integrity despite pressures to compromise	2.69
		Grand Mean	2.60

a way that honest ministry can be extended to the greatest number of people.

THE MINISTER AS A PERSON (NEGATIVE)

An analysis of what a denominational family finds most objectionable in a minister provides a commentary on its conceptions of piety. Disciples differ from other denominations in ranking four actions as more detrimental. They deal with the telling of dirty jokes, visiting nightclubs, smoking heavily in public, and gambling. Three of these same items appear as Core Cluster 51. The Disciples cluster that ranks as the most detrimental includes a hostile evaluation of gambling, occasional intoxication, the visiting of nightclubs, and involvement in illicit sexual affairs (one is reminded of the vices that frequently proved most destructive of home and community during the continent's pioneer past).

The Disciples also distinguish two specific negative characteristics, rather than the core group's single omnibus cluster, 54 ("Self-Protecting Ministry"). One (Disciples Cluster 39) centers on the avoidance of intimacy; it describes the minister who preaches abstractly, gossips, gives the impression of being in a hurry, and interprets criticism of programs as a personal affront. The other (Disciples Cluster 37) is a large cluster that describes a self-centered ministry; it revolves, interestingly, about the item "Talks as though unable to forgive self" (Item 574).

The five most detrimental qualities that can be found among ministers are described by Disciples in Table 9-11.

THE MINISTER AS A LEADER

The Disciples response implies an above-average sensitivity to the minister's role as leader. Disciples appear to place a higher premium on leadership than do the other denominational families (see Table 9-12). Four clusters unique to the Disciples are so highly valued that they outrank any of the core clusters dealing with leadership. The most highly ranked of the Disciples clusters dealing with leadership, "Skilled in Group Leadership," is a rich cluster that centers on facilitating greater understanding of changes that occur in the congregation and of controversial issues. However, the emphasis of this cluster is unmistakably on the encouragement of the broadest possible base of participation in congregational leadership. The following examples of items making up this Disciples cluster illustrate the desire by Disciples for such shared leadership: "In group discussion, stimulates many, not just a few, to participate" (Item 696); "Works to broaden the base of participation in the decision-making process of the

TABLE 9-11
Christian Church (Disciples of Christ) Clusters Relating to
"The Minister as a Person (Negative)"

Disciples Cluster No.	Disciples Cluster	Disciples Grand Mean	Disciples Rank Order
37	*Interpersonal Relations* Exercises ministerial authority in ways that are destructive to interpersonal relations, preventing growth in others as well as in self	−2.16	48
38	*Personal Lifestyle* Indulges in costly, personally debilitative activities that bring disrepute to the ministry	−2.12	47
39	*Avoidance of Intimacy* Does not deal honestly with people, is unable to relate positively to them, and does not take their needs seriously	−2.07	46
40	*Emotional Immaturity* Can respond positively only to persons who praise him/her, talks about personal problems openly, and "threatens" to leave ministry	−1.91	45
41	*Self-Centered* Unable to get self out of the way sufficiently to minister to other persons	−1.71	43

parish" (Item 729); "Shares leadership with lay leaders chosen by the congregation" (Item 695); "Helps people know why changes are being made and what they will be" (Item 718); and "Discourages use of stereo-typed sex roles in assigning responsible positions within the congregation" (Item 700). This cluster ranks highest of all the Disciples clusters concerning leadership skills; and it ranks fifth overall of the forty-eight Disciples clusters.

Another highly ranked cluster dealing with leadership concerns responsible church membership. It revolves about finding the real reasons for people's dropping out of church, and it includes teaching responsibility for the financial support of the congregation, as well as meeting with lay leaders to set goals consistent with their mission and potential.

TABLE 9-12
**Christian Church (Disciples of Christ) Clusters Relating to
"The Minister as a Leader"**

Disciples Cluster No.	Disciples Cluster	Disciples Grand Mean	Disciples Rank Order
42	*Skill in Group Leadership* Takes care that information is widely shared and understood, emphasizes lay participation in leadership	2.45	5
43	*Concern for Responsible Church Membership* Takes seriously the need of people to be responsible members of the church	2.39	9
44	*Mutual Trust* Stays close to members, does not dominate others, avoids "surprises" in exercise of own leadership	2.38	11
45	*Builds Sense of Community* Leads church in activities that build community and prepares congregation carefully for change; keeps low profile as a change agent	2.35	15
46	*Planning Strategy* Sees that plans are consistent with long-range goals, recruiting leaders carefully with clear criteria in mind	2.15	20
47	*Group Process Skills* Facilitates discussion in groups, deals with conflict constructively, keeps interpersonal relationships in the congregation open and honest	2.06	22
48	*Just Administration* Uses own authority fairly and treats colleagues and employees honestly and justly	1.78	29

The pragmatism noted earlier in this chapter is perhaps echoed in two other clusters in this section dealing with leadership. Neither ranks so highly as the two clusters just considered ("Skill in Group Leadership" and "Concern for Responsible Church Membership"); however, these two additional clusters are still viewed by Disciples respondents as "quite important." Each cluster is fairly short. The first emphasizes the importance of planning specific projects within the context of an overall parish strategy, recruitment and orientation of the most qualified persons for a particular task, and a continuous examination by groups of the reasons for the continued existence of their group. The second cluster, picking up again the theme of pragmatism, is composed of the same items as Core Cluster 59, although the items load in a slightly different fashion. In the core cluster, the central item is "Relates to staff in a manner consistent with own theology" (Item 711). In the Disciples cluster, the central item or locus is not one individual's theology, but rather a pressing of a governing board for fair treatment of church employees. The final item in this cluster stresses the importance of dealing in a direct and positive manner with a staff member whose services must be terminated.

Thus far the analysis has described the models of ministry that emerge from the Disciples responses. One other question can be asked with regard to the data: "How do Disciples responses vary from those of the other sixteen families of denominations when analyzed only on the basis of core clusters?"

As we scan all sixty-four dimensions, our first impression is that the Disciples tend to be similar to the mainstream of American Protestantism. The study, therefore, confirms the Disciples and several other mainline denominational families in most respects as "American" churches. Voluntarism in American religion makes denominations peculiarly vulnerable and responsive to "grass-roots" opinion. The test of ministry is essentially pragmatic practicality focused on the needs of the congregation. The three broad characteristics on which most agreement exists among all seventeen denominational families (and to which the greatest degrees of importance are attached) include an "Open, Affirming Style" (Factor 4), "Congregational Leadership" (Factor 8), and the ability of "Caring for Persons under Stress" (Factor 9). The personal and congregational orientation among both laypeople and ministers is strongly affirmed by the survey. This finding would not provoke surprise among Disciples—pragmatism and congregationalism are in this denominational family's blood.

One tangible evidence of Disciples accents on openness and response to congregational needs is the inclusion of programmatic courses within their seminaries. A generation ago, an acute need for ministerial leadership in religious education within local congregations was expressed. Each Disciples seminary responded with courses and faculty appointments in that area. Within the past twenty years, attention has been called to a need for skills in counseling. Today, each Disciples seminary has at least one, and in some instances two, full-time teachers in the area, and all seminaries have surrounded themselves with a core of skilled practitioners from hospitals and other community institutions for the clinical training of their students.

Robert Michaelsen (in a companion essay to that of Sidney Mead, referred to at the beginning of this chapter) pointed up the tendency of Protestant ministry in America to focus on the practical needs of people and of congregational leadership. "Ministerial education," he wrote, "has moved away from the classical pattern toward a greater emphasis on practical arts and vocational training."[7]

But voluntarism and congregationalism have not only resulted in a concept of ministry that is essentially pragmatic; that is, in judging ministers for their skills in meeting personal needs and their capacity to keep a congregation intact and vital. Voluntarism and congregationalism have also resulted in a close identification of the churches with the people of North America. American religions are religions of the people, reflecting their diverse cultural expressions and affirming their varied identifications within a pluralistic society. Ministers on this continent have been prevented from constituting themselves as a special class. This fact saves from absurdity the idea that one way to determine criteria of competence in ministry is to ask those people who minister and those to whom ministry is extended. Ministers and laypeople *are* the church, and what they think the church is and should be is crucial information for theological seminaries.

Historically, the Disciples seminaries have developed within a context of freedom from, and intimacy with, the denomination's ministers and congregations. They are not formally controlled by the churches, yet they are dependent on the churches for students and for money. Although there have been attempts at heresy hunts directed at particular seminaries, the denomination has no judicial nor financial structure through which such attacks could be made effective. The noncreedal Enlightenment tradition of the Disciples has proved sufficiently sturdy to provide autonomy of thought within the seminaries.

Yet pragmatic tests have been applied to the seminary graduates. Orthodoxy and loyalty to a denominational position have seldom been made tests of readiness for ministry. The leadership of a congregation and a cooperative and open spirit have been the measures of competence used by Disciples. This body has been free for decades from attacks on its seminaries by organizations of ministers or congregations. The issue of "control" has been raised when denominational funds have been in the process of being allocated, but the issue has been neither directed at the curriculum nor at faculty appointments, but rather at questions of capital needs, expansion of facilities, and endowments. Decisions within recent years to close seminaries were accompanied by no charges that they had been indifferent to the needs of the churches or that their graduates were incompetent. The money was not cut off at a central denominational spigot. The decisions were based on the assessment by their own governing boards that they could no longer afford to continue a viable seminary at current costs.

Accompanying this freedom is an intimacy between the denomination and its seminaries. Intimacy suggests frankness and sometimes confrontation between parties who recognize their mutual interdependence and commitment to one another. It is here that discussions about competency and curriculum take place. The seminaries continually receive feedback from their graduates, from ministers in their areas, and from laypeople.

In recent years, Disciples "restructure" has greatly increased the authority of Regional Ministers—the title (since 1969) for regional officials of the denomination—in the ordination and recommendation of ministers to congregations. The importance of this for the seminaries has not been overlooked. With at least one Disciples seminary, semiannual consultations have been regularly held between the seminary's administration and the Regional Ministers of its area. Faculty frequently have participated in these consultations. The experience has been one both of confrontation and of support. "Readiness for ministry" has been the recurring agenda. Definitions of competence have often been argued, along with questions of adequate financing in order that levels of competence might be reached. In the future, it may well be that the Disciples concept of ministry and its criteria for competence will find articulation in these meetings of seminary representatives and the Regional Ministers.

A theological seminary has several constituencies but none is more central to a Disciples seminary than the congregations to whom its graduates go and from whom its students come. Congregations make the final determination of a person's readiness for ministry. Disciples can understand that strange but inevitable mix between the *autonomy* that both seminaries and congregations accord to one another in the conduct of their own affairs and the *interdependence* by which they are held together. The seminaries know both ingredients in their relationship with congregations are of crucial importance to their continuing life and to the vitality of the church.

Alongside the expectations for ministry that they share with other American denominational families, Disciples are shown in their responses to exhibit certain distinctive characteristics. The most obvious may well be a greater-than-average concern with ministry to the community outside the walls of the organized church. There are five rather closely allied dimensions on which Disciples clergy evidence strong, although not statistically significant, support. (As noted earlier, due to the small number of responses from Disciples laypeople, it is not valid to isolate their responses as representative of laypeople within this denominational family.) However, because the pattern is consistent, one can read this as a definitely indicated trend, if not a statistical certainty. These five dimensions are the following: "Support of Unpopular Causes" (CC 50); "Support of Community Causes" (CC 15); "Active Concern for the Oppressed" (CC 16); "Aggressive Political Leadership" (CC 18); and "Coministry to the Alienated" (CC 26).

Undergirding this concept of ministry within the broader community, Disciples respondents rank among those denominational families attaching the greatest degree of importance to a beginning minister's "Promotion of Understanding of Issues" (CC 14), "Interest in New Ideas" (CC 33), and "Valuing Diversity" (CC 46). While not emphasizing the need of theological understanding, Disciples clergy consistently affirm the "Use of Broad Knowledge" (CC 30).

A second pattern in which the uniqueness of the Disciples responses appears deals with openness of style and leadership patterns. The Disciples vigorously affirm "Ecumenical and Educational Openness" (CC 8); the clergy give a relatively high ranking to "Sharing Congregational Leadership" (CC 57) and "Conflict Utilization" (CC 56).

Finally, the historic qualities of voluntarism and congregationalism still evidence themselves in the low rankings given by clergy and laity to the dimensions dealing with "Denominational Knowledge" (CC 32) and "Denominational Collegiality" (CC 49). The element of autonomy shows its continuing influence.

NOTES

1. See article by Sidney E. Mead, "The Rise of the Evangelical Conception of the Ministry in America: 1607–1850," in H. Richard Niebuhr and Daniel D. Williams, eds., *The Ministry in Historic Perspective* (New York: Harper & Row, 1956).

2. Quoted by D. Ray Lindley in "Types of Religious Leaders and the Church's Ministry," W. Barnett Blakemore, ed., in *The Renewal of the Church*, Vol. 3: *The Revival of the Churches* (St. Louis: Bethany Press, 1963), p. 145.

3. Clarence E. Lemon, "An Evaluation of Our Ministry in the Light of Our History," in W. Barnett Blakemore, ed., *The Renewal of the Church*, Vol. 1: *The Reformation of Tradition* (St. Louis: Bethany Press, 1963), p. 203.

4. Langdon Gilkey, *How the Church Can Minister to the World Without Losing Itself* (New York: Harper & Row, 1964), pp. 7–8.

5. Carroll C. Cotten, *The Imperative Is Leadership* (St. Louis: Bethany Press, 1973), pp. 39–40.

6. For example, 42 percent of the Disciples sampled, in contrast to 24 percent of other respondents, judged "Has thought through a theological stance regarding cooperation with

other denominations" as highly important. Even more striking is the response to "Partici-pates in ecumenical projects with ministers of other denominations." Forty-seven percent of the Disciples judged this as highly important, in contrast to only 17 percent of all other respondents.

7. Robert Michaelsen, "The Protestant Ministry in America: 1850 to the Present," in *The Ministry in Historic Perspective*, p. 274.

10

Orthodox Church

Stanley S. Harakas

Several of the authors representing denominational families participating in this study depict them as "typical American denominations." In contrast, the Eastern Orthodox Church refutes the notion of denomination and "perceives itself to be the 'Mother Church' of Christianity, identifying itself today with a tradition reaching back 2,000 years in unbroken continuity." Harakas notes, after examining the data, that they confirm to some extent at least the presence of a westernizing influence on the Orthodox Churches on this continent. Given the acknowledged emphasis within this church family on history and tradition (as well as a certain amount of resistance to change in matters of faith, worship and ethics), Harakas expects these data to be disconcerting to some readers, to the extent that the Orthodox share perceptions similar to those of other Christian groups in approximately one-half the dimensions.

In common with other groups, the Orthodox generally express "higher than average" expectations of their beginning clergy. Harakas also perceives a certain coalescence between Orthodox laity and the laity of other (predominantly Protestant) groups in the fact that differences of perception occur

Stanley S. Harakas is Dean and Professor of Christian Ethics at Holy Cross Greek Orthodox School of Theology, Brookline, Mass. He is the author of *Living the Liturgy* and *Contemporary Issues: Eastern Orthodox Perspectives*.

commonly where the difference is not based on denominational lines, but rather fixed according to one's classification as laity or clergy.

The Orthodox respondents differ from the other groups primarily in their attributing a sacramental-liturgical function to the priest. Such a function is foremost; the priest is set apart in the office of priest; the particular human who fits this role is of secondary importance. It is crucial to remember this primary conception of the priest's role when interpreting data from Orthodox respondents. For example, Harakas finds very little enthusiasm for priestly involvement in social issues and concerns, although lay involvement in such areas is acceptable. The Orthodox also attribute little importance to a role of the priest that is primarily juridical or organizational. The priest's role is liturgical; mutuality in the congregation can be derived from God's energies in the congregation and by human recognition of the common tradition shared by the Orthodox. From this primary conception of the priestly role also follows a diminished importance of the personal life or of personal expressions of religious commitment on the part of the priest. Harakas states that both clergy and laity of the Orthodox Churches have a rather closed view of the range and the sphere of priestly activities, as in closed communion, for example. Thus he does not find it surprising to find low ratings (relative to other groups) with regard to world mission or pastoral service to all. And, not surprisingly, Orthodox respondents have strong expectations that a priest be loyal to the Orthodox Church.

The Eastern Orthodox Church perceives itself to be the "Mother Church" of Christianity, identifying itself today with a tradition reaching back two thousand years in unbroken continuity.[1] In faith and worship, Orthodoxy claims to continue the life, practice and ecclesial unity of the apostolic and the patristic periods. The Orthodox Church perceives itself to be the continuation of the undivided church of the first nine centuries. Thus, in spite of obvious changes throughout its history, its roots are deeply set in the historical ground of Christianity.

This fact of self-understanding and self-perception is basic to understanding any aspect of the Orthodox Church, including the perceptions it has of the clergy role. However, this fact is not enough in itself. Difficult years during its more recent history have had their effects as well. Greek, Arabic, Romanian, and some Slavic Orthodox Churches show evidence of the 400-year-long subjugation to Moslem conquest. The Russian Orthodox Church was forcibly reduced to a department of the state in the time of Peter the Great in Imperial Russia and still suffers persecution and severe restriction in the Soviet Union.

As a result of this centuries-long oppression, certain aspects of church life, such as preaching, mission, and social outreach, have been rather more undeveloped than they might have been under more benign circumstances. The strong eucharistic and liturgical aspects of the Orthodox

Church have remained steady, but they have received heightened visibility due to the very inhibited growth of the social aspects. This has directly influenced the vision held in the Orthodox Church of the role of the clergyman, and especially the parish priest.

Another very important influence on this image is the monastic model commonly held by Orthodox Christians, including the clergy. The monastic image in Orthodoxy is a powerful force, providing an almost definitive determination of the context of Orthodoxy. The ancient struggle between diocese and monastery continues today in many guises. While no Orthodox Christian would wish to identify the parochial task with the monastic image, none would be willing, either, to separate them too far from one another.

The North American scene, however, provides its own ambiguities and nuances for the Orthodox Church. Chief among these is the increase of Orthodox church jurisdictions as a result, almost solely, of immigration. The ethnic dimension of Orthodoxy in the Americas cannot be overlooked or minimized, even though most members of the Orthodox Church clearly distinguish between their faith as Orthodox Christians and their ethnic heritage. The Americanization of the Orthodox Church in North America is occurring at varying rates for the different jurisdictions. Part of that process is due to the powerful forces of secularization. Another part is ecumenical in character; a combination of the religious spirit of America, locally dominant groups, and genuine ecumenism (although it operates primarily on an episcopal rather than a local parish level) have all served to influence Orthodox parish life in concrete and specific ways.

Thus, the local church, which theologically and historically is primarily a eucharistic community, has been expanded to embody some of those influences described earlier. This, of course, is reflected in the view of the priestly role, since the priesthood is almost incomprehensible, from an Orthodox Christian perspective, if separated from a worshipping community.

Given the Orthodox Church's emphasis on history and tradition, as well as its resistance to change in matters of faith, worship, ethics, and general ethos, it should be no surprise that the Orthodox Christian's expectations of the priest will have some unique configurations. However, for those who see the Orthodox as a people "totally apart" (and such views are held by some persons both within and outside of the Orthodox Church) it will be disconcerting to find many similarities to most Christian bodies with regard to understanding of readiness for priestly service. The Orthodox Church is unique, of course, but not to the degree that some might anticipate or desire.

We discover, with others, that almost half of the traits measured by the study (see Chapter 4 for an explanation of the instruments and the core clusters) are held in common by all groups. For example, members of the

Orthodox Church concur with the sixteen other denominational groups in rating as highly important in the new clergyman such traits as "Personal Responsibility" (Core Cluster, or CC, 42), "Positive Approach" (CC 44), and "Flexibility of Spirit" (CC 45). The Orthodox clergy and laity also agree with most other denominational families in designating as very detrimental to the priestly role such traits as "Alienating Activity" (CC 10), "Professional Immaturity" (CC 52), and a "Self-Protecting Ministry" (CC 54).

The data imply a common ground among North American Christians regarding certain basic expectations of their clergy. Not only do they seem to expect clergy to have various traditionally ascribed characteristics of the clerical role but also, even more important than the superficial aspects of that role, respondents communicate the desire for human, ethical, and professional standards that could be characterized as "higher-than-average" expectations. Certainly, this is a conclusion neither unexpected nor undesired! Lest one succumb to a sort of temporal myopia with regard to interpretation of the Readiness for Ministry Project data, it should be noted that the role of the clergy in the early church also was premised on "higher-than-average" human, ethical and professional standards. Tangible evidence of these elevated standards are to be found in the records of positive and negative canonical requirements of candidates for priesthood in the early church, in the self-image of the clergy themselves, and in the fact that nonpriestly services (the service of priest-physician) were offered by clergy to society.

Another interesting facet of this assessment is the difference in response between laity and clergy. The traditional laity-clergy distinction in Orthodoxy appears still to be very sharp. The understanding of the priest as one "set apart" in the Orthodox Church is conditioned theologically by the fact that ordination is considered to be a sacrament and by the perpetuity and indelible character of ordination. The concept of a priest being set apart is conditioned as well by the clearly distinctive liturgical role (the special vestments, the iconostasis, which separates the altar area from the congregation, and so on) assigned to the clergy by the rubrics which direct the conduct of the services. It is further conditioned by other factors, such as distinctive dress, social status of the priest (for example, in Greece the priest is often a peasant farmer taken from among the people themselves for services as priest to his own social equals, whereas in some Slavic countries the clergy often identify with the aristocracy), and the roles of hierarchy and church councils in the appointment and transfer of a priest from the parish.

In North America, however, a high level of congregational (church council) authority and control exists within the acknowledged context of a strong hierarchical structure. The presence of a congregational authority has served to create a coalescence of sorts between Orthodox laity and the laity of many other North American groups (primarily Protestant). Such coalescence is evidenced by the commonality of both lay perception and evaluation of various criteria of readiness for ministry—as distinguished from those of the clergy in general. Thus, transcending even the categories of denominational families, Orthodox laity concur generally with other laity in not considering as important as do clergy such traits as "Theological Reflection" (CC 29), "Support of Community Causes" (CC 15), "Enabling Counseling" (CC 22), or "Encouragement of World Mission" (CC 12).

It is interesting that the data inform a differentiation between clergy and laity of the Orthodox Church other than, and in addition to, that traditional one of role—that is, of the priest set apart for special sacramental and worship functions. The data seem to emphasize the importance in the minds of Orthodox laity of the office of priest; the specific human who fills that role is of less importance than the role itself. Thus, the expectations that denominations across North America use in assessing readiness for ministry can be applied also by Orthodox laity to their beginning priests. However, Orthodox laypeople frequently attach less importance to these expectations than do laypeople of other denominations, and Orthodox clergy are far more demanding than are their laity.

THE ORTHODOX PATTERN

The Orthodox Church family, not unexpectedly, identifies most completely with Model 2 discussed by Strommen in Chapter 4, with its sacramental-liturgical emphasis being perhaps the archetype for this pattern. The spiritual emphasis (Model 1) would be a second level of identification for the Orthodox clergy and laity. Significantly, at this point they are nearly always in agreement, both groups thus emphasizing the same basic attitudes of expectation. Lowest ranked among Orthodox Christians, and least representative, are dimensions relating to a broader ministry to the community and to social concerns (Strommen's Model 3).

Thus (and again, not surprisingly), the Orthodox Church finds itself more closely related in clergy expectations to such tradition-respecting churches as the Roman Catholic and the Anglican-Episcopal, and furthest away from a number of mainline Protestant groups. Surprisingly, in the areas considered least important (for example, those related to a sociopolitical ministry), the Orthodox Churches seem to have a measure of agreement with such conservative Protestant groups as Evangelical A and the Christian Church (not Disciples). The Orthodox Churches (particularly the laity) seem to agree frequently with the very conservative Protestants on what is least important to them: namely, "Initiative in Development of Community Services" (CC 13), "Support of Community Causes" (CC 15), "Interest in New Ideas" (CC 33), "Active Concern for the Oppressed" (CC 16), and "Aggressive Political Leadership" (CC 18). Orthodox laity concur with the laity of certain conservative evangelical groups on dimensions such as "Perceptive Counseling" (CC 21), "Enabling Counseling" (CC 22), and "Valuing Diversity" (CC 46). What emerges from this litany of core clusters is a fairly closed view of the Orthodox Church in which objective standards of faith and churchly function transcend personal and nonchurch considerations. Orthodox and conservative Protestants have a view of Christianity that is "given," "historical," and—in a measure—independent of current cultural and social realities. This is an empirical assessment, of course. In the following pages, I assess this perception of Orthodox Christianity in terms of its conformity to the content of Orthodox faith itself and raise, as well, the issue of the normative character of the Readiness for Ministry results for Orthodox theological education. Yet this empirical assessment points to a vision of the priesthood that is clearly function oriented; that is, the priest is essentially a servant of the institution, and the major, if not exclusive, focus is on acceptable form of function.

Some results of the clergy-laity assessment of the priestly role tend to gather at certain foci. As indicated earlier, the Orthodox Churches are not at all convinced that the clergy should be involved in *social issues and concerns*. Considering that over the past 500 years the churches have had to place a premium on survival, this is not surprising. Yet, this fact is not enough to explain the reluctance of the Orthodox Church in assigning a social activist role to the priest. The empirical evidence supporting priestly avoidance of such activity is consistent across several dimensions. Although not statistically significant, in the core cluster designated "Initiative in Development of Community Services" (CC 13), the Orthodox laypeople are second lowest of all responding groups (a standard score of 46.1); and Orthodox clergy rank lowest of all clergy groups in being expected to manifest "Active Concern for the Oppressed" (CC 16). In line with this tendency, both Orthodox laity and clergy affix less importance than all other groups to the core cluster designated "Support of Unpopular Causes" (CC 50—clergy standard score, 47.9; laity, 42.7).

Such findings must be interpreted specifically in terms of clergy role, and not necessarily as a position conceived as the current role of the church as a whole and especially of the laity. The key to a proper interpretation of this phenomenon is seen in the results reported for "Aggressive Political Leadership" (CC 18). Here, the Orthodox clergy and laity again rank lowest of all groups (clergy, 44.4; laity, 41.1). Yet, Orthodox laity do not necessarily hold to a position that political activity is inappropriate for the Orthodox Christian. On the contrary, many members of the Orthodox Churches find partisan political activity of great interest and importance. The key is that involvement in political activity is perceived to be an appropriate function of the layperson, while strongly rejected as inappropriate to the clergy.

In part, this rejection can be traced to the Byzantine pattern of church-state relationships in which emperor and patriarch were perceived ideally to be in an equal yet diverse yoking. The Orthodox doctrine of the *Symphonia* ("harmony") of church and state perceived the lay emperor as responsible to God for the external well-being of the people of God (a clearly spiritual and religious interpretation of the political function) and perceived the clergy patriarch as responsible to God for the inner well-being of the people of God (a role that often caused the patriarch to "whisper counsel into the ear of the emperor"). Theologically, the Orthodox Church may not be unconcerned with social questions that affect the ethical, social, and personal lives of the faithful. But it is not necessarily the exclusive, or even primary, task of the *priest* to exercise this function. Underlying this view is a very strong theology of the laity. Thus, the priest is specifically prohibited by rule and regulation from partisan political activity. The case of the ethnarch (that is, a clergyman political ruler of the nation) occurs only rarely, in an emergency situation of national crisis. In such cases it is not inappropriate for a bishop to assume political authority, but only for a short period of time until the crisis is resolved.[2] However, the average parish priest would hardly be seen as having to respond to such extraordinary situations.

The role of the priest is focused on the transcendent and holy. However, the role of the whole church is more inclusive. In Orthodox Christianity, the priest is not perceived to be the whole of the church, nor even a microcosm of it. It is the eucharistic community, the whole people of God—made up of both clergy and laity—that performs the broader role.

Within the Orthodox Church, there are also some interesting results concerning those characteristics roughly categorized as dealing with the *pastoral relationship to the congregation.* Underlying this configuration of clusters is Orthodox ecclesiology; thus, perhaps more than any other, data on this group of characteristics are surprising and disconcerting. A current emphasis in Orthodox ecclesiology identifies the Church with the local eucharistic community, presided over by a bishop. This theology, of course, needs to deal with the reality of the diocesan, national, and world-wide Orthodox Church as well as any implications for ecumenism. Yet, regardless of emphasis, the local church, where the Eucharist takes place, continues to be understood in Orthodox theology as the place where the church is manifested and where the reality of the church is most concretely experienced.

At the same time, The Orthodox Church is designated by its marks of unity, sanctity, universality, and apostolicity: The Church is One, Holy, Catholic, and Apostolic. In addition, all of the biblical and a few patristic metaphors for the church are taken as concretely descriptive of the Orthodox Church, for example, the Church as the body of Christ, the bride of Christ, the people of God, the chosen people. Most of all, the Church is a eucharistic community. The Divine Liturgy of St. John Chrysostom, the most widely used form of the Eucharist, is replete with expressions implying corporate and ecclesial unity. Thus, the litany prays for the "good estate of the holy churches of God and the union of all men." The Cherubic Hymn (sung in the Divine Liturgy before the Great Entrance) has the congregation identifying itself as "we who mystically represent the Cherubim." Before the Nicene-Constantinopolitan Creed is repeated, the congregation is instructed, "Let us love one another, that with one mind we may confess: Father, Son, and Holy Spirit; the Trinity one in essence and undivided"—the Church being seen as an icon of the Holy Trinity. Elsewhere it is prayed, "and grant us with one mouth and one heart to glorify and praise thine all-honorable and majestic name." Following Holy Communion, the response is one of corporate joy and triumph. All of these point to corporateness, community, sharing, and an experience of unity experienced in and by the church.

That is why, at first sight, the views of laity and clergy on the priestly role for community building come as a surprise. For example, the laity perceive the cluster of specific traits characterized as "Encouragement of Mutuality in Congregation" (CC 4) as being of lesser significance for the priestly role than do most other lay respondents; although the difference is not statistically significant, the Orthodox responses rank third lowest of all groups (clergy standard score, 47.3; laity, 45.7). Similarly, in Core Cluster 57, "Sharing Congregational Leadership," which is defined as "Active employment of lay leadership—regardless of sex—in establishing and executing an overall parish strategy," the Orthodox laity and clergy rank next to lowest of all groups. The laity do not perceive it to be an important task (relative to the values attached by other denominational families) for the priest to be responsible for securing the involvement of laity in the overall planning and executing of local church policy. Orthodox clergy value it only slightly more. Both are substantially under the average for all respondents (Orthodox clergy, 47.6; Orthodox laity, 45.2). An even more startling figure arises from the response to "Conflict Utilization" (CC 56), which is defined as "understanding conflict theologically and being able to utilize conflict as a means for airing differences and stressing concern and understanding." Here, of all responding groups, the Orthodox laity have the least desire or expectation that this be part of the clergy role, and there is a notable difference between Orthodox clergy expectations and those of their laity (clergy, 48.8; laity, 42.9).

On the face of it, these three core clusters viewed together would seem to deny the strong sense of corporateness and mutuality implied by Orthodox ecclesiological teaching and liturgical practice. Yet it may be that corporateness is not denied; it may be that the clergy role in the promotion of it is denied. There are several supporting explanations for such an interpretation. The first explanation questions the hidden assumption that the leadership of the priest is organizational and institutional, as in any secular group. This is not, in fact, the case with the Orthodox priest. His leadership is perceived to be liturgical, not primarily juridical or organizational. Furthermore, "Sharing Congregational Leadership" (CC 57) implies, for instance, that the priest possesses such leadership and may parcel it out to the laity. My guess is that the laity already feel they have a goodly portion of congregational leadership that is not the priest's either to mete out or redistribute! Finally, a core cluster such as "Encouragement of Mutuality in Congregation" (CC 4), which is described as "Developing a congregational sense of being a family of God where there is mutual sharing, worship, and broad participation," receives low ratings. Again, this is so because the priest is not perceived to be the source of mutuality in Orthodoxy. This characteristic is not perceived to arise out of an intentionally planned and organized campaign, directed by the priest. Practically, the mutuality of congregational life arises from identification with the tradition and the network of relationships of the church. Theologically speaking, membership, mutual sharing, unity of spirit, corporateness in worship are not the result of priestly initiative, campaigns, and organizational planning. Rather, they come about through God's energies in the life of the congregation and by immersion in a common tradition.

This emphasis on tradition and transmitted commonality thus relieves any one person (including the priest) from the expectation of initiating or promoting corporateness. It also explains why both Orthodox clergy and laity rank lowest of all groups in Core Cluster 46, "Valuing Diversity" (clergy, 44.0; laity, 40.5). For clergy to exemplify "acceptance and valuation of diversity in people and ideas" is a threat to the major unifying force in the congregation. Loyalty to a commonly held tradition and the network of relationships that creates in the membership is one of the chief means by which, humanly speaking, the church lives and perpetuates itself. To encourage diversity in people and ideas is to attack the very source of the unity and mutuality of the community, for it is the Transcendent Tradition that makes possible the unity and mutuality of the tradition, not the priest.[3] The priest is judged by that tradition as well, and the laity is prepared to make the evaluation. A "good priest" exemplifies the tradition, and praise and acclaim for him as a "good priest" on the part of the laity are a means of strengthening the mutuality and unity of the parish. Thus, Orthodox laity rank "Service in Humility" (CC 34), which includes a disregard of personal acclaim or recognition, lower than the majority of other denominational families. The priest, when he embodies the Orthodox ethos, is a paradigm for the church, encouraging identification with the tradition that provides the true source of the mutuality and corporateness of the local congregation. Paradoxically, acclaim and praise of the priest are a means used by the laity to strengthen the life of the local parish. The very process is an experience in mutuality, indirectly exercised.

Another aspect of the unique Orthodox configuration of clergy expectations appearing in the Readiness for Ministry results were those core clusters relating to the *personal lifestyle of the priest.* In many of the core clusters that reflect the personal lifestyle of the priest, the Orthodox do not vary significantly from all other respondents. The Orthodox respondents generally expect their priests to be responsible (CC 43), to have a positive approach to their work (CC 44), to have a measure of flexibility (CC 45), not to be alienating (CC 10), to be emotionally mature (CC 52), to be persons of personal integrity (CC 42), and to be Christian examples (CC 35).

However, there is a group of core clusters that indicates another trend or group of expectations. These expectations indicate that the personal life of the priest is differentiated in some significant measure from his priestly role. In one sense, this reflects the fourth-century Donatist controversy, in which some held that personal imperfections invalidated the sacramental validity of priestly actions. As is known, the early church rejected this correlation. While legislating in its canon law against all manner of priestly malfeasance and often punishing by defrocking, the church refused to consider sacramental acts of the personally unworthy priest as invalid. Thus there developed a certain tendency, within limits, to consider the priest's personal life as separate from the priestly role and function. A brief survey of some of these core clusters may prove of interest. In part they reflect the inappropriateness of some examples for the Orthodox ethos. Also, it should be noted that the range around the adjusted standard score figure of fifty is not extremely wide. Of the seven examples mentioned hereafter, most fall short of statistical significance; yet the trend is consistent. The Orthodox Church rates these qualities as less important than do the other denominational families.

For instance, in the core cluster entitled "Affirmation of Conservative Biblical Faith" (CC 31), Orthodox laity rank this attribute fourth lowest and the clergy third lowest among the denominational families (47.9 and 45.5, respectively). To interpret this, we must take into consideration the Orthodox understanding of Scripture as part of Holy Tradition, which forms the foundation of the faith. The wording of the items that form this core cluster has a distinctly Protestant sound to Orthodox ears. Often, in fact, it has a polemical ring to it, appearing sharply to contrast the Bible and its teaching with the teaching of the balance of Holy Tradition. In such a context, to "affirm biblical faith" takes on an anti-Orthodox color. Much of the ambiguity here is due to the context. Yet it may not be totally interpreted in this fashion. Although the Bible is central to doctrine, preaching, and worship, the personal life of the priest is not particularly validated in the eyes of others by an overt and public exhibition of biblical familiarity.

A similar pattern emerges in responses to Core Cluster 37, "Commitment Reflecting Religious Piety." Orthodox laypeople rank this dimension lower (47.9) than other lay respondents, with the exception of the Jewish and Unitarian family. Laypeople do not reflect as high an expectation of the priest's personal expressions of religious commitment as might be expected. Does this mean that the laity tend to see the priest more as a religious functionary than as a religious personality?

An affirmative answer to this question would seem to be strengthened by a group of core clusters that consistently imply lower expectations held by the Orthodox with regard to practices and traits centered on the personal life of the priest. For instance, Orthodox laity tend to attach less importance than do some other lay respondents to the priest's readiness to acknowledge his limitations (CC 36); Orthodox respondents, both lay and clergy, tend to downplay the importance of an open style on the part of the priest (CC 8). The Orthodox laity are among the least negative of all groups in terms of the detrimental effects they perceive implied by actions or traits included in Core Cluster 53, "Undisciplined Living." The ethical implications of this emerging pattern seem to indicate that Orthodox laypeople separate the personal worthiness of the priest from his role in the liturgical life of the church. Both Orthodox clergy and laity do not consider it important, relatively speaking, that the priest seek and accept the counsel of other people (CC 39). Here clergy are next to lowest and laity lowest of all respondents (clergy, 52.9; laity, 45.5). This may, in part, reflect the distance between clergy and laity engendered by the authority embodied for the faithful in the concept of the priesthood.

Finally, the same pattern is shown in the core cluster entitled "Self-Protecting Ministry" (CC 54). Orthodox clergy and laity are least negative in their assessment of these traits, which include people-repelling action or behavior such as a "critical, demeaning, and insensitive attitude." Here, only the Orthodox Churches and both Roman Catholic groups (Order and Diocesan) fall below 50 in the standard scores. Statistically, the variance is not perceived to be significant in denominational family contrasts. Yet the correlation with Roman Catholics tends to point, however inconclusively, to the traditional relative separation between the personal life of the priest and his sacerdotal identity.

In a large number of core clusters that refer generally to the *priestly role and skills,* the Orthodox Church has significant distinguishing profiles. The dominant view regarding the expectations of the clergy is the strong and powerful affirmation of the central place of the priest as a leader of sacramental worship. This dimension of the priesthood emerges as the most significant expectation regarding the priestly role and its concomitant skills. This emphasis emerges in two basic trends. The first is the clear-cut emphasis on skills related to the conduct of public worship. The second is the significant downplaying of other aspects of the priestly role not so clearly related to worship.

Thus, the Orthodox clergy and laity both accord more importance to the dimension entitled "Sacramental-Liturgical Ministry" (CC 9) than do all other responding groups. While Orthodox laypeople indicate their perception of its importance with a remarkable 58.9, the clergy score it even higher, with an even more remarkable 63.5—outdistancing even the Roman Catholic (Diocesan) response by a significant 4.9 points in the standardized scores. This obviously reflects the powerful eucharistic and sacramental orientation of Orthodox theology and doctrine. It may well reflect also the cultural history of many Orthodox national groups that have not permitted the church to function significantly in any other way. This poses the question of interpretation for the field of theological education, especially in a pluralistic, free, and demanding environment such as that of the Orthodox diaspora, the spread after World War I of Orthodox peoples to lands in which they had not previously settled. This conclusion is reinforced in the responses to Core Cluster 5, "Competent Preaching and Worship Leading"; the Orthodox give a higher ranking to this aspect of priestly skills than does any other group. That the Orthodox respondents give high ratings both to "Sacramental-Liturgical Ministry" (CC 9) and "Competent Preaching and Worship Leading" (CC 5) is interesting, for preaching is an integral part of liturgy and thus is sacramental. Liturgy is prayer, proclamation of the Word, and breaking of the bread. To isolate preaching from the liturgy would be a mistake. Preaching having been almost nonexistent in the Eastern Churches during the Ottoman Age (1453–1830), due to a lack of educated clergy, it is remarkable that this long absence of a preaching ministry has not permanently affected Orthodox perceptions of the importance of preaching.

Connected with the clear-cut sacramental role is a rather closed view of the range and sphere of priestly activities. The Orthodox Church holds officially to a closed communion. Theologically, the Eucharist manifests the church's existence and life in unity with the Holy Trinity. Membership in the church is defined both sacramentally (Baptism, Chrismation (Confirmation), Eucharist, and the other sacraments) and by doctrinal correctness (the term "Orthodox" may mean both "true belief" and "true worship" as well as loyalty to a canonical bishop). This means, for the Orthodox clergy and laity, that there is a strong, clear line drawn between Orthodox Christians and non-Orthodox Christians, and an even bolder line between Orthodox Christianity and other religions, or between Orthodox Christians and nonreligious people. This does not reach the point of total disengagement and rejection of others, of course. "Shunning" and exclusivism are not a part of the Orthodox ethos. Orthodox Christians, including priests, can and do relate to the world about them. Witness the ecumenical movement, in which Orthodoxy has long been involved. Yet one crucial distinction has to be noted: *Sacramental relations with non-Orthodox are always avoided.* Presence at a religious service may be tolerated, but it is always understood to be *nonsacramental*. When this background is related to the high regard in Orthodoxy for the sacramental role of the priest, the rationale restricting the priestly role to ministrations among the Orthodox flock is both consistent and an issue of integrity. Thus, Core Cluster 11, "Pastoral Service to All," and Core Cluster 12, "Encouragement of World Mission," are ranked by both Orthodox clergy and laity quite low, relative to other groups. On both these dimensions, the Orthodox Church differs significantly from some of the conservative evangelical Protestant groups in attaching less importance to these traits.

Accompanying this lesser concern for pastoral service to all and for encouragement of world mission is a strong expectation that the priest be loyal to the church. Thus Core Cluster 49, "Denominational Collegiality," is ranked quite high in importance by Orthodox clergy (54.9) and laity (52.9) as compared with other denominational families such as United Church of Christ or some of the conservative evangelical groups. Similarly, "Denominational Knowledge" (CC 32) ranks higher among Orthodox clergy than among any other group as an attribute needed by the priest (clergy, 55.2). Orthodox respondents attach approximately the same degree of importance to this cluster as do both Roman Catholic sub-groups, the Anglican-Episcopal, and some evangelical groups. It should be noted that Orthodox scores for this cluster are derived from the responses to the specific items that comprise it. The Orthodox Church does not consider itself a mere denomination, but the One, Holy, and Apostolic Church.

Two other clusters round out the picture. Both deal with the *priest's self-perception.* The Orthodox rank highest, with no differentiation between clergy and laity on the need for the "Acceptance of the Clergy Role" (CC 47) and rank "Priestly Commitment" (CC 41) second only to Roman Catholics. However, the obvious influence of the commitment to celibacy implied in the Roman Catholic response is not necessarily a central part of priestly commitment for the Orthodox, as it is for the Roman Catholics, since a priest in the Eastern Orthodox Church may be either married or celibate. This makes the requirement for "Priestly Commitment" all the more notable. This focus on the sacramental role for the priest shows also in a deemphasis on other aspects traditionally understood to be part of the clergyman's role. (See Table 10-1.) The counseling role in its more modern form is essentially deemphasized, as we see in Core Clusters 21, 22, and 25, especially by the laity; Orthodox clergy and laity rate the contents of the more traditional dimension, "Theologically Oriented Counseling" (CC 24), in a way that approaches an average response (clergy, 53.3; laity, 49.3). All these seem to be consistent with a view of the priestly role as essentially sacramental in character.

Several results are a bit puzzling and appear to require some interpretation. For instance, how are we to understand Core Cluster 60, "Intuitive

TABLE 10-1
Selected Clusters Ranked Low by Orthodox Respondents

Core Cluster No.	Core Cluster Name	Orthodox Rank	
		Clergy	Laity
25	Involvement in Caring	2nd lowest	lowest
21	Perceptive Counseling	—	lowest
22	Enabling Counseling	—	lowest
14	Promotion of Understanding of Issues	lowest	—
6	Encouragement of Spiritual Sensitivity	2nd lowest	2nd lowest

Domination of Decision Making," to which Orthodox clergy give the highest rating as compared to all other clergy? It would seem to be a reflection of the separateness and authority invested in the priest as a sacred person and would seem to fit the pattern described immediately preceding. Yet Orthodox clergy value "Effective Administration" (CC 58) more than does any other group of clergy or laity. This result does not seem to fit the pattern developed thus far. Significantly, efficiency seems to be much more important for Orthodox clergy than for the laity (clergy, 54.8; laity, 47.4), with more than seven standard scores difference. This is hard to understand if one is thinking in traditional categories; it might be understood as a rather unthreatening way of "modernizing" the priestly image. Another unusual aspect of the priestly role is the weight given to Core Cluster 23, "Caring Availability," which the Orthodox clergy rate higher than do all other respondent families. As is the case with "Effective Administration," this may be a safe and fitting way to modernize the priestly image ("We are as close to you as your telephone, a twenty-four-hour answering service"). Or it may be an attitude derived from the sacramental focus of the clergy. Special note should be made again of "Service in Humility" (CC 34). The results here do not, I believe, mean that clergy should be egotistical or self-aggrandizing. Rather, the clergyman is perceived to be the church community's spokesman. In my judgment, it arises from the need to assert the distinctiveness of the Orthodox Church as a religious group as unlike the Protestants and Roman Catholics in the pluralistic American milieu. It is reflected in the desire of many of the Orthodox (both clergy and laity), expressed several years back, to have the Orthodox Church proclaimed by state legislatures as "The Fourth Major Faith." Thus, the Orthodox Church in this country would hold that part of the priest's role is to focus attention on himself in the public eye, since he is a representative of the Orthodox community and the Orthodox faith. Yet we must also conclude that clergy think humble service significantly more important than do the laity (5.0 difference).

Orthodox clergy emphasize more than other groups the importance of "Caring Availability" (CC 23), "Effective Administration" (CC 58), and "Denominational Knowledge" (CC 32). However, Orthodox laity are not nearly so impressed by these indicators of readiness for ministry as are their clergy.

Orthodox laity show greater disinterest on some dimensions than do the laity of any other denominational family. They judge quite unimportant, in the role of the priest, such skills as "Conflict Utilization" (CC 56), "Enabling Counseling" (CC 22), and "Perceptive Counseling" (CC 21), as well as the need for the priest to acknowledge his limitations (CC 36). There exist extremely sharp differences between the perceptions of Orthodox laity and clergy on the core clusters dealing with counseling skills: 9.5 standard scores ("Enabling Counseling") and 7.4 ("Perceptive Counseling"). Clearly, Orthodox clergy see these as much more important than do the laity. There is a message here. Laity do not think the priest should be necessarily "reaching out to persons under stress with a perception, sensitivity, and warmth that is freeing and supportive" ("Perceptive Counseling," CC 21) nor that he be able to use "high levels of understanding and skill in aiding persons to work through serious problems" ("Enabling Counseling," CC 22). Rather, laity express an expectation that the priest be able to use "theologically sound counseling approaches to help people cope with personal problems, using resources of faith" ("Theologically Oriented Counseling," CC 24). There is much more unanimity here between Orthodox clergy and laity. This reflects the view of Orthodox sacramental theology, which indicates rich use of the spiritual, sacramental, and liturgical resources of the faith in counseling. Does this suggest that Orthodox clergy are seeking "professional identities" that at heart are not in harmony with the fundamental priestly image in the Orthodox Churches?

Finally, there is a group of differences that simply indicate particularly intra-Orthodox clergy-laity differences without any special correlation to other denominational families (see Table 10-2). Readiness for Ministry is perceived in a significantly different fashion by Orthodox clergy and laity in the following clusters: "Secular Lifestyle" (CC 51), "Theological Reflection" (CC 29), "Use of Broad Knowledge" (CC 30), and "Acknowledgment of Own Vulnerability" (CC 38). In all four cases, the clergy consider these items of greater significance than do the laity. The laity are not so concerned with the marks of a secular lifestyle among the clergy as are the clergy (a difference of 6.7 points). This may reflect what is often called the "priestly consciousness" among members of the Orthodox clergy. Appropriate lifestyle is also related to the priestly image as a sacred per-

TABLE 10-2
Significant Clergy-Laity Differences in the Orthodox Church Regarding Assessment of Clergy Readiness for Ministry

Core Cluster No.	Core Cluster Name	Standard Score		
		Clergy	Laity	Difference
22	Enabling Counseling	51.0	41.5	9.5
21	Perceptive Counseling	50.2	42.6	7.6
39	Acceptance of Counsel	52.9	45.5	7.4
58	Effective Administration	54.8	47.4	7.4
38	Acknowledgment of Own Vulnerability	50.6	43.3	7.3
51	Secular Lifestyle	51.7	45.0	6.7
56	Conflict Utilization	48.8	42.9	5.9
30	Use of Broad Knowledge	48.3	42.5	5.8
29	Theological Reflection	50.7	44.9	5.8
32	Denominational Knowledge	55.2	49.5	5.7
36	Acknowledgment of Limitations	53.2	47.9	5.3
50	Support of Unpopular Causes	47.9	42.7	5.2
34	Service in Humility	48.0	43.0	5

son. The evidence appears to support the conclusion that the priestly identity is more important to the clergy than to the laity, that the former are more exigent of themselves than are the laity of the clergy. The same dynamic seems to be at work in the results of Core Cluster 29, "Theological Reflection." A glance at the general denominational results shows a basically consistent pattern across the groups; the consistent disparity between laity and clergy results from the demands of the clergyman's self-perception, which laity cannot be expected to share. The difference between Orthodox lay and professional response is not out of the ordinary.

This is, however, not so in Core Cluster 38, "Acknowledgment of Own Vulnerability" (clergy, 50.6; laity, 43.3) and Core Cluster 30, "Use of Broad Knowledge" (clergy 48.3; laity, 42.5). In both cases, the Orthodox respondents reveal the greatest gap between clergy and laity of all denominational families (CC 38, 7.3; and CC 30, 5.8). Clergy are much more willing to see the need for the priest to acknowledge his limitations than are laity. In a sense, the laity too readily identify the exalted sacramental view of the priest with the personal capabilities of the priest and fail to recognize human frailties.

348 CHURCHES AND DENOMINATIONAL FAMILIES

The lesser emphasis by laity on the use of broad knowledge also indicates a differing perception of the priesthood. In the laity, it would seem to reflect both an older view, arising out of village orientations when the priest was not expected to be educated, and a "the priest ought to stick to religion" attitude. Unfortunately, this attitude is also shared by educated laity who, whatever their conception of religion's relationship to society, perceive the educated churchman as an antagonist. The educated priest is not so amenable to their control as the village priest may have been. The clergy probably value knowledge more highly not only as a result of their own education, but also from a more future-oriented perception of the priestly task, especially the demand to relate the truths of Orthodoxy and the Orthodox lifestyle to their congregations in an increasingly secular age.

I conclude this section with the observation that for the Orthodox respondents the sacramental-liturgical function of the priest is foremost in importance. This leads to a perception of the priest as a separate and sacred figure. The skills emphasized by the laity are those most clearly related to the sacramental life. These results support a conclusion I arrived at in my study of "The Orthodox Priest as Leader in the Divine Liturgy":

In the liturgical texts . . . the priest is not a leader in the usual sense of the word. He is neither dictator, nor charismatic, nor visionary, nor perfect personal example. His role is a derived one, dependent for all to see on a higher (reality). Even as an enabler, he admits freely that he himself must be enabled.

Yet in spite of all of these negations, the priest is a leader. But his leadership is clearly not of the kind which the world describes as such. . . . It is only in that paradoxical relationship of the priest at the altar that we can find the unique quality of the leadership of the priest of the liturgy. . . . His leadership consists of showing his people how to say to God with their whole lives: "The things that are thine are we offer to You according to all things and for all things" (said at the offering of the Divine Liturgy of St. John Chrysostom).[4]

In the Orthodox Church, the priest is expected primarily to be a priest.[5]

NOTES

1. For this study and the Readiness for Ministry material the denominational family name Orthodox Church, used interchangeably with Eastern Orthodox Church, subsumes both the Greek Orthodox Church in America and the Orthodox Church in America. For convenience, the term Orthodoxy is often used to describe the family, and "the Orthodox" is used to describe the family's respondents.
2. During the four or five centuries of Turkish domination, the role of the ethnarch was perpetually displayed by patriarch, bishops, and priests. It was imposed upon the first patriarch (and his associates) after the fall of Constantinople in 1453 by Sultan Muhummad II himself. This made the Orthodox clergyman a national leader, responsible for order to the Turkish authorities. The national involvement of the Eastern Orthodox clergy runs parallel

to the social and cultural involvements undertaken by the Western clergy after the collapse of the Western Roman Empire in 476 A.D. The church in the East and in the West filled, in a sense, the vacuum created by the absence of the Roman state.

3. This is not to imply that our understanding of "Transcendent Tradition" is rigidly immutable. The need to define "Tradition," in order best to apply it to the contemporary situation, still exists. Such a defining enterprise can be facilitated by dialogue with groups of other traditions. This need alone makes participation of the Orthodox Church in the ecumenical movement possible. Ultimately, the Church decides on "Tradition" and everything else is preparatory and tentative.

4. *The Greek Orthodox Theological Review,* Summer 1976, 21 (2), 163–176.

5. Beginning with a meeting on October 27, 1977, of the faculty of Holy Cross Greek Orthodox School of Theology, one of the two ATS-accredited Orthodox schools of theology in the United States, there have been many discussions on the results of the Readiness for Ministry Project as they have been particularized in the Orthodox criteria.

It has come as little surprise to us that clergy and laity together have agreed resoundingly about the sacramental-liturgical conception of the priesthood in Orthodoxy. Nor have we been surprised to see that Orthodox expectations of the priest in many cases have not been very different from those of other denominational families participating in the project. Our expectation that there would be more commonalities with the Roman Catholic and Anglican-Episcopal families than with other groups has proven correct.

However, there are some disturbing expectations and assumptions. In some cases, the core clusters themselves have developed in ways that have not properly represented Orthodox attitudes and that have run counter to what we have been doing as a school of theology in the task of preparing priests for the Orthodox priestly service. These seem to arise from an almost exclusive emphasis on the sacramental-liturgical dimension and a much less pronounced emphasis on other aspects of the priestly ministry. The faculty do not reject the centrality of the sacramental-liturgical role of the priest; however, we do reject sole reliance on such a conception for defining completely the nature of the Orthodox priestly calling. As a faculty, we perceive the issue theologically, and as churchmen we perceive it from the point of view of practical church life. Even were it a question of survival, we perceive a virtually exclusive reliance on this dimension as improper. What may have been the only possible course of action left to the church during the captivity under the Turks and during the enslavement of the church in Imperial Russia (and what may be the only alternative available to the church currently in the USSR) is not the only alternative available to the church in the diaspora, and specifically, the United States and Canada. (It should be noted, too, that the Russian anchorites [startzi] continued the tradition of freedom of the early desert fathers and that the Greek priests functioned additionally as teachers during the years of Turkish domination.)

In fact, theologically, the faculty feels that a much broader view of the priest's work is needed. As we survey the data, we feel that some very important theological foundations of the priestly ministry are being distorted and misrepresented. As central as the sacramental-liturgical role is for the Orthodox clergy and laity, the priest as teacher of his flock, as father and pastor, as leader of the Orthodox community, as missioner, and as example of Christian living also need to be emphasized.

On the one hand, a proper and healthy liturgical theology never restricts itself to an exclusive emphasis on the sacramental-liturgical dimension, narrowly understood. Sacramental theology, even when pursued as the key to Orthodox theology, always speaks of the "liturgy after the liturgy," meaning the life of the faithful outside the strictly eucharistic-sacramental experience. The sacramental-eucharistic approach, by its very presuppositions, demands not a narrow cultic approach to Christianity, but, rather, a sanctification of the whole of life. The priest shares in this broader sacramental life not only as the leader of worship and the sacraments, but also as teacher, preacher and counselor.

On the other hand, the sources of the Orthodox faith may be seen as transcending the strictly liturgical or even eucharistic orientation. As Orthodox theology surveys the tradition that serves as the source of its faith and practice, in reference to the priestly role, we do not find a monolithic corpus of teaching. In its rich variety, the Orthodox Church has many branches to its theology, which is firmly rooted in the Messiahship of Christ: the triune God, the Incarnate Son, the Holy Spirit, ecclesiology, eschatology, and *agape* love. The liturgy is not its only, much less chief, source. The Bible, patristic teaching, history, canon law, spirituality, monasticism, the ecumenical councils, all contribute to and inform the Orthodox understanding of the priesthood. All witness to the various dimensions of the priesthood, which include the roles of teacher, community leader, father, pastor, counselor, moral and spiritual guide, and personal example.

Hence, the faculty feel that the Orthodox criteria as reported in the Readiness for Ministry data dangerously underplay the importance of theological education, personal formation, pastoral skills, community building, communicative skills, mission, and social involvement. A well-rounded, and truly *Orthodox* priest is—as well as a theologian—an exemplar of personal Christian living, a counselor, a person responsible for the life of the church community, a representative of the Orthodox faith to the world, and an initiator, in the areas of both mission and social concern.

The Orthodox Church can understand these roles as derived from the sacramental-liturgical role. It is a common error to define too narrowly the richness of this prime role. Some of those roles derived from the sacramental-liturgical role can indeed be shared by both clergy and laity.

As change agent, the faculty is convinced that its task is to address the image of the priest held by clergy and laity alike, and to balance it and fill it out. As a result, we have been involved in a year-long curricular revision process whose main emphasis has been the improvement of education in the pastoral skills. The Readiness for Ministry criteria for the Orthodox priesthood have been useful to us, although the faculty would firmly reject using these criteria as a sole, normative base. The data have helped us receive an empirical view of the Orthodox Church's present attitude. This has led to a theologically based evaluation of the criteria. Consequently, we view the Orthodox profile neither as a purely normative directive nor as merely a descriptive statement. The "fact" bother us in some areas and confirm impressions in others. Yet, most of all, the Readiness for Ministry experience has helped us reflect on a picture of ourselves as a church and as a school serving the Orthodox Churches. It has already borne fruit, and we trust it will continue to do so.

Because of this experience, we have entered into the Readiness for Ministry assessment program for our students. We are hoping that some of the insights we have obtained for ourselves as a church and for Orthodox theological education will also be shared by our students on a personal and individual basis.

As the results of the Readiness for Ministry assessment and profile of Orthodox criteria become more fully known, we anticipate that they will also have some impact on the hierarchy, clergy, and laity of Orthodoxy in America, as well as on world Orthodoxy and theological education abroad.

11

Evangelical Churches

David Allan Hubbard and Clinton W. McLemore

The authors of this chapter acknowledge that the term evangelical *is applied to a broad variety of congregations and churches in North America. The chapter represents only a portion of those groups that are called* evangelical— *those whose theological schools are members of the Association of Theological Schools.*

In the original research design, evangelicals were to be grouped as a single denominational family; however, when the results of a pretest sample were analyzed, evangelicals divided into two clearly distinguishable groups (called for the purpose of the study, Evangelical A and B).

Hubbard and McLemore, after providing the reader with a broad, historical framework in which the term evangelical *can be viewed, examine the data from two vantage points. In the first major section, study results of each of the two evangelical groups are compared with the results generated by other*

David Allan Hubbard is President and Professor of Old Testament at Fuller Theological Seminary, Pasadena, California. From 1976–78 he served as President of the Association of Theological Schools in the United States and Canada.

Clinton W. McLemore is Associate Professor of Psychology in the Graduate School of Psychology at Fuller Theological Seminary and is the author of *Clergyman's Psychological Handbook*.

denominational families on the core clusters. The authors first predict what they might logically expect of evangelicals, then present the actual results.

In the second major section, in which Evangelical A and B are now viewed as a single group, the authors report and interpret those constructs that evangelicals use in rating the quality of ministry. In a concluding section, the authors compare the priorities of ten qualities of ministry most appreciated by evangelicals with those of the total Readiness for Ministry group. They hypothesize how the data might have differed had the entire evangelical movement been included in the study, then submit their forecasts about what these data augur for those evangelical groups that did participate in the study.

What is an evangelical Christian? This is no new question. The range of nuances the word *evangelical* has carried for centuries must have accustomed it to being the rope in ecclesiastic tug-of-war.

Luther and his followers claimed the term first to describe their commitment to a gospel whose truth and power they felt medieval Roman Catholicism had often obscured. For them, the evangelical church was that body of believers who taught and lived the evangelical doctrines of the Reformation: the authority of Scripture alone; grace, not works, as the ground of salvation; justification by faith in the saving work of Christ; and the full priesthood of all Christians.

Anglicans use the term to describe the movement within their church that has kept closest to their Reformation roots, particularly as expressed in the Thirty-Nine Articles of Religion of the Church of England (1563). In Anglican circles worldwide, *evangelical* is frequently used in contrast to "High Church" or "Anglo-Catholic." It describes those believers who stress evangelism and conversion as part of the church's mission and whose commitment to Christ centers more in the preaching of the gospel than in the sacraments.

In most of Latin America and other parts of the world where the Roman Catholic Church is dominant, *evangelical* is virtually synonymous with *Protestant*. In contrast to the emphasis on liturgy, hierarchy, religious celibacy, and adoration of the saints, evangelicals proclaim the word of the gospel.

For Christians in the United States, *evangelical* has had varied connotations. One of the most prominent has been the legacy of John Wesley (1703–1791) and the great revivals of George Whitefield (1714–1770). Spiritual vitality, warm piety, and concern for mission and evangelism worldwide were among their emphases. Not to be overlooked is the contribution of Alexander Campbell (1788–1866), whose followers in movements like the Christian Churches and Churches of Christ have become part of the larger evangelical stream.

Another American strand of evangelicalism originated in Scandinavia. There, especially in Sweden, the formalism of the state church, together with its ties with the government, provoked a response on the part of many believers that led to the forming of independent congregations. Frequently they met in houses, where they sang their gospel hymns, studied their well-worn Bibles, and prayed that the revival tides that had refreshed them would inundate their land. When the opposition of the state grew, they sought refuge in the New World, bringing the piety of their faith with them. The Evangelical Covenant Church in America, the Baptist General Conference, and the Evangelical Free Church (each of which was included in the research surveyed in this chapter) are part of their legacy to our generation. A similar pattern of opposition and even persecution in Holland, Germany, and Russia impelled Anabaptists such as the various Mennonite groups, to migrate to North America.

Evangelical can also be understood against the background of the theological liberalism that grew up within the church agencies and educational institutions of many denominations at the turn of this century. The term *fundamentalism* was more generally used to describe the movement, within and without those denominations, that refused to go along with the so-called modernizing of the Christian faith that the liberals supported. Fundamentalism held tenaciously to the basic doctrines of the church as expressed in the great creeds of the first four centuries and in the evangelical creeds of the Reformation era. Beyond that, it stressed what it regarded as biblical verities, such as the lostness of the human family apart from faith in Christ, the miraculous quality of his life—virgin birth, working of miracles, bodily resurrection, substitutionary nature of his death (more than a martyr's display of love and courage)—and the hope of his personal return.

For the past forty years or so, the term *evangelical* has described those American and Canadian Christians who viewed themselves as theologically conservative without necessarily espousing some of the more negative traits of fundamentalism: antiintellectualism that suspects scholarship and formal learning, especially when applied to the Bible or theology; apathy toward involvement in social concern, especially where political issues are in view; separation from all association with churches that are not, from the fundamentalist standpoint, doctrinally pure.

The National Association of Evangelicals (NAE), founded in 1942, was a concerted attempt to rally—for mission and fellowship—persons, congregations, agencies, and denominations who held to evangelical doctrines and who wanted to see evangelical influence deepened in the churches, the nation, and the world. The NAE and other evangelical alliances, often encouraged by the ministry of Billy Graham and his Evangelistic Association, have witnessed amazing experiences of evangelical unity. The Wesleyan, Scandinavian, Anabaptist, Reformed, Lutheran, and Pentecostal expressions of the evangelical movement have been brought together for great conclaves and strategies in the Berlin Congress (1966), the North American Congress of Evangelism (1969), Key '73, and, especially, the Lausanne Congress for World Evangelization (1974).

These concerted endeavors—together with the growth of Christian agencies such as World Vision International, Young Life, Campus Crusade for Christ, and Inter-Varsity Christian Fellowship—have resulted in an increase in evangelical vitality, which has caught much of the United States, especially the communications media, by surprise. Much of the support for these movements has come from laity and clergy who belong to the older churches. Almost every denomination, in fact, has seen a renewal fellowship formed within it to give expression and advocacy to an evangelical commitment. Conversion—being born again—is table conversation in thousands of households. The word *evangelical* is more and more a part of the national parlance.[1]

It should be clear from the outset that *evangelical* as used in the Readiness for Ministry study is a more narrow and precise term than this background sketch suggests. The evangelical movement has three centers of strength at the present: (1) evangelically oriented believers or organizations within the major Protestant denominations; (2) independent congregations and parachurch agencies for evangelism, education, and mission; and (3) denominations whose heritage and present confession are consciously evangelical. It is the third category whose findings are included in the present study—and from that category not every denomination that is consciously evangelical is included. No pentecostal denominations are represented, nor is the Christian Missionary Alliance, because institutions from those evangelical churches were not members of the Association of Theological Schools. How well the results reviewed in this chapter may reflect the larger evangelical scene receives comment later.

METHODOLOGY

The Denominational Groups Represented

For the first section of this chapter, we inspect the responses of two general families of denominations: Evangelical A and Evangelical B. Evangelical A, corresponding to group 16 on the cross-family core cluster plots (Chapter 5), consists of a total of 95 laypeople and 333 ministerial professionals selected mainly from the following denominational bodies:

Baptist General Conference
Baptist Missionary Association of America
Conservative Baptist Association of America
Evangelical Free Church of America
North American Baptist Conference

Evangelical B, corresponding to group 6 on the plots, consists of a total of 107 laypeople and 266 professionals from these bodies:

Church of God (Anderson, Ind.)
Church of the Nazarene
Church of the New Jerusalem (Swedenborgian)[2]
Churches of God, General Conference
Evangelical Congregational Church
Evangelical Covenant Church of America
Seventh-day Adventists

It is noteworthy that the original plan of research grouped all of these denominations together. The results of the survey, however, clearly indicate that there are two "camps" within these evangelical families. The response of the two "camps" differs significantly and frequently enough to encourage us to treat them separately under the labels Evangelical A and Evangelical B.

The Two Vantage Points of the Study

Our second section presents an analysis of how the two (A and B) evangelical families surveyed here compare and contrast with the other denominational families in rating the importance of the core criteria derived from the *entire ATS sample* (all families combined). As described earlier in this book, once all of the Readiness for Ministry questionnaires had been collected, all of them were combined and analyzed together, before more specialized analyses were conducted for particular denominational families. On the basis of this overall analysis, sixty-four "core clusters" were generated, and then sorted by a further analysis into larger groups reflecting "factors."

Clusters are sets of related items, and factors are basic dimensions or categories under which clusters can be subsumed. Clusters of items represent a fairly specific idea about some attribute of ministry, while factors capture more general or abstract ideas.

The value of comparing the responses of the various denominational families on a number of fixed criteria is that we may thereby discover how the families compare with each other. For a particular denominational group in the ATS Project, this means that we can determine whether its members value the attribute in question more, less, or the same as members of the other groups. We can, in effect, rank the denominations on each dimension according to how much their representatives endorse its importance. This is precisely what we attempt in the first section.

In the second section, by looking at the more specific information found in the clusters, we consider how the evangelical denominations in the survey construe the dimensions of ministry. The basic questions, then, are "Into what specific clusters do the items from the questionnaire group?" "What underlying ministerial characteristics are suggested by the clusters?" "What attributes are important to these evangelical churches?" And "How strongly do the evangelicals who were polled value the various characteristics of ministry included in the questionnaire?"

HYPOTHESES AND RESULTS: THE EVANGELICAL DENOMINATIONS RATE THE CORE CRITERIA

To keep the number manageable, we have chosen to deal with the more general category of *factors* rather than with the larger number of specific clusters. Our approach is first to state a hypothesis in each area described by a factor, then to test that hypothesis on the basis of the responses of the two evangelical families and those of the other denominational groupings. In our hypotheses, we attempt to make well-founded predictions based on what we know of evangelicals both from the literature that describes the movement and from our own personal acquaintance with it. Table 11-1 summarizes the results of our analysis.

If a difference in theology between the two groups is to be posited, it may be that some of the churches in Evangelical A have been more deeply influenced by Dispensationalism than those in Evangelical B. The Dispensational approach to biblical interpretation, pioneered by J. N. Darby (1800–1882), divides biblical history into seven eras, within each of which God's grace worked in a specific way. Among the by-products (to varying degrees at varying times) of Dispensational theology have been a suspicion of major denominations and ecumenical organizations, a concentration on the task of evangelization to the neglect of social and political action, and a conviction that Christian efforts at reform and renewal in society will not prove fruitful this side of Christ's second coming. Among the churches of Evangelical A, Dispensationalism has had a moderate influence on the Baptist General Conference and a substantial influence on the Conservative Baptist Association of America and the Evangelical Free Church of America.

It can be seen from the table that the evangelicals studied are notably appreciative of spiritual ministry that proceeds from a personal faith commitment (Factor 2) and that they are notably unappreciative of a ministry grounded in sacerdotal-sacramental belief and practice (Factor 7). Results on the other nine dimensions of ministry fall somewhere between these two extremes, with the clusters comprising a factor often yielding complex, if not conflicting, impressions.

TABLE 11-1
Summary of Evangelical Valuations of Factors
(Relative to Nonevangelical Valuations)

Factor No.	Factor Name	Evangelical Valuations	Comments
1	Ministry to Community and World	Low for EV-A; n.dif. for EV-B	EV-A relatively devalue aggressive political leadership and social action as well as intellectual and personal openness. EV-B highly value providing pastoral service to all, regardless of social class or church affiliation.
2	Ministry from Personal Commitment of Faith	High for EV-A and EV-B	EV-A and EV-B, along with other evangelically minded groups such as the Southern Baptists, greatly esteem biblically based piety, personal evangelism, and serious religious commitment stemming from an individual experience of spiritual regeneration ("born-again" Christianity).
3	Disqualifying Personal and Behavioral Characteristics	n.dif. for EV-A	Evangelicals are not distinctively troubled by negative psychosocial characteristics such as professional immaturity or insensitivity. Both EV-A and EV-B clearly devalue ostentatious "secularism," such as public drinking, heavy smoking, gambling, and telling off-color jokes.
4	Open, Affirming Style	n.dif. for EV-A; mixed results for EV-B	EV-B highly value personal integrity, realistic acknowledgment of limitations both intellectual and spiritual, and acceptance of the clergy role.
5	Development of Fellowship and Worship	Mixed results for EV-A and EV-B	EV-A is low on worship; EV-B is higher than EV-A on liturgical concerns; and EV-B is marginally high on congregational mutuality.

TABLE 11-1 — *CONTINUED*

Factor No.	Factor Name	Evangelical Valuations	Comments
6	Privatistic, Legalistic Style	Mixed results for EV-A and EV-B	Both EV-A and EV-B high on law orientation toward ethical issues and precedence of evangelistic goals
7	Priestly-Sacramental Ministry	Low for EV-A and EV-B	While not alone in their relative devaluation, evangelicals are clearly less appreciative of this dimension of ministry than are Anglicans, Orthodox, and Roman Catholics.
8	Congregational Leadership	n.dif. for EV-A; mixed results for EV-B	EV-B tend to value efficient administration.
9	Caring for Persons under Stress	n.dif. for EV-A or EV-B	EV-B tend to value, slightly more than others, ready and caring availability of the minister.
10	Theologian in Life and Thought	Mixed results for EV-A and EV-B	Relative to several other families, EV-B devalue self-disclosure; EV-A tend to give valuations similar to those of EV-B.
11	Denominational Awareness and Collegiality	Mixed results for EV-A and EV-B	Both groups value denominational knowledge more highly than the Christian Church (not Disciples). EV-A significantly lower than Presbyterian-Reformed. EV-B value denominational collegiality more highly than EV-A and four other groups.

Note: EV-A indicates Evangelical A respondents, and EV-B indicates Evangelical B respondents. n.dif. signifies "no consistent and statistically significant differences."

"Ministry to Community and World" (Factor 1)

This factor contains clusters of items ranging from those depicting the minister as exercising aggressive political leadership or serving as a champion of unpopular causes to those describing him or her as rendering pastoral service to all, regardless of social class or church membership.

Prediction

Because many contemporary evangelicals seem to have developed a reputation for political inactivity and separatism, we predict that, compared with other denominational families, they devalue the ministerial attributes reflected by this factor.

Results

Since the results in Factor 1 vary from cluster to cluster, we deal with several clusters in the attempt to check on our prediction. (The numbers in parentheses refer to the specific core cluster that emerges from the total Readiness sampling.)

1. *Aggressive Political Leadership* (Core Cluster, or CC, 18). This characteristic, though most devalued by the Orthodox respondents, is still valued significantly less by Evangelical B respondents than by representatives of the Free Church and Jewish and Unitarian families. The latter value such leadership more highly than do representatives of any other family. Evangelical A respondents rate it less favorably than those of fully eight other families: Free Church, Jewish and Unitarian, Lutheran, United Methodist, Presbyterian-Reformed, Roman Catholic (Diocesan), and United Church of Christ.

2. *Active Concern for the Oppressed* (CC 16). Evangelical A people rate this trait as less important than do persons in the Free Church, Jewish and Unitarian, United Methodist, Presbyterian-Reformed, and Roman Catholic (Diocesan) families, with Evangelical A clergy valuing such concern more than Evangelical A laypeople. Evangelical B ratings were about at the average of all families combined.

3. *Promotion of Understanding of Issues* (CC 14). The same sort of pattern obtains here, with the Evangelical A constituency valuing this cluster of items less than Christian (Disciples of Christ), Free Church, Jewish and Unitarian, Lutheran, United Methodist, Presbyterian-Reformed, Roman Catholic (Diocesan), and United Church of Christ families. Again, Evangelical A clergy seem to value the quality more than evangelical laypeople.

4. *Support of Community Causes* (CC 15). We see the same laity-clergy trend and once more find Evangelical A respondents awarding signifi-

cantly *lower* ratings than those of these families: Anglican-Episcopal, Southern Baptist, Christian (Disciples of Christ), Free Church, Jewish and Unitarian, Lutheran, United Methodist, Presbyterian-Reformed, Roman Catholic (Order and Diocesan). Evangelical B ratings are slightly below the general average.

5. *Initiation in Development of Community Services* (CC 13). Here all families are fairly close in their ratings—except Evangelical A, whose ratings are significantly lower than those of the Southern Baptist Convention, Free Church, Jewish and Unitarian, United Methodist, Presbyterian-Reformed, and United Church of Christ families. Evangelical B ratings are not especially low.

6. *Support of Unpopular Causes* (CC 50). Evangelical A respondents, next to Orthodox, most devalue this emphasis, and their ratings differ significantly from those of the family most esteeming it, the Jewish and Unitarian. Again Evangelical B ratings are approximately at the cross-family average.

7. *Ecumenical and Educational Causes* (CC 8). When it comes to "Openness in Style" (CC 8), Christian (Disciples of Christ) award the highest ratings and Evangelical A persons the lowest—significantly lower than persons in these families: Christian (Disciples of Christ), Free Church, United Methodist, Presbyterian-Reformed, and United Church of Christ. Evangelical B ratings, as before, are near the general average.

8. *Interest in New Ideas* (CC 33). Evangelical B ratings do tend to be low here. Yet only Evangelical A ratings are significantly lower than those of most other families.

9. *Pastoral Service to All* (CC 11). In this category, it is Evangelical B people who give deviant ratings. They value this *highly*, significantly more so than Orthodox and Jewish and Unitarian representatives.

Summary

It seems that we are accurate in our initial prognostication only with respect to the Evangelical A group of respondents. On the first eight of the nine core clusters, they give ratings significantly lower than those of at least one other denominational family, and usually of many more than one. The responses of Evangelical B are more surprising. Their ratings are significantly lower than those of two other families on the first cluster and significantly higher than those of two others on the last cluster. On the intervening clusters, there seems to be some slight tendency for their ratings to fall to the lower side of the mean, although not to a statistically significant degree. We are thus forced to offer the conclusion that for Evangelical B respondents our hypothesis stands unconfirmed. One cannot say with any certainty that they relatively devalue "Ministry to Community and World." Some possible reasons for the differences between Evangelical A and B are stated later.

Spiritual Ministry from Personal Faith-Commitment (Factor 2)

This factor contains clusters such as religious commitment, evangelistic witness, and affirmation of a biblical faith.

Prediction

These matters appear to be close to the hearts of all evangelicals, and so we predict that the denominations sampled value the ministerial characteristics more than other Christian traditions.

Results

Because of the stereotyped nature of these cluster results, we simply list the name of each along with the denominations from which Evangelical A or B significantly differs in its valuations.

1. *Commitment Reflecting Religious Piety* (CC 37). Evangelical A results differ from those of the Anglican-Episcopal, Jewish and Unitarian, United Methodist, and United Church of Christ families, while Evangelical B results differ from those of these families plus two others, Lutheran and Roman Catholic (Diocesan).

2. *Affirmation of Conservative Biblical Faith* (CC 31). Both evangelical bodies yield ratings that differ from those of the Anglican-Episcopal, Christian (Disciples of Christ), Jewish and Unitarian, United Methodist, Presbyterian-Reformed, Roman Catholic (Order and Diocesan), United Church of Christ, and United Church of Canada families. Each of the two also differs in its evaluations from one other family: Evangelical A from the Free Church family and Evangelical B from the Lutheran Churches.

3. *Theocentric-Biblical Ministry* (CC 2). Evangelical A differs from the Anglican-Episcopal, Free Church, Jewish and Unitarian, Lutheran, United Methodist, Roman Catholic (Order and Diocesan), and United Church of Christ families, and Evangelical B differs simply from the Anglican-Episcopal and Jewish and Unitarian families.

4. *"Born Again" Christianity* (CC 40). Evangelical A ratings differ from those of *every* other family except the Southern Baptist and Evangelical B, and the latter's rating show an identical comparison pattern except that they also fail to contrast with those of Christian (not Disciples) as well.

5. *Encouragement of World Mission* (CC 12). Evangelical A results differ only from Jewish and Unitarian ones, while those of Evangelical B differ from those of Anglican-Episcopal, Orthodox, Jewish and Unitarian, and Roman Catholic (Order). We should also note in passing that while the

lay-professional spread is negligible for the Evangelical B findings, within the ranks of Evangelical A the professional respondents award what seem to be substantially higher ratings; that is, they value missionary activity more than do their laity.

6. *Assertive Individual Evangelism* (CC 17). Here the results are more dramatic. Evangelical A differs from all families *except* Southern Baptist, Evangelical B, and the Christian Church (not Disciples). Evangelical B differs from all families *except* American-Canadian Baptist, Southern Baptist, Christian Church (Disciples), Evangelical A, and Christian Church (not Disciples).

7. *Christian Example* (CC 35). Ratings of Evangelical A respondents differ from those of Anglican-Episcopal, Jewish and Unitarian, Lutheran, United Methodist, Roman Catholic (Diocesan), United Church of Christ, and United Church of Canada. Groups from whose ratings those of Evangelical B's differ are identical, with the addition of Presbyterian-Reformed.

8. *Encouragement of Spiritual Sensitivity* (CC 6). Evangelical A differs from Anglican-Episcopal, Orthodox, Jewish and Unitarian, Lutheran, Roman Catholic (Order and Diocesan), and United Church of Christ, and Evangelical B differs from all of these, plus United Methodist and United Church of Canada.

9. *Theologically Oriented Counseling* (CC 24). Evangelical A ratings differ only from those of the Jewish-Unitarian family, while Evangelical B ratings differ from those of this family plus those of three others, Anglican-Episcopal, United Methodist, and United Church of Christ.

Summary

Clearly our hypothesis is confirmed for both Evangelical A and B denominations: Relative to most other families, they value highly a spiritual ministry that proceeds from a personal faith commitment. As even a quick inspection of the graphs in Chapter 5 will attest, a characteristic profile seems to emerge on these clusters: Evangelical A and B families, sometimes in concert with other groups such as the Southern Baptists, give the highest ratings, while the Jewish and Unitarian family gives the lowest. Ratings of the two evangelical families are routinely quite close to each other.

Disqualifying Personal and Behavioral Characteristics (Factor 3)

This factor groups together clusters of items having to do with such stances or traits as irresponsibility, immaturity, undisciplined living, and, most of all, a self-serving approach to ministry.

Prediction

Evangelicals tend to maintain fairly strict behavioral codes, and on this basis it seems reasonable to expect them, more than others, to value the *absence* of these behavioral traits in their clergy.

Results

A number of clusters—for example, "Self-Protecting Ministry" (CC 54), "Professional Immaturity" (CC 52), and "Undisciplined Living" (CC 53) reveal almost no differences among the denominational families, except that in the last cluster the Roman Catholic (Order) family's ratings are significantly different from those of the Southern Baptist, Free Church, and Evangelical A families, probably because the lead item in the cluster relates partly to extramarital affairs and thus has little meaning for a tradition whose clergy are celibate.

Secular Lifestyle (CC 51). Here we find a profile that resembles the pattern found in Factor 2 clusters. Its high point belongs to Evangelical A and its low point to the Jewish and Unitarian family. Evangelical B, on a par with the Southern Baptist family, is close to Evangelical A, whose ratings differ significantly from those of these families: Anglican-Episcopal, Orthodox, Jewish and Unitarian, Lutheran, Presbyterian-Reformed, Roman Catholic (Order and Diocesan), United Church of Christ, and United Church of Canada. Evangelical B ratings differ from those of all these families, *except* Orthodox, Presbyterian-Reformed, and United Church of Canada.

Summary

It appears that our hypothesis is confirmed only in the domain of such secular and observable actions as frequenting nightclubs and cocktail lounges, gambling, smoking, and telling off-color jokes (the items of CC 41). Evangelicals of either family are not more demonstrably troubled by negative interpersonal qualities (such as the harsh insensitivity of Cluster 54 or the generalized "neuroticism" of CC 52) than are representatives of the other denominational groups.

Open, Affirming Style (Factor 4)

This factor has to do with the minister's taking a positive approach to his or her job and acting, for example, with responsibility, flexibility, and integrity.

Prediction

We feel we have no basis for predicting whether evangelicals value such a style either more or less than nonevangelicals.

Results

The clusters "Positive Approach" (CC 44), "Fidelity to Tasks and Persons" (CC 43), "Flexibility of Spirit" (CC 45), and "Valuing Diversity" (CC 46) reflect no significant differences between evangelicals and the other families.

1. *Personal Responsibility* (CC 42). Results indicate that respondents of the Evangelical B group value personal responsibility more highly than do respondents of the Lutheran or Roman Catholic (Order or Diocesan) families. Evangelical B respondents, in fact, give items defining this attribute the highest absolute ratings of any of the denominational families.

2. *Acceptance of Clergy Role* (CC 47). Evangelical B people also esteem these items more highly than any other family and differ significantly in their ratings from Anglican-Episcopal and Roman Catholics (Diocesan) respondents. These items relate to the minister's not losing his or her composure under pressure, not using his or her authority as an interpersonal weapon, and not maintaining inappropriate personal ambitions.

3. *Acknowledgment of Limitations* (CC 36). Items in this category are also most highly endorsed by representatives of Evangelical B, whose ratings differ significantly from those in the Jewish and Unitarian family.

Summary

Persons representing Evangelical A do not seem to endorse the importance of an open, affirming style of ministry any more vigorously than do persons from other families. Our hypothesis, so far, goes unchallenged. A clear conclusion is more difficult to reach when we turn to Evangelical B results. While evangelicals in this family are not demonstrably more concerned with positiveness, responsibility, flexibility, or tolerance, of all the respondents in the survey they do award the highest absolute ratings of importance to integrity, role acceptance, and realistic modesty. In each case, these evangelical ratings differ significantly from those of at least one other family. We conclude, therefore, that several of the qualities subsumed under "Open, Affirming Style" are—contrary to prediction—especially important to Evangelical B people, perhaps because they are viewed as the fruit of piety that this tradition so values.

Development of Fellowship and Worship (Factor 5)

This factor has to do with a variety of qualities, ranging from conducting a sacramental-liturgical ministry, through relating well to children, to encouraging mutuality in one's congregation.

Prediction

No general prediction is made on this factor, although evangelicals are specifically expected to place high value on congregational mutuality and lower value on sacramental and liturgically oriented ministry.

Results

Clusters such as "Relating Faith to Modern World" (CC 1), "Competent Preaching and Worship Leading" (CC 5), and "Relating Well to Children and Youth" (CC 3) turn up no significant cross-family differences.

1. *Liturgical Sensitivity* (CC 7). Here Evangelical A respondents diverge from those of Evangelical B by placing much less importance on this quality than do the Evangelical B, Presbyterian-Reformed, and Roman Catholic (Diocesan) respondents, all of whom seem to take this quality to be desirable in their ministers.

2. *Sacramental-Liturgical Ministry* (CC 9). Evangelical A respondents value this emphasis significantly less than do those from the following families: Anglican-Episcopal, Lutheran, United Methodist, Presbyterian-Reformed, and Roman Catholic (Order and Diocesan). Evangelical B respondents value it significantly less than do members of the Orthodox and Roman Catholic (Order and Diocesan) families but significantly more than those of the Free Church Family.

3. *Encouragement of Mutuality in Congregation* (CC 4). Evangelical B respondents give significantly higher ratings than do Anglican-Episcopal respondents, whose valuation of this quality is markedly low.

Summary

While it seems clear that, as expected, evangelicals are relatively unappreciative of sacramental-liturgical ministry, we do not have clear warrant for claiming them to be demonstrably more concerned than others that their new ministers be able to facilitate fellowship, or *koinonia*.

Privatistic, Legalistic Style (Factor 6)

This is most characterized by resistance to community involvements and a law orientation to personal problems.

Prediction

Because of what is often described as "fundamentalist rigidity and separatism," together with the fact that the line between evangelical and fundamentalist is often a fuzzy one, it seems to us that evangelicals might value those qualities more highly than others.

Results

In "Total Concentration on Congregational Concerns" (CC 20), "Intuitive Domination of Decision Making" (CC 60), and "Alienating Activity" (CC 10), there is no appreciable difference between the Evangelical A and B groups and other families.

1. *Law Orientation to Ethical Issues* (CC 27). Both Evangelical A and B respondents tend to endorse this more than do people from the Anglican-Episcopal, Jewish and Unitarian, and United Church of Christ groups.

2. *Precedence of Evangelistic Goals* (CC 19). As one might expect, this stress is esteemed relatively highly by evangelicals. Evangelical B ratings are higher than those of the following families: Anglican-Episcopal, Christian (Disciples of Christ), and Jewish and Unitarian, Lutheran, United Methodist, Presbyterian-Reformed, Roman Catholic (Order and Diocesan), United Church of Christ, and United Church of Canada. Evangelical A ratings are higher than those of these denominations, plus two others, the American-Canadian Baptist and Free Church families.

Summary

It does seem that evangelicals are more prone toward endorsing some, but not all, of the attributes designated as "Privatistic, Legalistic Style," although one might question whether this title is entirely appropriate. That the minister place strong emphasis on evangelism does seem to be a characteristically evangelical concern. Both the use of legal norms in personal conduct and a concern for the evangelistic mandate probably stem from a doctrine of Scripture, as most evangelicals understand it.

Priestly-Sacramental Ministry (Factor 7)

Prediction

Evangelicals' traditional emphasis on preaching and personal conversion and piety should indicate a lower emphasis here than that found in several other denominational families.

Results

1. *Priestly Commitment* (CC 41). Both Evangelical A and B respondents give ratings significantly below those of the Anglican-Episcopal, Orthodox, Lutheran, and Roman Catholic (Order and Diocesan) families for this cluster. This recalls the even stronger results discovered in "Sacramental-Liturgical Ministry" (CC 9), as discussed earlier in Factor 5.

Congregational Leadership (Factor 8)

This area has to do with the sharing of congregational leadership, the building of community, and administrative effectiveness.

Prediction

Because all the denominations in Evangelical A and several in Evangelical B are congregational in organization (that is, primary authority is held by the local congregation rather than by denominational bodies or officials), we forecast that the evangelicals surveyed would highly value the contents of Factor 8.

Results

No clear interfamily differences appear with regards to "Conflict Utilization" (CC 56) or "Responsible Staff Management" (CC 59).

Sharing Congregational Leadership (CC 58). Both evangelical families give these relatively high ratings, although only those of Evangelical B are significantly higher than those of other families (specifically Anglican-Episcopal, Free Church, and Jewish and Unitarian).

Summary

While it seems that our hypothesis stands at least "softly" confirmed in relation to three of the five clusters for those denominational groups represented in Evangelical B, it remains to be substantiated for the denominations subsumed under Evangelical A. It may be that Evangelical A ministers are normally expected by their congregations to carry the bulk of the church's pastoral duties by themselves, without particular regard for dispersion of responsibility *throughout* the congregation or for interpersonally sensitive "management" (items of all five clusters are described in Chapter 5).

Caring for Persons Under Stress (Factor 9)

Prediction

The Great Awakenings seem to have come about not just through dynamic preaching, but also through pastoral care. "Discipling," as it is often called by evangelicals, is closely related to counseling, to meeting the psychosocial needs of others. We, therefore, predict that evangelicals would place a high premium on the "Caring for Persons under Stress."

Results

No interpretable differences appear on the first two clusters, "Perceptive Counseling" (CC 21) and "Cominstry to the Alienated" (CC 26), or on the last two clusters, "Enabling Counseling" (CC 22) and "Involvement in Caring" (CC 25). The items in "Caring Availability" (CC 23) are the most highly esteemed by the people in Evangelical B, whose ratings are significantly higher than those of the Anglican-Episcopal and of the Lutheran respondents.

Summary

Although no rigorous test of "significance" has been applied specifically to the laity-clergy rating differences for each of the two Evangelical samples, casual inspection of the profile graphs suggests that professional ministers in Evangelical A denominations value both "Perceptive Counseling" and "Enabling Counseling" more than do laypeople in the previously mentioned denominations.

Theologian in Life and Thought (Factor 10)

Prediction

This factor contains clusters of attributes that would seem to be dear to the hearts of many evangelicals. At the same time, large sections of the evangelical populace, both lay and clergy, probably still deserve their antiintellectual reputations. We correspondingly made no prediction.

Results

No significant interfamily differences are obtained on the clusters "Theological Reflection" (CC 29), "Service in Humility" (CC 34), and "Clarity of Thought and Communication" (CC 28). The sixth cluster, "Acceptance of Counsel" (CC 39), yields a few significant differences, but none of these involves Evangelicals A or B.

1. *Acknowledgment of Own Vulnerability* (CC 38). This primary cluster seems to capture what we think might best be described as a "self-disclosure ethic," a belief in the merits of revealing one's weaknesses and afflictions, spiritual and otherwise, to those in one's congregation. Evangelical B respondents do not seem to maintain this ethic close to their hearts. Their ratings of its importance are significantly lower than those of persons representing the Lutheran, Presbyterian-Reformed, and United Church of Christ families. Evangelical A ratings are very close to those of Evangelical B. While these evangelical-nonevangelical differences are not hard to accept as accurate, one wonders why evangelicals, who are steeped in a tradition of confession of sin, are anything less than fully committed to self-disclosure. A possible explanation may be that these evangelical groups interpret vulnerability as weakness not strength. Contributing to this interpretation may be the conviction that confession is made to God alone and is a personal matter between the believer and the Lord.

2. *Use of Broad Knowledge* (CC 30). Evangelical A ratings are notably low and differ significantly from the high ratings of the Jewish and Unitarian family. Evangelical B ratings are about at the average of the families. These results may reflect some antiintellectualism within Evangelical A ranks among both laity and ministers.

Denominational Awareness and Collegiality (Factor 11)

Both evangelical bodies, in common with the remaining denominational families, give significantly higher ratings than the Christian Church (not Disciples) family to the first cluster ("Denominational Knowledge," CC 32) of this factor. Furthermore, Evangelical A ratings are significantly lower than are those of the Presbyterian-Reformed family. This finding may reflect simple polity differences—since, in most of the evangelical denominations surveyed, unlike Presbyterian-Reformed or Anglican-Episcopal denominations, governance is centered in the local congregation rather than in a council of ordained elders or the local bishop—but it may also relate to a difference in how much members of the two families value historic confessional or creedal statements.

In terms of valuing "Denominational Collegiality" (CC 49), Evangelical B respondents rate it as significantly more important than do Southern Baptist, Jewish and Unitarian, United Church of Christ, Christian Church (not Disciples), *and* Evangelical A respondents, who also esteem it less than do the Roman Catholic (Diocesan) respondents.

Why the differences in response—and there are several—between Evangelical A and Evangelical B? History, polity, and (perhaps) theology seem to be the most significant explanations available.

Evangelical A respondents appear to be more theologically conservative than those of Evangelical B. This conservative trait shows up in Factor 1, "Ministry to Community and World," where social and political involvement are valued less highly by group A than B, and Factor 2, "Ministry from Personal Commitment of Faith," where, especially in Core Cluster 2 ("Theocentric Biblical Ministry"), A differs from many more families than does B.

Differences in historical background may account for part of this. It seems that with Evangelical A, the struggles of the liberal-fundamentalist controversy are yet alive. The Conservative Baptist Association of America, for one group, are still very conscious of their differences with the American Baptist Churches in the USA, from whom they separated about thirty years ago. Most of the churches in Evangelical B, in contrast, had their origins in pietistic revival decades before the battle with modernism reached its height. Several of them have not felt the need, therefore, to work within precise creedal frameworks. It should also be noted that the denominations in Evangelical A feel a closer kinship to the doctrinal precision of John Calvin than to the spiritual piety of John Wesley.

This concern for piety shows itself in a number of the Evangelical B responses. Factor 4, "Open, Affirming Style," contains an illustration of this in the exceedingly high value which Evangelical B places on integrity, acceptance of the role of minister, realistic modesty, and caring availability as pastoral attributes.

Differences in history may also account for the fact that Evangelical B values liturgical sensitivity more than does A. The Lutheran roots of the Evangelical Covenant Church of America, for instance, may account for some of this, whereas the Baptist groups in A may carry forward a "meeting house" heritage of directness and simplicity in worship.

Differences in polity should not be overlooked. The churches in Evangelical A are congregational in organization. The loyalties of both pastor and laity at the denominational level are less strong than those of Evangelical B, where both history and church government have forged stronger ties to the organized denomination.

RESULTS: EVANGELICALS RATE VARIOUS DIMENSIONS OF MINISTRY

What kinds of qualities in ministry do the evangelical denominations care about and how deeply? Those are the questions to which we turn in this section. Here we use only the responses of the evangelical group without regard to the comparisons with other denominational families that were the subject of the first section. In this section, no distinction is drawn between Evangelical A and B.

The level of value placed on any cluster or one of its items is expressed as a *mean* or average derived from the following scale:

	From	To
Highly important, essential or mandatory	+2.51	+3.00
Quite important, a major asset	+1.51	+2.50
Somewhat important, a minor asset	+0.51	+1.50
Neither important nor unimportant	−0.50	+0.50
Somewhat detrimental, a minor hindrance in ministry	−1.50	−0.51
Quite detrimental, a major hindrance in ministry	−2.50	−1.51
Highly detrimental, harmful, could destroy the effectiveness of ministry	−3.00	−2.51

Means, therefore, that are scored as 2.50 or better reflect strong endorsement.

The method of presentation begins with a table summarizing the importance that evangelicals attach (based solely on their data) to the various characteristics and emphases of ministry as they were described in the Readiness for Ministry questionnaires (Table 11-2). (The clusters that form from the evangelical patterns are unique; such clusters are not the same as the core clusters that form on the basis of the total Readiness group data.) Brief comments follow Table 11-2 attempting to analyze evangelical concerns and relate them to evangelical traditions and practices. Along the way, we keep an eye open for the places where evangelical laypeople respond differently from their clergy. Note that

1. In Table 11-2 and those that follow, these abbreviations are used: C = professional clergy of Evangelical A and B; L = evangelical laypeople; and T = total sample, both lay and clergy of Evangelical A and B.
2. Rank order shows how highly each cluster is valued in relation to the other clusters: 1 designates the most highly valued, 2 the second most highly valued, and so on.

TABLE 11-2
**Evangelical Clusters Related to "Ministries to
the Religious Community"**

Rank Order	Evangelical Cluster No.	Cluster Source	Grand Mean	Evangelical Cluster Title and Description
3.5	1	C	2.62	*Biblical Focus* Uses Scriptures to guide members, relates the gospel in understandable terms, and speaks of biblical events as real and important
11	2	C	2.48	*Christocentric Preaching* Through authoritative and dynamic preaching, awakens listeners to their need for Jesus Christ
12	3	T	2.40	*Nurture and Respect Toward Youth* Regards youth as thinking members, worthy of serious ministry, and encourages others who are in similar positions
19	4	C	2.25	*Communication of God's Love* Conveys God's nearness and forgiveness, inspires joy, facilitates conversion, and acts considerately
23(3)	5	T	2.20	*Facilitation of Community* Shares in members' daily lives, encourages mutuality during worship, and fosters gospel spirit of freedom and love
27	6	C	2.15	*Warm, Involved Manner* Effectively relates to people, including youth, actively participates in day-by-day activities, and supports innovators

3. The titles and descriptions of these clusters are our own attempts to capture their significance. They are based on the contents of evangelical response to the various questions in the Readiness questionnaire, but have not been correlated with the descriptions of core clusters that appear in Chapter 5 of this book.
4. The headings of this and the next seven tables refer to the section of the questionnaire from which the items that comprise the evangelical clusters in the table are drawn.

TABLE 11-2 — *CONTINUED*

Rank Order	Evangelical Cluster No.	Cluster Source	Grand Mean	Evangelical Cluster Title and Description
31	7	C	2.11	*Effective Teaching* Teaches in an organized, goal-directed, motivating manner and helps people determine their religious educational needs
48	8	C	1.54	*Esthetic Awareness* Appreciates and employs music and other worship aids that are liturgically and pastorally suitable, and maintains a balance between the formal and the personal
49	9	C	1.49	*Social Poise and Propriety* Shows respect for others' autonomy and sensitivity and interacts with ministers of other denominations
55	10	L	1.19	*Openness* Seeks congregation's evaluation of sermons and worship services and participates in ecumenical projects
57	11	T	0.78	*Sacramental-Liturgical View* Teaches meaning of sacraments; sees self as liturgist and ministry as sacramental; smoothly conducts all religious rites occurring in local setting
66	12	L	−1.50	*Constricted, Unloving Style* Acts emotionally "tight," plays favorites, pressures people toward belief, and uses pulpit to express irritation

The clusters summarized in Table 11-2 offer few surprises. We would expect ministers in evangelical denominations to have a strong biblical focus (Evangelical Cluster, or EvC, 1) and a desire to teach the Scriptures in a way that motivates people to discover the "religious educational needs in the congregation" and to "think through a theological stance regarding cooperating with other denominations" (EvC 7). Similarly, the demand for Christocentric preaching with the power and authority to encourage people to acknowledge their sin and their need of a savior (EvC 2) stands at the center of the evangelical heritage. It is also in keeping with this heritage that this cluster pictures the ministers' leading the way in repentance and faith by seeing themselves, along with their hearers, as being under God's judgment.

This call for biblical preaching and teaching seems to be asking for more than sterile dogma or doctrine that is merely objective. The nature of a minister's person and attitude is seen as critically important. For example, the communication of God's love (EvC 4) in both public worship and personal contacts (including a personal engagement in leading people to conversion and an ability to meet the needs of children in worship services) is highly valued; so, too, the ability to relate warmly and supportively to various subgroups in the congregation (EvC 6)—students, young adults, people with desire for change—is seen as crucial. This desire to avoid defensiveness also shows itself in the cluster that affirms openness to self-evaluation, congregational feedback, and participation in projects with ministers of other denominations (EvC 9).

Only two clusters turn up in the lay sampling under "Ministry to the Religious Community." This paucity of clusters may indicate that laypeople in the denominations surveyed have given less critical attention to the questions of such ministry than have their pastors. The laypeople, however, do register a firm interest in how their pastors behave: Positively, they express a fairly deep desire that ministers respect the personal autonomy of their hearers, conduct with poise the various aspects of the service, and participate in interdenominational projects, while weighing the theological implications of such cooperation (EvC 10); negatively, they strongly protest a style of ministry that is too formal, too highly structured, and too manipulative to encourage trust and respect (EvC 12).

Evangelicals may take some encouragement from the three clusters derived from the total group. Clergy and laity agree in their strong affirmation of a ministry that nurtures and affirms young people (EvC 3) and that seeks to build community by becoming part of the daily life of people, by creating an atmosphere enlivened by a spirit of freedom and love engendered by the gospel, and by leading the people in shared prayers (EvC 5). Laity and clergy also concur in their minimizing of a sacramental and liturgical view of worship and ministry—further evidence that the long-standing evangelical suspicion of a sacramental focus is yet alive.

Next we turn to Table 11-3, for evangelical responses on the theme of "Ministries to the Community and the World."

Two observations are prompted by Table 11-3. There is an unusual degree of similarity of perception between lay and clerical views of ministry to the community and the world, as evidenced by the eight total clusters; there is less intense concern among evangelicals for this focus of ministry than for, as an example, gospel preaching and Bible teaching—only two grand means are above 2.00.

TABLE 11-3
**Evangelical Clusters Related to "Ministries to the Community
and the World"**

Rank Order	Evangelical Cluster No.	Cluster Source	Grand Mean	Evangelical Cluster Title and Description
20.5	13	T	2.24	*Ministry to All* Shares God's love in Jesus Christ with everyone, regardless of class, geographical location, life circumstance, or church membership if any
33	14	T	2.01	*Dedicated, Outgoing Approach* Often goes beyond the call of duty, motivates youth, and visits the unchurched to share the faith
45	15	C	1.64	*Sociological Perspective* Understands the effects of social and psychological forces, on both individuals and groups, and urges members to understand and respond to community needs
47	16	C	1.56	*Social Responsibility* Speaks prophetically out of a conviction that the church is humanity's conscience and, in this vein, rejects violence and points to possible personal responsibility in causing world poverty
50	17	T	1.48	*Issues Orientation* Explores and points to theological, psychological, and sociological issues, influences, and implications
51	18	T	1.43	*Social Benefaction* Works to improve community services and practices and offers trustworthy civic leadership, based on theological understanding
53.5	19	T	1.34	*Anti-racism* Combats prejudice, bigotry, and racism, based on a sense of the church as society's conscience and on an understanding of minority groups and other oppressed people
58	20	T	0.36	*Precedence of Evangelistic Goals* Believes that efforts at direct societal betterment should be subordinated to evangelism

TABLE 11-3 — *CONTINUED*

Rank Order	Evangelical Cluster No.	Cluster Source	Grand Mean	Evangelical Cluster Title and Description
60	21	L	−0.38	*Civic Action* Takes active role in public affairs and works on behalf of minorities, older persons, exconvicts, rehabilitated alcoholics and drug addicts, and other outcasts
63	22	T	−1.07	*Aggressive Political Leadership* Works actively, sometimes using group pressure, to protest and redress social wrongs
65	23	T	−1.47	*Resistance to Community Involvements* Avoids social action out of doubt about its usefulness, fear of alienating members, and denial of responsibility

The ministers surveyed put moderate emphasis on both the need for knowledge of the social and economic forces that operate in society (EvC 15) and also the need for the pastor and the church to play a prophetic role in curtailing violence and world hunger (EvC 16). The single lay cluster (EvC 21) seems to suggest a cool response to social action as expressed by concern to know the background and hopes of ethnic groups, to work with community factions, to discuss public affairs, to care for the elderly, and to rehabilitate drug addicts and alcoholics. The lack of interest expressed in the grand mean (−0.38) may indicate that the renewed evangelical interest in social concern has thus far struck deeper roots among clergy than laity.

The deepest commitments registered in this section are to a ministry that shares Christ's love to all, regardless of race, station, or church membership (EvC 13), and to a pastoral style that goes the second mile in openness and outreach to young people and the unchurched (EvC 14). Here the compassionate outreach that Wesley described when he called the world his parish has found fresh expression among evangelicals.

Somewhat less fervent are the tangible expressions of this compassion in fighting racism and prejudice (EvC 19), in teaching congregations to express their social concerns (EvC 17), and in mobilizing them to pursue the cause of justice in their communities (EvC 18). The most affirmed item in this cluster, by the way, has to do with the minister's presentation of "a theological basis for the mission of the church," further evidence of evangelical occupation with biblical doctrine.

Among the most enlightening clusters to emerge in the entire study is one (EvC 20; grand mean, or GM, = 0.36) that specifies the extent to which evangelicals want their ministers to ignore human needs in their quests for spiritual vigor. Member items indicate that respondents are, on the whole, hesitant to allow that the task of proclaiming the gospel should overshadow the importance of relieving human physical, social, and economic suffering. Approaching strangers to inquire about the condition of their souls (issuing religious challenge in the absence of personal involvement) is given a mean rating of only 0.34 (although the mean for the entire group is significantly much lower yet). A strikingly low mean of −0.62 (although still significantly less negative than the total group) is given an item that implies a bifurcation between the sacred and the secular ("Insists that clergy should stick to religion and not concern themselves with social, economic, and political questions" Item 121). At the same time, the item with the highest mean rating (−1.04) is "Priorities in the use of time indicate the belief that the one and only way to build an ideal world society is to convert everyone to Christianity." So, while the evangelicals in the survey are manifestly unwilling to regard the sacred as mutually exclusive of the secular, they do tend to endorse a particular approach to human need; that is, the spread of Christianity. This mission, however, is always to occur in intimate conjunction with the doing of temporal good. Together with the clusters we mentioned earlier (for example, EvC 18 and 21), this small but telling group of items suggests that professional and lay evangelicals collectively are resistant to any sort of divorce that would advance faith or works at the expense of the other—apparently the two are seen as inextricably linked.

There seems to be an almost equal aversion to quietism on the one hand and radicalism on the other. Both lay and clergy oppose the use of the pulpit for political pronouncements and the use of church resources for lobbying with public officials, organizing nonunion laborers, or spearheading recall elections for incompetent public servants (EvC 22). The item in this cluster with the highest level of endorsement (0.28), although still modest, was "Organizes groups to change civil laws that seem in the light of Scripture to be morally wrong." It appears that the evangelicals surveyed are less reluctant to mobilize when society's legislation begins to controvert biblical teachings, as they understand them. At the same time, the people sampled regard as undesirable, and even detrimental, a minister's "expressing doubt about any good coming from social and political change," "not participating in community programs for fear of alienating members of the congregation," or "insisting that the betterment of society is not a responsibility of the congregation (EvC 23). If those evangelical denominations are not yet ready to plunge headfirst into a ministry of social concern, they certainly reflect little tendency to gather skirts of apathy around them in the midst of the suffering and injustice of our world.

Now we turn to the evangelical responses to the concept of "Ministries to People under Stress" (Table 11-4).

Table 11-4 speaks for itself in describing the intensity with which the pastors endorse the need for counseling skills (EvC 28) and perceptive empathy (EvC 25 and 27), together with the ability to refer needy people

TABLE 11-4
Evangelical Clusters Related to "Ministries to Persons under Stress"

Rank Order	Evangelical Cluster No.	Cluster Source	Grand Mean	Evangelical Cluster Title and Description
7	24	C	2.58	*Theological Perspective on Crisis* Turns crises into opportunities to cultivate faith and to draw on spiritual resources
10	25	C	2.50	*Perceptive Maturity* Counsels with warmth, ready availability, sensitivity, and good judgment, attending to feeling tones and addressing problems realistically and honestly
15.5	26	C	2.30	*Referral-Liaison Skills* Refers persons, when appropriate, to other professionals or to experienced laypeople
25	27	C	2.18	*Empathy* Tries to understand the sufferings of others, conveying an awareness of God's forgiveness, and respects others' autonomy
28	28	C	2.14	*Crisis Skills* Effectively intervenes in crises, particularly to those experiencing marital difficulties, illnesses, or estrangements
29	29	L	2.13	*Caring and Sensitivity* Based on a considered theology, freely and perceptively reaches out to help others
62	30	C	−0.72	*Legalistic Rigidity* Tries to solve all problems presented, emphasizing judgment and condemnation

to others who have the will and skill to help (EvC 26). It is in keeping with all that we have seen about the evangelical responses, that, in this section, the most highly affirmed cluster (EvC 24, grand mean 2.58) calls for a pastor who will "help people recognize ways God may be working in their lives"; who will lead people "to deepened spiritual growth and commitment"; who, when counseling will "sometimes confront people with the need to believe"; and who will "help people use the resources of faith in coping with personal problems." The single lay cluster (EvC 29) shows enthusiastic support for the theologically based and empathically expressed skill in counseling.

The cluster with the lowest grand mean (EvC 30, −0.72) seems to reveal some ambivalence in its items as regards to both a pastor's effort "to provide solutions for all personal problems present" (0.10) and the pastor's need to draw "attention to God's condemnation whenever wrongdoing is confessed privately" (−0.36). Strongly resisted by the professionals is the practice of labeling "suicides as deaths outside the kingdom of God" (−1.45).

Table 11-5 shows evangelical responses relating to "The Minister as Theologian and Thinker."

As shown in Table 11-5, both the professional and lay clusters show strong (although not overwhelming) support for a ministry with high intellectual training and interest (EvC 33). Yet the emphases are different: The professionals attach some importance to matters such as wide-ranging reading (EvC 35) and an acquaintance with other religions (EvC 37). The laity, however, gave high marks to clear thinking based on adequate information (EvC 32) and to a commitment to the theological and moral norms of the denomination (EvC 34). The laypeople's sense of dependence on the pastor seem to show up in their expectation of theological expertise (EvC 36), including the pastor's ability to use the biblical languages to identify modern forms of ancient heresies.

By far the cluster most strongly endorsed by both laity and clergy treats the minister's commitment to the Scriptures (EvC 31). The highest single item (mean = 2.95) in this cluster insists that the evangelical pastor "affirm that Jesus is the Son of God," while marks almost as high are awarded to items that deal with "continued and thorough study of the Scripture (mean = 2.85) and demonstration of "knowledge of Scripture." Do these evangelicals endorse a scholarly ministry? In large measure, the answer is affirmative; but they also insist that study of the Bible and a commitment to its teachings (including the acknowledgment of the presence and activity of a personal devil (mean = 2.40) be the primary focus of such scholarship.

Next we examine the evangelical responses to the theme, "The Minister's Personal Commitment of Faith" (Table 11-6).

TABLE 11-5
Evangelical Clusters Related to "The Minister as Theologian and Thinker"

Rank Order	Evangelical Cluster No.	Cluster Source	Grand Mean	Evangelical Cluster Title and Description
2	31	T	2.75	*Biblical Christianity* Affirms Jesus Christ as God's Son, diligently studies Scriptures, and acknowledges existence of a personal devil
34	32	L	1.96	*Cognitive Power and Balance* Evinces and encourages clear, critical thinking, seeks additional information when appropriate, and maintains effective integration of action and reflection
41.5	33	T	1.74	*Intellectual Capacity* Demonstrates awareness of current events, history, and other disciplines, and reflects deeply on the theological implications of these
43	34	L	1.72	*Theological-Denominational Awareness* Embodies and advocates denominational norms, understands youths' interests in other religions, and evaluates current trends in theology
46	35	C	1.60	*Intellectual Breadth and Confidence* Shows intellectual confidence, a wide range of literary interests, and the ability to work with members of other professions
52	36	L	1.40	*Theological Expertise* Uses Greek and Hebrew in private study, identifies modern versions of ancient heresies, and knows scriptural and theological roots of charismatic movement
56	37	C	1.12	*Theological Urbanity* Finds value in other religions, shows sensitivity to human needs and traditions in doing theology, and checks ideas against experience

The importance of the items in this category (Table 11-6) may be seen in the fact that five of the eight clusters have grand means of 1.87 and higher, while two of them show strong negative feelings in their grand means (EvC 44 and 45). The pastors strongly affirm approaches to ministry that seek to apply the gospel in positive Christian living and that show exemplary moral rectitude (EvC 40) and Christian humility in serving without public acclaim, acknowledging mistakes, confessing a need for renewal, believing that God is at work even in the midst of serious problems, and living with a sense of freedom in the gospel (EvC 41). The highest-ranking item in the first of the two clusters (EvC 40) is worth noting: Ministers value a marriage where the pastor's "spouse is a companion in the faith."

In Table 11-6, the two clusters that are formed by evangelical laity seem to complement each other. Evangelical laypeople participating in the study admire a pastor whose life and ministry are marked by a strong sense of the new birth, coupled with a firm call to ministry and a regular practice of prayer, meditation, and Bible reading (EvC 38). At the same time, the laypeople seem to accept the full humanity of their leaders who live "with a sense of daily forgiveness," confide in persons whom they trust, accept the ministries of another pastor or Christian friend, and acknowledge their own mistakes to their governing boards (EvC 42). Thus, daily dependence on God, with full openness to the help of others is a combination valued quite highly by the evangelical laity.

The two positive clusters formed by the total group seem to indicate something of the same balance. Both clergy and laity strongly value a vital Christian faith in ministers, a faith that is reflected sincerely in what they preach, that trusts God in the midst of problems, clings to a sense of call to ministry, depends on prayer in difficult decisions, and shows sensitivity to the Spirit's leading (EvC 39). Along with such a faith, although approved with less intensity, is an openness that means ministers may face up to doubts and temptations. Piety without pompousness or false self-sufficiency seems to be a prime desideratum for evangelical ministers.

The clusters rated negatively in Table 11-6 have to do with hostile or defensive behavior (EvC 44) and with sacramental practices that might be characteristic of Roman Catholic priests (EvC 45). Whatever ecumenical conversations may be taking place between evangelicals and Roman Catholics, the attitudes of both groups toward the use and role of the sacraments (especially the Sacrament of Penance and the Mass) are still poles apart.

Two tables deal with the minister as a person: Table 11-7 with the positive dimensions, and Table 11-8 with the negative.

The clergy clusters in Table 11-7 form an attractive portrait of the minister as a person. Evangelical pastors strongly endorse traits of integri-

TABLE 11-6
Evangelical Clusters Related to "The Minister's Personal Commitment of Faith"

Rank Order	Evangelical Cluster No.	Cluster Source	Grand Mean	Evangelical Cluster Title and Description
1	38	L	2.76	*Personal Orthodoxy* Believes self called to enter ministry, spends time daily in prayer and Scripture reading, and refers to self as "born again"
3.5	39	T	2.62	*Vital Christian Faith* Trusts God with human destiny, actively embraces the Gospel of Jesus Christ, and walks by faith and leading of Holy Spirit
6	40	C	2.59	*Exemplifies Gospel* In actions and words, shows the power of Christianity to positively affect lives, so that they are expressive of God's goodness
9	41	C	2.53	*Optimistic, Yet Humble, Service* Aware of personal limitations and trustful of God's redemptive power and intent, willingly gives of self to ministry
38	42	L	1.87	*Personal Freedom* Expresses sense of God's forgiveness through freedom to confide in others, acknowledges mistakes, and receives ministries of another pastor or friend
53.5	43	T	1.34	*Self-Disclosing Style* Openly, but with propriety, admits doubts, struggles, fears, frustrations, disappointments, and battles with temptation
67	44	T	−1.61	*Alienating Behaviors* Acts in ways that offend others, such as remaining aloof, fighting congregational structures, working at a secular job, and ignoring people in favor of work
77	45	T	−2.99	*Sacramental Sacerdotalism* Values and/or embraces such practices as receiving the Sacrament of Penance and expressing devotion to the Blessed Sacrament

TABLE 11-7
Evangelical Clusters Related to "The Minister as a Person (Positive Qualities)"

Rank Order	Evangelical Cluster No.	Cluster Source	Grand Mean	Evangelical Cluster Title and Description
13	48	C	2.34	*Psychological Maturity* Tolerates disagreement, performs even unpleasant duties, adapts well, is comfortable with highly successful persons, and tempers emotionality with objectivity
14	49	L	2.33	*Stability* Rebounds from setbacks, works autonomously when appropriate, and maintains integrity despite pressures to compromise
15.5	50	T	2.32	*Psychological Integrity* Retains a calm, positive orientation under stress and maintains commitments
20.5	51	L	2.24	*Interpersonal Sensitivity* Intuitively senses others' needs and concerns, shows flexibility and openness, and fosters a positive, caring atmosphere
32	52	C	2.07	*Comfort with Self* Positively accepts own sexuality, allows others leadership when appropriate, and eagerly tries out new possibilities
36(3)	53	C	1.92	*Intellectual Autonomy* Even in the face of adversity, freely expresses own opinions and maintains stands on issues
36(3)	54	C	1.92	*Accepts Diversity* Encourages valuation of diversity in cultures, lifestyles, ideas, and personal experiences
5	46	C	2.60	*Integrity and Security* Maintains commitments to family and others, despite contrary pressures, actively seeks to improve skills, and relates nondefensively to other ministers
8	47	C	2.55	*Healthy Emotionality* Bounces back after negative experiences and genuinely cares for each member

TABLE 11-7 — CONTINUED

Rank Order	Evangelical Cluster No.	Cluster Source	Grand Mean	Evangelical Cluster Title and Description
36(3)	55	L	1.92	*Personal Accessibility* Identifies with parishioners, seeks constructive criticism, does not use clerical role as a defense, and carries out even tasks that are disagreeable
41.5	56	C	1.74	*Peace with Authority* Relates effectively to superiors and denominational authorities and calmly maintains denominational regulations
59	57	L	0.29	*Aggressive Protest* Fights denominational policies, unhesitantly disobeys unjust laws, and supports unpopular causes without regard to social context
61	58	C	−0.44	*Celibacy and Clerical Clothes* Positively integrates celibacy into own life and wears clerical clothing

ty, resiliency, maturity, nondefensive self-acceptance, tolerance of diversity, courage to express one's own convictions, and amicable relationships to denominational structures and leaders.

The lay clusters in Table 11-7 actively support the needs for clergy who are stable in disposition and integrity, who are sensitive to the needs of others, and who do not let their ordination become a barrier to their relationships with others. Rated between detrimental and undesirable are items such as active countering of denominational policies and unhesitating disobedience to unjust laws "when the gospel or concrete situation dictates." At the same time, laypeople do acknowledge the importance of a minister's "supporting an unpopular cause, if own belief indicates it is right." Here we see the customary conservatism of evangelical laypeople at work in their queasiness about protest movements, although they do recognize the need for ministers to take unpopular stands where conscience dictates.

Table 11-8 describes evangelical responses to negative expressions of the minister's personality.

The lower ratings of the four clergy clusters (−1.89 to −2.25) may indicate that evangelical pastors have clearer definitions of the traits they

TABLE 11-8
Evangelical Clusters Related to "The Minister as a Person (Negative Qualities)"

Rank Order	Evangelical Cluster No.	Cluster Source	Grand Mean	Evangelical Cluster Title and Description
76	59	T	−2.48	*Flaunting of Transgressions* Flouts congregational expectations by indulging in offensive activities such as intoxication, infidelity, gambling, or heavy smoking
75	60	T	−2.26	*Social Insensitivity* Rarely reaches out to the infirm, attacks people through sermons, cannot apply learnings from books, and imposes his or her opinions *ex officio*
74	61	C	−2.25	*Harshness to Self and Others* Harshly judges self and others, and expresses condemnatory attitudes by moodiness, impatience, aloofness, and escapist behaviors
73	62	C	−2.23	*Compulsive Doubting and Rigidity* Shows ambivalence and indecisiveness, alternating with a need to retain control, a stiff unapproachability, and an inflexible manner
72	63	C	−2.17	*Authoritarianism* Behaves autocratically and judgmentally, always mindful of clerical status and manifesting a tight, abrupt, pessimistic, hurtful style
71	64	T	−1.95	*Occupational Maladjustment* Functions ineffectively in many areas, including socially, emotionally, and behaviorally, all of which signals poor job adjustment, at very least, and possibly psychological disturbance
70	65	C	−1.89	*Affective Constriction* Rushes about, rigidly unable to delegate authority, to consider alternative methods, to attend to advice from women, or to encounter other people authentically

TABLE 11-8 — *CONTINUED*

Rank Order	Evangelical Cluster No.	Cluster Source	Grand Mean	Evangelical Cluster Title and Description
69	66	L	−1.88	*Faulty Social Judgment* Personalizes criticisms of programs, publicly scolds congregation, fails to provide needed leadership at key times, and makes congregational decisions without consulting appropriate leaders
68	67	L	−1.69	*External Orientation* Relies excessively on public validation and translates need for approval into inappropriate career goals and manipulation of others

do not admire than do their laity. The pastors are on guard against harsh, rigid, overbearing, and tight patterns of behavior. And laypeople are quite sensitive to a critical or scolding spirit, particularly when that is coupled with lack of leadership or with arbitrariness in making decisions (EvC 66). Almost equally rejected by the lay sample are a minister's tendency to take credit for the congregation's accomplishments; to seek constant reassurance; to manipulate people to get things done; and to entertain "ambitions and dreams inconsistent with the ministerial calling" (EvC 67).

The cluster rated lowest and therefore most negatively in this category, shows the traditional evangelical concern with the habits of the clergy. Viewed as very detrimental are such items as repetitive intoxication, extramarital affairs or illicit sexual relationships, frequenting of nightclubs and cocktail lounges, gambling, and heavy tobacco smoking in public (EvC 59).

In general, it may be observed that the evangelical minister is expected to be a model of what he or she preaches, without becoming a pompous paragon of virtue. Emotional balance and sensitivity are highly valued traits. To those who have equated evangelical piety with legalistic lifestyles and attitudes, the appreciation of openness registered in these data may come as a surprise.

Leadership attributes are rated by evangelicals in Table 11-9.

The seven clergy clusters in Table 11-9 seem to suggest a substantial amount of consensus regarding sound managerial practices and a high

TABLE 11-9
Evangelical Clusters Related to "The Minister as a Leader"

Rank Order	Evangelical Cluster No.	Cluster Source	Grand Mean	Evangelical Cluster Title and Description
17	68	C	2.28	*Effective Group Management* Constructively manages conflicts, skillfully channels group process, protects rights of all members, and encourages group to reflect on its goals and strategies
18	69	C	2.26	*Good Information Flow* Actively solicits and distributes information, with a view toward evaluating church programs and keeping members adequately apprised
23(3)	70	C	2.20	*Arbitration and Negotiation Skills* Skillfully directs opposing factions toward creative solution, based on forthrightness, tact, and the ability to understand and clarify complex issues
23(3)	71	C	2.20	*Foresight and Planning* Anticipates the effects and understands the implications of changes under consideration, and relates specific plans to an overall congregational strategy
26	72	T	2.16	*Task-Social Leadership* Facilitates mutuality and trust in the congregation, exercising interpersonal skill, while at the same time effectively reaching concrete goals and evaluating programs
30	73	L	2.12	*Responsible Management* Administers fiscal resources openly and with a sense of stewardship and selects those who are truly the most qualified for particular tasks
39	74	C	1.85	*Acceptance of Dissent* Helps others feel comfortable in disagreeing and constructively airs conflicts of opinion

TABLE 11-9 — *CONTINUED*

Rank Order	Evangelical Cluster No.	Cluster Source	Grand Mean	Evangelical Cluster Title and Description
40	75	C	1.81	*Managerial Trustworthiness* Deals directly and positively with employees, for whom he tries to ensure fair treatment, and relates to staff in a way that is theologically consistent
44	76	C	1.67	*Delegation of Authority* Involves others in decision making, works to broaden the base of participation, and delegates tasks and powers when appropriate
64	77	T	−1.45	*Executive Superficiality* Fails to organize adequately or to appreciate the need for careful planning and glosses over human exigencies and differences

degree of commitment to their importance. Leadership is defined in terms of the abilities to manage group processes, to involve substantial numbers of laypeople in making and implementing decisions, to arbitrate conflict, to allow dissent, to show foresight in planning, to treat fairly the other members of the staff, and to delegate tasks effectively. The whole tone is less authoritarian than one might have guessed, given traditional evangelical response to strong, at times arbitrary, pastoral leadership.

The sensitivity to and regard for managerial style and competent people for the various tasks of ministry, sounds clearly and loudly whenever laypeople voice their concern to those who train their ministers.

CONCLUSION

Three issues need examination as we conclude this chapter: (1) The *priorities* that the evangelical denominations register, compared with the priorities derived from the sampling of all the denominational families; (2) *comparisons,* albeit conjectural, between the responses of the surveyed evangelicals and what might have happened had the Readiness study embraced the whole evangelical movement, as described at the beginning of the chapter; (3) forecasts about what the results of this study augur for the evangelical churches that took part.

The Priorities

A look is in order now at the differences and similarities between the clusters most valued or shunned by evangelicals and those highly regarded or rejected by the combined response of all denominational families in the Readiness study. Something about specific evangelical priorities ought to be discoverable from such a comparison. The evangelicals are paramountly concerned with the extent to which a minister personifies biblical Christianity, both in thought and action.

Evangelicals	*All Families*
1. *Personal Orthodoxy.* Believes self called to enter ministry, spends time daily in prayer and scripture reading, and refers to self as "born again"	1. *Service in Humility* (CC 34). Relying on God's grace, serves others without seeking personal reputation for success or infallibility
2. *Biblical Christianity.* Affirms Jesus Christ as God's Son, diligently studies Scriptures, and acknowledges existence of a personal devil	2. *Personal Responsibility* (CC 42). Honoring commitments by carrying out promises despite pressures to compromise
3. *Biblical Focus.* Uses scripture to guide members, relates the gospel in understandable terms, and speaks of biblical events as real and important	3. *Christian Example* (CC 35). Personal belief in the gospel, that manifests itself in generosity and a life of high moral quality
4. *Vital Christian Faith.* Trusts God with human destiny, actively embraces the gospel of Jesus Christ, and walks by faith and leading of Holy Spirit	4. *Acknowledgment of Limitations* (CC 36). Acknowledging limitations and mistakes and recognizing the need for continued growth and learning

After these more theological clusters, the emphasis among the evangelicals falls on the personal qualities of the pastor.

Evangelicals	All Families
5. *Integrity and Security*. Maintains commitments to family and others, despite contrary pressures, actively seeks to improve skills, and relates nondefensively to other ministers	5. *Building Congregational Community* (CC 55). Actions that will likely build a strong sense of community within a congregation
6. *Exempliifes Gospel*. In actions and words, shows the power of Christianity to affect lives positively, so that they express God's goodness	6. *Fidelity to Tasks and Persons* (CC 43). Showing competence and responsibility by completing tasks, relating warmly to persons, handling differences of opinion, and growing in skills
7. *Theological Perspective in Crisis*. Turns crises into opportunities to cultivate faith and to draw on spiritual resources	7. *Perceptive Counseling* (CC 21). Reaching out to persons under stress with a perception, sensitivity, and warmth that is freeing and supportive
8. *Healthy Emotionality*. Bounces back after negative experiences and genuinely cares for each member	8. *Positive Approach* (CC 44). Handling stressful situations by remaining calm under pressure while continuing to affirm persons
9. *Optimistic, Yet Humble, Service*. Aware of personal limitations and trustful of God's redemptive power and intent, willingly gives of self to ministry	9. *Theoncentric-Biblical Ministry* (CC 2). Drawing attention to God's word and person when preaching, teaching, and leading worship
10. *Perceptive Maturity*. Counsels with warmth, ready availability, sensitivity, and good judgment, attending to feeling tones and addressing problems realistically and honestly	10. *Enabling Counseling* (CC 22). Using high levels of understanding and skill in aiding persons to work through serious problems

Note that in comparing these two lists of ten clusters each, the names for the clusters were devised by the ATS researchers for the total sample clusters and by us for the evangelical clusters. Bear in mind also that evangelicals' response to the questionnaire factors into seventy-seven clusters, whereas the total group's response factors into sixty-four core clusters.

As to the positive list, the evangelicals clearly place a higher priority on their ministers' commitment to and use of the Bible than do the other families. At the same time, all the families in the survey concur in the need for integrity, humility, and maturity in their pastors.

Table 11-8 represents the nine ministerial characteristics viewed by evangelicals as least desired and most detrimental to ministry. These items are drawn from the category "The Minister as a Person (negative)." Ranking tenth from the bottom is "Priestly Commitments." For the evangelicals, this is the only lowest-ranked cluster that is not of a psychological character. If the evangelicals clearly treasure a ministry that is publicly and personally loyal to the Scripture, it is equally clear that what they most shun is not doctrinal heterodoxy but emotional angularity and insecurity.

The Comparisons

We can only conjecture how the evangelical responses might have differed if the total evangelical movement, including persons involved in independent churches, parachurch agencies, and major denominations (including Roman Catholic) had been surveyed. It is not likely that the differences would have been substantial.

Surely all who cherish the name *evangelical* would concur in the high marks given to personal orthodoxy, biblical Christianity and focus, and vital Christian faith, and would likewise shun, as do all Christians, the minister with obvious psychological disturbances.

In the clusters ranked in between the highest and the lowest, we might have found some differences. In denominational relationships and loyalties, for instance, the members of independent congregations and parachurch movements might well have rated significantly below the evangelical denominations surveyed. Even some evangelicals within the major denominations may have experienced sufficient conflict with their churchly structures during the turbulent 1960s and early 1970s to cause them to hold back from strong denominational participation.

We may well guess that greater importance would have been given to community involvement and other forms of social concern had the sampling been wider. There is a strong evangelical left, visible in publications like *Sojourners* and *The Other Side*, that is pressing evangelicals to deeper, more consistent involvement in causes of justice and relief. Furthermore, a number of parachurch agencies, such as World Vision International, Young Life, and Inter-Varsity Christian Fellowship, are giving high priority to these concerns. Beyond that, we can reasonably expect the host of evangelicals in major denominations to have benefited from the raising of Christian consciousness toward the biblical mandate of concern for the poor and the oppressed.

The Forecasts

Venturing forecasts of the future is even more risky than positing hypotheses about the present. There are nonetheless, some trends that need watching.

If the evangelical denominations in this study get the kind of leadership they have asked for, a number of things should follow. For one, there should be increasing *stability and harmony in congregational life,* thanks to pastors who are personally secure and administratively aware of the sound processes by which groups need to function.

For another, any feared trend toward liberalism or secularism in theology seems unrealistic. The commitment to the *centrality of the gospel and the authority of the Scriptures* looks solid. The survey showed these families to be every bit as evangelical in this regard as they purport to be.

For a third, *the piety of these groups seems wholesome.* Though obedience to the Bible and discipline in lifestyle are valued, there is little indication of fundamentalist legalism that would drive future generations into rebellion.

A fourth consideration seems to find these evangelical churches at a crossroads. Their understanding of *the biblical call to justice and their appreciation of the role of scholarship* in ministry seem less than virile. Does their lack of all-out commitment to justice and scholarship mean that they have not yet caught up with the implications of their faith, or does it mean that they are returning to the obscurantism that marked so much of fundamentalism in the 1920s and 1930s? Only an updating of this kind of study, for example, five years from now, will tell.

A fifth consideration may have *ecumenical consequences.* All in all, the differences between the evangelicals and the total sampling seemed fewer in number and smaller in scope than we might have guessed. Is this evidence that there is both a slight movement toward the left on the part of evangelicals and toward the right on the part of ecumenical Protestants? Surely the 1974 Lausanne Congress of evangelicals and the 1975 Fifth Assembly of the World Council of Churches at Nairobi seemed less far apart than did the 1966 Berlin Congress and the 1968 Fourth Assembly of the World Council of Churches at Uppsala.³

Finally, some of the issues most vital to evangelical ministry were not uncovered in the Readiness survey. Little in the survey is geared to investigate a style of leadership that contributes to the growth of congregations numerically and spiritually. The selection of denominations contributed to the lack of emphasis on church growth. Some of the fastest-growing churches—Assemblies of God and the Christian and Missionary Alliance, for example—were not included in the sampling.

Moreover, the items in the survey give inadequate attention to a number of factors that seem to contribute to church growth: the ability of a pastor to sense the needs and character of the constituency from which the congregation can most readily draw new members; an understanding of spiritual gifts and the ways that members can discover and nurture them; a recognition that every congregation is both a modality (an established, unified institution) and a set of sodalities (informal task forces and groupings according to interest, age, or calling); an awareness that the sodalities may be the key to mission, evangelism, and church growth; an insight that spots the subtle and persistent patterns of ingrownness that tend to shut out newcomers.

We have high hopes that the congregations whose pastors and members were surveyed will be agencies of renewal and outreach. But there is not much in the Readiness for Ministry Project that would predict this.

NOTES

1. For details and background of the contemporary evangelical movement in American Christianity, we refer the interested reader to a collection of essays edited by David F. Wells and John D. Woodbridge, *The Evangelicals: What They Believe, Who They Are, Where They are Changing* (Nashville, Tenn.: Abingdon Press, 1975), and to several other works of this genre: Donald G. Bloesch, *The Evangelical Renaissance* (Grand Rapids, Mich.: Eerdmans, 1973); Donald W. Dayton, *Discovering an Evangelical Heritage* (New York: Harper & Row, 1976); Millard Erickson, *The New Evangelical Theology* (Old Tappan, N.J.: Revell, 1968); Carl F. H. Henry, *Evangelicals in Search of Identity* (Waco, Texas: Word Books, 1976); John C. King, ed., *Evangelicals Today* (Guilford, Great Britain: Lutterworth Press, 1973); Bernard L. Ramm, *The Evangelical Heritage* (Waco, Texas: Word Books, 1973); and Richard Quebedeaux, *The Young Evangelicals: Revolution in Orthodoxy* (New York: Harper & Row, 1974). See also Sydney E. Ahlstrom, *Religious History of the American People* (New Haven, Conn.: Yale University Press, 1972).

2. Normally the Church of the New Jerusalem (Swedenborgian) would not be considered as part of the evangelical family. As Chapter 19 describes in detail this denomination empirically grouped with Evangelical B in regard to its conception of ministry. This does not suggest necessary agreement in regard to other theological or doctrinal questions.

3. The meetings at Berlin (1966) and Lausanne (1974) were convocations of evangelicals

from more than 100 countries. Assembled with the encouragement of the Billy Graham Evangelistic Association, the participants gave their attention to the task of evangelizing the world. The Assemblies of the World Council of Churches at Uppsala and Nairobi were part of the World Council of Churches' pattern of convening delegates from all the member churches every seven years.

12

Free Church Family

Warren F. Groff and Steven L. Tuttle

The research team has been aware from the beginning of this project of the difficulties Free Church respondents have in portraying their models of ministry using concepts that imply, to a greater or lesser degree, a view of the status and functions of clergy that is alien to the Free Church tradition. Within the Free Church family, people look for the gifts and responsibilities of ministry given by the Spirit to be shared and jointly administered by many members of the spiritual fellowship. The authors of this chapter have decided to organize the data around several key issues of the group's "heritage memory." These include (1) the role of service within the community as legitimating ministry, (2) the New Testament as the one rule of faith and practice, and (3) Christ's call to a community within the body of Christ—and thus, to the broader social community.

Warren F. Groff, theologian and author, is president of Bethany Theological Seminary in Oak Brook, Illinois. He serves as an ex officio member of the General Board of the Church of the Brethren and was Moderator of that denomination during 1978–79. He has served as a member of the Faith and Order Commission of the World Council of Churches.

Steven L. Tuttle was an M.Div. student at Bethany Theological Seminary at the time this chapter was written. He has served as project director in an effectiveness of treatment research program with the National Institute on Drug Abuse and the National Opinion Research Center. Tuttle is currently Pastoral Director of the Wholistic Health Center of Woodridge, Illinois.

The data confirm a high degree of consensus between the responses of the laity and the clergy of these churches. In fact, the Free Church family ranks first of all the denominational families in this degree of commonality between laity and clergy. Interestingly, the major point of disagreement concerns a law orientation to certain ethical issues, with ministers reflecting a more open stance. This issue further reflects one of the major concerns for this denominational family's future. Will a growing professionalization, through formal seminary education, of ministers polarize the two groups, laity and clergy?

In general, the data portray a group of churches wherein the minister's personal virtues and spiritual gifts authenticate his or her ministry far more than do theological knowledge or particular competencies. The data also seem to imply above-average concern among this group for the oppressed and for combatting social wrongs.

A composite description of the Free Churches as depicted by the religious and secular press would no doubt contain many of the following statements:

- They reject all creeds.
- They consider every member a minister.
- They are known for worldwide relief and rehabilitation efforts.
- They are called "peace churches" because they emphasize reconciliation.
- They exhibit sensitivity to social needs and are service oriented.
- They reject formalism in worship.
- They advocate disciplined Christian living.
- They stress simple living and conformity to secular standards.

Is the descriptive collage formed by these statements confirmed by the Readiness for Ministry data? What changes, if any, in specific images and overall impressions do the data demand?

These statements do reflect key Free Church accents or, to use a phrase coined by philosopher and ethnologist Michael Novak, the group's "heritage memory." Admittedly no one church family can lay exclusive claim even to its most distinctive emphases. Yet certain accents are not stated in the same way or with equal force by all the denominational families in the Readiness for Ministry Project, due to the distinctive experiences from which those accents spring. In this chapter, we have chosen to describe some of the distinctive accents of the Free Church family, which includes the following denominations: Brethren Church (Ashland, Ohio), Church of the Brethren, General Conference Mennonite Church, Mennonite Brethren Churches in North America, Mennonite Church, and Religious Society of Friends.

MINISTRY

Ministry has its legitimation and its service within community. It is rooted in the mission of the total laity. Ministry presupposes the enlivening gifts of the Spirit. These gifts are distributed freely and widely throughout the community, and in such a way that they are never domesticated by patterns of designated leadership. But the priority and the mobility of the Spirit's gifts also do not negate the need for "set-apart" ministers, or better, persons who are "specially positioned within" the body of believers. The task of these particular persons is to help each believer find his or her own identity, calling, and recommissioning as a minister within the community of faith; indeed, through a "set-apart" minister, the community is strengthened in its life and witness.

It can be argued that the Readiness for Ministry questionnaire does not provide an adequate means for describing this distinctive Free Church family accent. The following comments, written by Free Church respondents after taking the survey, show how keenly its members are conscious of the closeness of laity and clergy in Free Church congregations. Many feel the questionnaire items fail to give sufficient emphasis to this close relationship, saying, for example:

- "The pastor as 'equipper of the saints for the work of ministry' did not receive enough emphasis (in the questionnaire)."
- "I see the 'minister' as one of the gifts of the congregation, and would therefore see him or her functioning as one of those gifts. . . . Some of the things expected of the minister could better be supplied by other members of the congregation. This demands of the minister those qualities that permit cooperation, and so on. This means also that the minister must have the gifts to promote total involvement of the congregation."
- "The questionnaire is much too clergy oriented in terms of administration and function. It refers only to the minister's direct involvement rather than to the encouragement of . . . lay leaders and teachers."
- "No consideration was given to the possibilities of a congregation in which no 'ministers' exist, but where each member carries specific responsibilities in relation to his or her own specific gifts (Ephesians 4)."
- "The minister's role is to help all 'ministers' minister more effectively."

Despite the fact that the closeness between laity and clergy has not been explicitly highlighted in the questionnaire items, an implicit premising of that closeness can be seen as a thread that runs throughout the data of the Free Church family. The accent on mutuality is apparent, first of all, in many of the eighty clusters formed on the basis of data from Free Church respondents only.[1] Of these Free Church clusters, the ones indicated in Table 12-1 most directly reflect this closeness and mutuality.

Further evidence of this closeness between laity and clergy is found in the charts (in Chapter 5) that graph the differences between laity and clergy in the importance they accord the sixty-four core clusters. No other denominational family reflects less disparity between scores of laity and clergy than do the Free Churches. The only dimension for which the discrepancy between the two groups may be significant is "Law Orientation to Ethical Issues" (Core Cluster, or CC, 27). The difference in scores is 4.7 standard points, the only one that approaches statistical significance

TABLE 12-1
Rank Order of Free Church Clusters on Closeness and Mutuality

Free Church Cluster	Rank
Encouraging a shared leadership with wide participation	12
Respecting the freedom of persons to carry out assigned responsibilities, striving for a broad base of participation in decision making, and intervening before conflict becomes destructive	17
Identifying with all age groupings in the congregation, relating to persons in the midst of their daily activities, and facilitating their sense of belonging, their conficence, and their competence as they share their faith with one another	20
Nurturing a strong sense of community belonging, being attentive to the quality of relationships among all persons, helping to clarify goals and to devise appropriate implementing procedures, ensuring that tensions and conflicts serve to deepen rather than uproot interior covenants, cultivating shared leadership, and contributing overall efficiency and order to the affairs of the congregation	26
Mobilizing others to help persons with special needs, being open to learn from persons who are suffering, and knowing one's own professional limitations	27
Enabling others to be helping persons	42

(the Free Church laity accord more importance to such an orientation than do their professional clergy).

The close correlation of laity and clergy that runs as an integrating thread through the data is not in itself surprising when measured by the plumbline of long-standing Free Church assumptions about ministry. However, this distinctive accent cannot be blithely taken for granted, particularly in light of trends toward greater professionalism among Free Church clergy and toward the adoption of mainline college and seminary patterns of education for ministry. These trends, observable in recent years, might well have created a wider gap between laity and clergy than the Readiness for Ministry Project reveals. In fact, one wonders why this has not occurred.

Since the data provide no answers to this question, one can only suggest areas that might profitably be explored. Could it be that the style of education for ministry in the seminaries of the Free Church family differs from that of other educational institutions? If so, does that style influence the way in which ministers interpret their function? Are there significant differences among the denominations within the Free Church family with respect to this close agreement of laity and clergy?

Heritage understandings, which are so central in the formation of professionals, accent shared leadership styles, a concept supported by such teachings as "priesthood of all believers" and "distributed gifts for the equipping of all the saints for the work of ministry." Yet the trend towards greater professionalism is undeniable. Thus, the stage is set for potential misunderstanding, and even outright polarization, of laity and clergy, with one side crying "abnegation" and the other side shrinking back from the specter of "domination" in decision making. The data do not reveal a divergence, but the potential for division is there.

FAITH AND PRACTICE

The New Testament is the one rule of faith and practice in the heritage of the Free Church. The New Testament brings into view the purpose of God as revealed in the whole Bible and the ongoing tradition of the church. In the Free Church tradition, the New Testament centers life in Christ, provides direct guidelines for obedience, and opens members to the leading of Christ's Spirit. The New Testament in its dynamic fullness protects against creeds becoming rigid tests, preventing the unfolding work of the Spirit, or serving as instruments of coercion, especially when linked with either state or church powers of external enforcement. Christ is the "internal Word" of the Scriptures, the definitive, personal "symbol of faith" or "creed of creeds." He and the God who sent him forth form a unity that is like two pieces of wood joined so perfectly that the seams do not even show. In him, messenger and message, the one sending and the one sent, are united. Therefore, through him our salvation is secure.

Is this accent on the New Testament's being the one rule of faith and practice reflected in the Readiness for Ministry data? It is significant that the highest-ranked cluster derived from the responses of Free Church ministers and laity (Free Church Cluster, or FCC, 1) does emphasize this unity of belief and action (see Table 12-2). Three others (FCC 3, 14, 16) seem to underscore this emphasis.

More convincing, however, is the evidence found in a consistent pattern of elevated scores on the dimensions that comprise Factor 2, "Ministry from Personal Commitment of Faith" (see Table 12-3). These cluster scores for the Free Church family are elevated in comparison to the scores of many other denominational families. Note especially in Table 12-3 the dimension with the most elevated score, namely, "Encouragement of Spiritual Sensitivity" (CC 6). Members of Free Church congregations place high value on a spiritually sensitive ministry where the notes of forgiveness, freedom, and renewal are sounded. Noteworthy, too, is the higher degree of importance given to an affirmation of a strongly biblical faith in Jesus Christ—one that is informed by the gospel and conveyed through the Scripture (CC 31). The Free Church score is statistically significantly higher than the scores of three other denominational families—Anglican-Episcopal, Jewish and Unitarian, and United Church of Christ.

The importance of the New Testament as the basis for a unity of faith and practice applies also to a minister's personal life. Failure to follow the guidelines of the New Testament with respect to how one should live is considered detrimental to effective leadership in the Free Church. The

TABLE 12-2
Rank Order of Free Church Clusters on Faith and Practice

Free Church Cluster	Rank
Believing the Gospel and letting what one preaches shape priorities and fundamental attitudes	1
Continuing growth in faith and hope that shows itself in interpersonal relationships and a total life orientation	3
Combining theological clarity with doing, with freedom to seek additional information as needed	14
Reflecting theological soundness, consistency, and inclusiveness in all one's helping relationships	16

TABLE 12-3
Free Church Scores on "Ministry from Personal Commitment of Faith"

Core Cluster No.	Core Cluster	Free Church Standard Scores		
		Laity	Clergy	Total
6	Encouragement of Spiritual Sensitivity	53.0	53.8	53.4
40	"Born-Again" Christianity	54.0	51.3	52.65
12	Encouragement of World Mission	51.8	53.3	52.55
31	Affirmation of Conservative Biblical Faith	53.1	51.9	52.5
17	Assertive Individual Evangelism	52.7	51.6	52.15
37	Commitment Reflecting Religious Piety	51.9	52.4	52.15
24	Theologically Oriented Counseling	52.2	51.8	52.0
35	Christian Example	50.8	51.6	51.2
2	Theocentric-Biblical Ministry	50.9	51.1	51.0

importance of recognizing the detrimental and harmful aspects of certain types of behavior on the Free Church ministry is heavily underscored in the high scores given Core Cluster 51, "Secular Lifestyle" (see Table 12-4). The specific behaviors considered especially damaging include visiting local nightclubs and cocktail lounges (Item 543), gambling (Item 569), smoking tobacco heavily in public (Item 556), and telling jokes that hearers consider dirty (Item 526). Free Church laity and clergy give an evaluation of the detrimental effect of such actions that ranks with the highest scores found among the seventeen families. In fact, the Free Church family is significantly more negative with regard to a secular lifestyle than are nine of the sixteen remaining denominational families.

The Donatist tendencies of the Free Church family are evidenced in the fact that a minister's professional efficacy is called into question no matter how knowledgeable or competent he or she is, if the necessary personal virtues and spiritual gifts are lacking. Evidence of this is seen in the high level of Free Church concern over marks of undisciplined living and a self-serving ministry (CC 53).

COMMUNITY

In the heritage of the Free Church family, Christ's call is to community:

- To community whose foundation is the "one body and one spirit
  . . . one hope . . . one Lord, one faith, one baptism, one God and

TABLE 12-4
Free Church Scores on "Disqualifying Personal and Behavorial Characteristics"

Core Cluster No.	Core Cluster	Free Church Standard Scores		
		Laity	Clergy	Total
51	Secular Lifestyle	56.0	55.8	55.9
53	Undisciplined Living	52.4	52.3	52.35
54	Self-Protecting Ministry	51.7	52.2	52.0
52	Professional Immaturity	51.1	52.0	51.55

Father of us all, who is above all and through all and in all"
(Ephesians 4:4–6)
- To community within which persons cooperate in the coming into being of each other, in the naming and using and freeing of their own unique gifts for the strengthening of the whole body
- To community where concern for rectitude is not sacrificed, but where differences, even outright conflicts, are set within the context of a prior covenant
- To community marked by an open circle—not a closed clan—but a family open to all others who make up the larger family of God

The conclusions about community can be considered in two parts, the nature of community within the congregations of the Free Church family, and the scope of broader social community as perceived by Free Church members.

Do the Readiness for Ministry data reflect this traditional emphasis on community as a distinctive accent especially unique to the Free Church family? The answer is no. Measures related to a sense of community indicate that this accent is valued quite similarly by all other denominational families.

The one indication of a distinctive community accent concerns the broad definition of community and is found in the relatively elevated, although not statistically significant, Free Church scores on Factor 1, "Ministry to Community and World." The quite consistent pattern of scores above the mean of 50 strengthens empirically the notion that the Free Church family considers community an open circle that encompasses all humankind. Responses to some of the items validate the popular conception of the Free Church family as leaders in service projects and social action (see Table 12-5).

Two core clusters in "Ministry to Community and World" are especially important to the Free Church family: showing an active concern for the oppressed by working knowledgeably and earnestly on behalf of minority and oppressed peoples (CC 16) and giving aggressive political leadership by working actively with community groups to protest and change social wrongs (CC 18). Relative to all the laity in the Readiness for Ministry Project, Free Church laity especially value an active concern for the oppressed.

Perhaps the characteristics for which the Free Church family is best known are opposition to war and the assuming of a reconciliatory role. Where, if anywhere, are these characteristics evident in the Readiness for Ministry study?

The comments of some respondents in the survey suggest that the instrument used in the project makes inadequate provision for expressing these concerns; for example:

- "In general, there was too much use of traditional vocabulary, and therefore the questionnaire lacks Free Church options: for example, practices of an active peace witness."
- "There should have been more on a strong peace (nonviolent) emphasis and its implications."

TABLE 12-5
Free Church Scores on "Ministry to Community and World"

Core Cluster No.	Core Cluster	Free Church Standard Scores		
		Laity	Clergy	Total
16	Active Concern for the Oppressed	51.7	54.3	53
18	Aggressive Political Leadership	51.7	54.1	52.9
14	Promotion of Understanding of Issues	50.2	53.0	51.6
50	Support of Unpopular Causes	50.7	52.1	51.4
11	Pastoral Service to All	51.4	51.0	51.2
15	Support of Community Causes	49.8	51.7	50.75
13	Initiative in Development of Community Services	50.7	50.5	50.6

- "Our church understands, teaches, and preaches a strong service emphasis, including the way of suffering love, rather than of violence and killing."

An item on the questionnaire that does not cluster but is shown to be significant for the Free Church family is "Teaches people to reject violence in words and deeds as not being in accordance with the Gospel" (Item 159). Fifty-eight percent of Free Church respondents consider such teaching "highly important" compared with only 30 percent of the remaining group of respondents.

The emerging view of the Free Church family is that of a group with strong traditional accents on the community of believers, but one that also is increasingly influenced by values of mainstream American society. This is further reflected in the areas of ministry dealing with fellowship, worship, and service (Factors 5 and 7). The commonality with the rest of American Christendom is most apparent in the data. As the individual items form clusters, they tend to average out with much of the rest of Protestantism. Within this larger area of ministry, the Free Church family values a beginning minister who develops "a congregational sense of being a family of God where there is mutual sharing, worship, and broad participation" (CC 4). Not unexpectedly the Free Church family differs significantly from the Anglican-Episcopal family at this point.

Beneath this rather bland surface pulse greater differences. Note Table 12-6 in which the Free Church family responses to specific items are significantly different from that of other denominational families.

An understanding of ministry in the Free Church tradition opens more fully in an examination of the next area of ministry, "Caring for Persons under Stress" (Factor 9). A superficial or cursory survey of the data would report this group as undistinguished from the general mass of Protestantism. In general, both ministers and laypeople portray their desires for ministers who possess sensitivity and skill as they deal with people facing crises. But a careful look reveals more; it reveals not stark differences, but reflections of a style and outlook unique in the Free Church family (see Table 12-7).

Laity are the key to understanding the Free Church family. Their ministers who have completed college and theological seminary move closer to the mainstream. But people who basically have their roots in rural America and have perhaps thought less formally about ministry reflect expectations for a caring ministry that is different at three points. The first difference is in the high evaluation given by Free Church laity to a core cluster entitled "Involvement in Caring" (CC 25). Lay responses from this group rank the highest of any single group of laity or clergy. As indicated, the differences are not startling enough to be statistically significant but the pattern is so persistent that it demands recognition. The church desires

TABLE 12-6
**Selected Items in Which the Free Church Responses Differ
Significantly from Those of All Other Denominational
Families**

		Percentage Response "Highly Important"	
Item No.	Item	Free Church Family	All Other Denom- ational Families
43	Leads worship so it is seen as focusing on God	51	63
46	Uses biblical insights to guide members in making ethical or moral decisions	50	42
61	Explains the meaning of worship and liturgy	15	28
62[a]	People are converted as a result of his/her ministry[a]	74	66
78	Teaches the meaning of sacraments	20	42
85[a]	Preaches funeral sermons that acknowledge personal grief[a]	70	59
89	Demonstrates the skills needed to teach small children effectively	9	17
92	Understands and appreciates the dogmatic and liturgical foundations of prayer	11	24
107	Calls parishioners by their first names	22	10

Note: All responses are significant at the .001 level.
[a]Percentage includes both "highly important" and "quite important" responses.

the ministry of one who tries to learn the meaning of suffering, who encourages the ministry of those who, in the past, have struggled through a crisis, and who can, in turn, help someone else in a difficult situation. The church desires the ministry of one who can counsel in a caring, nondidactic fashion. The items that deal with suffering and the more intense grief situations most hint at the point where this group differs from mainstream Protestantism. Living now on the land, or having come recently from working with the soil and feeling close to nature, the people comprising the Free Church family perhaps live on more open terms with grief and death than members of other churches. People want to sense the reality of experience—rather than of theory or merely academic skills—in those on whom they place their hands in ordination.

TABLE 12-7
Free Church Scores on "Caring for Persons under Stress"

Core Cluster No.	Core Cluster	Free Church Standard Scores		
		Laity	Clergy	Total
25	Involvement in Caring	52.7	51.6	52.15
26	Cominstry to the Alienated	50.9	51.5	51.2
23	Caring Availability	51.7	49.4	50.55
21	Perceptive Counseling	49.7	50.7	50.2
22	Enabling Counseling	47.9	49.7	48.8

Secondly, the group has preserved particular means for ministering to those who are ill or in crisis. The Free Church family places significantly high value on the anointing of "the sick in a way that brings comfort and support" (Item 257). One senses that the Christian community itself is important in this process of ministering. The Free Church response is also significantly higher with regard to the most important item in "Enabling Counseling" (CC 22): "Helps persons test the implications of alternative decisions they are considering" (Item 261). Encouraging "the bereaved to talk through their grief" (Item 258) is valued significantly more by Free Church members than by the other groups of respondents.

Closely related to the first two points is the third distinction of the Free Church family in the context of caring ministry. In reading the responses of this group, one gets the impression that the members have perhaps a little less reverence for the specialist. They recognize the value of referral to a specialist when needed—but with significantly less enthusiasm than the others in the Readiness for Ministry Project. And they value a bit more highly than others a minister who respects a person's freedom to choose his or her own course of action. Convictions about God, who gives gifts to his people within the Body of Christ, play a clear role in shaping the Free Church family expectations for ministry in this area.

The areas of ministry dealing with the "Development of Fellowship and Worship" (Factor 5) and "Priestly-Sacramental Ministry" (Factor 7) can be examined together. The general pattern of Free Church expectations reflects motifs similar to those we have been examining (see Table 12-8).

Most Christian groups place similar values on many of the character-istics of ministry concerning competent preaching and leading of worship; namely, the ability to relate faith to life, and to minister to children and youth. The Free Church family attaches significantly less importance to

TABLE 12-8

Free Church Scores on "Development of Fellowship and Worship" and "Priestly-Sacramental Ministry"

Core Cluster No.	Core Cluster	Free Church Standard Scores		
		Laity	Clergy	Total
4	Encouragement of Mutuality in Congregation	50.9	52.3	51.6
3	Relating Well to Children and Youth	50.4	47.7	49.05
1	Relating Faith to Modern World	48.6	49.3	48.9
5	Competent Preaching and Worship Leading	48.6	48.2	48.4
7	Liturgical Sensitivity	46.8	48.1	47.5
9	Sacramental-Liturgical Ministry	46.1	45.3	45.7

an orientation that stresses the sacramental and liturgical aspects of worship than does the Roman Catholic, Anglican-Episcopal, Lutheran, Orthodox, Presbyterian-Reformed, Evangelical B, or United Church of Canada families. Within this broad area, the Free Church family values most highly the "Encouragement of Mutuality in Congregation" (CC 4), registering a ranking among the highest of the seventeen families in the Project.

The data in these two areas (Factors 5 and 7) support the traditional and popular concepts about the high value the Free Church family places on community. The churches' early emphasis on simple living seems to be still reflected in their patterns of worship. This is a good illustration of the high degree of agreement found between Christians, lay and ordained. The question of future change, of the possibility of an increasing distance between minister and laity is raised as one examines the directions and patterns of laity-clergy differences.

We shift our perspective now from areas of close agreement to some differences between Free Church laity and clergy. Are the differences ones we might expect in light of background heritage understandings? Do they reflect the shaping impact of contemporary patterns in the education of ministry, and are the directions ones educators intend?

"Law Orientation to Ethical Issues" (CC 27) is the core cluster on which there is the widest divergence between the attitudes of the Free Church clergy and the laity. This core cluster emphasizes both God's demands and his condemnation as a basis for solving personal problems. In all denominational families, a greater percentage of laity than professionals expect their minister to condemn wrongdoing, give solutions for all personal problems presented, and take a relatively hard line on matters such as suicide. This finding seems puzzling in view of the higher-than-average expectations of the Free Church family on "Active Concern for the Oppressed" (CC 16) and on "Involvement in Caring" (CC 25). Is it possible that members of the Free Church family have an open, accepting attitude toward non-Christian, but, because of high expectations for fellow Christians, a legalistic attitude toward church members? Further investigation might help clarify this apparent contradiction.

The discrepancy between clergy and laity in relation to law orientation seems to indicate that education is indeed having an effect and that clergy are moving more rapidly than the laity.

Another difference has to do with "Denominational Knowledge" (CC 32). Laity value knowing official polity statements somewhat less than do clergy. Laity also place slightly more stress on the value of "Denominational Collegiality" (CC 49). Another way of saying this is that laity give priority to the interiorized story of a given group, while clergy are clearer that the story as remembered needs the disciplining that comes from research and documentation. This suggests that education does influence attitudes among clergy and in ways that educators largely applaud.

Related areas of interest are "Theological Reflection" (CC 29) and "Clarity of Thought and Communication" (CC 28). Neither laity nor professionals in the Free Church family rank these characteristics very high as compared with other church families (see Table 12-9). On the former characteristic, the ranking falls in the middle range; on the latter, Free Church ministers rate this dimension lower than any other group of clergy. This is an understandable outcome in light of the Free Church heritage, with its emphasis on faith in life and action, accompanied occasionally by outright suspicion of things academic and intellectual. It is probably not the case that specialized knowledge in a minister is denigrated, but, rather, that such knowledge is not the crucial issue. The emphasis in the Free Churches has traditionally been on making the connection between possession of skills and their practical application, on the link between the abstract or intellectual and its practical embodiment. Here we surmise that contemporary educational patterns are designed to counter (albeit with less success than is likely to be desired) some of the heritage predispositions. To have clergy rate these qualities even slightly higher than laity is surely perceived by educators to be pointing in the right direction; that is, toward the goal that clergy and laity alike might give higher value to life-serving theological analysis and construction as part of strong continuing education disciplines.

One final area eliciting our comment deals with "Acceptance of Coun-

TABLE 12-9
Free Church Scores on "Theologian in Life and Thought"

Core Cluster No.	Core Cluster	Free Church Standard Scores		
		Laity	Clergy	Total
39	Acceptance of Counsel	54.9	58.1	56.5
38	Acknowledgment of Own Vulnerability	51.3	52.3	51.8
34	Service in Humility	48.0	49.0	48.5
30	Use of Broad Knowledge	48.2	48.4	48.3
28	Clarity of Thought and Communication	47.5	47.6	47.55
29	Theological Reflection	45.5	48.0	46.75

sel" (CC 39). It is almost misleading for us to deal with the issue under the rubric of differences between laity and clergy. Free Church clergy do assign somewhat higher value than laity to the need of the minister to accept the counsel and ministry of others in seeking to know God's will. But Free Church laity rate this dimension higher than do any other group of laity, and Free Church clergy rank second among all the clergy of the seventeen church families. We take this to be strong evidence that the Free Church heritage is having a continuing impact and that congregational as well as transcongregational educational patterns are forming lay and clergy responses in the direction intended.

In general, the data we have reviewed seem to confirm the picture of the Free Church sketched at the beginning of this chapter. It is not possible on the basis of the Readiness for Ministry data to determine whether simple living and nonconformity to secular standards are characteristic of the laity. The laity do, however, hold these expectations of their leaders. In a dimension entitled "Secular Lifestyle" (CC 51), Free Church members are significantly more negative than the Anglican-Episcopal, Orthodox, Jewish and Unitarian, Lutheran, Presbyterian-Reformed, Roman Catholic, United Church of Christ, and United Church of Canada families with regard to such "secular" habits as visiting local nightclubs, gambling, smoking, or telling dirty jokes.

The scores on "Ministry to Community and World" (Factor 1) support the popular conception of the Free Church as service oriented. However, one finds somewhat surprising the relatively low (that is, average) rankings on several dimensions such as "Service in Humility" (CC 34), as characteristics of ministers in a group that has emphasized the "servant" role of the church.

One can conclude from the data that root metaphors and teachings within the Free Church family continue to nurture a lofty vision of an obedient church and its ministry. Admittedly, this vision is far more an ideal than a steady state of affairs. The divisions that have plagued Free Church denominations through the years testify to the constant struggle to let the actual match the ideal. But, then, no single church family has privileged access either to the vision of life in covenantal community or to the struggle to achieve it.

NOTES

1. These eighty clusters were formed on the basis of data from Free Church respondents only.

Cluster No.	Description
1.	Believing the gospel and letting what one preaches shape priorities and fundamental attitudes
2.	Advising while respecting the freedom of persons to choose, helping persons discover ways faith relates to life, and listening for feeling tones
3.	Continuing growth in faith and hope that shows itself in interpersonal relationships and a total life orientation
4.	Serving without need for acclaim, acknowledging one's limitations, empowered by God's call
5.	Being a person of integrity in all relationships
6.	Having a sustaining sense of God's call and a nurturing spirituality
7.	Setting an example for others, strengthened by a supportive spouse
8.	Helping to keep conflict constructive
9.	Responding quickly, with genuine caring and with ability to mediate the resources of faith to persons coping with crisis situations
10.	Following through on commitments, stimulating positive expectations among persons, taking initiative, having a supportive spouse, facing up to unpleasant tasks, and standing up to those who disagree and those who are "symbols of success"
11.	Cultivating a broad base of financial support of the congregation, interpreting the reasons for and possible benefits of proposed changes, and helping all people understand controversial issues
12.	Encouraging shared leadership with wide participation
13.	Freely owning one's own limitations, maintaining a sense of humor, accepting the help of others, and encouraging youth to consider a ministerial vocation
14.	Combining theological clarity with doing, with freedom to seek additional information as needed
15.	Having relational and spiritual qualities, depth understanding, and counseling skills that make one a helping person
16.	Reflecting theological soundness, consistency, and inclusiveness in all one's helping relationships
17.	Respecting the freedom of persons to carry out assigned responsibilities, striving for a broad base of participation in decision making, and intervening before conflict becomes destructive
18.	Sharing and expressing feelings without loss of personal judgment
19.	Working for congregational renewal and identifying with persons in their daily affairs
20.	Identifying with all age groupings in the congregation, relating to persons in the midst of their daily activities, and facilitating their sense of belonging, their confidence, and their competence as they share their faith with one another
21.	Being open, adaptive, and a self-starter

22. Relating to persons who differ with acceptance and forthrightness
23. Teaching in a clear, interesting, and effective manner
24. Bringing helpful perspective and a reconciling spirit into conflict situations
25. Remaining level-headed and facilitating constructive attitudes among persons in conflict situations
26. Nurturing a strong sense of community belonging, being attentive to the quality of relationships among all persons, helping to clarify goals and to devise appropriate implementing procedures, ensuring that tensions and conflicts serve to deepen rather than uproot interior covenants, cultivating shared leadership, and contributing overall efficiency and order to the affairs of the congregation
27. Mobilizing others to help persons with special needs, being open to learn from persons who are suffering, and knowing one's own professional limitations
28. Having well-grounded faith convictions that are Christ-centered, Scripture based, and consistent with one's own denomination
29. Actively seeking ways to increase one's theological competency and to continue learning while ministering
30. Leading worship and preaching so that people experience the joy of having life centered in God and Christ
31. Valuing diversity, being willing to support an unpopular cause, and accepting the risks in change
32. Having an understanding of conflict as it relates to one's own theology, and helping the congregation to face into its tensions so as to strengthen community, while enlarging cultural interests, being aware of value implications of corporate discussions, and avoiding stereotyped sex roles within the group's own organizational life
33. Relating in a fitting professional manner to neighboring ministers and being secure in one's own ministerial identity
34. Being secure in one's ministry without excessive need for personal gain and recognition, working cooperatively with superiors
35. Being perceptive and thoughtful in one's beliefs, analytical when necessary, and able to communicate complex issues simply
36. Teaching nonviolence and speaking prophetically
37. Helping the congregation to avoid stereotyped sex roles within its own life, to enlarge its cultural interests, and to face its conflicts constructively; avoiding the launching of innovative projects without adequate congregational support
38. Preaching and leading worship in a manner that heightens the consciousness of God, strengthens the sense of community, and combines dignity with personal warmth, spontaneity, and pastoral appropriateness
39. Strengthening the unity of the body, dealing with differences by referring to Scripture and tradition, as well as to one's own inner life
40. Being an effective and trusted community leader
41. Contributing to the quality of the congregation's recordkeeping, office management, long-range planning, and delegation of authority
42. Enabling others to be helping persons
43. Lacking excessive concern about status as compared with other professions and having courage to take a stand on issues
44. Speaking knowledgeably and confidently about a variety of subjects, including the development of the church
45. Utilizing social awareness and analytical skills in support of community needs
46. Maintaining good colleague relationships with denominational leaders and other staff professionals, facing into disagreements rationally and calmly
47. Supporting persons willing to try something new, appealing to persons as those who are themselves socially responsible, and modeling a thoughtful cooperation with other denominations
48. Winning respect of society's outcasts, urging sacrificial giving, staying alert theologically from a world perspective
49. Helping persons experience the Scriptures as living
50. Openly admitting one's weaknesses and failings

51. Knowing denominational history, supporting attitudes of openness to other religions, and being informed biblically and theologically about the current charismatic movement

52. Enabling community and congregation to share concern for liberation of the oppressed

53. Spontaneously changed order of worship and encouraging congregational use of shared prayers

54. Contributing to the adequacy of the congregation's recordkeeping, planning process, and delegation of administrative responsibilities

55. Stimulating congregational singing, explaining meanings and changes in order of worship, and fostering an appreciation of music and other arts

56. Relating to staff and employees in a fair and straightforward manner

57. Using original languages, acknowledging activity of a personal devil, and accepting the Bible as final authority

58. Leading in the acceptance of persons who testify to a dramatic conversion experience

59. Working for racial integration and the welfare of the socially alienated

60. Combatting racism in church and community

61. Giving attention to persons needing social rehabilitation and to civil laws that should be changed

62. Being effective politically as an agent of social change

63. Thinking and functioning sacramentally

64. Organizing the congregation to reach particular political goals

65. Accenting personal conversion to the neglect of the gospel imperative that we serve the neighbor in need

66. Practicing fasting, experiencing the gift of tongues, and expressing antiestablishment views

67. Fostering decisions that favor buildings over people, underplaying importance of planning, glossing over real differences in order to preserve the appearance of unity, overplaying the place of intention and charisma in lieu of careful planning

68. Experiencing gift of tongues, practicing fasting, and earning a living through secular employment

69. Projecting negative attitudes toward the prospects of social betterment and place of the congregation in working toward that betterment

70. Using pulpit for personal ends, manipulating persons, and fostering congregational parochialism

71. Receiving the Sacrament of Penance regularly, celebrating Mass daily, and—as a priest—managing finances in a spirit of poverty

72. Being inflexible in face of unexpected demands, having ambitions inconsistent with ministry, constantly needing reassurance, intellectualizing as a way of avoiding emotions

73. Compulsively needing public acclaim, manipulating persons, consistently resisting unexpected demands, needing constant reassurance

74. Becoming overly deferential under pressure, being unable to accept one's mistakes and move on, worrying excessively about what others think, acting impulsively

75. Closing oneself off from wider community, being cold and impersonal, showing favoritism, measuring one's worth by salary, and taking criticism as an attack on one's office

76. Being status oriented; dominating group discussion; being frenetic, abrupt, and impatient in relationships; withdrawing when things do not go well; projecting pessimism, moodiness, and impatience; refusing to delegate responsibility; and using office to meet personal needs

77. Using sermons to attack and scold persons; failing to relate preaching and teaching to life, and projecting a confused sexual identity

78. Lacking regard for persons, being unable to adjust to other persons in close living situations, lacking self-forgiveness, and failing to give aggressive leadership when needed

79.   Ignoring persons, violating confidences, and taking criticism personally
80.   Occasionally becoming intoxicated, smoking heavily in public, gambling, becoming involved in extramarital affairs or illicit sexual relationships, and frequenting nightclubs

13

Lutheran Churches

George Lindbeck

Lindbeck first depicts Lutherans as defined by the empirical data. Then, in the latter half of his chapter, he reflects personally on possible practical implications of those traits distinctive to Lutherans—those characteristics that, although not the most highly valued aspects of ministry, define the unique traits that make Lutherans Lutheran.

The ministerial expectations articulated by Lutherans in this study are indeed somewhat eccentric within the context of North American Protestantism. Although Lutheranism, with its Christ-centeredness and its emphasis on sin and forgiveness, resembles to some extent what has come to be called "conservative evangelicalism," it is not, to the same degree, puritanical, literalistic, foreign-mission-minded, or revivalist. In some ways, therefore, Lutherans resemble those denominations that have moved farthest from their nineteenth-century evangelical embodiment toward greater liberalism and, possibly, toward more secularization. Lutherans continue to blend both "evangelical" and "catholic" (that is, sacramental, liturgical, and nonpuritanical) characteristics.

George Lindbeck is Professor of Theology in the Department of Religious Studies and the Divinity School, Yale University, New Haven, Connecticut. In addition to his teaching and writing, he is a member of the Management Committee of the Division of World Mission and Ecumenism of the Lutheran Church in America, and Co-chairperson of the International Roman Catholic—Lutheran Joint Study Commission.

Lutherans tend frequently to have more cluster scores in the middle range; however, a glib reading of the family as typically "religious Middle America" is inaccurate and misleading. As Lindbeck points out, given that the core clusters are derived from transdenominational data, Lutherans may have an average rating for a core cluster, but within that cluster they rate certain items significantly higher and others significantly lower than the total group rates them. Furthermore, Lutheran laity are quite often significantly more conservative than their clergy. Finally, the various bodies within the large family of North American Lutheran churches differ among themselves. Despite these difficulties implicit in the task of interpretation, Lindbeck maintains a broad perspective of the whole body and its current and potential place within the North American context.

Lutherans are frequently thought of as unique among major American Protestant bodies in the degree to which they take seriously their official doctrinal standards. It is generally supposed that in Lutheran responses to the Readiness for Ministry questionnaire one finds an expression of what is specifically Lutheran, of what constitutes Lutheran identity. We inevitably find ourselves asking, therefore, about the extent to which the understanding of Christianity and ministry reflected in the Lutheran responses to the Readiness for Ministry survey corresponds to the Lutheran Confessions (the official doctrinal writings of the Lutheran Churches), and the meaning of that correspondence or noncorrespondence.

Before raising questions, we must outline what the statistics indicate. This, however, is more hazardous an undertaking for Lutherans than it is for most denominational families. As regards expectations for young ministers, the three major bodies into which the North American family of Lutheran Churches are divided in some respects resemble other denominations more than each other. Based on factor analysis, the Lutheran Church in America reflects a concept of ministry similar to that of the United Methodist, Anglican-Episcopal, and United Church of Canada denominational families. The American Lutheran Church, however, shows an affinity with the United Church of Christ and the Reformed Church in America. The third Lutheran body, the Lutheran Church—Missouri Synod, reflects concepts parallel to those of the Christian Reformed Church and differs markedly with those of the Christian Church (Disciples of Christ). It follows from this that the ratings for Lutherans as a whole may apply with varying accuracy across the three bodies. Yet in this project we are confined to the overall ratings because more differentiated statistical analysis of the data has not been available. This indicates that the generalizations that follow must be treated with caution. They describe points of commonality among all Lutherans in North America; the data do not provide a portrait of any one of the three major Lutheran bodies.

Nevertheless, these generalizations do have their utility. When the Lutheran Churches as a whole differ markedly from others, including those bodies with which they are thought to have the closest affinities, one may justifiably surmise that a pandenominational trait of some importance to Lutheran identity is at work. Admittedly, such guesses need to be tested by more particularized studies, but surveys of the present kind are needed in order to identify the salient questions to be investigated later.

DESCRIPTION OF THE DATA

We must first describe the data before speculating about pertinent questions. The material in this initial, descriptive section is organized in terms of the eleven factors that emerge from the second-order factoring of the core clusters. The factors are not dealt with, however, in their sequential order, but rather in terms of increasing differentiation. Areas in which the denominations reflect similar expectations of beginning ministers are described before consideration of those areas in which the dissimilarities are greater.

More specifically, I start with views of what young ministers should or should not be as persons (Factors 4 and 3), leaders (Factors 6 and 8), and counselors (Factor 9). General qualities, rather than specifically ministerial ones, are for the most part grouped in these areas. Greater denominational divergence, but little that is distinctively Lutheran, becomes apparent when we turn to the factors that deal with the minister as educated person or as "Theologian in Life and Thought" (Factor 10) and as denominational functionary (Factor 11). The same holds true for "Priestly-Sacramental Ministry" (Factor 7), which chiefly serves to distinguish Roman Catholics from non-Roman Catholics. Uniquely Lutheran patterns of response become more evident, however, when we come to Factor 5, "Development of Fellowship and Worship"; and this distinctiveness increases in the last two factors, "Ministry to Community and World" (1) and "Ministry from Personal Commitment of Faith" (2), where political orientations and specifically religious convictions are salient.

The Minister as Person

Positive Traits: "Open, Affirming Style" (Factor 4)

The transdenominational agreement in this factor is remarkable. It is almost complete in three dimensions—"Fidelity to Tasks and Persons" (Core Cluster, or CC, 43), "Positive Approach" (CC 44), and "Flexibility of Spirit" (CC 45). And in those three clusters in which there are minor denominational variations, "Acknowledgment of Limitations" (CC 36), "Personal Responsibility" (CC 42), and "Acceptance of Clergy Role" (CC 47), or the one in which there are laity-clergy differences, "Valuing Diversity" (CC 46), Lutherans are for the most part not distinctive; they are solidly in the middle range. The only significant difference that occurs in this factor between the Lutheran Churches and the other sixteen families is that the Evangelical B family places higher total value on "Personal Responsibility" (CC 42) than do Lutherans. The American cultural consensus on what constitutes personal qualities is apparently a powerful one.

Yet there are two items in the cluster "Acknowledgment of Limitations" (CC 36) and one item in "Personal Responsibility" (CC 42) on which Lutherans, while considering those items important, fall significantly below the mean. Lutheran laity are less insistent than the total group that the young minister know when he or she needs help (Item 363), and laity seem less concerned that the young minister maintain "personal integrity despite pressures to compromise" (Item 513), although Lutherans still rate the trait as highly important.

Do Lutherans have lower standards in these matters? Or are they more likely to think that failure is inevitable either because of a particularly demanding definition of, for example, "integrity," or because of their doctrine of human sinfulness? Or do they perhaps have a concept of ministry as an objective task for which personal virtue is less important than for some other concepts? Given the differences between the denominational families that rank lowest in these dimensions, one suspects that here, as so often, diverse causes produce similar effects, but the available data do not provide any clear grounds for saying more than this. All we can do is note that here, as in certain of the following areas, a variety of interpretations is possible.

Disqualifying Personal and Behavioral Characteristics (Factor 3)

Certain types of behavior are disapproved across all denominational families. No one thinks young ministers should be self-protecting (CC 54), undisciplined in life (CC 53), or professionally immature (CC 52); and, furthermore, there is a remarkable degree of transdenominational agreement on what kinds of conduct are to be thus classified.

We should note, however, that Lutherans do tend to express themselves a bit more mildly than most respondents on many of the 42 items in these three clusters. This reaches statistical significance[1] at four points for Lutheran laity; namely, sermons containing personal attacks (Item 559), poor adjustment to those with whom the minister lives (Item 571), living beyond personal means (Item 560), and displaying mannerisms of the opposite sex (Item 550).

It is hard to know how to interpret this data. Possibly Lutherans on the whole really are somewhat more tolerant than most people of these defects in young ministers; however, conceivably their standards lead them to find these defects where others do not, with the result that they have more occasion to exercise the virtue of tolerance. One can ask, in short, whether the variation arises from differences in the definition of the behavior in question, or from a different attitude toward the behavior once it is defined. Nothing in the data provides an answer. It is thus impossible to draw any firm conclusions from the apparently less-condemnatory stance of Lutherans on these items.

However, there is a fourth group of generally disapproved actions, "Secular Lifestyle" (CC 51), regarding which Lutheran leniency is both statistically dramatic and for the most part unambiguous in interpretation. Drinking (Item 543), occasional gambling (Item 569), smoking (Item 556), and occasionally telling jokes "that hearers consider dirty" (Item 526) are the four items in this category. Lutherans are significantly less negative than the average on the first three points, and, taking the cluster as a whole, they rank far below most Protestants. Only the Anglican-Episcopal, United Church of Christ, United Church of Canada, Jewish and Unitarian, Roman Catholic (Order and Diocesan), and Orthodox families rank as low or lower. This is what most people would expect. Lutherans are widely reputed to be less puritanic (or, perhaps better, less Victorian) than the American Protestant mainstream, at least as far as nonsexual matters are concerned. It is reassuring to find general impressions confirmed.

Yet here, too, a difficulty of interpretation arises. Is Lutheran tolerance in this area to be explained by secularization—that is, accommodation to modern lifestyles—or is it an indication that Lutherans, like the Orthodox and the Roman Catholic families, are traditionalists who have been relatively unaffected by the puritanism and nineteenth-century evangelicalism of the wider American religious culture? The fact that Lutherans, as we shall see, are on many points more conservative than the Anglican-Episcopal, United Church of Christ, and United Church of Canada families suggests that the traditionalist answer is the correct one. But this leads to a further question: "Is Lutheran nonpuritanism attributable chiefly to theological convictions or to ethnic backgrounds?" On this question, the survey data provide no help. The data suggest that theological factors are operative, but no information bearing on the influence of ethnicity has as yet been isolated.

The Minister as Authority Figure

Negative Traits: "Privatistic, Legalistic Style" (Factor 6)

The transdenominational unanimity of Lutheran laity and clergy on two of the clusters in this area, "Alienating Activity" (CC 10) and "Total

Concentration on Congregational Concerns" (CC 20), is as great as anywhere. Two other clusters in this area show a marked difference between the responses of laity and clergy, but not between the Lutheran Churches and most other denominations. Lutheran laity are less critical than their clergy of a "Law Orientation to Ethical Issues" (CC 27) and of ministerial arbitrariness or "Intuitive Domination of Decision Making" (CC 60), but in these respects they are not denominationally distinctive. Laypeople are consistently and significantly less critical than their clergy of a legalistic orientation.[2]

A distinctively Lutheran emphasis does emerge, however, in a final dimension, "Precedence of Evangelistic Goals" (CC 19). The proportion of Lutherans who approve the items in this cluster is small but close to the mean except at one point. Lutherans as a whole are significantly more critical than the average respondent of the young minister who "frequently approaches strangers to ask about the condition of their souls" (Item 135).[3] This suggests that Lutherans have been less affected than most American Protestants, not only by the puritanism of nineteenth-century evangelicism, but also by its "conversionist," "revivalistic," or "born-again" emphasis. As we shall see, this suggestion is supported by other evidence.

Positive Traits: Congregational Leadership (Factor 8) and Caring for Persons under Stress (Factor 9)

Turning now to positive qualities in "Congregational Leadership" (Factor 8) and "Caring for Persons under Stress" (Factor 9), we note that trans-denominational agreement continues to prevail, and that in those clusters (six out of ten) in which one or more of the denominational families depart notably from the general consensus, the Lutherans remain in the middle range. Further, there are only eight individual items out of a total of 73 in which the Lutherans as a group depart significantly from the mean.

Only two of these exceptions have to do with the role of the minister as leader within the congregation. In the dimension of "Effective Administration" (CC 58), Lutherans place above-average stress on keeping parish records up to date (Item 672), while in the extremely large cluster of "Conflict Utilization" (CC 56), Lutheran laity (but not clergy) give significantly less than average weight to creating "a sense of community where members are concerned for each other" (Item 689). Polity presumably explains the first point, but Lutherans have a normal amount of concern for supportive interpersonal relations. Perhaps the word *community* is one to which they do not resonate so warmly as do most American church members.

This guess is possibly supported by scattered Lutheran deviations in the counseling area that could also be interpreted as reactions to words rather than as reflections of reality. The laity, in sharp distinction to Lutheran pastors, consider it less important than do most respondents that young ministers "listen for feeling tones" (Item 267), "convey warmth and concern by silence and physical presence" (Item 269), help "persons test the implications of alternative decisions they are considering" (Item 261), "learn the meaning of suffering from a person who suffers" (Item 247), and provide referrals to other professionals or specialists when needed (Items 259 and 277). On more traditional-sounding items related to divorce (Item 254), the terminally ill (Item 251), and in Core Clusters 23 ("Caring Availability") and 24 ("Theologically Oriented Counseling"), both laity and clergy tend consistently to be near or above the median. Whether this difference is to be accounted for chiefly by resistance to modern counseling emphases or simply by unfamiliarity and lack of sophistication is not clear from the data.

The Minister as Educator: Theologian in Life and Thought
(Factor 10)

That it might reflect a certain nonintellectual tendency within the Lutheran Churches is suggested by answers in another area that indicate that Lutheran laity, but not clergy, place somewhat less than usual emphasis on having ministers who are intellectually outstanding. Lutherans are below the mean on most of the items in "Use of Broad Knowledge" (CC 30),[4] where the profile peaks with the Christian Church (Disciples of Christ), Jewish and Unitarian, and the United Church of Christ families. In Core Cluster 28 ("Clarity of Thought and Communication"), Lutheran laity tend consistently to be lower than average, although they do not differ significantly. Interestingly enough, the clergy peak in this cluster occurs with that for the Southern Baptists. The Orthodox clergy, who were among the lowest-rating of the professionals in the previous dimension, rise, along with the Evangelical B group, to equality with the high-ranking Jewish and Unitarian family. Under the heading "Theological Reflection" (CC 29), Lutheran laity are significantly below average in the importance they give to young ministers' acknowledging the contribution of the Jewish past and present to an understanding of Christianity (Item 325), to thinking through the problems of "divorce, abortion, and suicide" (Item 327), and to his or her understanding the processes of ethical decision making (Item 326). For the dimension as a whole, however, Roman Catholic (Diocesan) ratings are the highest. It seems, given these variations in the denominational peaks, that different kinds of intellectuality are reflected in these three dimensions; Lutherans, it will be observed, are not outstanding in any.[5]

The three other dimensions in this factor of "Theologian in Life and Thought" have to do more with "life" than with "thought." Lutheran lay ratings continue, although to a lesser extent, to be somewhat low for items in two of the clusters. Take, for example, "Laughs easily even at self" (Item 333, from CC 34, "Service in Humility" or "Confides in a trusted person(s)" (Item 347, from CC 39, "Acceptance of Counsel"). By contrast, in the most heavily loaded cluster in this factor, "Acknowledgment of Own Vulnerability" (CC 38), Lutherans—and especially their clergy, along with those of the Christian Church (Disciples of Christ) and United Church of Christ—tend toward the high side. This reaction is not exclusive to Lutheran clergy; Lutheran laity stress even more the central item in the cluster; namely, "Openly admits to times of doubt and struggle over own personal faith" (Item 345). This perhaps reflects, not the influence of modern psychological insights (as may well be the case for other groups who rate high in this cluster), but rather the continuing effects of Luther's theological emphasis on the continuing effects of sin, even in the justified, for he spoke freely of his own attacks of anxiety and doubt even to the end of his life. The evidence is slight but seems to me to point in this direction.

The Minister as Functionary: Denominational Awareness and Collegiality (Factor 11)

When we turn to expectations concerning "Denominational Knowledge" (CC 32) and "Denominational Collegiality" (CC 49), we discover that the various families differ widely, but that Lutherans, together with the Anglican-Episcopal, United Methodist, and Presbyterian-Reformed families, fall within the middle range. In the cluster entitled "Denominational Knowledge," Lutheran professionals place somewhat more emphasis than their laity on knowing the historical background of confessions of faith (Item 316), but Lutherans as a whole are somewhat less inclined than the total group to stress knowledge of denominational polity and official statements (Item 323). In the second cluster, "Denominational Collegiality," they tend to avoid either pro- or antiestablishment extremes. Thus, for example, Lutherans are somewhat less likely than others to consider following "directives from denominational leaders" (Item 509) as either "highly" important or not important at all for a young minister. Lutheran clergy are less likely than their laity to judge this issue as "highly important." (The Lutheran mean rating for this item is, however, significantly higher than that of the total group.)

Two items that do not cluster should be noted. Lutherans are significantly more insistent than the average respondent that the young minister reflect "the teaching of the denomination" (Item 300),[6] but they are less concerned than the average that the neophyte identify "to parishioners the denomination's moral expectations" (Item 312). This difference can be construed as supporting the widespread view that Lutheran loyalties are focused on their sixteenth-century confessions (that is, "the teaching of the denomination") but not on what the currently organized denominations may say (that is, not on their "moral expectations"). It perhaps also reflects a Lutheran distrust of legalism and an insistence on the primacy of gospel over law.

In summary, Lutherans appear to want their young ministers to be moderately, but only moderately, good organization men and women. To be sure, given the newness of the Lutheran Church in America and the American Lutheran Church (both formed by mergers within the last two decades), and the disputes now rending the Lutheran Church—Missouri Synod, these responses perhaps indicate an unusual degree of underlying proclivities in favor of organization.

Lutherans Are Not Roman Catholics: "Priestly-Sacramental Ministry" (Factor 7)

Two dimensions in the area of "Priestly-Sacramental Ministry" are of little help in distinguishing non-Roman Catholic groups from one another. Lutherans, we discover from Core Cluster 41 ("Priestly Commitment") are very similar to other Protestants in their general aversion to such practices as receiving the Sacrament of Penance (Item 367), "daily celebration of Mass" (Item 349), and "devotion to the Blessed Sacrament" (Item 383), while from Core Cluster 48 we simply discover that a dimension entitled "Mutual Family Commitment" is much more important for groups with married rather than celibate clergy. A third cluster, "Sacramental-Liturgical Ministry" (CC 9) is more instructive for our purposes, but this is better dealt with in the next factor.

The Minister as Preacher, Celebrant, and Teacher: "Development of Fellowship and Worship" (Factor 5)

In Factor 5, at long last a distinctively Lutheran pattern of some magnitude is not only foreshadowed but clearly emerges. We learn, although scarcely to our surprise, that Lutherans are to a unique degree both "evangelical" (in the original sense of that term) and "catholic." They share with all Protestants (not including the Anglican-Episcopals) the view that the minister is fundamentally a preacher, a proclaimer of the Word, but the Lutheran Churches combine this concept with a more fixed and formal liturgy and a stronger emphasis on the sacraments than is typical of other Protestant denominations. Each item in this area on which Lutherans deviate markedly from the mean neatly illustrates one or more aspect of this pattern. Thus, under "Competent Preaching and Worship Leading" (CC 5), Lutheran laity place unusual stress on the preparation of people for "participation in Holy Communion" (Item 52). In a cluster on "Relating Faith to Modern World" (CC 1)—which does not exist as a distinguishable dimension in the Lutheran samples—the Lutherans show significantly more concern than does the remaining group that young ministers explain "any changes introduced into the worship service" (Item 45). In contrast, the encouragement of "participation of congregation in shared prayers" (Item 90) is of significantly less importance to Lutheran clergy. Finally, in "Sacramental-Liturgical Ministry" (CC 9), where Lutherans superficially resemble, for example, the United Methodist and Presbyterian-Reformed families, Lutherans place significantly greater weight than the total group on teaching the "meaning of sacraments" (Item 78). Lutherans, especially the laity, endorse to a significantly greater extent than the total group a conception of the ministry as sacramental (Item 76) rather than a view of the clergy as primarily liturgists (Item 65). With regard to the sacramental-liturgical dimension, Lutherans place significantly more weight on this cluster than do the American-Canadian Baptist, Southern Baptist, Free Church, Jewish and Unitarian, and Evangelical A families but significantly less importance than the Orthodox Churches and Roman Catholics (Diocesan). In worship, whatever might be true in other domains, Lutherans resemble high-church evangelicals.

Politics: "Ministry to Community and World" (Factor 1)

In this area, where political orientations are most prominent, clergy-laity differences reach their maximum for a large group of families, including the Lutheran Churches. The denominational contrasts are also sharp, although not so extreme as in the last factor, "Ministry from Personal Commitment of Faith," which we shall shortly consider. Amidst this diversity, Lutherans tend, as usual, to be in the middle range, but nevertheless in a distinctive fashion.

Their distinctiveness lies in the quietistic character of their affirmation (on which they are as emphatic as most) that the mission of the church include the service of the world. They agree that needy individuals should be helped no matter who they are and that worthy community causes should be supported, but the laity have an above-average reluctance to see the young minister involved in controversial issues. In short, Lutheran laypeople seem more inclined than most respondents to insist that the church not try to change systems, patterns, or structures. Rather, its social and political role should be ameliorative and supportive.

Responses to "Initiative in Development of Community Services" (CC 13) are in this respect symptomatic. Lutheran laity respond more positively than most to young ministers who work creatively with the youth (Item 114), but not (and this includes Lutheran clergy to a lesser degree) to those ministers who work actively "for justice in the local community" (Item 109). Similarly, Lutheran laypeople show average or above-average approval of the items in "Pastoral Service to All" (CC 11) and of those in the largely ecumenical cluster named "Ecumenical and Educational Openness" (CC 8). They are, however, consistently (although not significantly) below average in the dimension of "Active Concern for the Oppressed" (CC 16). This lay reticence reaches statistical significance in reference to young ministers who acquaint themselves with the needs of minorities (Item 157), recommend discontinuance of parish support for discriminatory institutions (Item 148), and speak "prophetically out of a conviction that the church is the conscience of humanity" (Item 156). Lutheran laity are especially resistant to the young minister who "speaks from the pulpit about political issues" (Item 117) and are significantly less positive than most respondents to the pastor who "takes an informed position on controversial community issues" (Item 126). In a cluster labeled "Support of Unpopular Causes" (CC 50), Lutheran laity fall below the mean in their approval of the beginning clergyperson who "supports an unpopular cause, if own belief indicates it is right" (Item 504)—although it should be added that the clergy are as willing as the median respondent to have him or her participate "vigorously in community causes as a private citizen" (Item 498). Finally, although Lutherans, especially clergy, are generally favorable to the "Promotion of Understanding of Issues" (CC 14) when this is a matter of using psychological and sociological knowledge for ordinary pastoral purposes, approval declines significantly among Lutheran laity.

It is especially perilous, however, to generalize about Lutheran positions in this area, not least because of the laity-clergy polarization. Lutheran pastors and laity are a significant 8.8 standard scores apart in the dimension of "Aggressive Political Leadership" (CC 18). This same gap is found among the United Methodist and American-Canadian Baptist families and is even greater for the United Church of Christ.

Why is this gap so great among Lutherans? The only suggestion that emerges from the data is that the general conservatism of the laity in this area is reinforced among Lutherans by a certain quietism, a special degree of insistence that the young minister avoid politically controversial issues, especially in the pulpit. This is combined with a greater-than-median insistence, especially among the clergy, on other aspects of the social mission of the church. One possible explanation for this disparity is that attitudes derived from a traditional, quietistic version of the "Two Kingdoms" theory (according to which the church should confine itself to preaching the gospel) continue to influence the laity but have largely disappeared among the professionals. Lutheran laity, therefore, lack the political activism characteristic of most American Protestantism. This activism comes from Reformed (Calvinistic) Puritanism, and can take conservative forms (for example, in the struggle legally to prohibit alcoholic beverages or enforce Sunday blue laws) as well as liberal forms. More data would be needed, however, either to confirm or disconfirm this hypothesis.

Fundamental Convictions: "Ministry from Personal Commitment of Faith" (Factor 2)

We turn now from laity-clergy polarization to the domain of greatest denominational contrasts. Traditional doctrinal differences are more influential here than anywhere else except for the Roman Catholic versus non-Roman Catholic disagreements registered in Factor 7. These differences affect not only the importance given to the various items but also the way they are interrelated.

Thus, there is nothing on the Lutheran side directly corresponding to the dominant or most heavily loaded core cluster in this area, "Commitment Reflecting Religious Piety" (CC 37). This divides into three distinct groups of Lutheran answers that differentiate a sense of sin and forgiveness, a sense of God's sustaining work and call in the carrying out of the Christian mission and of ministerial vocation. Further, the central item in the core cluster, "Shows sensitivity to the leading of the Holy Spirit" (Item 343), does not appear at all in these Lutheran clusters and is rated "very important" by significantly fewer Lutherans than by others. Yet Lutherans—especially clergy—are decidedly more insistent than the average on the importance of the young minister's living "with a sense of daily forgiveness" (Item 372). These are the two most notable Lutheran departures from the mean in the fourteen items of the cluster. The religiously committed person, they seem to say, is the forgiven sinner rather than the Spirit-led. One is reminded here of the historic Lutheran suspicion of the perfectionism and spiritualism of the sixteenth-century enthusiasts and of the Lutheran insistence that the justified are simultaneously sinners.

This same traditional opposition to perfectionism presumably helps explain the Lutheran reactions to the items that group under the concept of "Christian Example" (CC 35). The notion of the minister's setting a Christian example (Item 376) is theologically associated by Lutherans, not with "Behaves morally in a way that is above reproach" (Item 373) but, in a unique Lutheran cluster, with a sense of forgiveness and confession of sin (Items 372, 369). Indeed, the very idea of being "above reproach" is considered "very important" by notably fewer Lutherans than by others.[7]

It would be a mistake, however, to attribute this simply to antiperfectionism; that is, to Lutheran doubts that human beings can ever be morally above reproach. Lutherans, it seems, are also less inclined than the average to think of personal moral qualities as directly involved in the ministerial role. Lutheran laity consider it significantly less important than do others, for example, that the young minister "provide a personal witness to the Gospel by his own generosity" (Item 374).

The same "anti-Donatist" tendency to think of the ministry as the objective office or task of preaching the Word and administering the sacraments is also suggested by another pair of answers. Lutheran clergy in particular reverse the usual emphasis by stressing that the public call to the parish, rather than the personal decision to enter the ministry, is more important for young ministers to perceive as God's call (CC 37, Items 340 and 348). To be sure, a more refined analysis would perhaps show that there is, within Lutheranism, a conflict between a pietistic tendency to emphasize the inner call of the Holy Spirit and a nonpietistic inclination to think of God's call as coming through the church.

Interestingly enough, Lutherans associate the item on the public call (Item 340) with a sense of being sustained by God in carrying out Christian tasks (Item 337 and 332); while the second item, which stresses personal decision (Item 348), is grouped with such disapproved "pietistic" behavior as talking in social conversations "about what the Lord has done recently in the minister's own life" (Item 377). These help form a secondary Lutheran cluster that also includes two items central to the core cluster of " 'Born-Again' Christianity" (CC 40). In reference to these items, Lutheran laity are less negative to young ministers' speaking of themselves as being "sanctified" (Item 344) than are most respondents, but they are a little more negative (and the clergy are far more negative) to those who refer to themselves as "born-again" (Item 354).

Further evidence of opposition to revivalism emerges from an examination of "Encouragement of Spiritual Sensitivity" (CC 6). There is no corresponding Lutheran cluster. While Lutherans (especially clergy) place notably greater-than-average emphasis on the central item, "Enables people to sense the gift of forgiveness God conveys through his Word" (Item 59), this is in the context of worship that focuses on God (Item 43) and evokes consciousness of Jesus Christ (Item 47) rather than of services in which plans are changed spontaneously "in response to the leading of the Spirit" (Item 67). On this point and on the item, "Works for renewal in the church" (Item 91)—where Lutherans may tend to equate renewal with revivalism—the Lutheran answers are decidedly below the mean.

This coolness to revivalism is also indicated by the unusually negative reactions in the dimension of "Assertive Individual Evangelism" (CC 17) against the young minister who "frequently approaches strangers to ask about the condition of their souls" (Item 135) and, to a somewhat lesser degree, against the one who believes "that the one and only way to build an ideal world society is to convert everyone to Christianity" (Item 123). Lutheran clergy are, again, more critical of this latter attitude than are the laity. Yet Lutherans rank with the mean in the dimension as a whole because of their positive responses to, for example, the minister who "visits unchurched people to share the faith" (Item 116). This provides further evidence for the persistence within Lutheranism of an older, Reformation-type of evangelicalism that has been at least partly resistant to the nineteenth-century variety that has now largely appropriated the name.

The relatively small impact of this newer evangelicalism is perhaps also indicated in the scale of "Encouragement of World Mission" (CC 12). Lutheran laity are significantly low in their support for "world missions" (Item 146) and for the pastor who "urges parish to respond to critical needs in the world through sacrificial giving" (Item 120). Yet, as so often happens, Lutherans are median for the dimension as a whole; they are so in this case because they endorse as much or slightly more than the average such items as "pastoral service to all people with needs" (Item 147) and the "need for learning from Christians in other parts of the world" (Item 133).

We come now to a final set of significantly deviant responses found in the two dimensions of "Affirmation of Conservative Biblical Faith" (CC 31) and "Theocentric-Biblical Ministry" (CC 2). Lutherans are decidedly above average on the first three items in the stress they place on a minister who "interprets the authority of Scripture as being in the gospel message" (Item 308); on his or her affirming "that Jesus Christ is the Son of God" (Item 293); and on treating "the Bible, interpreted by the Church, as the final authority in all matters of faith" (Item 287). Yet they are close to average in their emphasis on the importance for the young minister of "continued and thorough study of the Scriptures" (Item 294), and of demonstrating "knowledge of Scripture" (Item 321). In the second cluster, "Theocentric-Biblical Ministry," they fall somewhat below the mean (with the laity significantly lower) on affirming a minister who "guides people by relating the Scriptures to their human condition" (Item 50), and decidedly below on his or her using "biblical insights to guide members in making ethical or moral decisions" (Item 46). Lutherans, it appears, remain at least to some extent influenced by Luther's dictum that the Bible is not to be used as a law book and that what is finally authoritative about it is not everything it contains, but its message of forgiveness through Christ.

Further evidence for this interpretation can be garnered from the pattern of responses to one of the few items in the questionnaire that raises the issue of biblical literalism: "Acknowledges the presence and activity of a personal devil (Satan)" (Item 313). Lutheran clergy are significantly less willing than the sample as a whole to say either that this is "very important" or that it is valueless or detrimental in a young minister. This suggests that many have the attitude that if such a belief can be scripturally supported, it should not be condemned outright, yet the mere fact that it is in Scripture does not make it important.

Many Lutherans like to think that their tradition is unique in emphasizing the Bible in a nonliteralistic, nonfundamentalistic way. Perhaps they are right. The evidence suggests, at any rate, that an unusually large proportion would like to maintain this combination. Once again, however, a more refined analysis would undoubtedly reveal great differences. A literalistic approach to the Bible is clearly a major issue within the Lutheran Church—Missouri Synod, even if it is not in the other two major Lutheran bodies.

Finally, it is imperative to note in reference to "Affirmation of Conservative Biblical Faith" (CC 31) that Lutherans place greater-than-average weight on young ministers affirming that "Jesus Christ is the Son of God" (Item 293), with a still heavier accent among the laity, than on any other item in the entire survey except one. The exception is "Believes the Gospel she/he preaches" (Item 338). These are the only two items that receive the rating of "very important" from over 90 percent of the Lutherans (the comparable scores for the total sample are 82 and 91 percent respectively). The next two "very important" ratings fall between 70 and 80 percent for both Lutherans and the total group, and constitute an analogous pair: "Demonstrates knowledge of Scripture" (Item 321—once again, from the "Affirmation of a Conservative Biblical Faith" cluster) and "Keeps own word—fulfills promises" (Item 505 from CC 42). It seems that what the respondents as a whole want, above all, are ministers of sincerity and integrity who believe in Jesus Christ and know their Bibles.

The only surprising thing about these desiderata is their utter traditionalism. They presumably also would have received top ratings in the North Africa of Augustine's day or the Europe of Luther, Calvin, and Ignatius Loyola.[8] On these points, Lutherans are not distinctive. They are simply part of a consensus that embraces most denominational families.

SUMMARY

Lutherans, as we have repeatedly noted, tend to fall in their core cluster scores in the middle range. Their profiles suggest that they are religiously "Middle American" to an even greater extent than United Methodists, who, although for the most part as close to the median as the Lutherans, diverge sharply in one dimension because of their greater puritanism ("Secular Lifestyle," CC 51).

This, however, is misleading. Lutherans, for example, are close to the extreme in the size of the gap between laity and clergy in the dimension of "Aggressive Political Leadership" (CC 18), but this is not reflected in the average or total group scores. An even more pervasive difficulty is that often core cluster profiles fail to disclose denominationally distinctive patterns or linkages of items. As we have seen, they fail to show that Lutherans, for example, emphasize the sacraments, but not the ministry as sacramental or liturgical; Lutherans emphasize sin and forgiveness, but not revivalistic techniques. They stress "bringing everyone to know God's love in Jesus Christ" (Item 150), but not conversion as a result of the pastor's ministry (Item 62); Lutherans emphasize the Bible, but not as a source of law. Lutherans, in other words, are not half-way between the extremes in their emphases on "Sacramental-Liturgical Ministry" (CC 9), " 'Born-Again' Christianity" (CC 40), and "Affirmation of Conservative Biblical Faith" (CC 31). Rather, they are in some respects high and in others low on what these dimensions normally mean within American Christianity. The patterns of their responses are distinctive, and *from the perspective of those patterns* they are not in the middle, they are not average, but rather, one suspects, consistently higher than other denominations.

Thus the data suggest that the Lutheran Churches continue in some measure to represent a form of Protestantism that is eccentric in the American context. This Lutheranism is like what has come to be called "conservative evangelicalism" in its Christ-centeredness and emphasis on sin and forgiveness, but it is not to the same degree puritanic, revivalist, foreign mission-minded or biblicist ("fundamentalist"). In these latter points (although the reasons are different), it resembles the liberal denominations, which, in adjusting to the modern world, have moved farthest beyond their nineteenth-century evangelical phase. However, the resemblance is in part superficial, for the Lutheran Churches are also liturgical and sacramental (as are the Anglican-Episcopal, Roman Catholic, and Orthodox families), doctrinal (as are Roman Catholics), quietistic —as far as the laity are concerned—in politics (as are the Orthodox), and more traditionalist (because the type of evangelicalism that they represent is older) than the conservative evangelicals themselves.

The continued discernibility of this pattern, however, says nothing about its current strength or long-term viability. Is it waxing, waning, or holding its own? How many Lutherans are consciously committed to maintaining it, and how strongly and how strategically are they placed to influence the future? Empirical answers to these questions would require surveys spread over a period of years and containing, in part, different items than the present ones. In short, we simply cannot tell on the basis of available information how significant the defining denominational characteristics are likely to be as tests of readiness for ministry in Lutheran churches during the coming decades.

Nevertheless, speculation on this question is unavoidable. The data we have reviewed, taken in conjunction with information and theories derived from other sources, will inevitably be used to help formulate policy recommendations. In the next section of this chapter, therefore, I suggest some of the possible practical implications. These suggestions are necessarily hypothetical. Their empirical confirmation or disconfirmation must be left to further research and to time.

REFLECTIONS

In focusing on the denominationally distinctive features of the Lutheran responses, I to some extent neglect the most important of all the Lutheran expectations for the ministry. Lutherans agree with others, it will be recalled, that young ministers above all should believe the gospel they preach, keep their word, know their Bibles, and accept Jesus Christ as Son of God. Yet, because these criteria are common to most churches, they will not be the center of attention. Our chief concern is with the defining Lutheran characteristics, even though these are from the Lutheran point of view of secondary importance.

At the same time, however, we must remember that a sharp line cannot be drawn between the universally Christian and the denominationally particular. A denominational tradition is not an extraneous husk enclosing an invariant Christian core, but is, rather, a distinctive way of being a Christian that influences all aspects of life and faith. Lutherans, for example, have their own perspective on what it means to "know the Bible" or to "accept Christ." Yet, although what is specifically Lutheran and what is more generally Christian cannot be isolated from each other, they can to some extent be separately considered.

What, then, are the strengths and weaknesses in the contemporary American scene of the distinctively Lutheran way of being a Christian? What can be done on the policy level to capitalize on the strengths and correct the weaknesses? How can the empirically ascertained expectations or criteria for ministry be met; or, if they cannot or ought not be met, what can and should be done to modify them?

These questions, obviously, are in part empirical ("What is the case?"), in part normative ("What ought to be the case?"), and in part practical ("What policies can help us move from the *is* to the *ought*?"). In what follows, I start with an interpretation of the empirical situation, turn to a consideration of norms, and lastly comment on policies. No attempt is made to give final answers. Rather, I try to indicate some of the factors to be taken into account when devising answers.

The Empirical Situation

Little can be directly inferred from the data reviewed in the first part regarding the actual strength or weakness of the Lutheran pattern of expectations for ministry. Consider, for example, the distinctively large gap between the clergy and laity in the dimension of "Aggressive Political Leadership" (CC 18). The survey by itself does not tell us when or how this gap developed or whether it is likely to expand or narrow. We must make use of other sources of information in order to draw conclusions on these points. These other sources, furthermore, rarely give us hard data. What knowledge they do supply is unmanageable, diffuse, and extensive and can be organized in a wide variety of interpretive frameworks. Whether the framework I have chosen is more or less adequate than alternatives is a question that cannot be discussed here.

An assessment of how strong the present Lutheran pattern is in contemporary North America must take into account both "social" and "faith" factors. One can ask, that is, about its ability to provide a sense of "belonging," on the one hand, and of "meaning," on the other, and about how the two are interrelated.[9] Where the sense of belonging is high and of personally appropriated meaningfulness is low, one has what might be called "low-intensity" religion. People may take membership seriously, but for traditional or social reasons rather than for reasons of personal faith. Where the reverse is true, enthusiasm may be high, but with little communal stability or permanence. When both the sense of belonging and meaning are intense, one has a sociologically sectarian group. From this perspective, mainline churches are normally composite. They contain nuclei[10] of communally loyal and religiously committed adherents within a very much larger mass of peripheral members, some of whom may be highly devout but identify little with the particular church to which they happen to belong; most are likely to be members largely for traditional or social reasons. These distinctions, it should be observed, do not correspond to that between active and inactive adherents. While nuclear Lutherans can be expected to be active, the religious-but-not-communal and the communal-but-not-religious groups consist of both the active and inactive.

From the viewpoint of this interpretive scheme, the strength of a denominational or confessional pattern depends in part on the degree to which it is supported by a distinctive cultural (such as ethnic) tradition or by wider social forces and, in part, on its appeal to those who are seeking for meaning, for salvation—for themselves or for the world. I return in a moment to the first part of this disjunction, but first let us glance at one reason why (within this schema) conservative evangelicalism, on the one hand, and Eastern cults and the "new religious consciousness," on the other, have been growing at the expense of the mainline denominations. The mainline denominations have lost appeal in part because of the widespread disenchantment with "the American way of life" and with the "establishment." Seekers for salvation have multiplied, but they have been most likely to listen to strident voices rather than to the muted proclamations of the larger churches. For the less alienated seekers, the answers, couched in the to-some-degree-familiar idiom of revivalistic, charismatic sectarian Christianity, have been the most intelligible and appealing; while the more thoroughly disenchanted questers (especially numerous among the youth of the better-educated classes) have often turned to non-Christian offers of salvation. It is uncertain how long or strongly the new religious movements will persist. They are often weakly institutionalized, and once the high-intensity phase is over and they are confronted with the difficult task of reproducing themselves in the next generation, they may lose their appeal and their ability to resist the pressures of the wider culture. History is full of religious movements that have initially been impressive but have vanished almost without a trace. It is therefore possible, although by no means certain, that in the long run the historic churches, including most of all the seventeen denominational families distinguished in the survey, will remain the major religious forces on the North American scene.

Change will, of course, continue within these varieties of Christianity. Conservative evangelicalism may continue to grow (and also to change its character), the Roman Catholic transformations started by the Second Vatican Council are not yet complete, the Orthodox will presumably become more and more another mainline American denomination, and the intellectual and cultural leadership of liberal and prestigious denominations such as the Anglican-Episcopal, Presbyterian-Reformed, and United Church of Christ families may well continue to decline. Their destiny is perhaps linked with that of the WASP elite within which they have historically been strongest, and the hegemony of this elite is passing. Ecumenical rapprochement and new denominational alignments may also make a difference. Our concern, however, is with the Lutheran Churches. What are the strengths and weaknesses of their distinctive denominational pattern within this shifting milieu?

It will be recalled that this pattern, as described in the first section of this chapter, is an "eccentric" one. It combines features that do not belong together in terms of the major American cultural patterns (although, obviously, the situation would be different in Germany or Scandinavia). It is both "evangelical" and "catholic" (that is, sacramental, liturgical, and nonpuritanic). It tends to be theologically conservative, but normatively not in its attitude toward the Bible. In the political realm, it is "this-worldly" rather than "other-worldly" in its basic view of the church's responsibility and involvement in the secular sphere, but it has been unusually quietistic.

These idiosyncracies could under some circumstances be a source of strength. Where Lutherans, for example, have a strong sense of belonging to an ethnic minority in which they take pride and whose distinctiveness they wish to preserve, their adherence to a special kind of religion is of great importance. The church legitimates their separateness, and their separateness sustains the church. This interplay between ethnicity and religion is a familiar theme to American historians and sociologists. Because of it, immigrant groups, including the Lutheran ones, have often become more, rather than less, insistent on their religion, and their confessional differences once they settled in this continent.

What was once an advantage, however, may now become a disadvantage. While it is true that most Lutherans have German or Scandinavian ancestors,[11] this proportion is declining. The desire to belong to churches with "our kind" of people remains strong, no doubt, but this phrase applies increasingly to the white middle classes in general, not primarily to those who have a similar ethnic background.

Lutherans do not seem likely to benefit, as Roman Catholics may, from the recent rise in ethnic consciousness.[12] There is little inducement for Protestants of North European background to stress their ethnic origins. They blend easily on the social and cultural level with other white Protestants and in some parts of the country even tend to get classified as "WASPs." Moreover, the role of Germans in twentieth-century history has not been such that Lutherans would be forward in claiming German ancestry. There seems, indeed, to be a programmatic commitment to not thinking of Lutheranism as in any way an ethnic denomination. Close to 90 percent of all Lutherans repudiate the notion that "Their German or Scandinavian origin makes Lutherans different from other Christians."[13] The mergers of the last two decades, furthermore, have eliminated almost all ethnically organized Lutheran church bodies. Except for certain small groups and for individual parishes, conscious stress on ethnicity will in the future be a handicap rather than a help to American Lutheranism.

This erosion of the ethnic base raises doubts, however, about the long-run viability of Lutheran distinctiveness. The problem is not simply that the Lutheran Churches are different (that is true of every denomination), but that they are different in a special way. They are a relatively small minority—8 percent of the total church constituency—that attempts to combine commitments which seem incompatible in the society as a whole. Their stance is likely to seem incoherent. When compared with the Catholic churches (Roman Catholic, Orthodox, and, in part, Anglican-Episcopal), they are obviously not Catholic—but from the viewpoint of the American Protestant mainstream they are also not fully Protestant.

Neither are they genuinely liberal or genuinely conservative on either theological or sociopolitical issues. This precarious paradox has perhaps contributed to the heavy loss in the past of originally Lutheran immigrants to other Protestant denominations and, to much lesser degree, to Catholic, especially Anglican-Episcopal, churches.

It also places Lutherans under pressure from the wider culture to resolve their apparent incoherences by becoming consistently Protestant or Catholic. Thus the Lutherans who arrived before the Revolution almost lost their confessional identity in the early part of the nineteenth century, before their ranks were swelled by masses of new immigrants from Europe. Similarly, the recent victory of conservatives in the Lutheran Church—Missouri Synod is seen by many as the triumph not of old-fashioned Lutheran orthodoxy, as its proponents claim, but of modern conservative evangelicalism. In both cases, Lutherans became and become more like other American Protestants. On the other side, when it comes to ecumenical discussions, Lutherans are particularly active in talking with Roman Catholics,[14] and they agree by a margin of 68 to 25 percent that they "are more like Roman Catholics than like Southern Baptists."[15] To repeat, the Lutheran characteristics seem peculiarly dissonant in terms of the cognitive habits of the wider culture and therefore particularly susceptible to attrition or revision.

This precariousness applies chiefly to the combination of evangelical and Catholic elements in Lutheranism, and to the blending of doctrinally conservative and biblically liberal attitudes. A third Lutheran oddity, that of a quietistic engagement with the world, may well be on the point of disappearing. Traditional Lutheran political quietism was thoroughly discredited as a result of the Nazi experience and is no longer supported as a matter of principle by theologians or church leaders anywhere in the world. Under these circumstances, it seems probable that whatever opposition to political activism continues to exist will lose its distinctively Lutheran character. This opposition will be the product of general cultural and sociological influences and will be legitimated by theological outlooks, such as those of premillennialism (which expects the early end of the world) or of the charismatic movement (with its emphasis on religious experiences such as speaking in tongues), which are not specifically Lutheran. The disappearance of this particular problem, it can be argued, will make it easier to defend Lutheran identity in other areas. Political activists no longer need feel that they are being disloyal to their tradition.

Yet the defense of defining Lutheran characteristics in the American milieu is not easy. The pressures are such that Lutherans are strongly disinclined to emphasize their distinctive identity. The data reported in *A Study of Generations* (a church-sponsored, cross-sectional survey of the attitudes of 5,000 Lutherans, published in 1972) indicate that they agree in the proportion of 77 to 19 that "Lutherans are not different from other

Christians." Further, the majority denies that "Lutherans believe more strongly in salvation by faith alone than other Christians do."[16] It may be that these self-descriptions are prompted by a desire to avoid the appearance of arrogance and intolerance, and that Lutherans are more distinctive than their own perceptions indicate. Whatever the truth on these points, however, it seems clear that they are resistant to attempts to raise their denominational self-consciousness. The characteristics may be precious, but Lutherans do not want to be reminded that they *are* defining characteristics. This, needless to say, augers ill for the future of Lutheran identity. A minority subject to majority pressures is unlikely to retain its distinctiveness unless it deliberately and self-consciously tries to do so.

A word more needs to be said about the character of these pressures. They are of peculiar intensity in a society, such as the American, in which religion is less and less a matter of familial or social tradition, and more and more a matter of individual preference or choice. A mass market develops. Success comes to those with the widest rather than the most discriminating appeals. Every church tries to serve the needs of everyone who has any chance of being attracted. Thus the mainline denominations, with their basically similar middle-class clientele, come to resemble each other more and more. It has been suggested that their products are basically the same and, like breakfast foods, are only marginally differentiated in order to give customers the illusion of choice,[17] but this by itself is excessively cynical. The command to preach the gospel to all seems to require, in a mass consumption society, that one aim the message at the common denominator of religious interests so that it will be accessible to everyone; none must be turned away. Thus the desire for institutional and communal expansion seems to combine with biblical imperatives to undermine denominational distinctiveness. The future of Lutheran eccentricities seems dim.

There are, however, countervailing forces. Some of these are at present operative, while others may be triggered by special circumstances.

First, what Lutherans lack in self-conscious identity, they in part make up for by geographical concentration.[18] In the upper Midwest and parts of Pennsylvania, they constitute half or more the churchgoing population in county after county. Among major Protestant denominations, only the Southern Baptists (in the South) and the United Methodists (in a scattered band of counties stretching from Maryland to the Great Plains) are at all comparable in this respect. Roman Catholics enjoy a similar status in large areas of the Northeast, the Great Lakes region, and the Southwest, but the three dominant denominations of early American history—the Congregational (now part of the United Church of Christ), the Anglican-Episcopal, and the Presbyterian-Reformed—have everywhere become a minority in the total population even while retaining great strength in the Protestant upper classes. Thus Lutherans, because of their quasi-majority status in certain geographical areas, have a sociological bias toward stability (and conservatism) that is an advantage in retaining historically distinctive traits. Lutherans, in other words, can more easily remain Lutheran where they represent a normal rather than aberrant form of Protestantism.

A second factor has to do with the structure of Lutheran identity. This is to a unique degree centered on confessional or doctrinal considerations. Polity has no role in determining who or what is or is not Lutheran, for Lutheran churches range from episcopal to congregational in their mode of organization. Nor can Lutheran identity be defined in terms of any single cultural, ethnic, spiritual, or even liturgical tradition. Not even the founder, Martin Luther, is peculiarly Lutheran property, for he has historically been claimed as progenitor by most Protestants (not to mention the possibility that he may some day be claimed as one of the fathers of faith by all Christians). There is only one possible way of identifying a church as Lutheran, and that is by whether it accepts in some fashion or other the confessional writings collected in the Book of Concord of 1580 or, at the very least, the (unaltered) Augsburg Confession of 1530 (which was the first and most influential Lutheran doctrinal standard).[19]

Given the ignorance of huge numbers of Lutherans, including clergy, of the contents of these confessions, this may seem like a wholly theoretical point, but it has empirically significant consequences. It places constraints much greater than exist in most Protestant denominations on the possibility of changing indefinitely, of losing distinctiveness, while still retaining the original name. There are definite points beyond which no professedly Lutheran body can accommodate to the tastes of the times or the environment without delegitimating itself. When a church goes too far, it becomes publicly implausible for that church to call itself Lutheran, and it loses the label or returns, as did nineteenth-century American Lutheranism, to a more confessional stance.[20] The necessity involved is quasi-logical and is rather like that which requires authorities elected on the basis of a constitution not openly to flaunt that constitution if they are to retain legitimacy. Lutheranism, in short, seems intrinsically less able than many other traditions to jettison its historic distinctiveness.

This lack of flexibility may well be a handicap at present, but it is not difficult to imagine circumstances in which this would no longer be the case. When religious bodies become too unfocused in their self-definitions and too promiscuous in the variety of answers to the question of salvation which they are willing to entertain, they lose the ability to provide a sense of belonging and of social and personal identity. Thus, if in the future, the middle-class clientele of the mainline churches come to feel a greater need for socioreligious location (not to mention definite answers to the question of salvation), the denominations that have retained distinctiveness may be best able to capitalize on the new needs. They will then maximize rather than minimize their defining characteristics, although these will, as hap-

437 Lutheran Churches   437

pens in every generation, be articulated in new ways. Yet, while such developments may be future possibilities, they are not present realities.

Ecumenical trends may also afford new opportunities. This would happen to the extent that mutual Roman Catholic-Protestant rapprochement became a serious interest—a rapprochement, that is, which involved, not only the reformation of Roman Catholicism, but the reintegration of Protestantism. Such a development would, in effect, be an affirmation of Lutheran identity, because Lutheranism originally defined itself as a reforming movement within the historic church rather than as a separate family of churches. It claimed that its expulsion was illegitimate and professed willingness to remain in communion with Rome, despite the latter's errors, providing only that it was allowed "freedom to preach the gospel." Admittedly, Lutherans have been no more interested than other Protestants in reunion with Rome during most of the last 400 years, yet the idea of reunion is part of official Lutheran tradition to a degree unique among Protestants.[21] To the extent that it becomes popular, if it ever does, Lutheranism would have a chance to develop a renewed and powerful sense of its distinctive character and mission.

One final, although distressingly vague, empirical question must be raised regarding the present situation. To what extent are the criteria for ministry that we have described behavioral and attitudinal and not merely verbal? We obviously cannot assume that answers articulated under survey conditions are identical to the day-to-day reactions of clergy and laity. In every area of life, words and conduct are often far apart. Economists, for example, often comment on the enormous gap between the rhetoric of competitive free enterprise favored by big business and the actual character of contemporary corporate capitalism. Similarly, may not the rhetoric of expectations for beginning ministry often contradict the actual expectations? Are Lutherans, for example, actually more tolerant than others of promise breaking in young ministers, or do they simply talk as if they are? Similarly, do they actually place more emphasis on living as a "forgiven sinner" and less on "Christian example" and "prophetic ministry," or have they simply been socialized into a distinctive use of language? Perhaps the operative criteria prevalent among Lutherans are closer to (or farther from) those of other denominations than their verbal responses would lead one to suppose.

It would be naive to deny the hiatus between words and behavior. At least since New Testament times, it has been recognized that religion and hypocrisy (whether conscious or unconscious) are often closely intertwined. What needs to be remembered, however, is that cognitive and linguistic patterns can have powerful consequences even when they are honored more in the breech than the observance. Hypocrisy, as the old aphorism says, is the tribute vice pays to virtue. This means, among other things, that what is rhetorically normative within a community embodies the standards by which it tries to justify or legitimate itself. Sometimes it may do so falsely (indeed, Lutheran churches are not always, or even usually, faithfully Lutheran), but the result is not just any kind of false consciousness or guilt, but a particular variety. Further, a normative rhetoric prescribes the character and possibilities of reform. It provides the standards and directives within which renewal takes place when and if consciences are awakened and circumstances are favorable. The prophets, it will be recalled, were sent to those who acknowledged at least verbally, even if not actually, the same covenant and law as they did. Lastly, the criteria for ministry that are in the long run most likely to be decisive are those which are important to the nuclear members of a denomination who, although usually few in numbers, have been most fully shaped and molded by the distinctive form of Christianity which that denomination represents. For all these reasons, the operative significance of verbally articulated criteria is far greater for a denomination as a whole than for the "average" members polled one by one. A community can survive, however miserable, as long as lip service is rendered to its ideals, but when even this vanishes renewal becomes impossible and communal identity disappears.

Yet in concluding these reflections on the contemporary situation I must return to my earlier suggestion that renewal of a distinctively Lutheran pattern does not seem likely as long as present trends continue. Erosion will continue apace. Denominationally distinctive criteria for ministry are more an embarrassment than a help, a source of weakness rather than of strength. Attempts to emphasize them would alienate many of those from non-Lutheran backgrounds whom the Lutheran churches are trying to attract and would also be a source of disaffection to many Lutherans who wish to think of themselves as "just like everyone else" (which sometimes means, "like conservative evangelicals," sometimes, "like liberal Protestants," and occasionally, "like high-church Episcopalians"). It is time, therefore, to turn to the normative question of what goals Lutherans should seek in such circumstances. Should they oppose current trends, or accommodate, and in what ways?

Normative Considerations

The norms for assessing criteria that we shall discuss are, needless to say, Lutheran ones. It would be difficult to make this distinction between norms and criteria in the case of some denominations. But in churches such as Lutheran ones, which have a well-defined body of official doctrines, the distinction is not only possible but necessary. As in the case of a country with a strong constitutional tradition, that which a minister (or, analogously, a president) should be is at times definably or even drastically different from popular expectations.

The highest authority for Lutherans, as for most Protestants, is the Bible, but with a qualification on which Lutherans insist more strongly (or, at least, more officially) than most. Scripture is authoritative only when it is interpreted in terms of the gospel of justification by the grace of Christ alone through faith, apart from works. The Confessions are a secondary norm. This implies in principle (even if not always in practice) that they are corrigible in the light of Scripture and of what Scripture says in changing historical circumstances.

Given these premises, there is only one supreme norm for ministry, in terms of which every particular criterion must be assessed. Does the criterion in question promote the communication of the gospel, of the new life in Christ, understood in accordance with justification by grace alone, by Christ alone, by faith alone? If it does and if the alternatives do not, it is mandatory. If not, it is prohibited or, if there are several alternatives, optional.

Thus the central norm is fixed, but the criteria are flexible. Lutherans, even those of a conservative persuasion, are accustomed to thinking that criteria may change with changing circumstances. We have already mentioned the historic openness to a variety of polities ranging from the episcopal to the congregational. More pertinently, it has now long been argued by many rigorously confessional Lutherans that a foreign-missions emphasis that was absent from early Lutheranism (as it was from sixteenth-century Protestantism in general) can now be seen, because of altered historical conditions, to be a biblical imperative. More recently, new groups of charismatic Lutherans have defended their departures from tradition on similar grounds; and activist ministers analogously maintain that the political quietism of the earlier period (to some extent reflected in the confessional writings), while understandable in the sixteenth-century context, must be abandoned for scriptural (and therefore ultimately for confessional) reasons. There is, clearly, no permanent pattern of normatively Lutheran criteria for ministry, although there is a permanent norm.

More radically, there is no normative necessity for a distinctively Lutheran pattern of any kind. It is the reality of justification by faith that counts, not formal doctrines, and Luther was emphatic in his insistence that the reality can be found apart from explicit doctrinal formulations such as his own. The reality, he said, was present even in the Roman communion of his day, despite what he regarded as its gross errors and corruption.[22] Error made the Reformation formulations necessary, but the formulations are to be regarded as corrective of specific distortions of Christian teaching and life, not as constitutive of the gospel (that is, the message or story) of Jesus Christ. One conclusion that some Lutherans are willing to draw from these considerations is that, when the particular errors against which the Reformation was directed are no longer the crucial ones, Lutheranism as a distinct movement can legitimately disappear. There is nothing sacrosanct about Lutheran identity from the point of view of normative Lutheranism; or, more precisely, the importance of empirical Lutheranism is, in terms of its own norms, merely conditional.

To be sure, those who hold this view generally maintain that the conditions that make the Lutheran corrective valuable continue to exist. While sixteenth-century forms of reliance for salvation not on God but on one's own good deeds may have largely vanished, cognate varieties of self-righteousness remain powerful, not only among Roman Catholics, but also among Protestants, including Lutherans. Thus the distinctive Lutheran witness retains its importance and the communities that embody it are needed by Christianity as a whole. If they were to disappear, Christianity would be impoverished and perhaps endangered. Lutherans, according to this argument, will continue to have a responsibility to the whole church for the foreseeable future to maintain their distinctive expectations for ministry.

Lutherans are unusual in the degree to which they give this kind of doctrinal definition to their specific role within the chorus of the churches, but there are at least three other reasons for maintaining identity that would be shared by most other denominations. One of them is now a commonplace within the ecumenical movement: Diversity is desirable, and uniformity is undesirable; ecclesial pluralism contributes to the richness, health, and creativity of Christianity. Reunion, therefore, should not eliminate variety, but rather allow it to flourish, and in the meantime the maintenance of defining denominational characteristics is a positive good as long as this is done nondivisively.

The second reason is more introverted. Denominations have a responsibility to those who have grown up within the traditions they represent and propagate. Thus the Lutheran Churches, for example, would be remiss in their duties if they neglected the special needs of the multitudes for whom the distinctively Lutheran form of Christianity is the most familiar and the most effective vehicle of grace. There are many whose experience of God in Christ has been shaped by liturgical and sacramental forms of worship, rather than, for example, by a revivalistic tradition. They may be gripped by a communion service and repelled by a testimony meeting. Their commitment to the cause of Christ is intertwined with loyalty to a particular group and heritage, and to attenuate this heritage may be to weaken the hold of Christianity itself on their lives. This makes it impossible for anyone with pastoral concern heedlessly to jettison denominational distinctiveness.

A third consideration is primarily organizational. No denomination can maintain its effectiveness if it does not evoke the loyalty of its adherents and, not least, of its professional leadership. In order to do this, however, it must stress its special features. The clergy, for example, need to have reasons for being ministers in this denomination rather than another. This is one of the reasons why they are drilled in the history and heritage of their tradition far beyond anything that most of them ever actually use in their pastoral work. Without this specialized education and the morale it helps generate, there is likely to be nothing to hold a denomination together except organizational loyalty; but this is quite inadequate—indeed, illegitimate—as a reason for committed service to a particular church body. A denomination must be seen not as the ecclesiastic equivalent of a business corporation but as a distinctive and significant form of Christianity. If not, it cannot legitimately mobilize the well-springs of Christian devotion.

Yet despite the strength of these reasons for cultivating denominational characteristics, they do at times conflict with what we have already identified as the supreme norm of ministry for Lutherans. Everything is to be judged by whether it promotes the communication of the gospel. When denominational distinctiveness impedes this communication, the distinctiveness must take second place. When salvation through faith alone can be better proclaimed by not reminding the hearers that this is Lutheran doctrine, the cultivation of self-conscious Lutheranism must be sacrificed. Because the central commitment is to the gospel, the only way to be authentically Lutheran is at times to minimize visible Lutheranism.

As a result, the Lutheran Churches, like other Christian bodies, are subjected to a double pressure, both sides of which have normative backing. On the one hand, there is the impulse to gain as many members as possible by weakening the denominational characteristics, and, while this can be a matter of sheer institutional self-interest, it is by no means always unjustified. It is wrong, for example, for Lutherans to stress their distinctiveness when this hinders them from serving a denominationally mixed population or, even more seriously, when it prevents them from reaching out to all classes and races and leaves them trapped in lily-white exclusiveness. Yet, on the other hand, the attenuation of distinctiveness decreases the ability of Lutherans to make their special contribution to the church at large or to nurture those who have grown up in the tradition. Ultimately it leads to a loss of morale and effectiveness that undermines the denomination's ability to serve even in nondenominational ways. The dilemma is acute, and all churches, not only the Lutheran ones, suffer from it. Denominational identitites often seem otiose or pernicious in the present situation, and, yet there are no available replacements for the denominational structures that provide the main means of communication and action beyond the local level.

As in the case of all genuine dilemmas, this one involves a conflict between genuine goods. Different and equally binding norms cannot always be simultaneously followed. The only way to resolve such problems is not by study and not by theory, but by decision. A choice must be made between incompatible imperatives. But when one makes such decisions one enters the practical domain of policy formation, and it is to this that I now turn.

Policies

The most that can be done in the compass of a brief discussion is to lay out the major options that have emerged from our description of the Lutheran situation and Lutheran norms. Here, as in all examinations of praxis, of what should actually be done, neutrality is impossible. It will be evident to the reader that I am taking sides.

There are four possible directions for North American Lutheranism to go. It can turn inward in an effort to repristinate the past, or it can move toward conservative evangelicalism, or liberal Protestantism, or toward rapprochement with Catholicism (chiefly Roman Catholicism but also to some extent the Anglican-Episcopal denominational family). The first strategy seems the least feasible. Ethnic enclaves have largely disappeared, thus there is neither sociological nor normative confessional support for reghettoization. Apparent cases of repristination (as, for example, in the right wing of the Lutheran Church—Missouri Synod) are perhaps best understood as instances for the second tendency. Many Lutherans are attracted by biblicistic and nonsacramental conservative evangelicalism of either charismatic or noncharismatic varieties and like to think of this as identical to the faith of their fathers. The third, liberal tendency to downgrade historic doctrines involves an even more decisive abandonment of Lutheran identity. It is favored by the rootlessness, pluralism, and relativism of modern society and is the culturally established position among those who are best educated. But as an option *for those who remain active in the church,* it seems to be losing its attractiveness. Theological liberalism appears to be losing its popularity at the grass-roots level even in those denominations where it has been strongest.

This leaves Catholic rapprochement as the remaining possibility. If this direction were pursued, it would involve the recovery in new forms of Lutheranism's original self-understanding and vocation as a reform movement within the Catholic Church of its day. Such a development, therefore, has normative support. It also has the advantage of strengthening Lutheran distinctiveness: no other confessional tradition officially professes the desire to be the evangelical wing of western Catholicism. (Some Anglican evangelicals perhaps come close to this, but they are a minor party within the Anglican-Episcopal denominational family.)

Yet the difficulties are formidable. Lutherans have not thought of themselves in these terms for 400 years. They have, like other Protestants, defined themselves in opposition to Rome, rather than as a part of one and the same holy, catholic, and apostolic church. Thus a major reformulation of psychosocial, even if not confessional identity, would be necessary if they were to start viewing themselves not primarily as Protestants but as evangelical Catholics. Needless to say, comparable changes are also necessary on the Roman Catholic side, but they do in fact seem to be under way since the Second Vatican Council.

It could be argued, however, that practical difficulties are not a reason for inaction, but only for patience and wisdom. Catholic rapprochement should not be pushed in such a way as to impede the communication of the gospel to those who are traditionally Lutheran; and the emphasis in addressing those who are from non-Lutheran backgrounds should be on the combination of the evangelical and catholic elements without emphasizing that this is peculiarly Lutheran.

This is not the place to go into further details. Specific policy decisions require attention to particularities of time and place that are much beyond the scope of this chapter. Nevertheless, if policies are to have a cumulative effect rather than dissolve into incoherence, they need to be developed within the context of general directives and overall goals. This holds true for policies related to criteria of readiness for ministry no less than in other areas of church life, and this is why my discussion of specifically Lutheran criteria has concluded with a consideration of the distinctively Lutheran role within the church universal.

NOTES

1. "Significant" (or "notable," "decided," or "striking") differences in this chapter are always those in which the probability of the chi-square is less than .0001.

2. With the exception of the Orthodox laity, all other laypeople are significantly less critical than their clergy of the leadership style described in CC 60.

3. Taking the cluster as a whole, Lutherans attach less importance to CC 19 than do the Southern Baptist Convention, Evangelical A and B, and the Christian Church (not Disciples).

4. They do not differ significantly in the cluster as a whole, however.

5. Since we are for the most part not at this point dealing with statistically significant contrasts, the tendency of Lutheran laity to rank slightly lower than average must be read as only a trend in this direction.

6. This item does not appear in the Lutheran clergy cluster.

7. While Lutheran laity rank Item 376 much higher than the total group, Lutheran ministers value the setting of a Christian example much lower than the entire group.

8. Biblical knowledge for priests, even if not for laity, was emphasized by the Counterreformation as well as by the Reformation.

9. Among others, Dean M. Kelley, *Why Conservative Churches Are Growing: A Study in Sociology of Religion* (New York: Harper & Row, 1972), discusses this issue.

10. The terminology, but not the exact concept of "nuclear" and "peripheral" members is borrowed from Joseph Fichter, *Social Relations in an Urban Parish* (Chicago: University of Chicago Press, 1954).

11. Merton P. Strommen, Milo L. Brekke, Ralph C. Underwager, and Arthur L. Johnson, *A Study of Generations: Report of a Two-Year Study of 5000 Lutherans Between the Ages of 15–65: Their Beliefs , Values, Attitudes, Behavior* (Minneapolis: Augsburg, 1972), pp. 30–32.

12. Gregory Baum and Andrew Greeley, *Ethnicity* (New York: Seabury Press, 1977).

13. Strommen, Brekke, Underwager, and Johnson, *A Study of Generations,* p. 109.

14. Some of the reasons for this are indicated in *Lutherans in Ecumenical Dialogue: An Interpretive Guide* (Division of Theological Studies, Lutheran Council in the USA, 360 Park Ave. S, New York, NY, 1977), pp. 13–18.

15. Strommen, Brekke, Underwager, and Johnson, *A Study of Generations,* p. 109.

16. Ibid.

17. Peter Berger, *The Sacred Canopy: Elements of a Sociological Theory of Religion* (New York: Doubleday, 1967), p. 148.

18. Douglas W. Johnson, Paul R. Picard, and Bernard Quinn, *Churches and Church Membership in the United States* (Washington, D.C.: Glenmary Research Center, 1974), insert.

19. As in the case of the Batak Church on the island of Sumatra, the acceptance may be indirect, for example, through membership in the Lutheran World Federation. See Vilmos Vajta, and Hans Weissgerber, eds., *The Church and the Confessions: The Role of the Confessions in the Life and Doctrine of the Lutheran Churches* (Philadelphia: Fortress Press, 1963), esp. pp. 119–147. In this case, the Batak Church formulated its own Confession of Faith to fit its own Third World situation, but this confession is in doctrinal agreement with the Augsburg Confession, and was acknowledged as such by the Lutheran World Federation when it admitted the Batak Church to membership.

20. For a description of "American Lutheranism," see Vergilius Ferm, *The Crisis in American Lutheran Theology* (New York: Appleton-Century-Crofts, 1927), pp. 117–184.

21. For a recent discussion of this ecumenical character of the early confessions, see Eric W. Gritsch and Robert W. Jensen, *Lutheranism: The Theological Movement & Its Confessional Writings* (Philadelphia: Fortress Press, 1976).

22. See, for example, "Concerning Rebaptism" (1528), *Luther's Works: American Edition,* Vol. 40, ed. and trans., Conrad Bergendoff (Philadelphia: Fortress Press), esp. pp. 231 ff.

14

United
Methodist Church

F. Thomas Trotter

Given the wide geographical distribution of the nearly 10 million members of the United Methodist Church, it is perhaps not surprising that the data elicited from them place the denomination generally in the middle of the spectrum of many expectations of a beginning minister. Methodists continue to affirm Scripture, tradition, reason, and experience as the underpinnings of their theological understanding and ministerial expectations.

Yet Trotter does find some surprises in the data that place in doubt conventional wisdom concerning United Methodists—for example, (1) they avoid polarities, normally falling into the middle range of opinions; (2) their churches do not appear more involved in the local community than other mainline Protestant churches; (3) concern for a learned ministry relates them to the Roman Catholic, Anglican-Episcopal, and Lutheran churches; and (4) the views of clergy and laypeople vary measurably, although not dramatically.

Trotter organizes his chapter around the sixty-four clusters formed solely on the basis of United Methodist responses. (These United Methodist clusters are not the same as the sixty-four core clusters that were generated by all the

F. Thomas Trotter is General Secretary of the Board of Higher Education and Ministry of the United Methodist Church and is based in Nashville, Tennessee. He was Dean of the School of Theology at Claremont, California, from 1961 to 1973.

denominational families participating in the study.) The United Methodist clusters are characterized by a self-consciousness of being professional. The vocabulary of interpersonal counseling, group dynamics, and educational psychology dominates the profile of ministerial expectations. These cause Trotter to raise serious questions: "Do such accents spring from traditional Scriptural and theological understandings?" "Has the earlier traditional sense of an evangelical movement simply given way to the demands of parish maintenance?"

The United Methodist Church is a "national" church, developed principally in the westward movement of the American frontier. Its character is reflected both in demography and ecclesiology.

Unlike denominations whose constituency may be defined somewhat regionally, the United Methodist Church is represented in most counties in the nation, although it is a majority in none.[1] The heaviest concentrations of United Methodists are in the Southeast and North Central regions of the nation, although substantial numbers of Methodist people are found in other sections as well.

The most recent statistics indicate that the denomination is the second largest Protestant denomination in America, with 9,785,534 members (1977).[2] (The Southern Baptist Convention lists 13,078,239 members for the same year.) It is worth noting that 3,813,452 members of the denomination live in the states of the Old Confederacy, while 62 percent of United Methodist members are northerners and westerners. With 353,326 black members (1973), it is the fifth largest black denomination in the United States. It has more Japanese, Chinese, Korean, and other Pacific people in its membership than any other Protestant denomination, and these people, along with Hispanics, are growing in membership in the church.

As recently as 1924, there were 1,023 foreign-language churches in the Methodist Episcopal Church, one of the precursor bodies to the United Methodist church.[3] While mostly German and Swedish at that time, Spanish-, Japanese-, and Korean-language churches now predominate.

The ecclesiology of the denomination has been shaped in part by its eighteenth-century origins. Methodism arose in America as a lay movement, a part of the evangelical revivals of that century. The first Methodist lay preachers became active in the colonies in the 1760s, although John Wesley himself had preached in Georgia in 1736–1737; and George Whitefield, beginning in 1736, had taken several trips to the colonies. These missions were not directly related to the organizational period of Methodism, which culminated in the founding of the Methodist Episcopal Church in Baltimore at Christmas 1784. However, the evangelical spirit of the early Methodists, their tradition of having lay preachers, and the revolutionary fervor of that period all combined to shape the Methodist ethos still visible today.

The denomination was born out of revolutionary necessity. The Tory sentiments of the Anglicans and of Wesleyan missionaries created problems in the administration of the sacraments for American Methodists who had considered themselves part of the Church of England. Furthermore, as the Methodist lay preachers moved farther into the wilderness, the practical urgencies of sacramental administration were heightened. The first General Conference of Methodist preachers (1784) established a style (borrowed heavily from the Wesleyans in England) that more nearly represented a revolutionary assembly than a church council. To this day, the quadrennial General Conference of the denomination is more like a revolutionary congress than a continuing body. Its members are elected by local conferences, and, for the days of the session, all the structures of the church are set temporarily aside, debated, redesigned, and restated for the next four years. The requirement that bishops must have the permission of the house in order to speak in the General Conference reflects an historical fear of autocracy in the church.

Since the denomination is nonconfessional, its theology, in a profound sense, is its ecclesiology. Its unamendable basis of authority includes the *Sermons* and *Explanatory Notes upon the New Testament* by John Wesley and the Twenty-Five Articles of Religion, taken from the Thirty-Nine Articles of the Church of England. The practical theology of the church has been expressed in the quadrilateral formula that affirms scripture, tradition, reason, and experience as the bases of theological understanding for members of the United Methodist Church.[5]

Because it was organized in the revolutionary period of the nation's birth and because of its national demographic character, the United Methodist Church has expressed itself in ways that reflect the nation's ethos and regionalism, its national attitudes and struggles. It broke with Anglicanism over independence, with Methodist Protestantism over the episcopacy, and was divided between North and South over slavery (1844). Jaroslav Pelikan has suggested that the Methodist Church "became so closely identified with the new nation that it was, and still is, thought of as the most American of churches, embodying many of the characteristics associated by both natives and foreigners with the typical American."[6]

Demography and ecclesiology, therefore, are strong influences within the character of the United Methodist Church. The denomination's national distribution subjects it to the necessity for compromise and tolerance in political attitudes. Its ecclesiology, shaped in revolutionary times, places extraordinary emphasis on consensus, flexibility, and order. At all times, the controlling principle is the "connection" (that is, the church's style) and not a confessional posture. This style is perceptible and influential in the Readiness for Ministry data.

The United Methodist Church's character is probably as representative a cross-sectional consensus of American national attitudes, both liberal and conservative, as any other social organization. It is therefore not surprising that the data elicited from United Methodists in the Readiness for Ministry Project locate the denomination approximately in the middle of the spectrum with regards to most attitudes and expectations, but with variations in a few significant areas.

Some of the conclusions suggested by the data may be surprising to United Methodists who have long had comfortable prejudices about their movement. Among the elements that emerge from the data are the following generalizations:

1. United Methodists do not appear to be at one end of the spectrum or the other and are, in fact, notable for their absence from extreme polar groupings thoughout the data. This may be a reflection of the denomination's style of ironic and tolerant belief.

2. Contrary to popular expectation, when compared with other denominations as a whole, the United Methodist churches do not appear more community involved or less isolated from the world than others in the middle group. The data do not indicate a distinctive emphasis on social activism.

3. With the presumed activism has followed an unspoken assumption that such activism implies a less reflective ministerial style; however, United Methodists are identified in the study with those groups stressing a learned clergy; namely, Roman Catholic (Order and Diocesan), Anglican-Episcopal, Lutheran, and United Church of Christ.

4. The United Methodist Church appears in the project to be a denomination in which the views of clergy and laity vary measurably, but not dramatically. The generally more liberal (and theologically trained) clergy and the more conservative and less activist laity tend to balance out in the middle-data positions articulated throughout this project.

THE UNITED METHODIST CLUSTERS

The respondents for the United Methodist Church in the study reflect a definition of ministry that parallels the general contours of ministry derived from the total sample of denominations (see Chapter 4). The analysis in this chapter presupposes that general framework. The factoring that developed the sixty-four clusters and the comparison of those clusters with the sixty-four clusters specific to the United Methodists presents a more pertinent index of denominational style. The generalization of the sectional data needs the particularity of the cluster analysis.

The sixty-four core clusters that form the basis for measuring readiness expectations across all forty-seven denominations are arranged in order of importance by average mean and reveal a priority of intensity or valuation of expectations. The clusters are arranged by descending order of the total group's grand mean, measured on a scale of expectations from $+3$ to -3:

	From	To
Highly important, essential or mandatory	+2.51	+3.00
Quite important, a major asset	+1.51	+2.50
Somewhat important, a minor asset	+0.51	+1.50
Neither important nor unimportant	−0.50	+0.50
Somewhat detrimental, a minor hindrance in ministry	−1.50	−0.51
Quite detrimental, a major hindrance to ministry	−2.50	−1.51
Highly detrimental, harmful, could destroy the effectiveness of ministry	−3.00	−2.51

United Methodist data, subsumed in the sixty-four core criteria in Chapter 5, are also factored to provide a subsidiary list of clusters (coincidentally, also 64) unique to United Methodists. This list may fairly be described as the expectation in readiness for ministry of the United Methodists participating in the project (see Chapter 4). Each ministry expectation or criterion represents a sufficiently similar response of the participants so that a cluster of agreements as to judgments was ordered and isolated. While the core clusters for the total project have been given very precise, terse titles, I have given the clusters for the United Methodists more descriptive titles, hopefully to make the total list more illustrative of the denomination's style. Table 14-1 lists the first 15 and the bottom 9 of the 64 United Methodist clusters ranked in order of average weight on scale.

ANALYSIS OF THE UNITED METHODIST CLUSTERS

These data reveal a very high valuation placed by the United Methodist respondents on interpersonal leadership and expectations in ministry. The more descriptive titles used in this section make comparison with the terse titles in the core criteria listing (see Chapter 5) difficult for the reader. However, the emphasis is unmistakable. Clusters for the United Methodist Church emphasize elements reflecting the prevalent pastoral model in the United Methodist Church. Interpersonal counseling, group dynamics, and the vocabulary of educational psychology dominate the responses of United Methodists. The significance of the expression in the data is the very high valuation attached to these clusters of items. Items whose means are in the 2.5–3.5 rank statistically as "highly important" to "quite important." The interpersonal pastoral model, which is an accent that draws a high valuation, runs through more than 50 percent of the total of sixty-four United Methodist clusters.

TABLE 14-1
United Methodist Clusters Ranked Highest and Lowest in Importance

Rank	United Methodist Cluster	Grand Mean
1(3)	Knows the parishioners well and encourages relationships of trust between self and congregation	2.46
1(3)	Shows honesty with self and congregation, reveals a human image of ministry	2.46
1(3)	Expresses respect, sympathy, and professional preparation in pastoral care	2.46
4(5)	Recognizes minister's commonality with spiritual problems of the congregation	2.41
4(5)	Speaks about theological issues in understandable language	2.41
6	Has ability to enable a congregation to experience opportunities for personal growth in spiritual enrichment	2.38
7	Demonstrates a style of lifelong learning, through continuing education, research, and study	2.34
8	Sees family life as a high priority and assumes his or her personal family style as consistent with ministry	2.32
9	Reflects a flexible, responsible, facilitative, and trusting style of leadership	2.29
10(11)	Gains financial support for the church while remaining sensitive to persons	2.27
10(11)	Assumes a nondefensive, professional role and is sensitive to matters of ministerial protocol	2.27
12	Encourages, recruits, and gives meaning to people for congregational tasks	2.26
13	Evidences personal growth and theological resources in counseling	2.25
14	Acts with openness, innovation, and eagerness to share the life of the community as a private citizen	2.24
15	Assumes a patient, hopeful, yet forceful role in dealing with people	2.24
56	Uses pietistic language in social conversation	−0.66
57	Separates evangelism from the work of building a humane, world society	−1.12
58	Perceives self to be the ultimate authority and basis of unity in parish	−1.28

TABLE 14-1 — *CONTINUED*

Rank	United Methodist Cluster	Grand Mean
59	Rejects sacerdotal definitions of ministry	−1.58
60	Demonstrates insecurity in entertaining ambitions inconsistent with ministerial calling and need for constant reassurance	−1.59
61	Fearful of participation in programs of social change	−1.77
62	Lifestyle involves occasional intoxication, heavy smoking, illicit sexual affairs, and gambling; questions whether he or she should be in ministry	−1.80
63	Shows coldness and immaturity, far more concerned with self than others, violates principles to protect self	−1.94
64	Frightens people off with dominating, superior attitude that is compulsive, condemning, sexist, demeaning, and pessimistic	−2.04

A quality that characterizes the total group core criteria is a self-consciousness of being professional. For instance, "Service in Humility" (which ranks first on the core criteria list) is the expression of a professional judgment as much as a pious expectation. One could hardly fault the cluster from any regard. But the United Methodist data reveal the degree to which the United Methodist respondents have been affected by a more defined kind of professionalism that emphasizes commonality with parishioners and not exceptionality, even in piety.

It is also interesting to note that the professional accents appear to be conditioned by the same interpersonal style. Therefore, Methodist Cluster 5 ("Speaks about theological issues in understandable language") suggests that theological issues are important, but urges speaking understandably. In other words, communication (a significant code word in the current jargon of educational psychology) may be the more significant accent.

Also significant for the very high location in the United Methodist ranking are United Methodist Clusters 6, 7, and 8, all bearing on the respondent's expectation that the personal life of the minister be considered a high priority in his or her professional self-understanding. These clusters accent the need and expectation of personal growth in the quality of family life (6); lifelong learning, professionally described as "continuing education" (7); and consistency in family and personal style with one's understanding and expression of ministry (8).

This accent is dramatically highlighted in the four items grouped in United Methodist Cluster 8. In each of these items, United Methodist data are significantly different from the data for the total project. For instance, 92 percent of the United Methodist respondents, as opposed to 71 percent of the total respondents, view Item 497 ("Keeps commitments to own children as consistently as professional appointments") as "quite" or "highly" important. Furthermore, while 13 percent of the total group think that this is an undesirable expectation, only 2 percent of the United Methodists indicate this as an undesirable expectation.

Equally significant variations in the comparison between total expectations and United Methodist expectations appear in Items 512 ("Schedules regular time to be alone with family") and 511 ("Spouse is sympathetic and committed to minister's vocation"). United Methodists place significantly more importance on these two items than does the total group. While this dimension ranks eighth in the United Methodist list, it ranks as 31 in the core cluster list, again indicating the greater value that United Methodist respondents place on family commitment.

The professionalism implicit in the United Methodist clusters emphasizes enabling types of ministries. Throughout the United Methodist list, one notes an emphasis on a ministry that is open, accepting, self-critical, patient, participatory, and exemplary. While this may appear to be a counsel of perfection, let it also be noted that there is an emphasis on self-criticism, as in high-ranking United Methodist Clusters 2, "Shows honesty with self and congregation, reveals a human image of ministry"; 4, "Recognizes minister's commonality with spiritual problems of the congregation"; 9, "Reflects a flexible, responsible, facilitative, and trusting style of leadership"; 11, "Assumes a nondefensive, professional role and is sensitive to matters of ministerial protocol"; and 14, "Acts with openness, innovation, and eagerness to share the life of the community as a private citizen." In other words, the respondents' expectations include *competence within the style of enabling openness* (my emphasis). This does not mean that the minister is expected to be soft or sentimental in leadership. It is clear that consistency, coherence, patience, risk taking, and efficiency are desired.

With regard to the classical priestly elements (for example, of a sacramental ministry), the United Methodist data are either ambiguous or silent. There are suggestions in the United Methodist clusters that preaching for conversion, providing leadership in prayer and worship, and inspiring others to an awareness of God, are clearly deemed important expectations. What seems to be missing, however, is attention to the sacramental life of United Methodists. While the denomination emphasizes the priestly mode of ministry in its more recent definitions (see the 1976 *Book of Discipline of the United Methodist Church,* Part 4, Chapter 1, Section 6), the respondents seem to have very little precise expectation in terms of sacerdotal leadership. The items simply do not appear in the United Methodist data or clusters.

The items that pertain most directly to the sacraments or to sacerdotal leadership are found in Core Cluster 9, "Sacramental-Liturgical Ministry." The United Methodist response to this cluster is significantly lower than the responses of the Orthodox and the Roman Catholic (both Order and Diocesan), and significantly higher than the Jewish and Unitarian and the Evangelical A families. With regard to the six items that comprise that cluster, the United Methodists differ significantly from the total group on only the most heavily loaded item in the cluster, "Considers his or her professional ministry as sacramental" (Item 76). United Methodists, more than the total group, shy from the extreme responses; that is, United Methodists are more likely than the total group to view this trait as "somewhat" or "quite" important in a beginning minister On three other items (63, 92, and 78) in this United Methodist cluster, the response falls a bit short of statistical significance, but a possible trend is visible: United Methodists appear to take a centrist sort of position with regard to items pertaining to the sacraments. United Methodists appear less likely than the total group to view these items as extremely important or as detrimental. Such a stance would seem to fit the general rationalistic style of United Methodists and their fourfold understanding of theology—Scriptures, tradition, reason, and experience.

Whereas the data indicate that United Methodist respondents generally share average expectations regarding ecumenism and other interdenominational and interreligious positions, it is significant that on Item 82 of Core Cluster 8, "Participates in ecumenical projects with ministers of other denominations," the United Methodist respondents had a significantly more positive response on ecumenical cooperation and participation than did most other respondents.

An additional area of exceptionality in the data revolves around two of the four items in Core Cluster 49, "Denominational Collegiality." United Methodists reflect significantly higher valuation of this trait (which relates to acceptance of denominational directives while maintaining collegial relationships with superiors and staff) than do the United Church of Christ and the Christian Church (not Disciples). United Methodists differ significantly from the total group in their less polarized valuation of two of these items: "Usually follows directives from denominational leaders" (Item 509) and "Works cooperatively with superiors" (Item 470). These items reveal a peculiar denominational style and expectation in the avoidance of extremes or, perhaps more positively, their predilection for a more centrist stance. United Methodists see themselves as a connectional church. Their denominational loyalties are related to a sense of the unity of the church, not to a system of management that assumes a directive kind of relationship.

The data reveal that the United Methodist laity tend to share with the clergy a fairly strong sense of social responsibility in the community. Characteristically, however, this manifests itself primarily in education and emphasis on social organization, rather than direct action. For example, United Methodists score significantly higher than the total group on all three items of Core Cluster 15, "Support of Community Causes." This means that the United Methodists rate it significantly more important than does the total group that a beginning minister actively support efforts to improve educational programs of the community (Item 144), that he or she serve on task forces or committees to improve conditions at school or in the neighborhood (Item 140), and finally, that the beginning minister work with different community factions (Item 158). For the cluster as a whole, however, United Methodists differ significantly only from the Orthodox and the Evangelical A families, which tend to attach less importance to this cluster.

United Methodists appear to recognize generally conservative methods of social pressure as appropriate; they stress education, information, and involvement in public education. Strongly emotive and connotative phrases such as "liberation of oppressed people" are more problematic and generally receive low scores, although United Methodist response does not deviate significantly from the total mean of a core cluster such as "Active Concern for the Oppressed" (CC 16). "Pastoral services" for all people with needs as well as community leadership "to awaken trust" are held to be important, but action in political modes is not thus esteemed.

The United Methodist clergy exhibit a high degree of confidence in the utility of social action, especially in racial integration (Item 155). Curiously, concern for minorities and the dispossessed is not expressed by clergy and laity in the same ways. In Core Clusters 16, "Active Concern for the Oppressed," and 18, "Aggressive Political Leadership," United Methodist clergy, together with clergy from each of the sixteen other denominational families, stress to a greater degree than do laity, the importance of fairly direct political and/or social involvement on the part of beginning ministers. The clergy view themselves as actors, but the laity see the clergy as commentators. Direct action by clergy is usually limited by laity to insistence on the importance for action. This may take the form of sacrificial giving (Item 120) as a response to critical missional needs, an action that satisfies both clergy rhetoric and lay reluctance by reassuring everyone that something has been done.

A FINAL OBSERVATION

In a project with the scope of the Readiness for Ministry design, it is apparent that limits have to be established. To suggest that respondents from forty-seven denominations find items that reflect the full range of their denomination's distinctive emphases is not realistic, and to suggest that there is sufficient commonality of theological and ecclesial language to provide equivalency in the responses is unduly optimistic. The design of the project and its necessary limits do minimize these variants. For United Methodists, the more subtle nuances of "connectionalism," "episcopacy," and "discipline," with their peculiarly United Methodist understanding, are not directly reflected in the data. While items dealing with the "priestly-sacramental" and "denominational collegiality" themes might be perceived as having elicited ambiguous United Methodist responses, this may reflect the peculiar fact that the denomination balances catholic and congregational styles. It may also reflect that United Methodists truly exhibit centrist tendencies relative to many denominations.

The United Methodist Church is a movement that participates in a variety of religious traditions. While it clings tenaciously to these several traditions, it seems to resist the temptation to be dogmatic about any. Equally affected by the Catholic roots of Anglicanism and the evangelical revival, it has no high- or low-church wings; rather, it accommodates these disparate elements in a style of openness and ease, valuing the unity of the church more than conformity. The "discipline" of the United Methodist Church is its order, but that discipline is a carefully prescribed statement of prerogatives and limitations in the management of the denomination, including the episcopacy and the clergy. So one will sense in the data a congregational authority, but also an acceptance of episcopal discipline.

Throughout the denomination, the same tolerance is apparent in theological variation. The United Methodist Church understands itself as a nondogmatic or nonconfessional church. It strives for unity within the faith, but without the urgency of uniformity. Coherence rather than conformity is the rule, as expressed in the denomination's understanding of the fourfold bases of authority: Scripture, tradition, reason, and experience. In some ways, the denomination understands itself best in its organization (theology as ecclesiology) and its hymnology (coherence and piety).

What seems to emerge from the study of the United Methodist data in this project are three questions:

1. Does the apparent emphasis on interpersonal modes of ministry, conditioned by cognate disciplines (such as psychology, social science, and therapeutic practice), spring from scriptural and theological understanding?
2. Has the Methodist sense of an evangelical movement been lost in the style of parish maintenance?
3. In what sense are the classical United Methodist themes now denominational rhetoric?

The data of this study suggest that the United Methodist respondents have a functional expectation of their beginning ministers; that is, their expectations are only remotely connected with denominational history. That may be a function of the study itself; or, the fact may be that United Methodist expectations of a beginning minister actually possess few explicit links to historically valued traits.

Since the denomination has emphasized coherence, empiricism, and piety, the style of openness makes for an extraordinary variety and tolerance (and, therefore, range of expectations) among United Methodist people. Often accused of not having "theology," United Methodists have emphasized openness as the context in which the church can do its work. Its "worldliness" is not seen as being disconnected from its understanding of the gospel. The world is the setting for the gospel. Evangelical piety and Arminianism are the countervalences to Catholic notions of priestly ministry and Reformation confessionalism. That is, for Methodists piety and energetic good works, as opposed to an emphasis on priesthood or confessionalism, have formed the denomination's character.

NOTES

1. Edwin S. Gaustad, *Historical Atlas of Religion in America,* rev. ed. (New York: Harper & Row, 1976).

2. Constant H. Jacquet, ed., *Yearbook of American and Canadian Churches* (Nashville, Tenn.: Abingdon, 1979).

3. Paul Douglass, "Bilingual Work and the Language Conferences," in *The History of American Methodism,* Vol. 2 (Nashville, Tenn.: Abingdon, 1964), p. 521

4. John Wesley, *Sermons* [from the Thomas Jackson edition of 1829–31] (Grand Rapids, Mich.: Zondervan, 1958); John Wesley, *Explanatory Notes upon the New Testament* [from the John Lawson edition] (London: Epworth, 1955). The Articles of Religion are found in *The Book of Discipline of the United Methodist Church,* 1976, Paragraph 68, p. 55.

5. *The Book of Discipline of the United Methodist Church,* 1976, Paragraph 69, Section 3, "Our Theological Task."

6. Jaroslav Pelikan, "Methodism's Contribution to America," in *The History of American Methodism,* ed. Emory Bucke, Vol. 3 (Nashville, Tenn.: Abingdon, 1964), p. 597.

15

Presbyterian-Reformed
Family

Arthur M. Adams, Dean R. Hoge, and Lefferts A. Loetscher

The responses of the Presbyterian-Reformed family place it generally in a centrist position relative to other denominations in North America. Where Presbyterian-Reformed respondents do express a distinctive position, Adams, Hoge, and Loetscher interpret this as a product of the Reformation and of historic Calvinistic Presbyterianism. Calvinistic Presbyterianism has traditionally been associated with an emphasis on God's initiative and sovereignty in human redemption. In recent generations, human decision and response have been increasingly emphasized. The commonalities with other Christian denominations are interpreted as results of more recent American influences.

This denominational family places greater-than-average emphasis on a beginning minister's having (1) a learned understanding and presentation of Christianity, (2) the use of Scripture in a nonfundamentalist fashion (particularly emphasized by clergy), (3) a slightly greater concern (again, particularly on the part of clergy) with political issues, (4) toleration for diversity of

Arthur M. Adams, former Dean of the Seminary and Professor of Practical Theology at Princeton Theological Seminary, Princeton, New Jersey, died prior to the publication of this book.

Dean R. Hoge is Associate Professor, Department of Sociology, Catholic University, Washington, D.C.

Lefferts A. Loetscher is Professor of American Church History, Emeritus, at Princeton Theological Seminary.

457

theological view within the denomination, and (5) a tendency to downplay denominational loyalty or collegiality.

Three other specific findings are noteworthy. First, the Presbyterian-Reformed family tends to conceptualize worship and teaching as a single facet of ministry. Second, no specific order (or content) of worship or liturgy is required. Third, data from this family form a cluster that could be named "Affirmation of Persons Amidst Stress"—concern with pastoral care, discipline, and leadership of groups troubled by disunity.

Unresolved issues for this group arise most sharply from the cleavage, reflected sharply in the data, between clergy and laity. As with many other denominational families, Presbyterian-Reformed laity are more conservative than their clergy in expectations or conceptions of ministry. Laity emphasize evangelism and religious experience, a more traditional, "historic Presbyterianism," in which Calvinistic influence is still apparent. The clergy, however, emphasize community and political causes; they frequently interpret the authority of Scriptures in a more liberal way than that of their laity. This disparity between lay and clerical perceptions may account for the sizable number of ministerial candidates who deliberately choose non-Presbyterian seminaries.

The Presbyterian-Reformed family in the Readiness for Ministry Project includes ten denominations, of which four are dominant (with 75.6 percent of the respondents): the United Presbyterian Church in the USA, the Presbyterian Church in the US, the Christian Reformed Church, and the Reformed Church in America. Smaller numbers of respondents come from the Associate Reformed Presbyterian Church (General Synod), the Cumberland Presbyterian Church, and the Presbyterian Church in Canada.[1] Our interpretations focus on the history of the largest Presbyterian and Reformed denominations.

The overall picture of Presbyterian-Reformed concepts of ministry, within the context of all North American Protestantism, is that of commonality rather than uniqueness. The Presbyterian-Reformed attitudes are quite centrist relative to the total body of opinion. In few areas are they unique, but the unique features do appear in a significant pattern. The distinctive Presbyterian-Reformed positions emerging in the data are largely the product of the Reformation era—either the conscious formulation of the Reformers or, perhaps less frequently, the unconscious product of the movement's early social settings. The much more numerous resemblances with the other Christian bodies clearly show influence from more recent and American sources. In other words, the differences are rooted basically in the era when the Presbyterian-Reformed groups originated, and those differences have been subjected to continuous erosion under the common impact of the new cultural and social forces in recent centuries, especially in America.

Our attention here is given to the areas of Presbyterian-Reformed distinctiveness and their historical roots. They merit the attention of people who aspire to ministry within this family and of people responsible for preparing ministers.

First, we note a distinctive emphasis on the importance of a learned grasp and presentation of Christianity. The Presbyterian-Reformed respondents stress an appropriate theological base for prayer and for church mission, and they want a minister to know the history of the church's confessions. They see as significantly more important than others that a beginning minister present "a theological basis for the mission of the church" (Item 110), understand and appreciate "the dogmatic and liturgical foundations of prayer" (Item 92), and know "the historical circumstances that shaped confessional statements of the denomination" (Item 316).[2] In cluster analysis within the Presbyterian-Reformed family, a large cluster (not found in the total data) emerges. It has high emphasis on Items 307, "Is clear about the theology that guides and informs his ministry"; 306, "Evaluates current trends in theological thought"; 314, "Teaches and preaches from a broad base of information"; and 318, "Reflects an awareness of current affairs reported in newspapers and periodicals." The Presbyterian-Reformed family is quite conscious of its desire for ministers with broad learning in the faith and in modern thought. The ideal of the minister as theologian and thinker lies at the center of the Presbyterian-Reformed self-image.

The responses stress historical learning more than is true in other denominational families. While the emphasis on history as such (at least in the contemporary view of history as process) is perhaps a more modern conception, the ideal of a ministry deeply grounded in the church's biblical and theological heritage is a characteristic emphasis of the Presbyterian-Reformed churches from their earliest days. The chief purpose of this is not personal prestige to the professional minister or the ability to influence and win the "right" people, but, rather, to present Christian truth correctly. It has not been enough, according to the Presbyterian-Reformed ideal, to have rediscovered full Christian truth "once and for all" and then merely to have transmitted this package. The church and especially its ministry must always be competent—ever anew—to evaluate and define what the gospel and Christian life really are; that is, the ideal of a church, both reformed and to be reformed. It is interesting that the Presbyterian-Reformed group seems preeminent in holding this ideal even to the present day.

A closely related finding is that the Presbyterian-Reformed family highly emphasizes Scripture. They accord significantly more importance than other respondents to Item 287, "Treats the Bible, interpreted by the church, as the final authority in all matters of faith"; Item 294, "Gives evidence of continued and thorough study of the Scriptures"; Item 321,

"Demonstrates knowledge of Scripture"; and Item 319, "In private study, uses original languages (Greek or Hebrew) to clarify obscure biblical passages." This emphasis on Scripture is not predominantly a twentieth-century "fundamentalist" view, as is shown by the finding that Presbyterian-Reformed ministers are generally inclined toward "mainline liberal" positions. There is no contemporary exact equivalent of precritical Presbyterian-Reformed biblical views. Modern critical views necessarily go beyond the biblical scholarship of the sixteenth century, but the reformers of that era did not teach the rigid and literalistic biblical views of twentieth-century fundamentalism. But the respondents' great emphasis on innovative scholarship and learning suggest that the modern Presbyterian-Reformed minister, with his or her continuing and now critical biblical scholarship, reflects, to a degree at least, the position of these Reformed forebears.

While there is a high degree of unanimity about the importance of Scripture in the work of ministry, the Presbyterian segment of this denominational family faces major questions regarding biblical interpretations. At its heart is a hermeneutical problem as to whether there is only one way in which we must interpret the Bible or whether a variety of ways are permissible. Clergy and laity alike report that the issue of how the Bible is to be accepted, interpreted, and applied is the most prevalent cause of conflict and controversy on all four levels—the session (local), presbytery (district), synod (regional), and General Assembly (national)—of the Presbyterian church today. Behind a whole range of problems ultimately stands the question of how authoritative the Scriptures are perceived to be with regard to making contemporary decisions. Concern is expressed that virtually every group within the church seeks to present its views as a legitimate outgrowth of historic Presbyterianism. This very strong emphasis on Scripture has caused an intense debate concerning the legitimacy of claims to biblical and historic Calvinistic support for a variety of contemporary issues.

Traditional "Calvinism" of the sixteenth and seventeenth centuries emphasized unforgiven sin as a barrier between humans and God. This emphasis continues to be reflected in the Readiness for Ministry study. Presbyterian-Reformed people stress more than others "When preaching, places self, as much as hearers, under God's judgment" (Item 53) and "Acknowledges there are times when he or she gives in to temptation" (Item 339). A minister who insists on the natural goodness of the human race will not be at home in this family.

Another important distinctiveness brought out in the survey is a broad concern for political issues, although it is limited by considerable divergence of views between ministers and members. The Presbyterian-Reformed respondents give greater importance to "Speaks from the pulpit about political issues" (Item 117) than does the remaining group. Whereas

47 percent of the total sample see this characteristic as being undesirable or detrimental to a beginning minister, only 36 percent of the Presbyterian-Reformed respondents say this. Also they give greater importance to "Makes contact with the political thought and life in the community" (Item 149) and "Insists that political struggle is a rightful concern of the church" (Item 128). On the last of these, 39 percent of the Presbyterian-Reformed respondents, contrasted with 28 percent of all respondents, say it is "highly" or "quite" important. The differences between Presbyterian-Reformed respondents and others on these items are some of the largest in the survey. However, it is crucial to remember that within this denominational family the clergy are significantly more concerned with political activism than are the laity (in general, the data show that Presbyterian-Reformed laypeople are far less "liberal" than their clergy).

The concern for political issues is borne out by the curricula in Presbyterian-Reformed seminaries and by the activism in churches and judicatories. It is related to early Reformed emphasis on God's role as Creator and Sovereign. Because the world and the structure of things are God's creation and because He rules over society and human affairs, it is an important part of the Christian's duty to be concerned with these things and to be involved in them. The Reformed concept of Christian vocation, in effect seeking to sanctify Renaissance emphasis on this world, has helped to make it a part of Christian duty also today to be involved constructively in all important human affairs. These ideas probably are rooted in the activities of the rising bourgeois class in the Reformation era—the "on the make," increasingly influential, dominant element in the Reformed churches. The Reformed ideal of higher education—particularly for the clergy—appears to have been not merely to give prestige and technical skill but also to give a broad knowledge of the world (especially the human aspects of the world and its affairs) in order that the gospel might be directly and effectively related to human affairs in their full range. Evidently, these ideals continue to influence clergy and laity in the Presbyterian-Reformed family.

Some would sharply debate this interpretation, suggesting instead that the present accent on involvement in social issues is motivated by concerns quite alien to historic Calvinism. An appeal to God's sovereignty is seen as a theological underpinning used to bolster decisions arising from radically different political and economic bases. As large numbers of theological students enter the Presbyterian-Reformed ministry from seminaries not directly related to the Presbyterian-Reformed churches, some clergy and laity are fearful that positions not compatible with historic Calvinism will increasingly be espoused. Denominational identity is becoming an issue that demands resolution.

Yet it is noteworthy that the Presbyterian-Reformed respondents show a degree of distinctiveness in their willingness to limit denominational loyalty and in their willingness to accept as fellow Christians people who hold diverse theological views. Presbyterian-Reformed people give greater emphasis than others to Item 322, "Encourages members to acknowledge one another as the body of Christ, even though they hold divergent theological views." Also, the cluster analysis within the Presbyterian-Reformed family fails to find a cognate to Core Cluster 49, "Denominational Collegiality." The core cluster is composed of items concerned with following denominational directives, working with superiors, and giving reasoned explanations of denominational policies to people; but the Presbyterian-Reformed respondents seem to see these issues as somewhat unrelated to each other.

The early Reformed faith, both on the European continent and in Puritan England, showed elements of what we today would call *ecumenicity*. Calvin's letter to Archbishop Cranmer, avowing a readiness to "cross seven seas" in the interests of Christian unity, has often been quoted. Calvin refused to endorse the outright rejection of the Anglican Prayer Book by the incipient Puritanism of his day, and Puritan Presbyterianism itself declared in the Westminster Confession of the 1640s that "the visible church . . . consists of all those throughout the world that profess the true religion, together with their children" (*Westminster Confession*, Chapter 25:2).

Of course, modern trends and the American environment have vastly extended this spirit of tolerance, but it is significant that the Readiness for Ministry Project finds the Presbyterian-Reformed group more tolerant of internal diversity than the average, since, of course, the other groups too have been subject to the same modern and American influences making for toleration of diversity. The deep and continuing commitment of this family to ecumenical concerns is rooted in its history but probably owes a good deal to modern leaders who have felt the urgency of unity. A minister serving this community must be aware that he or she stands in a tradition that has given the world such leaders as John A. Mackay (ecumenical leader and former President of Princeton Theological Seminary) and Eugene Carson Blake (General Secretary of the World Council of Churches).

Within this denominational family is the fear that this process is making the church more pluralistic and is moving the body from its historic position of connectionalism (centralized denominational unity) to a form of congregational polity that gives more local autonomy. This is one of the key issues identified within the United Presbyterian Church that demands attention now during the 1980s. While the church continues to profess connectionalism, some engage in practices that deny it, such as withholding monies from presbyteries, expressing open criticism of denominational policies and leaders, opting for non-Presbyterian curricula, and designating mission funds to outside agencies. The heart of the issue is whether, while honoring historic traditions and polity, the church is functionally moving toward positions that weaken its unique heritage.

Presbyterian-Reformed respondents, more than others, expect ministers to encourage lay leaders to make major decisions for the congregation. They give a higher-than-average valuation to "Encourages elected lay leaders to make major decisions affecting the congregation" (Item 703) and see as more detrimental than others "Seeks to be viewed as the ultimate authority in the parish" (Item 726). The crucially important office of lay elder is seen as having developed early among the Reformed churches of the continent, somewhat paralleling the representative political government already then developing among the bourgeoisie in free commercial cities, such as Zurich and Geneva. Adapted by the Scots under the leadership of John Knox, and taking firm root in America among Scottish Presbyterian immigrants, it remains today as a tradition of strong lay leadership. Leadership, however, poses another identifiable problem within the Presbyterian church. Historically the church body has sought to retain a degree of power among the lower governing bodies. Charges are raised that higher levels of church leadership have introduced changes into the decision-making process that have effectively shifted power to the highest levels of the synod and the assembly. Thus there are today within the Presbyterian-Reformed family contending forces moving both toward more central control and toward greater local autonomy.

It is interesting also to note that Presbyterian-Reformed respondents, more than the remaining group, tend to expect conscious planning by their leaders; they do not want pastors to substitute intuition and charisma for rational processes (as is shown in the cluster analysis). This is not at all surprising in a group so deeply influenced in its polity and procedures by Calvin, the gifted lawyer, and by the emerging business class, among whom careful, rational planning has always been very important.

The researchers carried out separate cluster analyses within each denominational family, and in so doing they found distinctive patterns in some families not found in the overall data. Such patterns identify different rubrics and categorizations of thought regarding ministry, not different priorities assigned to individual items. Already we have noted that in the Presbyterian-Reformed Family a uniquely large cluster of closely interrelated items have appeared, stressing historical knowledge, breadth of knowledge, and acquaintance with modern thought. The Presbyterian-Reformed respondents see these items as closely related, more so than do the other respondents. Also, we have noted that among Presbyterian-Reformed respondents no cluster concerned with "Denominational Collegiality" (CC 49) has appeared—suggesting that the items in this area are not perceived as comprising a distinct group.

Three other cluster analysis findings deserve mention. First, the Presbyterian-Reformed family has a large cluster that might be named "Competent Worship Leadership and Teaching" and that is unlike any cluster in the total data. The Presbyterian-Reformed respondents see worship and teaching to be so related that they comprise a single facet of ministry. Second, the Presbyterian-Reformed family has no cluster equivalent to Core Cluster 7, "Liturgical Sensitivity." Apparently, the core cluster closely identifies music with liturgy and with worship style; the Presbyterian-Reformed respondents do not see this close identification. This family has a heritage of negative positions on vestments and liturgy, a heritage reinforced by frontier conditions in America beyond the East Coast. Today the dislike of clerical collars in these denominations often follows geographical patterns. The recent ecumenical experience and dialogue, however, is opening the door to greater interest in art and music in the service of God. Third, the Presbyterian-Reformed cluster analysis has produced a large cluster that might be named "Affirmation of People Amidst Stress," with highest emphasis on such items as "Acts calmly during times of stress" (Item 501), "Helps others see the best in people" (Item 502), and "Remains positive and constructive toward cantankerous members" (Item 500). Calvin, tying pastoral concern and discipline closely together and revealing in his *Articles* (1537) and later in his *Ordinances* (1541) that he had been thinking about securing lay help (elders) in pastoral oversight, has left a heritage to the Presbyterian-Reformed family. Even today, concern with pastoral care, discipline, and leadership of groups troubled with disunity is strongly felt in the Presbyterian-Reformed family.

The researchers have scored each denominational family on the overall clusters uncovered in the total data set, and they have compared the families with each other. One result is the finding that the Presbyterian-Reformed laity (not clergy) rate among the highest of any Protestant group in the project on Core Cluster 3, "Relating Well to Children and Youth." The entire family differs significantly from others in placing far higher emphasis on seeing youth "as part of the congregation rather than a programmatic appendage" (Item 68). This reinforces our earlier comment on the concern that pastors be good teachers. Calvin's intense concern for the religious instruction of youth, reflected in his *Catechism* (1537) and reinforced in other Reformed catechisms and the long tradition of catechetical instructions, has helped to build a tradition of urgent concern for education. This must be acknowledged, whatever criticism may rightly be made today on psychological pedagogical grounds, of the catechetical method. Presbyterians believe that "Truth is in order to goodness," and they have not withheld the resources essential to give this conviction tangible shape. They have built institutions of higher learning all over America, establishing a tradition of having a number of students in a Presbyterian college within a generation after the organizing of a Presbyterian church in a community.

When clergy and laity are compared on the various clusters, a sharp rift appears in the Presbyterian-Reformed group, with the laity tending to emphasize evangelism (CC 19) and the clergy tending to emphasize community causes (CC 15). Clergy-laity gap in this family is the largest of any of the denominational families. Hoge, in his recent book, *Division in the Protestant House*,[3] reveals the same cleavage—especially within the United Presbyterian church—between those who emphasize personal religious experience and those who emphasize social concern (whom he calls "private Christians" and "public Christians," borrowing a phrase from Martin Marty). The Readiness for Ministry study has the same finding.

This last phenomenon seems to have more recent historical roots than those discussed earlier. It is the most difficult pattern to explain historically. Perhaps what we are seeing is an inability of the clergy to carry their constituency along with them into the more sophisticated interpretation of Christianity that modern knowledge requires. The laity may also be more economically and politically conservative than the clergy, hence hesitant to back church involvement in community issues. Hoge found both theological and social attitudinal differences behind Presbyterian division on this question. This divergence of view between pulpit and pew is a matter that invites very serious attention. It cannot be solved at the price of abandoning honest scholarship and ceasing to face courageously real intellectual and social questions. The Readiness for Ministry study finds, interestingly, that clergy-laity divergence about " 'Born-Again' Christianity" (CC 40) is even more acute among the Christian Church (Disciples of Christ) than among Presbyterian-Reformed respondents. That body has an early tradition of laying great stress on revivalism (although of a somewhat unemotional type) and also of disfavoring a professional ministry. Thus, as a professional ministry has developed within that church and quite rapidly become moderately "liberal," it is easy to see how a gap has emerged. The Presbyterian-Reformed group, on the other hand, has from the very beginning strongly emphasized a highly educated ministry. The apparent clergy-laity gap probably is the result of the relatively high education of the clergy and the difficulty that laity experience when attempting to follow them into the new critical views— especially when a ready escape is available to many laypeople by the simple refusal to leave the revivalistic tradition dominant in most of nineteenth-century American Protestantism.

Assuming a laity-clergy division, the issue becomes particularly acute at the point when the young lay Christian who has decided to enter the Christian ministry selects a seminary. The United Presbyterian Church, for instance, finds its candidates enrolled in sixty seminaries, with over 45 percent of the candidates attending non-Presbyterian seminaries. Many of these students have decided to enter the ministry as a result of a conversion experience during college years. While ultimately drawn to the ministry of the Presbyterian-Reformed churches in which they have been reared, they select their seminary on the more conservative recommendation of people in, for example, "Intervarsity Fellowship," "Navigators," or "Campus Christian Crusade," who have been influential in their renewed faith experience. In other cases, students are influenced by their own pastors, who are concerned with what they perceive as the church's movement away from historic (Calvinistic) Presbyterianism.

In conclusion, it is important to emphasize that the responses, as a whole, place the Presbyterian-Reformed family squarely in the center of the bodies comprising the Christian community, with far more important agreements than differences. Obviously, the distinctive views are survivals of the differences developed when the Presbyterian-Reformed family first had defined itself as a distinctive family in the Reformation era. The much larger body of convictions and practices held in common consist both of those common Christian elements that antedate the divisions of the Reformation, and thus are inherited by everyone, and also of those new insights and practices that have developed by the facing of common problems and by the using of common cultural resources. The recent convergence has occurred especially in mutual interchange and interrelationship.

NOTES

1. Three of the ten denominations in the empirically defined "family" are historically different from the other seven. They are the African Methodist Episcopal Church, the African Methodist Episcopal Zion Church, and the Moravian Church in America. They have joined the family "empirically," in that their responses resemble the responses of the Presbyterian and Reformed groups. The three comprise only 10.6 percent of the total respondents in the family, and it is impossible to describe them as a group from the data. Black churches are discussed in the introduction to this volume.

2. All differences noted in this chapter are significant at the .0001 level when the Presbyterian-Reformed family responses are compared with the total data.

3. (Philadelphia: Westminster, 1976).

16

Roman Catholic
Church

Francis A. Lonsway

Lonsway analyzes the Roman Catholic data (both Order and Diocesan) on the basis of the importance accorded by Catholic priests and laity to the eleven larger areas of ministry, the second-order factors. Roman Catholics represent a fairly large portion of the total response (approximately 12 percent or 592 people). They are atypical in that laity comprise 57 percent of the total group—whereas for most other denominational families professional clergy outnumber the lay portion of the sample. Because of the sheer size and variety of persons and values contained within this church, Lonsway warns us that it becomes difficult to draw many unqualified conclusions.

A major expectation held by Roman Catholics about beginning priests is that they manifest an openness in their ministerial style while remaining sensitive to the history and tradition of the church. A stereotype that focuses heavily on the sacramental and liturgical roles of the priest is destroyed, for a greater concern emerges that young priests relate the faith to daily life, preach well, and encourage the building up of the Body of Christ within their congregations. There is further a clear expectation that in their personal lives

---

Francis A. Lonsway, a Roman Catholic priest and Conventual Franciscan, is a member of the ATS Readiness for Ministry staff and an educational consultant for Roman Catholic orders.

priests give a genuine witness to the gospel and integrate their learning in the service of the parish.

In contrast to some of the Protestant denominations, Catholics tend to place less value on pastoral counseling, or sharing congregational leadership with laity, and on assertive personal evangelism.

Laity-clergy differences are significant at several points. Clergy place a greater emphasis than do laity on aspects of the church's tradition, denominational knowledge, theological reflection, and an active concern for the oppressed. The laity, however, express a greater desire for a more stringent handling of ethical issues, the religious nurture of their children and youth, and more responsibility in leading the parish. Lonsway suggests this diversity is inevitable and must be viewed within a greater unity of people who seek to treasure equally their history and their mission in the future.

The Roman Catholic Church is an intriguing object of study as much for its historical self-consciousness and view of its mission as for its size and complexity. While the ferment of theological inquiry adds nuances to the former and hence generally provides an enriched vision of its past and role in the world, the sheer size of its population very frequently makes generalizations about the church's views and ideals extremely complex. Size also brings tolerance, so that with a broad enough sample of Roman Catholics one would expect nearly every possible opinion regarding the church, its beliefs and practices, its strengths and weaknesses, its hopes and failures.

Therefore, we must be careful in this chapter to be faithful to the sample from which opinions were drawn to develop the portrait of the expectations of Roman Catholics for their young priests. The specific question to us was, "What do you consider most important in a beginning priest?"

The Roman Catholic Church is one of the forty-seven denominational families within the Association of Theological Schools (ATS). As with the others, careful samples were drawn from both the laity and the group that came to be known as "professionals" or "clergy." Clergy include members of theological faculties, bishops, ministers provincial and others within the hierarchy, pastors, and seminarians in their final year of studies before ordination. In the early phases of the project, data were separated for religious professionals and the laity they served (designated "Order") in contrast to diocesan professionals and their laity (designated "Diocesan"). While there are several significant differences between these groups, the overall pattern of expectations between the two groups is nearly identical. What is reported here, therefore, is their combined opinions about what Roman Catholics consider most important for those beginning the priesthood.

In the Readiness for Ministry study, the sample for Roman Catholics in North America comprised 339 laypeople and 253 clergy, or 57.3 percent laity and 42.7 percent clergy. These proportions provide a unique opportunity to interpret the data in quite an even-handed way. Simply put, the clergy group are not heard more strongly than the people to whom they have been called to minister. That seems a healthy benefit as we interpret our data.

The total, lay and clergy, usable responses to the Readiness for Ministry Survey were 4,995; the Roman Catholic total of 592 indicates that among all of the denominational families ours contributed 11.8 percent to the overall results of the study, a share second in size only to the sample of the Presbyterian-Reformed tradition.

Several strategies to organize the findings from the survey seem functional. There are sixty-four core clusters, formed mathematically through consistent patterns of response, called "core clusters." One could arrange the material by clusters or by the eleven second-order factors (larger groupings of core clusters). I have chosen to discuss the factors by rank order of their importance among Roman Catholics. This approach was chosen in order to more fully focus on the Roman Catholic view of beginning ministry for its priests in contrast to considering primarily the similarities and differences among the denominational families.

Table 16-1 provides the comparison between the rank order of the eleven factors by all denominations and by Roman Catholics. The differences begin to appear immediately. To illustrate, while the Roman Catholics share concern with all other denominations for the open, affirming style of its young churchmen, Roman Catholics treasure equally the denominational awareness and loyalty of their young priests, a characteristic that ranks fifth for all denominations. Whetted by this first finding, let us begin.

OPEN, AFFIRMING STYLE

The core clusters that comprise "Open, Affirming Style" (Factor 4), arranged in rank order by the means of Roman Catholic responses, include "Fidelity to Tasks and Persons" (CC 43), "Personal Responsibility" (CC 42), "Positive Approach" (CC 44), "Acknowledgment of Limitations" (CC 36), "Flexibility of Spirit" (CC 45), "Valuing Diversity" (CC 46), and "Acceptance of Clergy Role" (CC 47). This factor defines a feeling of ministry conducted responsibly, with integrity, sincerity, and in an atmosphere of flexibility. Among most denominational families, there is general agreement about the overall importance of these characteristics for the young priest or minister.

On the first of these clusters, "Fidelity to Tasks and Persons," however, Roman Catholics respond with the lowest valuation among all the denominations. This does not seem surprising. The characteristic focuses

TABLE 16-1
**Comparison of Means and Ranks Between Roman Catholics
and All Other Denominations**

Factor No.	Factor Title	Roman Catholics Grand Mean	Rank	All Other Denominations Grand Mean	Rank
4	Open, Affirming Style	2.11	1.5	2.18	1
11	Denominational Awareness and Collegiality	2.11	1.5	1.65	7
5	Development of Fellowship and Worship	1.99	3	1.79	6
9	Caring for Persons under Stress	1.95	4	1.98	2
10	Theologian in Life and Thought	1.91	5	1.88	4
8	Congregational Leadership	1.89	6	1.97	3
2	Ministry from Personal Commitment of Faith	1.75	7	1.82	5
1	Ministry to Community and World	1.42	8	1.32	8
7	Priestly-Sacramental Ministry	0.72	9	0.24	9
6	Privatistic, Legalistic Style	−1.25	10	−1.25	10
3	Disqualifying Personal and Behavorial Characteristics	−1.43	11	−1.80	11

on "honoring commitments by carrying out promises despite pressures to compromise." At first glance, this would seem to be an awkward response for Roman Catholics, given their highly refined ethical system. But for two reasons, it seems less than it might appear. First, it is a long-standing expectation that the clergy be responsible. The Roman Catholic tradition has generally prepared young priests who are responsible, and hence highlighting responsibility may not seem particularly urgent. Many priests and laity within the Roman Catholic Church might wonder, in fact, if the question were a serious one. Second, given the time of this study, the early 1970s, it may be that Roman Catholics were concerned about a number of other issues even more important to their lives in the church. For example, of greater concern were the dwindling numbers of priests (and religious) and the sense of loss of heritage or continuity with the past through many of the changes rapidly implemented during and after the

Second Vatican Council. These same phenomena could account for the equally high concern of Roman Catholics for denominational awareness and loyalty as for the open, affirming style of its young priests.

In approximately three-quarters (eight of eleven) of the factors, there occur some significant differences between the view of the laity and that of the clergy within the Roman Catholic Church (both Order and Diocesan). One such appears in "Acknowledgment of Limitations" (CC 36). Clergy value the characteristic more highly than do the laity. The implication, likely, is that such is a fundamental trait of servanthood inculcated early in the training of seminarians. Clergy view priesthood as a sign that they are to be witnesses and to be ever conscious that, while through ordination they might be considered "Alter Christus," they never lose their human frailty as followers of Christ.

The history of the Roman Catholic Church, with respect to ministry and priesthood, has not been an easy one. To many, Protestants have ministers and Roman Catholics have priests. To others, priesthood is essentially tied to the celebration of the Eucharist whereas ministry is applied to what others might do, such as reading of the scriptures or distribution of Communion during the liturgy. Furthermore, some priests have seen themselves as fundamentally above everyone else in the Church, so much so that there is but priest and people, and as such seek to be ministered to rather than to minister. Bernard Cooke, a noted Roman Catholic theologian, observes that we must not drive "too large a wedge" between the concepts of ministry and priesthood, since "the heart and culmination of Jesus' own ministerial service to his fellow humans undoubtedly came in his death and resurrection, which is also his supreme act of priestly sacrifice."[1]

DENOMINATIONAL AWARENESS AND COLLEGIALITY

Sharing with the expectation of "Open, Affirming Style" the position of being most valued by Roman Catholics, this factor, Denominational Awareness and Collegiality (Factor 11), includes only two clusters; namely, "Denominational Collegiality" (CC 49) and "Denominational Knowledge" (CC 32). The first focuses on acceptance of one's denomination's directives and regulations while maintaining a collegial relationship with superiors and staff, and the second is closely allied to this concept. This ranking by Roman Catholics is in sharp contrast to the overall assessment of the importance of such a background in the lives of Protestant ministers and Reform Jewish rabbis. Its overall ranking among all denominations places it seventh among the eleven second-order factors.

Both concepts suggest an appreciation for the past, its influence on the present, and its shaping of the future. With the long history of the Roman

Catholic tradition and its emphasis on the past as prologue, there should be no wonder that this characteristic is valued so highly in its young priests. As suggested earlier, this emphasis on the denomination was likely intensified within the church at the time of the survey (the 1970s), since many then felt (and a number continue to feel) adrift, cut away from their moorings.

On denominational knowledge, the clergy group views this more highly central to the life of the young priest than do the laity, in part, likely, because the clergy are the guarantors of the history, the living memory of the church's past.

One cannot leave this finding so quickly, however. While the emphasis of the clergy is understandable, there may very well be in this emphasis a wish that is not being fulfilled. It is quite one thing to expect young priests to have this sense of the church and quite another to see it exhibited in their ministries. Many feel that young priests are little different from the laity in their understanding of church history and in their appreciation for the notion of the "brotherhood of priests." Part of this can likely be traced to sterile teaching of church history but much more are the changes in formation to be cited. The personal freedom now emphasized often fails to acknowledge the common bonds with those already ordained, with the bishops, and, in a sense, with what the church teaches. Priesthood has consequently become for some a solo event, and a priest's ministry "his own." What I believe needs to be restored is an appreciation for the past of the Roman Catholic Church and for the present with other priests and religious, and a sense that one ministers personally or uniquely within those strong bonds of fraternity.

DEVELOPMENT OF FELLOWSHIP AND WORSHIP

Ranking third in importance for Roman Catholics is "Development of Fellowship and Worship" (Factor 5). The six clusters that comprise this factor are "Relating Faith to Modern World" (CC 1), "Relating Well to Children and Youth" (CC 3), "Competent Preaching and Worship Leading" (CC 5), "Encouragement of Mutuality in Congregation" (CC 4), "Liturgical Sensitivity" (CC 7), and "Sacramental-Liturgical Ministry" (CC 9).

The rank order of these clusters may be disquieting to Roman Catholics who value highly both what is pastorally suitable and inspiring in worship, as we see that "Liturgical Sensitivity" and "Sacramental-Liturgical Ministry" are not at the bottom of these priorities. Furthermore, characteristics ranked first, second, and third in this listing show no significant disagreements with other denominational families. It seems significant that for Roman Catholics what a young priest does to build the local church (developing within the congregation a sense of being the family of God and showing sensitivity and skill in ministering to children and youth), and what he preaches about, and how he holds the liturgical celebration together are all more important than either liturgical sensitivity or the sacramental-liturgical ministry. That is not to say that these latter characteristics are unimportant to us; the data show that we, along with the Anglican-Episcopal family and the Orthodox Churches, hold the sacramental and liturgical aspects significantly higher than any other denominational family.

There is no case being built, then, to suggest the unimportance of the liturgical and sacramental for Roman Catholics. There is, however, a new emphasis that I think we must consider. Argumentatively put, the new emphasis signals a diminished interest for the "sacramental technician." One does not need to travel far in both lay and clerical circles within the Roman Catholic Church to sense that this is happening. Laity are much more concerned about the quality of the homily and, in particular, what relevance the gospel has to their everyday lives.

It is helpful to look at some of the items that adhere to form those clusters ranked by Roman Catholics as more important; for example, "Helps laypeople relate Christian teachings to current issues and human needs"; "Presents the gospel in terms understandable to the modern mind"; "Sees youth as part of the congregation rather than a programmatic appendage"; "When preaching, holds the interest and attention of congregation"; and "Provides opportunities within the congregation for personal growth and spiritual enrichment." These suggest the concerns of both the Catholic laity and the clergy. For some priests, it is disturbing that people are not going to the sacraments as they have in the past and, hence, the shape of the priest's ministry must change. This has become a very serious issue for these men. Yet these changes enrich the texture of priesthood for those who are about to enter its service.

A significant difference between the laity and clergy within our tradition must be noted. The laity value the young priest's relating well to children and youth (Core Cluster, or CC, 3) significantly more important than do the fourth-year seminarians, the religious and diocesan officials, parish priests, and theological faculties. Is there not a message here?

CARING FOR PERSONS UNDER STRESS

For Roman Catholics, Factor 9, "Caring for Persons under Stress," ranks fourth in importance among the eleven factors; for the denominational families in general it ranks second. Its five clusters, in order of importance for Roman Catholics, are "Perceptive Counseling" (CC 21), "Caring Availability" (CC 23), "Enabling Counseling" (CC 22), "Involvement in

Caring" (CC 25), and "Coministry to the Alienated" (CC 26). There is no difference between the view of the lay and the professional group within the Roman Catholic tradition with regard to these clusters, whose titles leave no doubt about their emphasis.

When we consider that for Roman Catholics "Denominational Awareness and Collegiality" and the "Development of Fellowship and Worship" are both more important than "Caring for Persons under Stress," whereas this "caring under stress" factor is second among Protestant Christianity, more than a comment on rank comparisons is appropriate. There is no doubt about the pressure placed on seminaries by a variety of formal and informal organizations to develop offerings in counseling. When such offerings are devoid of theological content and the prospective priest is encouraged to behave like a therapist with a secular grounding, Roman Catholics will be concerned. They value more highly the personal practice of religion as the occasion for bringing together priest and the people who come to him.

Among course offerings within Roman Catholic seminaries, those in the pastoral skills areas are sometimes cited as "better" or "more interesting and useful" than those in areas such as systematic theology or Scripture. Part of the response can likely be due to quite different teaching styles. Some would say it is not so much that pastoral theology is not taught so well as that other theology is taught so poorly. My own judgment is that the pastoral area is innately more attractive and represents a much closer link to what young seminarians want to know in order to be effective priests. The challenge, then, is not an easy one, but those in "academic" theology must consider it a useful expenditure of time both to teach the connection between theology and priesthood and to live it as well.

These comments do not suggest that Roman Catholics might be corrupted by an emphasis on pastoral care within other denominations, nor even that Roman Catholics are being pressured into counseling, as if it were inappropriate for the young priest. What they do suggest, however, is that we must keep in mind that Roman Catholics do not as highly value "Caring for Persons under Stress" as either a sense of the history of our tradition and an understanding of how to work within this history, or the building up of the local congregation as the people of God and at worship, assembled in praise and thanks for his great work among us. And finally, we suggest that we must recognize that any counseling that does not have as its touchstone the commitment of faith, for both the priest and the laity, is certain to be inappropriate.

THEOLOGIAN IN LIFE AND THOUGHT

Ranked fifth by Roman Catholics (fourth by all denominational families), "Theologian in Life and Thought" (Factor 10) focuses on the young priest as he grows intellectually and uses his mental abilities in such practical ways as communication and staying informed both in theology and other areas. It also includes the characteristics of "Service in Humility," the most highly rated by the entire group sampled in the Readiness for Ministry study (CC 34). The other five clusters in this factor, by rank order among Roman Catholics include "Theological Reflection" (CC 29), "Clarity of Thought and Communication" (CC 28), "Use of Broad Knowledge" (CC 30), "Acknowledgment of Own Vulnerability" (CC 38), and "Acceptance of Counsel" (CC 39).

Many who are interested in the Readiness for Ministry assessment program are immediately drawn to this factor. It includes issues that closely reflect what we hope will be accomplished in theological education; namely, developed theological opinions regularly evaluated in the light of experience and current theology (CC 29), sharpened intelligence through continual theological study and attention to clarity in thought and expression (CC 28), and alertness to the world and ability to use a broad base of information to stimulate people to become thinking Christians (CC 30). While certainly this is not everything one hopes to see a young priest gain from his years of theological study, some skeptics of the system would be satisfied if this much occurred.

Three of six clusters in this factor focus on the integration of the theological experience—a cherished concept, to be sure. It is intriguing that the factor also reflects the personal self-effacing characteristics important to priesthood and ministry in general. "Service in Humility" and "Acknowledgment of Own Vulnerability" indicate a general openness within the young priest to admit his own humanity. He should be able not only to admit limitations and mistakes but also to laugh at himself. He is not as awesome as ordination might seem to make him, or as he might see himself to be. "Acceptance of Counsel" indicates a willingness to talk to trusted friends about matters that are central to his ministry.

A wholeness of person suggested by this factor says that the young priest ought to know himself well and that he should know how to get help in his own growth and to utilize the resources of his theological training for informing his ministry to others. Small wonder that this factor ranks high for laity and clergy among all denominations represented in the study.

Roman Catholic clergy value two clusters within this factor more highly than do the laity, namely, "Theological Reflection" and "Acceptance of Counsel." A point might be made with regard to the second. To talk about one's ministry with trusted friends is perhaps another way of saying, "I talk to my spiritual director." In the past each seminarian was assigned a spiritual director, and every priest was expected to avail himself of counsel throughout his life. Although the title for this function remains, the range of individuals whom a priest might consider his director has certainly broadened, as has the setting in which such counsel is given. For Roman

Catholic priests, in particular, this feature of their lives is constantly stressed as perhaps the most productive way by which they can grow in their calling. Article Two in the National Conference of Catholic Bishops' *The Program of Priestly Formation* (1976) describes the role of the spiritual director: "one of pastoral leadership in order to draw the entire seminary into a more generous response to the gospel message."[2]

CONGREGATIONAL LEADERSHIP

All other denominational families surveyed value "Congregational Leadership" (Factor 8) more highly (third among the eleven) than do Roman Catholics, who rank it sixth. The factor comprises five clusters: "Building Congregational Community" (CC 55), "Conflict Utilization" (CC 56), "Sharing Congregational Leadership" (CC 57), "Responsible Staff Management" (CC 59), and "Effective Administration" (CC 58). All indicate an emphasis on the working relationships that build within the congregation a sense of being the church. While there is likely theological agreement among all of the religious traditions within the study that the church is the "people of God, the body of the Lord, and the temple of the Holy Spirit,"[3] nevertheless, anyone living the Roman Catholic faith knows instinctively that he or she is more likely to "belong to the church" than "to be the church."

There is nothing inherently sinister in the notion of "belonging" (as opposed to "being"), but the difference in emphasis is important. For Roman Catholics, the church is likely to be seen as the body of Christ and the faithful, its members. The traditional emphasis on the hierarchy of the ordained clergy—pope, bishops, priests—is a very natural one, because they are representatives of Christ. As the Second Vatican Council's Dogmatic Constitution on the Church (*Lumen Gentium*) stated it, "They (the faithful) are fully incorporated into the society of the church who, possessing the spirit of Christ, accept her entire system and all the means of salvation given to her, and through union with her visible structure are joined to Christ, who rules her through the Supreme Pontiff and the bishops."[4] If one is the representative of Christ, and on the local level this is preeminently the pastor of the parish, then one is alert to his leadership, to his style, and to his method of operation.

This point is even stronger in light of the contrasts between Roman Catholics and a number of other religious traditions in "Sharing Congregational Leadership" (CC 57). Roman Catholics value this trait among its young priests as significantly less important than 40 percent of the denominational families. Contrasting groups include the Evangelical B, Free Church, United Methodist Church, Presbyterian-Reformed, United Church of Christ, and United Church of Canada families.

The reasonableness of the difference in emphasis is made obvious by citing key statements from the Readiness for Ministry survey that yielded this cluster; for example, "Meets with lay leaders chosen by the congregation" and "Seeks adequate congregational support before launching innovative projects." Our lay leadership is emerging, and we have begun to implement this direction. But, given our respect for the role of the hierarchy, we are not likely to move fully to the coministerial form suggested by this factor.

This phenomenon cannot comfort those who want reality to be other than it is, but it explains, in part, the dismal failure of many experiments in team ministry. Some of these have simply become groups with special turf and therefore not cooperative, but as competitive as pastors and assistants and laity have always been. Some dioceses and religious communities are developing detailed guidelines for the formation of teams. This accents, I believe, the experimental nature of such efforts, and it will be only with a number of good working experiments that there will be a chance for a gradual share by laity in the development of the church.

There are no differences in judgment between the Roman Catholic laity and its clergy on any of the clusters forming "Congregational Leadership."

MINISTRY FROM PERSONAL COMMITMENT OF FAITH

The factor on which the Roman Catholics differ consistently with many of the denominational traditions is "Ministry from Personal Commitment of Faith" (Factor 2). There are no significant differences between Roman Catholic laity and clergy within the entire factor. Catholics rank it seventh among the eleven factors.

Nine clusters comprise the factor. In order of importance for Roman Catholics, they are "Christian Example" (CC 35), "Commitment Reflecting Religious Piety" (CC 37), "Theologically Oriented Counseling" (CC 24), "Theocentric-Biblical Ministry" (CC 2), "Affirmation of Conservative Biblical Faith" (CC 31), "Encouragement of Spiritual Sensitivity" (CC 6), "Encouragement of World Mission" (CC 12), "Assertive Individual Evangelism" (CC 17), and " 'Born-Again' Christianity" (CC 40). In total, they describe a ministry that emerges from a personal faith commitment, is centered in biblical affirmation, and emphasizes the evangelistic and mission goals of God's people.

On every one of these nine clusters, Roman Catholics differ with at least one denominational tradition. On a third of them, they differ with at least seven and as many as eight denominations. The groups with which they most frequently differ are the Southern Baptists, the Evangelical A and B families, and the Jewish and Unitarian group. The fewest differences among denominations are detected in "Theologically Oriented Counseling," "Theocentric-Biblical Ministry," "Encouragement of World Mission," "Commitment Reflecting Religious Piety," and "Christian Example." There are nonetheless consistent differences within these five clusters that involve a number of other denominations as well. For example, the Jewish and Unitarian family consider less important an emphasis on using the resources of faith, which is integral to the concept "Theologically Oriented Counseling" (CC 24), than do either the Roman Catholics or ten other families. The point is that, while there are some differences within these first five clusters for Roman Catholics and a few other denominational traditions, some of these same traditions differ with a considerable number of other families than the Roman Catholic.

However, the clusters that involve the greatest number of differences between Roman Catholics and others frequently have a fundamentalistic ring to them. Those clusters include " 'Born Again' Christianity," "Assertive Individual Evangelism," "Affirmation of Conservative Biblical Faith," and "Encouragement of Spiritual Sensitivity." Given our centuries of theological reflection, we would generally be less inclined to take the basics as the major part of any theological discussion. From our point of view, such would deny the richness and complexity of our faith.

" 'Born-Again' Christianity" (CC 40) introduces the four clusters that seem to highlight the more fundamentalistic aspects of Christianity. The item most highly rated in this cluster describes the cluster well: "In social conversation, talks about what the Lord has done recently in own life." The Jewish and Unitarian family values this characteristic least among the denominations and differs significantly from all others in this regard. Roman Catholics, as do Anglican-Episcopals, the Orthodox, Lutherans, and others, value this less than do those in Southern Baptist Churches and the Evangelical A and B families.

This is not to suggest that there are no Roman Catholics who are "born again." The strength and presence of the charismatic movement, in particular, would give lie to such a statement. Rather, for Roman Catholics in general, such is not their experience of faith nor their expectation for the life of faith in their young priests.

"Assertive Individual Evangelism" is valued lowest by the Jewish and Unitarian family, which differs significantly from every other family in its judgment on this cluster. Roman Catholics, also, value this same characteristic less than do the Southern Baptist Convention, the Evangelical A and B families, the Presbyterian-Reformed, the American-Canadian Baptist family, the Free Church family, and the Christian Church (not Disciples). The description of this characteristic suggests adequately the reason for the lack of Roman Catholic enthusiasm. It represents an "aggressive approach to strangers and the unchurched, hoping to convert some to Christianity." The valuation of this trait would certainly be different in missionary lands or even in the United States if answered by such home mission groups as the Glenmary Home Missioners or the Josephite Fathers.

"Affirmation of Conservative Biblical Faith" (CC 31) yields much the same pattern, likely for much the same reason. The Jewish and Unitarian family values it least among all the denominations; many of the groups that differ from the Roman Catholics in "Assertive Individual Evangelism" nevertheless value this dimension of a young minister's work more highly.

What about the "Encouragement of Spiritual Sensitivity" (CC 6)? Some of the central items that comprise the cluster include "Preaches sermons that awaken listeners to their sinfulness and need for a savior"; "When preaching places self, as much as hearers, under God's judgment"; and "Will spontaneously change plans during a worship service in response to the leading of the Spirit." The last item is less than likely within our tradition (unless it be outside the context of the celebration of the Eucharist). The earlier two reflect a moment or two within our heritage, but not the current moment. The phrases have the ring of the "fire and brimstone" that a number of Roman Catholics might remember from their youth but that is not a common preaching style now. Many Roman Catholic priests are trying to become biblical preachers, using the liturgical texts for the Eucharist assigned for Sundays, weekdays, and feasts. Many of these readings lend themselves more to preaching the unfolding of the mystery of the presence of God with creation and, as such, lead from death to resurrection and union.

The differences the data show between Roman Catholics and others seem to be understandable. Our emphasis is on the historical development of God's presence and the living out of that history across time. This does not deny the evangelical in any sense, but rather suggests that such is the beginning of a history of the life of a person with Christ and not the end.

MINISTRY TO COMMUNITY AND WORLD

Nine clusters comprise "Ministry to Community and World" (Factor 1). In order of importance as viewed by Roman Catholics surveyed in this study, they include "Initiative in Development of Community Services" (CC 13), "Pastoral Service to All" (CC 11), "Ecumenical and Educational Openness" (CC 8), "Support of Unpopular Causes" (CC 50), "Promotion of Understanding of Issues" (CC 14), "Support of Community Causes" (CC 15), "Active Concern for the Oppressed" (CC 16), "Interest in New Ideas" (CC 33), and "Aggressive Political Leadership" (CC 18).

At first glance, it might appear that "Interest in New Ideas" is not particularly germane to this factor with its eight other clusters clearly focused on involvement beyond the local church. Several items in the cluster, however, would indicate that, while the fit might not be conceptually perfect, it at least seems appropriate. For instance, two items from the cluster suggest it is important that the young priest "encourages the belief that some other religions of the world make worthwhile contributions to humanity" and "advocates a 'liberation theology' because of its implication for oppressed people."

The social encyclicals awakened within Roman Catholics the special poignancy of looking beyond themselves to see the larger world and their mission to bring Christ present to the lives of all people. Justice was the emphasis of these works, peace their fulfillment. The encyclical letters of John XXIII, *"Mater et Magistra"* (1961) and *"Pacem in Terris"* (1963) rekindled the special message of these earlier works. The Second Vatican Council in the Pastoral Constitution on the Church in the Modern World (*"Gaudium et Spes,"* 1965) put it urgently: "In our times a special obligation binds us to make ourselves the neighbor of absolutely every person and of actively helping him when he comes across our path."[5]

On a number of these dimensions, the Evangelical A family consistently views the social outreach beyond their denominations less important than do most other groups, including Roman Catholics. Three significant differences occur between the laity and the clergy within the Roman Catholic tradition itself. In each, the clergy value the trait higher in the young priests than do the laity. These include "Interest in New Ideas," "Aggressive Political Leadership," and "Active Concern for the Oppressed." Such an emphasis is fitting, certainly, for it rests principally with those in the professional group—bishops, religious superiors, pastors, teachers, and men ready for ordination—to carry the message of the church's concern for social justice and peace.

Again, however, I believe that we are more in the realm of the ideal than the real. I think that both clergy and laity are to be indicted; neither can lay the fault at the other's doorstep. I admit that there are structures that call us to a concern for peace and justice. Nearly every diocese and religious order and many parishes have such commissions or committees. Most of us would also admit that much of what is done is to collect clothes on an annual basis, or to earmark some small contribution to a wandering missionary known personally or through a letter. Groups such as the Center for Concern in Washington, D.C., are trying to tackle our inertia, but it is slow work. For Roman Catholics, at least, the area of social justice and peace is a clear case of sound theology, carefully developed, but the practice is often far from the ideal.

PRIESTLY-SACRAMENTAL MINISTRY

"Priestly-Sacramental Ministry" (Factor 7) is formed by three clusters: "Sacramental-Liturgical Ministry" (CC 9), "Priestly Commitment" (CC 41), and "Mutual Family Commitment" (CC 48). The last, which focuses on the relationship of the minister to spouse and children, will not be discussed other than to note that Roman Catholics, lay and clergy, differ significantly with every other denominational tradition in their low valuation of this characteristic for young priests.

"Sacramental-Liturgical Ministry," included in the factor on "Development of Fellowship and Worship," as well, yields significant differences between Roman Catholics and every other denominational tradition in the study except the Anglican-Episcopal family, who value it nearly the same as do Roman Catholics. The Orthodox churches consider such ministry as significantly more important than do the Roman Catholics; the remainder of the traditions consider this feature of ministry much less important.

"Priestly Commitment," which focuses in part on the sacramental life of the young priest and in part on his lifestyle, proves to be significantly different for Roman Catholics than for all other denominational traditions. The Anglican-Episcopal and Orthodox Churches value this characteristic as more important than do all other groups of Protestants, and the Roman Catholic community values it more highly than either of these.

It is quite natural, given our history, the development of the sacramental theology, and of the celebration of the Eucharist, for Roman Catholics to look closely at such characteristics as "Sacramental-Liturgical Ministry" and "Priestly Commitment" for signs of strength in the bonds with our heritage. It is important to point out, however, that neither of these two clusters is in the top thirty of the sixty-four clusters most valued by laity and clergy alike within the Roman Catholic tradition. An examination of Table 16-2, which lists the ten most valued, is instructive.

Those characteristics that are most important of all, "Service in Humility," "Christian Example," and "Commitment Reflecting Religious Piety," suggest a witness to priesthood that is considerably more important for Roman Catholics than the young man's sacramental ministry. The remainder focus variously on relating learning to his work as a priest ("Relating Faith to Modern World," "Theologically Oriented Counseling," "Clarity of Thought and Communication," "Theological Reflection," and "Perceptive Counseling") and again, on witness or style of priesthood ("Fidelity to Tasks and Persons," "Personal Responsibility," and "Positive Approach").

In sum, then, there are two overall patterns suggested by this table, both of which, in the responses of Roman Catholics, are valued more highly than the young priest's sacramental ministry, namely, a genuine witness

TABLE 16-2
Rank Order of Roman Catholic Clusters

Rank	Mean	Cluster	Title
1	2.62	34	Service in Humility
2	2.36	35	Christian Example
3	2.31	37	Commitment Reflecting Religious Piety
4	2.29	1	Relating Faith to Modern World
5	2.27	24	Theologically Oriented Counseling
6	2.25	43	Fidelity to Tasks and Persons
7.5	2.24	28	Clarity of Thought and Communication
7.5	2.24	29	Theological Reflection
7.5	2.24	42	Personal Responsibility
10.5	2.20	21	Perceptive Counseling
10.5	2.20	44	Positive Approach

to the gospel and the integration of learning with his mission of service to the people.

It is easy to be upset should we expect the "sacramental priesthood" to be preeminent in the life of the young priest. Comments were made earlier regarding this position. Positively viewed, what the Roman Catholic data encourage us to consider is the radical grounding of the priest in Christian witness and in the integration of learning for his ministry. Put another way, the integrity of the young priest is more basic than his function. What can be said for the young priest, par excellence, is what Hans Küng wrote as final words to his massive work, *On Being a Christian:*

> By following Jesus Christ
> man in the world of today
> can truly humanly live, act, suffer and die:
> in happiness and unhappiness, life and death,
> sustained by God and helpful to men.[6]

PRIVATISTIC, LEGALISTIC STYLE

The final (and overall lowest-rated) factor for Roman Catholics is "Privatistic, Legalistic Style" (Factor 6). It contains some interesting findings, in particular, the largest difference between the laity and the clergy within our church on any single cluster of the whole study. The five clusters that comprise this factor, in rank order for Roman Catholics are "Law Orientation to Ethical Issues" (CC 27), "Precedence of Evangelistic Goals" (CC 19), "Intuitive Domination of Decision Making" (CC 60), "Total Concentration on Congregational Concerns" (CC 20), and "Alienating Activity" (CC 10).

On only the first two of these clusters are there any significant differences among the denominations. Hence, we can assume basic agreement among the traditions with respect to their valuation of a minister's deciding what is best for the congregation (CC 60), his resistance to involvements beyond the local church (CC 20), and on being apart from the church he serves (CC 10). No denomination values these characteristics highly. The Roman Catholic lay group, however, views the "Intuitive Domination of Decision Making" in a significantly different way than does their professional group of priests, bishops, and fourth-year theological students. They value it more highly, thereby revealing a consistent way of looking at the role of the priest as unquestioned head of the parish. If change is to come about in this regard, and most agree that it must, then it is good that the clergy group itself consider the role less desirable and by their actions, over the course of time, aid in reducing the view that the parish priest is above being questioned. To some extent, this has begun to happen here and there in our parishes in North America.

The Orthodox and the Jewish and Unitarian families differ with both Roman Catholics and a number of other traditions on "Law Orientation to Ethical Issues" (CC 27). The Orthodox value this more highly than any other group; the Jewish and Unitarian respondents, lower. Within the Roman Catholic tradition, the largest laity-clergy difference occurs on this trait. The laity are more insistent than the clergy to place an "Emphasis on God's demands and condemnation as a basis for solving personal problems." Hence, it seems clear that our laity expect a much harder line than priests may be inclined to provide. In our preaching and confessional practice, the dramatic movement to the note of forgiveness is likely to be causing the very people we serve some discomfort. More likely, though, it seems that the clergy are not clear enough about ethical issues considered significant by the laity; for example, suicide as death outside the kingdom of God, one of the items that comprises this cluster. And there are probably other issues, such as methods of birth control, married clergy, ordination of women, sterilization, and euthanasia. Many priests, I am certain, are questioned on these issues and are pressed for both unequivocal positions and uniform practice.

The "Precedence of Evangelistic Goals" (CC 19) also reveals a number of differences. The separation occurs fairly much like some of the more "fundamental," personal conversion areas that formed part of "Ministry from Personal Commitment of Faith" (Factor 2). This cluster fits here because its emphasis is on what is right and proper for a young priest or minister to do, namely, "stick to religion." We regard this emphasis as much less important than the American-Canadian Baptist family, the Southern Baptist Convention, the Evangelical A and B families, and the Christian Church (not Disciples). Lowest in its valuing such a characteristic is the Jewish-Unitarian family.

DISQUALIFYING PERSONAL AND BEHAVIORAL CHARACTERISTICS

Four negative clusters form Factor 3, "Disqualifying Personal and Behavioral Characteristics": "Self-Protecting Ministry" (CC 54), "Undisciplined Living" (CC 53), "Professional Immaturity" (CC 52), and "Secular Lifestyle" (CC 51).

"Self-Protecting Ministry" suggests the type of person who defends himself through his office—fundamentally insecure, psychologists would say. "Professional Immaturity" indicates just that, namely, that the priest or minister has not quite grown up enough for the office of pastoral ministry. Evaluation of these traits reveals no differences among the denominational families.

Of all denominational families, Roman Catholics are least concerned about the self-indulgent priest. Let us be careful here; this is not to say that such traits are thereby endorsed, but only that, in the overall evaluation of this trait, Roman Catholics score lowest. They are significantly lower, however, than three families: the Southern Baptists, the Free Church, and Evangelical A families. It is at least curious to note that among the laity-clergy differences within the Roman Catholic tradition, the professional group differs more sharply here than in any of the other differences found between the two groups in this study. They are far more concerned than the lay group about "Undisciplined Living" (CC 53). It may be that the laity do not judge their priests in this way or that fellow priests are more sensitive to its reality.

However, Roman Catholics, both laity and clergy, differ significantly from a number of denominational traditions on "Secular Lifestyle" (CC 51). They (along with the Anglican-Episcopal family for nearly every difference), indicate less concern for this trait in their young priests than do the American-Canadian Baptists, the Southern Baptist Convention, the Evangelical A and B families, the Free Church family, the United Methodist Church, and the Christian Church (not Disciples). The interpretation is probably forthright: It is not forbidden or a matter of discipline for a Roman Catholic priest to visit a cocktail lounge, to gamble occasionally, or to smoke heavily. (These are among the key items that comprise this particular cluster.)

REFLECTIONS

Roman Catholics are a complex group, as the Readiness for Ministry survey has detected, and, to the extent that this study was accurate in gaining a balanced sample of the Roman Catholic membership, it is neither mysterious nor alone among the denominational families. It expects a high standard of behavior and wholesome characteristics from the young priests who are engaged in pastoral ministry.

Roman Catholics have a strong concern that their young priests have an openness in their ministerial style and in the same breath demand that they have a sense of church history and process, a feature more highly cherished by Roman Catholics than by others within this study. While some within and outside the denomination would make much of sacramental and liturgical concerns, it is clear that, while important, these are secondary to the fundamental requirements that young Roman Catholic priests relate the faith, preach well, and encourage the building up of the Body of Christ within their congregations. Furthermore, in their personal lives, Roman Catholics expect them to give both genuine witness to the gospel, and, through the integration of their learning, to serve the parish.

While other traditions emphasize counseling roles, shared congregational leadership styles, and forthright efforts to convert others, these are noticeably less important for Roman Catholics.

Roman Catholics do not always move in unison. Some significant differences between the laity and their priests, bishops, ministers provincial, pastors, and fourth-year theological students do occur. The latter group definitely emphasize major parts of the Roman Catholic "tradition," denominational knowledge, theological reflection, interest in new ideas, and active concern for the oppressed. The young priests likewise are expected to acknowledge their limitations and to accept counsel. The laity, however, stress keener interest in a firmer handling of ethical issues by their young priests, increased responsibility for leading the parish, and greater concern for the religious nurturing of children and youth.

While these expectations are real, as are the differences, they nevertheless have a hopeful rather than a fulfilled quality about them. They may be more cherished than realized. High ideals can prod Roman Catholics to achieve them; for example, to be both unique individuals who minister and share common bonds with all who minister, ordained and not ordained, and to begin living their concern for social issues and for peace.

The Roman Catholic Church, then, should be seen as a union of Christians who nearly equally treasure both its history and its future. One might, therefore, predict that there will likely never occur easiness between where we have been and where we are to go. With the vast size of the Roman Catholic Church, its disparate membership, its breadth of opinion and belief, it nevertheless has a wholeness about it that adds the richness of color to its fabric. It moves forward, sometimes uneasily, but forward with concern that its young men be holy ministers, inheritors, and servants, conscious of the past and concerned for the people they serve—who are the Roman Catholic Church's gift to the future.

NOTES

1. Bernard Cooke, *Ministry to Word and Sacraments: History and Theology* (Philadelphia: Fortress Press, 1975), p. 197.

2. National Conference of Catholic Bishops, *The Program of Priestly Formation* (Washington, D.C.: National Conference of Catholic Bishops, 1976), p. 37.

3. Walter M. Abott, ed., *The Documents of Vatican II* (New York: Herder and Herder, 1966), p. 37.

4. Abott, *The Documents of Vatican II*, p. 33.

5. Abott, *The Documents of Vatican II*, p. 226.

6. Hans Küng, *On Being a Christian* (New York: Doubleday, 1976), p. 602.

17

United Church
of Christ

Thomas C. Campbell

This chapter is subdivided into four basic sections: an overview of the general pattern of United Church of Christ response, an examination of similarities between it and other denominational families, a look at unique or distinctive characteristics of the United Church of Christ, and, lastly, a consideration of the extent to which the findings confirm or refute commonly held assumptions about the denomination's identity.

The United Church of Christ, the result of a twenty-year-old merger of two denominations (representing both an early American wing of congregationalism as well as a church that resulted from German migrations to this country during the nineteenth century), is a complex blend of differing attitudes and backgrounds. The data seem to depict it as a "typical American denomination," as Campbell concludes. The responses imply a certain "averaging out" of these heterogeneous backgrounds. The United Church of Christ differs significantly from at least one other denominational family in about 40 percent of the core expectations. Campbell argues, however, that one should focus as much on the commonality expressed as on the unique characteristics. He notes

Thomas C. Campbell, until his untimely death during the final months of the preparation of this book, was Academic Vice-President and Professor of Theology and Culture, United Theological Seminary of the Twin Cities (Minneapolis and St. Paul, Minnesota).

that generally the United Church of Christ differs by desiring less than other denominations any particular dimension of ministry.

What is the identity of this relatively new church in the American scene? It emerges from the study as a "liberal," autonomous church body that affirms a critical examination of Scripture, concern for the whole person without directly confronting sinful nature, freedom to make local applications of program and style, a "human" as opposed to a "priestly" clergy, and a free worship focus. Yet strong social activism is not characteristic of this otherwise liberal group.

The United Church of Christ is in one sense the youngest major denomination in the United States. Officially formed only twenty years ago as a merger of the Congregational Christian Churches and the Evangelical and Reformed Church, it is also the only major denomination in the United States that has in recent history brought together congregations differing in polity and in ethnic and theological traditions. However, on the North American continent these distinctions must take second place to those of the United Church of Canada. While the United Church of Canada and the United Church of Christ are unions of approximately the same number of parishioners, the United Church of Canada has preceded the United Church of Christ by more than thirty years and represents a merger of three different denominational traditions rather than two, as in the case of the United Church of Christ. As we proceed with the analysis of the Readiness for Ministry data in this chapter, we see the relevance of this comparison between these two major mergers of diverse denominational traditions.

In the United Church of Christ merger, the Congregational Christian Churches represented an "American" church tracing its history back to Pilgrim and Puritan ancestors. It had a relatively radical interpretation of the "congregational" form of church polity and was a denomination that drew its constituency mainly from the more privileged social strata of the society and from a theological tradition centered primarily in various forms of the Calvinistic and Zwinglian reformed heritage. The Evangelical and Reformed Church, however, represents a denomination heavily identified with a particular ethnic migration group, the Germans; it had a modified form of presbyterian organization; its constituency represented a much more average social class position; and its theological heritage combined certain strains of Lutheran as well as Calvinistic and Zwinglian traditions.

Given the Evangelical and Reformed polity, all the congregations of that denomination were officially a part of the new United Church of Christ once it was formed, whereas the individual congregations of the Congregational Christian Churches needed to vote individually to become a part of the new denomination. This difference in polity meant that all Evangelical and Reformed congregations immediately tended to change the sign "out front" to United Church of Christ, while Congregational churches often chose to keep the "old name" and to call themselves First Congregational Church (United Church of Christ). Early in the merger, there was also a tendency to be very self-conscious about how many denominational officials were Evangelical and Reformed in background and how many were Congregational Christian. While some persons have been of the opinion that these subtle (and sometimes less than subtle) differences have persisted in many ways, others are of the opinion that in twenty years the denomination has matured and begun to develop its own self-conscious, unique style and identity.

The Readiness for Ministry Project has been carried out at a very interesting time in the life of the United Church of Christ. It provides an opportunity to evaluate the broad expectations of the denomination's laity and clergy with respect to the qualities and competencies desired in beginning ministers. The project is limited to general denominational expectations, inasmuch as the statistics represented in this study average the responses of persons with differing points of view. The data reflect measures of tendency rather than specific portrayals of the particular expectations of any one congregation, much less of any one member or clergyperson of that denomination. In twenty years, it seems likely that the former Evangelical and Reformed congregations and former Congregational Christian memberships have actually blended several denominational backgrounds.

It is on the uniqueness of that blend that the data throw some light. Thus the general findings from this project ought to give us clues concerning the views of the types of people who are attracted to congregations bearing the label United Church of Christ.

In one sense, it is unfortunate that the data collected do not permit us to compare, for example, respondents from former Evangelical and Reformed congregations with those from former Congregational Christian groups. Such a comparison could give some clues on the extent to which the denomination is truly merged, or how much it remains an alliance between persons of somewhat differing perspectives. However, sociologists have long demonstrated that in the American scene the members of a single congregation may consist of people from many denominational backgrounds; thus any denominational perspective may well be a blending of several divergent points of view.

A word is appropriate at this point concerning the subtle complexity of the blending of people from different denominational backgrounds into single congregations or particular denominational labels. Certain denominations, such as the Lutheran Churches, for example, continue to have a strong ethnic commonality. Thus when a Lutheran moves from one place to another, that person tends to join another Lutheran church even if it represents a different specific Lutheran denomination (The American Lutheran Church rather than the Lutheran Church in America, for example). Other denominations have less clear ethnic identities, and people affiliated with such denominations may feel freer to change denominational identification when experiencing geographical mobility. While I do not have the statistics to support my assumption, I would hazard the opinion that former Evangelical and Reformed members, on moving into a new community, are more likely than former Congregational Christian members to join a United Church of Christ congregation (especially if that congregation was formerly an Evangelical and Reformed church). Ethnic loyalty may continue to operate for one strand within the United Church of Christ while not for the other strand. If we add other factors to this argument concerning loyalty to ethnic tradition—factors such as loyalty to confessional stance, liturgical patterns, or polity issues—we receive a complex picture of both homogenization and denominational particularization. Indeed, we should not be surprised to find (if a study were carried out that traced denominational particularities over a time period) homogenization of opinion across denominational families, as well as distinctive denominational patterns between denominational families.

This chapter begins by giving a general overview of the United Church of Christ findings; it then outlines ways in which the United Church of Christ is a typical American denomination; that is, its similarities with other denominational families represented in the project. The third section focuses on the unique characteristics of the United Church of Christ responses, and the chapter closes with a consideration of the extent to which the findings support and/or deny commonly held views about the identity of the United Church of Christ.

THE GENERAL PATTERN

In the fourth chapter of this book, findings point to four dominant models of ministry among which the denominational families could be placed. The evangelistic model finds the United Church of Christ among the denominations that stress this to the lowest degree. Likewise, in the model that emphasizes sacramental and liturgical aspects, the United Church of Christ is again among the denominations stressing this least. In partial contrast, the third pattern, which highlights social concern and action, places the United Church of Christ above the mean in emphasis. If one stands back from the data for a broader view, it seems that the United Church of Christ puts relatively more emphasis on the ministry of the church to the world and less on denominational loyalty, sacraments, liturgy, and the more conservative expressions of the Christian life. This may not seem very surprising to anyone who has been identified with the

United Church of Christ for any period of time. The denomination has a tendency, especially among its most active clergy and laity at the state and national levels, to view itself as socially concerned, relevant, and change oriented. Especially during the late 1960s and early 1970s, many programs and "voted emphases" have stressed concern for the oppressed, outcast, and needy. The denomination was among the first to develop a contemporary Statement of Faith as a liturgical confession of faith.[1] The denomination has women clergy and leaders, having abolished many years ago the traditional pattern of separate organizations for laywomen and laymen. Thus, while the findings tend to support the dominant official self-image and understanding of the denomination, it is interesting to note the extent to which this image is supported, the specific content of the clusters and items that support it, and the denominations that most closely resemble the United Church of Christ.

To put into perspective the general pattern just outlined, it is necessary to discuss the patterning of core clusters where the United Church of Christ differs in a statistically significant way from other denominational families. First of all, let us examine the number of clusters where there is a significant difference between the United Church of Christ responses and responses from other denominations. In order to do this, we will place each of the second-order factors in rank order in terms of the grand mean for each (see Chapter 4 for a discussion of denominational contrasts). The number of clusters included in each factor will be noted, plus the number of clusters in which there is a statistically significant difference noted between United Church of Christ responses and those of other denominational families. The factors order themselves as follows (with United Church of Christ differences from other denominations noted).

1. *"Open, Affirming Style" (grand mean 2.18)* Differs from only one other denomination in one of the seven clusters
2. *"Caring for Persons under Stress" (grand mean 1.98)* Differs from no other denomination in any of the five clusters
3. *"Congregational Leadership" (grand mean 1.97)* Differs from only one other denomination in one of the five clusters
4. *"Theologian in Life and Thought" (grand mean 1.88)* Differs from one other denomination in two of the six clusters
5. *"Ministry from Personal Commitment of Faith" (grand mean 1.82)* Differs from other denominations in all eleven clusters
6. *"Development of Fellowship and Worship" (grand mean 1.79)* Differs from four other denominations in one of the six clusters
7. *"Denominational Awareness and Collegiality" (grand mean 1.65)* Differs from other denominations in both of the two clusters included in this factor (in cluster "Denominational Collegiality," differs from eight denominations)

8. *"Ministry to Community and World" (grand mean 1.32)*   Differs from other denominations in five of the eight clusters
9. *"Priestly-Sacramental Ministry" (grand mean 0.24)*   Differs from other denominations in all three clusters
10. *"Privatistic, Legalistic Style" (grand mean −1.25)*   Differs from other denominations in only two of the five clusters
11. *"Disqualifying Personal and Behavioral Characteristics" (grand mean −1.80)*   Differs from other denominations in only one of the six clusters

Several matters of note emerge from this listing of the clusters and how the United Church of Christ differs from other denominations. The first is that the differences are confined primarily to the clusters that fall in the mid-range of emphasis. That is, the differences emerge among the clusters where there is, overall, neither strong general approval nor strong disapproval. It is important to situate this chapter in such a context, since the chapter tends to concentrate on an analysis of differences between the United Church of Christ and other denominations. In such a context, there is a grave danger that commonalities with other denominations will be forgotten or ignored. Thus, while the data show that United Church of Christ clergy and laity are more likely than most denominational families to expect a minister to give more stress to community concerns and to give less stress to issues of personal faith commitment, these expectations are not the only expectations; in fact, they are not even the most important expectations. The United Church of Christ respondents to the study have many expectations that parallel those of other denominations. These other shared expectations are of a higher order of priority for the clergy and lay respondents than are the matters of community concern and faith commitment.

A second important finding emerges from this analysis: the clergy and laity of the United Church of Christ differ significantly from at least one other denomination in twenty-six of the sixty-four clusters. Thus, in about 40 percent of the clusters considered in this study the denomination has some element of distinctive identity. In other words, the expectations of ministry within this denomination are very similar to other denominations about half of the time, and the other half of the time they have some degree of noteworthiness or uniqueness. Again, however, it should be stressed that the special characteristics of United Church of Christ expectations of beginning ministers are largely confined to those matters and issues where there is neither strong positive nor strong negative emphasis.

In Table 17-1, the clusters are grouped within the second-order factors of the study, and for each cluster the number of denominations that differ statistically from the United Church of Christ responses is noted.

TABLE 17-1
Comparison of United Church of Christ Responses with Other Denominational Families

Factor Grand Mean	Factor No.	No. of Denominational Families Differing with United Church of Christ	Rank Order Cluster	Core Cluster Number	Factor and Core Cluster
2.18	4				Open, Affirming Style
		0	8	44	Positive Approach
		0	6	43	Fidelity to Tasks and Persons
		0	16.5	45	Flexibility of Spirit
		0	2	42	Personal Responsibility
		0	28.5	47	Acceptance of Clergy Role
		0	4	36	Acknowledgment of Limitations
		1	20.5	46	Valuing Diversity
1.98	9				Caring for Persons under Stress
		0	7	21	Perceptive Counseling
		0	42	26	Cominstry to the Alienated
		0	12(3)	23	Caring Availability
		0	10	22	Enabling Counseling
		0	36	25	Involvement in Caring
1.97	8				Congregational Leadership
		1	18	57	Sharing Congregational Leadership
		0	5	55	Building Congregational Community
		0	34.5	58	Effective Administration
		0	16.5	56	Conflict Utilization
		0	39	59	Responsible Staff Management

TABLE 17-1 — *CONTINUED*

1.88   10   Theologian in Life and Thought

1	43	38	Acknowledgment of Own Vulnerability
0	25.5	30	Use of Broad Knowledge
0	27	29	Theological Reflection
0	1	34	Service in Humility
0	14	28	Clarity of Thought and Communication
1	45	39	Acceptance of Counsel

1.82   2   Ministry from Personal Commitment of Faith

6	12(3)	37	Commitment Reflecting Religious Piety
11	20.5	31	Affirmation of Conservative Biblical Faith
4	9	2	Theocentric-Biblical Ministry
0	28.5	61	Evangelistic Witness
0	37	62	Accepting Mutual Intercession
8	51	40	"Born-Again" Christianity
1	22	12	Encouragement of World Mission
9	49	17	Assertive Individual Evangelism
5	3	35	Christian Example
4	23.5	6	Encouragement of Spiritual Sensitivity
2	15	24	Theologically Oriented Counseling

1.79   5   Development of Fellowship and Worship

0	30	5	Competent Preaching and Worship Leading
0	19	3	Relating Well to Children and Youth
0	38	7	Liturgical Sensitivity
0	12(3)	1	Relating Faith to Modern World
4	48	9	Sacramental-Liturgical Ministry
0	23.5	4	Encouragement of Mutuality in Congregation

1.65   11   Denominational Awareness and Collegiality

1	41	32	Denominational Knowledge
8	33	49	Denominational Collegiality

TABLE 17-1 — *CONTINUED*

1.32	1	Ministry to Community and World	

2	52	18	Aggressive Political Leadership
0	47	16	Active Concern for the Oppressed
1	44	14	Promotion of Understanding of Issues
0	46	15	Support of Community Causes
1	31.5	13	Initiative in Community Service
0	34.5	50	Support of Unpopular Causes
1	40	8	Ecumenical and Educational Openness
1	50	33	Interest in New Ideas
0	25.5	11	Pastoral Service to All

0.24	7	Priestly-Sacramental Ministry	

4	63	41	Priestly Commitment
4	48	9	Sacramental-Liturgical Ministry
2	31.5	48	Mutual Family Commitment

−1.25	6	Privatistic, Legalistic Style	

0	56	20	Total Concentration on Congregational Concerns
3	54	27	Law Orientation to Ethical Issues
0	55	60	Intuitive Domination of Decision Making
6	53	19	Precedence of Evangelistic Goals
0	57	10	Alienating Activity

−1.80	3	Disqualifying Personal and Behavioral Characteristics	

0	62	54	Self-Protecting Ministry
0	64	53	Undisciplined Living
0	60	64	Irresponsibility to the Congregation
0	61	52	Professional Immaturity
0	59	63	Pursuit of Personal Advantage
6	58	51	Secular Lifestyle

SIMILARITIES: THE UNITED CHURCH OF CHRIST AS A "TYPICAL" AMERICAN DENOMINATION

As was stated earlier, it is important to look first at the ways in which the United Church of Christ responses are similar to those from other denominational families, for in the majority of the clusters (about 60 percent) the United Church of Christ expectations for persons entering ministry are not statistically different from the expectations of any other denomination.

This matter of similarity is even more dramatic when one considers that in only fourteen of the sixty-four clusters (about 20 percent) do the United Church of Christ responses differ from more than two other denominations. While I have not done a similar analysis for all of the denominational families, it is my hunch that few of the denominational families would differ so seldom from the other families (see Chapter 4 for denominational contrasts). The findings from this study would tend to argue that the United Church of Christ expectations of readiness for ministry make it a truly "American" denomination.

The following summary of the way in which these "typical" findings order themselves portrays the United Church of Christ general expectations:

1. The highest expectation concerns the positive personal characteristics of the minister him- or herself. Contrary to many professions, the expectation of those served is first for the kind of person the minister is, and only then does the concern move to the professional skills and content of the ministry itself.
2. The clergy and laity expect the clergyperson to have primary concern for personal and internal forms of ministry. It appears that only after the individual persons in need within the congregation have been ministered unto is it even possible for the minister to give attention to the internal group life of the congregation.
3. The sharing of congregational leadership with the laity is third in order of priority.
4. The content and interpretation of the faith proclaimed emerges as fourth in order of importance. Those of us in seminaries who spend most of our time stressing to ministerial candidates the importance of theological knowledge and interpretation may well be disheartened that this area of competence did not rank higher.
5. Evangelistic functions of ministry emerge as relatively low in United Church of Christ priority.
6. Forms of worship and certain professional skills emerge next in order of priority.
7. United Church of Christ responses give relatively low priority to denominational loyalty or collegiality.

8. Social concerns and community ministry follow in priority, with some relative increase in concern among United Church of Christ respondents.
9. Priestly ministry and a legalistic orientation to ministry are of the lowest priority.

Persons who have been engaged in ministry during the 1960s and early 1970s will not be unduly surprised by this listing of similarities between the United Church of Christ responses and those of other denominational families. However, it is important to remember that these statistics were gathered in the early 1970s. At that time, many, perhaps especially within the United Church of Christ, expected that the church was becoming an "institution for others." Apparently, institutions that are voluntary organizations do not move very rapidly into social forms of ministry without certainty that personal needs of the members are first attended to. As one who has deep concern for the social aspects of ministry, I can add that this is a very hard lesson to learn, but these statistics appear to indicate that it is an essential lesson.

Having outlined the ways in which the United Church of Christ is similar to other denominational families, it is now important to examine just which denominational families the United Church of Christ most resembles and which least. Table 17-2 organizes the data from Table 17-1 in a different fashion. In this table, we have included only the clusters where there is any statistically significant difference between United Church of Christ responses and those of other denominational families.

The reader will notice (Table 17-2) that in the great majority of cases the other denominational families desire more emphasis on almost all of the clusters. If one ignores the differences related to the Jewish and Unitarian family, there are only nine cases where another denominational family wants less emphasis on a cluster than does the United Church of Christ. This is a very interesting finding, for it indicates that the United Church of Christ responses portray a denomination where, if there is a difference with another denomination, it is most likely a difference where United Church of Christ members want less emphasis on whatever ministerial characteristics are being considered! Is this denomination, which I have called a "typical American denomination," simply a more secularized version of American Christianity? Some would clearly answer yes. Because of theological reasons related to church-culture issues, I would not be quite so quick to give an affirmative answer to the question.

Table 17-3 represents another interesting way to organize findings related to denominational similarities and differences, that of listing the denominations in order of their similarity to the United Church of Christ findings.

Several interesting issues emerge from an examination of Table 17-3.

TABLE 17-2

Statistically Significant Differences Between United Church of Christ Responses and Those of Other Denominational Families

No. of Differences	Core Cluster No.	Anglican-Episcopal	Am.-Can. Baptist	Southern Baptist	Christian (Disciples)	Orthodox	Evan. B	Free Churches	Jewish-Unitarian	Lutheran	United Methodist	Presb.-Reformed	R. Cath. (Ord.)	R. Cath. (Dioc.)	U.C. Canada	Evan. A	Christian
No. of Differences:		2	7	9	0	7	13	5	11	3	2	5	4	6	0	15	5
4	2			+			+		−							+	
4	6			+			+		−							+	
1	8															−	
4	9					+			−				+	+			
1	12								−								
1	13															−	
1	14															−	
9	17		+	+			+	+	−		+	+				+	+
2	18			−												−	
6	19		+	+			+	+								+	+
2	24						+		−								
3	27					+	+									+	
11	31		+	+			+	+	+	−	+	+		+		+	+
1	32																+
1	33															+	
5	35		+	+			+		−							+	
6	37		+	+			+		−			+				+	
1	38						+										
1	39								−								
8	40		+	+			+	+	−	+		+				+	
4	41	+				+							+	+			
1	46					−											
2	48												−	−			
8	49	+				+	+			+	+	+	+	+			
6	51		+	+			+	+								+	+
1	57															−	

Note: (+) = denominational family desires more emphasis than United Church of Christ; (−) = denominational family desires less emphasis.

TABLE 17-3
Number of Significant Differences Between United Church of Christ and Others by Denominational Family

Denominational Family	No. of Differences in Responses to the 64 Core Clusters
Christian Church (Disciples of Christ)	0
United Church of Canada	0
Anglican-Episcopal Churches	2
United Methodist Church	2
Lutheran Church	3
Roman Catholic Church (Order)	4
Presbyterian-Reformed Family	4
Free Church Family	5
Christian Church (not Disciples)	5
Roman Catholic Church (Diocesan)	6
American-Canadian Baptist Family	7
Orthodox Churches	7
Southern Baptists	9
Jewish and Unitarian Family	11
Evangelical B	13
Evangelical A	15

First, two denominational families—the United Church of Canada and the Christian Church (Disciples of Christ)—do not differ significantly from the United Church of Christ on any of the core clusters. Earlier in this chapter, it was pointed out that the United Church of Canada resembled the United Church of Christ in terms of being a merger of several denominational groups that differed in polity, ethnic background, and theology. It appears that such mergers are the ones most likely to produce "North American" characteristics. This hypothesis is further strengthened when one considers that the Christian Church (Disciples) also forms a denominational family especially indigenous to America. It was founded by Americans, in America, for Americans. It is interesting at this point to note that the United Church of Christ and the Christian Church (Disciples) are presently engaged in formal conversations about the possible merger of the two groups. It appears that these two groups do not differ significantly in their expectations of clergy, whatever other differences they might have. Furthermore, the Readiness for Ministry findings would seem to support a thesis that in the not-too-distant future someone will propose that there be a new denominational merger known as the United Church of North America consisting of the United Church of Canada, the United Church of Christ, and the Christian Church (Disciples).

There are also two families—the United Methodist Church and the Anglican-Episcopal Churches—that differ from the United Church of Christ in only two clusters. This would seem to make these two families good candidates for proposed mergers as well. However, in this case we must examine the cluster content where differences emerge. In the case of the United Methodists, the differences are centered in the following two clusters: "Assertive Individual Evangelism" (CC 17) and "Denominational Collegiality" (CC 49). These are two of the four clusters where the United Church of Christ differs from eight or more of the denominations. These characteristics appear to be issues that make the United Church of Christ distinct by their absence. Therefore a merger with a group that places more emphasis on those two clusters would seem to hold little likelihood of success. The very same point remains true for the comparison with Anglican-Episcopal responses. The two clusters where differences emerge are "Denominational Collegiality" (CC 49) and "Priestly Commitment" (CC 41). Again, in both clusters the United Church of Christ would seem to be distinct in not affirming those clusters; thus, any conversations with denominational families affirming those clusters would appear likely to experience early failure.

One could go on to discuss other denominational families that also differ from the United Church of Christ responses in only a few clusters (Lutherans, three clusters; Presbyterian-Reformed, four clusters; and Roman Catholic (Order), four clusters). But the findings reveal that, as in the case of the United Methodist Church and the Anglican-Episcopal Churches, the differences, while not numerous, are in fact fairly fundamental differences. More of these matters will be discussed in the following section.

We turn now to a consideration of those differences where, on the basis of the Readiness for Ministry data, the unique identity of the United Church of Christ appears to emerge.

DIFFERENCES: DOES THE UNITED CHURCH OF CHRIST HAVE AN IDENTITY?

Considering the large number of similarities to other denominations already pointed out in the previous section, it is not surprising that many of the clergy and leaders of the United Church of Christ are currently asking just what identity the United Church of Christ has. While the Readiness for Ministry data can hardly be expected to give conclusive answers to such a search for identity, the data can nevertheless be examined for whatever clues they might yield.

In Table 17-4, various clusters are organized in terms of the number of denominational families where statistically significant differences emerge. The table includes only clusters where more than two denominational families differ statistically from the United Church of Christ.

An examination of the titles of the clusters included in Table 17-4 seems to reveal the United Church of Christ as a strange church indeed! Its clergy and laity are less likely to affirm a biblical faith, do not have a strong belief in evangelism, are not collegial, affirm a more secular lifestyle for their clergy, do not seem to emphasize that their clergy have a pious religious commitment, are less likely to want a Christian example from their clergy, are less interested in the sacraments and liturgy, are less likely to encourage spiritual renewal, and are less likely to want "priests" as ministers. Not one cluster from second-order Factor 1 ("Ministry to Community and World") appears in this list.

What possible sense of identity could be built from such a seemingly negative list? One must look at the items that make up the clusters listed. If one engages in that task from my theological perspective, a somewhat different picture emerges. "Affirmation of a Conservative Biblical Faith" (CC 31) is a set of items most of which have a tendency to affirm the more conservative end of the continuum in the fundamentalist-modernist debate. From my perspective, the content of the items tends toward the

TABLE 17-4
Denominational Families Differing with the United Church of Christ on Core Clusters

Core Cluster No.		No. of Denominational Families Differing
31	Affirmation of Conservative Biblical Faith	11
17	Assertive Individual Evangelism	9
49	Denominational Collegiality	8
40	"Born-Again" Christianity	8
19	Precedence of Evangelistic Goals	6
51	Secular Lifestyle	6
37	Commitment Reflecting Religious Piety	6
35	Christian Example	5
9	Sacramental-Liturgical Ministry	4
2	Theocentric-Biblical Ministry	4
6	Encouragement of Spiritual Sensitivity	4
41	Priestly Commitment	4

danger of biblicism rather than toward their being an exposition of the central tenets of the biblical faith. "Assertive Individual Evangelism" (CC 17) is a set of items that I interpret as rather narrowly focused on concern for personal decisions and not for people's wholeness. "Good News" for persons in need may not be to ask them about the condition of their souls but rather to seek to listen to their hurts and needs. "Denominational Collegiality" (CC 49) has at least two items within it which, from my perspective, point to subservience of local clergy to denominational authority figures. Such a style would hardly be welcome to a church whose clergy stand in the tradition of the Pilgrims!

Similar points could be made by an examination of the remaining clusters and the items they contain. These first few clusters, however, are sufficient to reveal the direction in which I would see United Church of Christ identity emerging from the Readiness for Ministry data.

In summary then, the United Church of Christ is a denomination that affirms critical examination of the Scriptures, concern for the whole person without confrontation with his or her sinful nature, local clergy and congregations seeking local application of program and style, a "human" clergy as opposed to a "priestly" clergy, a free worship form, and contemporary forms of communication in expressing the content of the Christian faith and witness.

To many, the list that has just been given is a definition of a "liberal" denomination, and so it is. The Readiness data (when one examines the United Church of Christ "differences") do reveal the United Church of Christ as a liberal denomination, with one exception. Normally one includes social activism among the defining characteristics of a liberal church, but this characteristic is notable by its relative absence in the Readiness data generated from the United Church of Christ.

CONSIDERING UNITED CHURCH OF CHRIST MYTHS AND REALITIES

As an ordained minister within the United Church of Christ, I found the examination of the Readiness data to be a fascinating exercise in confirming and denying "myths" by which the members of the United Church of Christ explain their denomination. These myths exist in all denominations, and they are one other way to explain denominational identity. The list of myths that will be considered in this section is not intended to be exhaustive, and it is necessarily somewhat subjective. It could hardly be otherwise—no one would be able to outline fully the myths of such a liberal, autonomous denomination. However, the following list includes many common understandings that would probably be shared by a majority of United Church of Christ clergy and laity.

1. *The United Church of Christ uniquely emphasizes lay leadership.* The findings from the Readiness Project bring this myth into serious question. Nothing in second-order Factors 8 ("Congregational Leadership") or 5 ("Development of Fellowship and Worship") point to a distinctive emphasis on lay leadership on the part of the United Church of Christ over other denominations. It appears that all denominations in America have about as much concern for shared leadership as does the United Church of Christ.

2. *The United Church of Christ affirms an educated ministry.* This myth is both affirmed and questioned. Second-order Factor 10 ("Theologian in Life and Thought") is not peculiarly emphasized by the United Church of Christ responses, and yet second-order Factor 2 ("Ministry from Personal Commitment of Faith") shows the United Church of Christ respondents to want a form of Christian communication that would seem to demand an educated clergy.

3. *The United Church of Christ is a "uniting" denomination.* This myth is also affirmed and denied. It is affirmed in the sense that the United Church of Christ is very much like at least two other denominations in its expectations of clergy, and it also reveals itself as a denomination that has a majority of its responses following patterns similar to other churches. Yet there remains a series of issues (largely related to the fundamentalist-modernist debate) revealing that it would have great difficulty uniting with a good many of the other denominations. It is also characterized by a desire for "low doctrines" of clergy and worship. This too would keep it apart from several denominations.

4. *The United Church of Christ is a "free church" in worship and thought.* This myth would largely be affirmed. (It is a paradox how a free church ever establishes identity, since its identity is in its diversity!)

5. *The United Church of Christ is a "liberal" church.* Again, this is a largely affirmed myth.

6. *The United Church of Christ is a socially active church.* This myth is more questioned than it is affirmed. While the United Church of Christ respondents do indeed distinguish themselves modestly in terms of affirming second-order Factor 1 ("Ministry to Community and World"), they are by no means the most outstanding denominational family in this regard. That distinction clearly belongs to the Jewish and Unitarian family.

In summary, the Readiness for Ministry Project both confirms and denies the myths about themselves that most United Church of Christ clergy believe. The study reveals expectations that clergy and laity have for new persons entering the ministry in this denomination. Such a potential clergyperson would be well advised to examine all of the United Church of Christ findings carefully. They would show him or her certain areas where expectations are nearly universal and where denial of them on his or her part would probably spell disaster in terms of long-term leadership. Yet examination of the data will also help the potential (and practicing) clergyperson know where to focus emphasis for change, where to expect disagreement within congregations, and where to seek new life. As one clergyperson in that denomination, I come from the examination of the data with a new commitment to a personal agenda for future ministry, and look forward to finding ever new and constructive contemporary ways to tell an old, old story of what God in Christ has done for humans to enable new life!

NOTE

1. The Statement of Faith was adopted by the General Synod of the United Church of Christ in July 1954. It is contained in *The Hymnal—The United Church of Christ* (p. 11) and is used as a confession of faith along with the other historic confessions of this church.

18

United Church
of Canada

William O. Fennell

William Fennell prefaces his presentation of those ministerial expectations that emerge from the data as distinctive of the United Church of Canada with his own normative analysis, based on theological statements of his church body that he considers crucial. The position of this analysis at the front of the chapter is an indication of Fennell's perception of how the data are to be interpreted and used. Their major usefulness is "to raise questions about ministry in the church, and to advise and warn the (ministerial) candidate about the church's expectations of its ministers, so that he or she might be prepared to be supported or challenged in his or her own understanding of what ministry requires." He employs the data to raise critical questions regarding the nature of ministry and of preparation for it.

The picture that emerges is that of a "liberal" denomination, as opposed to "evangelical" and/or "reformed." The denomination holds consistently positive views concerning areas of social concern or social action and consistently responds less positively to traits dealing with personal piety and evangelical concern.

Fennell's reaction to such a portrait of his church body is partially one of

William O. Fennell is Professor of Systematic Theology and Principal of Emmanuel College, Toronto, Ontario. He was ordained to the ministry of the United Church of Canada in 1942 and is a member of its General Council.

505

skepticism—in fact, a second, larger sampling of United Church of Canada respondents was taken (with very similar results to the first) in order to allay any fears that the initial sample was too small to be valid. If Fennell grants the validity of this general portrait, he admits deep concern over the lower-than-average estimate accorded by respondents to what he considers central affirmations of the Christian faith.

In this chapter I shall portray the distinctive characteristics of the United Church of Canada as they emerge from an analysis of the questionnaire results. My primary concern is with the differences between the United Church of Canada and other denominations, as well as with the differences between the professional leadership and the laity of this church family. Even a quick analysis of the data shows the large amount of overall agreement that exists among the church families with regard to both the mission of the church and the task of ministry, but that is not my focus here.

It would have been interesting to compare the United Church of Canada's responses with those of denominations with which it traditionally has had very close ties—the United Methodist, the Presbyterian, the United Church of Christ. It would also have been of interest, in view of recent church-union discussions, to seek out the similarities and the differences between the United Church of Canada, the Anglican-Episcopal Churches, and the Christian Church (Disciples of Christ). Often the United Church of Canada responses appear to be in very close correlation with the responses of these other denominational families; sometimes they are in surprising deviation. Despite the interest there would be in such comparisons, our task is to attempt, with rather stark strokes and in rough outline, a sketch of the United Church as it emerges from an interpretation of the Readiness for Ministry data. Since the interpretation includes both a descriptive account of the expectations held by clergy and laity of the United Church of Canada and critical comment about them, it might prove helpful to state first the normative understanding presupposed in making the critique.

A basic presupposition that lies behind the following analysis is that the church is the body of the living Christ and that it is served through a special ministry chosen by Him through an interior call. To quote the confessional standard of the United Church: "We believe that Jesus Christ, as the Supreme Head of the Church, has appointed therein a ministry of the word and sacraments, and calls men and women to this ministry; that the Church under the guidance of the Holy Spirit, recognizes and chooses those whom He calls, and should thereupon duly ordain them to the work of the ministry" (Basis of Union: Article XVII).

From this perspective, the United Church of Canada is not seen as a society whose primary reason for being is to promote ethical culture and practical good works in the world. Nor does it exist for the cultivation of religious experience or the enrichment of personality as primary goals of its mission and life. The Church is essentially a community of faith and love, constituted and preserved by the Word and Spirit of the living God. As community of faith, it lives in the power and freedom of the good news of God's forgiving love in Jesus Christ. As community of life, it seeks through the enablement of God's presence in Word and Spirit to dwell in love and to perform the works of love both within the church as a family of God and within the world whose God-given mission it is to serve.

The ordained ministry of the Church is a unique service whereby God's truth is announced so as to call forth faith (Romans 10:14). Such announcement is made in both forms of proclamation traditionally known as the Word and the sacraments. The minister is primarily and preeminently the minister of the Word and the sacraments. He or she is also, in a third traditional way of speaking, a minister of pastoral care.

In all three forms of this ministry, ministers are called to be knowledgeable exponents of God's truth and exemplary servants of God's love. If true to their calling, they live and serve from sources and resources not their own. Their vocation is not self-originating or self-imposed. Nor is it simply originated or imposed by the church into whose service they are called. The Church is indeed Christ's servant, through which they are called, and it does indeed test their calling to determine if, in its judgment, that calling originates in Jesus Christ. Moreover, the Church also tests the gifts needed for a proper exercise of ministerial calling. In advance of such testing, the Church provides for the cultivation of these gifts through education before authorizing, in the name of Christ and through ordination, their exercise. The Church's authorization to perform ministry is not done in its name only, but in the name of Him who is the source of its own being and life. And what the Church seeks from the minister, thus understood, is not simply something of which he or she is the origin—wise thoughts and counsel, ethical guidance and inspiration, friendly companionship, and an example in life of noble things. The "simply" in that sentence is thoughtfully used. For good fortune, it is if the minister be a whole person, realizing in himself or herself (and as an example to others) the filled-out human life God wills for all His children. Moreover, the human offenses of poor judgment, ethical aberrance, want of friendliness and a cultured style of life could seriously impede, and even prevent, effective service of the Gospel. An awareness of this fact has led to many of the questions included in the questionnaire that touch on preparedness for ministry. But it still remains true that it is the Gospel that the minister is primarily, in manifold and diverse ways, called on to serve. Or perhaps better put, he or she is called to be a human servant through whom Jesus Christ serves in the fulfillment of His promise to draw all men unto Himself and to create in the proclamation of His name a Church that nothing can destroy. Within the constitution, expansion, edification, and mission-oriented expression of *that* Church's life, the ordained minister has special serving functions to perform.

From the perspective outlined in the foregoing, the basic tests of readiness for ministry are:

1. A profound conviction in the would-be minister that Christian obedience for him or her must take the form of lifelong commitment to the ordained ministry of Jesus Christ

2. An informed faith that will enable her or him to lead the community to an ever deeper understanding of the faith it lives by and which it professes

3. An ability to relate the Church's faith to other claims to knowledge and truth encountered in the sciences, arts, and religions of mankind

4. An informed, sensitized conscience that will enable him or her to help the community to discover love's demand, both in its life and work as community within, and in its outward-turning service in the world

5. An eager acknowledgment of the fact that together with him or her are equally dedicated, if diversely called, lay ministers of the church, and also persons of goodwill in the world, with whom it is essential for him or her to work and from whom to learn

6. A profound conviction that above and beyond all carefully planned and executed preparation for ministry, and above and beyond all cooperation and support given to and derived from those just mentioned, there are resources for ministry, hidden but very real, in the One who has called into ministry and who has promised to give His Spirit as strengthener and guide to the end

The United Church of Canada that appears in the Readiness for Ministry data seems to be markedly "liberal" in character as distinguished from "evangelical" and/or "reformed." The answers of its representatives, lay and clergy alike, are consistently high in the areas of social concern and low in relation to questions dealing with personal piety and evangelical concern. Later we shall raise some questions about the difficulty of knowing exactly how to interpret some of these findings. But of these findings themselves, there would seem to be clear statistical evidence.

For example, in assessing the desirability of a young minister's being committed to work actively for justice in the local community (Item 109), 72 percent of United Church of Canada respondents consider it essential or a *major* asset, as compared with 58 percent of all other respondents. Similarly, 67 percent of the United Church respondents judge it of some degree of importance that ministers speak from the pulpit about political issues (Item 117), as compared with 53 percent of all others. When "mission-mindedness" of a congregation is interpreted in terms of "response to world need," the professional respondents of the United Church score relatively high (CC 12). These examples demonstrate a higher-than-average expectation that beginning ministers manifest social concern.

Yet the data reflect a remarkable tendency to downgrade the importance of assertive, individual evangelism. For instance, 90 percent of United Church of Canada respondents (versus 68 percent of the remaining group) believe it undesirable or detrimental to an effective ministry that a beginning minister approach strangers "to ask about the condition of their souls" (Item 135). Only 16 percent of United Church of Canada respondents, as opposed to 33 percent of the remaining group, consider it highly important that a beginning clergyperson "visit unchurched people to share the faith" (Item 116). United Church respondents are significantly more negative (73 percent versus 57 percent) than the remaining group about a view of ministry wherein a belief is evidenced that "the one and only way to build an ideal world society is to convert everyone to Christianity" (Item 123). And, in the last item of Core Cluster 17, "Assertive Individual Evangelism," United Church respondents attach significantly less importance than does the remaining sample to a young minister's seeking "to bring everyone to know God's love in Jesus Christ" (Item 150).

In a similar vein, United Church of Canada respondents rank significantly lower than several denominational families in the characteristic entitled "Affirmation of a Conservative Biblical Faith" (CC 31). In the most highly emphasized item of this cluster, United Church respondents are significantly less likely than the remainder of the total sample (32 percent versus 47 percent) to rate it as highly important that a beginning minister interpret "the authority of Scripture as being in the Gospel message" (Item 308). A surprising 29 percent actually rate it as undesirable that a minister think along such lines. And in a cluster that describes religious experience that manifests itself in verbal expression regarding the activity of God in daily life (" 'Born-Again' Christianity," CC 40), United Church of Canada respondents are significantly less likely, on four of the five items that comprise the cluster, to rate these items as important or valuable to an effective ministry. Only 15 percent of the denomination's respondents, as compared with 32 percent of the remaining group, consider it highly important that a young minister talk, in the course of "social conversation about what the Lord has recently done in her or his own life" (Item 377). In fact, nearly half (43 percent) of the United Church of Canada respondents consider such talk negative for a minister.

We wish to ask later what exactly is being denied (or, at least, not forcefully affirmed) in such reserved responses to fundamental issues of Christian faith and life. Why do some United Church members resist affirming what "evangelical" Christians regard as essential to Christian life; namely, to manifest the quality of such a life in Christ by giving verbal expression to God's presence and action in that life? Do the United

Church of Canada evaluations signal a Christian church that is becoming eccentric with respect to its evangelical base? Have a significant number of persons within that denomination ceased to be Christocentric in their beliefs? In their sensitivity to the demands of Christian love to seek a humane and just social order, have they become insensitive to the "serious call to a devout and holy life"? Or is another interpretation possible? Could it be that what we have here is reaction, perhaps overreaction, to perverted or distorted forms of pietism and/or "orthodoxies" of every sort? Or is it that United Church of Canada respondents are reacting negatively to the actual phrasing of the questionnaire items?

Whatever may be the answer to these questions, it does seem that the United Church of Canada's responses point in the direction of a church committed to prophetic witness both in word and deed aimed at social reform, not a church primarily concerned to increase and upbuild itself as a community of faith founded on a gospel of personal salvation and committed to live by its offerings and demands. Judging by this evidence, it does not seem that the present-day United Church of Canada has managed to preserve in its thought and life a balance or creative dialectic between "evangelical" and "social" concerns such as it signified in the past by naming one of its major departments the "Department of Evangelism and Social Service."

It may be for this reason, among others, that there has recently come into being in the United Church of Canada a vigorous group of evangelical clergy, which names itself "Church Alive", concerned for the integrity of the faith of the church and committed to the preservation of that faith and its renewal in the church's life. Some will find it surprising to find so little evidence of the concerns of this group in the answers to the questionnaire. I find it even more surprising to find so little evidence of the influence of the theological revival, associated with the names of Karl Barth, Emil Brunner, Reinhold Niebuhr, and the like, that occurred in important educational centers of the United Church of Canada. These theologians challenged forcefully the kind of "liberal" church of the 1920s and 1930s that seems still to be reflected in our data. Did the United Church generally not feel the impact of that challenge? I would have liked to interpret the data as being the result of faulty sampling; however, after a second large sampling of United Church of Canada respondents confirm what a first sampling had indicated, this is not possible. I concede that my initial reluctance to trust the data probably grows out of my reluctance to accept findings that depict a denominational church family that one must consider somewhat aberrant in its self-understanding and its expectations concerning ministry, at least when looked at from certain theological perspectives.

It does not come as too much of a surprise to me, a theological educator who has long felt troubled and frustrated by it, to find both an antiintellectual and an antitheological bias reflected in the answers of United Church of Canada laity. These are tendencies sufficiently widespread to be caught in any net of random sampling. It is interesting to note the very different evaluations placed by laity and clergy groups on intellectual gifts, theological discernment, and the acquired capacity to think theologically in ministry. Take, for example, "Promotion of Understanding of Issues" (CC 14). Here, in assessing the desirability of ministerial leadership defined as "developing, using, and encouraging theological, sociological, and psychological understandings in ministry," the lay response is 7.7 standard scores lower than that of clergy (45.3 versus 53). With regard to specific items in that cluster, the laity are significantly lower than their clergy on the following: "Demonstrates understanding of the influence of social and psychological forces on people" (Item 138), "Explores theological issues underlying current social movements" (Item 131), and "Identifies sociological characteristics of congregation and community" (Item 145).

Is it an antiintellectual or an antitheological bias that is reflected in the low lay scores recorded in the answers to questions in Core Cluster 29, "Theological Reflection"? The laity show a standard score of only 42.6, compared with 50.9 for the clergy. On the most central item in this cluster ("Regularly reflects theologically on own ministerial experience," Item 324), 39 percent of the laity rate this trait as "highly" or "quite" important in the beginning minister, whereas 84 percent of clergy perceive it as such.

It is ironic, given the significantly lower rating that laypeople seem to attach to theological and intellectual gifts, to note that the United Church of Canada has a "continuing education" requirement for ministers that is second to none on the continent, mandatory for all in the pastorate, and generously supported financially. To what ends is it employed, given this assessment of a minister's intellectual and theological requirements for ministry? Surely it is cold comfort to find that other denominations that traditionally have placed an emphasis on the need for a "learned clergy" and that continue to require educational achievements of a high order as prerequisite for ordination, reflect similar disparity in ratings between their laity and their clergy.

While on the subject of differences in assessment of intellectually related characteristics of ministry between clergy and laity, it is of interest to note other examples of laity-clergy disparity in the United Church of Canada answers to the questionnaire. Table 18-1 contains those clusters that reflect a divergency of five or more standard scores, which could be regarded as a significant difference.

Five of the core clusters (CC 14, 15, 16, 18, and 33) in Table 18-1 belong to the broad area of ministry that is defined as socially conscious, issue-oriented, concerned for the oppressed, and actively attempting to rectify social wrongs (Factor 1, "Ministry to Community and World"). Five of the

TABLE 18-1
Core Clusters on Which United Church of Canada Laity and Clergy Differ by Five or More Standard Scores

Core Cluster No.	Core Cluster Title	United Church of Canada Standard Scores		
		Laity	Clergy	Difference
14	Promotion of Understanding of Issues	45.3	53.0	7.7
15	Support of Community Causes	45.0	52.1	7.1
16	Active Concern for the Oppressed	47.1	53.1	6.0
18	Aggressive Political Leadership	44.7	55.8	11.1
26	Coministry to the Alienated	45.0	50.0	5.0
27	Law Orientation to Ethical Issues	51.0	44.5	6.5
29	Theological Reflection	42.6	50.9	8.3
32	Denominational Knowledge	43.6	50.4	6.8
33	Interest in New Ideas	46.3	53.8	7.5
59	Responsible Staff Management	44.4	50.6	6.2

nine core clusters in this first factor reflect a significant disparity between the ratings of United Church of Canada lay and clergy respondents. United Church clergy, like the clergy of every other denominational family, place more importance on these facets of ministry than do their laypeople. The highest-loading (most crucial) dimension in this area is "Aggressive Political Leadership" (CC 18). On this dimension, the gap between laypeople and clergy of the United Church of Canada is 11.1 standard scores, a difference larger than that of any other denominational family (as well as representing the point of greatest difference between laity and clergy of the United Church of Canada). And laypeople are considerably less enthusiastic than their clergy with regard to a beginning minister's own involvement in work on behalf of minorities or oppressed people ("Active Concern for the Oppressed," CC 16); or his or her active attempts, from within formally established social structures, to improve the community ("Support of Community Causes," CC 15). In assessing the desirability of ministerial leadership demonstrated by "developing, using, and encouraging theological, sociological, and psychological under-standings in ministry" (CC 14), laypeople of the United Church, like laypeople of the remaining denominational families, place significantly less value on such leadership than do their clergy (45.3 versus 53.0, or 7.7 standard score difference). The last cluster in this broad area on which United Church of Canada laity and clergy differ significantly with each other is "Interest in New Ideas" (CC 33). The clergy of the United Church, along with others, value an attitude of openness to current ideas. But it is interesting that the laity rate the importance of this attitude a significant 7.5 standard scores lower than their clergy.

What is the explanation of these lower estimates? One cannot explain away the importance of these data for the United Church of Canada by noting that the clergy of the remaining denominational families also consistently rate these dimensions as more valuable than do laypeople. Is resistance to current ideas, for example, simply another example of antiintellectualism? Or is it born of conservative attitudes generally? Is it perhaps fear of a negative impact of modern, secular ideas on the layperson's faith? If the latter should be the case, one might venture the opinion that a greater degree of commitment on the part of the church to intellectual and theological endeavor in matters of faith would lead to a spirit of openness to challenging ideas from whatever sources they come. Paradoxically enough, perhaps a more "orthodox" theology, and a more Christocentric Christian life than that reflected in the United Church of Canada responses to the questionnaire, would lead the laity of the church to a more open and venturesome dialogue with secular culture and possibilities for human good within it.

The other four core clusters on which United Church of Canada laity and clergy differ significantly by five or more standard points are "Coministry to the Alienated" (CC 26), "Law Orientation to Ethical Issues" (CC 27), "Denominational Knowledge" (CC 32), and "Responsible Staff Management" (CC 59). Each of these four clusters comprises one part of four different, broader areas of ministry, and within that broader area each is the single cluster in which significant disparity between United Church laity and clergy exists. For example, "Coministry to the Alienated" is part of Factor 9, "Caring for Persons Under Stress." Laypeople and clergy of the United Church of Canada agree basically with each other on four of the five core clusters in Factor 9; it is only with regards to "Coministry to the Alienated" (CC 26) that a gap exists. And this gap is due primarily to one item within the cluster; nearly one-half (47 percent) of United Church of Canada lay respondents versus 21 percent of the clergy believe that it would be harmful or detrimental for a beginning minister to train groups to carry out specialized ministries, such as rehabilitation, crisis intervention, legal and medical aid, and financial counsel (Item 265).

"Law Orientation to Ethical Issues" (CC 27), part of the broader area entitled "Privatistic, Legalistic Style" (Factor 6), is the only cluster for which significant difference between United Church of Canada clergy and laypeople exists and in which the laity place a higher valuation on the dimension than do clergy (laity, 51.0; clergy, 44.5). It is interesting to examine the responses to the specific items that comprise Core Cluster 27. Neither clergy nor laity want the beginning minister to treat suicides as deaths outside the Kingdom of God (Item 255), nor do they want a minister to draw attention to God's condemnation whenever wrongdoing is privately confessed (Item 281), although the laity are slightly less negative than their clergy. It is the third item in this cluster that calls forth significantly different responses from the two groups. Of the clergy, 82 percent condemn as harmful or detrimental to an effective ministry attempts by a minister to provide solutions for all personal problems presented (Item 250); however, only one-third of the lay respondents agree with the clergy. In fact, 38 percent of United Church laity deem it "highly" or "quite" important that a beginning minister make such attempts.

Why do the laity seem more reluctant than clergy to recognize a minister's humanity and proneness to failure? The implicit assumption of omnipotence that seems to be attached by laity to their clergy with regards to Item 250 (attempting to provide solutions for all personal problems) is perhaps echoed in the response of laity to "Acknowledgment of Own Vulnerability" (CC 38) and "Acceptance of Counsel" (CC 39). In the most crucial item of Cluster 38, over two-thirds (71 percent) of United Church of Canada clergy believe it "highly" or "quite" important that a minister admit openly to times of doubt and struggles over his or her own personal faith. Only two-fifths (41 percent) of laypeople accord similar importance to such an admission. And in the most crucial item, "Acceptance of Counsel," clergy attach significantly more importance than do laity to a minister's seeking the opinions of other people as one way of knowing the will of God (Item 355). Seventy-three percent of clergy, compared with 38 percent of laypeople, perceive this action as "highly" or "quite" important. Does this reflect a sense of insecurity on the part of lay members of the congregation that can be dealt with only by thinking of their clergy as always self-confident and self-assured? Is it a feeling that, although laypeople may be weak in faith and in fidelity to principles of the Christian life, the clergy must always be strong and good? If so, there is nothing in such data that a more profound theology, a more intelligent and realistic understanding of life as seen in the light of the truth that is in Jesus Christ, and the forgiveness and hope that are in Him, will not cure.

Having noted where United Church of Canada laity and clergy have different perceptions, let us return to our attempt to sketch unique characteristics of the United Church by examining where this denomination differs significantly from other denominational families. The greatest number of significant differences between the United Church of Canada and other denominations is provoked by "Assertive Individual Evangelism" (CC 17). The United Church of Canada response differs in being significantly lower than the American-Canadian Baptist, Southern Baptist, Evangelical A and B, and Christian Church (not Disciples) groups. Like every other denomination, the United Church of Canada values this dimension more than the Jewish-Unitarian group. Those groups that rate "Assertive Individual Evangelism" significantly higher than the United Church also differ, not surprisingly, on Core Cluster 19, "Precedence of Evangelistic Goals." This cluster is defined as implying a "strong belief that efforts for the betterment of society are of minor importance by comparison with the evangelization of all humankind." For a group that consistently rates social action and social concern quite highly compared with other denominations, this is not surprising—although it may still be a bit distressing, to some who believe that evangelism can definitely imply social action, that the two are not mutually exclusive.

United Church of Canada members differ with five other families on two other clusters. "Secular Lifestyle" (CC 51) provokes significantly more negative feelings among the Southern Baptists, Evangelical A and B, and the Free Church family than among United Church of Canada respondents; whereas the Jewish and Unitarian family is significantly less negative than the United Church of Canada. And "Sacramental-Liturgical Ministry" (CC 9), which is defined as an orientation toward worship that stresses the sacramental and liturgical aspects of the faith, finds the United Church differing significantly with five families. The Orthodox Churches and the Roman Catholic Church (Diocesan) rank this as significantly more important; the Free Church, Jewish and Unitarian, and Evangelical A families rate this dimension significantly less important than does the United Church of Canada.

Significant differences between United Church of Canada perceptions and those of other denominational families are summed up in Table 18-2. (The definitions of the core clusters, and the items that comprise them, are found in Chapter 5).

Data generated by specific items in the questionnaire permit a glance at other distinctively United Church of Canada perceptions. For example, since the United Church has always thought of itself as a "uniting church," it is not surprising to find its members showing a positive attitude toward, and commitment to, ecumenical concerns. The United Church of Canada respondents place significantly more emphasis on two items related to such concerns: "Participates in ecumenical projects with ministers of other denominations" (Item 82) and "Alerts members to their need for learning from Christians in other parts of the world" (Item 133).

Most of those items on which United Church (particularly clerical) response is significantly higher than that of the total sample group belong to "Aggressive Political Leadership" (CC 18) or "Interest in New Ideas"

TABLE 18-2

Significant Differences Between United Church of Canada Perceptions and Those of Other Denominational Families

Denominational Family	Core Cluster No.'s on Which United Church of Canada and Denominational Family Differ Significantly	Total No. of Differences
Anglican-Episcopal	4, 41	2
American-Canadian Baptist	17, 19	2
Southern Baptist	17, 19, 31, 35, 37, 40, 51	7
Christian (Disciples)	—	0
Orthodox	9, 18, 27, 41	4
Evangelical B	6, 17, 19, 24, 27, 31, 33, 35, 37, 40, 51, 61	12
Free Churches	9, 51	2
Jewish and Unitarian	2, 6, 9, 12, 17, 24, 27, 31, 35, 37, 39, 41, 51, 61, 62	15
Lutheran	—	0
United Methodist	—	0
Presbyterian-Reformed	—	0
Roman Catholic (Order)	41, 48	2
Roman Catholic (Diocesan)	9, 41, 48	3
United Church of Christ	—	0
Evangelical A	2, 6, 9, 17, 19, 27, 31, 33, 35, 37, 40, 51, 61	13
Christian (not Disciples)	17, 19, 32, 33, 49	5
	Grand Total	67

Note: Significance is at the .0001 level.

(CC 33). Table 18-3 contains those items to which United Church of Canada persons respond significantly more positively and that could be classed as expressions of "liberal" social concern.

If the United Church of Canada responses to the preceding items are interpreted as those of a "liberal" denomination, one is not astonished to note those items on which the United Church of Canada is significantly less emphatic than the total group of respondents. As remarked earlier, social action and concern seem to exist at the expense of traditional, evangelistic actions and attitudes. Table 18-4 illustrates the lesser emphasis that the United Church places on evangelism, "born-again" concepts, mission concerns, literal interpretations of the Bible, and other "conservative" affirmations. The titles of some of the core clusters from which these items are drawn give the reader a preliminary intimation of what the

TABLE 18-3
**Items in Which United Church of Canada Responses Are Significantly
More Positive Than Those of Total Group**

Item No.	Item	Core Cluster No.	Mean United Church of Canada	Total Group
109	Actively works for justice in the local community	13	1.89	1.63
117	Speaks from the pulpit about political issues	18	0.36	−0.14
128	Insists that political struggle is a rightful concern of the church	18	1.08	0.14
130	Pressures public officials on behalf of the oppressed	18	0.98	0.12
143	Is willing to risk arrest to protest social wrongs	18	−0.52	−0.72
160	Makes individuals aware of their possible part in causing world poverty	16	1.78	1.16
288	Encourages the belief that some other religions of the world make worthwhile contributions to humanity	33	1.88	1.43
303	Regularly attends the theater and cinema (from G to X)	33	−1.11	−1.18
328	Advocates a "liberation theology" because of its implication for oppressed people	33	1.04	−0.28
700	Discourages use of stereotyped sex roles in assigning responsible positions within the congregation	57	2.06	1.76

Note: Significance is at the .0001 level.

United Church of Canada respondents, particularly clergy, are downplaying: "Precedence of Evangelistic Goals" (19), "Affirmation of Conservative Biblical Faith" (31), " 'Born-Again' Christianity" (40), and "Evangelistic Witness" (61).

It is important to note that those specific items (and core clusters) on which the United Church of Canada response differs significantly from the total group or from various denominational families are not those which the United Church (or the total group, for that matter) most or least stress. In other words, the United Church of Canada differs distinctively on those items that belong to a sort of middle ground, where one does not find those items the United Church of Canada or other denominations consider the most important or the most detrimental to an effective ministry. In forty-one of the sixty-four core clusters, the United Church of Canada does not differ significantly with any one denominational family. It is for the most part in this middle ground that one must seek to find any uniquely United Church of Canada characteristics. Although the United Church may be significantly more positive than the total group about a minister's speaking from the pulpit about political issues, this action still ranks as "somewhat," not "highly" important. United Church of Canada respondents are significantly less negative than the total group about such actions as wearing casual clothes, even for professional activities; making impulsive decisions; visiting local nightclubs or cocktail lounges; and displaying mannerisms commonly associated with members of the opposite sex. However, United Church persons still consider these actions undesirable or detrimental to an effective ministry. Moreover, the mean scores presented here represent a weighted average (50:50) of United Church of Canada laity and clergy. In some cases, especially those which concern overtly political or social action, the clergy of the United Church of Canada (like the clergy of most other denominations) are far more "liberal," more positive with regard to such action than are their laity.

In conclusion, I would like to return to the question I raised earlier about the difficulty of knowing how to interpret the findings of the questionnaire. How authentic a picture of the United Church of Canada today do the findings provide? What is their significance as a normative guide to ministerial education? Before addressing these questions directly, I offer a general comment on the character of the report as a whole that may have some bearing on the answers to be given to them.

Without denying the questionnaire's sociological importance in providing a description of a Christian denomination such as the United Church of Canada, one can ask how authoritative a picture it allows when its respondents have been selected randomly. When the United Church of Canada meets in council to make crucial decisions in matters of faith and practice, it chooses representative persons not by random selection, but on the basis of judgments made concerning personal gifts and leadership

TABLE 18-4
Items in Which United Church of Canada Responses Are
Significantly Less Positive Than Those of Total Group

| | | | Mean | |
Item No.	Item	Core Cluster No.	United Church of Canada	Total Group
56	Develops educational ministries with persons of other races and cultures	8	−0.38	1.09
62	People are converted as a result of his/her ministry	61	1.33	1.65
64	Preaches sermons that awaken listeners to their sinfulness and need for a Savior	6	1.35	1.54
75	Quotes much Scripture from memory when preaching or teaching	61	0.02	0.54
121	Insists that clergy should stick to religion and not concern themselves with social, economic, and political questions	19	−1.41	−1.18
123	Priorities in use of time indicate the belief that the one and only way to build an ideal world society is to convert everyone to Christianity	19	−1.14	−0.50
134	Holds that the church's task of proclaiming the gospel by preaching and teaching over-shadows in importance the task of helping to eliminate physical sufferings of people	19	−0.92	−0.56
135	Frequently approaches strangers to ask about the condition of their souls	17, 19	−1.64	−1.18

TABLE 18-4 — *CONTINUED*

Item No.	Item	Core Cluster No.	United Church of Canada	Total Group
			Mean	
136	Works to make sure that all people are free to buy property in areas of their choice	18	−1.67	−0.74
287	Treats the Bible, interpreted by the church, as the final authority in all matters of faith	31	1.19	1.30
313	Acknowledges the presence and activity of a personal devil (Satan)	31	−0.12	1.14
346	Practices fasting as important to spiritual growth	40	−1.47	−1.01
354	Refers to self as a "born-again" Christian	40	−0.62	0.28
373	Behaves morally in a way that is above reproach	35	*2.06	2.22

Note: Significance is at the .0001 level.

qualities. Therefore, a less "scientific" but perhaps a more "authoritative" account of the ecclesial nature of the denomination might be obtained by a selective process of choosing respondents from, as an example, the membership of this denomination's general council. Of course, if it is simply a picture of the actual church that is desired, more descriptive than normative in character, the method adopted is a good one (and one cannot totally ignore those areas where clergy and laity differ significantly). But then it is important to regard the answers from a descriptive rather than a normative point of view.

Yet we have found some difficulty in knowing precisely how to interpret the responses made, even as a basis for describing the United Church of Canada. We do not know with any degree of certainty what the questions meant, precisely, for those who were asked to answer them. How were the questions themselves being interpreted and understood? I must confess to being very disturbed at the relatively low estimate accorded by United Church of Canada respondents to central affirmations concerning Christian truth and life and their bearing on ministry. My comments are not designed to deny the general impression of a church that is "liberal," humanitarian, somewhat antitheological, and perhaps somewhat less than biblical in orientation, as sketched by the overall answers to the questions asked. But I do want to raise the question of whether one is receiving historically conditioned reactions to false interpretations of what may be basic to Christian thought and life (and therefore ministry) rather than resistance to what should be regarded as essential to Christian truth and goodness.

There are other problems: "Are too many of the questions directed toward a "person-centered" rather than a "goal-centered" conception of ministry? As such, do they imply a person-centered view of theological education? Some might think this desirable, but it is an assumption and not a theologically argued conclusion. Again, do the questionnaire and the replies to it beg the questions of what criteria of "effectiveness" in a ministry should be? It can, of course, be argued that all that is sought is a description of what expectations do exist, not a normative determination of what expectations are appropriate. But how is it possible to resist the pull in the direction of accepting a description of expectations for what "should be"? Again, it can be argued, as I have anticipated earlier, that the study's major usefulness is to raise questions about ministry in the church and to advise and warn the candidate about the church's expectations of its ministers, so that he or she might be prepared to be supported or challenged in his or her own understanding of what ministry requires. This is, in my opinion, beyond everything else the major contribution to theological education that the Readiness for Ministry study can make—this raising of the critical question in churches and theological schools about the nature of ministry and about the nature of education for it.

It is possible, from this perspective, to look at the United Church of Canada profile as we have drawn it not as an authoritative, dependable guide to its essential reality as church. If it *were* to be so regarded, one would have to ask whether the answers before us are not more psychologically or sociologically than theologically motivated. They provide an instrument for interpreting what generally the church's membership understands by the church and its ministry. As startling, even disillusioning, as one may find them to be in terms of normative, theological understanding, the results of the questionnaire provide a useful pole of reference (both in churches and theological schools) for raising critical theological as well as pragmatic questions about what constitutes ministry and its effectiveness today.

III

Research
Methodology

19

How Criteria for
Assessing Readiness for Ministry
Were Identified and Analyzed

Milo L. Brekke

The validity of any endeavor's outcome largely depends on the care taken in its execution. This is an account of how major early phases of the project were conducted. Because of the magnitude and complexity of the project, not all documents and detail can be included here. Some of this description also assumes readers' acquaintance with Schuller, Strommen, and Brekke's earlier statement of rationale and method.[1]

This description of method covers the first three of four somewhat overlapping phases of the project: the preparatory phase (May 1973 through September 1973), the criterion identification phase (October 1973 through January 1975), and the criterion analytic phase (February 1975 through August 1978).

THE PREPARATORY PHASE

Among the nearly 200 member schools of the Association of Theological Schools (ATS) and their respective denominations, there are numerous

---

Milo L. Brekke, a Lutheran clergyman and psychologist, is Principal Research Scientist at Search Institute and a member of the Readiness for Ministry Project team. His previously published works include *A Study of Generations, How Different Are People Who Attended Lutheran Schools,* and *Ten Faces of Ministry.*

definitions of what constitutes readiness to begin professional ministry. Such definitions are not "reflections" of reality but are conceptual schemata. The task of the research team, therefore, was *not* to impose its conceptualization by attempting to define readiness for ministry beyond the general statement of the antecedent ATS task force: that readiness consists of the basic competence required to perform acceptably the work of ministry plus the ability to develop professionally by learning from experience outside the school context. The challenge in the first half of the project was to identify criteria appropriate for use in assessing readiness to enter professional ministry across the association and within various subgroups. The project proposal clearly stated that the criteria used in assessing readiness were to be empirically derived, based on the judgments of five groups of evaluators from each of the forty-seven denominations represented in the ATS: seminary professors, lay constituents, fellow professionals (including new ministers), denominational officers responsible for placement, and ministerial students. Furthermore, work previous to the project had led to assumptions that some criteria would be common to all denominations, some to certain families of denominations, and still others only to single denominations; that some criteria would be common to all, while others would be distinctive to specific settings for ministry; and that a variety of criteria would be common across the range of evaluators while other criteria would be peculiar to a single group such as the laity.[2]

Therefore, during the five-month preparatory phase the research team laid groundwork for a statistical identification of criteria for readiness by reviewing relevant literature, enlisting an advisory committee, conscripting and visiting technical consultants, securing a sample of cooperating seminaries, and defining limits.

Review of Relevant Literature

An extensive search of literature concerning assessment of competence in any profession was conducted particularly to identify sources of both criteria and methods. This review, briefly summarized in the previously mentioned statement of rationale and method,[3] included literature primarily of three types:

1. Research in theological education concerning assessment of performance in ministry
2. Lists of criteria for evaluating ministerial effectiveness developed by individuals, theological faculties, and denominational boards or judicatories

3. Reports of similar efforts in evaluation of competency in other helping professions such as law, medicine, social work, teaching, nursing, and clinical psychology[4]

Major conclusions relevant to the identification of criteria suggested that:

1. No other profession had empirically identified criteria for readiness to begin practice, although those involved in evaluation generally tended to recognize that need as a foundation for development of relevant means of assessment.
2. Criterion analysis should emphasize many discrete behaviors and characteristics rather than global definitions.
3. Measures of these behaviors and characteristics should be as similar to the criteria themselves as possible. Means of assessing readiness should, whenever possible, attempt to elicit an actual work sample or sample of criterion performance, rather than something known or assumed to be predictive of the criterion.
4. Criterion-referenced[5] measures are to be preferred to the more traditional norm-referenced measures.

Conscription of Special Consultants

Advisory Committee

A relatively small group of people was invited by the ATS staff to become an advisory committee, meeting at least annually to perform especially two functions: (1) critical monitoring of the direction the project would take in relation to the overall church and seminary scene, and (2) interpretation of the needs and concerns of schools and denominations to the research team, and of the project to the schools and denominations. The committee membership was chosen to be representative geographically and denominationally, of theoretical and practical concerns, and of majority and minority perspectives.

Denominational Meetings

The advisory committee could pursue issues in greater depth, but not all of the diversity just noted could be represented in a small group. Therefore, each year a much larger gathering for information and counsel was convened of denominational executives responsible for theological education or ministerial placement.

Technical Consultants

Early plans included the formation of a technical panel of consultants with special expertise in such matters as research design, conceptualization, measurement, sampling, and statistics. As plans matured, it was found to be more practical and efficient to seek out individual technical consultants when special issues arose.

Drawing a Sample of Seminaries

Because this is an ATS project, the member seminaries (rather than, for example, the denominations) were viewed as the appropriate access to necessary information such as descriptions of the settings in which fledgling ministers first begin to function, criterion ratings from the five evaluator groups, evaluations and responses from faculty and students to preliminary forms of assessments, and evaluations of the usefulness of the results of newly developed assessment tools. Since asking any one seminary to provide all of this information might unduly strain the resources of that school, the research team decided to draw a representative sample of schools for the identification of criteria, to draw a second representative sample to help with development of assessments, and to spread other opportunities for assistance among the schools not included in either sample.

During the preparatory phase, seventy-nine schools were chosen as the first representative (random) sample, which was stratified by size[6] and by denominational family.[7] Rather quickly, seventy-eight of the seventy-nine sample schools agreed to participate.

Defining Limits

The first request for data from the sample schools required that a number of limits of the project be described concerning readiness and ministry.

Readiness to Begin the Practice of Professional Ministry

The scope was not defined as broadly as assessment of "effectiveness in ministry." Rather, the project was clearly limited to assessment of "readiness to begin ministry"—the brief period in time at the end of preliminary preparation and the beginning of professional practice. The focus, then, was on a kind of "take-off point" on the preparation curve. We sought to identify the criteria that the range of evaluators use or believe should be used to assess readiness *to enter into* professional ministry.

Ministry

A definition of professional ministry was also required. The research team adopted the following minimal working definition of professional ministry:

1. An office or task that an individual fulfills or performs in relation to some community of faith or institution of the church or synagogue involving appointment, ordination, or commissioning by some authorized sector of the religious community
2. Work that includes one or more functions such as leader of worship, preacher, teacher, counselor, as well as other direct or enabling service to an intentional community of people

Contexts for Beginning Ministry

The full range of professional practice of ministry is not represented among the first positions entered by new ministers. Therefore, the first data requested from sample schools was used to identify the finite number of contexts in which new clergy begin to minister. The term *context* was used, rather than *setting*, to denote an environment broader than geographic location.[8] A total of thirteen types of contexts for beginning ministry were identified among graduates of sample schools in the year 1973 and were the foci people used when determining the importance of criteria.[9]

THE CRITERION IDENTIFICATION PHASE

The months of October 1973 through February 1975 were devoted to developing a pool of criterion items and a preliminary criterion-rating instrument, administering the preliminary instrument and analyzing the data it produced, revising the preliminary instrument, administering the final criterion-rating instrument, deriving clusters common to all denominations (core clusters), and deriving second-order factors (families of criteria).

An Initial Pool of Criterion Items

A pool of more than 1,200 sentence descriptions of possible criterion characteristics or actions were developed from two major sources: (1) lists of criteria found in the review of literature and current related projects, and (2) descriptions of real-life critical incidents submitted by both lay and clergy observers.[10]

Preliminary Taxonomy of Criteria

These statements were then organized into a taxonomy of logically inter-related categories and subcategories.[11] This taxonomy provided structure for the later development of a criterion-rating instrument, and one concep-tualization of readiness criteria against which to compare the results of an empirically derived taxonomy based on the ratings of thousands of evaluators.

Writing Items

Questionnaire items were developed that described a single criterion char-acteristic or skill that was behaviorally observable, that could be rated as to its positive or negative importance for a ministry context, and that reflected one aspect of the taxonomic categories. Items were written by the members of the research team assisted by six ministers' spouses of various Protestant persuasions.[12]

Criticizing the Item Pool

Approximately 2,000 items in the pool were submitted to a heterogeneous group of experts for reaction and criticism.[13] They suggested deletions, additions, and modifications after examining the item pool for repetitions, omissions, ambiguity, equivocality, bias, and lack of the accents of par-ticular religious traditions. As a result of their critiques, 834 highly modi-fied items survived and were included in the preliminary criterion-rating instrument.

A Preliminary Criterion-Rating Instrument and Its Data

An instrument was needed that would allow evaluators to rank the criteria they use in making judgments about the readiness of candidates for pro-fessional ministry. The objective was to develop a criterion-rating instru-ment sufficiently comprehensive that every evaluator could find the criteria currently used, but short enough to complete.

Structure of the Instrument

The 834 items included in the preliminary form of the criterion-rating instrument consisted of 8 items requesting personal data, 147 general criterion items, and 679 specific criterion items. The 147 general items were the categories and subcategories of the initial taxonomy. The 679 specific items were from the item pool that survived the process of criticism.

The four major sections of the instrument paralleled the four major categories of the initial taxonomy. Each section consisted of both general and specific criterion items. A seven-point scale was provided for rating the specific criterion items. The scale was used to determine how desirable or detrimental for ministry each criterion characteristic or skill was considered to be by the evaluators. The seven possible ratings were "absolutely necessary," "desirable," "somewhat helpful," "somewhat detrimental or harmful," "undesirable," "should be avoided," and "does not apply." A three-point scale—"extremely important," "important," and "of little or no importance"—was provided for rating the general criterion items. Each respondent was asked to select one of the thirteen ministry contexts as a frame of reference for responding to all items in the questionnaire, both general and specific.

Administering the Preliminary Instrument

Collecting Data

The preliminary form of the instrument was administered to each of five evaluator groups during December and early January 1974. A very careful design was used for selecting two- and three-stage probability (random) samples, depending on the evaluator group involved. The previously described sample of 79 schools from ATS was the first-stage sample. The second-stage samples selected from within those schools included faculty (both part- and full-time), seniors, and alumni—all stratified by denominational family. The third-stage sample consisted of a fraction of lay members stratified by size of congregation from a random subset of the congregations served by the alumni drawn in the second-stage sample.

The sample of denominational executives responsible for placement was a simple first-stage random sample within denominational families. Due to the extreme variety in denominational polity, the populations sampled for denominational executives responsible for theological education or placement were chosen by ATS staff and in some instances by executives of denominations.

It was recognized that the relative proportions of the five evaluator groups would influence the results of the survey. Furthermore, the leadership of the different denominations would likely want different weights given to their groups of evaluators. Both the advisory committee and the denominational representatives accepted the recommendation of the research staff that sampling be performed in such a way that (1) laity and (2) the four combined groups of professional (clergy) evaluators would each comprise 50 percent of the samples. (The professional group was technically not all clergy, since it included senior seminary students and some faculty who were not ordained. For ease of expression, however, we refer to this combined group as "clergy" throughout this book.) Sample sizes were calculated such that, if a high rate of response (approximately two-thirds) were consistently secured, separate data analyses could be performed with reasonably reliable results for laypeople and professionals alone, and in some denominational families for each evaluator group.[14]

Samples by denominational family were not strictly proportionate to size nor were they exactly equal. Samples of the larger denominational families were two and occasionally three times as large as the equal numbers drawn for the rest of the denominational families, in order that the immense variability to be expected in the large families might be adequately represented.

Even though very large total samples of approximately 5,500 were drawn, disproportionately large numbers of members of minority groups were oversampled and invited to participate (for example, Hispanic-American clergy and laity, women clergy, and black clergy).

Sampling and collection of criterion-rating data were basically carried out through seminaries (faculty, seniors, alumni, and laity) using denominational contacts primarily to collect data from denominational officials.[15]

Approximately 5 percent of the respondents were instructed to be questionnaire critics. Instead of rating criteria in the usual fashion, they criticized the instructions, structure, and content of the entire questionnaire. All others who answered the questionnaire were urged to use the comment sheet for criticism of the content and form of the instrument.[16]

The primary purpose of collecting these data using the preliminary version of the criterion-rating instrument was to secure from a representative sample reactions to the initial list of criteria and their suggestions as to what was missing, offensive, ambiguous, equivocal, biased, or otherwise unclear or incomplete.

Respondents willing to contribute additional time beyond the approximately three hours required for criterion ratings were requested to submit abbreviated yet highly specific descriptions of critical incidents of very effective or ineffective ministry observed by them.

Analytic Design

The preliminary survey produced three types of data: usable ratings of both specific and general criteria from 2,011 respondents (461 laypeople and 1,550 clergy);[17] 1,400 paragraphs of comments recommending deletions, additions, or modifications of instructions, ministry contexts, response possibilities, or criterion items; and slightly more than 800 additional critical incidents.

These data were needed to answer the following questions regarding the research design: "Can core criteria (statistically and rationally homogeneous clusters of criterion items) be identified by the cluster and factor analytic techniques using evaluator ratings of criterion items? If so, does their structure parallel the organization of the research team's a priori taxonomy of criteria? Do core criteria or rankings of individual items systematically vary by denominational families, by evaluator group, by ministry context? and Which of the preceding three classifications is the greatest source of variation?"

The data were also needed to answer questions regarding the adequacy of the instrument: "Was the range of criterion items adequate for all evaluators? Did the items exhibit the necessary variety of frame of reference regarding ministry? What items could be deleted or added? Was the questionnaire length manageable? Were the response possibilities sensible and adequate? Did the ministry contexts have face validity? Were the instructions clear and adequate? Were there problems of sex bias? Was use of a standard, mark-sense answer sheet too confusing? Were closed-ended response possibilities tolerable and minimally restrictive? Was there evidence of need for separate lay and clergy questionnaires? Must the number of items be so reduced as to demand items that use a higher level of abstraction in order to cover the range of criteria?"

Analysis of Data

Ratings of criterion items were analyzed as follows. The percentages of people giving each rating for all items in the entire questionnaire were calculated separately for each of the five evaluator groups, for all laypeople, for all clergy (faculty, seniors, ministers, and denominational officials combined), for each of the thirteen ministry contexts, and for each of the seventeen denominational families. These distributions of ratings were used to identify items that discriminated among evaluator groups; particularly between laypeople and clergy; among faculty, seniors, and denominational executives; among denominational families; and among ministry contexts.

Rating data were used also to perform both cluster and factor analyses[18] separately for all of the items in each of the four major sections of the questionnaire and separately for three different groups of people: laypeople alone, clergy alone, and laypeople and clergy combined (all 2,011 respondents).[19] Results of these cluster and factor analyses were used particularly to determine whether empirically derived clusters of criterion items would be meaningful. They were used also to identify redundant criterion items and small homogeneous sets needing additional items to balance the content of the questionnaire.

The 1,400 paragraphs of evaluative comments were classified by section, questionnaire item, and nature of the criticism (concerning additions, ambiguities, bias or imbalance, insulting absurdities, hermeneutic or theological issues, problems concerning instructions, design, response possibilities, ministry context, general form, and so on). These data were used as a basis for examining every line of the criterion-rating questionnaire for possible revisions or deletions. All discrete new criterion items as suggested by the 800 critical incidents were written afresh and added to the pool for possible inclusion in the final rating instrument.

Preliminary Conclusions

Conclusions drawn from the analyses of preliminary data were considered strictly tentative. They included the following five conclusions:

1. Meaningful core criteria can be derived by these methods. A number of quite homogeneous and readily interpretable, unidimensional clusters were formed from the data.[20] Many of the clusters were large and often rather amorphous. Clusters formed from the same section of the questionnaire by the two different methods often overlapped in a small, common set of items but differed considerably in the rest of their content. It was decided that these inadequacies stemmed primarily from the imprecision and ambiguity of many of the items. The procedures for deriving core criteria were apparently adequate, but the rating instrument required major revisions, both in content and form.

2. The greatest differences in perspective on readiness for ministry are between laypeople and clergy. Although differences among professional (clergy) subgroups did appear, with theological professors the most variant group, these differences were clearly minimal by comparison with the laity-clergy differences. Nevertheless, results of cluster and factor analyses of data from lay and clergy groups separately showed some clusters nearly identical for both groups.

3. Ministry context might prove to be a greater source of variation than denominational family. The results were inconclusive because samples from certain denominational families were too small for reliable comparisons.

4. The preliminary rating instrument was too long and lacked an adequate range of item content and response opportunity.

5. Respondents would need additional assistance and reminders throughout the final questionnaire in order to keep the focus of their ratings on the beginning minister.

Revising the Criterion-Rating Instrument

The general plan for revision was to make modifications and additions based on the data[21] and to shorten the expanded instrument on the basis of a great number of criteria, including the revised taxonomy; the factor and cluster results; item discrimination among evaluators, denominations, and ministry contexts; and critiques of content imbalance. Both expansion and reduction procedures were partially governed by some thirty-four logical continua found among the items, relative to the activity and environment of ministry.[22]

Use of Consultant Critics

One hundred fifty items were significantly modified; 195 items were discarded due to their ambiguity. With the addition of suggested new items and items created from new critical incidents, the total number of criterion items potential for the final instrument rose to more than 1,100. This pool, organized by taxonomy and with each item identified as to origin (old, revised, or new), was then submitted to a battery of consultant critics carefully selected to represent a very wide variety of ministry specialties, ministry contexts, and special concerns.[23] Consultant critics were instructed to recast the written text and not just criticize, to respond as representatives of a specific stance or group, to evaluate the appropriateness of the language for their group or area of specialty, and to add what yet seemed to be missing.

Special invitations for additional criterion items were extended to and accepted by two groups: faculty and students from interdenominational schools, and clergy and laity from black parishes and denominations. Both groups, in criticizing the preliminary questionnaire, said they could not find a profile of ministry in the questionnaire to which they could subscribe. Not only were their suggested new items included, but it was largely on the basis of complaint, particularly from the first of these two groups, that an additional response possibility ("I reject this item; I find it meaningless or irritating") was added to the final questionnaire.

The Nature of the Major Revisions

Typeface, overall layout, organization, general instructions, ministry contexts, response possibilities, and criterion items were all significantly revised. The research team attempted to (1) give better balance for diverse expressions of theological views regarding church and ministry; (2) better represent those dissenting from traditional views of ministry; (3) shorten the first questionnaire; (4) redress the overemphasis on psychological guidelines; (5) hone each item to remove ambiguity, bias, and blandness; and (6) link the instrument more closely to the real-life situations from which it grew and to which it was addressed.[24]

Field Testing the Revised Instrument

A semifinal version of the instrument was field tested in early March 1974 to secure data about an audiotaped oral introduction, sequence and timing of sections, range and balance of criterion items, and new response possibilities and descriptions of ministry contexts.[25] The semifinal field test was limited to ten locations in Minnesota: four seminaries and six congregations. Nine denominational families, nine ministry contexts, and wide ranges of age, socioeconomic status, race, and geography were represented in the sample.

Analyses of Field Test Data

There were respondents who both answered and criticized the questionnaire. As before, frequency distributions of ratings of all items by all people were calculated, and cluster and factor analyses were made for each section based on the combined data from all participants. The much greater clarity and precision of the criterion items showed in the larger number of quite homogeneous and readily interpretable clusters of items, even though a very small but heterogeneous sample was used.

The transcribed oral introduction was rejected as unnecessary and impersonal. Knowing the purpose and use of the data was judged to be much more important than the sequence in which items were presented for rating. Range was generally considered to be adequate. The use of different response possibilities for different sections of the questionnaire was generally found unnecessary and confusing.

Final Selection of Items

The entire research team was involved in the final selection of every item, and the members of the advisory committee were given one final opportunity to review the selected set.

An item tended to be selected if it discriminated among ministry contexts, denominational families, or evaluator groups; was one of the three prime variables forming the core of a cluster; was not repetitious of other items; represented a distinctive concern of a divergent racial, theological, ethnic, or special interest group;[26] included distinctive language of a denominational family; represented readiness to begin ministry versus effectiveness in ministry in general, or in any other profession; was the only item representing a given taxonomic subcategory; was concrete and specific; or was necessary to provide a full spectrum of positions on a continuum.

An item tended *not* to be selected if it did not discriminate (almost everyone tended to rate it the same); did not cluster or was near the periphery of a very large cluster; received a strong negative reaction from recent item review critics; was ambiguous or double headed; was global or highly abstract; was stated in absolute terms; or was the least discrete or clear of a set of items within a given taxonomic subcategory.

Survey Using the Final Criterion-Rating Instrument

Selection of the sample for five evaluator groups and administration of the final criterion-rating instrument was completed essentially in the same fashion as for the preliminary survey with the following exceptions: (1) the sample was twice as large, with slight oversampling of underrepresented constituencies of ATS (especially Hispanics and women clergy); (2) no respondents were asked to be questionnaire critics, although the final instrument did include a comment sheet allowing for criticisms or additional criteria; (3) laypeople were only from congregations being served by beginning ministers;[27] (4) the research team did not usually participate in the administration of the survey; (5) the period of data collection was longer; (6) greater effort was expended in following up nonrespondents to encourage their participation;[28] (7) a strike of Canadian postal employees ruled out participation of many in Canada; (8) data were collected on selected characteristics of nonrespondents; (9) greater efforts were made to standardize administration across all evaluator groups and denominations.

Participation

A total of 5,169 persons responded in some fashion to the final criterion-rating instrument (other than providing notification of refusal to participate). As shown in Table 19-1, data from 4,895 were usable; that is, they were received in time for all data analyses and were complete enough to pass a very careful edit for significant errors and omissions.[29]

Table 19-1 also shows that the percentages of answer sheets returned by laity and clergy varied widely by denominational family, making possible some variation in the reliability or representativeness of data from different groups. There was, of course, no way of correcting for possible unrepresentativeness from small absolute numbers. Imbalance of subgroup size was corrected in data analyses by weighting the subgroups (lay and clergy, and families) so that each contributed equally to results of any analyses where they were combined (described later).

TABLE 19-1

**Numbers of Data Sets Used in Derivation of Core Criteria, and
Corresponding Percentages of Survey Returns, by Evaluator
Group and Original Denominational Family**

	Data Sets Used			Percentages of Return		
Denominational Family[a]	Laity	Clergy	Total	Laity	Clergy	Total
1. Anglican-Episcopal	92	167	259	44	48	46
2. American-Canadian Baptist	59	265	324	65	37	41
3. Southern Baptist	106	148	254	53	39	44
4. Christian-Disciples of Christ	17	94	111	74	57	59
5. Orthodox	48	74	122	28	21	23
6. Evangelicals	129	408	537	35	40	39
7. Free Churches	121	199	320	45	47	46
8. Jewish	53	39	92	29	16	21
9. Lutheran	340	221	561	42	59	47
10. United Methodist	89	229	318	37	66	54
11. Presbyterian-Reformed	192	359	551	43	64	55
12. Roman Catholic (Order)	42	120	162	14	33	25
13. Roman Catholic (Diocesan)	297	133	430	64	38	53
14. United Church of Christ	65	135	200	50	55	53
15. United Church of Canada	30	133	163	77	46	50
16. Others (outside ATS affiliation)	32	122	154	97	81	84
17. Others (affiliated with ATS)	94	243	337	39	50	46
Total	1,806	3,089	4,895[b]	43	45	45

[a]When core criteria were derived, the slightly different denominational families, to which the rest of the book refers, had not yet been identified empirically. The criterion rating sample was stratified and core criteria were derived on the basis of these seventeen families, which represent the a priori judgment of the ATS staff. See note 7 and the section "Empirical Identification of Denominational Families" in this chapter.

[b]Other than here, this publication reports 4,995 because a second, much later sampling of the United Church of Canada yielded 263 respondents (an additional 100). See the last page of the section entitled "The Analytic Phase" in this chapter.

The research team investigated the question of sample representativeness by conducting a follow-up study of nonrespondents. Seminary alumni (beginning ministers) who were either unable or unwilling to allow or involve members of their congregations in the survey were the greatest source of nonparticipation in that they were the gatekeepers to the third-stage samples of laypeople. The two most frequent reasons for not participating cited by them and all nonrespondents were lack of time for such a long survey or lack of interest. No other systematic differences between respondents and nonrespondents were identified. Therefore the research team concluded that the samples were biased by consisting of a higher proportion of people more highly interested in the issue of readiness for ministry and/or who were or perceived themselves as less busy. The team interpreted this to mean the samples likely contained a disproportionately large number of people either very highly committed to, or dissatisfied with, the ministry of the churches—and that the possibly counterbalancing emphases from such groups might not be particularly detrimental to the purpose of identifying criteria for readiness.

Deriving Criteria Common to All Denominations (Core Clusters)

The basic plan of analyzing the ratings in order to identify criteria that are generally accepted across all denominations (common or core criteria) was (1) to both cluster and factor analyze the ratings of all items by all respondents, and (2) then to identify the *single* criterion (characteristic or skill) described by *all* the items in *each* cluster that was derived jointly by both methods of analysis.

Settling on the details of this analytic design required taking a definite stand on a number of methodological issues. Those stands were taken not only on the basis of logic and theory but also on the basis of experimentation with data.

The following decisions were made regarding grouping of data:

1. To perform *three separate sets of analyses* based on data from all laypeople only, from all clergy only, and from the total group (laypeople and clergy combined)[30]
2. *Not* to divide each of these three groups (lay, clergy, and total group) into two random halves to further validate the generalizability of the analytic results[31]
3. In the set of total group data, to *weight laypeople and clergy equally* as groups[32]
4. In the sets of data from laypeople only and clergy only, to weight the *denominational families equally*[33]
5. *Not to weight* the denominations within each family,[34] or the four kinds of evaluators among clergy,[35] or the ministry contexts[36]

6. To analyze data from *one section of the questionnaire at a time* (not to combine several sections of items in one analysis)[37]
7. To perform final cluster and factor analyses of the set of all leftover items from the entire questionnaire that did not find their way into clusters during the section-by-section analyses[38]

The following decisions were made regarding the scoring of data:

1. To give the seven possible ratings the *numerical values of 7 to 1* as follows: "highly important" = 7, "quite important" = 6, "somewhat important" = 5, "undesirable" = 4, "detrimental" = 3, "I reject this item" = 2, and "does not apply" = 1 (therefore neither empirically scaling, resequencing, nor omitting any of the ratings)[39]
2. *Not to transform* the distributions of ratings[40]

The following decisions were made regarding the clustering and factoring techniques:

1. To use hierarchical clustering[41] and the method of principal components analysis[42]
2. To extract independent rather than correlated factors[43]
3. Not to completely factor, but to derive only those factors that contained more information than a single item[44]

Selecting a Discrete Set of Clusters

From each of the three data sets (laity only, clergy only, and total sample), at least fifty clusters were formed. Counterparts of most total-group clusters were derived also from laypeople and professionals. However, some lay and clergy clusters had no parallels.

One parsimonious set of clusters from all three groups was selected as follows:

1. Selection proceeded one section of the questionnaire at a time.
2. Clusters of total-group origin were preferred over lay or clergy clusters, unless
   a. There was no similar lay or clergy cluster (suggesting that the total-group cluster was a statistical artifact).
   b. A similar lay or clergy cluster was statistically more cohesive.
   c. A similar lay or clergy cluster was much richer (consisted of the same items plus a number more that gave much added meaning to the whole cluster).
3. Similar clergy and lay clusters, for which there was no similar total group cluster, were rare. Cohesiveness, richness of meaning, and lack of items that overlapped with already selected clusters were used as criteria for selection in those rare instances.

4. Finally, unique lay and clergy clusters were selected.

Two researchers made independent selections, compared results, and reconciled differences through discussion. The third researcher reviewed their joint selections and contested all apparent inconsistencies with the decision rules stated earlier until agreement was reached.

Rank-Ordering the Criteria

To know that "having brown eyes" is used as a criterion (an untrue example) is one thing; to know just how beneficial or detrimental "having brown eyes" is by comparison with other criteria is quite another. Each of the sixty-four clusters of items describes a single criterion (a skill, property, or characteristic like "having brown eyes"). Just how significant each criterion is generally viewed to be throughout the denominations was estimated by calculating the average rating of each cluster.[45] Arranging the average ratings of all clusters from highest to lowest provided a ranking of the significance of each of the core criteria for readiness—as viewed by laity, clergy, or both, depending on the source of the criterion.[46]

Naming and Describing Clusters

Again, two members of the research team worked independently giving titles and sentence descriptions to clusters, reconciled their differences through discussion, and subjected their work to the criticism of the third team member. The resulting titles and sentence descriptions of all common or core criteria were then submitted for written criticism to teams of denominational executives who attended the second yearly meeting. Their critiques are reflected in intermediate names and descriptions of core clusters. The refinement process, as it continued, is described in a later section of this chapter.

Deriving Second-Order Factors (Families of Criteria)

In the initial analyses, described earlier, 440 items were factored to produce sixty-four clusters (first-order factors). Then the sixty-four clusters were factor analyzed to produce eleven themes or families of clusters (second-order factors). However, one factor analysis of the interrelationships among all sixty-four clusters did not seem reasonable. It would have required calculating scores for individuals on clusters that were not derived from their data (for example, scoring laypeople on clusters that were derived from and really represented the frame of reference of clergy only).[47] Therefore three factor analyses were performed,[48] and the results were combined into a "best judgment" of what would have resulted had a single analysis of interrelationships among all clusters been legitimate.

Selecting the Discrete Set of Second-Order Factors

Each of the three analyses resulted in a separate set of second-order factors —the total-group analysis based on total-group clusters, the lay analysis based on total-group plus lay clusters, and the clergy analysis based on total-group plus clergy clusters. Total-group clusters were common to all three sets of results.

The task was to select a parsimonious and discrete set of second-order factors as they would likely have formed had a single analysis of all sixty-four clusters simultaneously been legitimate. It was done in much the same fashion as the selection of the discrete set of core clusters:

1. All three analyses (lay, clergy, and total group) resulted in essentially the same seven sets of total-group clusters. (Just as first-order factoring resulted in clusters of items, so second-order factoring resulted in sets of clusters.) The clergy analysis resulted in four unique sets of clergy clusters, but the rest of the clergy clusters were scattered as obvious additions to the common sets of total-group clusters. The lay analysis resulted in no separate sets of lay clusters, but rather in a scattering of all of the lay clusters, also as obvious additions to the common sets of total-group clusters.

2. This was taken as evidence that had only one factor analysis of the interrelationships of all sixty-four clusters been possible, it would have resulted in four factors consisting almost entirely of clergy clusters, and in nine more factors consisting predominantly of total-group clusters with a few clergy and/or lay clusters in each set.

3. In a very few instances where a given cluster was almost equally related to more than one factor, it was reported with the factor to which it was most logically related.

4. Names given to the second-order factors were tentative, since at that time they were the judgments of the research team only. As those names were used by more and more people within the association over time, and more people became familiar with the content of the second-order factors, suggestions for improved names were forthcoming from a variety of sources. The names now used in this book therefore reflect the judgments of a wide variety of people far beyond the research team.

Empirical Identification of Denominational Families

When at the outset it was necessary to draw a stratified random sample of schools through which to secure samples of evaluators, members of the

ATS staff judged the schools to fall into fifteen denominational families plus a group of interdenominational schools and a miscellaneous category. Evaluators who completed the criterion-rating instrument were categorized into those fifteen families plus the two "other" categories, making a total of seventeen families, as listed in Table 19-1. In deriving core criteria, data were weighted equally for each of those seventeen families.

The research team decided to attempt to verify empirically those judgments of the ATS staff regarding denominational groups (see Note 7 in this chapter). Selection of a single author to represent each family's viewpoint further compelled this study to see if, indeed, there was close agreement about criteria for readiness among denominations classified in the same family. Considering the eventual results of that empirical identification, it is important to note that at the beginning of the entire project, one member of the ATS staff had predicted two quite distinct groups of evangelicals, which he delineated, but about which the entire team was not then sufficiently convinced to use as an additional subgrouping for sampling and early analyses.

Factor analysis that would identify groups based on patterns of denominational ratings of the criteria was used as the means of empirically verifying the a priori denominational families as follows: A matrix of intercorrelations was calculated among all denominations across average denominational ratings of every item. That matrix of intercorrelations was analyzed by the method of principal components. Factors were extracted by varimax rotation (an orthogonal procedure, that is, one that leads to maximally independent factors) of only those factors that contained more information than a single denomination; correlated factors were also extracted by oblique rotation as a means of checking that the orthogonal rotation did not substantially constrain or violate the data. Similar enough results were obtained by both methods for the team to conclude that the orthogonally extracted factors were not artifactual (spurious) but a reasonable representation of the data.

First separate analyses were performed using lay data alone and clergy data alone. The results from lay data alone were quite distinct and articulate; those from clergy data were especially specific and distinct, with the exception of the first factor, which seemed to be something of a large conservative-liberal continuum. Since the lay and clergy results were quite different, and factors other than the first few were often less than immediately apparent or familiar, and since especially the lay samples of many denominations were very small, an analysis based on the total sample (laity and clergy equally weighted) was performed.

Results based on the total sample closely replicated a number of the a priori families, although some of the factors were bipolar. Again, hesitating to rely heavily on results concerning denominations with smaller samples, the team decided to stay with the a priori groupings except where they were strongly contradicted by logically consistent outcomes[49] that included some denominations with larger samples. Those exceptions, which were incorporated into the organization of a new set of families, included the following: (1) the formation of two evangelical groups generally replicated the prediction of the one ATS staff member; (2) a Christian Church (not Disciples) group formed separate from A Priori Family 4 (see Table 19-1); and (3) various denominations originally in one of the two "other" categories were located in identifiable families (most notable of these was the empirical location of Unitarians with Jews). Table 4-1 shows the fourteen new families of denominations, each of which is relatively homogeneous in its perspective on readiness for ministry. As in the a priori categorization, a number of the families consist of only a single large denomination.

All denominational family distinctions mentioned in this book, other than the weighting used in deriving the core clusters, refer to these new families that differ slightly from the a priori groupings.

Deriving Criteria Common Only to Each Denominational Family

Another hope at the outset was to derive not only criteria common to all forty-seven denominations but also criteria distinctive of each of the denominational families, and even those idiosyncratic to specific denominations. Ideally, that meant repeating the procedures used in deriving the core criteria: using data separately from each of the denominational families, and using data separately from each of the denominations. When the original sampling was being planned, such analyses were considered. It was determined that they would require minimum simple random samples of at least 30,000 people and, with only some proportional representation of denominations by size, would require a minimum of well over 100,000 people. Since costs prohibited securing such large numbers, samples were originally drawn with no intent of ever having sufficient numbers to derive criteria that would be distinctive of single denominations (except as a single denomination might be classified as a denominational family). But the original samples were drawn so that, with ideal rate of response, criteria distinct to each denominational family could be derived.

Therefore, as many sets of cluster and factor analyses were performed for each denominational family as there were family datasets (laypeople only, professionals (clergy) only, or total group) that each included at least 100 people.[50] For one-third of the families, all three sets of analyses were performed, as in the derivation of core clusters. For another third, only total-group and either lay or professional sets were performed; and for the rest, only a total-group set of analyses was completed.

Wherever more than one set of analyses was performed, the same set of procedures for selecting a discrete set of clusters was followed, as described earlier regarding core criteria.

This discrete set of family-distinctive criteria was given to the author of the respective denominational family chapter. In addition, each author was given the following data: (1) frequency and percentage distributions of response to all individual items by the total of all people in that denominational family compared with the total of all other people, (2) the same kind of compared frequency distributions for demographic variables, (3) results of statistical tests[51] indicating whether the differences in sample distributions were extreme enough to warrant drawing the conclusion that people in that denominational family as a whole would tend to respond significantly differently from people in the other families, and (4) graphed results of the laity-clergy within-family analyses of variance described in the following analytic section.

A few authors requested and received additional data (especially Lutheran and Roman Catholic). These data usually included the additional criterion clusters not included in the discrete set of criteria selected by the research team, and sometimes included denominational-family average ratings of core clusters (denominational family ratings were provided with each of the discrete-set denominational family criteria).

Authors usually made one or two sets of comparisons, often with the help of a team of people representative of the variety of perspectives within their own denominational families: (1) how the family rating of core criteria or items differed from the pandenominational rating, or from that of specific other families, and/or, (2) how distinctive family criteria compared with core criteria in content. The first of these comparisons assumed the core criteria as a common frame of reference for the author's own denominational family as well as all other families. The importance given to each item or criterion was the point of comparison. In the second type of comparison, the question was the degree to which the frame of reference of the author's denominational family differed from that of the common core. Results of these comparisons varied considerably by family. (See preceding chapters for details.)

THE ANALYTIC PHASE

In all of the analyses described so far it was assumed that laity-clergy status and denominational family demark important subgroups whose average criterion ratings might be expected to differ significantly. This assumption was not made without careful study of the relationship of all demographic and personal data variables to the distributions of item, cluster, and second-order factor ratings.

Identifying Significantly Different Subgroups

It is one thing to make the claim that people with certain specifiable characteristics tend on the average to give significantly higher or lower ratings to particular criteria. Such descriptive claims are reasonable to make from such cross-sectional data (data collected at one point in time). It is quite another thing to claim that one or more of those specifiable characteristics cause the higher or lower rating. Cross-sectional data such as these do not provide sufficient evidence for such causal claims.

A causal analysis, with the intent of being able to make explanatory statements, typically concentrates on interrelationships among variables. In this case, seventeen characteristics of criterion raters were available for examination as possible predictors of variance in the significance attributed to criteria. Typical analyses attempt to determine whether hypothesized predictors have any effect, and, if so, whether they each act independently or interact with each other in some complex fashion.

Descriptive analyses typically consist of isolating subgroups of people who tend to rate a particular criterion or set of criteria in much the same way and then to identify the distinctive characteristics of each subgroup of people (for example, they might be mostly clergy, or almost all above a certain age, or almost all of a particular denominational family).

Both approaches were taken to some degree, but with the ultimate goal of being descriptive rather than making causal claims. The research team did not attempt thorough analysis of the relative effects of variables on the different ways in which persons rated the criteria (causal approach) for a number of reasons: (1) Data were cross-sectional rather than longitudinal, and very little was known about the characteristics of the variables to be analyzed; for example, whether or not variables such as ministry context or occupation or frequency of worship met the assumptions underlying most causal-analytic methods was unknown; (2) there were financial restraints; (3) all seventeen variables rarely accounted for more than 10–20 percent of the variation in criterion ratings, so even a thorough causal analysis could not lead to results explaining the preponderance of variation in ratings; (4) even a sample of 4,895 people is small and offers very limited degrees of freedom when one is attempting to analyze simultaneously the possible effects of as many as fifteen or more variables; (5) exploratory analyses showed little confounding or interaction among variables (primarily independent or substitutive effects); and (6) exploratory analyses showed that even within the small percentages of variance that the seventeen known characteristics of raters could account for, two or three variables so predominated that systematic and thorough analyses of all seemed potentially unproductive.

Nevertheless, a number of exploratory analyses were performed among the seventeen characteristics of criterion raters that might be related sytematically to different ratings of items, criteria, or second-order factors. The characteristics were denominational family, evaluator group, laity-professional status, laity-clergy presently serving congregations status, sex, age, ministry context, race, frequency of worship attendance, whether or not the rater was a relative of a minister, amount of formal education, family income, type of occupation, geographic region, size of community, size of congregation or parish, and, if Roman Catholic, whether Order or Diocesan ministry setting.

Factor Analyses of Demographic and Personal Data

Principal components analyses (with orthogonal rotation) among the seventeen demographic and personal variables were performed separately with each of three samples (laity, professionals, and total group). This was done to identify intercorrelated sets of variables and/or sets of variables that might be called by different names or descriptors but for all practical purposes were the same (for example, laity-clergy status and amount of theological education).

Multiple-Regression Analyses

A few multiple linear regression analyses were performed to secure preliminary ideas of the amount of variation in criterion ratings controlled independently by a few sets of intercorrelated variables. The majority of demographic and personal variables were found to show little relationship to variations in criterion ratings. Denominational family and laity-clergy status stood out by contrast, but even they rarely accounted for any more than 10 percent of the variance with exceptions such as their relationship to second-order Factor 7, "Priestly-Sacramental Ministry," where denominational family alone accounted for better than 60 percent of the variations in ratings of the importance of that area of ministry.

Since multiple linear regression has rather stringent assumptions and is best suited for precise hypothesis testing, and thus requires careful and detailed structuring, this method was set aside in favor of one more efficiently suited for broad-scale exploratory analyses.

Automatic Interaction Detection (AID)

The relationships of all seventeen characteristics of raters to each other and to each of the eleven second-order factors was pursued systematically through use of automatic interaction detection. AID is a large-scale computer program that simulates a researcher with a prestated and reproducible strategy investigating a large body of data for the predictors that increase one's ability to account for the dependent variable (in this case, ratings of criteria and second-order factors).[52] The basic strategy uses a nonsymmetrical branching process, based on repeated one-way analyses of variance, to divide the data set into a series of subgroups that maximize the researcher's ability to predict values of the dependent variable.[53] (Linearity and additivity assumptions characteristic of multiple regression techniques are not required, although the criterion is reduction of error, not statistical significance.) It is rather ideal as a technique by which a relatively large number of predictor or potential "effector" variables with a wide variety of relatively unknown characteristics and interrelationships can be analyzed in simultaneous relationships to one dependent or criterion variable after another.[54]

Correlation between predictors is easily seen when two would reduce error variance about the same amount. If, when one is chosen, the other no longer offers any (or significantly less) explanatory power in relation to the resulting subgroups of persons, the two contending predictors are obviously correlated; one is about as good as the other. In this way, the more powerful of the correlated predictors serves as a control against the other. Therefore, if a predictor in the beginning is highly correlated with a dependent variable but never makes a split, it has been "beaten out" by other predictors that are correlated with it, but are more highly correlated than it with the dependent variable.

It was on the basis of this possibility that AID was used, both to identify homogeneous subgroups of raters who attributed unusually large or small importance to given criteria or second-order factors, and to identify the distinctive common characteristics of the members of each subgroup.[55] Usually no more than two or three characteristics of raters were found to be significantly related to variations in ratings of second-order factors. Sometimes individual criteria had to be used as the dependent variable before any consequential relationship was found with any characteristics of the raters. Denominational family, laity-clergy status, and frequency of church attendance were by far the most common best predictors of variations in ratings of all second-order factors.

Considering the negligible effect of most demographic and personal variables on ratings of most areas of ministry, and the largely independent effect of most variables significantly related to ratings of criteria for readiness, the research team decided to concentrate further analysis on (1) the few variables controlling most of the variance and (2) a few variables such as gender and age that both laity and clergy tend to believe are the bases on which people differentially evaluate criteria.

Analyses of Variance

Attention was therefore concentrated on denominational family, laity-clergy status, sex, age, frequency of church attendance, size of parish, and ministry context. These were analyzed one at a time, or in sets of two, in one- and two-factor analyses of variance. Thus, several series of analyses were performed in which the relationships between one or two characteristics of raters at a time and significantly high or low ratings of each of the sixty-four criteria were identified.[56]

Chapter 4 of this book is based on the results of one series of two-way analyses of variance in which laity-clergy status and denominational family (completely crossed independent variables) were analyzed in relation to ratings of each of the sixty-four criteria (dependent variables).[57]

Statements were made in Chapter 3 about a variety of distinguishing characteristics of people who tended to emphasize or deemphasize the importance of specific second-order factors and criteria. Those were based both on the series of analyses of variance and on the AID analyses described earlier. Throughout all of those analyses, so few complex relationships among characteristics of raters (significant interactions) were identified that the author of Chapter 3 chose to act as if there were none at all, and reported only independent relationships (main effects) between rater characteristics and ratings given to criteria.

During the writing of this book, denominational executives in the United Church of Canada, with the cooperation of the research team, decided to attempt to secure a new larger, and, they hoped, more representative, sample of their membership as the basis for their denominational family criterion ratings. They were successful in securing the cooperation of a sample of laity and professionals that was larger than the original by 100 people. Usable data from their previous sample, as reported in Table 19-1, were replaced by data from their new sample (thus increasing the total criterion rating dataset to 4,995 persons). Their denominational family distinctive criteria were rederived on the basis of that new sample, and the two-way analysis of variance otherwise reported in Chapter 4 (laity-clergy status by denominational family) was repeated using their new data. The criteria emphasized or deemphasized by the United Church of Canada by contrast with some or all other denominations were identified anew as a result of that analysis, and what is now reported throughout the book reflects these latter analyses based on a new and larger United Church of Canada sample collected and analyzed at their expense. The resulting differences were few but tended to present a slightly more conservative perspective on what is most significant in ministry among members of that denominational family.

PREPARATION OF DATA FOR PRESENTATION IN THIS BOOK

Despite the best conceptualization, careful planning, and consistent execution, what occurs in a project of several years' duration is a gradual evolution of better ways to summarize and report the data. *Readiness for Ministry*, Volume I: *Criteria* and Volume II: *Assessment*, which were produced midway in the project to communicate findings as rapidly as possible, illustrate this point. Produced in paperback, they were intended to serve as limited interim publications, later to be superseded by this book. Feedback from those volumes enabled the project team to discover what was meaningful, what was confusing, and what carried potential for misunderstanding and misinterpretation.

The writing of this book became an occasion for reexamining a number of issues, including how data were presented. This reexamination was done with full awareness of the need for continuity with past presentations and publications, but was matched by a concern for improvement in clarity and accuracy and for coordination of information with what is being used in ongoing assessment procedures. Our decisions have modified some of what appeared in earlier publications.

The goals were (1) to clear up imprecisions and errors (whether of judgment or action) and (2) to present data in forms less conducive to misunderstanding or misinterpretation and applicable to a variety of purposes. We determined to follow procedures in handling, organizing, and presenting data that, with the benefit of hindsight, the team would follow in any future replication of this work for comparison or update.

Specific Decisions

Consistent Use of Average Total-Group Ratings

In early presentations of average ratings of criteria and second-order factors, we used only the group from which a criterion was derived when calculating average ratings. (For example, only the ratings of laypeople were used in calculating the average rating of the criterion clusters resulting only from that group.) It was assumed that if a particular criterion cluster of items was not evident in the data from the other subgroup, then an average rating of items that included that subgroup would not be very reliable.

Later, the research team tested this rationale empirically by also calculating reliability estimates of the ratings of criteria by the group not originating them. In most instances, the two reliabilities were inconsequentially different (average differences $= -.023$), and in only four instances did the two estimates vary by more than $\pm.10$ on a possible range from 0.00 to 1.00. Because of these results, the average criterion and second-order factor ratings were recalculated using total-group averages. In these computations, data from both laity and professionals were equally weighted, and also denominational families were equally weighted.

Organization by New Empirical Denominational Families

The seventeen denominational families that were given equal weight in the derivation of criteria and second-order factors, were the families based on the a priori judgments of the ATS staff at the outset of the project. Although those judgments were reasonably accurate when tested empirically as reported earlier, the empirically identified families were judged to be an improvement for several reasons including: (1) denominations originally placed in the two "other" categories (because it was originally *schools* that were being categorized in terms of their denominational affiliation, some of which were interdenominational) were sorted out among specific families and (2) on the basis of the data provided by each denomination the empirically identified families were generally each more homogeneous in their distinctive view of ministry. Therefore data for this book were analyzed and/or organized in terms of families of denominations adjusted by the empirical findings. These families are based on perceptions of the relative importance of beliefs, attitudes, activities, and skills of ministry. The same denominations might organize into different families on the basis of other doctrines, polity, or something else.

A New Criterion-Rating Scale from +3.00 to −3.00

Earlier presentations of average ratings of items, criteria, and second-order factors were in terms of a seven-point scale: 7 = highly important, 6 = quite important, 5 = somewhat important, 4 = undesirable, 3 = detrimental (2 = rejection of item, 1 = item does not apply to denomination or ministry context). A limitation of this scale consisted in one's not being able to identify a helping or hindering form of ministry, by seeing only its average rating. Furthermore, the ranks from 1 to 64 tended to be in danger of misinterpretation because differences in ratings in the top ranks tended to be very small (sometimes only .01 of a point), while at the bottom of the rank order average ratings were rather widely separated (criterion ratings were very skewed toward the lower end).

Therefore, the research team decided to deemphasize rank orders and to present average item, criterion, and second-order factor ratings throughout this book in terms of a new numeric scale from +3.00 to −3.00, with 0 as mid-point between desirability and undesirability (the range from +0.50 to −0.50 bounds the category of "little or no consequence").

In this process of rescaling ratings, a number of matters were corrected or reconciled, all of which made for slight readjustments of many previously reported data:

Items Describing Criteria versus Items in Scales

During the criterion definition phase of the project, the goal was to identify sets of items, each of which was relatively homogeneous in terms of the ratings people gave to them and each of which therefore described a single criterion of readiness for ministry. For that description, the larger the set of items the better. Therefore, in order to specify the nature of each criterion as fully as possible, the research team used a relatively low standard for including items in a cluster (identification by both methods of analysis, and factor loadings equal to or greater than .30). Average criterion ratings as originally presented were based on all items so identified and placed in criterion clusters.

Later during the analytic phase, the criteria were used as dependent variables, having been made into scales for which raw and standardized scale scores were calculated. In investigations of patterns of emphasis and deemphasis of different criteria by denominational or other subgroups such as reported in Chapter 4, the situation was not necessarily one of "the more items in a cluster, the better." To include in such analyses items only very peripherally related to the core of a given criterion would only make the discrimination of different patterns of emphasis the more difficult. Therefore, when the analytic dataset was created and standard scale scores were calculated, items that had been included earlier for descriptive purposes (but known to be almost equally related to more than one criterion) and items with factor loadings less than .45 generally were deleted. Thus scale scores were calculated only on the basis of items that at least correlated with the core of a criterion at a level $\geq$ .45.

For descriptive purposes, completeness was more important. But for analytic purposes internal consistency—that is, tight homogeneity or unidimensionality—was more important. That same need to accentuate discreteness was relevant in the presentation of interdenominational and denominational family expectations on assessment profiles. Therefore, expectations were presented on profiles calculated from the analytic dataset.

In calculation of the average ratings of items, criteria, and second-order factors in the new scale from +3.00 to −3.00 for this book, the analytic dataset was also used. Since in that dataset a few items used in original calculations of core criterion ratings were omitted, findings presented in this book in a few instances vary slightly from those presented in earlier publications.

Handling of Missing Data

Persons completing the criterion-rating questionnaire occasionally omitted items, either inadvertently or deliberately. Answer sheets with less than 80 percent of all items rated were not used. Rarely did any individual omit more than 5 percent of the items and rarely did more than 5 percent of the people fail to respond to a given item (usually 1–2 percent).

In complex analytic procedures such as used in this project, blanks or missing data are very troublesome sources of great additional complexity and cost. Therefore, it is common practice when small numbers of data are missing to substitute a best estimate for them. Thus, when the analytic dataset was created, missing data were given the value of the average rating of the particular item involved (if you must guess what a person who did not respond would have done had the item not been omitted, one best estimate is the average of what everybody did). Thus, the analytic dataset was created with literally no blanks or missing data, and additional costs and analytic complexity were avoided. However, in the earlier criterion identification stage, computer programs were used that treated missing data as zeros without reducing the denominator used in calculating average ratings by the number of persons with zero scores. This procedure, which tended slightly to deflate average item and criterion ratings, was corrected by use of the analytic dataset for calculation of all average item, criterion, and second-order factor ratings presented in this book.

Furthermore, during the criterion identification stage great difficulty was encountered when attempting to derive criteria from the section of the questionnaire entitled "The Minister as Person (Negative)." Raters apparently found it more difficult to discriminate well among different degrees of undesirability. When the frequency distributions of those items were studied, a few people (varying by item) were found to rate generally rejected behavior as acceptable and sometimes contributing greatly to effective ministry, and sometimes many raters rejected items or declared that certain items did not apply. Therefore, the research team decided to attempt to derive negatively perceived personal criteria using data only from people who discriminated some degree of undesirability or hindrance. That approach was successful, and original average ratings of criteria from that section were calculated on the basis of that reduced number of raters—in keeping with the rationale that average ratings be based only on data from people from whom the criteria were derived. Later when that rationale was tested and rejected, the analytic dataset (with average response values substituted for missing data) was used in the recalculation of average item, criterion, and second-order factor ratings on the new seven-point scale.

Variations resulting from these two changes in procedure (different general handling of missing data, and the special situation in the one section of the questionnaire) were never more than .10 of a point except for criteria derived from the " . . . Person (Negative)" section of the questionnaire.[58]

Reconciling Different Sets of Response Possibilities

Three slightly different sets of response possibilities were used in different sections of the criterion-rating questionnaire.[59] In original calculations of average criterion ratings, those slight differences were ignored, and, since seven response possibilities were offered in every section, those that were offered were given the same values of 1 through 7.

Two years later, when Readiness for Ministry Assessment profiles were being developed, a very careful decision was made not to present students' scores from assessment instruments in numeric form, both for ease of interpretation and to discourage overinterpretation. The same decision was made regarding the presentation of interdenominational and denominational family expectations on those same profiles. It therefore became important to equate identical or comparable *meanings* of expectations (a common set of meanings for average ratings of criteria from different sections of the questionnaire was required). The procedures used in that equating process were later used in the rescaling of average item, criterion (core clusters), and second-order factor ratings in terms of a ± 3.00 scale for this book.

Therefore, rescaling to ± 3.00 did not consist merely of subtracting 4.00 from each value, so that 7 became 3, 6 became 2, and so on. Rather, to the maximum degree possible, the same score value was attached to responses with essentially the same meanings.[60] That procedure included some numeric interpolation that resulted in some minor changes in average ratings. In some instances, that led to minor changes in rank order of criteria from what was initially reported. However, average ratings now reported in this book are more representative of what evaluators originally intended, and data reported in this book coincide with ranges of expectation presented on assessment profiles.

Regarding Interpretation

This willingness on the part of the research team to make the modifications just described emphasizes how important it is that writers, readers, and users not overinterpret data even though they are presented here in numeric form. For example, great care should be taken in any use of rankings to compare different groups, because differences at the top of the rank order are typically very slight, while often considerable at the bottom. To illustrate further, interpreters of criterion ratings should ignore small differences and those based on single comparisons and should pay attention only to large differences and consistent patterns of differences in the average rating of *groups* of criteria. It is important to set numeric data within the larger framework of meaning expressed in words. For example, one criterion rated, on the average, 1.51 and another criterion rated 2.50 both fall within the general category of "quite important, a major asset."

Therefore, if editors have leaned in any direction, it has been to avoid overinterpretation and to provide appropriately conservative presentations of the data and their meanings.

NOTES

1. David S. Schuller, Merton P. Strommen, and Milo L. Brekke, "The Assessment of Readiness for the Practice of Professional Ministry: Rationale and Method," *Theological Education,* 1973, *10*, 1, 50–65.
2. The project proposal presented the challenge as follows:

> *There is in fact no one definition of readiness;* many definitions will exist and must be provided for in the criteria and measurement procedures. The study must therefore identify the most important *areas* included in these many definitions, find the different *criteria* used by evaluators in these areas, and develop *measures* for these criteria.
>
> To put the problem of the study in a different way, a process must be constructed with sufficient flexibility to allow persons charged with assessing readiness for ministry to use its components like building blocks to see how well the criteria of their choice are met by the candidate. Here again, faced with the impossibly large variety of evaluators, we must hypothesize an underlying simplicity of structure, a limited number of areas and of criteria in those areas that will serve the vast majority of evaluators' needs.

3. Schuller, Strommen, and Brekke, "The Assessment," 51–55.
4. This third survey of literature was the most extensive and resulted in a separate publication by the scholar who was asked to conduct this portion of the review: See Robert J. Menges, *Assessing Readiness for Professional Practice,* Occasional Paper of the Center for the Teaching Professions (Evanston, Ill.: Northwestern University, 1973); also published in revised form under the same title in *Review of Educational Research,* 1975, *45,* 173–207.
5. In norm-referenced uses of measurements, the performance of each assessee is compared and reported with reference to the performances of some other group of assessees who are taken as a standard or norm. With this approach, unless the performance of the norm group can be described and interpreted in reference to some absolute standard of performance, knowing that a certain testee performs better or worse than a certain proportion of the norm group is minimally meaningful.

In criterion-referenced uses of measurements, each assessee is *not* compared with other assessees; rather, the performance of each assessee is compared and reported with reference to some specific and clearly describable set of actions or performances, a standard of performance, a criterion.

6. Size of school was determined by number of students seeking their first theological degrees, such as M.Div. or B.D., but not degrees in, for example, church music.
7. Stratification assures better representation than might sometimes occur with a simple random sample. Thus, ideally stratification would have been by the forty-seven denominations (forty-eight, counting Roman Catholic Order and Diocesan schools separately). However, that would have required selecting just about every school (4 sizes $\times$ 48 denominations = 192 cells in the sampling frame, with only 196 in the association). Therefore, as a compromise, the ATS first grouped the schools by denominational affiliation into seventeen families according to staff experiences and hypotheses of distinctive perspectives on ministry among denominations. Fifty-six schools were drawn in a (4 $\times$ 17) stratified random sample (there were no schools in some of the 68 categories). Then, since 23 denominations were still not directly represented, an addendum group of one more school from each of these denominations was selected at random, bringing the total sample to 79.

The seventeen denominational families were (1) Anglican-Episcopal, (2) Canadian-American Baptist, (3) Southern Baptist, (4) Christian-Disciples of Christ, (5) Orthodox, (6) Evangelical A and B, (7) Free Churches, (8) Jewish, (9) Lutheran, (10) United Methodist, (11) Presbyterian-Reformed, (12) Roman Catholic (Order), (13) Roman Catholic (Diocesan), (14) United Church of Christ, (15) United Church of Canada, (16) Interdenominational, and (17) Other. Plans were then made to test this a priori grouping of families later through factor analyses of average criteria ratings by denomination to see if, indeed, there was closer agreement about criteria for readiness among denominations classified in the same family.

8. The staff person responsible for placement in every sample seminary was asked to provide seven to nine different situation descriptions (paragraphs of 50–75 words each) that would illustrate kinds of places to which their graduates were going (not including those continuing their education). They were asked to include at least the following factors in each description: (1) setting of ministry (congregation, chaplaincy in hospital or other setting, missionary, and so on); (2) size of institution (membership of church or size of hospital); (3) position (pastor, associate or assistant, minister of education, and so on); (4) community location of institution (core or inner-city urban, suburban, village, open country); and (5) description of population served (race, average age, socioeconomic level, three to five major occupations represented, general level of education). Each was asked also to indicate a rough approximation of the proportion of the school's graduates going to that type of situation.

9. Descriptions, one to a card, were sorted by three members of the research staff into sets that each independently judged to be homogeneous. Differences of opinion were reconciled through discussion, and the twelve most common contexts and a miscellaneous category were agreed on. Each researcher then independently wrote a descriptive title and paragraph for each category. Again through discussion, the best title or description of each category was selected and edited into a consistent style. For validation of the categories (contexts), five research assistants independently resorted all cards into the thirteen categories after thorough study of the titles or descriptions. These titles and descriptions were later criticized by many of the people who answered the preliminary criterion-rating instrument and were revised again for the final rating instrument. Titles of the thirteen contexts are (1) "Grassroots General Practice"; (2) "Homogeneous, Urban-Suburban"; (3) "Ethnic Congregation"; (4) "Transitional Community"; (5) "Inner-City Struggle"; (6) "Subsidized Mission"; (7) "Prospering Urban-Suburban Congregation"; (8) "Educational or Youth Ministry in a Parish"; (9) "Educational Ministry—Academic"; (10) "Ministry in and to the Community"; (11) "Therapeutic Ministry in an Institution"; (12) "Evangelism"; and (13) "Other."

10. Written descriptions of actual incidents of effective and ineffective ministry were requested from representative samples of people who observe ministers at work in a broad spectrum of situations. Forms for writing descriptions of both effective and ineffective ministry were mailed to the following:

	No. of Forms
Academy of Parish Clergy	200
Association of Clinical Pastoral Education	200
Church Women United	96
The Association of Church Administrators	100
Selected Black Clergy	88
Benedictine Women Religious	30
Newly Ordained Roman Catholic Priests	100

Respondents were asked to describe the incident in detail giving the setting, roles of the people involved, exactly what was said or done that constituted effective or ineffective ministry, and why they judged the incident to be effective or ineffective ministry.

To gain greater specificity, senior students and recent graduates of two Roman Catholic seminaries were interviewed on critical incidents, having had several days of opportunity for preparatory recall.

11. Each of the 1,200 sentence descriptions was written on a 3 × 5 card. Two of the primary members of the research team each independently organized the 1,200. After the fact observations showed that one tended to organize by function and the other by ministerial role. Discussion led to a composite organization that was validated by the third member of the research team developing a satisfactory descriptive label for each of the categories. Major categories of the taxonomy were:

  I. The Minister in a Profession
     A. The Human Side of the Profession
     B. The Realm of Ideas
     C. Religious Commitment
     D. Clergy as Theologians
 II. The Minister as a Person
     A. Stability of Spirit and Attitude
     B. Positive Spirit
     C. Psychologically Free to Serve Others
     D. Alert and Open to New Possibilities
     E. Able to Live and Act as an Autonomous Person
     F. An Exemplar
III. The Minister as a Skilled Leader
     A. Skilled in Relating to People
     B. Skilled in Conflict Resolution
     C. Skilled Leader of Group Discussion
     D. Skilled Administrator in Effecting Change
     E. Skilled as Trainer, Educator, and Theologian in Developing the Resources of People
     F. Skilled in Encouraging Mutuality
     G. Skilled as a Manager
 IV. The Minister in Professional Roles
     A. Leader of Public Worship
     B. Community Leader
     C. Prophet
     D. Preacher
     E. Evangelist
     F. Educator
     G. Counselor
     H. Ecumenical Leader

12. Each writer was given the cards from several subcategories of the taxonomy and was asked to write at least one criterion-rating item for each card. Each newly written item was examined by a minimum of two other members of the research team as to its relevance to the area of ministry described on the card. Great care was taken to preserve the language of the source in the newly written item in order that a maximum of the perspectives and persuasions might be maintained and a minimum of bias might be introduced by the writer. Authors were also instructed to write items that were more concrete than the material on the more than 1,200 cards.

13. Critics included the professional staff of ATS and the advisory committee for the Readiness for Ministry Project, the entire professional staff and board of directors of the Youth Research Center, a certified consulting psychologist, a director of psychological services at a major county hospital, a professor of clinical pastoral counseling, a seminary academic dean, and a specialist in content analysis at a major university.

14. Probabilities of a given member of a specific evaluator group being drawn into one of the samples were not equal across denominational families because of the extreme range of differences in size among the seventeen denominational families. However, probabilities were equal within each family. In other words, samples of evaluator groups were stratified by denominational family.

15. With instruction from the research team, a project representative from each sample school drew all samples, except laity and denominational officials, and arranged for group administration of the preliminary instrument at the seminary to faculty and seniors. The preponderance of group administrations was conducted by ATS staff members, who also led discussion about the instrument after its administration.

Samples of alumni and denominational officials were invited to participate by letter from the research team. Lay samples were drawn and invited to participate by the person serving them as minister. Faculty and seniors at first choosing not to participate were followed up through personal contact by the project representative at each school. Nonparticipating alumni and denominational officials were reapproached by letter from the research team and occasionally from an especially interested denominational official or project representative. Laypeople, faculty, and seniors absent from group administrations were sometimes encouraged to complete the survey in private.

16. By the end of December, it had been demonstrated that the questionnaire was too long for the average group. Therefore the remaining schools were instructed to direct respondents to omit the rating of general criteria, with the exception of one individual from each group who was instructed to rate *only* the general criteria.

17. At least 40 percent of the sample responded. Of those, 2,011 people completed at least 95 percent of the survey and provided usable data for analyses of the ratings of criterion items.

18. Homogeneous keying was the method of cluster analysis used. The theory undergirding this technique is provided by Jane Loevinger, "A Systematic Approach to the Construction and Valuation of Tests of Ability," *Psychological Monograph,* 1947, *61,* iii–49. Details of the technique and an actual research example are provided in Philip H. DuBois, Jane Loevinger, and Goldine C. Gleser, "The Construction of Homogeneous Keys for a Biographical Inventory," *Research Bulletin, 52–18,* 1–19. (USAF Human Resources Center, Lackland Air Force Base, San Antonio, Texas) The technique begins with a variance-covariance matrix of the initial pool of items and produces clusters with two properties: (1) relative independence or having low correlations with remaining clusters and (2) maximum homogeneity or internal consistency reliability.

The method of factor analysis used was principal components analysis followed by normal varimax rotation. Details concerning these methods can be found in the following:

Harold Hoteling, "Analysis of a Complex of Statistical Variables Into Principal Components," *Journal of Educational Psychology,* 1933, *24,* 198–250; R. J. Rummel, *Applied Factor Analysis* (Evanston, Ill.: Northwestern University Press, 1970); and Henry Kaiser, "The Varimax Criterion for Analytic Rotation in Factor Analysis," *Psychometrika,* 1958, *23,* 187–200.

19. Rating data were factor and cluster analyzed by sections of items for several reasons. The first purpose was to discover if *meaningful* clusters of criterion items could be derived *at all* by these methods. Second, some subgroupings of items had to be used. Even with a very powerful computer (IBM 370, Model 158, with 2,500,000 bytes of memory and virtual [selective] storage) no factor analysis program available could analyze more than 200 variables at a time. Third, these items were already logically organized by section. Since definitive core criteria (clusters of items) were not being sought at this time, analysis by section of the questionnaire would not provide undue restriction on the formation of clusters relevant to questionnaire revision. Both cluster and factor analyses were performed as a means of cross-validating results. Both theory and previous experience indicated that both methods should produce essentially the same results. Using only clusters produced by both methods guards against placing undue confidence in core criteria that are method- or sample-specific.

20. Internal consistency reliability of the most readily interpreted dozen clusters ranged from .80 to .97.

21. Fortunately most critical comments not only identified what was wrong but also proposed what would make it right. Furthermore, rarely did only one critic identify a particular problem. Usually there were several who gave similar suggestions for its correction. Nevertheless, a clearly needed modification was made sometimes on the basis of only one critic.

22. For example, age of the mentioned recipient of ministry. Care was taken that not all items descriptive of teaching referred only to teaching children but also to teaching other age groups.

23. Again, the full professional staff of ATS was involved, together with the members of the advisory committee for the Readiness Project, the full professional staff of the Search Institute (SI) together with SI board members in addition to another dozen specialists in school and parish settings including professors, students, clergy, and laity.

24. Critical incidents served two more important functions. First, they described not only the "what" of ministry but also the "where." The new categories that emerged from a classification of the critical incidents provided a new basis for sectioning the questionnaire:

I. Ministries to the Religious Community
II. Ministries to the Community and World

III. Ministries to Persons under Stress
IV. The Minister as Theologian and Thinker
V. The Minister's Personal Commitment of Faith
VI. The Minister as a Person
VII. The Minister as a Leader

Second, a number of critics underscored the difficulty of rating certain criterion items describing ministers' behavior "because it depends so much on the circumstances." To provide a general, real-life context and frame of reference for each of the major sections of the final questionnaire, abbreviations or quotations from four or five critical incidents were chosen to introduce each of the seven sections of items.

25. Throughout the use of all forms of the instrument, clergy and laity were instructed to select and use the ministry context most nearly like the congregation of which they were members; faculty, students, and denominational executives were instructed to select and use the ministry context with which they were most familiar, assuming that would be easiest for them to maintain as a frame of reference throughout the entire questionnaire.

26. After the criterion-rating instrument had been finalized, a copy was sent to the Dean of Hebrew Union College at Cincinnati, who developed a revised version, "Readiness for Ministry/Rabbinate Survey," which was used in the Jewish community.

27. This was to sharpen the focus on readiness. For the preliminary questionnaire, laity came from a random sample of all types of congregations served by alumni of all ages. This was consistent with the intent to secure as wide a range of input concerning criteria as possible from respondents to the preliminary, developmental questionnaire. The objective for the final questionnaire was to concentrate the rating process on the criteria relevant for use in assessing the beginning minister. Therefore, the final lay sample was limited to those parishes in which new ministers were serving and where laypeople, because of their recent experience of being served by a new minister, might more readily maintain the frame of reference of readiness.

28. From three to five follow-up contacts with each nonrespondent were made, depending on the evaluator group and the thoroughness of the work of each project representative and 1973 graduate. In an attempt to increase participation, data collection was held open from mid-April through early September 1974 (the first-round mailing of questionnaires was completed in late June).

29. A high-speed optical scanner was used to transfer the responses of each person from answer sheets to a single record on magnetic tape that could be processed by computer. During this transfer, two additional processes were completed. The seven possible ratings for each item were given numerical values from 1 to 7. Second, the total record of responses for each person was subjected to a careful edit for possible errors and omissions, including the following: answer sheet markings beyond the range of possible responses, missing personal data, obvious errors in the sequence of marking answers (since certain sections of the standard answer sheet required skipping), mismatching of the two answer sheets, or less than 80 percent of the answer sheet completed. Answer sheets with significant errors or omissions were rejected, corrected when possible, and resubmitted. Of all the answer sheets, 4,895 sets survived this process.

30. The groups of people that are combined to provide data for a single-factor analysis should be reasonably homogeneous in their perspectives—in this case, their ratings of the set of criterion items. If they are too heterogeneous, the results of the factor analysis will be spurious and not characteristic of any of the heterogeneous groups present in the data. The samples of evaluators were drawn equally from laypeople and clergy under the assumption that laypeople and professionals would each use or recommend some criteria that the other would not, while there would likely be a majority of criteria common to both. Thus the appropriateness of analyses of lay and clergy data both separately and combined.

31. If two analytic methods produce essentially the same results, the probability is considerably less that the results are idiosyncratic to a specific method. Likewise, if two random samples produce essentially the same results, the probability is considerably less that the results are sample-specific.

To examine this issue, the data from one denominational family were divided into two random halves, and both halves were factor and cluster analyzed independently. The results of the two sets of analyses were essentially the same. Therefore, to conserve time and other resources, further analyses were not performed on two random halves.

32. Equal numbers of laypeople and clergy were drawn in the sample but, of course, equal numbers did not participate. When some of the total-sample data were analyzed, both unweighted and with various weights given to laypeople and clergy, significantly different results were obtained. In order that neither group might predominate, the data from laypeople and clergy were weighted as if exactly the same number had participated from each group.

33. Likewise, experiments with various weightings of denominational families led to strikingly different results. To assure that no one denominational family might dominate the results, data were weighted to produce results as if the same number of people had participated from each denominational family.

34. By definition, all denominations in a given family were assumed to share the same perspective on ministry. Whether more data within a given family came from a particular member denomination should be irrelevant. A subsequent empirical (factor analytic) derivation of denominational families did not produce results different enough to cause the research team concern about this assumption. (See section entitled "Empirical Identification of Denominational Families" in this chapter.)

35. The same argument (as in Note 34) applies to the four subgroups of professional evaluators. As with the preliminary data, item by item comparisons of the distributions of ratings by each of the five evaluator groups showed some significant differences among professionals on specific issues. But they were far smaller and less frequent than the differences between laity and clergy. This pattern of differences was found in trial analysis of data from two denominational families as well as in the total sample.

36. In the same type of item by item comparison of distributions of ratings, ministry context did not show itself to be nearly as significant a source of variance as, for example, denominational family and laity-clergy status.

37. Computer programs allowed simultaneous analysis of up to 200 items. Experimental analyses combining data from as many as four sections of the questionnaire were performed using three sources of data: (1) preliminary data from clergy only, (2) final data from a single denominational family, and (3) final total-sample data from a variety of sections. Verifying the taxonomic divisions prepared by the research team, factor and cluster analytic results in each case essentially reidentified the original sections of the questionnaire. Therefore, to proceed with analyses one section at a time apparently would lead practically to no constraint on the analytic results.

38. Fourteen additional clusters were derived from that across-section analysis of leftover items. Each cluster still tended to consist almost entirely of items from a single section of the questionnaire—additional validation of the decision to analyze by section in the first place.

39. On first inspection, the "I reject this item" and "Does not apply" responses do not seem to be part of the same continuum as the rest of the ratings. But several experiments with scoring showed that the seven ratings scaled as a single dimension and that ratings scored 7 through 1 tended to produce the clearest and most meaningful clusters. Apparently, despite the logical disjuncture, most respondents used "I reject this item" and "Does not apply" as their most negative ratings. (See also section entitled "Handling Missing Data" in this chapter.)

40. Distributions of ratings consistently tended to be negatively skewed (with a disproportionately smaller number of low ratings). Factor analysis assumes multivariate normal distributions. However, the researchers concluded that transformation of the data to change the shape of the distribution presented a greater risk of artifactual results than proceeding with somewhat skewed distributions.

41. Because of idiosyncracies of computer programs, hierarchical clustering was chosen to replace homogeneous keying as the clustering method, when the decision was made to weight the data. Experiments (with two random halves of the data from the most variable section of the questionnaire from a single denominational family) showed the results of homogeneous keying and hierarchical clustering to be identical. For discussion of the algorithm and examples, see Stephen C. Johnson, "Hierarchical Clustering Schemes," *Psychometrika*, 1967, *32*, 241–254.

42. Principal factor analysis, which is iterative and based on only common variance instead of total variance, was considered. It was rejected because experiments with it using the same data (Section IV of the questionnaire; lay, professional, and total group) produced

essentially the same results as principal components analysis, but the process was many times more expensive to perform.

43. The goal of the project was to develop an efficient set of assessment instruments. A comprehensive set of independent measures would be most efficient. Therefore independent clusters were sought as bases for assessments. Factor solutions were submitted to orthogonal (varimax) rather than oblique rotation.

44. One of the objects of cluster and factor analyzing was to organize the data in units of information that would be more succinct and reliable than was already available from the ratings of individual items. To limit the process to the identification of factors with eigenvalues greater than 1.00 theoretically assured that each factor would summarize more information from the data than contained in a single item. (Here, an eigenvalue is the total variance in ratings explained by a factor, on a scale where the variance of each item in the analysis has been standardized to 1.00.) Conclusions drawn from information based on more than one question are characteristically more reliable than those based on information from just a single question. Criteria based on factors that summarize information from more than one interrelated question should therefore be more reliable than any single-criterion item.

45. The average rating given each item in a cluster was calculated (giving equal weight to each denominational family). The average cluster rating was calculated by averaging all of the average ratings of items in the cluster.

46. For example, to use data from clergy in calculating average ratings for clusters (that is, criteria) not characteristic of clergy seemed inappropriate and potentially misleading. As a result, the average cluster ratings were based in each case only on the ratings of the evaluator group from which the cluster was derived—laypeople only for lay clusters, clergy only for clergy clusters, and both for total-group clusters. (See also section entitled "Consistent Use of Average Total Group Ratings" in this chapter.)

47. A score for a given cluster for a specific individual was calculated by simply adding up the numerical values (from 1 to 7) of the individual's rating of each of the items in that cluster. The following cluster scores were calculated:

1. For *laypeople* on all total-group and lay clusters
2. For *clergy* on all total-group and clergy clusters

48. Three sets of intercorrelations were calculated as a basis for the three factor analyses of clusters:

1. Intercorrelations among total-group clusters, based on cluster scores of the sample (both laypeople and clergy)
2. Intercorrelations among total-group and lay clusters, based on cluster scores of laypeople only
3. Intercorrelations among total-group and clergy clusters, based on cluster scores of clergy only

49. Some outcomes, although speculatively interesting, were unusual enough for the team to hesitate to base all future analyses on them. For example, the three Lutheran bodies did not group together. The Lutheran Church in America correlated most highly with a group including rather non-conservative mainline protestants; The American Lutheran Church related most closely to the United Church of Christ and the Reformed Church in America; and the Lutheran Church—Missouri Synod most closely resembled the stance of the Christian Reformed Church. The stability of these results needs verification in future empirical studies.

50. An absolute requirement for usable factor analytic results is that there be as many people as variables included in the analysis; ideally, there should be two to three times as many people as variables. Even with small numbers of variables, analyses based on data from less than 100 people tend to be unstable and highly sample-specific. For this reason, a decision rule of a minimum of 100 people per sample was used. At no point did the number of variables exceed the number of people included in any analysis. Furthermore, in the selection of the discrete set of criteria for a family, whenever the number of people in a given analysis approached only 100, special emphasis was given to the results of the total-group analysis of which that subgroup was a part.

51. Chi-square tests of association were performed. The skewed distributions of response

to large numbers of the items led to many expected frequencies that would violate the assumptions underlying the statistic. Therefore, for most of the items, frequency distributions were collapsed across some of the least-used categories of response. Most authors received only the collapsed frequency and percentage distributions.

52. Second-order factor scores were calculated by weighting each criterion rating by its orthogonal factor load (correlation) on the second-order factor to which it was most highly related. Such weighted scores for all criteria defining a given second-order factor were summed to produce a second-order factor score.

53. Results are reproducible in that a rerun using the same specifications for both the dependent variable and the predictors on the same data will produce identical results. A similar run on a comparable dataset will probably give similar results for at least the first few splits of the dataset into subgroups of subjects.

54. Datasets of at least 1,000 subjects are advisable; a dependent variable must be specified, preferably continuous, but satisfactorily dichotomous if no more imbalanced than 80 to 20 percent. Up to 200 predictors may be specified, each with two or more classes that preferably form a single dimension. The following strategy parameters must be specified.

The program begins by examining the entire dataset in relation to every predictor and searches for the predictor, and two sets of the classes of that predictor, that if used as a basis for splitting the dataset into two subgroups, will reduce or "explain" the most error variance. The program therefore begins by calculating the subgroup means and the ratio of between sums of squares to total sums of squares (BSS:TSS) for every possible split of the dataset on the basis of every combination of two sets of classes of each predictor. If the classes of a predictor have a natural order, such as age, that order can be preserved. Otherwise the classes are reordered by the levels of the subgroup means on the dependent variable. The "best" predictor for first splitting of the dataset into two subgroups is the predictor with the two sets of its classes that provided the best BSS:TSS ratio. The dataset is then split on the basis of classes of that predictor. As soon as the first split takes place and two subgroups are formed, the search process begins again with the subgroup with the most variance. A given predictor can be chosen as the basis for a split as often as it offers the best BSS:TSS ratio.

This branching process of splitting the dataset into more and more subgroups increasingly homogeneous in terms of the predictors is continued until one of the user-specified parameter limits is reached. The researcher must specify (1) the minimum reduction in error variance to justify an additional split (some prestated fraction of the original variance around the mean, such as .006, or 0.6 percent of TSS); (2) the minimum size of allowable subgroup (such as twenty people); and (3) the total number of splits allowed (such as twenty-five, which would allow twenty-six final groups and fifty subgroups altogether). These parameter limits are for making sure the process stops before unreliable reduction in variance occurs.

55. The AID program offers the possibility of introducing sets of predictors into the running, in sequential order. Predictors can be given ranks from 0 through 9. Those ranked at 0 are not allowed to produce splits. The information about what they might have done is produced. All predictors ranked 1 are allowed to produce all the splits of which they are capable before any ranked 2 are given a chance, and so on through Rank 9. Generally, however, in these eight analyses all predictors were allowed to run free without being given the preference of rank.

56. Two-variable analyses included the following groupings: laity-clergy status and denominational family, laity-clergy status and sex, laity-clergy status and age, laity-clergy status and frequency of church attendance, evaluator group and frequency of chuch attendance, and evaluator group and sex. Size of parish and ministry context were analyzed separately in one-way analyses of variance, since they had earlier been observed to be relatively uncorrelated with the other variables used in these series.

57. For that series and all others, criterion ratings were standardized to a mean of 50 and standard deviation of 10, based on the data from the group from which the criterion was derived. In other words, criteria derived from laypeople only were standardized on the basis of the lay mean and standard deviations; criteria derived from professional data only were standardized on the professional mean and standard deviation. Therefore, in the graphs that appear in relation to Chapter 4, lay and professional group scores do not always average to a mean of 50. They will average to a mean of 50 only in the cases of criteria derived from total-group data where standardization was to the total-group mean and standard deviation.

58. One notable exception was Core Cluster 41, "Priestly Commitment." The average rating of that criterion, as derived by these latter procedures, is an artifact. It is caused by the fact that more than 40 percent of the raters indicated that the items that constitute that criterion do not apply for them. Therefore, a special average rating of Cluster 41 was calculated and reported in earlier chapters based only on evaluations given by persons who found those items applicable—largely, but not entirely, persons from the Roman Catholic Church (Order and Diocesan), the Anglican-Episcopal Churches, and the Orthodox Churches.

59. All sections of the criterion-rating questionnaire, with the exception of the two concerning "The Minister as Person," offered the following response possibilities: 7 = "highly important (absolutely essential)," 6 = "quite important (major asset)," 5 = "somewhat important (minor asset)," 4 = "undesirable," 3 = "detrimental," 2 = "reject," and 1 = "does not apply." Section 6A, entitled, "The Minister as Person (Positive)," offered these response possibilities: 7 = "highly important (absolutely essential)," 6 = "quite important (major asset)," 5 = "somewhat important (minor asset)," 4 = "not important," 3 = "undesirable," 2 = "reject," and 1 = "does not apply." Section 6B, entitled, "The Minister as Person (Negative)," offered the following response possibilities: 7 = "does not apply," 6 = "reject," 5 = "desirable," 4 = "not detrimental," 3 = "somewhat detrimental," 2 = "quite detrimental," and 1 = "highly detrimental." (See also Note 39.)

60. The rows of the following table show the general correspondence between the original response possibilities and the meanings of ratings now scaled from +3.00 to −3.00:

Core Clusters 51–54, 63–64	*Core Clusters 42–50*	*Core Clusters 1–41, 55–62*	*New (Final) Scale of All Core Clusters 1–64*
7 Highly detrimental	1 Does not apply	1 & 2 Does not apply & reject	−3 Highly detrimental
6 Quite detrimental	2 Reject	3 Detrimental	−2 Quite detrimental
5 Somewhat detrimental	3 Undesirable	4 Undesirable	−1 Somewhat detrimental
4 Not detrimental	4 Not important	4.5	0 Little or no consequence
3 Desirable	5 Somewhat important (minor asset)	5 Somewhat important (minor asset)	+1 Minor asset
2 Reject	6 Quite important (major asset)	6 Quite important (major asset)	+2 Major asset
1 Does not apply	7 Highly important (absolutely essential)	7 Highly important (absolutely essential)	+3 Absolutely essential

20

Criterion Items That Did Not Cluster

Merton P. Strommen

It is impressive that 85 percent of the 444 criterion statements organized themselves into clusters. As a result, we have three levels of core criteria:

377 criterion items
64 criterion clusters (core clusters)
11 criterion families (second-order factors)

But what about the 67 items that were not drawn into a cluster? They cannot be ignored as discards, inasmuch as they have been identified as part of the domain of criteria people use when judging clergy. They have an importance as single items that ought not be ignored.

Assuming that the nonclustering items do touch important facets of ministry, the question naturally arises: "Why did they fail to cluster? Were the activities, attitudes, or qualities they describe considered unimportant by the evaluator groups?" The answer is no. Fully a third of the items drew either high ratings because they describe major assets for a beginning minister or low ratings because they identify something detrimental. They reflect the same range and intensity of importance as those drawn into one of the sixty-four core clusters.

What are the reasons for their not clustering? Four possibilities can be mentioned.

1. *No counterparts.* A few have no other items with which to cluster. In

a sense, each one is a cluster in itself and reflects a dimension for which there were no additional items (such as "Is frequently ill"). Had other related items been available, they likely would have clustered with them. The possibility of more criterion clusters underscores the need for continually revising and updating the present taxonomy.

2. *Noncontroversial nature.* Some of the nonclustering criterion statements represent criteria that are widely accepted and appreciated. As a result, the range of ratings for these items is narrow, meaning that almost everyone tended to give these items similar ratings. However, the people who agreed on their importance apparently differed quite radically in how they rated other criterion items. Since clusters are formed by similar rating patterns, these items did not cluster.

Significantly, half of the noncorrelating items are found in two sections: "The Minister as Theologian and Thinker" and positive qualities of "The Minister as Person." More than a fourth of the items found in these two areas failed to cluster.

By way of contrast, almost all the items in three other sections of the survey formed clusters: "Ministries to Community and World," "Ministries to Persons under Stress," and negative qualities of "The Minister as Person." Only one in twelve of these criterion statements remains outside a cluster. It is likely that individuals responded to these statements in more consistent and systematic patterns, representing varying opinions about the item's importance. The resulting pattern of responses, with their systematic variations and broad range, encouraged more of these items to cluster.

3. *Denominational variation.* Some denominations view certain criteria as integral to a pastor's ministry, and others do not. As a result, items that would cluster for a given denomination lack the correlational strength to form a cluster when all forty-seven denominations are involved. An example of this is found in an item relating to financial leadership: "Teaches a sense of responsibility for the financial support of the congregation." This item correlates reasonably well ($R = .48$) with a number of other items on finances: "Understands a financial statement of assets and liabilities" (Item 684), "Causes people to feel they are needed in the ongoing work of the parish" (Item 712), "Informs congregation of how its money is being spent" (Item 677), and "Maintains an appreciation for the relationship between the budget and program needs" (Item 681).

While these items lacked the intercorrelational strength to form a cluster across all denominational families, one such cluster did form when the data for a specific denomination were cluster analyzed. This "almost a cluster" phenomenon illustrates how later analyses of denominational and subgroup data may provide clusters that do use some of the nonclustering items. Already our analyses of denominational data have shown subtle differences in the composition of clusters that reflect the subtle but real distinctions among denominations. In the opinion of denominational leaders, their unique combination of items has been an accurate reflection of their respective denominational traditions.

When analyses are made of data from such populations as female clergy, ethnic groups, laity of certain denominations, clergy in specialized ministries, and each evaluator group, the likelihood is that new and interesting criterion clusters for ministry will form.

4. *Ambiguity.* Some items lack specificity and concreteness. Their level of abstraction and generality makes it possible for them to be interpreted quite differently by various individuals. Because they can be viewed from so many different perspectives, they fail to draw a consistent or systematic response. Rather than being part of one cognitive notion, they are made a part of several notions. A possible example is the item, "Earns a living through secular employment in order to serve as a minister without salary" (Item 382).

These four reasons provide some insight into the clustering process and draw attention to the possible significance of nonclustering items in future analysis. Because they are part of the original domain definition and because some may later feature unique emphases of certain subgroups, a complete listing of these items with their mean ratings is shown in Table 20-1.

TABLE 20-1
Items That Did Not Cluster, Ranked by Total Group Mean

Rank No.	Item No.	Item	Total Group Mean
1	272	Advises in a way that respects a person's freedom to choose his own course of action	2.44
2	304	Seeks additional information when ideas are not clear	2.37
3	72	Teaches with objectives clearly in mind	2.32
4	496	Expresses honest opinions in the face of opposition	2.31
5	458	Shows an intuitive ability to sense the concerns and needs of people	2.29
6	723	Allows persons freedom in carrying out assigned responsibilities	2.29
7	722	Discourages groups from making decisions in the heat of emotional conflict	2.26
8	724	Intervenes in group conflict before it becomes destructive	2.22
9	88	Leads worship in a way that encourages a sense of being a community of faith	2.22
10	719	Teaches a sense of responsibility for the financial support of the congregation	2.22
11	283	Shows compassion and understanding of people usually condemned by society	2.21
12	459	Participates in educational retreats, workshops, and seminars to increase own effectiveness	2.18
13	461	Converses easily with the opposite sex	2.13
14	58	When preaching on a social issue, shows respect for the listeners' sense of personal responsibility	2.12
15	322	Encourages members to acknowledge one another as the body of Christ, even though they hold divergent theological views	2.07
16	478	Lets others "run the show" when they are in charge	2.05

TABLE 20-1 — *CONTINUED*

Rank No.	Item No.	Item	Total Group Mean
17	728	Administers with a sense of stewardship the monies and properties assigned to his jurisdiction	2.05
18	80	Provides adequate education for lay teachers	2.04
19	86	Encourages youth to rethink and restate ageless truths about themselves	2.04
20	721	Often anticipates where conflict may arise among members	1.88
21	341	Accepts guidance and judgment of superiors willingly	1.87
22	153	Provides community leadership in ways that awaken trust	1.87
23	302	Shows confidence in own intellectual ability	1.86
24	282	Service to another is not dependent on a hoped-for religious response	1.83
25	472	Seeks constructive criticism of own work wherever available	1.81
26	375	Spouse is a companion in the faith	1.81
27	477	Shows positive acceptance of own sexuality	1.79
28	460	When possible, clears with neighboring clergy before ministering to their members	1.78
29	305	Advocates keeping in balance the two emphases of preaching the gospel and working to improve the material well-being of people	1.75
30	159	Teaches people to reject violence in words and deeds as not being in accordance with the gospel	1.73
31	462	Does not draw attention to self	1.72
32	84	Determines where people are in their understanding of Christian doctrine	1.66

TABLE 20-1 — *CONTINUED*

Rank No.	Item No.	Item	Total Group Mean
33	309	On controversial issues, shows sensitivity to the relationship between Scripture and tradition	1.65
34	350	Encourages selected young people to consider the ministry as a vocation	1.56
35	312	Clearly identifies to parishioners the denomination's moral expectations	1.53
36	300	Own beliefs reflect the teachings of denomination	1.49
37	320	Is informed on the scriptural and theological background of the current charismatic movement	1.43
38	342	If unmarried, functioning is not impaired by an overwhelming loneliness	1.38
39	688	Works to enlarge the cultural interests of the congregation	1.33
40	98	Fosters an appreciation and use of music and arts	1.29
41	87	Engages groups in evaluating the worship services	1.27
42	378	Actively tries to change the traditional shape of ministry to fit the future better	1.25
43	83	Occasionally provides for group discussion of the sermon (homily)	1.19
44	149	Makes contact with the political thought and life in the community	1.07
45	471	Lives, eats, and dresses no better than parishioners	1.03
46	253	Shows discernment in the questions asked during times of confession	1.03
47	107	Calls parishioners by their first names	1.03
48	301	When teaching, identifies ancient heresies in contemporary disguise	1.01
49	319	In private study, uses original languages (Greek or Hebrew) to clarify obscure biblical passages	1.00

TABLE 20-1 — *CONTINUED*

Rank No.	Item No.	Item	Total Group Mean
50	112	Requests members to hire exconvicts and rehabilitated alcoholics and drug addicts	.59
51	475	If unmarried, integrates celibacy into own life in a positive way	.37
52	489	Disobeys unjust laws unhesitantly when the gospel or concrete situation dictates	.24
53	494	Is open to pentecostal charismatic renewal in the parish	.17
54	97	Views self primarily as a change agent in the church	−.34
55	291	Defines the mission of the church independent of the surrounding society's customs and cultures	−.42
56	486	Regularly wears clerical collar or other distinctive clothing	−.61
57	479	Actively protests against denominational policies	−.76
58	522	Wears casual clothes even for professional activities	−.97
59	527	Is frequently ill	−1.26
60	549	Allows job responsibilities to take priority over family	−1.27
61	524	Appears humiliated over mistakes made in public	−1.29
62	368	Often so engrossed in work, does not enjoy good conversation at dinner	−1.48
63	329	Seldom relates God's activity in history to everyday life and happenings	−1.58
64	532	Wonders in conversation with members whether he/she should be in ministry	−1.59
65	381	In relation to the church, expresses anti-establishment views	−1.68

TABLE 20-1 — *CONTINUED*

Rank No.	Item No.	Item	Total Group Mean
66	106	Forms close friendships with selected members of the parish	−1.71
67	382	Earns a living through secular employment in order to serve as a minister without salary	−2.01

Index

Abortion, 239
Accountability, 5
Adams, Aruthur M., 457
Administration, effectiveness of, 34; commonalities in ministry, 86–87; denominational family comparisons, 211; Lutheran Churches, 419; Orthodox Church, 345; profile of, 210–11; Southern Baptists, 274
Advisory committee, 527
Affirming style. *See* Open, affirming style
Age as variable used in study, 28
Alcoholic beverages. *See* Secular lifestyle
Aleshire, Daniel O., 23
Alienated, coministry to, 33; commonalities in ministry, 83; denominational family comparisons, 145; profile of 144–45; Southern Baptists, 281; United Church of Canada, 513
Alienating activities: commonalities in ministry, 81; denominational family comparisons, 113; Lutheran Churches, 418; Orthodox Church, 335; profile of, 112–13
Ambiguity, 8
American Baptist Churches, 246, 370
American-Canadian Baptist family, 245–64, 268
American Lutheran Church, 415, 422
Analytic design, 532–33
Anglican-Episcopal Churches, 64, 227–44; sacramental-liturgical ministry, 65–66; Southern Baptists, compared with, 268
Anglicans, 352
Assemblies of God, 393
Assertive individual evangelism, 38;

denominational family comparisons, 127; Evangelical Churches, 362; Lutheran Churches, 426–27; profile of, 126–27; Roman Catholic Church, 478; United Church of Canada, 509, 514–15; United Church of Christ, 500, 502
Associate Reformed Presbyterian Church, 458
Association of Theological Schools (ATS), 9, 15, 525–26; members of, 351, 354; Roman Catholic Church and, 468; underrepresented constituencies of, 537
Attendance at worship or mass, frequency of, 27, 37, 39
Augsburg Confession of 1530, 436
Automatic Interaction Detection (AID), 547–48
Average total-group rating, consistent use of, 550

Baptism, 260
Baptists, 89; American-Canadian Baptist family, 245–64, 268; Black Baptists, 264; general conference, 353–54, 356. *See also* Southern Baptists
Baptist Federation of Canada, 246–47
Baptist Missionary Association of America, 354
Barth, Karl, 510
Becker, Edwin L., 65–66, 307
On Being a Christian, 482
Believer's baptism, 260
Bereavement, 406
Berlin Conference (1966), 353, 393
Bible, 4; Christian Church, 317; interpretation of, 460; and literalism,

572